The Post-Development Reader

ABOUT THE EDITORS

Majid Rahnema was born in Tehran in 1924. A career ambassador for much of his life, he represented Iran at the United Nations for twelve successive sessions. Among the many posts he held were UN Commissioner for Rwanda and Burundi (1959), Chairman of the Fourth (Decolonization) Committee of the General Assembly (1965), Member of the Executive Board of UNESCO (1974–78) and of the Council of the United Nations University (1974–80). In 1967 he was asked to form his country's first Ministry of Science and Higher Education, a post from which he resigned in frustration four years later. He subsequently founded an Institute for Endogenous Development Studies, which, inspired by the educational ideas of Paulo Freire and the bottom-up vision of pioneers of the time, worked in several neglected villages to try to discover alternatives to the authoritarian and top-down development pursued by the Shah. Having left Iran some time before his country's revolutionary upheavals, he was invited by Bradford Morse, the UNDP Administrator at the time, to become the UNDP's Representative in Mali, and later his special advisor for Grassroots and NGO Matters, in which role he sought to open a window on the concerns of the drop-outs in the development process. Following his retirement in 1985, he was a Visiting Professor at the University of California at Berkeley for six years. He has held a similar position at Pitzer, Claremont Colleges since 1993. He is currently a visiting professor at the American University of Paris.

Victoria Bawtree was born in Australia. Educated in England, she has a degree in economics from London University. She has spent over thirty years of her life in Italy, during most of which time she edited *Ideas and Action*, a journal of the Food and Agriculture Organization. In the late 1950s she joined the social reformer Danilo Dolci in Sicily as a volunteer, after which she spent two years in the USA working as a speech-writer with the Iranian and Egyptian Missions to the United Nations. In the early 1970s she founded the Human Rights Information Group for FAO staff; during this time she actively supported the African liberation movements and participated in the work of the International Tribunal on the Rights and Liberation of Peoples. In 1979 she became a founding member of the Research and Information Centre on Eritrea (RICE), and in the early 1980s set up the '1% for Development Fund' in Rome. She now lives in the Alpes de Haute Provence, in Southern France, where she has helped to create an association to promote local social, cultural and ecological issues.

The Post-Development Reader

EDITED BY **MAJID RAHNEMA**

WITH **VICTORIA BAWTREE**

ZED BOOKS
London & New Jersey

UNIVERSITY PRESS LTD
Dhaka

FERNWOOD PUBLISHING
Halifax, Nova Scotia

DAVID PHILIP
Cape Town

The Post-Development Reader was first published in 1997 by:

In Bangladesh:
The University Press Ltd, Red Crescent Building,
114 Motijheel C/A, PO Box 2611, Dhaka 1000.

In Southern Africa:
David Philip Publishers (Pty Ltd), 208 Werdmuller Centre,
Claremont 7735, South Africa.

In Canada:
Fernwood Publishing Ltd, PO Box 9409, Station A,
Halifax, Nova Scotia, Canada B3K 5S3.

In the rest of the world:
Zed Books Ltd, 7 Cynthia Street, London N1 9JF, UK, and
165 First Avenue, Atlantic Highlands, New Jersey 07716, USA.

Second impression 1998.

Cover design by Andrew Corbett.
Designed and typeset in Monotype Bembo by
Lucy Morton & Robin Gable, Grosmont.
Printed and bound in Malaysia by Forum.

Library of Congress Cataloging in Publication Data

The post development reader / compiled and introduced by Majid Rahnema with Victoria Bawtree.
p. cm.
Includes bibliographical references and index.
ISBN 1 85649 473 X (hb).—ISBN 1 85649 474 8 (pbk.)
1. Subsistence economy. 2. Economic development.
3. Acculturation. 4. Economic anthropology. I. Rahnema, Majid, 1924– . II. Bawtree, Victoria, 1934–
GN448.2.P67 1997 96–25685
306.3—dc20 CIP

Canadian Cataloguing in Publication Data

The post-development reader.
Includes bibliographical references and index
ISBN 1–895686–84–9
1. Subsistence economy. 2. Economic development.
3. Acculturation. 4. Economic anthropology. I. Rahnema, Majid, 1924–
II. Bawtree, Victoria, 1934–
GN448.2.P67 1997 306.3 C97–950060–5

A catalogue record for this book is available from the British Library

ISBN 1 85649 473 X (Hb)
ISBN 1 85649 474 8 (Pb)

Bangladesh: ISBN 984 051389 3 Pb
Southern Africa: ISBN 0 86486 331 4 Pb
Canada: ISBN 1 895686 84 9 Pb
Rest of world: ISBN 1 85649 473 X Hb; 1 85649 474 8 Pb

CONTENTS

PART THREE THE VEHICLES OF DEVELOPMENT

PART FOUR DEVELOPMENT IN PRACTICE

ACKNOWLEDGEMENTS

The editors would like to express their appreciation to all those who have made this Reader possible. We are especially grateful to the authors, *all* of whom have agreed to waive their copyright for the occasion, for without this generous gesture the Reader would never have seen the light of day. A special word of thanks must go to Professors Serge Latouche and Teodor Shanin, and to Rajni Kothari, who kindly wrote articles specially for the Reader, and to Professor Ivan Illich, who agreed to share his current thoughts on development with us all. The Reader also includes a number of articles and thoughts (in boxes) which appear in the English language for the first time: Pierre de Senarclens, Eduardo Galeano, Emmanuel N'Dione, Ignacio Ramonet, Hassan Zaoual, as well as Pierre Bungener, Joseph Ki-Zerbo, Edouard Lizop, José Nun, Marie-Dominique Perrot, Gilbert Rist, Claude Roy, Michel Serres, Dominique Temple, Philippe Thureau-Dangin.

We should also like to express our gratitude to the following publishers for freely giving us permission to reproduce excerpts from their books: Aldine Publishing Co., New York; Cambridge University Press, Cambridge; Communitas Inc. Manchester, Connecticut; Doubleday & Co. Inc., New York; Editions d'En Bas, Lausanne; ENDA-GRAF, Dakar; Gunnars Publishing Co., Winnipeg; International Institute for Sustainable Development, Winnipeg; Macmillan, London; Oxford University Press, Oxford, New York, New Delhi; Peter Lang, New York; Pluto Press, London; Presses Universitaires de France, Paris; Princeton University Press, Princeton; Simon & Schuster, New York; Stockholm Studies in Social Anthropology, Stockholm; The Sierra Club, San Francisco; Vintage Books, New York; Yale University Press, New Haven; Zed Books, London.

We also appreciate the ready co-operation of the editors of the following journals and magazines: *The Ecologist*, *Resurgence*, *Interculture*, *Development* (SID), *Le Monde Diplomatique*, *Political and Economic Weekly* (Bombay), *IFDA Dossier*; as well as that of the Dag Hammarskjöld Foundation.

Finally, we thank Anne Rodford of Zed Books, and Robin Gable and Lucy Morton, for their work on production, as well as all those people, too numerous to mention, who gave us inspiration and encouragement while we were preparing this Reader.

INTRODUCTION

Majid Rahnema

The disintegration of the colonial empires brought about a strange and incongruous convergence of aspirations. The leaders of the independence movements were eager to transform their devastated countries into modern nation-states, while the 'masses', who had often paid for their victories with their blood, were hoping to liberate themselves from both the old and the new forms of subjugation. As to the former colonial masters, they were seeking a new system of domination, in the hope that it would allow them to maintain their presence in the ex-colonies, in order to continue to exploit their natural resources, as well as to use them as markets for their expanding economies or as bases for their geopolitical ambitions. The myth of development emerged as an ideal construct to meet the hopes of the three categories of actors.

For quite a long time, this temporary meeting of otherwise highly divergent interests gave the development discourse a charismatic power of attraction. The different parties to the consensus it represented had indeed their own differences as to the ways development had to be implemented. For an important group, *economic* development was the key to any kind of development. For another, *culture* and the social conditions proper to each country had to prevail in any process of development. On another plane, an animated debate witnessed major differences between people who wanted an expert-based and professionally managed development and others who were for an 'endogenous', 'human-centred', 'participatory', 'bottom-up' or, later, 'sustainable' form of development. These 'policy-oriented' divergences seemed, however, too weak to question the ideology of development and its relevance to people's deeper aspirations. In the 1960s, when an 'outsider' like Ivan Illich set out to challenge the very idea of development as a threat to people's autonomy, his stand was perceived by many as sheer provocation. Development, even more than schooling, was then such a sacred cow that it appeared totally irresponsible to question its relevance.

This almost unanimous support for development was somehow significant of the very gap it had started to produce in societies in which it had been introduced. For now it appears clearly that such a unanimity was far from being shared at the grassroots level, where it was supposed to reach the suffering populations. Only the 'authorities' who were speaking on behalf of their 'target populations' claimed that such was the case. The voices that, here and there, were heard across the barriers separating the rulers from the ruled, showed that the latter had never been seriously consulted.

It may well be said that when the 'national' leaders of various anti-colonial struggles took over the movements emerging from the grassroots, they succeeded in making them believe that development was the best answer to their demands. As such, for all the victims of colonial rule, it did appear for a while as a promising mirage: the long-awaited source of regeneration to which they had been looking for so long. But the mirage ultimately transformed into a recurring nightmare for millions. As a matter of fact, it soon appeared to them that development had been, from the beginning, nothing but a deceitful mirage. It had acted as a factor of division, of exclusion and of discrimination rather than of liberation of any kind. It had mainly served to strengthen the new alliances that were going to unite the interests of the post-colonial foreign expansionists with those of the local leaders in need of them for consolidation of their own positions. Thanks to these alliances, societies that had invented modernized poverty could now extend it to all 'developing' countries.

This is how, under the banner of development and progress, a tiny minority of local profiteers, supported by their foreign 'patrons', set out to devastate the very foundations of social life in these countries. A merciless war was waged against the age-old traditions of communal solidarity. The virtues of simplicity and conviviality, of noble forms of poverty, of the wisdom of relying on each other, and of the arts of suffering were derided as signs of 'underdevelopment'. A culture of 'individual' success and of socially imputed 'needs' led younger men to depart their villages, leaving behind dislocated families of women, children and older men who had no one to rely on but the promises of often unattainable 'goods' and 'services'. Millions of men and women were thus mortally wounded in their bodies and souls, falling *en masse* into a destitution for which they had never been culturally prepared.

For the development establishment and its beneficiaries, this unprecedented tragedy was interpreted only as the inevitable price to be paid for a good life for all. Even now, when, with a few localized exceptions, the famous economic gap between the 'haves' and the 'have-nots' continues to reach ever more intolerable proportions, development ideologists attribute its failures only to political or other causes external to the development ideology. The very fact that, only recently, on the occasion of the United Nations' fiftieth anniversary, delegates were unanimous in giving it their full support shows that development, like the nation-state it serves and the educational systems it promotes, has become one of the founding pillars of the modern 'global village' programmed for the twenty-first century. Similarly, the majority of books and articles published on development continue to talk about what it needs to grow rather than the threats it poses to its 'target populations'. For a long time, even students trying to see 'the other side of the moon' had difficulty hearing the voices of the great losers and their friends.

The idea of a collection of essays that would make it possible for such students to hear those voices originally started some twelve years ago, when I was invited by the University of California at Berkeley to teach a course on 'The Myth and the Reality of Development'. Thus, a first Reader was put at the disposal of the students, soon followed by a larger one in two volumes, which was compiled from a great number of xeroxed texts. These materials and manuscripts were largely either unknown or inaccessible to students. The papers were all selected with the aim of giving them a view of development and its practices from the perspective of the grassroots populations. The unexpected demand for the two Readers showed that not only Berkeley students but also many outsiders, including development activists, welcomed the idea.

Yet I owe to Robert Molteno, the inspiring editor at Zed Books, the suggestion (in 1991) that a Reader of the same kind be published, in order to reach the growing number of development students who, both inside and outside the universities and other academic centres, were eager to have a view of development from the perspective of the 'losers' and their friends. For various reasons, it took us much longer to implement the idea than we had initially planned. Not only had the number of serious writers witnessing the agonies of development considerably increased in the meantime, but more impressive evidences and reports were now published, so that a complete revision and updating of the materials included in the original Readers was required. Moreover, the first appearance of the word 'Post-Development' some six or seven years ago[1] made it necessary, henceforth, to take into account the practices and thoughts that were actually shaping the period following the demise of the development ideology. Finally, as Robert and I were trying to redesign the entire project, in the light of all those elements, Victoria Bawtree, a dear friend and former editor of *Ideas and Action* (a well-known FAO magazine which was doomed to disappear because of many of its 'subversive' grassroots positions) joined in the endeavour, bringing to the task her valuable knowledge and experience and the contagious energy of an old development insider.

As in the Berkeley Reader, the texts presented here have at least three qualities in common. They are *subversive*, not in the sense attributed to this adjective by modern inquisitors, but as Cardinal Arns, of São Paulo, defined it in his courageous statement before an annual meeting of the Society for International Development, in 1983: 'Subvert', he said, 'means to turn a situation round and look at it from the other side'; that is, the side of 'people who have to die so that the system can go on.'

Hence, the selections are also *human-centred*; that is, they represent a perception of reality from the perspective of the human beings involved in the processes of change. As such, the concern of the contributors to this Reader is not for 'progress', 'productivity', or any other achievement *per se* in the scientific, technological or economic fields. It is rather to find out whom these serve or exclude, and how they affect the human condition and the relational fabric of the society into which they are introduced. If some spectacular technological advance delights a minority of individual 'winners' to the detriment of an increasing number of 'losers', the contributors to this anthology are eager to convey what these losers think about it, and how their lives are affected by it.

Finally, the ideas presented here are *radical*, not in the polemical sense often intended by the use of this adjective to discredit free thinking, but in the etymological sense of the word: that is, going to the roots (Latin *radix*) of the questions, 'pertains to, or affects what is fundamental'.

The contributors to this volume inhabit a vast spectrum of cultures with all their differences. They represent different horizons of thought. They are also persons who have occupied very different 'social positions'. There are, amongst them, not only 'developers' and activists or 'agents of change' but also philosophers, psychologists, sociologists, economists, anthropologists, journalists, anarchists, dreamers, artists, poets, and you name it – Dadacha, for example, one of our most exceptional guests, is an 'illiterate' sage. Yet, not only do the contributors share the qualities just mentioned; they have been requested to present their views because of the particular respect we have towards them, as thinkers and often as friends. In fact, we acted from the beginning as if we were inviting them to a gathering of *friends*, who would come around a table just to enjoy a friendly conversation. It was important for us to think that even when they disagreed with each other, they did so as friends, not as experts or specialists.

One further feature is common to most of the guests at this gathering. They belong to a generation that went quite far to defend the great ideologies that marked the present century, most drawing their strength from the deeply *humanistic* traditions of all the world's cultures. Progress, socialism and development were their names. As a rule, the majority of the contributors to this Reader have, at some moment of their personal itinerary, bitterly experienced the disillusions intrinsic to such ideologies. Yet, that does not seem to have driven them to discredit the virtues often associated with the birth of such ideologies, but to discover their extraordinarily corrupting possibilities, particularly when they tend to colonize one's autonomous capacity to search for the Truth.

The contributions to this Reader have been classified in five parts.

Part One pictures a number of world societies in the pre-development era. It starts with excerpts from Marshall Sahlins' *Stone Age Economics*. In this revolutionary text, which has now become a classic, the author, basing himself on recent anthropological findings, shows how the economistic bias has served to give a totally distorted picture of life in the so-called archaic or primitive societies. According to Sahlins, hunters/gatherers were not *poor*. Rather, they were *free*. They were indeed leading quite a simple and frugal life. Yet, as a rule, the people's material wants were satisfied. The fraction of people who went to bed hungry every night was paradoxically much smaller than in the present world of 'affluence' where it is still one-third to one-half of the population.

Helena Norberg-Hodge shows, in turn, how the preservation of the cultural sap had enabled another society, this time in Ladakh, to continue enjoying a good life until development broke in forcefully. Here again, an unbiased testimony shows how a population, internationally labelled as one of the poorest and least developed of the world, can still give the most 'developed' lessons of wisdom and virtue in every walk of life.

For Hassan Zaoual, a major reason why the development ideology has failed to grasp the rich complexity of the non-economized societies is its blindness to the specificity of their sites, in particular their symbolic dimensions. On the African sites, notices the Moroccan economist, 'the economic logic rests on the native social soils' and 'the rational is nothing but the relational.' These sites, which have been culturally produced with a view to saving the African way of life, are today threatened with total destruction by 'the missiles of development'. People's resistance to development should be studied in the context of their will to protect their local symbolic sites from destruction.

A testimony coming from a totally different geographic site, that of the American Indians of the Ojibway Nation, shows that the cultures of the world, despite their great diversity, have many things in common. Linda Clarkson, Vern Morrissette and Gabriel Regallet describe how, here as elsewhere, great traditions of wisdom and virtue, and millions of individual and group experiences, have converged to develop 'customs, beliefs, institutions and methods of social control' that cannot be dismissed, or worse, replaced from outside.

The taped interview of Gemetchu Megerssa with Dadacha, an elder of the Ethiopian Borana tribe, reveals other aspects of these sites. In this truly extraordinary document, Dadacha points his finger at the heart of the question. What is important to his sisters and brothers is *fidnaa*, a concept based on the 'necessary harmony between God and people', which 'does not end with growth' but with 'something else which we call *gabbina*' (well-being and splendour) and 'is similar to that of a ram's horn growing in a spiral'. The *limaati*, or the new concept of development, that is proposed to the people not only reduces their perception of a good life to an abstract economic formula but threatens to destroy 'the flow of civilized life'.

In the small 'boxes' illustrating the main themes of Part One, many inspiring thoughts articulated by well-known thinkers, from Marcel Mauss to Jerry Mander, as well as less famous but even more significant people like the anonymous Inouit, show how the rich world of societies labelled as 'underdeveloped' continues to be misrepresented.

Part Two discusses the different aspects of the development paradigm – paradigm being taken here as the sum of the assumptions underlying the concept, and the beliefs or the world-view it both prescribes and proscribes. Teodor Shanin starts the discussion by examining the genealogy of the paradigm, which goes far back to the idea of progress. For Professor Shanin, this attractive ideology soon became 'an immensely "energizing" tool of policy and counterpolicy', 'a particular expert style' which took away from the majority 'the right to choose and even to understand why their own experience was increasingly being negated'.

For Marshall Berman, Faust can be traced as the first developer, after he sells his soul to Mephistopheles and decides, at any cost, to develop an entire region around him. The arrogance that grows with his ambition to develop his services leads him to ask his new friend Mephistopheles to kill Philemon and Baucis, the sweet old couple who were offering hospitality to shipwrecked sailors and wanderers, and who refuse to sell him their little cottage. This tragic blindness to others' feelings leads him ultimately to pronounce his own death sentence.

Using Foucault's methodology to dissect the development discourse, Arturo Escobar shows how the discourse made it possible for the rulers 'to subject their populations to an infinite variety of interventions, to more encompassing forms of power and systems of control', including 'killing and torturing [and] condemning their indigenous populations to near extinction'.

As Ivan Illich was perhaps one of the first thinkers who, as early as the late 1960s, had perceived most of the dangers inherent in the development discourse, 'Development as Planned Poverty' is inserted here as a prophetic message. For him, 'underdevelopment' is 'the surrender of social consciousness to prepackaged solutions', a phenomenon that was actually fostered by development. Focusing on the school system as it was introduced in the 'Third World', he shows how 'schools rationalize the divine origin of social stratification with much more rigour than churches have ever done.'

A quarter of a century later, we see the flowering of Illich's earlier thoughts in the interview he granted us specially for this Reader. The gist of his message, as I understand it, places a totally different type of responsibility, and perhaps a much heavier one, on the shoulders of every one of us: 'The possibility of a city set up as the milieu that fosters a common search for good has vanished... Dedication to each other is the generator of the only space that allows what you ask: a mini-space in which we can agree on the pursuit of the good.'

My own essay on 'Development and the People's Immune System' closes this discussion on the development paradigm by taking up the history of *homo oeconomicus* as one of the main agents of development, and the way he historically introduced himself in vernacular niches, as the HIV does in the

T4 cell, replacing the genetic codes of the latter by its own. In all economized societies, the stage now seems set for *homo oeconomicus* to 'become' his victims. To what extent, and how, could they resist the invasion? Are there 'fields of power' still left to the people exposed to the new 'virus', which may be reinforced in order to help them drive it back or destroy it? What could each of us do in the David-and-Goliath-like struggles that lie ahead? These questions can be better addressed if one gains a clearer notion of the institutions or the vehicles used by development in achieving its goals.

It is in Part Three of the Reader that some of these 'vehicles' are discussed. The articles in this section deal with economy, the nation-state, education, science, the colonization of minds, the hegemony of 'the one and only way of thinking', the media, and the international organizations.

Addressing the role of economy, as one of the most important vehicles of development, Serge Latouche defines development as 'the trickle-down effect of industrial growth'. He submits that, for mainstream thinking, growth has been identified with 'the good'. But the good it claims to represent 'is not the quality of life, but the quantity of gadgets considered as useful by the mere fact that they are being produced and consumed'.

The *problematique* of the nation-state, another fundamental vehicle of development, is described in all its complexities and ambivalences by Rajni Kothari. As a thinker who, through all his writings, has denounced the abuses committed by the modern repressive nation-state in the name of development, he notices that, at a time when the state is being rendered weak and disembodied by the overriding forces of technology and the world market, it is facing another major challenge from a totally opposite direction: the assertion of cultures, ethnicity, nationalities, pluralism and the violence of terrorism and fundamentalism. 'It is also ceasing to be an embodiment of civil society and a protector of the poor, the weak and the oppressed.'

The various aspects of education as a factor of 'cultural defoliation' are then discussed in a 'multi-voice' report by five authors well versed in the impacts of the imported school system on indigenous populations. They include Cheikh Hamidou Kane of Senegal, the author of *The Ambiguous Adventure*, and the Burkinabé historian Joseph Ki-Zerbo.

Vandana Shiva follows with an analysis of science and its 'reductionist and universalizing tendencies' that tend to destroy local knowledge. For her, it is not just development that is a source of violence to women and nature, but 'at a deeper level, scientific knowledge, on which the development process is based [which] is itself a source of violence'.

In societies abruptly exposed to processes which systematically produce at all levels modern needs and expectations, these different vehicles of development have been highly instrumental in extending the old forms of colonization to the mind of their victims. Ashis Nandy's analysis of the colonization of the mind gives a vivid picture of this new and pernicious type of control. At the level of the very societies that have been mainly responsible for such a colonization, the same processes have led to the institution of 'the one and only way of thinking'. Ignacio Ramonet sees in this phenomenon an 'intimidating force that stifles all attempts at free thinking.' On another plane, James Petras discusses the role of the media in the cultural domination of societies exposed to development. Finally, Pierre de Senarclens discusses the role of the United Nations system and international assistance in prolonging the 'colonial' type of development.

Part Four starts with a forceful demonstration by Susan George of the ways 'the poor are developing the rich', thanks to development practices. Eduardo Galeano follows by telling us the sad story of those who are programmed to die of hunger 'on the altar of productivity', 'during the last chapter of the televised serial of history'. At the end of a poignant testimony on what Latin America has gone through in order to 'be like them', he asks himself whether the Goddess of Productivity 'is worth our lives'.

Other concrete examples of development practices are then given from the perspective of the grassroots populations. James Ferguson addresses the case of development in Lesotho, which, in his view, constitutes an 'almost unremitting failure'. The tragic effects of the transmigration project in Indonesia are then discussed by Graham Hancock. Pam Simmons then shows how recent efforts, particularly by the aid agencies, to integrate women into mainstream development theory and practice constitute a serious threat to much of what the women's struggle for freedom and dignity has stood for, especially in the South. This is followed by Peter Bunyard's testimony on the 'other side of the story' in the case of the Tehri dam in the Himalaya region, and how 'the misguided obsession with prestigious projects, such as large dams, is missing the point that denuded lands urgently need rehabilitation.'

To bring a note of almost black humour into the picture, Leonard Frank gives us, finally, an inside story of how development projects are generally prepared. Consultants familiar with the type of mission he describes would have no difficulty in agreeing in private that Leonard Frank's account is not an unusual one.

The last section of the Reader, Part Five, is intended to give an idea of the arts of resistance that 'losers' all over the world continue to refine in order to build for themselves different and more humane futures. They are designed to show wayfarers that the most promising roads are, to paraphrase Machado, the ones that they discover by themselves as they move ahead. There is no point in taking old roads which lead to undesirable destinations. In such a context, it becomes imperative for all wayfarers to learn, from their own traditions and from each other, the arts of resistance most adequate to the conditions of their journey. It is also important for them not to fall into ideological traps, the false promises of which often prevent their followers from seeing things around them *as they are*, and to learn from their own experiences.

To this end, this last part of the anthology starts with some inspiring thoughts on the ways different cultures have learned to resist domination.

These theoretical reflections are then followed by some examples illustrating the various types of resistance.

Gustavo Esteva and Madhu Suri Prakash open up the discussion by dissecting the fashionable slogan 'Think globally, act locally'. They find it misleading to the extent that it does not prevent the harmful effects of 'thinking big'. Grassroots populations engaged in movements such as Community Supported Agriculture (CSAs) do not deny the reality of the internationalization of economy. But they seek to oppose globalism with radical pluralism. The Zapatista movement in Chiapas reflects people's choice 'to live, to think as well as to act on the human scale'. And that does not prevent them from circulating their news through three different e-mail networks.

For Wolfgang Sachs, after forty years of development, the world has indeed developed, but in two opposite directions. The 8 per cent of the world population who own a car now compose a global middle class that is socially excluding the remaining majority. The demise of development has brought about a crisis of justice and a crisis of nature, in an inverse relationship to each other. Three perspectives are proposed to address the double crisis: the 'fortress perspective', the 'astronaut's perspective' and the 'home perspective'.

The Chiapas rebellion was a historic signal to the extent that it represented this last perspective, as the report by Gustavo Esteva shows. Like the Narmada Valley movement, it signifies that the conventional development idea has to be abandoned in the name of justice. Similarly, the 'efficiency revolution' should be complemented by a 'sufficiency revolution'; that is, a mix of 'intelligent rationalization of means and prudent moderation of ends'. Such a revolution cannot, however, be programmed or engineered. For in the home perspective, the discourse amounts to an invitation, rather than to a strategy.

Mahatma Gandhi's citations remind the reader that the quest for simplicity, advocated by the previous authors, actually belongs to a deep-rooted tradition of vernacular societies. David Shi goes on to indicate how simple living has had similar roots in the history of the West, from the early Greeks to modern Americans. 'Like the family, simplicity is always said to be declining but never disappears.'

The question remains as to how the victims of unjust and dehumanizing regimes go about exercising their power – that is, 'act over other's actions' – as Foucault has defined power. For James Scott, whose book *Domination and the Arts of Resistance* is a landmark in the understanding of this subject, it is crucial to decipher the 'hidden transcript' of the subordinate groups's resistance. This is enacted in a host of down-to-earth, low-profile stratagems designed to minimize appropriation. This form of resistance continually presses 'against the limit of what is permitted on stage, much as a body of water might press against a dam'.

Focusing on the grassroots movements in India, D.L. Sheth submits that these movements have now turned their backs on 'received' theories of any kind. What appeals to them is 'concrete and specific struggles' aimed at their own empowerment and at 'redefining economic demands in terms of political and cultural rights.'

The 'power of the powerless', particularly under a post-totalitarian system (a term he uses to describe the political regimes of East Europe in the late 1970s) is then forcefully explored in Václav Havel's contribution. Taking up the case of a greengrocer who places in his window, among onions and carrots, the slogan 'Workers of the World Unite!', the president of the Czech Republic imagines the day when the same greengrocer stops putting up the slogan and refuses to submit himself to the 'blind *automatism* which drives the system'. This revolt is for him a crucial decision to *live within the truth.* For that is tantamount to breaking 'the exalted façade of the system' and saying the emperor is naked! No wonder that such simple gestures are actually perceived as a fundamental threat to systems whose main pillar is living a lie.

At the end of his essay, Havel's message, based on his own personal experience, reveals a fact common to many great social changes and takes a prophetic dimension: 'The moment ... a single person breaks the rules of the game, thus exposing it as a game – everything suddenly appears in another light and the whole crust seems then to be made of a tissue on the point of tearing and disintegrating uncontrollably.'

The essay by Karen Lehman reminds us how such novel approaches to the emergence of a world of friendship and gift make it imperative for everyone to focus on more fundamental issues, such as the relationship between the 'space within' and the 'structure around it'. The space within, she notices, is shrinking with the economization of life, as it places a market value on such gifts as childbearing and housekeeping. The post-development era would not be different from the present one if the space within was still forced to fit the economy. A new kind of relation should be imagined in order to create a relation between the two 'that supports both and damages neither'.

Could such a relation lead to what Judith Snow, another contributor concerned with friendship and the preservation of the unique gift incarnated by everyone, calls the 'inclusion society'? For her, one creates the possibility of meaningful interaction by offering one's gift to the community. And the millions who are now trying to regenerate the old ideal of a community under modern conditions do it mainly by creating and broadening such possibilities.

And that is perhaps why they continue singing. We sing, Mario Benedetti tells us,

> because the sun recognizes us
> and the fields smell of spring
> and because in this stem and that fruit
> every question has its answer.

Depending on the oppressive regimes to which the subjugated belong – be they developmentalist, totalitarian, 'post-totalitarian' or fundamentalist –

people indeed have their different ways of preparing for the day when they all together cry out 'the emperor is naked!' It remains true, however, that the ends are always affected by the means. That perhaps explains the reason why Gandhiji refused, as early as the 1930s, to invite his fellow companions to 'seize' power, or to choose violence for reaching their ends. Thus did Sunderlal Bahuguna in India, Vaclav Hável in former Czechoslovakia, Subcomandante Marcos and Superbarrio in Mexico, or the Chodak team in Dakar who later learned, from their own experiences, that it was more important to *modify* the nature of political power than to *seize* a power that ultimately corrupts *all* its holders. 'Reinventing the Present', the essay presented by Emmanuel N'Dione and his Chodak team, is a fascinating report on how a relationship of friendly complicity between insiders and outsiders can lead to increasing refinement in the arts of helping each other.

Now, a final word on the 'boxes' that appear throughout this anthology. They have been chosen to represent some of the most interesting thinkers of all cultures, whose insights and words of wisdom illuminate the questions raised in the Reader. We view these as messages from absent friends or teachers who were either too far away or too busy to spend more time around the bigger table where the main conversation was being held. And we welcome their 'messages' as their gifts to us; they add new dimensions to the ongoing dialogue. References to their works have, however, been given in each case so that the more inquiring students can meet their authors at their convenience. We recommend strongly that readers use the boxes of their choice as signposts for the particular roads they are inclined to explore.

I take it as a good omen that the last box contains Fe Remotigue's moving poem on the power of resurrection, that which from the Christ to the smallest, most forgotten 'architects of dream' – like Garitoy – gives life its fullest meaning. 'One body down, one spirit up…'

NOTE

1. The first international meeting organized under this name was the Colloquium sponsored by the Eckenstein Foundation in Geneva together with the *Institut d'Etudes sur le Développement*, in 1991. A report of the meeting was published the following year in Lausanne. See Gilbert Rist, Majid Rahnema and Gustavo Esteva, *Le Nord perdu: Repères pour l'après-développement*, Editions d'en bas, Lausanne, 1992.

PART ONE

THE VERNACULAR WORLD

The one who by rediscovering the old can contribute to the new is indeed worthy to be called a teacher.

Confucius, *The Analects*, 2:11

1

THE ORIGINAL AFFLUENT SOCIETY

Marshall Sahlins

The popular view of life in a tribal society with a subsistence economy has always been that it was terribly difficult and unpleasant. This assumption was well established in anthropology for many years, and it still underlies the thinking of many development planners. Even evolutionary anthropologists assumed that technological progress was driven by material necessity and retarded by ignorance. The simpler the economy, the more precarious the existence.

The possibility that simple hunter-gatherers, organized in bands, might actually enjoy a good life was officially recognized by anthropologists at the 'Man the Hunter' symposium held in Chicago in 1965. This conference brought together seventy-five researchers from around the world, including many who had conducted fieldwork among hunter-gatherers. A variety of dramatic new perspectives on hunting and gathering emerged from the conference papers and the discussion. The paper presented by Marshall Sahlins proposing that simple hunter-gatherer bands represented the original 'affluent society' has become a classic. Sahlins reverses conventional wisdom and proposes that evolution has been downhill in terms of human welfare. An expanded version of this argument appears as the first chapter of Sahlins' book *Stone Age Economics*, published in 1972.

The above presentation is taken from 'Notes on the Original Affluent Society', in Richard Lee and Irven DeVore, eds, *Man the Hunter*, Aldine Publishing Co., New York, 1968. The following text is an abridged version of an article (itself based on Chapter 1 of *Stone Age Economics*) entitled 'The Original Affluent Society', published in *Development: Seeds of Change* (journal of the Society for International Development [SID], Rome), vol. 3, 1986.

MARSHALL SAHLINS is Professor of Anthropology at Chicago University. His many contributions to anthropological literature include *Islands of History* (Routledge, London, 1987), (with Patrick Vinton Kirch) *Anahulu: The Anthropology of History in the Kingdom of Hawaii* (2 vols, University of Chicago Press, Chicago, 1992), and *How 'Natives' Think: About Captain Cook, for Example* (University of Chicago Press, Chicago, 1995).

If economics is the dismal science, the study of hunting and gathering economies must be its most advanced branch. Almost universally committed to the proposition that life was hard in the palaeolithic age, our textbooks compete to convey a sense of impending doom, leaving one to wonder not only how hunters managed to live, but whether, after all, this was living? The spectre of starvation stalks the stalker through these pages. His technical incompetence is said to enjoin continuous work just to survive, afford him neither respite nor surplus, hence not even the 'leisure' to 'build culture'. Even so, for all his efforts, the hunter pulls the lowest grades in thermodynamics – less energy per capita per year than any other mode of production. And in treatises on economic development he is condemned to play the role of bad example: the so-called 'subsistence economy'.

The traditional wisdom is always refractory. One is forced to oppose it polemically, to phrase the necessary revisions dialectically: in fact, this was, when you come to examine it, the original affluent society. Paradoxically, that phrasing leads to another useful and unexpected conclusion. By common understanding, an affluent society is one in which all the people's material wants are easily satisfied. To assert that the hunters are affluent is to deny, then, that the human condition is an ordained tragedy, with man the prisoner sentenced to the hard labour of living with the perpetual disparity between his unlimited wants and his insufficient means.

For there are two possible courses to affluence. Wants may be 'easily satisfied' either by producing much or desiring little. The familiar conception, the Galbraithean way, makes assumptions peculiarly appropriate to market economies: that man's wants are great, not to say infinite, whereas his means are limited, although improvable: thus, the gap between means and ends can be narrowed by industrial productivity, at least to the point that 'urgent good' becomes plentiful. But there is also a Zen road to affluence, departing from premisses somewhat different from our own: that human material wants are finite and few, and technical means unchanging but on the whole adequate. Adopting the Zen strategy, a people can enjoy an unparalleled material plenty – with a low standard of living.

That, I think, describes the hunters. And it helps explain some of their more curious economic behaviour: their 'prodigality', for example – the inclination to consume at once all stocks on hand, as if they had it made. Free from market obsessions of scarcity, hunters' economic propensities may be more consistently predicated on abundance than our own. Destutt de Tracy, 'fish-blooded bourgeois doctrinaire' though he might have been, at least compelled Marx's agreement on the observation that 'in poor nations the people are comfortable', whereas in rich nations 'they are generally poor'. This is not to deny that a pre-agricultural economy operates under serious constraints, but only to insist, on the evidence from modern hunters and gatherers, that a successful accommodation is usually made. After taking up the evidence, I shall return in the end to the real difficulties of the hunting-gathering economy, none of which are correctly specified in current formulas of palaeolithic poverty.

SOURCES OF THE MISCONCEPTION

'Mere subsistence economy', 'limited leisure save in exceptional circumstances', 'incessant quest for food', 'meagre and relatively unreliable' natural resources, 'absence of an economic surplus', 'maximum energy from a maximum number of people' – so runs the fair average of anthropological opinion of hunting and gathering.

> The aboriginal Australians are a classic example of a people whose economic resources are of the scantiest. In many places their habitat is even more severe than that of the Bushmen, although this is perhaps not quite true in the northern portion... A tabulation of the foodstuffs which the aborigines of northwest central Queensland extract from the country they inhabit is instructive... The variety in this list is impressive, but we must not be deceived into thinking that variety indicates plenty, for the available quantities of each element in it are so slight that only the most intense application makes survival possible. (Herskovits, 1952, pp. 68–9)

But the traditional dismal view of the hunters' fix is also pre- and extra-anthropological, at once historical and referable to the larger economic context in which anthropology operates. It goes back to the time Adam Smith was writing, and probably to a time before anyone was writing.[1] It was probably one of the first distinctly neolithic prejudices, an ideological appreciation of the hunter's capacity to exploit the earth's resources most congenial to the historic task of depriving him of the same. We must have inherited it with the seed of Jacob which 'spread abroad to the west, and to the east, and to the north', to the disadvantage of Esau who was the elder son and cunning hunter, but in a famous scene deprived of his birthright.

Current low opinions of the hunting-gathering economy need not be put down to neolithic ethnocentrism, however. Bourgeois ethnocentrism will do as well. The existing business economy, at every turn an ideological trap from which anthropological economics must escape, will promote the same dim conclusions about the hunting life.

Is it so paradoxical to contend that hunters have affluent economies, their absolute poverty notwithstanding? Modern capitalist societies, however richly endowed, dedicate themselves to the proposition of scarcity. Inadequacy of economic means is the first principle of the world's wealthiest peoples. The apparent material status of the economy seems to be no clue to its accomplishments; something has to be said for the mode of economic organization (see Polanyi, 1947, 1957, 1959; Dalton, 1961).

The market industrial system institutes scarcity, in a manner completely unparalleled and to a degree nowhere else approximated. Where production and distribution are arranged through the behaviour of prices, and all liveli-

A Western Shoshone Educator Asks Himself: Has the White Man Programmed the Universe for Destruction?

In Indian terms there is no equation in dollars for the loss of a way of life... you cannot equate dollars to lives. The redmen are the last people on Earth who speak on behalf of all living things. The beast, the deer, the sagebrush have no one else to speak for them. The animals and plants were put here by the Great Spirit before he put the humans here... There is a story that the old people tell about the white man. They are like children. They want this and that, they want everything they see, like it's the first time on Earth. The white men have all these tools but they don't know how to use them properly. The white people try to equate national defense with human lives. There can never be an equation between dollar bills and living things – the fish, the birds, the deer, the clean air, clean water. There is no way of comparing them ... The white people have no love for this land. If we human beings persist in what we are doing, we will become like a bad cancer on Mother Earth. If we don't stop ourselves, something will stop us. We are destroying everything. The way things are fouled by nuclear waste, nothing can live on it. After we have made the earth uninhabitable, will the human beings take this to other planets? If we take these ways of destruction to other planets, we will be the worst cancer in the universe. The universe will be programmed for destruction. We will wipe out the whole galaxy with our filth.

Glen Wasson, *Newe Sogobia: The Western Shoshone People and Land*, quoted in Jerry Mander, *In the Absence of the Sacred: The Failure of Technology and the Survival of the Indian Nations*, Sierra Club Books, San Francisco, 1991, p. 318.

hoods depend on getting and spending, insufficiency of material means becomes the explicit, calculable starting point of all economic activity.[2] The entrepreneur is confronted with alternative investments of a finite capital, the worker (hopefully) with alternative choices of remunerative employ, and the consumer... Consumption is a double tragedy: what begins in inadequacy will end in deprivation. Bringing together an international division of labour, the market makes available a dazzling array of products: all these Good Things within a man's reach, but never all within his grasp. Worse, in this game of consumer free choice, every acquisition is simultaneously a deprivation, for every purchase of something is a forgoing of something else, in general only marginally less desirable, and in some particulars more desirable, that could have been had instead.

Yet scarcity is not an intrinsic property of technical means. It is a relation between means and ends. We should entertain the empirical possibility that hunters are in business for their health, a finite objective, and that bow and arrow are adequate to that end.

'A KIND OF MATERIAL PLENTY'

Considering the poverty in which hunters and gatherers live, in theory, it comes as a surprise that Bushmen who live in the Kalahari enjoy 'a kind of material plenty', at least in the realm of everyday useful things, apart from food and water.

> As the !Kung come into more contact with Europeans – and this is already happening – they will feel sharply the lack of our things and will need and want more. It makes them feel inferior to be without clothes when they stand among strangers who are clothed. But in their own life and with their own artifacts *they were comparatively free from material pressures*. Except for food and water (important exceptions!) of which the Nyae Nyae !Kung have a sufficiency – but barely so, judging from the fact that all are thin though not emaciated – they all had what they needed or could make what they needed, for every man can and does make the things that men make and every woman the things that women make... *They live in a kind of material plenty* because they adapted the tools of their living to material which lay in abundance around them and which were free for anyone to take (wood, reeds, bone for weapons and implements, fibers for cordage, grass for shelters), or to materials which were at least sufficient for the needs of the population... The !Kung could always use more ostrich egg shells for beads to wear or trade with, but, as it is, enough are found for every woman to have a dozen or more shells for water containers – all she can carry – and a goodly number of bead ornaments. In their nomadic hunting-gathering life, travelling from one source of food to another through the seasons, always going back and forth between food and water, they carry their young children and their belongings. With plenty of most materials at hand to replace artifacts as required, the !Kung have not developed means of permanent storage and have not needed or wanted to encumber themselves with surpluses or duplicates. They do not even want to carry one of everything. They borrow what they do not own. With this ease they have not hoarded, and the accumulation of objects has not become associated with status. (Marshall, 1961, pp. 243–4, emphasis added)

Analysis of hunter-gatherer production is usefully divided into two spheres, as Mrs Marshall has done. Food and water are certainly 'important exceptions', best reserved for separate and extended treatment. For the rest, the non-subsistence sector, what is said here of the Bushmen applies in general and in detail to hunters from the Kalahari to Labrador – or to Tierra del Fuego, where Gusinde reports of the Yahgan that their disinclination to own more than one of each of the utensils frequently needed is 'an indication of self-confidence'. 'Our Fuegians', he writes, 'procure and make their implements with little effort' (1961, p. 213).[3]

In the non-subsistence sphere, the people's wants are generally easily satisfied. Such 'material plenty' depends partly upon the ease of production, and that upon the simplicity of technology and democracy of property. Products are homespun: of stone, bone, wood, skin – materials such as 'lay in abundance around them'. As a rule, neither extraction of the raw material nor its working up take strenuous effort. Access to natural resources is typically direct

Gifts

For the Bushman, 'The worse thing is not giving presents. If people do not like each other but one gives a gift and the other must accept, this brings a peace between them. We must give what we have. That is the way we live together.'

Lorna Marshall, 'Sharing, Talking and Giving: Relief of Social Tensions among !Kung Bushmen, *Africa* 31, 1961, p. 245.

– 'free for anyone to take' – even as possession of the necessary tools is general and knowledge of the required skills common. The division of labour is likewise simple, predominantly a division of labour by sex. Add in the liberal customs of sharing, for which hunters are properly famous, and all the people can usually participate in the going prosperity, such as it is.

But, of course, 'such as it is': this 'prosperity' depends as well upon an objectively low standard of living. It is critical that the customary quota of consumables (as well as the number of consumers) be culturally set at a modest point. A few people are pleased to consider a few easily made things their good fortune: some meagre pieces of clothing and rather fugitive housing in most climates;[4] plus a few ornaments, spare flints and sundry other items such as the 'pieces of quartz, which native doctors have extracted from their patients' (Grey, 1841, vol. 2, p. 266); and, finally, the skin bags in which the faithful wife carries all this, 'the wealth of the Australian savage' (p. 266). For most hunters, such affluence without abundance in the non-subsistence sphere need not be long debated. A more interesting question is why they are content with so few possessions – for it is with them a policy, a 'matter of principle' as Gusinde says (1961, p. 2), and not a misfortune.

Want not, lack not. But are hunters so undemanding of material goods because they are themselves enslaved by a food quest 'demanding maximum energy from a maximum number of people', so that no time or effort remains for the provision of other comforts? Some ethnographers testify to the contrary, that the food quest is so successful that half the time the people seem not to know what to do with themselves. On the other hand, *movement* is a condition of this success, more movement in some cases than others, but always enough to depreciate rapidly the satisfactions of property. Of the hunter it is truly said that his wealth is a burden. In his condition of life, goods can become 'grievously oppressive', as Gusinde observes, and the more so the longer they are carried around. Certain food collectors do have canoes and a few have dog sleds, but most must carry themselves all the comforts they possess, and so only possess what they can comfortably carry themselves – or perhaps what the women can carry; the men are often left free to react to the sudden opportunity of the chase or the sudden necessity of defence.

As Owen Lattimore wrote in a not too different context, 'the pure nomad is the poor nomad'. Mobility and property are in contradiction.

That wealth quickly becomes more of an encumbrance than a good thing is apparent even to the outsider. Laurens van der Post was caught in the contradiction as he prepared to make farewells to his wild Bushmen friends:

> This matter of presents gave us many an anxious moment. We were humiliated by the realization of how little there was we could give to the Bushmen. Almost everything seemed likely to make life more difficult for them by adding to the litter and weight of their daily round. They themselves had practically no possessions: a loin strap, a skin blanket and a leather satchel. There was nothing that they could not assemble in one minute, wrap up in their blankets and carry on their shoulders for a journey of a thousand miles. They had no sense of possession. (1958, p. 276)

A necessity so obvious to the casual visitor must be second nature to the people concerned. This modesty of material requirements is institutionalized: it becomes a positive cultural fact, expressed in a variety of economic arrangements. Lloyd Warner reports of the Murngin, for example, that portability is a decisive value in the local scheme of things. Small goods are in general better than big goods. In the final analysis 'the relative ease of transportation of the article' will prevail, so far as determining its disposition, over its relative scarcity or labour cost. For the 'ultimate value', Warner writes, 'is freedom of movement'. And to this 'desire to be free from the burdens and responsibilities of objects which would interfere with the society's itinerant existence', Warner attributes the Murngin's 'undeveloped sense of property', and their 'lack of interest in developing their technological equipment' (1964, pp. 136–7).

Here, then, is another economic 'peculiarity' – and I will not say it is general, and perhaps it is explained as well by faulty toilet training as by a trained disinterest in material accumulation: some hunters, at least, display a notable tendency to be sloppy about their possessions. They have the kind of nonchalance that would be appropriate to a people who have mastered the problems of production, even as it is maddening to a European:

> They do not know how to take care of their belongings. No one dreams of putting them in order, folding them, drying or cleaning them, hanging them up, or putting them in a neat pile. If they are looking for some particular thing, they rummage carelessly through the hodgepodge of trifles in the little baskets. Larger objects that are piled up in a heap in the hut are dragged hither and yon with no regard for the damage that might be done them. The European observer has the impression that these [Yahgan] Indians place no value whatever on their utensils and that they have completely forgotten the effort it took to make them.[5] Actually, no one clings to his few goods and chattels which, as it is, are often and easily lost, but just as easily replaced... The Indian does not even exercise care when he could conveniently do so. A European is likely to shake his head at the boundless indifference of these people who drag brand-new objects, precious clothing, fresh provisions, and valuable items through thick mud, or abandon them to their swift destruction by children

> and dogs... Expensive things that are given them are treasured for a few hours, out of curiosity; after that they thoughtlessly let everything deteriorate in the mud and wet. The less they own, the more comfortable they can travel, and what is ruined they occasionally replace. Hence they are completely indifferent to any material possessions. (Gusinde, 1961, pp. 86–7).

The hunter, one is tempted to say, is 'uneconomic man'. At least as concerns non-subsistence goods, he is the reverse of that standard caricature immortalized in any *General Principles of Economics*, page one. His wants are scarce and his means (in relation) plentiful. Consequently he is 'comparatively free of material pressures', 'has no sense of possession', shows 'an undeveloped sense of property', is 'completely indifferent to any material pressures', and manifests a 'lack of interest' in developing his technological equipment.

In this relation of hunters to worldly goods there is a neat and important point. From the internal perspective of the economy, it seems wrong to say that wants are 'restricted', desires 'restrained', or even that the notion of wealth is 'limited'. Such phrasings imply in advance an Economic Man and a struggle of the hunger against his own worse nature, which is finally then subdued by a cultural vow of poverty. The words imply the renunciation of an acquisitiveness that in reality was never developed, a suppression of desires that were never broached. Economic man is a bourgeois construction, as Marcel Mauss said, 'not behind us, but before, like the moral man'. It is not that hunters and gatherers have curbed their materialistic 'impulses': they simply never made an institution of them. 'Moreover, if it is a great blessing to be free from a great evil, our [Montagnais] Savages are happy; for the two tyrants who provide hell and torture for many of our Europeans, do not reign in their great forest – I mean ambition and avarice ... as they are contented with a mere living, not one of them gives himself to the Devil to acquire wealth' (LeJeune, 1897, p. 231).

We are inclined to think of hunters and gatherers as *poor* because they don't have anything; perhaps better to think of them for that reason as *free*. 'Their extremely limited material possessions relieve them of all cares with regard to daily necessities and permit them to enjoy life' (Gusinde, 1961, p. 1).

SUBSISTENCE

When Herskovits was writing his *Economic Anthropology* (1958), it was common anthropological practice to take the Bushmen or the native Australians as 'a classic illustration of a people whose economic resources are of the scantiest', so precariously situated that 'only the most intense application makes survival possible'. Today the 'classic' understanding can be fairly reversed – on evidence largely from these two groups. A good case can be made that hunters and gatherers work less than we do; and, rather than a continuous travail, the food quest is intermittent, leisure abundant, and there is a greater amount of sleep in the daytime per capita per year than in any other condition of society.

Some of the substantiating evidence for Australia appears in early sources, but we are fortunate especially to have now the quantitative materials collected by the 1948 American–Australian Scientific Expedition to Arnhem Land. Published in 1960, these startling data must provoke some review of the Australian reportage going back for over a century, and perhaps revision of an even longer period of anthropological thought. The key research was a temporal study of hunting and gathering by McCarthy and McArthur (1960), coupled to McArthur's analysis of the nutritional outcome.

The most obvious, immediate conclusion is that the people do not work hard. The average length of time per person per day put into the appropriation and preparation of food was four or five hours. Moreover, they do not work continuously. The subsistence quest was highly intermittent. It would stop when the people had procured enough for the time being, which left them plenty of time to spare. Clearly in subsistence as in other sectors of production, we have to do with an economy of specific, limited objectives. By hunting and gathering, these objectives are apt to be irregularly accomplished, so the work pattern becomes correspondingly erratic.

In the event, a third characteristic of hunting and gathering was unimagined by the received wisdom: rather than straining to the limits of available labour and disposable resources, these Australians seem to underuse their objective economic possibilities.

> The quantity of food gathered in one day by any one of these groups could in every instance have been increased. Although the search for food was, for the women, a job that went on day after day without relief, they rested quite frequently, and did not spend all the hours of daylight searching for and preparing food. The nature of the men's food gathering was more sporadic, and if they had a good catch one day they frequently rested the next… Perhaps unconsciously they weigh the benefit of greater supplies of food against the effort involved in collecting it, perhaps they judge what they consider to be enough, and when that is collected they stop. (McArthur, 1960, p. 92)

It follows, fourthly, that the economy was not physically demanding. The investigators' daily journal indicates that the people pace themselves; only once is a hunter described as 'utterly exhausted' (McCarthy and McArthur, 1960, pp. 150f.). Neither did the Arnhem Landers themselves consider the task of subsistence onerous. 'They certainly did not approach it as an unpleasant job to be got over as soon as possible, nor as a necessary evil to be postponed as long as possible' (McArthur, 1960, p. 92). In this connection, and also in relation to their underuse of economic resources, it is noteworthy that the Arnhem Land hunters seem not to have been content with a 'bare existence'. Like other Australians (see Worsley, 1961, p. 173), they become dissatisfied with an unvarying diet; some of their time appears to have gone into the provision of diversity over and above mere sufficiency (McCarthy and McArthur, 1960, p. 192). In any case, the dietary intake of the Arnhem Land hunters was adequate – according to the standards of the National

Other Societies, Other Values

People for instance who only possess as much as what they can easily carry along for a certain distance – i.e. the instruments necessary for hunting and gathering – are not necessarily poor, even if, according to our standards, they live at the edge of greatest poverty: for they own but very few objects. According to their standards, however, they are living in affluence: they have all they need in abundance, namely nourishment and clothing, and they only need to 'work' in order to obtain it. People who – even if they have time and leisure – do not work until they have everything which we consider absolutely necessary for a worthwhile life, are not necessarily *lazy*. Perhaps, they attribute to *leisure* a greater value than we do. People who do not accumulate stock, although they might – according to our view – have at certain periods great need of it, but rather use their surplus for festivities, thus dissipating their riches, are not necessarily *frivolous* or *short-sighted*. They may have learned from experience that there is a certain security in sharing their surplus with others – neighbours, close-by tribes or villages – rather than accumulating stocks which might perish or get eaten by animals. For neighbours may return the generosity when it is their turn to have a good crop, a good catch or when they have caught an especially big animal. People who do not switch to agriculture and livestock farming, but rather maintain their traditional hunting and gathering or maybe nomadic animal husbandry in spite of the evidence of centuries, even millennia, of the so-called blessing of a high cultural level of agriculture and sedentary life, are not necessarily primitive or backward.

They may know that their lifestyle allows for more leisure or that their survival chances are greater in their particular kind of region because they do not exploit to the full the possibilities of their ecological niche, that is to say, they are *underproductive*, thus living with a certain margin of security in case of climatic changes or other unforeseeable fluctuations.

Peasants who stubbornly refuse to plant modern, more productive hybrid cereals instead of their traditional mixed crops, are not necessarily bound by blind prejudices. One could say the same of the persistence concerning the traditional division of land into many small, even tiny plots which hinder any kind of rational agricultural modernization. Here, too, we may find an insight which can no longer be formulated, which has been desymbolized and only lives on in traditions and rules, an insight into what, in modern scientific language, is meant by a strategy of risk minimization....

The Pakots, nomadic shepherds in Western Kenya, together with other Nilotic tribes, all in all around three million people, resisted until well into the 1950s all attempts by the British colonial administration to change their tribal ways of life in favour of European/American notions and concepts in the political, economic or religious realms; contrary to their Bantu neighbours, herdsmen like them, who partly 'successfully' modernized.

However, contrary to the Bantus who also till fields and do not rely to such a degree on cattle raising, the subsistence economy of the Pakots depends almost exclusively on cattle. Their lifestyle is ecologically so embedded and their social and political integration has reached such a high standard that no single element may be taken out of its global context without the danger of provoking a chain reaction threatening their very existence.

In terms of the present treatise, the resistance of the Pakots to innovations could be described in the following way: the pastoral production techniques represent the best risk minimization strategy for the Pakots, for even in the event of recurrent cattle plague, their resources are less threatened by sickness in general or drought than if they were to live primarily by crops. In the region of their pastures, rainfall and the degree of humidity vary a great deal. The nomads are mobile and can adapt to change of weather. The same would not be true for agriculture. Leisure preference, too, plays a decisive part because almost as important as the fact that cattle fit their risk minimization strategies better than agriculture is the fact that, according to Harold Schneider, 'cattle, sheep and goats increase by themselves and need comparatively little attention.'

Dieter Groh is Professor at the Philosophy Faculty, University of Konstanz, Germany. The extract is from *Development: Seeds of Change* (SID), no. 3, 1985.

Research Council of America. Mean daily consumption per capita at Hemple Bay was 2,160 calories (only a four-day period of observation), and at Fish Creek 2,130 calories (eleven days).

Finally, what does the Arnhem Land study say about the famous question of leisure? Much of the time spared by the Arnhem Land hunters was literally spare time, consumed in rest and sleep. The main alternative to work, changing off with it in a complementary way, was sleep:

> Apart from the time (mostly between definitive activities and during cooking periods) spent in general social intercourse, chatting, gossiping and so on, some hours of the daylight were also spent resting and sleeping. On the average, if the men were in camp, they usually slept after lunch from an hour to an hour and a half, or sometimes even more. Also after returning from fishing or hunting they usually had a sleep, either immediately they arrived or whilst game was being cooked. At Hemple Bay the men slept if they returned early in the day but not if they reached camp after 4.00 p.m. When in camp all day they slept at odd times and always after lunch. The women, when out collecting in the forest, appeared to rest more frequently than the men. If in camp all day, they also slept at odd times, sometimes for long periods. (McCarthy and McArthur, 1960, p. 193).

The failure of Arnhem Landers to 'build culture' is not strictly from want of time. It is from idle hands.

So much for the plight of hunters and gatherers in Arnhem Land. As for the Bushmen, economically likened to Australian hunters by Herskovits, two excellent recent reports by Richard Lee show their condition to be indeed the same (Lee, 1968; 1969). Lee's research merits a special hearing not only because it concerns Bushmen, but specifically the Dobe section of !Kung Bushmen, adjacent to the Nyae Nyae, about whose subsistence – in a context otherwise of 'material plenty' – Mrs Marshall expressed important reservations. The Dobe occupy an area of Botswana where !Kung Bushmen have been living for at least a hundred years, but have only just begun to suffer dislocation pressures. (Metal, however, has been available to the Dobe since 1880–90.) An intensive study was made of the subsistence production of a dry season camp with a population (forty-one people) near the mean of such settlements. The observations extended over four weeks during July and August 1964, a period of transition from more to less favourable seasons of the year, hence fairly representative, it seems, of average subsistence difficulties.

Despite a low annual rainfall (6 to 10 inches) Lee found in the Dobe area a 'surprising abundance of vegetation'. Food resources were 'both varied and abundant', particularly the energy-rich mangetti nut – 'so abundant that millions of the nuts rotted on the ground each year for want of picking' (Lee, 1969, p. 59).[6] His reports on time spent in food-getting are remarkably close to the Arnhem Land observations.

The Bushman figures imply that one man's labour in hunting and gathering will support four or five people. Taken at face value, Bushman food collecting is more efficient than French farming in the period up to World War II, when more than 20 per cent of the population were engaged in feeding the rest. Confessedly, the comparison is misleading, but not as misleading as it is astonishing… In the total population of free-ranging Bushmen contacted by Lee, 61.3 per cent (152 of 248) were effective food producers; the remainder were too young or too old to contribute importantly. In the particular camp under scrutiny, 65 per cent were 'effectives'. Thus the ratio of food producers to the general population is actually 3:5 or 2:3. But these 65 per cent of the people 'worked 36 per cent of the time, and 35 per cent of the people did not work at all' (Lee, 1969, p. 67).

For each adult worker, this comes to about two and one-half days' labour per week. ('In other words, each productive individual supported herself or himself and dependants and still had three-and-a-half to five-and-a-half days available for other activities.') A 'day's work' was about six hours; hence the Dobe work week is approximately fifteen hours, or an average of 2 hours 9 minutes per day. Even lower than the Arnhem Land norms, this figure however excludes cooking and the preparation of implements. All things considered, Bushmen subsistence labours are probably very close to those of native Australians.

Also like the Australians, the time Bushmen do not work in subsistence they pass in leisure or leisurely activity. One detects again that characteristic palaeolithic rhythm of a day or two on, a day or two off – the latter passed desultorily in camp. Although food collecting is the primary productive activity, Lee writes, 'the majority of the people's time (four to five days per week) is spent in other pursuits, such as resting in camp or visiting other camps' (Lee, 1969, p. 74):

> A woman gathers on one day enough food to feed her family for three days, and spends the rest of her time resting in camp, doing embroidery, visiting other camps, or entertaining visitors from other camps. For each day at home, kitchen routines, such as cooking, nut cracking, collecting firewood and fetching water, occupy one to three hours of her time. This rhythm of steady work and steady leisure is maintained throughout the year. The hunters tend to work more frequently than the women, but their schedule is uneven. It is not unusual for a man to hunt avidly for a week and then do no hunting at all for two or three weeks. Since hunting is an unpredictable business and subject to magical control, hunters sometimes experience a run of back luck and stop hunting for a month or longer. During these periods, visiting, entertaining and especially dancing are the primary activities of men. (Lee, 1968, p. 37)

The daily per-capita subsistence yield for the Dobe Bushmen was 2,140 calories. However, taking into account body weight, normal activities and the age–sex composition of the Dobe population, Lee estimates that the people require only 1,975 calories per capita. Some of the surplus food probably went to the dogs, who ate what the people left over. 'The conclusion can be drawn that the Bushmen do not lead a substandard existence on the edge of starvation as has been commonly supposed' (Lee, 1969, p. 73).

Taken in isolation, the Arnhem Land and Bushmen reports mount a disconcerting if not decisive attack on the entrenched theoretical position. Artificial in construction, the former study in particular is reasonably considered equivocal. But the testimony of the Arnhem Land expedition is echoed at many points by observations made elsewhere in Australia, as well as elsewhere in the hunting-gathering world.

RETHINKING HUNTERS AND GATHERERS

> Constantly under pressure of want, and yet, by travelling, easily able to supply their wants, their lives lack neither excitement nor pleasure. (Smyth, 1878, Vol. 1, p. 123)

Clearly the hunting-gathering economy has to be re-evaluated, both as to its true accomplishments and as to its true limitations. The procedural fault of the received wisdom was to read from the material circumstances to the economic structure, deducing the absolute difficulty of such a life from its absolute poverty. But always the cultural design improvises dialectics in its relationship to nature. Without escaping the ecological constraints, culture would negate them, so that at once the system shows the impress of natural conditions and the originality of a social response – in their poverty, abundance.

What are the real handicaps of the hunting-gathering praxis? Not 'low productivity of labour', if existing examples mean anything. But the economy is seriously afflicted by the imminence of diminishing returns. Beginning in subsistence and spreading from there to every sector, an initial success seems only to develop the probability that further efforts will yield smaller benefits. This describes the typical curve of food-getting within a particular locale. A modest number of people usually sooner than later reduce the food resources within convenient range of camp. Thereafter, they may stay on only by absorbing an increase in real costs or a decline in real returns: rise in costs if the people choose to search farther and farther afield; decline in returns if they are satisfied to live on the shorter supplies or inferior foods in easier reach. The solution, of course, is to go hunting somewhere else. Thus the first and decisive contingency of hunting-gathering: it requires movement to maintain production on advantageous terms.

But this movement, more or less frequent in different circumstances, more or less distant, merely transposes to other spheres of production the same diminishing returns of which it is born. The manufacture of tools, clothing, utensils or ornaments, however easily done, becomes senseless when these begin to be more of a burden than a comfort. Utility falls quickly at the margin of portability. The construction of substantial houses likewise becomes absurd if they must soon be abandoned. Hence the hunter's very ascetic conceptions of material welfare: an interest only in minimal equipment, if that; a valuation of smaller things over bigger; a disinterest in acquiring two or more of most goods; and the like. Ecological pressure assumes a rare form of concreteness when it has to be shouldered. If the gross product is trimmed down in comparison with other economies, it is not the hunter's productivity that is at fault, but his mobility.

Almost the same thing can be said of the demographic constraints of hunting-gathering. The same policy of *débarrassement* is in play on the level of people, describable in similar terms and ascribable to similar causes. The terms are, coldbloodedly: diminishing returns at the margin of portability, minimum necessary equipment, elimination of duplicates, and so forth – that is to say, infanticide, senilicide, sexual continence for the duration of the nursing period, and so on, practices for which many food-collecting peoples are well known. The presumption that such devices are due to an inability to support more people is probably true – if 'support' is understood in the sense of carrying them rather than feeding them. The people eliminated, as hunters sometimes sadly tell, are precisely those who cannot effectively transport themselves, who would hinder the movement of family and camp. Hunters may be obliged to handle people and goods in parallel ways, the draconic population policy an expression of the same ecology as the ascetic economy. More, these tactics of demographic restraint again form part of a larger policy for counteracting diminishing returns in subsistence. A local group becomes vulnerable to diminishing returns – so to a greater velocity of movement, or else to fission – in proportion to its size (other things being equal). In so far as the people would keep the advantage in local production and maintain a certain physical and social stability, their Malthusian practices are just cruelly consistent. Modern hunters and gatherers, working their notably inferior environments, pass most of the year in very small groups widely spaced out. But rather than the sign of underproduction, the wages of poverty, this demographic pattern is better understood as the cost of living well.

Hunting and gathering has all the strengths of its weaknesses. Periodic movement and restraint in wealth and population are at once imperatives of the economic practice and creative adaptations, the kinds of necessities of which virtues are made. Precisely in such a framework, affluence becomes possible. Mobility and moderation put hunters' ends within range of their technical means. An underdeveloped mode of production is thus rendered highly effective. The hunter's life is not as difficult as it looks from the outside. In some ways the economy reflects dire ecology, but it is also a complete inversion.

Reports on hunters and gatherers of the ethnological present – specifically on those in marginal environments – suggest a mean of three to five hours per adult worker per day in food production. Hunters keep bankers' hours, notably less than modern industrial workers (unionized), who would surely settle for a 21–35 hour week. An interesting comparison is also posed by recent studies of labour costs among agriculturalists of neolithic type. For example, the average adult Hanunoo, man or woman, spends 1,200 hours per year in swidden cultivation (Conklin, 1957, p. 151); which is to say, a mean of 3 hours 20 minutes per day. Yet this figure does not include food gathering, animal raising, cooking and other direct subsistence efforts of these Philippine tribesmen. Comparable data are beginning to appear in reports on other primitive agriculturalists from many parts of the world. The conclusion is put conservatively when put negatively: hunters and gatherers need not work longer getting food than do primitive cultivators. Extrapolating from ethnography to prehistory, one may say as much for the neolithic as John Stuart Mill said of all labour-saving devices; that never was one invented that saved anyone a minute's labour. The neolithic saw no particular improvement over the palaeolithic in the amount of time required per capita for the production of subsistence; probably, with the advent of agriculture, people had to work harder.

There is nothing either to the convention that hunters and gatherers can enjoy little leisure from tasks of sheer survival. By this, the evolutionary inadequacies of the palaeolithic are customarily explained, while for the provision of leisure the neolithic is roundly congratulated. But the traditional formulas might be truer if reversed: the amount of work (per capita) increases with the evolution of culture and the amount of leisure decreases. Hunters' subsistence labours are characteristically intermittent – a day on and a day off – and modern hunters at least tend to employ their time off in such activities as daytime sleep. In the tropical habitats occupied by many of these existing hunters, plant collecting is more reliable than hunting itself. Therefore the women, who do the collecting, work rather more regularly than the men, and provide the greater part of the food supply. Man's work is often done. On the other hand, it is likely to be highly erratic, unpredictably required; if men lack leisure, it is, then, in the Enlightenment sense rather than the liberal.

Hunters and gatherers maintain a sanguine view of their economic state despite the hardships they sometimes know. It may be that they sometimes know hardships because of the sanguine views they maintain of their economic state. Perhaps their confidence only encourages prodigality to the extent that the camp falls casualty to the first untoward circumstance. In alleging that this is an affluent economy, therefore, I do not deny that certain hunters have moments of difficulty. Some do find it 'almost inconceivable' for a man to die of hunger, or even to fail to satisfy his hunger for more than a day or two (Woodburn, 1968, p. 52). But others, especially certain very peripheral hunters spread out in small groups across an environment of extremes, are exposed periodically to the kind of inclemency that interdicts travel or access to game. They suffer – although perhaps only fractionally, the shortage affecting particular immobilized families rather than the society as a whole (see Gusinde, 1961, pp. 306–7).

Still, granting this vulnerability, and allowing the most poorly situated modern hunters into comparison, it would be difficult to prove that privation is distinctly characteristic of the hunter-gatherers. Food shortage is not the indicative property of this mode of production as opposed to others; it does not mark off hunters and gatherers as a class or a general evolutionary age. Lowie asks:

> But what of the herders on a simple plane whose maintenance is periodically jeopardized by plagues – who, like some Lapp bands of the nineteenth century were obliged to fall back on fishing? What of the primitive peasants who clear and till without compensation of the soil, exhaust one plot and pass on to the next, and are threatened with famine at every drought? Are they any more in control of misfortune caused by natural conditions than the hunter-gatherer? (Lowie, 1938, p. 286)

Above all, what about the world today? One-third to one-half of humanity are said to go to bed hungry every night. In the Old Stone Age the fraction must have been much smaller. This is the era of hunger unprecedented. Now, in the time of the greatest technical power, is starvation an institution. Reverse another venerable formula: the amount of hunger increases relatively and absolutely with the evolution of culture.

This paradox is my whole point. Hunters and gatherers have by force of circumstance an objectively low standard of living. But taken as their *objective*, and given their adequate means of production, all the people's material wants usually can be easily satisfied. The evolution of economy has known, then, two contradictory movements: enriching but at the same time impoverishing, appropriating in relation to nature, but expropriating in relation to man. The progressive aspect is, of course, technological. It has been celebrated in many ways as an increase in the amount of need-serving goods and services, an increase in the amount of energy harnessed to the service of culture, an increase in productivity, an increase in division of labour and increased freedom from environmental control. Taken in a certain sense, the last is especially useful for understanding the earliest stages of technical advance. Agriculture not only raised society above the distribution of natural food resources; it allowed neolithic communities to maintain high degrees of social order where the requirements of human existence were absent from the natural order. Enough food could be harvested in some seasons to sustain the people while no food would grow at all; the consequent stability of social life was critical for its material enlargement. Culture went on then from triumph to triumph, in a kind of progressive contravention of the biological law of the minimum, until it proved it could support human life in outer space – where even gravity and oxygen were naturally lacking.

Other men were dying of hunger in the marketplaces of Asia. It has been an evolution of structures as well as technologies, and in that respect like the mythical road where for every step the traveller advances his destination recedes by two. The structures have been political as well as economic, of power as well as property. They developed first within societies, increasingly now between societies. No doubt these structures have been functional, necessary organizations of the technical development; but within the communities they have thus helped to enrich, they would discriminate in the distribution of wealth and differentiate in the style of life. The world's most primitive people have few possessions, *but they are not poor*. Poverty is not a certain small amount of goods, nor is it just a relation between means and ends; above all, it is a relation between people. Poverty is a social status. As such it is the invention of civilization. It has grown with civilization, at once as an invidious distinction between classes and more importantly as a tributary relation – that can render agrarian peasants more susceptible to natural catastrophes than any winter camp of Alaskan Eskimo.

NOTES

1. At least to the time Lucretius was writing (Harris, 1968, pp. 26–7).
2. On the historically particular requisites of such calculations, see Codere, 1968 (especially pp. 574–5).
3. Turnbull similarly notes of Congo Pygmies: 'The materials for the making of

shelter, clothing and all other necessary items of material culture are all at hand at a moment's notice.' And he has no reservations either about subsistence: 'Throughout the year, without fail, there is an abundant supply of game and vegetable foods' (1965, p. 18).

4. Certain food collectors not lately known for their architectural achievements seem to have built more substantial dwellings before being put on the run by Europeans (see Smyth, 1871, vol. I, pp. 125–8).

5. But recall Gusinde's comment: 'Our Fuegians procure and make their implements with little effort' (1961, p. 213).

6. This appreciation of local resources is all the more remarkable considering that Lee's ethnographic work was done in the second and third years of 'one of the most severe droughts in South Africa's history' (1968, p. 39; 1969, p. 73n).

REFERENCES

Conklin, Harold C., *Hanunóo Agriculture*, Food and Agriculture Organization of the United Nations, Rome, 1957.

Dalton, George, 'Economic Theory and Primitive Society', *American Anthropologist* 63, 1961, pp. 1–25.

Grey, Sir George, *Journals of Two Expeditions of Discovery in North-West and Western Australia During the Years 1837, 38, and 39*, 2 vols, Boone, London, 1841.

Gusinde, Martin, *The Yamana*, 5 vols, Human Relations Area Files, New Haven, Conn., 1961 (German edn 1931).

Herskovits, Melville J., *Economic Anthropology*, Knopf, New York, 1952.

Lee, Richard, 'What Hunters Do for a Living, or, How to Make Out on Scarce Resources', in R. Lee and I. DeVore, eds, *Man the Hunter*, Aldine, Chicago, 1968.

——— '!Kung Bushmen Subsistence: An Input–Output Analysis', in A. Vayda, ed., *Environment and Cultural Behavior*, Natural History Press, Garden City, N.Y., 1969.

LeJeune, le père Paul, 'Relations of What Occurred in New France in the Year 1634', in R.G. Thwaites, ed., *The Jesuit Relations and Allied Documents*, vol. 6, Burrows, Cleveland, 1897 (first French edn 1635).

Lowie, Robert H., 'Subsistence', in F. Boas, ed., *General Anthropology*, Heath, Boston, Mass., 1938.

——— *An Introduction to Cultural Anthropology* (2nd edn), Rinehart, New York, 1946.

McArthur, Margaret, 'Food Consumption and Dietary Levels of Groups of Aborigines Living on Naturally Occurring Foods', in C.P. Mountford, ed., *Records of the Australian–American Scientific Expedition to Arnhem Land*, vol. 2: *Anthropology and Nutrition*, Melbourne University Press, Melbourne, 1960.

McCarthy, Frederick D. and Margaret McArthur, 'The Food Quest and the Time Factor in Aboriginal Economic Life', in C.P. Mountfort, ed., *Records of the Australian–American Scientific Expedition to Arnhem Land*, vol. 2: *Anthropology and Nutrition*, Melbourne University Press, Melbourne, 1960.

Marshall, Lorna, 'Sharing, Talking and Giving: Relief of Social Tensions among !Kung Bushmen', *Africa* 31, 1961, pp. 231–49.

Mauss, Marcel, 'Essai sur le don: Forme et raison de l'échange dans les sociétés archaïques', in *Sociologie et anthropologie*, Presses Universitaires de France, Paris, 1966 (first published 1923–24 in *L'Année Sociologique*).

——— *Manuel d'Éthnographie*, Payot, Paris, 1967 (first published 1947).

Polanyi, Karl, 'Our Obsolete Market Mentality', *Commentary* 3, 1947, pp. 109–17.

——— 'The Economy as Instituted Process', in K. Polanyi, C. Arensberg and H. Pearson, eds, *Trade and Market in the Early Empires*, The Free Press, Glencoe, 1957.

——— *The Great Transformation*, Beacon Press, Boston, Mass., 1959 (first published by Rinehart, New York, 1944).

Smyth, R. Brough, *The Aborigines of Victoria*, 2 vols, Government Printer, Melbourne, 1878.

van der Post, Laurens, *The Lost World of the Kalahari*, Morrow, New York, 1958.

Warner, W. Lloyd, *A Black Civilization*, New York, Harper & Row, 1964 (first edn 1937).

Woodburn, James, 'An Introduction to Hadza Ecology', in R. Lee and I. De Vore, eds, *Man the Hunter*, Aldine, Chicago, 1968.

Worsley, Peter M., 'The Utilization of Food Resources by an Australian Aboriginal Tribe', *Acta Ethnographica* 10, 1961, pp. 153–90.

2

LEARNING FROM LADAKH

Helena Norberg-Hodge

Learning from Ladakh is the subtitle of Helena Norberg-Hodge's book *Ancient Futures.* She feels that Western society has much to learn from the traditional style of life of the Himalayan people of Ladakh, which she first visited in 1975. In the first part of the book, under 'Tradition', she describes the agricultural cycle of the society, the relationships between members of the community, their attitudes to health and illness, and their religious beliefs (the Ladakhis are Buddhists). All through she stresses the 'joie de vivre' that seemed to pervade the whole community, despite its harsh environmental setting and lack of material comforts. It is difficult to excerpt from this book, which illustrates so well the main thesis of our own anthology. We have chosen to reproduce here Chapter 4, 'We Have to Live Together', which depicts how people in a society at peace with itself and with nature relate to each other, and how tolerance and harmony are held as supreme values.

The second part of the book, entitled 'Change' recounts a sad story. It describes how, over the last two decades, external forces have descended on Ladakh like an avalanche, causing massive and rapid disruption of the society, especially in the capital, Leh. The process of change started in the mid-1970s, when the Indian Government opened up the region to tourism, and to development – which, of course, means Western-style development. Roads, energy, medicine and education have undoubtedly brought some benefits to the Ladakhis – but at what cost! Part Three, 'Looking Ahead', consists of the most searing indictment of development and its impact on the Ladakhis. The author contrasts the vernacular Ladakh, where people had no notion of poverty, to the emerging one, where the new economic paradigms have introduced modernized poverty, and where the breakdown of the old community ties and values is causing irreversible damage.

Ancient Futures: Learning from Ladakh, is published in the USA in 1991 by The Sierra Club (730 Polk Street, San Francisco, CA 94104), and in the rest of the world in 1992 by Rider Books (Random Century, London).

HELENA NORBERG-HODGE has studied numerous cultures at varying degrees of industrialization: in Bhutan, rural France and Spain, as well as twenty years in Ladakh. She helped found the local Ladakh Ecological Development Group (LEDeG), which seeks to adapt change to Ladakh's decentralized community structures without sacrificing cultural values or ecological stability. The author also founded

the International Society for Ecology and Culture (21 Victoria Square, Clifton, Bristol BS8 4ES, UK) to promote discussion of the social and environmental impact of economic development and globalization.

'WE HAVE TO LIVE TOGETHER'

Even a man with a hundred horses may need to ask another for a whip.

Ladakhi saying

'Why can't you give us a room? We'll pay a reasonable price.' Angchuk and Dolma looked down, indicating that they were not going to change their minds. 'You talk to Ngawang', they repeated. 'But we're already renting rooms from him, and it's getting quite noisy. There's no reason why we should rent yet another one from him.' 'You're staying with Ngawang now, and he might be offended if we offer you a room.' 'I'm sure he wouldn't be so unfair! Please go ahead and give us a room, won't you?' 'Talk to him first – we have to live together.' I was spending the summer of 1983 with a team of professors doing socio-ecological research in the village of Tongde in Zanskar. After a month or so, some of them felt the need for an extra room for quiet study. Since the house where we were staying was full of young and boisterous children, we thought we would ask the neighbours. At first I felt annoyed at Angchuk and Dolma's stubborn refusal. To me, with my emphasis on individual rights, this seemed so unfair. But their reaction, 'We have to live together', made me think. It seemed that to the Ladakhis the overriding issue was coexistence. It was more important to keep good relations with your neighbour than to earn some money.

Another time, Sonam and his neighbour had asked the carpenter to make some window frames; they were both building extensions to their houses. When the carpenter was finished, he brought all the frames to the neighbour. A few days later, I went with Sonam to collect them. Some were missing; his neighbour had used more than he had ordered. This was a considerable inconvenience to Sonam since he could do no further construction work until the frames were in place, and it was going to take several weeks to have new ones made. Yet he showed no signs of resentment or anger. When I suggested to him that his neighbour had behaved badly, he simply said, 'Maybe he needed them more urgently than I did.' 'Aren't you going to ask for an explanation?' I asked. Sonam just smiled and shrugged his shoulders. '*Chi choen*?' ('What's the point?'). 'Anyway, we have to live together.'

A concern not to offend or upset one another is deeply rooted in Ladakhi society; people avoid situations that might lead to friction or conflict. When someone transgresses this unwritten law, as in the case of Sonam's neighbour, extreme tolerance is the response. And yet concern for community does not have the oppressive effect on the individual that one might have imagined. On the contrary, I am now convinced that being a part of a close-knit community provides a profound sense of security.

In traditional Ladakh, aggression of any sort is exceptionally rare – rare enough to say that it is virtually nonexistent. If you ask a Ladakhi to tell you about the last fight he can remember, you are likely to get mischievous answers like 'I'm always beating up my neighbour. Only yesterday, I tied him to a tree and cut both his ears off.' Should you get a serious answer, you will be told that there has been no fighting in the village in living memory. Even arguments are rare. I have hardly ever seen anything more than mild disagreement in the traditional villages – certainly nothing compared with what you find in the West. Do the Ladakhis conceal or repress their feelings?

I asked Sonam once, 'Don't you have arguments? We do in the West all the time.' He thought for a minute. 'Not in the villages, no – well, very, very seldom, anyway.' 'How do you manage it?' I asked. He laughed. 'What a funny question. We just live with each other, that's all.' 'So what happens if two people disagree – say, about the boundaries of their land?' 'They'll talk about it, of course, and discuss it. What would you expect them to do?' I didn't reply.

One means of ensuring a lack of friction in traditional Ladakhi society is something I call the 'spontaneous intermediary'. As soon as any sort of difference arises between two parties, a third party is there to act as arbiter. Whatever the circumstances, whoever is involved, an intermediary always seems to be on hand. It happens automatically, without any prompting; the intermediary is not consciously sought and can be anyone who happens to be around; it might be an older sister, or a neighbor, or just a passing stranger. I have seen the process function even with young children. I remember watching a five-year-old settling a squabble between two of his friends in this way. They listened to him willingly. The feeling that peace is better than conflict is so deeply ingrained that people turn automatically to a third party.

This mechanism prevents problems from arising in the first place. The spontaneous intermediary, it seems, is always around in any context that might possibly lead to conflict. If two people are involved in trade, for example, they can be sure that someone will be there to help them strike a deal. This way they avoid the possibility of direct confrontation. In most situations, the parties already know one another. but if someone unknown to the others intervenes, it is not seen as meddling – the help will be welcomed.

One spring I was traveling on a truck from Kargil to Zanskar. Since snow still covered the road, the journey was taking longer than usual, but though it was rough and uncomfortable, I was enjoying the experience. It was fascinating observing our driver. He was exceptionally large and burly for a Ladakhi and had become a bit of a hero in the short time since the road had been built. Everywhere along the way, people knew him. Travelling up and down the road every few weeks, he had become an important personage in the eyes of the villagers – sending messages, delivering parcels and carrying passengers.

He had brought a sack of rice, for which he wanted some of the famous creamy Zanskari butter. As he approached an old woman, a large crowd gathered around. Suddenly a young boy no more than twelve years old was taking charge. He was telling this King of the Road how much to expect, what was reasonable. The whole affair lasted fifteen minutes, the driver and the old woman bartering through the young lad, never directly with each other. It seemed incongruous, this big tough man meekly following the advice of a boy half his size, yet so appropriate.

Traditional Ladakhi villages are run democratically, and, with few exceptions, every family owns its own land. Disparities in wealth are minimal. About 95 per cent of the population belong to what one might call a middle class. The remainder is split more or less evenly between an aristocracy and a lower class. This latter group is made up primarily of Mons, the early settlers of Ladakh, who are usually carpenters and blacksmiths. Their low status is attributed to the fact that extracting metals from the earth is thought to anger the spirits. Differences between these three classes exist, but they do not give rise to social tension. In contrast to European social boundaries, the classes interact on a day-to-day basis. It would not be unusual to see a Mon, for instance, joking with a member of the royal family.

Since every farmer is almost completely self-sufficient, and thus largely independent, there is little need for communal decision-making; each household essentially works its own land with its own resources. Many activities that would otherwise require the whole village to sit down and draw up plans – like the painting of the village monastery or arrangements for *Losar* (New Year) – have been worked out many generations ago and are now done by rotation. Nonetheless, sometimes matters have to be decided on a village level. Larger villages are divided up into *chutsos*, or groups of ten houses, each of which has at least one representative on the village council. This body meets periodically throughout the year and is presided over by the *goba*, or village head.

The *goba* is usually appointed by rotation. If the whole village wants to keep him on, he may hold his position for many years, but otherwise after a year or so the job will pass on to another householder. One of the *goba*'s jobs is to act as adjudicator. Though arguments are unusual, from time to time some differences of opinion arise that need settling.

Visiting the *goba* is a relaxed occasion, with little formality. Often the parties involved sit in the kitchen and discuss the problem together with the help of a little tea or *chang* (a kind of beer made from barley). I have spent a lot of time in the house of Paljor, the *goba* in the village of Tongde, listening as he helped to settle disputes. Since my research in Tongde focused on child-rearing practices, I would often sit in the kitchen with Paljor's wife, Tsering, who had just had a baby. People would come in from time to time to talk to Paljor.

Once two villagers, Namgyal and Chospel, came to the house with a problem. Namgyal started telling us what had happened: 'My horse, Rompo, got loose this morning. I had tied her to a big stone while I went in to talk to Norbu about his broken plough. I don't know how she got loose, but somehow she did.' 'I saw her from my rooftop', Chospel continued. 'She was munching away at my barley; she had already chewed off a whole corner of the field. I threw a stone to scare her off, but then I saw her fall; I must have hurt her.'

Throwing stones, often with a yak-hair sling, is the way in which Ladakhis usually keep their animals under control, and they can throw with astonishing accuracy. I have seen them control whole flocks of sheep nearly half a mile away with a few deftly placed stones. But this time, Chospel's aim had been off, and he had hit the horse just below the knee, injuring her leg. Who should compensate whom? And for how much? Although the horse's injury was more serious than the loss of the barley, Namgyal was guilty of an offence that could not be overlooked. To protect their crops, Ladakhis have agreed on strict rules about stray animals, and each village has someone, called a *lorapa*, specially appointed to catch them and collect a fine from the owner. After much discussion, the three men decided that no compensation was necessary either way. As Paljor told Namgyal: 'Hurting Rompo's leg was an accident, and you were careless in letting her go loose.'

Before coming to Ladakh, I had always thought that the best judges were the ones who were in no way connected with the individuals they were judging; maintaining this neutrality and distance, it seemed, was the only way of administering real justice. Perhaps it is, when you are talking about a society on the scale of our own. But, having lived in Ladakh for many years, I have had to change my mind. Though no system of justice can be perfect, none is more effective than one that is based on small, close-knit communities and that allows people to settle their problems at a grassroots level, by discussion among themselves. I have learned that when the people settling disputes are intimately acquainted with the parties involved, their judgement is not prejudiced; on the contrary, this very closeness helps them to make fairer and sounder decisions. Not only do smaller units allow for a more human form of justice, they also help prevent the sort of conflict that is so much a part of larger communities.

In fact, the more time I spent in Ladakh, the more I came to realize the importance of scale. At first, I sought to explain the Ladakhis' laughter and absence of anger or stress in terms of their values and religion. These did, no doubt, play an important role. But gradually I became aware that the external structures shaping the society, scale in particular, were just as important. They had a profound effect on the individual and in turn reinforced his or her beliefs and values. Since villages are rarely larger than a hundred houses, the scale of life is such that people can directly experience their mutual interdependence. They have an overview and can comprehend the structures

Popular Traditions of Frugality

Popular traditions of frugality were not ideologies, they were living practices. They were the way the ordinary women and men carried out their daily lives and taught their children to follow them. That all this should have been discarded overnight was a grievous loss, and grievously we are paying for it. To want to re-evaluate and revalue these traditions has nothing to do with a desire to return, to inflict a life of penny-pinching misery and privation upon the people. It is rather to wish to restore a sense of balance against the celebration of waste, the sanctification of the superfluous. That we have developed a capacity to see this as normal, even as essential, is an indication of immeasurable losses; loss of judgement and discrimination among them.

Trevor Blackwell and Jeremy Seabrook, *Revolt Against Change: Towards a Conserving Radicalism*, Vintage, London, 1993, p. 78.

and networks of which they are a part, seeing the effects of their actions and thus feeling a sense of responsibility. And because their actions are more visible to others, they are more easily held accountable.

Economic and political interactions are almost always face to face; buyer and seller have a personal connection, a connection that discourages carelessness or deceit. As a result, corruption or abuse of power is very rare. Smaller scale also limits the amount of power vested in one individual. What a difference between the president of a nation-state and the *goba* in a Ladakhi village: one has power over several millions of people whom he will never meet and who will never have the opportunity to speak to him; the other coordinates the affairs of a few hundred people whom he knows intimately, and who interact with him on a daily basis.

In the traditional Ladakhi village, people have much control over their own lives. To a very great extent they make their own decisions rather than being at the mercy of faraway, inflexible bureaucracies and fluctuating markets. The human scale allows for spontaneous decision-making and action based on the needs of the particular context. There is no need for rigid legislation: instead, each situation brings forth a new response.

Ladakhis have been fortunate enough to inherit a society in which the good of the individual is not in conflict with that of the whole community; one person's gain is not another person's loss. From family and neighbours to members of other villages and even strangers, Ladakhis are aware that helping others is in their own interest. A high yield for one farmer does not entail a low yield for another. Mutual aid, rather than competition, shapes the economy. It is, in other words, a synergistic society.

Co-operation is formalized in a number of social institutions. Among the most important is the *paspun*. Every family in the village belongs to a group of households that help each other out at the time of birth, marriage and death. The group consists of between four and twelve households, sometimes from different villages. Generally they share the same household god, who is believed to protect the families from harm and disease. At New Year, offerings are made to the god at a small shrine on the roof of each house. The *paspun* is most active at the time of a funeral. After death, the body is kept in the family house until the day of cremation (usually a week or so later), but the family does not need to touch it. The *paspun* members have the responsibility to wash and prepare the body; from the moment of death until the body has been totally consumed by fire, it is they who arrange most of the work so that the relatives are spared unnecessary distress.

A monk comes to read from the *Bardo Thodol*, the Tibetan *Book of the Dead*, for the period before the funeral. The consciousness of the dead person is told of experiences in the afterlife and urged not to be afraid of demons, but to turn instead toward the pure white light, the 'clear light of the void'.

On the day of the cremation, hundreds of people gather at the house, bringing the customary gifts of bread and barley flour. The relatives of the deceased, in particular the women, sit in the kitchen wailing the mourning chant over and over between tears: '*Tussi loma, tussi loma* ...'('Like falling autumn leaves, the leaves of time'). Neighbours and friends file past, expressing sympathy: '*Tserka macho*' ('Don't be sad'). The sounds of the monks' music and chanting fill the house.

The first funeral I attended was in the village of Stok, when a friend's grandfather died. Just after midday we were served a meal. The *paspun* members were in a sense acting as hosts. When they were not stirring the giant thirty-gallon pots of butter tea, we could see them dashing around with plates of food in their hands, making sure everyone was served. In the early afternoon, while the women stayed behind at the house, the monks led the funeral procession to the cremation site. Wearing brightly coloured brocade and tall headdresses with thick black fringes hanging down over their eyes, they emerged from the chapel with a great flurry of drums and shawms. They walked slowly through the fields toward the edge of the village. Behind them came the *paspun*: four men carrying the body on a litter, with the others bringing wood for the fire. After them followed a long line of male friends and relatives. As the monks performed the 'burning of offerings' beside the small clay oven, the *paspun* alone remained with them, tending the fire.

The *paspun*, just like the *chutso*, brings a sense of belonging to an intimate group that remains together for life, united by a common purpose. In traditional Ladakhi society, people have special links not only with their own family and immediate neighbours, but with households scattered throughout the entire region as well. Again, human scale allows for flexibility. If, for instance, a *paspun* member happens to be in the middle of the harvest or some other crucial work when a funeral is to take place, no unbending rule says that he must drop his work and go. If he cannot be there, he may talk with other *paspun* members and make arrangements for someone else to take his place.

Much farming work is shared, either by the whole community or by smaller subgroups like the *chutso*. During the harvest, for instance, farmers help one another to gather their crops. This works well since fields ripen at different times even in the same village. With everyone working together, the harvest can be gathered in quickly as soon as it is ripe. *Bes*, as shared work of this sort is called, often incorporates more than one village, and the reasons for it are not always purely economic. Some farmers will stagger the harvest, even when two fields are ripe at the same time, just so they can work together. You almost never see people harvesting alone; instead, you find groups of men, women and children all together in the fields – always with constant laughter and song.

Rares (literally, 'goat turn') is the communal shepherding of animals. It is not necessary for someone from each household to go up to the mountains with the animals every single day; instead one or two people take all the sheep and goats from several households and leave everyone else free to do other work.

Private property is also shared. The small stone houses up at the *phu* (grazing land), though owned by one household, will be used by many, usually in exchange for some work, or milk or cheese. In the same way, the water mills used for grinding grain are available to everyone. If you do not own one yourself, you can make arrangements to use someone else's; and only in late autumn, when water is very scarce and everyone is trying to grind as much grain as possible for winter, might you compensate the owner with some of the ground flour.

At the busiest times of the agricultural year, farm tools and draft animals are shared. Especially at the time of sowing – when the earth is finally ready after the long winter and farmers must work hard to prepare the fields – families pool their resources to enable everything to be done as quickly as possible. Again this practice is sufficiently formalized to have a name, *lhangsde*, but within this formal structure, too, a high degree of flexibility is possible.

Once I was in the village of Sakti at sowing time. Two households had an arrangement whereby they shared animals, plough and labour for the few days before sowing could start. Their neighbour, Sonam Tsering, who was not a part of the group, was ploughing his own fields when one of his *dzo* (a hybrid between the local cow and a yak) sat down and refused to work any longer. I thought at first that it was just being stubborn, but Tsering told me that the animal was ill and that he feared it was serious. Just as we were sitting at the edge of the field wondering what to do, the farmer from next door came by and without a moment's hesitation offered his own help as well as the help of the others in his *lhangsde* group. That evening, after they had finished their own work, they all came over to Tsering's fields with their *dzo*. As always, they sang as they worked, and long after dark, when I could no longer see them, I could still hear their song.

3

THE ECONOMY AND SYMBOLIC SITES OF AFRICA

Hassan Zaoual

The following text is taken from the second chapter of 'The Economy and the Symbolic Sites of Africa',[1] which appeared as the Winter 1994 issue of the quarterly journal *Interculture*, edited by Robert Vachon and published by the International Institute of Montreal (4917 St Urbain, Montreal, Quebec H2T 2W1).

Robert Vachon, in his presentation of this 42-page document (of which he is the translator), explains how Zaoual, after years of study and reflection on development issues, came to appreciate the deep roots of Mahgreb, Moroccan and African culture and to understand why the 'transfer of technology and development in general is a failure – even an impossibility'. The first chapter, entitled 'The Methodology of Symbolic sites', explains how every human being belongs to a symbolic site – that is, to a concrete culture or all-encompassing matrix. He then describes 'the archeology, the geology and architecture of symbolic sites', distinguishing their three layers and using, to do so, the pedagogical devices of

- the black box – the beliefs, the un-said, the un-thought;
- the conceptual box – ways of thinking;
- the tool box – outward behaviour.

'He tells us, in sum, that the behaviour and paradigms of societies always come from their deep beliefs, their "divinities", their mythical complexes, their "symbolic software", their "steady compass" etc. He also stresses how the latter screens, adapts, transforms what it receives. He shows the importance of taking seriously into account and respecting the different symbolic sites that exist throughout the world.'

Using a highly original analyis, Zaoual shows how and why so many of the endeavours caried out in the name of development are doomed to failure from the start.

Hassan Zaoual is described by Robert Vachon as 'one of those rare, unorthodox economists who believe that the economy is not primarily an economic problem, but a cultural one. He is a realist. He refuses to reduce reality, and hence culture itself, to economics, i.e. to a market value, to calculus. He thinks of economics from the perspective of culture and not vice-versa. Thus, he speaks of "the culture of development" as being one culture among many others, and which is not simply

transferable to "Third World" countries, since the latter, like the culture of development itself, have their own "culture software", their own "symbolic sites", their own "deep cultural matrices" which he calls "black boxes".

As indicated by Vachon, ethno-economics for Zaoual consists of trying to understand the economic behaviour of peoples from the specific ground of the symbolic systems at work in their respective contexts. This is what he attempts to do with regard to the relationships between the culture of development on the one hand and the African/Mahgreb culture on the other.'

HASSAN ZAOUAL is professor in the Faculty of Economics and Social Services at the University of Lille and Maître de Conferences at the Institute of Technology, Littoral University, Dunkirk. He is a founder and administrator of the North–South Network 'Culture and Development', whose quarterly journal *Quid Pro Quo* has published a number of his articles, also in English. He recently completed a doctoral thesis on 'The Role of Beliefs in Economic Development'.

THE CULTURES AND ECONOMIES OF AFRICAN MICRO-ORGANISMS

The implicit meaning behind social practices always has a quasi-religious character. Symbolic sites are imperatives. In Africa this postulate is amply verified by the daily actions of its peoples, both at the individual and collective levels. Communities and groups can only maintain their cohesion and their ways of functioning because they are embedded in their own symbolic sites. This is what Emmanuel N'Dione calls the magico-religious dimension of people's conceptual system,[2] even of those who, theoretically, are in the urban and modern arena. (In spite of their transplantation to the world of the urban periphery, people reproduce their rural models of social organization.) To African eyes, each place has its '*genii*' or 'spirits' who watch over the security of their people, protecting them against curses, spells, bad omens and the uncertainties of life. Their veneration serves to focus people on a whole set of symbolic reference points which are useful for the cohesion of African socio-economic organizations.

'All environmental elements, animals, things and people', writes N'Dione, 'bask in a world of symbolic representations and are systematically listed according to the role they play to ensure the integration of mankind and its security, or to annihilate or destroy those whose intentions are contrary to the normal functioning of the cosmos.'[3] This pervasiveness of local symbols confirms the hypotheses of the methodology of symbolic sites. Since they are the deep guides of behaviour, the symbolic sites have a power which is more real than is believed by the experts of social systemic change. The empirical research done by the ENDA team (Senegal), of which N'Dione is a member, clearly indicates that economic logic rests on the native social soils,[4] which in turn are based on the collective beliefs that pervade African networks.

Economic activities are not exempt from the deep influence of such local symbols. Hence it is inconceivable that their workings can be adequately grasped without considering these attitude-generating myths. Upon closer scrutiny, African beliefs are seen to be a code which holds the secret to the logic behind the practices. The latter, when we care to observe them differently, reveal a religious life which is the source of all their efforts to master their environment and thus to produce their own reality. Throughout their interrelations, they commune with the divinities of their site. These attitudes also ensure the coherence of the various organizational forms (material and immaterial) of the social groupings. The African exchange systems are thus an inextricable mixture of economic, social affective, symbolic, mythic facts, explicit or implicit.[5] 'In that perspective', writes N'Dione at the end of his book, 'economic phenomena must not be isolated from the rest. They are an integral part of the environmental system.'[6]

Awareness of the deeply pervasive influence of symbolic sites on both individual behaviour and community networks makes us relativize values and knowledge which claim to be universal. 'Truth for developers, error for the people',[7] as N'Dione says in his book. Thus, it is almost as if all the development projects were meant to be diverted towards another purpose. Working on the basis of different logics, the project and the milieu disappear from sight and lose touch with each other, so that we cannot understand exactly what is happening. The result of such interactions remains an enigma.

What seems certain is that the projects, along with the business management models, are 'diverted' because they tend to standardize the African sites in the image of the world's great capitalist society. But the local milieux work, quite to the contrary, on the principle of diversification of social links. This process at work within African reality is an economic principle that is inherent to a culture of relationship, sharing and solidarity. The African actors know or believe they know what they are doing; for the advantage of African economic rationality resides in the fact that it improves the security of the group's members by reducing hazards and risks. On the other hand, the individualistic rationality of the Western economic model makes individuals more fragile and can, at any moment, plunge them into absolute poverty.[8] In other words, relational investment results for the African investor in a multiplication of what N'Dione calls 'drawers', which are used according to the investor's evolving situation and needs. F.R. Mahieu has codified this same phenomenon with the notion of communitarian transfer.[9] In fact, it is the re-enactment of the system of reciprocity[10] which is jammed by the irruption of Western democracy. The theoretical and the empirical studies based on African field work indicate that, for the African actor, *the rational is nothing but the relational.*

Contrary to the Western model or way of seeing things, the paradigm that emerges from the cosmogonies of the African site would seem to be characterized more by relations between human beings than by utilitarian, individual,

The Gift Society

The water, wells, and springs that are given ensure against thirst; the clothes, gold, and sunshades, the sandals that allow one to walk on the scorching-hot ground, come back to the giver both in this life and the next. The land given away that yields its harvests for others causes the affairs of the donor to prosper both in this world and in the next as well as in future rebirths. 'As the waxing of the moon increases day by day, likewise the gift of land once made grows from year to year, from one harvest to the next.' (Book XIII of the *Mahabharata, Anuçasanaoarvan*) The earth produces its harvests, its income and taxes, mines and cattle. The gift of it once made enriches both giver and recipient with these same products....

In any case here one can see how a theory of alms can develop. Alms are the fruits of a moral notion of the gift and fortune on the one hand, and of a notion of sacrifice on the other. Generosity is an obligation, because Nemesis avenges the poor and the gods for the superabundance of happiness and wealth of certain people who should rid themselves of it. This is the ancient morality of the gift, which has become a principle of justice. The gods and the spirits accept that the share of wealth and happiness that has been offered to them and had been hitherto destroyed in useless sacrifices should serve the poor and the children ... The Arab *sadaka* originally meant exclusively justice, as did the Hebrew *zedaqa*: it has come to mean alms. We can even date it from the Mishnaic era, from the victory of the 'Poor' in Jerusalem.

Marcel Mauss, *The Gift*, trans. Douglas Hall, W.W. Norton, New York, 1990, pp. 56, 18.

economic functions. A Senegalese proverb expresses this perfectly: 'Man is a remedy for Man.' This suggestive maxim helps us to understand the endogenous African economy as an economy of affection. Unlike the management ideas that are in vogue in the West, in Africa and in the Arabo-Islamic world people tend to invest primarily in human beings. Unlike mountains, human beings meet, says a Maghreb proverb. All this confirms the solidity of social networks in that part of the world. It poses a formidable problem to economic analysis, which wants, at all costs, to isolate its theoretical objects (money, investment, production, consumption, market exchange, and so on) from the rest. Yet in African organizations, economics 'dissolves itself into the religious, symbolic and political dimensions of segmentary societies'.[11]

In Africa, the relevance of the relational shows the importance of the group with regard to the individual. In African sites there are no really anonymous individuals. All African individuals are *persons*, embedded in relationship to each other. This is what makes N'Dione talk about clusters (*grappes*). The group guarantees the smooth running of the communitarian link-economy. Through this communitarian constraint,[12] suffered or accepted by the agents of the site, the group creates the moral and economic conditions for the interplay of 'drawers'. This mechanism is not always perceptible to the eye of a foreign intervenor. Indeed the latter can be taken in by the subtle logic of the African site and not notice it. The foreigner is also immediately perceived as a future drawer that the African tries to connect to the whole network to which he belongs, as African logic constantly spins a web within its territories. Everything seems to be linked together, including what comes from outside.

Many NGOs undergo this process of 'getting caught', without being able to draw the lessons – theoretical and procedural – in order to identify the conditions for a real endogenous dynamic of African economic and social organizations. This rigidity can readily be explained by the weight of the mythology of development that burdens development workers. However, such is less and less the case for an NGO like ENDA-Tiers Monde, which operates permanently from Dakar, and which has become aware of the cultural limits of the economic presuppositions of the developers. As N'Dione has underlined:

> Paradoxically, while we consider the aid that we grant as disinterested, the people think the opposite, namely that their participation must bring a material or symbolic reward. Therefore they expect to be coopted in our own network and to benefit from financial or relational support: employment of kin or friends, and regular participation in the family ceremonies.[13]

This is the attitude of African logic. Take it or leave it!

Thus marked by their traditional mentalities, African organizations develop collective and individual behaviour which comes from the economics of the gatherer. Networks and social links serve that purpose. This is confirmed by views held by local communities. While sojourning in a Mauritanian camp, N'Dione and his team asked the elders and the children: 'Where are the men? Have they left with the animals?' In a single voice they answered: 'No, they are all in the new pastures.' The team, surprised, asked everybody: 'It has rained somewhere?' 'No,' said the elders and the children, 'the new pastures is Nouakshott' (the capital). N'Dione infers from this that the actors in African society see the world as a great pasture from which they draw their means of existence, present and future;[14] a great storage bin or reserve from which they can draw. And N'Dione clarifies the point: 'Among the things that can be drawn are of course resources and money, but especially relational ties, which remain the best way to store for the future.'[15]

In brief, everything indicates that the human essence of African endogenous economies is not founded on limitless production and accumulation, but on redistribution within the framework of the cohesion of the group and of the whole society. These 'twine-type' economies embed African Man in belief sites that can coexist and cohabit with capitalism without being able to develop the latter in a truly endogenous way. Thus, the capitalistic economy

The Meaning of a Good Life in Thagaste in the Year 354

When [St] Augustine was born there, in 354, the town of Thagaste [modern Souk Ahras, in Algeria] had existed for 300 years ... The area was then going through a period of great prosperity. The most typical memorial of this period comes from an inscription at Timgad, a town far to the south of Thagaste, in what are now the desolate highlands of southern Algeria: '*The hunt, the baths, play and laughter: that's life for me!*'

Quoted in Peter Brown, *Augustine of Hippo: A Biography*, Faber & Faber, London, 1967.

finds itself at the periphery of this 'magma of endogenous African relations'. African sites, due to their defence mechanisms, marginalize projects as they do capitalism as a whole. This is reinforced by the errors in the conventional theory of social change, which scrutinizes the African human and physical landscape, hoping to convince people that well-defined projects will be sufficient to spark the 'big bang' of development.

Albagli draws up the following balance sheet:

> It is not enough to create units of productivity. One must understand the framework in which they are set. The failure to do so hides the real motivation behind them. Doing so would avoid not only some disappointments, but also repeated and useless financial injections. The development of the 1960s was built on a mind-set that favoured three key notions: the State, the plan, the factory. Today, however, the state through its omnipotence has sparked defiance; the plan obviously does not prefigure the future, and the factory is no longer the cathedral of development.[16]

THE SPONTANEOUS ORDERS OF THE AFRICAN SITES

The obstacles to the spirit of capitalism in Africa obviously reside, in part, in the self-protecting layers developed by the symbolic sites of that continent. Contrary to the spirit of accumulation of the culture of development, the theoreticians of capitalistic management note that 'the regulatory element of the African system is expenditure',[17] the latter being a consumption and an investment in relationships. In fact, the essential motivations of the economy of African sites are consumption and the affection of the group. In other words, money circulates at the service of expenditure for self and others. As N'Dione underlines: 'The upkeep and maintenance of the social network is the surest strategy to protect oneself from life's uncertainties.'[18] This is a way of rediscovering the principle of reciprocity explained by Polanyi: 'What is given today will be compensated by what will be received tomorrow.'[19]

In order for the whole of this co-ordination system to work perfectly, each site, through its social conventions, sets 'procedures that are meticulously articulated and perfectly preserved, thanks to elaborate methods of publicity, to magical rites ... which bind the group through mutual obligations', as Polanyi has stated.[20] The economic functions have their primordial source in the rites of the site. In that sense, they are completely determined, 'by the very concrete experiences which offer a superabundance of non-economic motivations for each act which is accomplished within the framework of the entire social system.'[21] Thus the light of the symbolic site is present in each act, which is highly ethical. The site constantly reaffirms its existence[22] in order to safeguard its integrity. As a whole, its system of functioning is self-contained. Its processes of adaptation tend ultimately to realize the social equilibrium which the site's intelligence is seeking. Theoretically, Polanyi goes on to say, 'all social obligations are reciprocal in the long run.'[23] Everything happens as though the African social micro-organisms are seeking – through their spontaneous orders emerging from their world-views – to safeguard their existence and their mythical and practical coherence. In that sense, it is not only the great industrial and market society which is blessed with an auto-regulated and spontaneous order.[24] The world of the market society has its own, and the African sites have their own too.

It is for this reason that N'Dione notes from the field that one must not impose the norms of a system on persons who function according to the norms of another system.[25] Each site – modern or not – has its own collective unconscious from which derive its rules of functioning, around which aggregate, mechanically as it were, all the individual behaviours. The world has an infinite variety of 'site clocks' which co-ordinate human beings, each in its own way. This variety of conventions thus reveals that market exchange, whose essential motive is both utilitarian and individualistic (seeking maximum individual well-being), is not the only procedure to which human beings have recourse, at all times and in all places. Even in the society from which it comes, when the market expands and pervades every pore of society, the latter tends to implode. Moreover, Western capitalism can in fact only work in the presence of a specific culture and minimal public interventionism. The system holds together thanks to the cohesion of many factors, possessing very different and even contradictory characteristics according to the pure economic theory of the market. The principle of diversity or mixtures retards for a while, or at least attenuates, the entropy inherent in the exclusiveness of a uniform and totalizing order.

Given such a vision of societal dynamics, one can understand why the African sites seek a mixture in inter-individual and inter-network relations, all the while orchestrating the rationality of the market economy that comes from outside. In this context of a pluralistic world, Africans have at their disposal a stabilizing diversity within the site of reciprocity, as they do outside of it (state, market, NGOs, and so on). The last three are decoded from the angle of reciprocity, which is intrinsic to the deep cultural layers of local sites. Like a sponge, the world of reciprocity thus absorbs all the vectors that come from the Western site. The invisible hand of liberal economies, for example, is both crushed and recuperated by communitarian embraces. There is undoubtedly a phenomenon of decomposition and recomposition which takes place without the awareness of those who do not want or cannot face reality.

As a practical figure of the African site, reciprocity is a sort of programme that seeks to achieve communitarian cohesion. Essential reality being what it is, reciprocity will tend, each time, to stamp its quasi-genetic message on the foreign regulators of the market and of the state. As the latter are invaded by local realities, they have trouble in attaining their theoretical ends (Western rationality and capitalistic development). It is not always easy to replace one world by another, especially when rejecting local customs. There is therefore conflict, tension and searching in the fog of the local harmony of the site and in a perturbed world. With its 'spirit of the given thing',[26] reciprocity, or 'African welfarism', more or less successfully beats its own ethical and economic path, by mixing its own immanent rules with the ingredients of development. In such a context, development in its theory and in its economic practice is not an essential reference point in the collective and individual trajectory of Africans. Rather, it is reduced to smithereens which can be used again within the logic of the local sites. The latter, even while being destabilized by the irruption of foreign elements, pull themselves together and tend to rebuild their own universe. We are therefore dealing with social beings endowed with extremely adaptive and flexible qualities that disconcert the most vigilant theoretician. The so-called informal sectors of African reality are a choice terrain for these mechanisms of adaptation.

The African sites are in a restless state of equilibrium since they are forced to adapt continually to an environment brought about, from the outside, by development. Even if the latter does not succeed, it messes things up by the debris strewn from its crash. This gives way to complex worlds within which the African sites work out arrangements where stability and change are inextricably mixed. The 'informal' dynamics express this state of affairs very well. It is as if they incorporate, in homeopathic doses, the ingredients of development. This, on the other hand, allows them to safeguard the local symbolic sites from total destruction by the 'missiles of development'. If, hypothetically, total destruction were to happen, the target society would be totally absorbed into a black hole. In other words, the'informal' dynamics fill the ever-growing black holes that development leaves behind. They thus seem to be the result of a foreign perturbation, a source of disorder at the symbolic and economic levels. Furthermore, these dynamics, often microscopic, stabilize the society and answer its most pressing needs that official society does not meet, either on the symbolic or the economic level. While accommodating some elements of a still-born development, the adaptation dynamics of local sites cannot be reduced to a capitalistic form. We are dealing here with forms that reinvent themselves and are different from those that are essentially characteristic of capitalism. They are pregnant with a meaning that the selective and excluding eye of the pan-economic paradigm cannot detect. The utilitarian and productivist paradigm of development is like a telescope through which the West sees only itself, when it thinks it sees the Third World. It cannot do otherwise because it is an instrument made to measure itself and no one else. Inevitably there is confusion because this looking from outside considers that it is looking from inside.[27] It has always been important for Western science to look at things from the outside, even if it is an empty shell when seen from the inside. This is the limitation of the science of economics, which refuses to take into account the subjectivity of the people under scrutiny. It is this same analytical rigidity that is found in those approaches to informal dynamics that are triggered by the interactions between transposed development and African sites.

NOTES

1. Vachon explains that '"sites" in English is a literal translation of the French word *sites*, the originals of which in Latin and Greek are *situs* and *topos*. Symbolic sites refer here, according to the author, to the invisible but unique stable core, "motor", axis, "hard disk" of the reality of any given culture, which resists all standardization and uniformity, but which is open, in that it adapts all foreign incoming elements to itself. The assumption here is that the human being is not a placeless being, that he or she is always rooted in a concrete culture, that cultures are not simply conceptual systems and signs but also invisible symbolic realities, "implicit meanings" that constantly subvert or break open our rationalizations. In other words, reality is pluralistic and escapes the so-called universality of science; hence the limits of the latter. The author's method … is based on this fact and insists on taking this into account in any study – economic or otherwise – of social reality.'
2. Emmanuel S. N'Dione, *Le Don et le recours: Resorts de l'économie urbaine*, ENDA-Editions, Dakar, 1992.
3. Ibid., pp. 176–7.
4. The notion of native social soil in N'Dione's terminology is close to the notion of symbolic site that we are using here.
5. N'Dione, *Le Don et le recours*, p. 182.
6. Ibid., p. 199.
7. Title of a section of N'Dione's book; ibid., p. 184.
8. As Karl Polanyi remarked: 'By not following the accepted honour and generosity code, the individual cuts himself off from the community and becomes an outcast' (*The Great Transformation*, Beacon Press, Boston, Mass., 1957).
9. See François Régis Mahieu, *Les Fondements de la crise économique en Afrique*, L'Harmattan, Paris, 1990. For more details of the author's approach, see commentary in the *Canadian Journal of Development Studies*, vol. 12, no. 1, 1991, Ottawa.
10. See Dominique Temple, 'Economicide', *Interculture*, vol. 22, no. 1, 1988.
11. P. Batifoulier, I. Cordonnier and Y. Zenou, 'L'Emprunt de la théorie économique à la tradition sociologique: le cas du don et du contre-don', *Revue Economique*, vol. 43, no. 5, September 1992, p. 921.

12. This notion is taken from Mahieu, *Les Fondements.*
13. N'Dione, *Le Don et le recours*, p. 190.
14. Ibid., p. 192.
15. Bringing this hidden logic of African economic behaviour out into the open reveals African society as being dominated by intense movements of communitarian transfers. These transfers – monetary or other – in favour of those who belong to the group are enormous. They also go in all directions (city–country, urban–rural, within a zone, from one social position to another, and so on). They can be unequal or find compensation in different ways. That is how cohesion is maintained. The important thing to note, as Mahieu does, is that 'to satisfy one's collective duties fully is a precondition to pursuing one's individual economic interests' (*Les Fondements*, p. 35). In other words, the communitarian constraints (rights and obligations) largely determine the economic behaviour of the African actor.
16. C. Albagli, 'Esprit d'entreprises, unités de production et organisations internationales', in *L'Entreprenariat en Afrique francophone: culture, finance et développement*, a collective project directed by Georges Hénault and Rachid M'Rabet, edited by John Libbey Euro-text, AUPELF/UREF, London and Paris, 1990, p. 169.
17. See, for example, B. Traoré, 'La dimension culturelle de l'acte d'entreprendre en Afrique', in *L'entreprenariat*, p. 9.
18. N'Dione, *Le Don et le recours*, p. 114.
19. Polanyi, *The Great Transformation*, p. 80.
20. Ibid., p. 76.
21. Ibid., p. 77.
22. The site one belongs to is constantly watching the individual's behaviour, which must follow the norm. That is why, writes B. Traoré, 'the facts must obey the patriarch, not vice-versa.' See 'La dimension culturelle', p. 11.
23. Polanyi, *The Great Transformation.*
24. See, for example, the criticisms that Ragip Ege formulates concerning Hayek, the great theoretician of ultra-liberalism, in 'Emergence du marché concurrentiel et évolutionisme chez Hayek', in *Revue Economique*, vol. 43, no. 6, November 1992, pp. 1007, 1036.
25. N'Dione, *Le Don et le recours*, p. 185
26. The formulation of Marcel Mauss, who also says that 'the given thing bears traces of the donor, of its original site and possesses a history of its own which tends to give it a soul' (*Sociologie et Anthropologie*, PUF, Paris, 1985, p. 147).
27. These optical problems remind us of the words that the novelist Italo Calvino put into the mouth of his character Palomar, when he was meditating on scientific truth: 'We can know nothing about what is outside us, if we overlook ourselves ... the universe is the mirror in which we can contemplate only what we have learned to know in ourselves' (Italo Calvino, *Mr Palomar*, trans William Weaver, Picador, London, 1986, p. 107). Earlier, the author says the same thing: 'The thought even of a time foreign to our experience is impossible.' In other words, the reality of the other remains unimaginable to ourselves. Yet the Third World's symbolic sites need to be looked at differently – that is, from within – with categories capable of thinking the unconfessed, the tensions, the misery and riches of each one. This is a necessary revolution because 'underdevelopment' – synonymous here with human and ecological destruction, as is 'development' – is a chaotic process which proliferates in proportion to the supposedly correct means of struggle for treating it. It unceasingly manufactures itself, on the model of products from mass industries.

4

OUR RESPONSIBILITY TO THE SEVENTH GENERATION

Linda Clarkson, Vern Morrissette and Gabriel Regallet

The following text is taken from *Our Responsibility to the Seventh Generation: Indigenous Peoples and Sustainable Development*, published in 1992 by the International Institute for Sustainable Development (161 Portage Avenue East, 6th Floor, Winnipeg, Manitoba R3B 0Y4, Canada). As the report states, there is an interesting paradox in that, on the one hand, Indigenous peoples everywhere have been pushed to the fringe of society and marginalized economically, while on the other, there is a growing appreciation of the relevance, for today's world, of their long-held views on the need for society to be sustainable. The report aims to encourage people to listen to the voices of Indigenous peoples direct, rather than receiving their message filtered through mainstream perspectives. It shows the suffering and pain caused by the cumulative effect of colonial policies, short-sighted development patterns, and the denial of Indigenous values and lifestyles.

LINDA CLARKSON and VERN MORRISSETTE are Indigenous people from Winnipeg (Manitoba); GABRIEL REGALLET was programme officer of the International Institute for Sustainable Development, co-ordinating their 'listen and learn' process on Indigenous people and sustainable development.

Indigenous people have always been intimately aware of their symbiotic relationship with the earth based upon a delicate balance between all living things on Turtle Island. This is the name we use for the land that derives its history from the creation story of the Ojibway people – this story is similar in many respects to the creation story of other Indigenous nations. This understanding did not arise from a romanticized version of our relationship to the earth; it developed before contact with other societies and was based upon the basic law. This law was, quite simply, life and death. Indigenous understandings of this have always been quite clear. Through the process of cultural evolution, we have developed our customs, beliefs, institutions and methods of social control; our sense of belonging and connectedness to the earth – all are based upon the original law.

There is a teaching passed down from our ancestors that crystallizes our sense of responsibility and our relationship to the earth that arises out of the original law. It is said that we are placed on the earth (our Mother) to be the caretakers of all that is here. We are instructed to deal with the plants, animals, minerals, human beings and all life as if they were a part of ourselves. Because we are a part of Creation, we cannot differentiate or separate ourselves from the rest of the earth. The way in which we interact with the earth, how we utilize the plants, animals and the mineral gifts, should be carried out with the seventh generation in mind. We cannot simply think of ourselves and our survival: each generation has a responsibility to 'ensure the survival of the seventh generation'.

NATURAL LAW AND SPIRITUALITY

Indigenous people occupied the land for thousands of years before contact with Europeans. During this period of pre-contact, our ancestors developed ways and means of relating to each other and to the land based upon a very simple and pragmatic understanding of their presence on this earth. If they failed to consider what the environment had to offer, how much it could give, and at what times it was prepared to do this, they would simply die. This basic law held for every living thing on the earth. All living creatures had to be cognizant of the structure of the day, the cycle of the seasons and their effects on all other living matter. If the plant world tried to grow in the winter it would die; the earth was not prepared to give life at this time. If the animal world did not heed the changing of the seasons and prepare themselves, by leaving the immediate environment for a more hospitable one or by storing fat for the winter, they would die. If the people were to deplete the animal or plant resources of their immediate environment, pain and suffering could be expected. This understanding gave rise to a relationship that is intimately connected to the sustainability of the earth and its resources.

Our ancestors tell us that the cycles of the seasons were in themselves full of meaning. The changing of the seasons reflected and paralleled the changes in our lives from birth to old age. Spring was a time of renewal, of new life and new beginnings, as in the birth of a child. Summer was a time of plenty, a time to explore and to grow, as in the time of youth. Fall was the time to incorporate the teaching of the previous two cycles and to harvest and crystallize the knowledge that we had been given, as in the middle years of life. Winter was the time of patience and understanding and the time to teach and to plan for the next cycle of life, the time of old age. Not only did the seasons provide us with lessons, but the animals also provided us with teaching about ourselves and our role.

Each animal and plant had something to teach us about our responsibility to the earth. For example, the tiny mouse teaches us to focus, to observe the world with all our energy and our being and to appreciate the wonder of our world. The bear teaches us to walk quietly upon the earth and to live in harmony with the cycles. One had only to observe and to take the time to see with more than our eyes and our mind. These teachings were heeded very solemnly by our ancestors. The institutions and the relationships that developed over thousands of years of interdependence have become tied perennially to our psyche as Indigenous people.

The consequences of this relationship with the earth and its gifts are a profound, intimate and respectful relationship with all living things and a deep reverence for the mystery of life. In our ways, spiritual consciousness is the highest form of politics. When we begin to separate ourselves from that which sustains us, we immediately open up the possibility of losing understanding of our responsibility and our kinship to the earth. When we view the world simply through the eyes of human beings we create further distance between ourselves and our world. When the perceived needs of one spirit being is held above all others, equality disappears. We can view the things of the earth as 'resources' to be used for our own benefit. We can take without thought for the consequences. We can trick ourselves into believing that our life and the life of others has improved. While doing all of this, we can quite readily forget that at some point in time the earth will no longer be able to give and we will no longer be able to take. As the separation between human beings and the earth widens, so the chances of our survival lessen.

From this basic understanding our ancestors assumed their role as the spiritual guardians of the earth. One of the most significant illustrations of this is the central belief that the whole of Creation is a sacred place. Because of this we are directed to exercise respect at all times for the gifts that are bestowed upon us all – not simply for those gifts that sustain our life, but also for the lessons that the Creation provides us with each and every day. At the first level of understanding we can see the relationship between humans and their basic biological needs as they relate to the earth. The second level creates the relationship that ties the biological need to the spiritual. This is a dialectical relationship. More than ingesting the fruits of our labour through one orifice and discharging them through another, it is a fundamental alliance with the earth.

THE EVOLUTION OF INDIGENOUS INSTITUTIONS

The basic law that was the driving force behind the development of our culture is reflected in the institutions and systems of our people. Because of the social nature of human beings, life since time immemorial has been the

Were Savage Indians the Experts Who Helped Draft the Constitution of the United States?

Virtually all traditional tribal people share three primary political principles: (1) all land, water, and forest is communally owned by the tribe; private ownership of land or goods beyond those of the immediate household is unthinkable; (2) all tribal decisions are made by consensus, in which every tribal member participates; and (3) chiefs are not coercive, authoritarian rulers, as we tend to think of them; they are more like teachers and facilitators, and their duties are confined to specific realms (medicine, planting, war, relationships, ceremonies)...

[According to Professor Donald Grinde, Jr., of the University of California at Riverside, in his book *The Iroquois and the Founding of the American Nation*,] the colonists saw freedom widely exercised by American Indians. Even the cultural arrogance and racism of English colonists could not fully disguise their astonishment at finding Native Americans in such a free and peaceful state ...

It is surely one of the most closely guarded secrets of American history that the Iroquois Confederacy had a major role in helping such people as Benjamin Franklin, James Madison, and Thomas Jefferson as they attempted to confederate a new government under democratic principles. Recent scholarship has shown that in the mid-1700s Indians were not only invited to participate in the deliberations of our founding fathers, but that the Great Binding Law of the Iroquois Confederacy became the single most important model for the 1754 Albany Plan of Union, and later the Articles of Confederation and the Constitution.

Jerry Mander, *In the Absence of the Sacred: The Failure of Technology and the Survival of the Indian Nations*, Sierra Club Books, San Francisco, 1991, pp. 227, 233, 230.

story of group process. The hunting and gathering activities aimed at the survival of the group demanded co-operation between individuals to acquire food, materials for shelter and clothing, and implements for hunting and gathering. While the basic law was the driving force, nature was the theatre in which the development of our culture occurred. In this theatre, our ancestors organized themselves into communal groups that were egalitarian, self-sufficient and intimately connected to the land and its resources.

Our ancestors had a capacity for educating their children, outlining social responsibilities, acquiring the necessities for their survival, and for establishing and maintaining relationships among themselves and other bands. All of this occurred inside of a system of organization that derived its parameters from nature – the clan system.

While the ancestors in our territories developed social structures based on hunting and gathering in communal bands, the social structure of other communal-band societies varied. Indigenous people in what is now eastern Canada developed an agricultural economy and a matriarchal system of governing; with its implementation in the longhouse. The West Coast Nations developed different, more elaborate social structures and a higher level of productivity. These differing forms of communal-band society were a reflection of the variation in the resource base, which was a function of climate. The more temperate coastal and southern areas gave rise to more abundant resources which could support a larger population. A larger population required different means of regulating the social, economic and political life of the group. But they shared an understanding about their relationship to the earth with our ancestors and their economy was characteristically the same. They produced to meet their survival needs and did not accumulate. The development of social institutions and mechanisms of social control were premissed upon the same understanding of their relationship to the earth.

The clan system arose from observation of the natural world. The earth was full of knowledge about the way each piece of the environment contributed to the balance of the whole. Each animal and plant had a function that was intimately connected to another aspect of the environment. Our ancestors observed these relationships and based their understanding of themselves on the lessons of the earth. Each animal possessed a gift, a way of living in the total environment that allowed it to fulfil its obligation to the larger order. At the most obvious level, the wolf was considered to be an example of strength and determination with allegiance to the pack and special prowess as a hunter. Those who were born into this clan were expected to understand the wolf and its characteristics in order to understand better their role with respect to the community.

Today, wolf mythology paints a fierce and bloody picture of the life of the wolf. We know him differently. Our Creation story tells of our relationship to the wolf as our first relative. During the time of Creation, the first human was very lonely. Because of this, the wolf was sent to walk with the human until the task of exploring and understanding the Creation was complete. When this was done, the wolf and human were told that they would always walk separate but parallel paths. The strong relationship and dependence on the land and its gifts for survival is the same for the wolf and for humans. As the wolf is threatened, so too is the human.

The clan forms the guidelines for action and for socialization in the group. The responsibilities of each clan laid down the requirements for all aspects of band life. There were medicine people who followed one clan, hunters who followed another, and leaders who followed yet another. At this level, there was opportunity to ensure that the social, economic and political needs of the community were fulfilled in the context of the relationship to the environment. The observations of the animal world illustrated to our ancestors the

A Yupik from Alaska Talks about the Creation of Poverty in His Land

'Poverty' has only recently been introduced to Native communities... for thousands of years people subsisted from the land and ocean along the west coast of Alaska. It was a hard life, but it had none of the frustrations and stigmas of poverty, for the people were not poor. Living from the land sustained life and evolved the Yupik culture, a culture in which wealth was the common wealth of the people as provided by the earth, whether food was plentiful or scarce among the people. This sharing created a bond between people that helped ensure survival. Life was hard then, but people found life satisfying. Today life is getting easier, but it is no longer satisfying.

...With the first Russian traders came the idea of wealth and poverty. These new people added to the process of living the purpose of accumulation. Whether it was furs, money, land or the souls of the converts, lines were drawn between people on the basis of what they had accumulated.... The new economic system ... began replacing food and furs with cash, cooperation with competition, sharing with accumulating.

...White men brought diseases like measles and syphilis, which killed thousands of people.... It is not so well known that the economic impact of western civilization was every bit as devastating to the well-being and spirit of the people ... these new ways of doing things can be as disturbing to the life of a person or of a culture as the measles infection is to the life of a body. Fortunately a cure has been found for measles. A cure has not been found for our 'poverty'.

From Art Davidson (ed.) and the Association of Village Council Presidents, *Does One Way of Life Have to Die So Another Can Live?*, Yupik Nation, Bethel, Ala., 1974.

ways and means by which the earth sustained itself in a manner that established a sense of order and relatedness. Through understanding the animals and their relationship to the earth and their connectedness to other animals and plant life, our ancestors integrated themselves into this natural order.

At another level, each individual could expect to be connected to a large group of extended-family members. That is, it was not simply the mother, father and children that formed the nucleus of the family. The family usually consisted of aunts, uncles, cousins, nieces, nephews and grandparents as members active in the daily operations of family life. Additionally, it was not unusual to 'adopt' new members into the family for various reasons. This would happen whenever a child was orphaned or when a family was unable to care for a child; or whenever there was great respect for someone, so that person would be adopted as a brother or sister.

This kind of family system is different in form and substance from the nuclear family in Western family structures. Inside these extended family systems, the roles and responsibilities were shared. For example, in our system it was not always the role of the mother and father to provide discipline. Rather, it was often the aunts, uncles and cousins who performed this duty. Additionally, each member shared responsibility for educating the children, caring for the sick or injured, providing shelter and obtaining the necessary food requirement for survival.

This understanding of our shared responsibilities and our need to co-operate for survival were the guidelines that further substantiated and solidified our roles inside our family systems. These family systems worked toward the development of the day-to-day survival requirements of our people. The clan system was based upon the observations of the earth and its creations and became reflected in the manner in which we defined and understood ourselves. The communal aspect of family life solidified the meanings of sharing and co-operation among the members of the band and made them an integral part of survival.

DECISION-MAKING AND THE DIVISION OF LABOUR

At the macro-level, when decisions had to be made that affected the whole community, each clan would sit around a central fire with all the other clans. Decisions the clans made together might include when to move, conservation of the resources of the territories, the striking of alliances and relationships with other nations, and how to implement these decisions. Usually, after much discussion and further consultation with clan members, decisions would be made that would respect the interests of all clans and their members. Decisions were not arrived at in the same manner as in Western society, through majority vote. When decisions had to be made, it would be accomplished through a process of consensus. Everyone had to agree with the course of action, or no action was taken.

It might seem that there would be a danger of doing nothing at all, putting the community at risk. But because all people shared an understanding of the survival needs of the community and the patterns of life on the land, this did not usually occur. For example, the decision to move camp to a different part of the territories, because of the changing of the seasons, was one arrived at without great discussion and debate. Survival depended on it and experience had proven to be the best teacher. Decisions arrived at in this manner were then carried through with respect to the responsibilities of each clan and its members. When it was time to implement a decision for the community, each member took their responsibility very seriously and with equal respect for the other's task.

In terms of the division of labour, another aspect of clan politics was reflected in the way the leadership was chosen. While the clan was represented at the central fire, it was not always represented by the same person. In fact, who was there was dependent upon the decision to be made. If it had to do with assessment of the resources of the immediate territory, the clans would send their best hunters and medicine people to discuss the issue at hand. Quite simply, they were the best barometers of resources and could make informed discussion on the subject. Medicine people were used to forecast the potential of resources from their knowledge of the seasons, changes in patterns, and their intimate relationship with the spirit world. If it were a decision that related to contact with another band, warriors and statesmen would be sent to discuss the matter. When we call people warriors, consider it in the context of protectors of the people, not in the sense of a standing army that is the reality of today.

In terms of the decision-making role of the central fire through the clan system, it was not always a static body politic that convened at regular intervals and attempted to answer all the questions of the community. Rather, it was leadership appointed by experience and representation and convened at those times when decisions would have to be made. The Elders of the community were consistently present. It was, and still is, the belief of our people that Elders are to be held in high esteem. They alone have the experience and wisdom of the years and the deep understanding of our roles as Indigenous people and our relationship to Creation.

At the micro-level, the division of labour with respect to the clans and their roles was based upon need, survival and family structure. This was the arena of everyday decision-making affecting each member of the clan and extended family. Each member had a role to play in acquiring the substance of survival. Men were the hunters and the warriors of the community, while women performed the role of teachers and transmitters of values – they were the socializers of the children. The children themselves were teachers to the younger siblings and relatives as well as performing tasks around the camp. The old people were the transmitters of the stories and legends that kept alive our direct connection to the natural order of things and the natural law.

Anthropological studies have often portrayed the life of Indigenous women as hard and laborious, while the lives of men were full of gamesmanship and revelry. It was certainly true that life was hard, but it is obvious in this interpretation that ethnocentric bias rears its head. Men hunted out of survival necessity; not simply as an opportunity to be out in the bush for a wilderness experience. Today, modern man waits for the season, then slips into hunting regalia and sets off to the bush where he pits his skills against the wily creatures of the forest. In true sportsmanlike fashion, he kills the beast, wrenches his trophy from the still warm carcass of the animal and discards the rest to rot in the forest. This was not the case with the Indigenous hunter. With crude instruments by today's standards, the Indigenous hunter entered the forest in communion with nature. Prayers were offered to the spirit of the animal, asking for pity for the hunter and his family so that the animal would give up its life in order to feed and clothe them. Oftentimes the men would return empty-handed and hunger was the outcome. The importance of the women's role as gatherers took on greater significance at this time; without them the family and the community would starve. So the romantic and ethnocentric version of the division of labour in Indigenous societies is quickly relegated to the Western novel and the Western bias from which it arises.

Women's roles centred around the camp. The tasks associated with this are considered, by today's Western standards, as those less appreciated, less worthwhile. Western thought considers this interpretation of women's roles to be sexist and demeaning. In Indigenous societies, it was a survival requirement. Women were the ones who had the ability of creation; they could bring life into the world. Their role was defined by their biology to some degree. As the creators of life, they were charged with the sacred responsibility of caring for the needs of the next generation. This meant that much of the work contributed by the women was in the context of the immediate environment of the camp. However, it is important to note that the work women performed was not devalued as it is in Western society. In fact, we are told that women should be afforded the utmost respect, for it is only they who have the capacity to create new life. They are closer to the Creator than men could ever hope to be. Balance is natural to them, whereas men struggle each day of their lives to achieve and maintain this. The reality was one of survival based upon necessity and co-operation of all members, male and female alike. The manner in which women are treated today in Indigenous communities is not a function of our history, but is more a function of our contact with Western society.

The role that children played with respect to the family and the clan was important to the survival of the group in a significant way. While children were given the opportunity to explore and grow with their gifts, there was an expectation that they would participate in the life of the family and community in more than a playful and inquisitive way. As they grew and learned about their environment, they would be expected to provide a frame of reference for the younger children. Additionally, the older children would be expected to contribute to the family through the gathering of fuel, foodstuffs and materials for the maintenance of the camp.

The old people played a central role in many aspects of the daily life of the people. They were first and foremost the transmitters of the culture itself. Through legends and stories they would impart to all members, including the children, the history of the people and the deep understanding of our relationship to our Mother the earth. They would provide advice and guidance when we became unsure of our role or when we did not know what to do. They watched over the children and protected them from harm. They watched over the parents and ensured that they were doing their part in the care and maintenance of the family and the clan. They advised the appointed leaders by calling upon their years of experience and knowledge of their role and relationship to the Creation.

RESPECT AS THE BASIS OF OUR RELATIONSHIP TO THE EARTH

Sustaining an existence in an environment that changes from season to season, cycle to cycle, has had significant impact on the evolution of culture. The life of the people became a reflection of the life of the earth, and our ancestors became intimately connected to and inseparable from these natural realities. Through many years of experience, trial and error, hunger and hardship, our ancestors learned that the depletion of plant and animal life in their immediate environment meant starvation and death. The practical outcome of this was the movement of the people to match the changes of the season and the cycle of the earth and its gifts. The ways in which our ancestors organized themselves through the clan system and designation of roles and responsibilities were always in relation to the earth and our responsibility to its maintenance and care for future generations. The practical realities of survival gave rise to an understanding of this role as sacred and intimately connected to the Creation. Additionally, the patterns of life could be seen as a circular relationship. Everything that the people did today would have repercussions for tomorrow and for their own survival and the survival of future generations.

As for the sacredness of the land, seeing the world in relationship to ourselves and containing the same essence (spirit) that connected all of us to the Creation excluded the possibility of assuming ownership over Creation or any aspect of it. As Oren Lyons states:

> We native [Indigenous] people did not have a concept of private property in our lexicon, and the principles of private property were pretty much in conflict with our value system. For example you wouldn't see 'No hunting' or 'No fishing' or 'No trespassing' signs in our territories. To a native person such signs would have been equivalent to 'No breathing' because the air is somebody's private property. If you said to the people, 'the Ontario government owns all the air in Ontario, and if you want some, you are going to have to go and see the Bureau of Air', we would all laugh.[1]

All of life had rights of access and use of the land and its gifts within reason. Reason, of course, was based on the reality that exploiting the land to extinction would ultimately mean your own extinction. Although there were distinct and known boundaries of territories marked by rivers, mountains and valleys, these boundaries usually represented some aspect of the territories' ability to sustain the people. That is, it could be expected that the people would utilize several different territories over the course of the seasons. This seasonal migration was a natural conservation technique that was based on the land's ability to sustain life. People did not own the land; they simply used it and moved on, allowing the land and the plant and animal life to regenerate itself.

This understanding held for all living things of the Creation. As there were plant and animal matter in the Creation, there were also people living in the territories, whose life was dependent upon the respectful use of the gifts of the land. Our ancestors were careful to respect the use of the territories and to ensure that they did not infringe upon the livelihood of another people. It is true that differences of opinion occurred between the different Nations, but these matters were usually settled without bloodshed. The reality faced by all peoples of the land was that most energy should be expended in surviving from season to season. Fighting was an unnecessary expenditure of energy where negotiations and discussion would accomplish the same ends. Indigenous people all shared the same understanding of the Creation and the realities of survival. To deviate from this would be a transgression of the role that they had been assigned. Further, the long history of the relationship to the land had ordered the nations so that each sustained their livelihood with respect to the territories and their different gifts. The buffalo hunters maintained their territories, and the hunters of moose and deer maintained theirs. There was more than enough for all the nations to acquire their livelihood from the earth.

NOTE

1. Oren Lyons, *Spirituality, Equality and the Natural Law: Pathways to Self-Determination*, University of Toronto Press, Toronto, 1984.

5

THE SPIRAL OF THE RAM'S HORN: BORAN CONCEPTS OF DEVELOPMENT

Gudrun Dahl and Gemetchu Megerssa

The book *Kam-Ap, or Take-off: Local Notions of Development*, from which the following extract is taken, is the result of a research programme in the Department of Social Anthropology at Stockholm University, which aimed at analysing how the concept of development (and closely related concepts such as progress, modernity, civilization) is used, interpreted, questioned and reproduced in various social contexts in different parts of the world.

In addition to the article reproduced here, the book contains five other studies that could be of interest to students of the development ideology. The first, by Don Kulick, describes how 'Kam-Ap' means 'development' in Gapun, the language of a village in Papua New Guinea, and shows how the ninety inhabitants of this isolated village, due to their perception of development, have shifted away from their vernacular language, Taiap, to Tok Pisin, one of the country's official languages. The villagers link Christianity with 'Kamap' (from 'coming up' or development) and feel that only if and when they become morally good Christians will they become 'developed' like white people in other countries and possess all the worldly goods that white men control. Another article, by Minou Fuglesang, addresses 'Women's Notions of "Development and Modernity" in Lamu Town, Kenya'. Yet another study, by Annika Rabo (who co-edited the volume with Gudrun Dahl and wrote the Introduction), considers 'The Value of Education in Jordan and Syria'.

Kam-Ap, or Take-off: Local Notions of Development was published in 1992 by Stockholm Studies in Social Anthropology (SSSA) and distributed by Almqvist & Wiksell, PO Box 4627, 11691 Stockholm, Sweden.

GUDRUN DAHL is a Swedish anthropologist who, over the last twenty years, has written a number of monographs about societies in the Horn of Africa, particularly pastoral communities. GEMETCHU MEGERSSA is an Oromo from Ethiopia who has specialized in research into Oromo culture and society.

'Development' is an abstract notion, the use of which is ambiguous even in the industrialized and urbanized West. Translation between the expressions used in the dominant Western European languages is difficult enough. The aim of comparing different notions of 'development' between cultures and languages which are distant in terms of space, origin and social context is thus futile. When do we find the notions similar enough to merit comparison at all? When do we classify a concept as corresponding to that of development? Would we include all ideas of a directed historical change in the state of society and its resources? Or do we only refer to concepts relating to the content of that direction in Western thinking – industrialization, rationalization, technological improvement, the acquisition of a Western political and administrative system, literacy, or whatever else 'development' may contain?

People in rural Africa, Asia and Latin America experience 'development' in several ways. They experience in practice processes that are described to them as development, in terms of official discourse inspired by or dressed up in an idiom of Western origin. They can evaluate these processes for themselves in terms of material loss and gain, as well as set them in relation to the values they themselves have for what is a good life. But they also get the ideological message itself. They scrutinize it for its validity in relation to local ideas and also for its consistency with the practical process they have seen. Do the ideal claims of development agree with the praxis? Much of this evaluation is a collective process, interwoven with the routines of daily life. However, there is also a place in the process for the individual thinker, the local intellectual.

In the present chapter, Dadacha, an elder of the Borana tribe, will share with us his ideas of man's place in the historical process and how this process fluctuates between good and bad. We shall also learn of Dadacha's interpretation of the messages about development that he has received as a citizen of Ethiopia and Kenya. These are messages that have reached him partly through his observation and evaluation of actual government practices in Boran areas, and partly through listening to the rhetoric of representatives of the government as it occurs on the local scene or is broadcast on the Kenyan and Ethiopian radio.

The Boran heartland lies in Ethiopia, mainly between the three towns of Moyale, Arero and Tertelle. This is the area where Boran traditions have been maintained most strongly, and which the Borana regard as their cultural centres. Many Borana today live at Marsabit and Waso in Kenya, or as refugees in Nairobi or Somalia. Traditionally, most Borana were pastoral nomads, specializing in cattle, sheep and goats.

This chapter draws mainly on material from two taped interviews undertaken by Gemetchu Megerssa, one concentrated on development issues, the other on ecology.[1] Dadacha, who in real life has another name, has spent most of his life in the border area between Kenya and Ethiopia, but is currently living in exile. His personal background is as a local specialist in

Boran law, custom and ritual. He was educated to hold a high position within the traditional legal organization of the Borana, but has only a couple of years' formal education. He worked as a policeman for a few years. Now he mainly subsists on trade in livestock in one of Ethiopia's neighbouring countries, maintaining in his present setting the role of local sage for the exiled Borana. The interviews were undertaken after thorough discussion between Gudrun Dahl and Gemetchu Megerssa about the issues to be raised, but the general character of the relationship between Gemetchu and Dadacha is that of disciple and teacher, and the interviews have been undertaken in this spirit. They were conducted in Oromo and later translated into English by Gemetchu. It should be recognized that the material presented here represents the views of a man who, even if he has almost no formal schooling, is used to intellectual reflection on societal matters, and to expressing his ideas in a well-organized form. Thus they may be more elaborate and formalized than would be the case if we had tried to depict the ideas of the Boran common man as they can be extracted from the stream of daily life and talk. In other respects, we feel that they are fairly representative. Dadacha's thoughts reflect the norms of a very Boran idea of what generates a beneficial flow of life.

IDEAS OF SOCIETAL AND COSMOLOGICAL ORDER

Before venturing into more specific discussion of 'development', it is necessary to explain some of the general principles around which Dadacha's discourse is normally organized in his lectures to his disciples, particularly in relation to the character of law and its relation to the natural and social order. Borana have a monotheistic idea of God. Waaqa, the heavenly God, can however also be seen as a unity in which are joined a number of cosmic principles, *ayaana*. These are themselves immaterial but have material manifestations in this world.[2] Such manifestations can be characteristics tied to particular calendar days, human personalities and tasks in life, the collective fates of specific groups of people, and so on. Although these *ayaana* are immaterial, they are basic to the order of things and to everyday life. Ideas about them are closely linked to astrology and the use of the human body as a social and cosmological metaphor.

Asked to give the Boran equivalent of the Ethiopian concept of *limaati* and the Kenyan concept of *maendeleo*, both expressions which are abundantly and conventionally used in government discourse as translations of the English word 'development', Dadacha immediately suggests the concept of *fidnaa*. This concept, the full meaning of which is broader than that suggested by 'development', has been discussed by Aneesa Kassam in her article 'The Fertile Past: the Gabbra Concept of Oral Tradition'.[3] Searching for a suitable term for 'oral tradition', Kassam came across *finn duri*, which she translates as 'fertility of long ago'. The basic meaning, she claims, is human, animal and vegetational 'fertility'. However, she also offers a number of applications which suggest a different meaning of *finna* or *fidnaa*. These refer to the mental and psychological states connected with a fertile environment, and with the absence of conflict, dissatisfaction, hunger, disease, and so on. They also imply a fertile exchange of ideas, stimulating and absorbing friendship, and other positive values. As the concept is used by Dadacha, alternative translations might be 'tradition', 'way of life', 'culture' or 'civilization'. A comprehensive translation might be 'the flow of civilized life in the spiritual and material sense'. Dadacha explains:

> When we talk of *fidnaa*, it begins from that of the individual family, then that of different families that make up the grazing community. And that by which the *gadaa* [tribal government] leads the whole people can be generally summed up in that single word *fidnaa*. *Fidnaa* could be seen as existing at higher and lower levels. To begin with the lowest we call it *guddina* [growth]. Then we say it does not end with growth, it leads to something else which we call *gabbina* [well-being and splendour]. Well-being leads to another thing which we call *ball'ina* [expansiveness]. This is linked with what we call *bad'd'aad'a*, a harmony between God and people. This ties up with *hormaata* [capacity for reproduction]. Fertility leads to what we call *dagaaga* [stable and even growth], similar to that of a ram's horn growing in a spiral. Even growth finally leads to what we call *daga-hora* [expanding cultural and political influence]. None of these has in itself any end stage, but we can outline it thus in order to show how it is viewed. This is how we view what you call *maendeleo*.

Dadacha then continues by pointing out that the concepts for growth, well-being and so on all have a very concrete meaning, but that a perceptive person can easily see how they can be applied to more abstract values.

> In order to get to where we are today man had to multiply. Whether we think of livestock or of mankind, they reached their present state through their capacity for reproduction. If there was no such capacity or if it was something that could come to an end, then life would have ended a long time ago. It is the same with the process of *fidnaa*. If the outgoing *gadaa* government had not handed over the knowledge, experience and other *fidnaa* to the incoming rulers then there wouldn't have been anything to continue to build on. This is why we say this thing is something that has growth, splendour, stability and even expansion, which implies expanding political and cultural influence, and so on. To make it clearer let us take what we call *gadaa*. By *gadaa*, we are referring to the body of people who lead the people in general by going in front of them. They are just like the one we call *mangisti* or *sirkaalaa* [Swahili: *serikali*, i.e. the government]. Our Government also has its law. Our law is something similar to what they call *shariya*, by which present-day governments regulate community life, and by which the coexistence of the whole world is regulated. Our law is precisely of this nature, and regulates how people live together. So what keeps this *fidnaa* alive is that the law promotes fertility and access to the necessities of life and comfort, and furthers the reproduction of wealth and the rebuilding of family resources. Laws and custom keep 'development' alive, help it continue, and protect it. A closer look shows that law and custom are themselves part and parcel of 'development'.... Nor can they exist without 'development'. All these things are intertwined...

If we scrutinize Dadacha's arguments, we see that there are a few concepts he returns to. The first is growth and reproduction, the multiplication of riches. The re-creation of vital resources is a central value in many cultures, but the question is whether the relation between growth and continuity in reproduction is particularly characteristic of any economy such as the Boran one. Life flows from God, through the rain that impregnates the soil and fills up the wells. It flows through the sprouting grass and through the mineral water that nourishes the cattle so that their bellies are filled with calves and their udders with milk. This is a flow which is very visible to the Borana and is elaborated upon culturally. If the chain is broken, even only temporarily, the consequences are far-reaching. In a shorter time perspective, human subsistence, mainly based on milk, is very vulnerable to disturbances in reproduction. In a longer perspective, the total survival of the Boran society and culture depends on the survival and rebirth of their herds. Access to many animals and to a large number of children are a concrete insurance of continuity and ongoing well-being.

The second theme in Dadacha's thinking about 'development' is that of a necessary harmony between God and people. This condition is characterized by rain, peace, growth, lack of fear and hunger, and freedom from worries about one's nearest and dearest, by simple and unambiguous legal rules and by a stable, egalitarian and expanding social order that extends to neighbouring peoples. Other traits are the presence of honest and dedicated leaders, and the absence of human and animal disease and of external threats. The local 'ecological' interpretation, so to speak, emphasizes that peace brings rain. Human harmony is most easily achieved when people are satisfied: that in turn brings Divine Harmony, which will re-create good natural conditions.

The third important theme is a view of law as in itself at once divine and created from the consensus of the people. We would suggest that this view is consistent with the general view of divine nature that we have outlined above. As each individual through his personal *ayaana* represents cosmic principles, the sum of individual wills represents the wishes of God. It also represents something which has been handed down from the ancestors but yet is contemporaneously created.

CONSENSUS

The interviewer asks Dadacha to expand his ideas on the concept of *gabbina*, which is translated here as 'splendour' or 'well-being'. The literal meaning of the term is 'the radiance of a well-fed and carefree person'. Dadacha replies that *gabbina* in this context refers to something completely different, to something which is decided communally.

We are talking of the law you set as a point of departure, or something which you agree to achieve. You may agree on the rule of the *gadaa* and then on the law by

> which it should rule. This law protects the water resources from vanishing, protects the kindred and the clan and guarantees that the ponds and the wells are safe, protects even the wild animals and sees to it that the roads do not disappear, that the threshold board of the well does not break ... Such an initial idea of *fidnaa* is presented to the group and they agree on it. When this idea is agreed on without opposition, without excluding anybody, and with no faction wanting to challenge the majority's decision, when it is implemented without distortion, whether in respect of water, war, clanship, roads, wells, the threshold board of the well, or the place where you dispose of waste ... If all matters have been considered, both inside and outside the family context ... then we say the *fidnaa* has splendour. Still it may not yet have growth. Growth comes after this ... whatever will be added to make it larger than before, whether big or small. But if a significant number of people oppose the idea then the *fidnaa* is said to be lacking in splendour and we cannot talk of growth.

Dadacha here picks up one of his main themes, that of a good flow of life as necessarily related to egalitarian consensus and participation. In connection with this theme, he is asked for his general opinion about the present state of the Borana in particular and of the Oromo in general.

> Any human being, whether an individual, group or people, is in *fidnaa* ... our people cannot be outside it, yet there are two types of *fidnaa*. Our people are not in a good *fidnaa* (*fidnaa danssaa*); they are rather in an evil *fidnaa* (*fidnaa hamaa*). To live is not a choice one makes since life is given by God ... But when we say *fidnaa*, it is either one that you as a people make for yourselves or else you live in one made for you. Furthermore, there is also that which is made against you. Our people find themselves in the latter, which is an evil *fidnaa*.

Asked to describe an evil *fidnaa*, Dadacha reiterates:

> First there is the *fidnaa* that you did not make yourself for yourself but which is made for you or forced upon you ... Second, there is the *fidnaa* that you made for yourself or the one that you participated in making. That is another form of *fidnaa* and hence has its distinct character. It does not matter how good or how bad that *fidnaa* may be. When we say our people are in an evil *fidnaa* we are not referring to a *fidnaa* the Oromo made for themselves, but which went evil. Nor are we referring to a *fidnaa* which the Oromo participated in making, but which later went wrong. Rather we refer to the type of *fidnaa* which others made to their own advantage and against the Oromo, and imposed on the latter by force.

As we shall see, free will and participation make up one of the main dimensions used by Dadacha in his evaluation of the messages of 'development' that reach the Borana from the modern state administrations, and how these messages relate to Borana conceptions of *fidnaa*.

CRITICISM OF DEVELOPMENT

The interviewer asks Dadacha to reflect on the fact that both the Ethiopian and the Kenyan governments claim to improve the living conditions of ordinary people. He also asks him to say what he himself thinks should be done. Dadacha's evaluation can be read at different levels. First, it reflects a consciousness of the difference between the ideals claimed and the praxis:

> It is clear that the two views, that of the governments and our view of development, are contradictory. They claim that they are doing everything towards developing us. In contrast the people feel that everything is being done towards our destruction. They have already destroyed us: they are working for our total eradication. The claim of the governments that we are all together, and have everything in common, is a plain lie. They claim that we live for one another. They claim that we have a *fidnaa* in common which they proclaim as though people have agreed to it. It is obvious that he who does evil things never admits that he is doing evil, and as a matter of fact he usually covers it up.

Borana often express a cynical attitude to the practices even of their own leaders. Yet truthfulness is an important aspect of a leader's legitimacy in Boran terms. *Duga* (truthfulness) is the opposite of *chubbu* (sinfulness), and a basic condition of ritual purity. The moral and ritual status of leaders reflects back on the political conditions of human society, but also has a direct bearing on Divine Harmony and hence on God's benevolence in terms of rain, grazing, fertility, and so on.

Apart from this general observation of a divergence between what is done and what is said, it is possible to get a picture of what Dadacha interprets as the content of the governments' claims about themselves as developers. How does he regard these claims in the light both of new development ideals and of his own traditional ideas about the good life? The unfulfilled promises, according to Dadacha, concern, among other things, concrete reforms such as communications and health services, but also technological innovations that could in practice make pastoralism more efficient:

> If it were genuine development, they would have built us roads, they would have taught us how to improve our ways of cultivation and of keeping livestock, how to resist and survive drought, how we could co-operate among ourselves.

In the interview on ecological issues, he raises the same examples:

> If the government had helped in the rehabilitation of the old water wells, had helped people to have enough land according to the grazing communities (*reera*) by advising them not to overgraze in any particular area; if it had supplied them with the necessary medical service for the animals; if it had taught the herdsmen how to give injections to sick animals; if those who milk had been taught how to look after the calves and how to create the conditions that could provide animals with enough water and pasture and see to it they were not overcrowded; if the government had provided the people with educational and medical services whereby they could learn the new ways and after that had left them alone – then we could have regarded it as assistance. But as things stand now, most of the land does not even have a road passing through it. The majority of the people, let alone their animals, have never seen medicine even for human beings. There are people who have never

> heard the sound of a car; there are some who would faint if they saw such a moving metal object! There are those who have never seen what corrugated iron roofs are and who would vomit if they saw them. So why talk about wild animals? These people who are deliberately excluded are still wild animals themselves. First of all the government did not care to make human beings out of these people. So why expect it to protect land, and wild or domestic animals? That is simply not what it is aiming at.

On these issues, apparently, Dadacha does not challenge the prevalent 'modern' ideas about what, in concrete terms, development should actually be about, even slipping into an animal metaphor in describing those people who are excluded from development. In the interview on the environment, however, his complaint is not only that the promised material benefits are just not there; he also takes a more critical attitude towards what modern economic change has implied for the resource basis of the Borana, by emphasizing issues such as the soil erosion caused by extended cultivation and the expansion of tree felling due to urban needs for fuel. Ethiopian attempts at establishing grazing reserve are (probably rightly) discarded as intended to 'create a place where they can fatten the animals which they purchase cheaply from us and send to the land of the Arabs in order to make a profit'. He also objects to the tax demands that the government imposes on the citizens.

> The aims of *limmaati* or *maendeleo* they talk of have always fallen short of reaching our people. Yet they force us to pay for developing their own area. They rob us day and night in the name of development. They do not charge the husband and leave the wife. They do not charge the mother and leave the children. They do not charge you for the cattle and leave the goats. They do not charge you for the horse and leave the mule. They do not charge you for the donkey and leave the camel. The worst form of robbery in the name of development is the fact that, apart from the dog, there is no domestic animal for which we are not taxed. Despite the fact that the land is ours! Despite the fact that we are not traders who bring in commodities from outside!

EDUCATION, LANGUAGE AND CULTURE AS PART OF FIDNAA

At a certain stage in the development interview, the discussion becomes more polemical, and our informant becomes more specifically concerned with the Ethiopian regime (referred to as 'the enemy'). We are talking about imperial as well as revolutionary rule: both are seen as dominated by Amharic interests.

The issue that engaged Dadacha most was education. This is also a field of unfulfilled promises; schools are scarce in the rural Boran areas of Ethiopia. According to him, they can only be found in a few towns, they cater only for the urban population and, in addition, follow an irrelevant curriculum. While the pupils seem to be learning things which are useful for the government, such as Amharic, they learn little of actual use for their own development. Dadacha's criticism on this issue, however, is not only yet another complaint that the government's practice does not live up to the pretensions of its propaganda but also one which relates to a breach in the continuity of *fidnaa* in the sense of a civilized and fertility-enhancing tradition.

> The so-called education, in short, consists of lessons which sustain and strengthen the rule of such evil. In my view, this is not education, I think of it as a device whereby the enemy is out to make people forget what they already know. The device whereby he destroys our age-old wisdom, by making it impossible to pass it down to the younger generation. In such schools, our children, far from studying their own language, are thrown out of school for using it …
>
> What we see being taught in the enemy's schools is the following: in the field of customs, Christianity is what he [the enemy] emphasizes. Christianity is a custom which is strange to our land, one which they [the Amhara] borrowed from the Europeans [*faranji*] since they do not have one of their own. God [*Waaqa*] is my witness that as a people they did not have any culture of any sort. Hence they borrowed. Worst of all is that they also force our young to abandon our own customs and to adopt this borrowed one along with them. In this way our great customary system [*aadaa*] is denied its natural place. The young people no longer learn it. The grown-ups who know it are afraid and are constantly threatened if they use it…

What, in Dadacha's view, constitutes Borana as human beings and as a nation, is their history, language and legal system.

> Our people were not people who lived like wild animals in the bush or in caves. They were not like cattle who were led in any direction, or like birds, and they did not live in trees. Our people are people who have had a *seera* [customary system], an *aadaa* [law], *fidnaa* [traditions/development], language and history of their own … In the days when the white men made the black men stand in line, and shared them out among themselves like cattle rounded up in a ride, or like a loaf of bread broken into pieces and shared, then the Amhara succeeded in enslaving our people under the arms and protection of the white man. From the very beginning the devices used have been clumsy and utterly vicious. In terms of colour the enemy is not white, he is as brown as I am. Yet he has denied the fact that he is of black origin … With the superiority he acquired through the white man's firearms, he massacred our future and present rulers … The enemy hunted down anyone suspected of being the custodian of our wisdom. Any young man suspected of having learnt or inherited wisdom from his father was hunted down and butchered. Only women and children below the age of any type of knowledge were left … That was the beginning of our dark age, the day we were reduced from a people of wisdom to a society of enslaved women and children, who were then given new names and shifted around from the place they originally knew. Between our two settlements the enemy settled his own people. That was the day and the way our people's *fidnaa*, our people's identity and pride, were struck down by the arms of the enemy. That was the day he buried our law, custom, language, history and *fidnaa* in general. Then, on the grave of my image, my identity and my values, he planted a false remembrance tree relating to his own image.

The metaphor that Dadacha uses here refers to the fact that the Oromo usually plant trees on graves. Dadacha means that the Amhara make a false claim to heritage in a common tradition by arguing that Ethiopia is an ancient name. The message is that continuity is important, but not false continuity. Also, identity, wisdom and heritage should be handed down from father to son; in the Boran conception, men are the transmitters of culture and society.

In the passage quoted and in other parts of this interview, Dadacha emphasizes the centrality of language as the transmitter of identity, and the need to guard the knowledge inherited.

> The right to keep our identity as a people is the foundation without which we will have no standing. Even if my *fidnaa* had been bad for me, so that the other one was doing me a favour by forcing me into his, they shouldn't have campaigned against such precious things as my language, history and identity.

LAW OR DISORDER

In the Boran view, equality, democratic consensus, legal regulation and ordered social relations are regarded as necessary to economic welfare. These are concepts which many adherents of the dominant Western ideology of development would agree on, but it is important to note that Dadacha does not refer to them as a way of evaluating 'modern development' in its own terms. He refers to them because the Boran versions of these concepts are essential to him, and because he sees them as absent from the way the government practices development. He has no experience of Western development thinking except as it is filtered through this practice, and through local political rhetoric. There is no reason why he should have insight into such thinking as a body of coherent and formalized ideas.

> To develop the land and the people, they should develop the foundations of the latter's kin system [*golaa]* and the customs of their clans [*gossa*], approved by the people's consensus, making use of that which the people already have, their customary system of voluntary and obligatory contributions, the practices that pertain to water resources and livestock, those belonging to the incense burner and the bed, those of burial and marriage, those of sadness and joy! That customary system which embraces everything including the wild animals, the wild and domestic stock, both with hooves and with cloven feet! Such a great customary system that the world seeks after it, one which is unique, one from which even those who claim to be advanced may learn some things! The enemy campaigned against us, a people with such a *fidnaa*, without giving place to any of our customs in his rule, or offering any reason why these customs had to be rejected! They campaigned to destroy our customs and replace them by their own! That which cared for the high and the low, that which cared for those who have and those who have not, is being destroyed. My *fidnaa* is being made to disappear, the one in which leaders are elected by the people. Instead, people are ruled by mere force of arms. Such is the government that rules us now, a government which has no legal basis for taking over political power but does so by violence.

For Dadacha, violence is not a way to solve societal conflicts. Social order rests on each person knowing his or her place in society, keeping a respectful distance from other social categories, and leaving their position to successors at the appropriate time. It rests on a discussion of what has been handed down by tradition and weds creative change with continuity. To Dadacha, the contrast between the old and the new is therefore to a great extent between an old order based on reason and consensus and one which is based upon the language of violence.

> Moreover, you are debarred from participation in making the *fidnaa* you are forced to live in and at the same time totally denied the right to make one of your own. Once it is decided for you, you have no say in the matter but must obey. This is what does not suit me, as an Oromo. What I would have preferred would have been either to participate in the making of the common *fidnaa*, or to have the right to speak out about what I feel is good and bad for me. If someone else is supposed to make *fidnaa* for me, it would have made sense if the new *fidnaa* were to be based on the one I already have. Had there been any kind of dialogue in order to amalgamate the two sides, so as to build the new *fidnaa* on a ground common to both parties, then I would have said that we made it together. But the other side denies me any say in the whole affair and rejects the *fidnaa* that I had already made for myself. He denies me the right to live according to it, and instead forces me to go in an opposite direction to that which was mine. You know that, unless forced, nobody will leave his own *fidnaa* and follow that of another.

Continuity is a critical issue in pastoral production. The right amounts of rain at the right moments; the recuperation of vegetation struck by drought; the fecundity and regrowth of livestock herds; the production of milk over the seasons – all these are fragile assets. Material well-being among pastoralists is not only assumed by religious precepts to be very vulnerable to disturbances in the social order. Such disturbances are a very real threat to the necessary input of motivated and knowledgeable labour in sufficient quantity. When political unrest or poverty – caused by warfare and drought – force young men to turn temporarily away from involvement in herding to wage labour in agricultural or urban areas, the physical reproduction of the herds under proper management suffers. So also does the transmission of the necessary husbandry knowledge from generation to generation. Poverty, insecurity and labour shortage may force the herdsmen to desert vital pastures; however temporary such desertion may seem to be to begin with, these areas are then easily lost to competing neighbours or to innovative forms of arid land use such as tourism or irrigation. These dimensions of continuity are common to all pastoral societies and visible to the external observer.[4] The Borana do not elaborate on all of them, but for them the development of material well-being cannot be separated conceptually from social and cultural aspects of 'the flow of civilized life'. It is continuity in orderly social relations, in the guardianship of traditional wisdom and growth of knowledge and in political consensus-making that re-creates good conditions for livestock, and hence for people. Law, language and history are fundamental to this: peaceful human life is the creative force that carries development on until one day bad *fidnaa* follows upon good *fidnaa*, as surely as night follows day.

NOTES

1. The interview was undertaken in 1988 and the specific government referred to was that of the Derg in Ethiopia.
2. G. Megerssa, 'The Concept of *Ayaana* and Its Relevance to the Oromo World-view', unpublished research report, Department of Anthropology and Sociology, School of Oriental and African Studies, University of London, 1990.
3. A. Kassam, 'The Fertile Past: The Gabra Concept of Oral Tradition', *Africa*, vol. 56, no. 2, 1986.
4. G. Dahl and G. Megerssa, 'The Sources of Life: Boran Conceptions of Wells and Water', in G. Palson, ed., *From Water to World-making*, Scandinavian Institute of African Studies, Uppsala, 1990.

PART TWO

THE DEVELOPMENT PARADIGM

6

THE IDEA OF PROGRESS

Teodor Shanin

TEODOR SHANIN is Professor of Sociology at the University of Manchester. He is the author of numerous books and articles on peasants and peasant culture, including *Introduction to the Sociology of 'Developing Societies'* (Penguin, London, 1971), *Late Marx and the Russian Road: Marx and the Peripheries of Capitalism* (Monthly Review Press, New York, 1983) and (with Hamza Alavi) *The Roots of Otherness: Russia as a 'Developing Society'* (Macmillan, London, 1984).

The following text was written specially for this Reader.

Answering Nilu

The idea of progress is the major philosophical legacy left by the seventeenth to nineteenth centuries to the contemporary social sciences. The idea was secular, departing from the medieval mind-set where everything could be explained by God's will, and it offered a powerful and pervasive supra-theory that ordered and interpreted everything within the life of humanity – past, present and future. The core of the concept, and its derivations and the images attached to it, have been overwhelmingly simple and straightforward. With a few temporary deviations, all societies are advancing naturally and consistently 'up', on a route from poverty, barbarism, despotism and ignorance to riches, civilization, democracy and rationality, the highest expression of which is science. This is also an irreversible movement from an endless diversity of particularities, wasteful of human energies and economic resources, to a world unified and simplified into the most rational arrangement. It is therefore a movement from badness to goodness and from mindlessness to knowledge, which gave this message its ethical promise, its optimism and its reformist 'punch'. The nature of the interdependence of the diverse advances – economic, political, cultural and so on – has been the subject of fundamental divisions and debate; for example, is it the growth of rationality or of the forces of production which acts as the prime mover? What was usually left unquestioned was the basic historiography of the necessary sequence and/or stages along the main road of progress as the organizing principle on which all other interpretations rest.

It is important to acknowledge that the idea of progress – its conceptual apparatus as much as the values, images and the emotions it attracted – was not restricted to the philosophers and to the philosophizing community of scholars, but penetrated all strata of contemporary societies to become the popular common sense, and as such resistant to challenge. Consequently even when some actual experience challenged that vision (as it often did), such evidence was usually brushed aside as accidental or transitional while the belief in progress and its implications held firm. The wording changed with fashion: 'progress', 'modernization', 'development', 'growth', and so on. So did the legitimizations: 'civilizing mission', 'economic efficiency', 'friendly advice'. Yet the substantive message proved remarkably resilient.

This power of the idea of progress – as indicated by a popularity and plausibility which survived so well for two centuries – should be considered before turning to its impact on human thought and action. This in part reflected the onset of the so-called 'Industrial Revolution', and the first flush of triumphal belief in the ceaseless production of endlessly proliferating material goods, making humanity happy. But, as significant and yet mostly disregarded, the idea of progress, I would suggest, was generated as an ambiguous and yet, to its authors and consumers, remarkably satisfying solution to two major riddles the Europeans faced at the dawn of what later came to be called 'modernity'.

The first was the rapid growth of evidence concerning the diversity of humanity. The established assumptions as to what is self-evident and 'natural' in human interaction and in the ways societies are arranged, based on the simple device of 'looking at ourselves', crumbled as European travellers and conquerors progressively discovered new lands, new people and new ways. The old conceptual duality of the civilized versus the barbarian (or Christians versus the infidels) was proving wholly inadequate to the volume of everyday experience that challenged it. The endless and growing diversity of human societies that was perceived had to be made sense of, or at least ordered and categorized, in a way acceptable to its discoverers.

The second riddle that historical experience presented to Europe's secular minds concerned the changing perception of time. For most of written history, the dominant model in this sphere was a cyclical one: the biological metaphor of the youth, maturity, old age and death of societies and empires which organized human understanding; the myth of eternal return, present in religion and legend.[1] In that model, the end was the beginning; and while humans and societies lived by it, the structure and the essentials of such a world remained intact – Plutarch or Cicero read as true to the eighteenth century European literati as a contemporary. However, in the period which interests us here, the dawn of a new era was increasingly being felt. The old images of time and of the natural repetition of events were out of joint. The end was no longer the beginning, but was something else: a linear perception of time and a shift into an as yet uncharted future reflected what centuries

Fraud, Luxury and Pride: The Causes of Prosperity

The problem of the relationship between economics and morality was acutely – indeed, explosively – posed by Mandeville at the beginning of the [eighteenth] century.

Bernard de Mandeville, born in the Netherlands, settled in London as a physician. In 1705 he published a sixpenny satire in verse called *The Grumbling Hive; Or, Knaves Turn'd Honest*. This poem in doggerel verse grew into a book by the addition of 'Remarks' and other pieces in two successive editions (1714, 1723), under the title, *The Fables Of The Bees; or, Private Vices, Publick Benefits* (Kaye's edition: Mandeville, 1924). The sub-title summarizes the argument of the poem: a hive, presented as a mirror of human society, lives in corruption and prosperity. Harbouring some nostalgia for virtue, it prays to recover it. When the prayer is granted, an extraordinary transformation takes place: with vice gone, activity and prosperity disappear and are replaced by sloth, poverty and boredom in a much reduced population…

Moreover, of the trio of vices, 'Fraud, Luxury and Pride', that are given in the poem as the causes of prosperity and greatness, ('The Moral', 1924, p. 23, vs 7), the first, Fraud, was finally retained only as one of the 'inconveniences' that accompany a brisk trade, like the dirt in the streets of London. Only Luxury and, more fundamentally, Pride, maintain their status as causal factors….

…In Hume, justice owes its origin, on the one hand, to the egoism and limited generosity of men, on the other, to the fact that the nature of relations to things over the relations between men cannot be more forcibly and naively expressed. This is the decisive shift that distinguishes modern civilization from all others, in which primacy is given to the economic view in our ideological universe. It is this shift that, whatever his intimate convictions may have been, Mandeville has described, for us, as well as for his contemporaries, in *The Fable of the Bees: or Private Vices, Publick Benefits*.

Louis Dumont, *From Mandeville to Marx, The Genesis and Triumph of Economic Ideology*, University of Chicago Press, Chicago, 1977, pp. 63–4, 81. Louis Dumont has written another seminal work: *Homo Hierarchicus: Le Système des castes et ses implications*, Gallimard, Paris, 1979 [1967].

later would be called a 'take-off' period for Europe. It was a time of puzzlement.

The idea of progress was the dramatic resolution of two great riddles by linking them. What produced diversity? The different stages of development of different societies. What was social change? The necessary advance through the different social forms that existed. What is the task of social theory? To provide an understanding of the natural sequence of stages from past to future. What is the duty of an enlightened ruler? To put to use the findings of scholars and to speed up the necessary 'advance', fighting off regressive forces which try to stop it. The new orientation within the complex world of human endeavours carried the immense promise and optimism of the belief that, once understood, the human world could be reformed scientifically, that is, by taking into account knowledge of the necessary and the objective. What boosted confidence and optimism was that those who first adopted the notion of progress presented their own understanding as the highest achievement of progress to date, and consequently projected the shape of the coming future to the rest of mankind – as an example to all, a natural leader of all. This lent the idea its immense arrogance.

Once it was established as the major means of orientation in a complex human world, the idea of progress developed a life of its own. It interacted powerfully with the 'Industrial Revolution' and urbanization, as much as with the spread of colonialism, giving them for a time an almost metaphysical meaning – an image of the unilinear and the necessary which was also universally right and positive in the unfolding of human history. Knowledge of the world was classified accordingly: some societies as 'developed', others as 'underdeveloped', in need of help, tutelage, and so on. The 'advanced' societies were showing to all the rest their own futures. The argument was about the correct indices and triggers of 'development', not about the significance of existing divisions. This fed into the various political visions and, moving with the times, entered the newly created academic disciplines of the social sciences – Sociology, Anthropology, Economics – taking the form of modernization theories, 'strategies of development', and programmes of 'growth'. The Kautskian Marxism of the Second International and the eventual adoption of a version of it as the obligatory ideology of the Soviet Union shows the overriding nature of the idea of progress, whatever the party politics involved. The only questions that remained to be asked were: Who is the most progressive? Who is to set the example to the others? Which utopia will bring about human bliss?

The impact of the idea of progress (involving, as it did, modernization theory, development strategy, the goal of economic growth, and so on) was threefold: as a general orientation device, as a powerful tool of mobilization, and as an ideology. On the face of it at least, its contribution as an interpretation of social reality – the ordering, classification and comprehension of the complexities of human reality – has stood up to the endless proliferation of information. In many ways it promoted understanding by focusing on interconnections and on the causes of the social changes observed. What is more, it made social planning possible, intellectually respectable and indeed necessary, due to its foundation in objective – that is, established, necessary and repetitive – patterns of history, which scientists and technicians could mathematize and computerize. It became, accordingly, also an immensely 'energizing' tool of policy and counterpolicy, as well as serving to mobilize the devotion and readiness of its followers, who were often prepared to sacrifice much – often life itself – to help speed up the inevitable approach of the necessary and glorious future.

The idea of progress, with its many derivations, has also become an important ideology – a blinker on collective cognition. Up to a point, it became the 'normal science' as defined by Kuhn where, once established, a field of knowledge defines its own questions, brushing aside as illegitimate other questions, and evidence, which do not fit its assumptions.[2] That was not all, for service to progress became an important justification employed by both development experts and hardened politicians, enabling them to override whatever did not fit their vision – views and people alike – and to award themselves massive privileges of power, status and well-being, while most people were turned into objects of manipulation (for their own good, of course). There developed a particular expert style: brash, smart, detached. For the majority, the cause of progress took away, for the sake of scientific planning, the right to choose and even to understand why their own experience was increasingly being negated. Endless planning disasters followed, while the planners earned their promotions and moved on.

The most significant 'material' representation and instrument of the idea of progress has been the modern state, with its legitimation as the representation of the nation, its claims to bureaucratic rationality and to an understanding of the objectively necessary ways humans are managed, and its strategies resting on a notion of progress linked to the power to disburse privileges and to enforce ways and means. While the struggle for power and the choice between alternatives increasingly became a battle between interest groups for the control of the state machinery and its resources of intervention and enforcement, it was usually disguised as debate about the interpretation of the objective laws of progress. 'Progress', 'development', 'growth' and so forth became the main ideological *raison d'être* for statehood, the governability of people, and the enforcement of privileges. As such, the pre-1991 East–West division was remarkably limited in fact, which partly explains why so little changed with the end of the Cold War. Neither did the spread of multinationals and indirect US dictatorship via the International Monetary Fund over the weaker parts of the global community change substantively the progress-and-statehood ideologies justifying the advantage of the privileged and the major irrationalities perpetrated by the guardians of official rationalism. It is not accidental that the major expressions of widespread anger and defiance, in East and West, North and South, have taken the form of deep, virulent anti-statism. The image of the Great Brother, the brute enforcer and all-invasive presence in human life which makes it unbearable, has never been so pertinent as it is now, even though disaffection is largely expressed in apathy and counter-manoeuvre rather than in open rebellion.

Thus the idea of progress eventually became a powerful ideology of disenfranchisement, and often generated remarkable acts of cruelty, accepted as 'insignificant in the long term' and therefore permissible – indeed a duty – to the elite of 'those who know'. The remarkable, often fanatical will with which the idea of progress was realized in the high-speed reform programmes bears comparison with the Christianity of the Middle Ages. Its message of mutual love – and we do not doubt its positive significance for European civilization – was turned into absolute truth and universal historiography for the human race. To speed up the Second Coming, crusades carried war and murder through the world, while the Holy Inquisition disposed of doubters and deviants. Life itself was sacrificed for the necessary future. To paraphrase Acton: absolutist theory (and unrestricted zeal) corrupts absolutely (and the remarkable cruelty it engenders is made palatable to its perpetrators and victims).

The limitations of the progressivist became increasingly apparent. This severely limited or delayed knowledge of extensive evidence which did not fit the particular model of progress – be it Islamic revival, 'minorities' (which are majorities in an increasing number of populations), communism which exploits, capitalism which stifles economic development, and so on. Ideas of limitless linear growth blinded us to the complexity of the social world – to the diverse and parallel forms which operate side by side without being transitory; the so-called informal or expolary[3] family economies of survival within the 'post-industrial' world. Such ideas also delayed our understanding of ecological issues. Real human history, accounting for the complexity of forms rather than their conforming to a pre-defined process of universalization and simplification, was being lost. The blueprint of progress/development/growth offered blank cheques to repressive bureaucracies, both national and international, to act on behalf of science and to present as objective matters which are essentially political, thereby taking choice away from those influenced most by such decisions.

As often happens with overarching conceptualizations in retreat, the ideas of progress have not been replaced at once by a new vision. What has come instead over the last decade is various forms of capitulation on the part of intellectuals: amounting to the view that nothing can any longer be seen as comprehensive. Within the current critique of modernity and its explanations by the postmodernists, with everything turned relative except relativity itself, the idea of progress reaches its peculiar final stage of impact through negation. Nevertheless, the rhetoric of 'progress' will not disappear so long as it serves powerful interest groups. Those who find the unmasked consequences of the idea of progress reprehensible depart for the most part into private lives, while 'the masses' can proceed with life in a consumer society of goods and entertainments, amid fears of incomprehensible global 'markets' and global 'unemployment', while society's centre becomes increasingly empty of human content.

Those who wish to face up to the substantive failure of one total theory that mankind adhered to in the last two centuries, and to do so without surrender, should probably begin where it all began to disintegrate: with the issue of the human content of social structures and entrenched ideologies – that is, matters of choice. We all know the limitations of human choice within contemporary society. We have to comprehend better and learn to put to use the limits of such limitations.

NOTES

1. M. Eliade, *The Myth of the Eternal Return*, Arkana, Harmondsworth, 1989; Princeton University Press, Princeton, N.J., 1992.
2. T. Kuhn, *The Structure of Scientific Revolutions*, University of Chicago Press, Chicago, 1970.
3. For 'expolary', see T. Shanin, 'Expolary Economies: A Political Economy of Margins', paper delivered to Colloquium on Alternative Economies, Toronto, May 1988.

The Loss of All Meaning

Never has the individual been so completely delivered up to a blind collectivity, and never have men been less capable, not only of subordinating their actions to their thoughts, but even of thinking. Such terms as oppressors and oppressed, the idea of classes – all that sort of thing is near to losing all meaning, so obvious are the impotence and distress of all men in the face of the social machine, which has become a machine for breaking hearts and crushing spirits, a machine for manufacturing irresponsibility, stupidity, corruption, slackness and, above all, dizziness.

The reason for this painful state of affairs is clear. We are living in a world in which nothing is made to man's measure; there exists a monstrous discrepancy between man's body, man's mind and the things which at the present time constitute the elements of human existence; everything is in disequilibrium. There is not a single category, group or class of men that is altogether exempt from this destructive disequilibrium, except perhaps for a few isolated patches of more primitive life; and the younger generation, who have grown and are growing up in it, inwardly reflect the chaos surrounding them more than do their elders....

This disequilibrium is essentially a matter of quantity. Quantity is changed into quality, as Hegel said, and in particular a mere difference in quantity is sufficient to change what is human into what is inhuman. From the abstract point of view quantities are immaterial, since you can arbitrarily change the unit of measurement; but from the concrete point of view certain units of measurement are given and have hitherto remained invariable, such as the human body, human life, the year, the day, the average quickness of the human mind. Present-day life is not organized in the scale of all these things; it has been transported to an altogether different order of magnitude, as though men were trying to raise it to the level of the forces outside nature while neglecting to take their own nature into account. If we add that, to all appearances, the economic system has exhausted its constructive capacity and is beginning to be able to function only by undermining, little by little, its own material foundations, we shall perceive in all its simplicity the veritable essence of the bottomless misery that forms the lot of the present generations.

Simone Weil

Simone Weil (1909–1943) was an extraordinarily lucid witness of our time: T.S. Eliot called her 'a kind of genius, akin to that of the saints'. Yet, strangely enough, she is little known, even now, to the public at large. Her prophetic thoughts, published mostly in the 1950s, after her death, are however amazingly relevant to our present-day realities. The above excerpts are from a study she wrote in 1934, *Reflections Concerning the Causes of Liberty and Social Oppression*, which she considered her principal work. Camus praised it as being unequalled, since Marx's writings, in its social, political and economic insights. The English version of the excerpts is taken from *The Simone Weil Reader*, David McKay, New York, 1977, p. 29. See also Suggested Readings.

7

FAUST, THE FIRST DEVELOPER

Marshall Berman

The book *All That Is Solid Melts into Air: The Experience of Modernity* (Verso, London and Penguin, New York, 1983), from which this extract is reproduced, takes its title from a sentence used by Karl Marx to describe the universe of 'modern bourgeois society', which the author of *The Communist Manifesto* compares to 'the sorcerer who is no longer able to control the powers of the underworld that he has called up by his spells'. 'Goethe's *Faust*: The Tragedy of Development' forms Part One of the book. Chapters 1–3 deal with the three metamorphoses of Goethe: the first as a 'dreamer', the second as a 'lover', and the third as a 'developer'. The final chapter of this part ends with an epilogue on the 'Faustian and Pseudo-Faustian Age'.

MARSHALL BERMAN is Professor of Political Science at the City College, New York. He formerly taught at Stanford and at the University of New Mexico. His other publications include *The Politics of Authenticity: Radical Individualism and the Emergence of Modern Society* (Atheneum, New York, 1970), *Coming to Our Senses: Body and Spirit in the Hidden History of the West* (Simon & Schuster, New York, 1989), and many articles, including in *The Nation*, *Partisan Review* and *Dissent* (of which he is a member of the Editorial Board).

The vital force that animates Goethe's *Faust*, that marks it off from its predecessors, and that generates much of its richness and dynamism, is an impulse that I will call the desire for *development*. Goethe's Faust tries to explain this desire to his devil; it isn't all that easy to explain. Earlier incarnations of Faust have sold their souls in exchange for certain clearly defined and universally desired good things of life: money, sex, power over others, fame and glory. Goethe's Faust tells Mephistopheles that, yes, he wants these things, but these things aren't in themselves what he wants... What this Faust wants for himself is a dynamic process that will include every mode of human experience, joy and misery alike, and that will assimilate them all into his self's unending growth; even the self's destruction will be an integral part of its development.

One of the most original and fruitful ideas in Goethe's *Faust* is the idea of an affinity between the cultural ideal of *self*-development and the real social movement toward *economic* development. Goethe believes that these two modes of development must come together, must fuse into one, before either of these archetypally modern promises can be fulfilled. The only way for modern man to transform himself, Faust and we will find out, is by radically transforming the whole physical, social and moral world he lives in. Goethe's hero is heroic by virtue of liberating tremendous repressed human energies, not only in himself but in all those he touches, and eventually in the whole society around him. But the great developments he initiates – intellectual, moral, economic, social – turn out to exact great human costs. This is the meaning of Faust's relationship with the devil: human powers can be developed only through what Marx called 'the powers of the underworld', dark and fearful energies that may erupt with a horrible force beyond all human control. Goethe's *Faust* is the first, and still the best, *tragedy of development*...

THIRD METAMORPHOSIS: THE DEVELOPER

...Now Faust takes on what I call his third and final metamorphosis. In his first phase, as we saw, he lived alone and dreamed. In his second period, he intertwined his life with the life of another person, and learned to love [Gretchen]. Now in his last incarnation, he connects his personal drives with the economic, political and social forces that drive the world; he learns to build and to destroy. He expands the horizon of his being from private to public life, from intimacy to activism, from communion to organization. He pits all his powers against nature and society; he strives to change not only his own life but everyone else's as well. Now he finds a way to act effectively against the feudal and patriarchal world: to construct a radically new social environment that will empty the old world out or break it down.

So far this is a typical theme of romantic melancholy, and Mephisto hardly notices. It's nothing personal, he says; the elements have always been this way. But now, suddenly, Faust springs up enraged: Why should men let things go on being the way they have always been? Isn't it about time for mankind to assert itself against nature's tyrannical arrogance, to confront natural forces in the name of 'the free spirit that protects all rights'? Faust has begun to use post-1789 political language in a context that no one has ever thought of as political. He goes on: it is outrageous that, for all the vast energy expended by the sea, it merely surges endlessly back and forth – 'and nothing is achieved!' This seems natural enough to Mephisto, and no doubt to most of Goethe's audience, but not to Faust himself:

> This drives me near to desperate distress!
> Such elemental power unharnessed, purposeless!
> There dares my spirit soar past all it knew;
> Here I would fight, this I would subdue!

Faust's battle with the elements appears as grandiose as King Lear's, or, for that matter, as King Midas's whipping of the waves. But the Faustian enterprise will be less quixotic and more fruitful, because it will draw on nature's own energy and organize that energy into the fuel for new collective human purposes and projects of which the archaic kings could hardly have dreamt.

As Faust's new vision unfolds, we see him come to life again. Now, however, his visions take on a radically new form: no longer dreams and fantasies, or even theories, but concrete programmes, operational plans for transforming earth and sea. 'And it is possible! … Fast in my mind, plan upon plan unfolds.' Suddenly the landscape around him metamorphoses into a site. He outlines great reclamation projects to harness the sea for human purposes: man-made harbours and canals that can move ships full of goods and men; dams for large-scale irrigation; green fields and forests, pastures and gardens, a vast and intensive agriculture; waterpower to attract and support emerging industries; thriving settlements, new towns and cities to come – and all this to be created out of a barren wasteland where human beings have never dared to live. As Faust unfolds his plans, he notices that the devil is dazed, exhausted. For once he has nothing to say. Long ago, Mephisto called up the vision of a speeding coach as a paradigm of the way for a man to move through the world. Now, however, his protégé has outgrown him: Faust wants to move the world itself.

We suddenly find ourselves at a nodal point in the history of modern self-awareness. We are witnessing the birth of a new social division of labour, a new vocation, a new relationship between ideas and practical life. Two radically different historical movements are converging and beginning to flow together. A great spiritual and cultural ideal is merging into an emerging material and social reality. The romantic quest for self-development, which has carried Faust so far, is working itself out through a new form of romance, through the titanic work of economic development. Faust is transforming himself into a new kind of man, to suit himself to a new occupation. In his new work, he will work out some of the most creative and some of the most destructive potentialities of modern life; he will be the consummate wrecker and creator, the dark and deeply ambiguous figure that our age has come to call 'the developer'.

Goethe is aware that the issue of development is necessarily a political issue. Faust's projects will require not only a great deal of capital but control over a vast extent of territory and a large number of people. Where can he get this power? The bulk of Act Four provides a solution. Goethe appears uncomfortable with this political interlude; his characters here are uncharacteristically pale and flaccid, and his language loses much of its normal force and intensity. He does not feel at home with any of the existing political options and wants to get through this part fast. The alternatives, as they are defined in Act Four, are: on one side, a crumbling multinational empire left over from the Middle Ages, ruled by an emperor who is pleasant but venal and utterly inept; on the other side, challenging him, a gang of pseudo-revolutionaries out for nothing but power and plunder, and backed by the Church, which Goethe sees as the most voracious and cynical force of all. (The idea of the Church as a revolutionary vanguard has always struck readers as far-fetched, but recent events in Iran suggest that Goethe may have been on to something.)

We should not belabour Goethe's travesty of modern revolution. Its main function is to give Faust and Mephisto an easy rationale for the political bargain they make: they lend their minds and their magic to the Emperor, to help him make his power newly solid and efficient. He, in exchange, will give them unlimited rights to develop the whole coastal region, including *carte blanche* to exploit whatever workers they need and displace whatever indigenous people are in their way. 'Goethe could not seek the path of democratic revolution', Lukács writes.[1] The Faustian political bargain shows Goethe's vision of 'another way' to progress: 'Unrestricted and grandiose development of productive forces will render political revolution superfluous.' Thus Faust and Mephisto help the Emperor prevail. Faust gets his concession, and, with great fanfare, the work of development begins.

Faust throws himself passionately into the task at hand. The pace is frenzied – and brutal. An old lady, whom we will meet again, stands at the edge of the construction side and tells the story:

> Daily they would vainly storm
> Pick and shovel, stroke for stroke;
> Where the flames would nightly swarm
> Was a dam when we awoke.
> Human sacrifices bled,
> Tortured screams would pierce the night,
> And where blazes seaward spread
> A canal would greet the light.

The old lady feels that there is something miraculous and magical about all this, and some commentators think that Mephistopheles must be operating behind the scenes for so much to be accomplished so fast. In fact, however, Goethe assigns Mephisto only the most peripheral role in this project. The only 'forces of the underworld' at work here are the forces of modern industrial organization. We should note, too, that Goethe's Faust – unlike some of his successors, especially in the twentieth century – makes no striking scientific or technological discoveries: his men seem to use the same picks and shovels that have been in use for thousands of years. The key to his achievement is a visionary, intensive and systematic organization of labour. He exhorts his foremen and overseers, led by Mephisto, to 'use every possible means/ To get crowds and crowds of workers here./ Spur them on with enjoyment, or be severe,/ Pay them well, allure or repress!' The crucial point is to spare nothing and no one, to overleap all boundaries: not only the boundary between land and sea, not only traditional moral limits on the exploitation of labour, but even the primary human dualism of day and night. All natural and human barriers fall before the rush of production and construction.

Faust revels in his new power over people: it is, specifically, to use an expression of Marx's, a power over labour-power:

> Up from your beds, my servants! Every man!
> Let happy eyes behold my daring plan.
> Take up your tools, stir shovel now and spade!
> What has been staked must at once be made.

He has found, at last, a fulfilling purpose for his mind:

> What I have thought, I hasten to fulfil;
> The master's word alone has real might!...
> To consummate the greatest work,
> One mind for a thousand hands will do.

But if he drives his workers hard, so he drives himself. If church bells called him back to life long ago, it is the sound of shovels that vivifies him now. Gradually, as the work comes together, we see Faust radiant with real pride. He has finally achieved a synthesis of thought and action, used his mind to transform the world. He has helped mankind assert its rights over the anarchic elements, 'bringing the earth back to itself./ Setting the waves a boundary,/ Putting a ring around the ocean.' And it is a collective victory that mankind will be able to enjoy once Faust himself is gone. Standing on an artificial hill created by human labour, he overlooks the whole new world that he has brought into being, and it looks good. He knows he has made people suffer ... But he is convinced that it is the common people, the mass of workers and sufferers, who will benefit most from his great works. He has replaced a barren, sterile economy with a dynamic new one that will 'open up space for many millions/ To live, not securely, but free for action [*tatig-frei*].' It is a physical and natural space, but one that has been created through social organization and action.

Walking the earth with the pioneers of his new settlement, Faust feels far more at home than he ever felt with the friendly but narrow folk of his home town. These are new men, as modern as Faust himself. Emigrants and refugees from a hundred Gothic villages and towns – from the world of *Faust, Part One* – they have moved here in search of action, adventure, an environment in which they can be, like Faust himself, *tatig-frei*, free to act, freely active. They have come together to form a new kind of community: a community that thrives not only on the repression of free individuality in order to maintain a closed social system, but on free constructive action in common to protect the collective resources that enable every individual to become *tatig-frei*.

These new men feel at home in their community and proud of it; they are eager to put their communal will and spirit against the sea's own energy, confident they will win. In the midst of such men – men whom he has helped to come into their own – Faust can fulfil a hope he has cherished ever since he left his father's side: to belong to an authentic community, to work with and for people, to use his mind in action in the name of a general will and welfare. Thus the process of economic and social development generates new modes of self-development, ideal for men and women who can grow into the emerging new world. Finally, too, it generates a home for the developer himself.

Thus Goethe sees the modernization of the material world as a sublime spiritual achievement; Goethe's Faust, in his activity as 'the developer' who puts the world on its new path, is an archetypal modern hero. But the developer, as Goethe conceives him, is tragic as well as heroic. In order to understand the developer's tragedy, we must judge his vision of the world not only by what it sees – by the immense new horizons it opens up for mankind – but also by what it does not see: what human realities it refuses to look at, what potentialities it cannot bear to face. Faust envisions, and strives to create, a world where personal growth and social progress can be had without significant human costs. Ironically, his tragedy will stem precisely from his desire to eliminate tragedy from life.

As Faust surveys his work, the whole region around him has been renewed, and a whole new society created in his image. Only one small piece of ground along the coast remains as it was before. This is occupied by Philemon and Baucis, a sweet old couple who have been there from time out of mind. They have a little cottage on the dunes, a chapel with a little bell, a garden full of linden trees. They offer aid and hospitality to shipwrecked sailors and wanderers. Over the years they have become beloved as the one source of life and joy in this wretched land. Goethe borrows their name and situation from Ovid's *Metamorphoses*, in which they alone offer hospitality to Jupiter and Mercury in disguise, and, accordingly, they alone are saved when the gods flood and destroy the whole land. Goethe gives them more individuality than they have in Ovid, and endows them with distinctively Christian virtues: innocent generosity, selfless devotion, humility, resignation. Goethe invests them, too, with a distinctively modern pathos. They are the first embodiments in literature of a category of people that is going to be very large in modern history: people who are in the way – in the way of history, of progress, of development; people who are classified, and disposed of, as obsolete.

Faust becomes obsessed with this old couple and their little piece of land: 'That aged couple should have yielded./ I want their lindens in my grip,/ Since these few trees that are denied me/ Undo my worldwide ownership. Hence is our soul upon the rack,/ To feel, amid plenty, what we lack.' They must go, to make room for what Faust comes to see as the culmination of his work: an observation tower from which he and his public can 'gaze out into the infinite' at the new world they have made. He offers Philemon and

Baucis a cash settlement, or else resettlement on a new estate. But what should they do with money at their age? And how, after living their whole long lives here, and approaching the end of life here, can they be expected to start new lives somewhere else? They refuse to move. 'Resistance and such stubbornness/ Thwart the most glorious success/ Till in the end, to one's disgust/ One soon grows tired of being just.'

At this point, Faust commits his first self-consciously evil act. He summons Mephisto and his 'mighty men' and orders them to get the old people out of the way. He does not want to see it, or to know the details of how it is done. All that interests him is the end result: he wants to see the land cleared next morning, so the new construction can start. This is a characteristically modern style of evil: indirect, impersonal, mediated by complex organizations and institutional roles. Mephisto and his special unit return in 'deep night' with the good news that all has been taken care of. Faust, suddenly concerned, asks where the old folks have been moved – and learns that their house has been burned to the ground and they have been killed. Faust is aghast and outraged, just as he was at Gretchen's fate. He protests that he didn't say anything about violence; he calls Mephisto a monster and sends him away. The prince of darkness departs gracefully, like the gentleman he is; but he laughs before he leaves. Faust has been pretending not only to others but to himself that he could create a new world with clean hands; he is still not ready to accept responsibility for the human suffering and death that clear the way. First he contracted out all the dirty work of development; now he washes his hands of the job, and disavows the jobber once the work is done. It appears that the very process of development, even as it transforms a wasteland into a thriving physical and social space, re-creates the wasteland inside the developer himself. This is how the tragedy of development works.

But there is still an element of mystery about Faust's evil act. Why, finally, does he do it? Does he really need that land, those trees? Why is his observation tower so important? And why are those old people so threatening? Mephisto sees no mystery in it: 'Here, too, occurs what long occurred:/ Of Naboth's vineyard you have heard.' Mephisto's point, in invoking King Ahab's sin in I Kings 21, is that there is nothing new about Faust's acquisition policy: the narcissistic will to power, most rampant in those who are most powerful, is the oldest story in the world. No doubt he is right; Faust does get increasingly carried away by the arrogance of power. But there is another motive for the murder that springs not merely from Faust's personality, but from a collective, impersonal drive that seems to be endemic to modernization: the drive to create a homogeneous environment, a totally modernized space, in which the look and feel of the old world have disappeared without a trace.

To point to this pervasive modern need, however, is only to widen the mystery. We are bound to be in sympathy with Faust's hatred for the closed, repressive, vicious Gothic world where he began – the world that destroyed Gretchen, and she was not the first. But at this point in time, the point where he becomes obsessed with Philemon and Baucis, he has already dealt the Gothic world a death blow: he has opened up a vibrant and dynamic new social system, a system oriented toward free activity, high productivity, long-distance trade and cosmopolitan commerce, abundance for all; he has cultivated a class of free and enterprising workers who love their new world, who will risk their lives for it, who are willing to pit their communal strength and spirit against any threat. It is clear, then, that there is no real danger of reaction. So why is Faust threatened by even the slightest traces of the old world? Goethe unravels, with extraordinary penetration, the developer's deepest fears. This old couple, like Gretchen, personify all the best that the old world has to give. They are too old, too stubborn, maybe even too stupid, to adapt and to move; but they are beautiful people, the salt of the earth where they are. It is their beauty and nobility that make Faust so uneasy. 'My realm is endless to the eye, behind my back I hear it mocked.' He comes to feel that it is terrifying to look back, to look the old world in the face. 'And if I'd rest there from the heat, their shadows would fill me with fear.' If he were to stop, something dark in those shadows might catch up with him. 'That little bell rings, and I rage!'

Those church bells, of course, are the sound of guilt and doom and all the social and psychic forces that destroyed the girl he loved: who could blame him for wanting to silence that sound forever? Yet church bells were also the sound that, when he was ready to die, called him back to life. There is more of him in those bells, and in that world, than he likes to think. The magical power of the bells on Easter morning was their power to put Faust in touch with his childhood. Without that vital bond with his past – the primary source of spontaneous energy and delight in life – he could never have developed the inner strength to transform the present and future. But now that he has staked his whole identity on the will to change, and on his power to fulfil that will, his bond with his past terrifies him.

> That bell, those lindens' sweet perfume
> Enfolds me like a church or tomb.

For the developer, to stop moving, to rest in the shadows, to let the old people enfold him, is death. And yet, to such a man, working under the explosive pressures of development, burdened by the guilt it brings him, the bells' promise of peace must sound like bliss. Precisely because Faust finds the bells so sweet, the woods so lovely, dark and deep, he drives himself to wipe them out.

Commentators on Goethe's *Faust* rarely grasp the dramatic and human resonance of this episode. In fact, it is central to Goethe's historical perspective. Faust's destruction of Philemon and Baucis turns out to be the ironic climax of his life. In killing the old couple, he turns out to be pronouncing a death sentence on himself. Once he has obliterated every trace of them and their world, there is nothing left for him to do. Now he is ready to pronounce the words that seal his life in fulfilment and deliver him over to death: *Verweile doch, du bist so schoen!* Why should Faust die now? Goethe's reasons refer not only to the structure of *Faust, Part Two* but to the whole structure of modern history. Ironically, once this developer has destroyed the premodern world, he has destroyed his whole reason for being in the world. In a totally modern society, the tragedy of modernization – including its tragic hero – comes naturally to an end. Once the developer has cleared all the obstacles away, he himself is in the way, and he must go. Faust turns out to have been speaking truer than he knew: Philemon and Baucis's bells were tolling for him after all. Goethe shows us how the category of obsolete persons, so central to modernity, swallows up the man who gave it life and power.

Faust almost grasps his own tragedy – almost, but not quite. As he stands on his balcony at midnight and contemplates the smouldering ruins that will be cleared for construction in the morning, the scene suddenly and jarringly shifts: from the concrete realism of the construction site, Goethe plunges us into the symbolist ambience of Faust's inner world. Suddenly four spectral women in grey hover towards him, and proclaim themselves: they are Need, Want, Guilt and Care. All these are forces that Faust's programme of development has banished from the outer world; but they have crept back as spectres inside his mind. Faust is disturbed but adamant, and he drives the first three spectres away. But the fourth, the vaguest and deepest one, Care, continues to haunt him. Faust says, 'I have not fought my way through to freedom yet.' He means by this that he is still beset by witchcraft, magic, ghosts in the night. Ironically, however, the threat to Faust's freedom springs not from the presence of these dark forces but from the absence that he soon forces on them. His problem is that he cannot look these forces in the face and live with them. He has striven mightily to create a world without want, need or guilt; he does not even feel guilty about Philemon and Baucis – though he does feel sad. But he cannot banish care from his mind. This might turn out to be a source of inner strength, if only he could face the fact. But he cannot bear to confront anything that might cast shadows on his brilliant life and works. Faust banishes care from his mind, as he banished the devil not long before. But before she departs, she breathes on him – and with her breath strikes him blind. As she touches him, she tells him that he has been blind all along; it is out of inner darkness that all his visions and all his actions have grown. The care he would not admit has stricken him to depths far past his understanding. He destroyed those old people and their little world – his own childhood world – so that his scope of vision and activity could be infinite; in the end, the infinite 'Mother Night', whose power he refused to face, is all he sees.

Faust's sudden blindness gives him, in his last scene on earth, an archaic and mythical grandeur: he appears as a peer of Oedipus and Lear. But he is a distinctively modern hero, and his wound only drives him to drive himself and his workers harder, to finish the job fast:

Deep night now seems to fall more deeply still,
Yet inside me there shines a brilliant light;
What I have thought I hasten to fulfil;
The master's word alone has real might!

And so it goes. It is at this point, amid the noise of construction, that he declares himself fully alive, and hence ready to die. Even in the dark his vision and energy go on thriving; he goes on striving, developing himself and the world around him to the very end.

NOTE

1. Georg Lukács, *Goethe and His Age*, trans. Robert Anchor, Merlin Press, London, 1968.

The 'Clandestine Passengers' in the Development Discourse

There are those who feel that 'development' is such a huge and vague notion that it is absurd to reject it totally and that it can very well be used to stimulate 'alternative projects' which go against the dominant trend. Marie-Dominique Perrot shows that everything depends on the existence of presuppositions, the 'clandestine passengers in the text': these are shared by intergovernmental organizations (UNDP) transnational corporations (CIBA-Geigy) and non-governmental organizations (the French Catholic Committee against Hunger and for Development). All of them accept that 'development' exists, that it is known, desirable and universal. From there on, the discourse closes up on itself, but not before it has trapped the critical interlocutor: whoever accepts the implicit facts (that is, the presuppositions given by the text) can only legitimize, in turn, the need for 'development' to resolve the 'problems of the Third World.'

If, in sum, 'development' is synonymous with life (or, which comes to the same thing, with 'meeting basic needs'), who can question it? It is enough, then, to undertake any activities (including commercial ones) 'in the name of development' for them to be seen as such and for our perception to become a 'reality'. And this is all the more difficult to verify because the organizations usually have a monopoly over information about their 'projects' and they are seldom asked whether the 'signs of development' (factories, wells, tractors, etc.) have any real meaning for the 'target populations'.

Gilbert Rist

'I work for development therefore I develop; I develop therefore I am a development organization. What's more, I speak the truth, because I can prove it.' (Taken for granted is the fact that the evidence of it all is constituted by the material effects of development.) A small but disturbing question keeps nagging: 'what confirms that my proof is to be trusted?' In order that this question remain hidden, the discourse must be legitimate and authoritative, with the reader taking it on trust. These three factors – legitimacy, authority and faith – provide the ground on which a power relationship develops between the producers and the receivers of the development discourse, in favour of the former.

The former have the legitimacy and the authority, while the latter are expected to show their faith. Implicitly, the fact of being there and of practising in the field is understood as bringing about automatically, and somehow naturally, reliable knowledge about the situation on the one hand, and appropriate activities on the other. Put more simply, through their development discourse the development organizations affirm: we are in the field, *therefore* we know; we have practical experience, *therefore* we contribute to development. These simplistic conclusions have an almost magical effect: mere presence brings about knowledge and almost any old activity is equivalent to 'doing development work'.

Obviously nobody will admit to reasoning like this. Nevertheless, it is precisely what the reader or the donor is expected to believe. How can one explain that the implicit meaning of peremptory affirmations about development is accepted without question (except when there is a financial problem, which happens now and again)? The answer lies partly in the efficacy of this 'terrorist effect'. The power of the development discourse helps to maintain the illusion that practice *per se* results in development: all the more so as it is indeed unseemly, given the situation in the Third World, to ask too many questions about those working in this field.

On the other hand, development organizations benefit from the distance factor, both geographically and culturally, which means that they have established a field of activity that is protected from any criticisms, save those they themselves choose to make. When the chips are down we know very little about what is happening except what has been filtered by the organizations. Nor is it easy to get access to the files and to the accounts of development projects and of the organizations themselves. And even these files do not tell the whole story of the work in the field: they produce some sort of 'directions for use' that impose a selective reading of reality that depends on the development logic followed by the project. The lay person thus has virtually no means of getting informed except by asking the institutions that have an interest in disseminating a specific kind of information. True, it seems better to choose one organization rather than another, but this choice will be based mainly on the principles promoted by their discourse, the obscurities of which remain intact. It is true that the organizations do have to 'show' concrete results, but what often happens is that they do not explain what is actually going on in the field; usually they are satisfied just to assure the donors, in very general and positive terms, that *something* is happening. They pick on all signs of what, in their eyes, are positive changes and present them as heralding development.

These discourses usually have a prophetic connotation, which makes it possible to accept an indefinite postponement of the achievements that they have predicted and are continuing to pursue. But, as development as an objective does not seem to materialize, the obstacles are presented as justifying *a fortiori* the existence of these very development organizations, at the same time as bestowing the aura of heroes upon them.

The failure of a project, in fact, is seldom presented as such, still less as being the responsibility of the organization. Instead of talking about failure or mere problems that inevitably arise, an organization usually prefers to dwell on the obstacles to development. Everything preventing development from taking place can be placed in that category so that, in the end, responsibility for failure is not attributed to the organization. Given all the phenomena that can be considered as 'obstacles', the organization's image appears both more impressive (hence acquiring more legitimacy) and more vulnerable (therefore needing more support). The ambivalence of this image helps it to organize its own reproduction successfully.

Marie-Dominique Perrot

From Gilbert Rist and Fabrizio Sabelli, *Il était une fois le développement*, Editions d'En-Bas, Lausanne, 1986, pp. 104–6. Translated by V.B.

Gilbert Rist is professor at the Institute Universaire d'études du Développement, Geneva, and the author of several books challenging the development concept, the last of which is *Développement: histoire d'une croyance occidentale*, Presses des Sciences-Po, Paris, 1996. Marie-Dominique Perrot is professor at the same Institute; she has written extensively on development and the presuppositions underlying the concept. See Suggested Readings.

8

THE MAKING AND UNMAKING OF THE THIRD WORLD THROUGH DEVELOPMENT

Arturo Escobar

The following text is extracted from Chapter 2, 'The Problematization of Poverty: The Tale of Three Worlds and Development', of *Encountering Development: The Making and Unmaking of the Third World*, Princeton University Press, Princeton, N.J., 1995. The book poses a number of fundamental questions. For example, why did the industrialized nations of North America and Europe come to be seen as the appropriate models of post-World War II societies in Africa, Asia and Latin America? How did the postwar discourse on development actually create the so-called Third World? The book shows how development policies became mechanisms of control that were just as pervasive and effective as their colonial counterparts. The development apparatus generated categories powerful enough to shape the thinking even of its occasional critics, while poverty and hunger became widespread. 'Development' was not even partially 'deconstructed' until the 1980s, when new tools for analysing the representation of social reality were applied to specific 'Third World' cases. The author deploys these new techniques in a provocative analysis of development discourse and practice in general, concluding with a discussion of alternative visions for a post-development era.

ARTURO ESCOBAR is a Colombian anthropologist who is currently teaching at the University of Massachusetts, Amherst. He is one of the first thinkers to have attempted analysis of the development discourse using Foucauldian methodology.

THE DISCOURSE OF DEVELOPMENT

What does it mean to say that development started to function as a discourse, that is, that it created a space in which only certain things could be said and even imagined? If discourse is the process through which social reality comes into being – if it is the articulation of knowledge and power, of the visible and the expressible – how can the development discourse be individualized and related to ongoing technical, political and economic events? How did development become a space for the systematic creation of concepts, theories and practices?

An entry point for this inquiry on the nature of development as discourse is its basic premisses as they were formulated in the 1940s and 1950s. The organizing premiss was the belief in the role of modernization as the only force capable of destroying archaic superstitions and relations, at whatever social, cultural, and political cost. Industrialization and urbanization were seen as the inevitable and necessarily progressive routes to modernization. Only through material advancement could social, cultural and political progress be achieved. This view determined the belief that capital investment was the most important ingredient in economic growth and development. The advance of poor countries was thus seen from the outset as depending on ample supplies of capital to provide for infrastructure, industrialization, and the overall modernization of society. Where was this capital to come from? One possible answer was domestic savings. But these countries were seen as trapped in a 'vicious circle' of poverty and lack of capital, so that a good part of the 'badly needed' capital would have to come from abroad.... Moreover, it was absolutely necessary that governments and international organizations take an active role in promoting and orchestrating the necessary efforts to overcome general backwardness and economic underdevelopment.

What, then, were the most important elements that went into the formulation of development theory, as gleaned from the earlier description? There was the process of capital formation, and the various factors associated with it: technology, population and resources, monetary and fiscal policies, industrialization and agricultural development, commerce and trade. There was also a series of factors linked to cultural considerations, such as education and the need to foster modern cultural values. Finally, there was the need to create adequate institutions for carrying out the complex task ahead: international organizations (such as the World Bank and the International Monetary Fund, created in 1944, and most of the United Nations technical agencies, also products of the mid-1940s); national planning agencies (which proliferated in Latin America, especially after the inauguration of the Alliance for Progress in the early 1960s); and technical agencies of various kinds.

Development was not merely the result of the combination, study, or gradual elaboration of these elements (some of these topics had existed for some time); nor the product of the introduction of new ideas (some of which were already appearing or perhaps were bound to appear); nor the effect of the new international organizations or financial institutions (which had some predecessors, such as the League of Nations). It was rather the result of the establishment of a set of relations among these elements, institutions and practices and of the systematization of these relations to form a whole. The development discourse was constituted not by the array of possible objects under its domain but by the way in which, thanks to this set of relations, it was able to form systematically the objects of which it spoke, to group them and arrange them in certain ways, and to give them a unity of their own.[1]

To understand development as a discourse, one must look not at the elements themselves but at the system of relations established among them. It is this system that allows the systematic creation of objects, concepts and strategies; it determines what can be thought and said. These relations – established between institutions, socio-economic processes, forms of knowledge, technological factors, and so on – define the conditions under which objects, concepts, theories and strategies can be incorporated into the discourse. In sum, the system of relations establishes a discursive practice that sets the rules of the game: who can speak, from what points of view, with what authority, and according to what criteria of expertise; it sets the rules that must be followed for this or that problem, theory or object to emerge and be named, analysed, and eventually transformed into a policy or a plan.

The objects with which development began to deal after 1945 were numerous and varied. Some of them stood out clearly (poverty, insufficient technology and capital, rapid population growth, inadequate public services, archaic agricultural practices, and so on), whereas others were introduced with more caution or even in surreptitious ways (such as cultural attitudes and values and the existence of racial, religious, geographic or ethnic factors believed to be associated with backwardness). These elements emerged from a multiplicity of points: the newly formed international organizations, government offices in distant capitals, old and new institutions, universities and research centres in developed countries, and, increasingly with the passing of time, institutions in the Third World. Everything was subjected to the eye of the new experts: the poor dwellings of the rural masses, the vast agricultural fields, cities, households, factories, hospitals, schools, public offices, towns and regions, and, in the last instance, the world as a whole. The vast surface over which the discourse moved at ease practically covered the entire cultural, economic and political geography of the Third World.

However, not all the actors distributed throughout this surface could identify objects to be studied and have their problems considered. Some clear principles of authority were in operation. They concerned the role of experts, from whom certain criteria of knowledge and competence were asked; institutions such as the United Nations, which had the moral, professional and legal authority to name subjects and define strategies; and the international lending organizations, which carried the symbols of capital and power. These principles of authority also concerned the governments of poor countries, which commanded the legal political authority over the lives of their subjects, and the position of leadership of the rich countries, which had the power, knowledge, and experience to decide on what was to be done.

Economists, demographers, educators, and experts in agriculture, public health and nutrition elaborated their theories, made their assessments and

Silence! We Are Developing!

A certain mystifying discourse soon spread all over Africa. 'Partisan divisions are over. Everyone should unite behind the leader in the struggle for economic development. ' In short: 'Silence! We are developing!' And in the process we have lost both development and democracy: 'Silence! We are killing!' Both through the open violence of the kalashnikovs and the deaf violence of structures. Stabilization funds aimed at protecting peasants from world price fluctuations have, in fact, served to accumulate surpluses during the good years, without rebates to the producers during the poor years. Thus, they often became the private safes of leaders who used them to build up their personal foreign accounts, hence contributing to the disinvestment and the plundering of their own country. As for the cadres, they migrate in masses. Why? Because an educational system inherited from the colonizer, which has not been fundamentally reformed, combined with an economy in which industrialization is structurally blocked by the absence of a sizeable market and an effective demand, have turned the African school into a factory to produce the unemployed. But also because the political conditions are often suffocating, almost suicidal, for the intellectuals. Africa, which contains 50 per cent of the world's refugees, suffers from a veritable collective cerebral haemorrhage. Eighty-five per cent of the research on Africa takes place outside the continent.

Joseph Ki-Zerbo, from his preface to Ahmadou A. Dicko, *Journal d'une défaite*, L'Harmattan/Dag Hammarskjöld Foundation, 1992. (Translated by M.R.) Ki-Zerbo is president of the Centre des Recherches pour le Développement Endogène (CRDE), BP 606, Ouagadougou, Burkina Faso. See also pp. 153–4 below.

observations, and designed their programmes from these institutional sites. Problems were continually identified, and client categories brought into existence. Development proceeded by creating 'abnormalities' (such as the 'illiterate', the 'underdeveloped', the 'malnourished', 'small farmers', or 'landless peasants'), which it would later treat and reform. Approaches that could have had positive effects in terms of easing material constraints became, linked to this type of rationality, instruments of power and control. As time went by, new problems were progressively and selectively incorporated: once a problem was incorporated into the discourse, it had to be categorized and further specified. Some problems were specified at a given level (such as local or regional), or at various of these levels (for instance, a nutritional deficiency identified at the level of the household could be further specified as a regional production shortage or as affecting a given population group), or in relation to a particular institution. But these refined specifications did not seek so much to illuminate possible solutions as to give 'problems' a visible reality amenable to particular treatments.

This seemingly endless specification of problems required detailed observations in villages, regions and countries in the Third World. Complete dossiers of countries were elaborated, and techniques of information were designed and constantly refined. This feature of the discourse allowed for the mapping of the economic and social life of the countries, constituting a true political anatomy of the Third World.[2] The end result was the creation of a space of thought and action, the expansion of which was dictated in advance by the very same rules introduced during its formative stages. The development discourse defined a perceptual field structured by grids of observation, modes of inquiry and registration of problems, and forms of intervention: in short, it brought into existence a space defined not so much by the ensemble of objects with which it dealt but by a set of relations and a discursive practice that systematically produced interrelated objects, concepts, theories, strategies, and the like.

To be sure, new objects have been included, new modes of operation introduced, and a number of variables modified (for instance, in relation to strategies to combat hunger, knowledge about nutritional requirements, the types of crops given priority, and the choices of technology have changed); yet the same set of relations among these elements continues to be established by the discursive practices of the institutions involved. Moreover, seemingly opposed options can easily coexist within the same discursive field (for instance, in development economics, the structuralist school and the monetarist school seem to be in open contradiction – yet they belong to the same discursive formation and originate in the same set of relations; it can also be shown that agrarian reform, Green revolution, and integrated rural development are strategies through which the same unity, 'hunger', is constructed).... In other words, although the discourse has gone through a series of structural changes, the architecture of the discursive formation laid down in the period 1945–55 has remained unchanged, allowing the discourse to adapt to new conditions. The result has been the succession of development strategies and substrategies up to the present, always within the confines of the same discursive space.

It is also clear that other historical discourses influenced particular representations of development. The discourse of communism, for instance, influenced the promotion of those choices which emphasized the role of the individual in society, and, in particular, those approaches which relied on private initiative and private property. So much emphasis on this issue in the context of development, so strong a moralizing attitude, probably would not have existed without the persistent anti-communist preaching that originated in the Cold War. Yet the ways in which the discourse organized these elements cannot be reduced to causal relations.

In a similar vein, patriarchy and ethnocentrism influenced the form development took. Indigenous populations had to be 'modernized', where modernization meant the adoption of the 'right' values – namely, those held by the white minority or a mestizo majority and, in general, those embodied in the ideal of the cultivated European; programmes for industrialization and agricultural development, however, have not only made women invisible in their role as producers but have also tended to perpetuate their subordination. Forms of power in terms of class, gender, race and nationality thus found their way into development theory and practice. The former do not determine the latter in a direct causal relation: rather, they are the development discourse's formative elements.

The examination of any given object should be done within the context of the discourse as a whole. The emphasis on capital accumulation, for instance, emerged as part of a complex set of relations in which technology, new financial institutions, systems of classification (GNP per capita), decision-making systems (such as new mechanisms for national accounting and the allocation of public resources), modes of knowledge, and international factors all played a role. What made development economists privileged figures was their position in this complex system. Options privileged or excluded must also be seen in light of the dynamics of the entire discourse – why, for instance, the discourse privileged the promotion of cash crops (to secure foreign exchange, according to capital and technological imperatives) and not food crops; centralized planning (to satisfy economic and knowledge requirements) but not participatory and decentralized approaches; agricultural development based on large mechanized farms and the use of chemical inputs but not alternative agricultural systems, based on smaller farms, ecological considerations, and integrated cropping and pest management; rapid economic growth but not the articulation of internal markets to satisfy the needs of the majority of the people; and capital-intensive but not labour-intensive solutions. With the deepening of the crisis, some of the previously excluded choices are being considered, although most often within a developmentalist perspective, as in the case of the sustainable development strategy.

Finally, what is included as legitimate development issues may depend on specific relations established in the midst of the discourse: relations, for instance, between what experts say and what international politics allows as feasible (this may determine, for instance, what an international organization may prescribe out of the recommendations of a group of experts); between one power segment and another (say, industry versus agriculture); or between two or more forms of authority (for instance, the balance between nutritionists and public health specialists, on the one hand, and the medical profession, on the other, which may determine the adoption of particular approaches to rural health care). Other types of relations to be considered are those between sites from which objects appear (for instance, between rural and urban areas); between procedures of assessment of needs (such as the use of 'empirical data' by World Bank missions), and the position of authority of those carrying out the assessment (this may determine the proposals made and the possibility of their implementation).

Relations of this type regulate development practice. Although this practice is not static, it continues to reproduce the same relations between the elements with which it deals. It was this systematization of relations that conferred upon development its great dynamic quality: its immanent adaptability to changing conditions, which allowed it to survive, indeed to thrive, up to the present. By 1955 a discourse had emerged which was characterized not by a unified object but by the formation of a vast number of objects and strategies; not by new knowledge but by the systematic inclusion of new objects under its domain. The most important exclusion, however, was and continues to be, what development was supposed to be all about: people. Development was – and continues to be for the most part – a top-down, ethnocentric and technocratic approach, which treated people and cultures as abstract concepts, statistical figures to be moved up and down in the charts of 'progress'. Development was conceived not as a cultural process (culture was a residual variable, to disappear with the advance of modernization) but instead as a system of more or less universally applicable technical interventions intended to deliver some 'badly needed' goods to a 'target' population. It comes as no surprise that development became a force so destructive to Third World cultures, ironically in the name of people's interests.

The crucial threshold and transformation that took place in the early post-World War II period discussed [above] were the result not of a radical epistemological or political breakthrough but of the reorganization of a number of factors that allowed the Third World to display a new visibility and to irrupt into a new realm of language. This new space was carved out of the vast and dense surface of the Third World, placing it in a field of power. Underdevelopment became the subject of political technologies that sought to erase it from the face of the earth but that ended up, instead, multiplying it to infinity.

Development fostered a way of conceiving of social life as a technical problem, as a matter of rational decision and management to be entrusted to that group of people – the development professionals – whose specialized knowledge allegedly qualified them for the task. Instead of seeing change as a process rooted in the interpretation of each society's history and cultural tradition – as a number of intellectuals in various parts of the Third World had attempted to do in the 1920s and 1930s (Gandhi being the best known of them) – these professionals sought to devise mechanisms and procedures to make societies fit a pre-existing model that embodied the structures and functions of modernity. Like sorcerers' apprentices, the development professionals awakened once again the dream of reason that, in their hands, as in earlier instances, produced a troubling reality.

At times, development grew to be so important for Third World countries that it became acceptable for their rulers to subject their populations to an infinite variety of interventions, to more encompassing forms of power and systems of control; so important that First and Third World elites accepted the price of massive impoverishment, of selling Third World resources to the most convenient bidder, of degrading their physical and human ecologies, of killing and torturing, of condemning their indigenous populations to near extinction; so important that many in the Third World began to think of themselves as inferior, underdeveloped and ignorant and to doubt the value of their own culture, deciding instead to pledge allegiance to the banners of reason and progress; so important, finally, that the achievement of development clouded awareness of the impossibility of fulfilling the promises that development seemed to be making.

After four decades of this discourse, most forms of understanding and representing the Third World are still dictated by the same basic tenets. The forms of power that have appeared act not so much by repression as by normalization; not by ignorance but by controlled knowledge; not by humanitarian concern but by the bureaucratization of social action. As the conditions that gave rise to development became more pressing, it could only increase its hold, refine its methods, and extend its reach even further. That the materiality of these conditions is not conjured up by an 'objective' body of knowledge but is charted out by the rational discourses of economists, politicians and development experts of all types should already be clear. What has been achieved is a specific configuration of factors and forces in which the new language of development finds support. As a discourse, development is thus a very real historical formation, albeit articulated around an artificial construct (underdevelopment), which must be conceptualized in different ways if the power of the development discourse is to be challenged or displaced.

To be sure, there is a situation of economic exploitation that must be recognized and dealt with. Power is too cynical at the level of exploitation and should be resisted on its own terms. There is also a certain materiality of life conditions that is extremely preoccupying and that requires great effort and attention. But those seeking to understand the Third World through development have long lost sight of this materiality by building upon it a reality that, like a castle in the air, has haunted us for decades. Understanding the history of the investment of the Third World by Western forms of knowledge and power is a way to shift the ground somewhat so that we can start to look at that materiality with different eyes and in different categories.

The coherence of effects that the development discourse achieved is the key to its success as a hegemonic form of representation: the construction of the poor and underdeveloped as universal, preconstituted subjects, based on the privilege of the representers; the exercise of power over the Third World made possible by this discursive homogenization (which entails the erasure of the complexity and diversity of Third World peoples, so that a squatter in Mexico City, a Nepalese peasant, and a Tuareg nomad become equivalent to each other as poor and underdeveloped); and the colonization and domination of the natural and human ecologies and economies of the Third World.[3]

Development assumes a teleology to the extent that it proposes that the 'natives' will sooner or later be reformed; at the same time, however, it reproduces endlessly the separation between reformers and those to be reformed by keeping alive the premiss of the Third World as different and inferior, as having a limited humanity in relation to the accomplished European. Development relies on this perpetual recognition and disavowal of difference, a feature identified by Bhabha[4] as inherent to discrimination. The signifiers of 'poverty', 'illiteracy', 'hunger' and so forth have already achieved a fixity as signifieds of 'underdevelopment' which seems impossible to sunder.

NOTES

1. The methodology for the study of discourse used in this section follows that of Michel Foucault. See especially M. Foucault, *The Archeology of Knowledge*, Harper Colophon Books, New York, 1972; and 'Politics and the Study of Discourse', in Graham Burchell, Colin Gordon and Peter Miller, eds, *The Foucault Effect*, University of Chicago Press, Chicago, 1991, pp. 53–72.
2. The loan agreements (Guaranteed Agreements) between the World Bank and recipient countries signed in the late 1940s and 1950s invariably included a commitment on the part of the borrower to provide 'the Bank', as it is called, with all the information it requested. It also stipulated the right of Bank officials to visit any part of the territory of the country in question. The 'missions' that this institution periodically sent to borrowing countries was a major mechanism for extracting detailed information about those countries.
3. The coherence of effects of the development discourse should not signify any sort of intentionality. As with the discourses discussed by Foucault, development must be seen as a 'strategy without strategists', in the sense that nobody is explicitly masterminding it; it is the result of a historical problematization and a systematized response to this.
4. Homi K. Bhabha, 'The Other Question: Difference, Discrimination and the Discourse of Colonialism', in Russell Ferguson et al., *Out There: Marginalization and Contemporary Cultures*, New Museum of Contemporary Art, New York and MIT Press, Cambridge, Mass., 1990, pp. 71–89.

9

DEVELOPMENT AS PLANNED POVERTY

Ivan Illich

In his introduction to Illich's *Celebration of Awareness*, Erich Fromm said of his writings (see Suggested Readings) that 'they represent humanistic radicalism in its fullest and most imaginative aspect. The author is a man of rare courage, great aliveness, extraordinary erudition and brilliance ... whose whole thinking is based on his concern for man's unfolding – physically, spiritually and intellectually ... [His thoughts] have a liberating effect on the mind by showing entirely new possibilities.' Ivan Illich has continued to refine the human and intellectual qualities to which Fromm refers all along his pilgrimage on the path to his Truth. He is currently teaching at Bremen University and at Penn State University, Philadelphia. This text is reproduced from Chapter 11 of *Celebration of Awareness* (Marion Boyars, London, 1971), a dozen essays that address social and educational questions.

It is now common to demand that the rich nations convert their war machine into a programme for the development of the Third World. The poorer four-fifths of humanity multiply unchecked while their per-capita consumption actually declines. This population expansion and decrease of consumption threaten the industrialized nations, who may still, as a result, convert their defence budgets to the economic pacification of poor nations. And this in turn could produce irreversible despair, because the ploughs of the rich can do as much harm as their swords. United States trucks can do more lasting damage than United States tanks. It is easier to create mass demand for the former than for the latter. Only a minority needs heavy weapons, while a majority can become dependent on unrealistic levels of supply for such productive machines as modern trucks. Once the Third World has become a mass market for the goods, products and processes which are designed by the rich for themselves, the discrepancy between demand for these Western artefacts and the supply will increase indefinitely. The family car cannot drive the poor into the jet age, nor can a school system provide the poor with education, nor can the family refrigerator ensure healthy food for them…

THE 'PACKAGE DEALS' DESIGNED BY INSTITUTIONS

We have embodied our world-view in our institutions and are now their prisoners. Factories, newsmedia, hospitals, governments and schools produce goods and services packaged to contain our view of the world. We – the rich – conceive of progress as the expansion of these establishments. We conceive of heightened mobility as luxury and safety packaged by General Motors or Boeing. We conceive of improving the general well-being as increasing the supply of doctors and hospitals, which package health along with protracted suffering. We have come to identify our need for further learning with the demand for ever longer confinement to classrooms. In other words, we have packaged education with custodial care, certification for jobs, and the right to vote, and wrapped them all together with indoctrination in the Christian, liberal or communist virtues.

In less than a hundred years industrial society has moulded patent solutions to basic human needs and converted us to the belief that man's needs were shaped by the Creator as demands for the products we have invented. This is as true for Russia and Japan as for the North Atlantic community. The consumer is trained for obsolescence, which means continuing loyalty toward the same producers who will give him the same basic packages in different quality or new wrappings.

Industrialized societies can provide such packages for personal consumption for most of their citizens, but this is no proof that these societies are sane, or economical, or that they promote life. The contrary is true. The more the citizen is trained in the consumption of packaged goods and services, the less effective he seems to become in shaping his environment. His energies and finances are consumed in procuring ever new models of his staples, and the environment becomes a by-product of his own consumption habits. The design of the 'package deals' of which I speak is the main cause of the high cost of satisfying basic needs...

DEVELOPMENT, AS DEFINED BY THE RICH

Rich nations now benevolently impose a straitjacket of traffic jams, hospital confinements and classrooms on the poor nations, and by international agreement call this 'development'. The rich and schooled and old of the world try to share their dubious blessings by foisting their prepackaged solutions onto the Third World. Traffic jams develop in São Paulo while almost a million northeastern Brazilians flee the drought by walking five hundred miles. Latin American doctors get training at The Hospital for Special Surgery in New York, which they apply to only a few, while amoebic dysentery remains endemic in slums where 90 per cent of the population live. A tiny minority gets advanced education in basic science in North America – not infrequently paid for by their own governments. If they return at all to Bolivia, they become second-rate teachers of pretentious subjects at La Paz or Cochabamba. The rich export outdated versions of their standard models.

The Alliance for Progress is a good example of benevolent production for underdevelopment. Contrary to its slogans, it did succeed – as an alliance for the progress of the consuming classes, and for the domestication of the Latin American masses. The Alliance has been a major step in modernizing the consumption patterns of the middle classes in South America by integrating them with the dominant culture of the North American metropolis. At the same time, the Alliance has modernized the aspirations of the majority of citizens and fixed their demands on unavailable products.

Each car which Brazil puts on the road denies fifty people good transportation by bus. Each merchandized refrigerator reduces the chance of building a community freezer. Every dollar spent in Latin America on doctors and hospitals costs a hundred lives, to adopt a phrase of Jorge de Ahumada, the brilliant Chilean economist. Had each dollar been spent on providing safe drinking water, a hundred lives could have been saved. Each dollar spent on schooling means more privileges for the few at the cost of the many; at best it increases the number of those who, before dropping out, have been taught that those who stay longer have earned the right to more power, wealth and prestige. What such schooling does is to teach the schooled the superiority of the better schooled.

All Latin American countries are frantically intent on expanding their school systems. No country now spends less than the equivalent of 18 per cent of tax-derived public income on education – which means schooling – and many countries spend almost double that. But even with these huge investments, no country yet succeeds in giving five full years of education to more than one-third of its population: supply and demand for schooling grow geometrically apart. And what is true about schooling is equally true about the products of most institutions in the process of modernization in the Third World.

Continued technological refinements of products which are already established on the market frequently benefit the producer far more than the consumer. The more complex production processes tend to enable only the largest producer to replace outmoded models continually, and to focus the demand of the consumer on the marginal improvement of what he buys, no matter what the concomitant side effects: higher prices, diminished life span, less general usefulness, higher cost of repairs. Think of the multiple uses for a simple can opener, whereas an electric one, if it works at all, opens only some kinds of cans, and costs one hundred times as much...

UNDERDEVELOPING THE THIRD WORLD

In most Third World countries, the population grows and so does the middle class. Income, consumption and the well-being of the middle class are all growing while the gap between this class and the mass of people widens. Even where per-capita consumption is rising, the majority of men have less food now than in 1945, less actual care in sickness, less meaningful work, less protection. This is partly a consequence of polarized consumption and partly caused by the breakdown of traditional family and culture. More people suffer from hunger, pain and exposure in 1969 than they did at the end of World War II, not only numerically but also as a percentage of the world population.

These concrete consequences of underdevelopment are rampant; but underdevelopment is also a state of mind, and understanding it as a state of mind, or as a form of consciousness, is the critical problem. Underdevelopment as a state of mind occurs when mass needs are converted to the demand for new brands of packaged solutions which are forever beyond the reach of the majority. Underdevelopment in this sense is rising rapidly even in countries where the supply of classrooms, calories, cars and clinics is also rising. The ruling groups in these countries build up services which have been designed for an affluent culture; once they have monopolized demand in this way, they can never satisfy majority needs.

Underdevelopment as a form of consciousness is an extreme result of what we can call, in the language of both Marx and Freud, reification. By reification I mean the hardening of the perception of real needs into the demand for mass manufactured products. I mean the translation of thirst into the need for a Coke. This kind of reification occurs in the manipulation of primary human needs by vast bureaucratic organizations which have succeeded in dominating the imagination of potential consumers.

Let me return to my example taken from the field of education. The intense promotion of schooling leads to so close an identification of school attendance and education that in everyday language the two terms are interchangeable. Once the imagination of an entire population has been 'schooled', or indoctrinated, to believe that school has a monopoly on formal education, then the illiterate can be taxed to provide free high school and university education for the children of the rich.

Underdevelopment is the result of rising levels of aspiration achieved through the intensive marketing of 'patent' products. In this sense, the dynamic underdevelopment that is now taking place is the exact opposite of what I believe education to be: namely, the awakening awareness of new levels of human potential and the use of one's creative powers to foster human life. Underdevelopment, however, implies the surrender of social consciousness to prepackaged solutions.

The process by which the marketing of 'foreign' products increases underdevelopment is frequently understood in the most superficial ways. The same man who feels indignation at the sight of a Coca-Cola plant in a Latin American slum often feels pride at the sight of a new normal school growing up alongside. He resents the evidence of a foreign 'licence' attached to a soft drink which he would like to see replaced by 'Cola-Mex'. But the same man is willing to impose schooling – at all costs – on his fellow citizens, and is unaware of the invisible licence by which this institution is deeply enmeshed in the world market.

WHEN SCHOOLS CREATE INFERIORITY

The higher the dose of schooling an individual has received, the more depressing his experience of withdrawal. The seventh-grade dropout feels his inferiority much more acutely than the dropout from the third grade. The schools of the Third World administer their opium with much more effect than the churches of other epochs. As the mind of a society is progressively schooled, step by step its individuals lose their sense that it might be possible to live without being inferior to others. As the majority shifts from the land into the city, the hereditary inferiority of the peon is replaced by the inferiority of the school dropout who is held personally responsible for his failure. Schools rationalize the divine origin of social stratification with much more rigour than churches have ever done.

Until this day no Latin American country has declared youthful underconsumers of Coca-Cola or cars as lawbreakers, while all Latin American countries have passed laws which define the early dropout as a citizen who has not fulfilled his legal obligations. The Brazilian government recently almost doubled the number of years during which schooling is legally compulsory and free. From now on any Brazilian dropout under the age of sixteen will be faced during his lifetime with the reproach that he did not take advantage of a legally obligatory privilege. This law was passed in a country where not even the most optimistic could foresee the day when such levels of schooling would be provided for only 25 per cent of the young. The adoption of international standards of schooling forever condemns most Latin Americans to marginality or exclusion from social life – in a word, underdevelopment…

THE NEED FOR A PROFOUND REVOLUTION

The Third World is in need of a profound revolution of its institutions. The revolutions of the last generation were overwhelmingly political. A new group of men with a new set of ideological justifications assumed power to administer fundamentally the same scholastic, medical and market institutions in the interest of a new group of clients. Since the institutions have not radically changed, the new group of clients remains approximately the same as that previously served …

Underdevelopment is at the point of becoming chronic in many countries. The revolution of which I speak must begin to take place before this happens.

Education again offers a good example: chronic educational underdevelopment occurs when the demand for schooling becomes so widespread that the total concentration of educational resources on the school system becomes a unanimous political demand. At this point the separation of education from schooling becomes impossible.

The only feasible answer to ever-increasing underdevelopment is a response to basic needs that is planned as a long-range goal for areas which will always have a different capital structure. It is easier to speak about alternatives to existing institutions, services and products than to define them with precision. It is not my purpose either to paint a Utopia or to engage in scripting scenarios for an alternative future. We must be satisfied with examples indicating simple directions that research should take.

Some such examples have already been given. Buses are alternatives to a multitude of private cars. Vehicles designed for slow transportation on rough terrain are alternatives to standard trucks. Safe water is an alternative to high-priced surgery. Medical workers are an alternative to doctors and nurses. Community food storage is an alternative to expensive kitchen equipment. Other alternatives could be discussed by the dozen...

Defining alternatives to the products and institutions which now pre-empt the field is difficult, not only, as I have been trying to show, because these products and institutions shape our conception of reality itself but also because the construction of new possibilities requires a concentration of will and intelligence in a higher degree than ordinarily occurs by chance. This concentration of will and intelligence on the solution of particular problems regardless of their nature we have become accustomed over the last century to call research.

A COUNTERRESEARCH FOR FUNDAMENTAL ALTERNATIVES

I must make clear, however, what kind of research I am talking about. I am not talking about basic research either in physics, engineering, genetics, medicine, or learning. The work of such men as F.H.C. Crick, Jean Piaget and Murray Gell-Mann must continue to enlarge our horizons in other fields of science. The labs and libraries and specially trained collaborators these men need cause them to congregate in the few research capitals of the world. Their research can provide the basis for new work on practically any product.

I am now speaking here of the billions of dollars annually spent on applied research, for this money is largely spent by existing institutions on the perfection and marketing of their own products. Applied research is money spent on making planes faster and airports safer; on making medicines more specific and powerful and doctors capable of handling their deadly side effects; on packing more learning into classrooms; on methods to administer large bureaucracies. This is the kind of research for which some kind of counterfoil must be developed if we are to have any chance to come up with basic alternatives to the automobile, the hospital, the school, and any of the many other so-called 'evidently necessary implements for modern life'.

I have in mind a different, and peculiarly difficult kind of research, which has been largely neglected up to now, for obvious reasons. I am calling for research on alternatives to the products which now dominate the market; to hospitals and the profession dedicated to keeping the sick alive; to schools and the packaging process which refuses education to those who are not of the right age, who have not gone through the right curriculum, who have not sat in a classroom a sufficient number of successive hours, who will not pay for their learning with submission to custodial care, screen and certification or with indoctrination in the values of the dominant elite.

This counterresearch on fundamental alternatives to current prepackaged solutions is the element most critically needed if the poor nations are to have a livable future. Such counterresearch is distinct from most of the work done in the name of the 'year 2000', because most of that work seeks radical changes in social patterns through adjustments in the organization of an already advanced technology. The counterresearch of which I speak must take as one of its assumptions the continued lack of capital in the Third World.

The difficulties of such research are obvious. The researcher must first of all doubt what is obvious to every eye. Second, he must persuade those who have the power of decision to act against their own short-run interests or bring pressure on them to do so. And, finally, he must survive as an individual in a world he is attempting to change fundamentally so that his fellows among the privileged minority see him as a destroyer of the very ground on which all of us stand. He knows that if he should succeed in the interests of the poor, technologically advanced societies still might envy the 'poor' who adopt this vision.

There is a normal course for those who make development policies, whether they live in North or South America, in Russia or Israel. It is to define development and to set its goals in ways with which they are familiar, which they are accustomed to use in order to satisfy their own needs, and which permit them to work through the institutions over which they have power or control. This formula has failed, and must fail. There is not enough money in the world for development to succeed along these lines, not even in the combined arms and space budgets of the superpowers.

An analogous course is followed by those who are trying to make political revolutions, especially in the Third World. Usually they promise to make the familiar privileges of the present elites, such as schooling, hospital care, etc., accessible to all citizens; and they base this vain promise on the belief that a change in political regime will permit them to sufficiently enlarge the institutions which produce these privileges. The promise and appeal of the revolutionary are therefore just as threatened by the counterresearch I propose as is the market of the now dominant producers.

In Vietnam a people on bicycles and armed with sharpened bamboo sticks have brought to a standstill the most advanced machinery for research and production ever devised. We must seek survival in a Third World in which human ingenuity can peacefully outwit machined might. The only way to reverse the disastrous trend to increasing underdevelopment, hard as it is, is to learn to laugh at accepted solutions in order to change the demands which make them necessary. Only free men can change their minds and be surprised; and while no men are completely free, some are freer than others.

Aimé Césaire on Colonialism

I hear the storm. They talk to me about progress, about 'achievements', diseases cured, improved standards of living.

I am talking about societies drained of their essence, cultures trampled underfoot, institutions undermined, lands confiscated, religions smashed, magnificent artistic creations destroyed, extraordinary *possibilities* wiped out.

They throw facts at my head, statistics, mileages of roads, canals, and railroad tracks.

I am talking about thousands of men sacrificed to the Congo-Océan [railroad]. I am talking about those who, as I write this, are digging the harbor of Abidjan by hand. I am talking about millions of men torn from their gods, their land, their habits, their life – from life, from the dance, from wisdom.

They dazzle me with the tonnage of cotton or cocoa that has been exported, the acreage that has been planted with olive trees or grapevines.

I am talking about natural *economies* that have been disputed – harmonious and viable *economies* adapted to indigenous population – about food crops destroyed, malnutrition permanently introduced, agricultural development oriented solely toward the benefit of the metropolitan countries, about the looting of products, the looting of raw materials.

They pride themselves on abuses eliminated.

I too talk about abuses, but what I say is that on the old ones – very real – they have superimposed others – very detestable. They talk to me about local tyrants brought to reason; but I note that in general the old tyrants get on very well with the new ones, and that there has been established between them, to the detriment of the people, a circuit of mutual services and complicity...

[Our old societies] were communal societies, never societies of the many for the few.

They were societies that were not only ante-capitalist, as has been said, but also *anti-capitalist*.

They were cooperative societies, fraternal societies.

I make a systematic defense of the societies destroyed by imperialism.

They were the fact, they did not pretend to be the idea; despite their faults, they were neither to be hated nor condemned. They were content to be. In them, neither the word *failure* nor the word *avatar* had any meaning. They kept hope intact.

From *Discourse on Colonialism*, trans. Joan Pinkham, Monthly Review Press, New York, 1972, pp. 21–3. The great Martinican poet and playwright was a descendant of slaves deported from Africa. His thirst for freedom and his extraordinarily colourful French contributed to the richness of the surrealist movement in France, to which he belonged: André Breton called *Cahier d'un retour au pays natal* (1939) 'nothing less than the greatest lyrical monument of this time'.

10

TWENTY-SIX YEARS LATER

Ivan Illich in conversation with Majid Rahnema

Majid Rahnema Ivan, I was already 'contaminated' by many of your ideas on development and education, when I first read your talk on 'Development as Planned Poverty', later followed by your other great essay on the Epimethean Man.[1] Like your other writings, those papers continued to display the laser quality of your mind which allowed you to pierce through many of the opacities of our times. Yet, the 'developer' in me was then in great difficulty, considering your attack on the new myth as nothing more than a skilful provocation. But now their prophetic dimensions have prompted me to bring at least one of them to the attention of the younger generation as an important contribution to the history of the present. Yet, as I was coming to see you here in Bremen, I felt it would be a more exceptional gift to the readers if I could offer them your views on development, some twenty-six years later, especially as the Reader is intended to help them better understand the post-development era. And now that you have so kindly agreed to break your long silence on development and allowed me to engage in a friendly yet open conversation on the matter, I would like you to satisfy my curiosity on a couple of questions.

If I am correct, you have never been interested in the kind of actions in which missionaries, developmentalists or Marxist and other social intervenors generally take pride; namely, to extend care or assistance to those who are presumed to suffer or need help. Unlike them, you seem to consider this attitude as both unloving and unrealistic, arrogant and counterproductive. By contrast, you have always been concerned with the art of suffering, in particular the history of different cultures in coping with their sufferings. And you have deplored the fact that modernity has affected this art very negatively, while it has created new and perhaps more intolerable forms of suffering. This position has led some of your critics to argue that you are interested more in the history of the arts of suffering than in actions aimed at reducing or eventually eliminating different forms of sufferings. Hence, the following set of questions: To what extent do you believe that human solidarity implies that one has to somehow respond to suffering, eventually with a view either to reducing it, or to transforming it into an elevating exercise that is the opposite of its dehumanizing forms? And if so, could these be achieved in a meaningful and dignified manner?

Ivan Illich Majid, there is something unsettling about your inquisition. Here we are, seated on my futon with a steaming samovar in front of us, relaxing in my mansard in the Bremen house of Barbara Duden: you soon to depart to celebrate the seventy-fifth birthday of Dadaji;[2] I to teach one more class on the history of iconoclasm at the university. Just last night, with my students who are also your readers, we celebrated *your* seventieth birthday. Thus I cannot very well reject your request. Further, I speak with pleasure, for your questions are a poignant reminder of a conversation that has been a true enquiry. I know this is so because I remember it as controversial and polemical in character. Now we are both older; each of us had to advance along his own road to reach a level where we can find ourselves in agreement.

You are correct in your belief that I had qualms about the notion of economic development early on. From my very first encounter with it, when I became vice-chancellor in charge of 'development' at a university in Ponce, Puerto Rico, I had doubts. That was exactly forty years ago, twelve years before you were made Minister of Education, seventeen years before each of us overcame his timidity and we met in Tehran, where we sucked on an *ablambú*, a huge pomegranate, at our first meeting. Intuition guided my initial rejection of development. I only learned to formulate true reasons gradually, over the stretch of time that coincides with our growing friendship.

During a decade or more, my criticisms focused on the procedures used in the attempt to reach goals that I did not then question. I objected to compulsory schooling as an inappropriate means to pursue universal education – which I then approved (*Deschooling Society*). I rejected speedy transportation as a method to increase egalitarian access (*Energy and Equity*). In the next step, I became both more radical and more realistic. I began to question the goals of development more than the agencies, education more than schools, health more than hospitals. My eyes moved from the process toward its orientation, from the investment toward the vector's direction, toward the assumed purpose. In *Medical Nemesis*, my main concern was the destruction of the cultural matrix that supported an art of living characteristic of a time and place. Later, I increasingly questioned the pursuit of an abstract and ever more remote ideal called health.

Majid, it is only after those books to which you just referred – that is, since the 1970s – that my main objection to development focuses on its rituals. These generate not just specific goals like 'education' or 'transportation,' but a non-ethical state of mind. Inevitably, this wild-goose chase transforms the good into a value; it frustrates present satisfaction (in Latin, enough-ness) so that one always longs for something better that lies in the 'not yet.'

M.R. This morning, I conveyed to you the message of a younger friend who asked me to thank you for having left a deep mark on his life, since the first time he learned from you the need constantly to question his certainties. Although the lesson had enriched this friend's inner life in many ways, it has also, I guess, acted on him as a destabilizing factor, actually discouraging him from continuing to take an active part in social life, as he did before. Thinking of him, I sometimes wonder whether the joy and indeed the inner clarity gained by this type of questioning does not sometimes hinder one's capacity to relate to the outer world and to participate in a meaningful social life.

To help you grasp the depth of my question, I think of a beautiful answer you gave to David Cayley when he asked you, 'Once one has laid bare these certainties and become aware of "needs", "care", "development" – whatever these cherished concepts are – once one has investigated them, once one has seen ... how destructive they may be, what next? Is your counsel to live in the dark?' You emphatically said 'No' to him, and then added: 'Carry a candle in the dark, be a candle in the dark, know that you're a flame in the dark.' To me, this is a Buddhist answer, the kind of comment which makes me sometimes believe that, despite your resistance to the idea, you often come close to the Buddhists in some important areas of thinking and action. But, closing this parenthesis, I remembered you saying yesterday that Buddhists who use meditation or other 'spiritual' exercises tend to focus more on their navels than upon the possible consequences of their belief in their oneness with the world. So, in the name of eliminating the causes of sorrow, you said, they actually sever themeselves from other people's sufferings rather than experiencing them.

Now, coming back to your advice to David, how do you think one could be a candle in the dark and still develop, at a social level, the type of compassion and love of the world which permeates all your thinking? I know that, for you, friendship is perceived as a way of reconciling the two, but is it possible to extend the grace of friendship to everyone?

I.I. Majid, your queries are like challenges, more stimuli than questions. Now you ask something which just fits the sense with which we concluded our first session. Tell your friend the story of Saadi's Golestan, the story you related at the celebration last night: 'In the annals of Ardashîr Bâbakân, it is told that he asked an Arabian physician how much food one should eat daily. He replied, "A hundred dirham's weight would suffice." The king pressed him further, "What strength will this quantity give?" The physician answered, "*This quantity will carry you; and that which is in excess of it, you must carry.*"'

'Enough' is like a magic carpet; I experience 'more' as a burden, a burden that during the twentieth century has become so heavy that we cannot pack it on our shoulders. We must load it into lorries that we have to buy and maintain.

The story is true of things, be they food, or ideas, or books. But it does not apply to friends. Friendship cannot be true unless it is open, inclusive, convivial – unless a third is fully welcome. The candle which burns in front of us also lights our pipe; a match would serve just as well. But a match would not let us see the continual reflection of a third one in both our pupils, would not remind us of this persistent presence.

Now, back to your questions. I worry about minds, hearts and social rituals being infected by development, not only because it obliterates the unique beauty and goodness of the now, but also because it weakens the 'we'. As you know better than I, most languages have several differently sounding words for the first person plural, for the we, the us. You use a different expression for saying, 'You and I, we two,' the Greek or Serbian *dualis*, and another for designating 'those of us who sit around this table' – to the exclusion of others; and yet another to refer to those with whom you and I live our daily lives together.

This refinement of the first-person experience has been largely washed away wherever development has set in. The multiple 'we' was traditionally characteristic of the human condition; the 'first person plural' is a flower born out of sharing the good of convivial life. It is the opposite of a statistical 'we', the sense of being jointly enumerated and represented in a graphic column. The new voluntaristic and empty 'we' is the result of you and me, together with innumerable others, being made subject to the same technical management process – 'we drivers', 'we smokers', 'we environmentalists'. The 'I' who experiences is replaced by an abstract point where many different statistical charts intersect.

Assure your friend that neither navel-gazing nor flight from the city is appropriate; rather, only a risky presence to the Other, together with openness to an absent loved third, no matter how fleeting. And remember that there is no possibility of achieving this so long as the candle near our samovar stands for 'everyone'. The most destructive effect of development is its tendency to distract my eye from your face with the phantom, humanity, that I ought to love.

M.R. You were amongst the first to reject development as an irrelevent, unethical and dangerous form of intervention into other people's lives. I then believed, like most intellectuals of the so-called Third World, that development represented a justified claim of the victims of the colonial order. As it seemed to us as a prerequisite for their full achievement of their independence, your attitude appeared then to us as an outright provocation. Many of us now believe that you were basically right, for development did ultimately serve purposes that had nothing to do with people's sufferings. It was actually used as a 'cultural defoliant' and a rather powerful means for the destruction of the victims' defence immune systems. Worse, what appears to me as the new AIDS soon developed to such an extent that even the grassroots seem now to have been co-opted in the process. In these circumstances, (a) do you see any chance for the victims to change their mind, or to find a meaningful alternative to their present state? And if so, what could be the conditions? (b) Is your outright rejection of development still based on its unethical aspects, its irrelevence to people's suffering, its false claims to represent an act of solidarity, or as a part of your wider philosophical stand that any institutionalization of the Good Samaritan gesture is doomed to become a disastrous failure?

I.I. Majid, in Puerto Rico I resigned rather than expand the university at the cost of less support for public elementary schools. Later, I faced serious injury through my attempts to stop missionaries of development from invading Latin America. You asked that we reflect together on the roads we have both travelled. Now let us go one step further. In a first stage, I took as my model the pamphleteers of the Enlightenment. During the 1950s, I called on people to recognize the surreptitious injustices implicit in publicly financed professional organizations of teachers, social workers and physicians. In my battles against invasion by volunteers, I appealed to reason. *Celebration of Awareness* expresses this attempt. In a second stage, my rhetoric was inspired by the stories of myth. I called attention to the engineering of new mentalities in which thirst demands, 'I'll have a Coke', 'good' means 'more', and desire becomes mimetic. I would like to have been a dramatist like Sartre or Beckett. Then I could have put a necktie on Sisyphus, and placed Prometheus in front of a computer – as I put the death-denying physician in a white coat. In my battles against delusional and therefore destructive goals, I tried to tell stories, like *Energy and Equity* or *Shadow Work*. In a third stage, I risked losing my audiences rather than write replays of dramas I had already offered to the public in the 1960s. The performances of schooling, medicalization, human garaging and shipment by motorized transport were now produced on many stages.

You were then among those who urged me to do for law or social work what I had done for the institutions of education, transportation and health care. I refused. I refused to restrict my analysis to the unwanted technical and social consequences of education, health and productivity. I thought I should look at these fantasies as at a frightful Greek ogre, a fateful destiny in the pursuit of which all but some of the rich or protectively credentialed are highly likely to be ground up by the rituals created to reach it.

Now you ask me how we can avoid blaming the victims of development. I do not think that we can, or that we should. The enterprise to transform *la condition humaine* has been crowned by success. And this 'human' condition is and remains bound up with development, despite the fact that the latter is a disastrous failure. Your task and mine can only be to explore how to trust and love and suffer in a milieu that drowns out our voices and makes our sparks invisible. Given who we are, two very privileged people who have been far too slow in recognizing the truth, we now ought to bear witness to what we have come to know.

Now back to the 'victims' of development. They are not all of one kind. So I must ask: do you have in mind Charlie's father in Ghana? With his large chicken farm, he still went bankrupt to send his son through the missionaries' schools to learn techniques which, in the meantime, have become obsolete. Or do you think of my former colleague at the University of Bremen? Too late, he tried to unhook himself from the tortures of chemotherapy in order to die a peaceful death, soothed by a few grains of opium. These and their like got what they asked for; their fate was not imposed on them. They were 'victims' because, in some way, they were privileged: Charlie's father because he was close to the missionary; my colleague because he was well insured.

Or perhaps you are not thinking of the privileged, but of the 'mass', of those processed into modernity, of those railroaded into dependence on antibiotic consumption or into the replacement of their traditional seed stocks by 'improved' varieties. Or you may be thinking of those who are subject to compulsory school attendance laws, but have no chance to go; of all those countless persons who have been disembedded from their cultures, only to progress into the worldwide majority of underconsumers.

Majid, over the years we have known one another we have both learned a lesson in powerlessness. Once we felt powerless 'to do'; now we recognize that we are powerless even to recommend. We have both found out that the 'social responsibility' that once motivated us was itself the result of a belief in the same progress that spawned the idea of development. Social responsibility, we now know, is but the soft underbelly of a weird sense of power through which we think ourselves capable of making the world better. We thus distract ourselves from becoming fully present to those close enough to touch. We had to pierce the illusion of responsibility – which, in a non-legal sense, has not been around for more than a century – in order to accept the lesson of powerlessness.

We had to learn the lessons of our powerlessness in order truly to renounce development. This means that we recognize that we are no more powerful than our grandfathers: yours, a historically influential holy man of Islam in Iran; and mine, a Jew, financing a string of German Lutheran schools with money made by destroying Bosnian forests.

M.R. Some four years ago, in a declaration prepared by you and a group of friends concerned with the environment, you defined virtue as 'that shape, order and direction of action informed by tradition, bounded by place, and qualified by choices made within the habitual reach of the actor'; and you noted that 'such virtue is traditionally found in labour, craft, dwelling and suffering supported not by an abstract earth, environment, or system, but by the particular soil these very actions have enriched with their traces.'

For me, that declaration expressed the essence of your objections to development, not only as a war against people's regenerative ties with that soil, but also as a foolish attempt to destroy that virtue and replace it by scientific methods of management and control over resources. Since your first essays on the dangers of the development project, even 'virtuous' NGOs and grassroots-oriented organizations have finished by dis-valuing virtue in the hope of finding more 'resources' in order to have the benefits of development trickle down towards the excluded. In the meantime, in the North, virtue seems to have gone through a democratically processed type of mutation. It is replaced by a universally defined type of care or assistance cooked up by politicians and their selected teams of experts and professionals.

In these circumstances (which you had already foreseen in the 1960s), do you think that there are still some untapped spaces left, in both vernacular and industrialized societies, where the old species of virtue have a chance to grow safely? Spaces which could point at what you once called 'a major change of direction in search of a hopeful future'? And, if you answer in the affirmative, could you elaborate on that? Please, consider that I am not asking you this question in the context of some possible management of another planned future, but, to use a Foucauldian expression, thinking of you as a historian of the present.

I.I. Majid, the answer is simple. Yes, there are such spaces. Most of us, no matter how poor our circumstances, can still claim or mark a threshold. We can also do this with the memory of someone absent. For each other, we can be a source of clarity and goodness; that, plus spaghetti, is all we have to share.

Majid, as I look at your face, I guess that you are thinking of the disappointment, or even disdain, on the faces of future readers. They are decent people who want to do good, and might allow that friendship could be a germ from which political action grows. I recognize that their political interpretation of friendship stands in a venerable tradition. This notion distinguishes Aristotle from his teacher, Plato. For two millennia, this political understanding of friendship has been strong enough to illumine the Western practice of politics. But that time is past. The possibility of a city set up as the milieu that fosters a common search for the good has vanished. You have often spoken to me of the times when Islam could still shape an ethical city. However, in the East as well as the West, we now live 'after ethos', or, as Alasdair MacIntyre notes, 'after virtue'.

Commitment to progress has extinguished the possibility of an agreed setting within which a search for the common good can arise. Techniques of information, communication and management now define the political process, political life has become an empty euphemism. Political friendship, which for Aristotle was the outcome of civic virtues practised in the household and on the forum, is, therefore, inevitably corrupt, however lofty the intentions of those who promote it. In a world set on development, no matter the economic stage reached, the good can only come from the kind of personal complementarity which Plato, not Aristotle, had in mind. Dedication to each other is the generator of the only space that allows what you ask: a mini-space in which we can agree on the pursuit of the good.

NOTES

This conversation is reproduced for the first time in this Reader.

1. The first, reproduced in this Reader, appeared in 1969 in the first edition of *Celebration of Awareness* (Doubleday, New York), and the second in 'Rebirth of Epimethean Man', Chapter 7 of *Deschooling Society*, Penguin, Harmondsworth, 1971, pp. 106–16.
2. See Chapter 10 n. 21, p. 129 below.

11

DEVELOPMENT AND THE PEOPLE'S IMMUNE SYSTEM: THE STORY OF ANOTHER VARIETY OF AIDS

Majid Rahnema

Since the plague in the Middle Ages, no disease has haunted the collective imagination of a whole epoch as much as AIDS. The syndrome has already given birth to metaphors which many a writer has studied as a mirror of our deeply troubled times. Susan Sontag, in her brilliant essay on the subject, has shown how the syndrome has turned out to be one of the most meaning-laden of diseases.

In most of the metaphoric descriptions found to explain the disease, the cause is generally attributed to an enemy, an infectious agent that comes from outside. Even the very young history of the disease is affected by this metaphor, itself witnessing the controversy over present world tensions. For Randy Shilts, 'Patient Zero' was an airline steward who infected large numbers of men across North America.[1] In Susan Sontag's words,

> many doctors, academics, journalists, government officials, and other educated people believe that the virus was sent to Africa from the United States, an act of bacteriological warfare (whose aim was to decrease the African birth rate) which got out of hand and has returned to afflict its perpetrators. A common African version of this belief about the disease's provenance has the virus fabricated in a CIA-Army laboratory in Maryland, sent from there to Africa, and brought back to its country of origin by American homosexual missionaries returning from Africa to Maryland.[2]

Thus, the AIDS epidemics has served 'as an ideal projection for First World political paranoia. Not only is the so-called AIDS virus the quintessential invader from the Third World. It can stand for any mythological menace.' The metaphors associated with AIDS were used by Susan Sontag as a key to deciphering the language of modern dominant institutions, and the ways it is used to achieve their ends. This same metaphoric language helped me to understand an exceptionally important feature of development ideology to which little attention had been paid to date: the loss of the last thing left to 'target populations' for regenerating their life space.

I had already used a number of modern metaphors to convey, in a more 'familiar' way, some of the aspects of vernacular societies that were more difficult for outsiders to understand. I had talked of their 'genetic codes' to express those very specific particularities that constituted their cultural roots, that made them say and do and flourish in the unique ways they do. Similarly, I had used the medical metaphor of 'immune defence system' to describe how the same societies maintain and defend the very foundations of their life against different odds originating from 'outside'. These ideas were the basis for a paper I presented at a series of seminars held at Stanford University, which explored how the language used to describe the AIDS syndrome could illustrate the processes of a socio-cultural variety of AIDS – call it AIDS II – to which vernacular societies were exposed during the modern age.[3] The present essay is a fully revised version of that paper, which has been prepared especially for this Reader.

I

Vernacular societies,[4] at the group and the individual levels, exhibit a very complex configuration of ways and means that allow them to maintain and defend themselves against all dangers or 'foreign bodies' threatening their integrity. It is the totality of these devices that I refer to as their socio-cultural immune systems.

Societies' immune systems at work

Each culture or social entity proceeds in its own particular way in shaping its 'immune system', depending on the flavour and the specific characteristics of the culture. The lessons of its own experience are the ones that count. They are also the ones on which its members rely more than any other, to maintain or improve the quality of their life. From a first look at the history of how these immune systems came to be formed, it appears that life and its protection have always gone hand in hand.

In the biological world, the formation of cell membranes, for example, represents both a logical step towards greater metabolic efficiency, and a means of protection. It allows each cell to keep the outside out and the inside in, thus maintaining a measure of stability. Similar functions are served by the membranes of molecules and enzymes within each cell. In societies, the need for protective cultural 'membranes' has equally been a major and constant concern, both for the community and for its constituent households. These socio-cultural membranes are constituted in order to distinguish the community or household member from the stranger, and to create, within the protected cell, the necessary conditions for everyone to participate in the shaping of their common cultures.

Characteristics of vernacular spaces

A vernacular space, such as a village or a community, may look simple or even primitive from the outside. But it actually represents a microcosm, a different and highly complex universe of its own. It is a living and complex web of human solidarities which have been woven, throughout the ages, between the members of a social group. It often exudes a sense of belonging and adherence to the group, to which the great historian Ibn Khaldun has given the Arabic name of *'asabīyah* (see Box on page 126) The *'asabīyah* of the community serves to dissolve everyone's 'I' into a 'We' from which is drawn one's identity and sense of self. The particular microcosm of signs and symbols, of ways of doing and talking, of beliefs and myths, of customs and traditions, and the common language which serves every vernacular community to represent and 'decode' the world in its own way, defines the group's *'asabīyah*, making it different from another, and yet allowing them to relate to each other, in their own ways.

Vernacular societies differ, indeed, in many ways, from modern 'economized' societies:

1. They have a certain organic consistency: in other words, their structures are a living tissue of social and cultural relations defining the activities of their members and protecting them against possible dangers. It is this tissue of human solidarities that preserves the community's immune system.

2. They are generally formed by communities with a limited number of members.

3. The cultural and material needs of these communities are, as a matter of principle, simple and restricted. What is considered to be necessary and desirable for them to live in dignity is defined both by tradition and by their collective capacity to meet their culturally defined needs. A vernacular society does not believe that it must, at all costs, maximize its 'resources', for its functionality is not based on the idea that the needs of its members are without limits. On the contrary, greed being perceived as a vice, it considers that the restriction of needs to the minimum dictated by the socio-economic and natural environment ensures the cohesion of the social tissue, to the benefit of everyone.

4. Although the activities recognized as economic or 'productive' play a leading role in the functioning of vernacular societies, they are always 'embedded' in socio-cultural relations. Their economy is a social affair in which the actors are involved with a view to strengthening the group's immune system. On another level, 'the usual stimulus of a worker is not

profit, but reciprocity, competition, pleasure of work and the approval of society.'[5]

5. The 'resources' that these societies consider to be essential for their life are defined and produced locally.

Altogether, the 'immune system' of vernacular societies tends to preserve and constantly increase their own autonomous capacity to live and defend themselves against foreign aggression. As such, it focuses on the long-term health of the community, rather than on spectacular interventions aimed at curing advanced cases of disease. Moreover, all human activities within a vernacular space have a multi-purpose dimension: they not only serve to meet specific needs related to that activity; they also serve to strengthen the cohesion of the community and its immune system.

Yoga, both as a philosophy and as an art, provides a striking example of the basic features of most vernacular immune systems. With almost no additional 'resource', it enables everyone to develop the gifts they have received in life, and eventually become their own teacher – and doctor! Without imposing a 'model' of achievement, it seeks to give everyone the possibility of knowing themselves, trusting themselves and fully blossoming 'like a flower from a bud.'

Yet vernacular societies should not be idealized. They constitute challenging spaces, often full of strongly conflicting fields of interest, loaded with mutual fears, suspicions and violence. Deprivations of all kinds, different forms of domination and of subjugation, of imposed as well as voluntary servitude, have been the constant companion of men and women in these societies. And in many of them, pathological fears have unleashed tragedies which resemble the body's behaviour in certain cases of cancer, allergy, or other 'auto-immune' disease, producing antibodies that decoy all the rest of its immune system into making the wrong fight in the wrong place. Likewise, when too emotional a sense of self-preservation, or too fear-laden a suspicion of the 'other' or the non-traditional, leads the body social to mistake its own parts for 'foreign bodies', the confusion results in senseless and ultimately self-destructive mobilizations against imaginary enemies. 'Fundamentalist' reactions, and ethnic or 'religious' confrontations of this nature, thus produce severe damage to the body social, rather than preserving its integrity.

In practical terms, the 'immune system' of each vernacular society is preserved and reinforced by a unique set of practices and approaches. However, some themes appear to be common to all. For example: the minimization of risks, ecological vigilance, the diversification of resources, prudent attitudes towards innovation, and the multi-dimensional aspect of all life's activities.

The minimization of risks As a rule, the necessity to secure, in the first place, the subsistence needs of the community leads its members to minimize risks, which means that the 'trial and error' process of learning is desirable and possible only up to a certain point. Risks which could endanger the community's survival are generally avoided. The 'moral economy' of peasants, as described by James C. Scott, Michael Watts and others[6] is an expression of this same principle that some consider, not without reason, as the hard core of the social logic of pre-modern societies.

Ecological vigilance Vernacular societies have another trait in common: a kind of instinctive care of the physical environment and attention to messages from Mother Nature. The concern for a clement environment is, however, very different from the modern concept of 'ecology'. For, here, nature is not perceived as an additional super-resource which has to be managed in a 'scientific' and 'cost-effective' fashion. It is rather a god-given source of life without which it would be unimaginable for anyone to live. In the Chipko case,[7] the preservation of trees gained such an importance for women that they paid for them with their lives.

Diversification of resources The diversification of resources, a corollary of the principle of minimizing risks, is another aspect of the self-protecting or 'immune' systems characteristic of vernacular societies. It seems to have led to a double strategy: scattering and the optimal mixture of resources.

Prudent attitudes towards innovation The vernacular societies' approach to innovation, whether technological or organizational, demonstrates another aspect of the way they tend to protect themselves against unfamiliar or unpredictable processes which they are not in a position to control. Change is justified only when it is perceived as a way of doing things better, and to the benefit of the entire community.

The 'holistic' and multi-dimensional aspects of human activities Their 'holistic' and multi-dimensional approach to life is another significant feature of vernacular societies, and of their immune system.

In a vernacular space, most activities have a multi-purpose aspect, and are an opportunity for everyone to learn from others. Life organized around them often becomes the space for a collective apprenticeship, where the younger and the elder, each in their own way, learn from each other. Children may not be sent to institutions specializing in education, but they are much less 'infantilized' than their urban peers, whose world is reduced mostly to schools. While mixing with people of different ages, they too discover new ways of strengthening their immune systems, like their ancestors before them.

Similarly, vernacular 'technologies' are never just a collection of tools or of imported 'gadgets'. They are organically incorporated into people's way of life. And they often require the co-operation of ever-widening human groups, beginning with the members of the household. Far from being crutches leading to new forms of dependency, they are tools that correspond to a profound need to be autonomous; not only an extension of people's hands and brain, but also a constant reminder of their need for conviviality and for reinforcing the immune systems necessary for protecting the communal niche.

II

The tragedy of development can be understood as a parallel to the tragedy of AIDS. In the metaphoric presentation that is commonly made of AIDS, the syndrome is explained in the following terms.[8]

AIDS is a disorder of the immune system in the human body. But the disorder is not due to a genetic, inherited condition. It is acquired by infection. That is why it is called the acquired immune deficiency syndrome. The agent of this infection is a virus called HIV. It has a very insidious way of entering the body. It bypasses the array of large cells called macrophages, which are mobilized whenever a 'foreign body' tries to get in. After having evaded these first defenders, the invader homes in on the master co-ordinator of the immune system, the helper T-cell. It stays on the surface of that cell until it finds a receptor into which one of its proteins fits perfectly, like a key into a lock. Docking with the cell, the virus then penetrates the cell membrane, shedding its protective shell in the process.

After taking up permanent residence in the cell, the naked virus, with the help of an enzyme it carries with it, converts its RNA into DNA, the master molecule of life. The molecule penetrates the cell nucleus, inserts itself into a chromosome and takes over part of the cellular machinery, directing it to produce more HIV viruses.[9] In other words, once the invader succeeds in bypassing the immunological defences of the body, it takes over the cellular mechanism of the immune system to produce the alien products necessary to its ultimate collapse.

A genealogical profile of *homo oeconomicus*, the 'invader' in 'AIDS II'

In the case of AIDS II – that is, the socio-cultural variety – the 'invader', called development, operates roughly in the same way. Yet, to understand its particular mode of operation, it is helpful to trace its genealogy, which starts with the birth of *homo oeconomicus*, the founder of the family.

In the history of the human species, 'economic man' represents a novelty. He developed, indeed, in the womb of early capitalism, and his identity card could have been stamped with the words 'white', 'European' and 'male'. Yet he took pride in proclaiming his 'freedom' from belonging to any particular tribe or community, roots or culture, village or oasis. He was an a-cultured, uniform and substitutable person. He perceived himself as an 'individual' rather than a 'member of the community', a self-centred and self-made person

We Should Have Thought Small!

'Drought is a catalyst rather than a cause', says a Mauritanian senior civil servant who wishes to remain anonymous. 'If, in 1960, more attention had been paid to agricultural policies instead of believing that the economy would take off through the exportation of iron ore, we would not be in this mess today. But we had to sell iron, to build an army, to maintain an administration, embassies, schools ... The sector which provides a living for 80 per cent of the population was neglected. We copy economic models without knowing if we can handle them. Everywhere, you see money petrified in the form of tractors and machines of all sorts, abandoned and beyond repair. The Europeans who sold them to us (in exchange for iron ore) built concrete buildings for us. We entered into the world of machines, of fuel and fertilizers, yet we will never be able to produce all these things ourselves. What is more, agricultural machines are disastrous for our country, where the layer of topsoil is so thin, so fragile that, when it is worked too deeply, it turns into dust and is carried off by the wind. We ought to have protected the environment. Think small! At the present moment, the logic of foreign financing means that the population continues to get poorer. When you say this, the governments think they are being attacked. In fact, they are up against a brick wall. In the Third World, as in the West, they are caught up in a system. Humanity is powerless and the desert will continue to advance. The most frightening thing is that it could swallow up the River Senegal, and we could all starve to death!'

Jacques Girardon, 'Drought is a Catalyst Rather than a Cause', *Sciences et Avenir*, no. 445, March 1984. Translated by M.R.

committed to gain and personal 'freedom' rather than to subsistence and to a community's *'aṣabīyah* or *gabbina*.[10] Even his name was composed of two words that had meant totally different things before.

To start with the epithet defining *homo oeconomicus*, the etymon *oekonomia*, which is the Greek word for 'householding', meant production for one's own use. As Karl Polanyi has brilliantly analysed, before the appearance of a self-regulated system of markets called market economy, all human formations represented self-sufficient units where goods were produced, stored and used. The essence of householding was production for use rather than for gain. Labour was also never separated from other activities of life. Economy was 'embedded' in social relations. By contrast, the 'economy' epitomized by *homo oeconomicus* was a totally different and unprecedented concept of the organization of society, representing a new economic system, no longer 'embedded' in social relations but seeking always to shape the latter according to its own needs.[11] For Polanyi,

> to separate labour from other activities of life and to subject it to the laws of the market was to annihilate all organic forms of existence and to replace them by a different type of organization, an atomistic and individualistic one … In practice, this meant that the noncontractual organizations of kinship, neighbourhood, profession, and creed were to be liquidated since they claimed the allegiance of the individual and thus restrained his freedom.[12]

Homo oeconomicus started his meteoric ascent in the eighteenth century, when he coupled the ideology of a self-regulating market with the full use of newly invented machines, with a view to shaping the emerging industrial society. He personified the startling change that substituted the motive of subsistence with that of gain, and the transformation of 'the natural and human substance of society into commodities'. All social structures and institutions which stood in the way of profit and productivity had to be removed. In fact, he did not start his career in the colonies and against the 'coloured' people, but against white populations in their own homelands.

Homo oeconomicus and the economization of colonialism

In the colonies, however, 'economic man' could fully realize his own objectives only *after* the political collapse of colonialism, with its economization, under the banner of development. Before that, his relations with the colonial rulers had been ambiguous. Although he was needed to foster the economic viability of the Empire and military conquests, the expansion of geopolitical power and the maintenance of 'law and order' remained the privilege of the 'Crown'. To achieve its ends, the colonial administration opted for local rulers as their 'natural' allies. By 'respecting' their status, by giving them a small part of their booty, the colonial powers strengthened the position of the traditional, local exploitative leaders, to the detriment of the oppressed. Power and political control were their main concern, not development.

Thus, all through the colonial period, economy remained, as it were, 'embedded' in colonial social relations. Important investments were eventually made to foster the colonial objectives. They included projects of a 'developmental' nature, such as building roads, setting up plantations, creating schools, and so on. A host of other economic, socio-cultural and administrative infrastructures were created to pave the way for an eventual 'transfer of power' to the emerging generation of 'national' leaders. Yet the colonial administrators preferred, as a rule, to achieve their imperial objectives *through* the local social institutions rather than upsetting them.

It was therefore after the collapse of political colonialism that *homo oeconomicus* chose 'development' as a mask aimed at giving a human face to an even more pernicious form of colonialism. Freed from the tutelage of political colonialism, he could now fully use the colonial machinery to destroy the basic institutions of local populations, which he considered to be detrimental to economic growth. The operation was indeed much more deceitful. For *homo oeconomicus* was now coming as a friend and a saviour, as a grave-digger of colonialism, wearing the mask of liberation. The development he was proposing was not only to bring back to the victims what they had lost under foreign rule, but also to help them 'catch up' with their previous masters, in a couple of generations. It even reassured them that they could have the fruits of progress without necessarily destroying their own modes of life.

The fundamental difference between colonialism and development

To go back to the metaphoric language of AIDS, it is only when the invader 'docks' with the cell and penetrates the membrane that it strips off its protective shell and takes up permanent residence. From now on, the body's own cell *becomes* the invader. Similarly, *homo oeconomicus* transforms all his prey into 'economic men', like himself, substituting their motives of subsistence and their sense of belonging to the community with those of gain and of full 'individual freedom'.

This is the point that makes the fundamental difference between political colonialism and development. The former subjugates through a traditional master–slave relationship, where the otherness of each is maintained. By contrast, development aims at colonizing from within. It acts as the 'intimate enemy',[13] setting out to change every vernacular person into an economic agent, able to produce and make more money in order to meet all one's 'needs'. It seeks to teach people how to explore the exhilarating universe of these 'needs', free from any obligation toward others. It helps them learn a new art of living, based on the economic principle of maximizing their own possibilities of accumulating wealth, in order to meet all their growing needs. It finally aspires to make its target populations 'freely participate' in their mutation. Its ends are achieved only when its own perception of reality, and its underlying assumptions, are transferred to its victims and fully internalized by them.

III

The 'power' of development, like that of the AIDS virus, lies in its internalization by the host. Amongst the different areas through which it penetrates into people's minds, I consider three as its most effective strategies: the school system, the production of addictive needs, and the dis-valuation of indigenous know-how. I shall start with the educational area.

The school system: a nursery for the processing of minds

When Mahatma Gandhi, already in 1937, dissected the negative aspects of the imported school system and proposed to his countrymen his *Nai Taleem* (Basic Education) scheme,[14] he was amongst the few at that time who saw the heart of the problem. His ideas were highly relevant and original, and welcome to the participants of the Wardha meeting (see Box on p. 121). But immediately after independence, they were shelved. Even his closest disciples, including the Cambridge-educated Nehru, considered them to be too naive to meet the 'educational needs' of a great emerging nation. Meanwhile, the commodity called 'education' had been successfully marketed as a highly valued scarcity, and the public was quick to clamour for its 'democratization' and extension to the entire population. As a result, the Western school system, which colonial rule had introduced as a powerful tool for 'defoliating' local cultures and converting the colonies' potential 'elites' to its own world-view, became the most pressing demand of everyone everywhere. Paradoxically, the 'drop-outs' and the excluded were the most eager to clamour for it.

The case is typical of the ambiguous methods used by development to achieve its ends. Schooling is first offered as a scarce commodity reserved for the few. On the other hand, development does everything to give the school graduates social prestige and economic rewards. As a result, the commodity creates a need, one which responds less to the urge to learn than to a craving to be recognized by the system, and, for some, to beat the system on its own ground. Yet, once the school doors are open to its new consumer, the system surreptitiously corrupts these motivations. Many of its consumers start developing a love–hate, an ambiguous and addictive, relationship with the school. They are led to consider it as a means for gaining personal achievement and social acceptance. The 'angry man' of the early school days is often easily co-opted by the system, on his way to becoming either an 'honourable member of the opposition' or its future corporate executive. And last but not least, the system fails to keep its legitimizing promises of providing the nation with the 'human resources' it needs.

The production of addictive needs

A second area privileged by development for its own form of colonization is the production of addictive 'needs'. The process consists in occupying people's life spaces with a paraphernalia of goods, services and representations, all of which are designed to addict their target populations. Adopting 'pusher-dealer' techniques used to attract potential drug users, development rapidly creates markets for all kinds of new commodities and services, from canned food, radios and washing machines to institutionally provided education and health. Once people are 'hooked', and a compulsive sense of scarcity is created, the most deprived are the first to claim more. The process leads to the modernization of poverty, a structural phenomenon which everywhere accompanies the gap produced between the rapid multiplication of needs and services, and a much slower increase in people's income.

In the so-called developing countries, the disruptive effects of this phenomenon are much more rapid and devastating. For here, it also upsets some of

Nai Taleem: The Gandhian Scheme of Education Aimed at Nurturing the Heart, the Head and the Hands

Nai Taleem, the Hindi phrase for 'Basic Education' was a scheme proposed by Mahatma Gandhi in 1937, at a conference he had organized at his Wardha ashram. At this meeting, in which most of the Congress Party leaders participated, Gandhiji advocated a radical reorientation of educational policy in India, on the following grounds:

> The educational system introduced by the British was a poisonous gift to the people of India. Not only was it irrelevant to the learning needs of the millions, but it constituted a major colonial instrument for their enslavement and the destruction of their cultural roots. Its main function was to create a new class of the 'educated' to provide clerks and specialists for colonial administration. 'The system', he thought, 'is surreptitiously detaching its consumers from the main stream of life in India, making them strangers in their own land.' It was conditioning them to compete for personal gain, unpolluted by the misery of the poor and the 'illiterate'. The object of this education was called 'Progress', although it represented new processes of isolation, destitution and dependency for the grassroots.

For Gandhiji, the imported system was a travesty of education:

> Instead of serving the 'all-around development' of human faculties, it 'misdirects the mind' and hinders its full development. True education addresses the intellect, the heart and the body, as it ensures co-ordination and harmony amongst them. As such, it should develop through concrete action, mainly a handicraft, such as the spinning wheel. For it is a craft that sets problems to the learner, draws out his intellectual potential, builds up his character and develops his artistic and creative sensibilities. A craft-centred education ensures at the same time that the learner's growth is rooted in his natural, social and cultural environment. It does not isolate him from his life realities.

As India lives in her villages and her culture has a rural setting, one of the main targets of the colonial rule was, according to Gandhi, to destroy the ancient village organization and what that represents in terms of conviviality, self-reliance, self-support and other human values proper to Indian life.

The new education was serving the objectives of a society based on violence, 'loot, robbery and vandalism'. What the Indian people needed was an education aimed at promoting the ideals of non-violence, love of freedom, pluralism and tolerance – in short, of human dignity.

The Wardha Conference endorsed the main ideas of Gandhiji's scheme on Basic Education in a resolution containing, *inter alia*, the following recommendations:

- education should be imparted in the mother-tongue;

- education should be based on constructive and productive activities and imparted in a natural and social environment;
- teachers should be able to meet their day-to-day expenses through the sale of school products.

The Wardha Conference triggered one of the most innovative and inspiring grassroots movements of our century. In 1958 eight states had prepared and introduced integrated syllabuses in their areas with a view to orienting primary education on the lines of Basic Education and to stopping dualism in education. But for various political and administrative reasons, the movement declined and events turned it into a different direction.

As Basic Education and primary schools were brought under one administrative officer, and various bureaucratic, professional, political and other pressures led the authorities in charge to reinforce the main educational system as inherited from the British, in most *Nai Taleem* programmes productive work gradually stopped. Activities such as community living, common prayer, *safai* work, the cultural programme, village service, which formed an integral part of Basic Education, were also stopped. As a result, except for some private agencies in Gujarat, West Bengal, Bihar and Tamil Nadu, Basic Education is not working anywhere in India.

M.R.

A well-documented report of the movement is contained in Dwarika Singh's book, published by the Indian Council of Basic Education in Bombay in 1981, under the title *Basic Education – Then and Now, 1937–1978.* The author was himself a pioneer in the field of Basic Education.

the most resilient foundations of social life – that is, the rigorously maintained principle that needs should not exceed society's capacity to meet them, and the traditions of simplicity, frugality and solidarity which had always helped the noble poor from falling into destitution. Above all, it soon leads to frustrating and sometimes catastrophic situations. For the rate of increase in demand for the addictive new 'drugs' runs far ahead of the economic possibilities of their consumers. At the same time, the latter's dependency on these new imputed needs makes it much harder for them to survive on their own means of subsistence. As a result, most people have to live in debt, a fact that has already impaired the nature of traditional relationships within communities. At both individual and national levels, their increasing dependency on credit institutions seriously impairs their autonomy.[15]

'Dis-valuation' of the indigenous know-how and knowledge systems

The world of representations and of the imaginary is another area targeted for colonization by development strategists. Here, the main goal is the 'dis-valuation' of the vernacular cultures. Coined by Ivan Illich, the word 'dis-value'[16] 'bespeaks the wasting of commons and culture with the result that traditional labour is voided of its power to generate subsistence'. In fact, suggests Illich, 'economic value accumulates only as the result of the previous wasting of culture, which can also be considered as the creation of disvalue.' The dis-valuation attempts aim not only at denigrating traditional knowledge and know-how, but also the world-views and concepts underlying them. This is achieved through both the language and the practices of development.

The language of development is pseudo-scientific, technocratic and expert-based, composed of words that are ambiguous, confusing and manipulative, particularly to the local people. Some terms are chosen to denigrate attitudes and modes of life in which the communities concerned have always taken pride. The term 'primitive economy' is used instead of conviviality. A community which produces just what it needs, leaving the rest of its time to leisure and other artistic activities,[17] is labelled 'unproductive'. Many terms are technical; they appear to convey important conceptual or 'scientific' truths, which are generally obscure to the uninitiated, – 'economic growth', 'reducing the gap', 'GNP', 'macro-economy', 'ecoscience' or 'ecosystem', 'cost-effective', 'priorities' and so on. Expressions are fabricated with a view to creating programmed illusions, and further 'needs'; that is, sustainable or bottom-up development, full employment, income-generating projects, and so forth. Almost all are intended, indirectly or directly, to inculcate in the minds of the 'underdeveloped' the hard 'truth' of their existential and historical inferiority, the fact that unless they think and do as the 'developed' think and do, there is no hope of salvation for them or for their children.

The language of the development establishment is, however, only one aspect of the dis-valuing war it wages against the people's vernacular universe. Another, much less subtle, aspect comes with every important project of 'technical' or financial 'assistance', which composes the bulk of development activities. Here, whole armies of international experts and consultants work together to demonstrate, in all fields, the scientific and superior aspects of modern technology, modern management and modern economy. No occasion is missed to prove that monetarized economy and professionally devised technology (whether high-tech or 'appropriate') are essential for human survival, under the present conditions. Even when the dearth of means and resources makes it sometimes economically valid for certain projects to follow local ways of doing things, these are recognized only when they are approved on 'expert advice'.

The balance sheet of the new global colonization

The HIV type of invasion undertaken by development goes far beyond any previous form of colonization. Beside the differences already mentioned, it is not directed against a particular country or people. It rather seeks to accomplish a global mission, legitimized and justified by its claims to represent the latest in the stages of mankind's evolution, to be democratic and scientific, and to help all peoples of the world to gain a place in the sun.

To refute these claims as totally unfounded is not the point. Development, like any other institution, can be credited with some technical or social 'achievements'. All national governments or international organizations of technical assistance can insist, sometimes with convincing evidence, that, here and there, very 'useful' things have been done with development and aid money. But *at what price*? And are the few 'success stories' of development worth the possible loss of a society's socio-cultural immune system or some of its basic virtues? That is the question which remains central to the populations targeted by development to be saved or assisted.

IV

The euphoria of seropositivity in the victims of AIDS II

All AIDS patients perceive their disease as a tragedy. They are stunned and overwhelmed when they learn about their seropositivity. Not only do they see it as an unjust doom; it also gives many of them a sense of shame. Most are reluctant to admit to their condition in public, for fear of being rejected and isolated.

There are, however, cases where tragedy also produces staggeringly regenerative effects.[18] In a recent study, victims cited new reasons to start afresh, and a startling desire to be stronger than death. 'I have the feeling that I am born a second time', says a 28-year-old dancer. 'I became conscious of what life was really about', says another; 'the disease made me understand love.' A third comments: 'Seropositivity brought me much stability.' Says a fourth, 'It allowed me to encounter myself. Which is far from being a bad encounter.' For one, finally, 'AIDS shows up all that no longer functions.'

In the case of AIDS II, reactions are very different, depending on the cultural background and the socio-economic groups of its victims. Generally speaking, very few, particularly amongst city-based or 'modernized' populations, perceive development as a 'disease', or a threat to one's health. Quite the contrary. It is often welcomed as a boon and a promise of the good life. And as the addictive effects of goods and services increase the material 'comfort' of their consumers, the imperceptible replacement of one's individual or community immune mechanisms by megasystems of 'security' – be they secure 'jobs', bank accounts, investment or interest-rate portfolios, or dependence on health, education, transport or other services such as insurance, police or prisons – is appreciated by most. Not only does the advancing socio-cultural seropositivity provide its subjects with feelings of euphoria, similar to those produced by heroin and morphine, but the contaminated tend to perceive their addiction as a universal model of life, good for all the non-addicted.

In vernacular spaces that are still alive and reactive, there is a wholly different set of reactions. At one end of the spectrum, there appears the so-called fundamentalist or ultra-nationalistic reactions to the 'invader'. Many a victim displays aggressivity and often blind forms of violence which tend eventually to destroy them rather than the intruders.

In the larger, middle part of the spectrum, reactions are ambiguous. That of the 'upper' and 'middle' classes, generally more addicted to development-induced needs, is similar to that of the populations of 'developed' societies. The addiction is often perceived as a blessing and a privilege, seldom as a threat. The degree of euphoria it gives the contaminated depends on the positions and privileges they hold in society. As to the populations, whose induced needs increase much faster than their economic resources, they are subject to mimetic effects of all kinds. The least conscious, who seek to be socially recognized, get satisfaction – and sometimes feel pride – in following the 'winners'. Many others are led to compromise with the invading forces, either out of sheer resignation to their fate, or in the hope that, some day, they too would be admitted to the winners' camp.

Only at the other extreme end of the spectrum can totally different forms of regenerative and liberating reaction be recognized. They remind one of those young victims of AIDS I, mentioned above, who become suddenly 'conscious of what life could mean' and find enough strength in their own self to challenge all forms of death.

The difficulties of preserving one's integrity

In a world increasingly exposed to AIDS II in its different forms, a world where anonymous institutions, assisted by professionals, acquire the power to decide for the people and to 'protect' their rights, in the name of rationality, economic affluence and their own freedom, healthy and 'biophilic' reactions to the syndrome tend to be suffocated. The vernacular immune systems described in this chapter, which living cultures have created for themselves throughout the ages, continue to show that they cannot so easily be destroyed by man-made institutions. Even under the worst conditions, new human formations and alliances appear, which try to defend people's roots and their desire to live in autonomy, and which use a language basically different from that of development. The *problématique* of the emerging post-development era will be marked by the outcome of the struggles, at all levels, between the biophilic forces of human awareness and creativity, and the manipulative strategies of economistic and professionalized institutions.

I should confess that, ten years ago, when I started my intuitive search to identify the biophilic forces of resistance to development, the refreshing vibrations I received from some of them resulted in an overflow of optimism and of 'wishful thinking' on my part. Not that my assessment of their vital strength was unfounded. But the messages of popular creativity and non-

'Aṣabīyah, or the Communal Ethos of the Bedouins

'*Aṣabīyah*, a term used extensively by Ibn Khaldun, has been translated into 'group feeling' (Rosenthal), 'communal ethos' or 'social solidarity' (Muhsen Mahdi), 'esprit de corps' (De Slane). For the great Arab historian of the fourteenth century, whom Arnold Toynbee considered to be the founder of modern history, '*aṣabīyah* constituted the key to the preservation of earlier communities, and its loss the major cause of their destruction. This is exemplified by the story in the Qur'an about Joseph's brothers. They said to their father: 'If the wolf eats him while we are a group, then, indeed, we have lost out.' This means that one cannot imagine any hostile act being undertaken against anyone who has his '*aṣabīyah* to support him.

When a tribe has achieved a certain measure of superiority with the help of its '*aṣabīyah*, it gains control over a corresponding amount of wealth and comes to share prosperity and abundance with those who have been in possession of these things [for a long time] ... [But when members of the tribe] are merely concerned with prosperity, gain and a life of abundance [and] lead an easy, restful life … adopt royal habits in building and dress, a matter they stress and in which they take more and more pride, … their '*aṣabīyah* (group feeling) and courage decrease in the next generations. Eventually, group feeling is altogether destroyed. They thus invite [their] own destruction. The greater their luxury and the easier the life they enjoy, the closer they are to extinction … When group feeling is destroyed, the tribe is no longer able to defend or protect itself, let alone press any claims. It will be swallowed by other nations.

Whenever we observe people who possess group feeling ('*aṣabīyah)* and who have gained control over many lands and nations, we find in them an eager desire for goodness, and good qualities, such as generosity, the forgiveness of error, tolerance toward the weak, hospitality toward guests, the support of dependants, maintenance of the indigent, patience in adverse circumstances, faithful fulfillment of obligations, liberality with money for the preservation of honor, respect for the religious law and for the scholars who are learned in it, observation of the things to be done or not to be done that [those scholars] prescribe for them, thinking highly of [religious scholars], belief in and veneration for men of religion and a desire to receive their prayers, great respect for old men and teachers, acceptance of the truth in response to those who call to it, fairness to and care for those who are too weak to take care of themselves, humility toward the poor, attentiveness to the complaints of supplicants, fulfillment of the duties of the religious laws and divine worship in all details, avoidance of fraud, cunning, deceit, and of not fulfilling obligations, and similar things.

Abdel Rahman Ibn Khaldun, *The Muqaddimah*, trans. Franz Rosenthal, Pantheon Books, New York, 1958, pp. 286–7, 292–3.

economistic efficiency I received from them led me to conclusions that were perhaps more emotional than realistic. I shall try to reformulate my thoughts in the light of observations I have made since then.

In the original paper on the socio-cultural variety of AIDS, I reported what I had witnessed in India and Mexico, from my personal contacts with some grassroots movements. I expressed my enthusiasm for the ways they were producing new forms of 'antibodies', aimed at rejecting their modern invaders. Together with the emergence of new types of non-cooperative, non-violent movements, I had also witnessed that new alliances were in the making, everywhere and at all levels, which deserved to be carefully analysed. These, I submitted, were bringing 'to the grass-roots movements, thousands of deprofessionalized intellectuals, university professors, teachers and students, members of liberal professions, government officials and others. Their contacts with the real life of their people make them discover a new world of compassion, kindle new fires in their hearts and minds, and lead them to discover their own possibilities of self-liberation, free from the vulgar tyranny of economic possessions.'

I continue to believe, as then, that in real life humans have more than one trick up their sleeves. An impressive number of individuals and communities are re-examining what they need in non-economic terms and in the context of a simple and humanly rewarding life. They realize how rewarding it is for them to substitute their induced compulsive needs with creative activities and different resourceful types of interactions. And more people come to rediscover how simple human gifts such as friendship, solidarity and compassion can indeed enrich and transform their lives, and how the economistic bias can be a threat to their true blossoming.

Some of the movements that caused me at that time to make these comments were Chipko and Lokayan[19] in India, and Anadeges[20] in Mexico. Since then, I had the personal privilege of getting a much closer look at movements such as Swadhyaya[21] in India, Chodak[22] in Senegal, and Longo Mai[23] in France, and many others which were brought to my attention. Many of them represented genuine types of search for a better life, based on such universally recognized virtues as compassion, friendship, human solidarity and hospitality. In different degrees, social, cultural and political events such as the massive Zapatista movement in Chiapas, the colourful Superbarrio[24] phenomenon after the Mexico City earthquakes in 1985, or the latest manifestations against the French nuclear tests in Muroroa, appear to me as the expression of the same biophilic, regenerative reactions to what 'the victims of progress' perceive as an aggression against their integrity as human beings. To all these reported expressions of resistance should be added the thousands, if not millions, of persons and small groups of simple friends who have no other name but their own, who do not 'form' any particular association or organization, and yet fully but modestly participate in genuine processes of regeneration, trying to relate, to think and to work together as *friends*. I know personally many who have discovered new meanings to their life, new ways of posing the old questions and are weaving living communities of a novel kind.

To come back to the regenerative forms of resistance to the AIDS II syndrome, there is no doubt that they develop in the context of a David–Goliath type of struggle. The modern Giant has at its disposal the most sophisticated means and resources required to manipulate, to lure, to addict, to buy, or actually to conquer or destroy the minds and bodies of its opponents. Yet the contradictions unleashed by modernity and the development processes are also so great that new and quite unpredictable forms of David-like victory should by no means be discarded. The paths to that victory are not, however, easy to trace or take. Those who do so should be under no illusion as to the difficulties ahead. The only chance for future Davids to thwart the modern Goliath is not only to understand both the true nature of development's objectives and cunning strategies, but, even more important, to engage in the demanding work of self-exploration, which requires faith in one's own truth and strength. If they do not do so, there is a serious risk that they will become the agents of their own destruction before they even begin to confront the forces they seek to overcome.

NOTES

1. R. Shilts, *And the Band Played On*, St Martin's Press, New York, 1987.
2. Susan Sontag, *Illness As Metaphor/AIDS and Its Metaphors*, Doubleday, New York, 1988, p. 140 (also published in the UK by Penguin in 1990).
3. The draft, entitled 'From Aid to AIDS', was the basic paper for a seminar held at the School of Education, Stanford University. A first version of it was published in *Alternatives* (XIII, 1988, pp. 117-36), under the title: 'A New Variety of Socio-Cultural AIDS and Its Pathogens'. A second version appeared, in French, as a chapter in the book by Gilbert Rist, Majid Rahnema and Gustavo Esteva, *Le Nord Perdu, Repères pour l'Après-développement*, Editions d'En-Bas, Lausanne, 1992.
4. The word 'vernacular' is used here instead of 'traditional' or 'subsistence' societies, for it seems to me that the two latter expressions have reductionist connotations. *Vernaculum* in Latin designated everything that was brought up, woven, cultivated and fabricated at home, as opposed to what was received through exchange. A vernacular language thus reflects 'home-made' words and expressions proper to the people using them naturally, as opposed to a language cultivated and borrowed from elsewhere.
5. Karl Polanyi, *The Great Transformation* (1944), Beacon Press, Boston, Mass., 1957, p. 270.
6. See James C. Scott, *The Moral Economy of the Peasant: Rebellion and Subsistence in Southeast Asia*, Yale University Press, New Haven, Conn., and London, 1976; and Michael Watts, *The Silent Violence*, University of California Press, Berkeley, 1983.
7. The Chipko movement has been quite extensively studied. See, in particular, Vandana Shiva, *Staying Alive*, Zed Books, London and New Jersey, 1989; also Peter Bunyard, 'Tehri: A Catastrophic Dam in the Himalayas', No. 25 in this Reader.
8. For the sake of brevity, I have combined here a presentation of the syndrome used in my earlier paper (*Alternatives*, XIII, 1988, pp. 117-36) with quotations used by Susan Sontag in her essay.

9. Sontag, *Illness As Metaphor/AIDS and Its Metaphors*, p. 106.

10. On *gabbina*, see G. Dahl and G. Megerssa, 'The Spiral of the Ram's Horn', No. 5 in this Reader.

11. Polanyi, *The Great Transformation*, p. 57.

12. Ibid., p. 163

13. The expression was first coined by Ashis Nandy. See his 'Colonization of the Mind', No. 16 in this Reader.

14. See Box on pp. 121–2 of this Reader.

15. See Susan George, 'How the Poor Develop the Rich', No. 20 in this Reader.

16. See Ivan Illich, 'Disvalue', in *In the Mirror of the Past*, Marion Boyars, London, 1992. The chapter is an edited version of a paper presented at the first meeting of the Entropy Society, Keyo University, Tokyo, 9 November 1986.

17. See Marshall Sahlins, 'The Original Affluent Society', No. 1 in this Reader.

18. See 'Vivre séropositif', an enquiry by Nicole Leibowitz, Jean-Yves Le Talec and Prof. Christine Katlama, in *Le Nouvel Observateur*, 23 February–1 March 1995, pp. 6–13.

19. *Lokayan* means dialogue in Hindi. This movement was created around the Indian Centre for the Study of Developing Societies, three of whose members, Rajni Kothari, D.L. Sheth and Ashis Nandy, are represented in this Reader. Lokayan has founded its activities on a continuing and sustained dialogue between suffering populations, particularly in the rural areas, and different groups of 'intellectuals' ready to respond to their needs. The movement publishes a regular bulletin bearing the same name (13 Alipour Road, Delhi 110054).

20. This innovative movement called ANADEGES (from the Spanish words for Analysis, Decentralism and Management), started in the 1980s in Mexico. It considers itself as a 'hammock' for peasants, marginals and 'deprofessionalized intellectuals'. Around 500,000 persons are said to be involved in this 'hammock', whose discourse and practices take the opposite course to those of 'development'. The movement has become known to the outside world thanks to one of its most vocal architects, Gustavo Esteva. See, in particular, his articles 'A New Call For Celebration', *Development* [SID, Rome], no. 3, 1986, pp. 92–8; and 'Regenerating People's Space', *Alternatives* XII, 1987, pp. 125–52.

21. Swadhyaya is a most original grassroots movement which was started in India, some forty years ago, by Dadaji (an affectionate nickname for the Reverend Pandurang Athvale Shastri) with only nineteen persons, and is said to have now over 3 million followers. The word *swadhyaya* means self-knowledge or self-discovery. The movement is entirely self-reliant and based on the Vedic belief that there is a God within each person. Besides the impressive changes Swadhyaya has already brought to the daily life of its members and to the human quality of their relationships with each other and with the outside world (including, indeed, nature), it has also generated great material wealth without any outside assistance. The 'family' has been using that 'wealth' and its regenerated relationships to improve the condition of its poorer members in a most ingenious and graceful manner. See Majid Rahnema, 'Swadhyaya, the Unknown, the Peaceful, the Silent, yet Singing Revolution of India', *IFDA Dossier* 73, April 1990; also, an important collection of essays, edited by Raman Srivastava, of the Centre for the Study of Developing Societies in Delhi (forthcoming).

22. An excellent presentation of Chodak, written by its main architects, is 'Reinventing the Present: The Chodak Experience in Senegal', No. 37 in this Reader.

23. Longo Mai is a network of rural co-operatives in different parts of Europe, the main one being in Upper Provence with others in France, Switzerland, Austria and Germany. Set up in 1973, the co-operatives, which are both agricultural and artisanal, aim at revitalizing abandoned rural areas, while they also receive and train young people in self-reliant skills. Address: B.P. 42, 04300 Forcalquier, France.

24. See Box on pp. 130–31 of this Reader.

Who is Superbarrio?

This is how the Uruguayan writer Eduardo Galeano has presented Superbarrio, the man dressed as a Superman who, some time after the Mexican earthquake in 1985, appeared in his new outfit and became a living myth overnight.

Half a century after the birth of Superman in New York, Superbarrio appeared in the streets and the roofs of Mexico City. The prestigious steel man of North America, a universal symbol of power, lived in a city named Metropolis. Superbarrio, like any flesh and bone Mexican, hero of the poor, lives in a suburb called Nezahualcoyotl.

Superbarrio has a belly and crooked legs. He uses a red mask and a yellow cap. He does not fight against mummies, or ghosts, or vampires. In one end of the city, he confronts the police and saves some starving people from eviction; at the other end, he heads a demonstration for women's rights, or against air pollution; and at the same time, down town in the centre, he invades the National Congress and starts a discussion denouncing the dirty tricks of the Government.

The following is an excerpt from a talk Superbarrio had with the writer-journalist Carlos Nuñez:

I was a professional wrestler; but for some years I had been inactive and retired. As a child, I had suffered eviction. In September and October 1985, I started participating in the organizations of the people who had suffered from the earthquake and entered the Assembly of the Barrios. In April 1987, there was a complaint on behalf of a number of people belonging to the Assembly. They were on the point of being evicted from their houses by the landlord who had already sued them and cut their electricity off. These were problems which I particularly resented because I had lived through similar situations.

When I heard those people, I felt great concern for them. When I saw that people's belongings had been thrown out on the street, many questions came to my mind: what to do, how to fight, how to co-operate with others in order to put an end to this ... For many months, these questions kept coming to my mind: I asked myself what to do, but I really could not come up with a clear idea of how to respond to this situation.

In June 1987, I was leaving my house for work (I am a peddler in Mexico City), when the door opened suddenly, and a very intense red and yellow light came in, with a lot of wind. The light was so strong that I could no longer see anything else, and the wind was whirling all around the little room where I was living. This really alarmed me. And when the light disappeared, and the wind stopped whistling, I was there as you see me now, and I heard a voice saying to me: 'You are Superbarrio, the scourge of the landlords and defender of the poor tenants, and this will be your task.'

Then I understood that this was a response to my anguish. And when I presented myself in this dress to comrades of the Assembly of the Barrios and explained to them why I was dressed like that, what my name was and what I intended to do, the people supported and applauded me. They felt that there was now somebody who was going to help them without any conditions. Now, whenever there is an eviction, they throw three firecrackers, and well, we do our best to come and prevent a family being thrown into the street.

...I do not want to substitute myself for the fighting spirit of the people. But I say that we all are Superbarrios: I, as an individual, cannot solve all the problems – that is, I have neither the strength nor the desire to solve them in a violent way. I also do not want to be the individual who does it. Our identity is a mask, and it does not matter who is behind that mask. That can be anyone, anybody who fights and is really committed to the cause of the poor.

...In the beginning the struggle was basically around questions of housing – tenants and landlords. But I think that the symbol and the idea of the personage has now gone much beyond these mere questions of housing. For instance, there are now peasants who tell you: Well, why only the tenants? Why should you not think of all the peasants and the people who have suffered from injustices outside the housing world? Or the street peddlers, the students, the workers' movements? Or the teachers who come and say: This is a symbol of everybody's struggle, not only that of the people's fight about housing alone. I am, for instance, very glad that in Veracruz there now exists 'Ecologista I', which is a symbol of the people's anti-nuclear struggle in that state. We are creating what is called a legion of Superamigos. This intention to create a symbol reflecting the image of the people's struggle and resistance, has been important. We have earned a place and a presence amongst the people, who have now given us recognition.

Extracts from CEAAL and CEASPA Panama, *De Superman a Superbarrios*, Encuentro Latinoamericano de Cultura y Comunicación Popular, Panama, 10–15 September 1989. Translated by M.R.

PART THREE

THE VEHICLES OF DEVELOPMENT

12

PARADOXICAL GROWTH

Serge Latouche

SERGE LATOUCHE is a professor of Economics at the University of Paris XI, and the author of *The Westernization of the World* (Polity Press, Cambridge, 1996) and *In the Wake of the Affluent Society* (Zed Books, London and New Jersey, 1995).

It is good form these days to scoff at the per-capita gross national product (GNP) as an indicator of the well-being and the standard of living of populations. The methods used in the calculations are too arbitrary and they reduce social reality to its purely economic aspects. Now, therefore, the fashion is for human development indicators and other sophisticated statistics. One can only be thankful. However, it is always a question of variations, more or less subtle, on the theme of standards of living, thus of numbers of dollars per head.

These criteria are not sufficiently criticized and the alternatives proposed are derisory. You cannot reject the myth of children being born in a cabbage patch and then say that it is the storks that bring them. The search is always for criteria for indicators enabling situational evaluations to be made – all of course objective – which will be genuinely universal and transcultural, the per-capita GNP being recognized as having too narrow a focus. But by making these changes, the vision of Western economics has not been discarded. It is like looking for the white blackbird. For lack of a critique of the ethnocentric bias of economistic and Western assumptions, the new universality is just as vitiated by common ethnocentrism as the old one was. This goes for the human development indicators (HDI) as for its variants.

For its advocates the HDI is a universal index of real wealth and real poverty. In order to construct it, there has been an effort to combine commonsense evidence, of the no-development-with-poverty-growth kind, with other evidence provided by economic analysis: in other words, a collection of Western prejudices put together. In particular, growth of the GNP is a good thing and the condition for all other improvements. Therefore the serious people, such as the experts of the International Monetary Fund or the World Bank, but also others (the economists of the development NGOs, for example), once the humanitarian gloss has been stripped off, consider the level and growth of the GNP as the ultimate criterion for evaluating human societies. This follows from the logic of modernity, as the economization of the world enables Western economic criteria to function.

In sum, all the governments of the world, if not their populations, interiorize the GNP criterion as a basis for evaluating themselves. Willingly they participate in the Olympic Growth Games, in the hope of ending high up in the honours list. In spite of the pathos of the call for 'the development of man and of all men' (*Populorum progressio*), development effectively depends on growth. The only serious basis, at least in appearance, of the social, human and even ecological effects of development as it really exists is the trickle-down effect, or the spin-off effects of vigorous growth. Social development, as discussed at the UN Social Summit in Copenhagen in March 1995, still depends on such growth taking place thanks to the alms dispensed by the rich – in the same way that sustainable development has been waiting for serious financial support since the UN Earth Summit in Rio de Janeiro in June 1992. This involves paradoxical thinking which results in a dangerous mystification of economic growth.

After having shown how growth acts as a mainstay in the ideology of modern society, we shall illustrate the different paradoxes that it conveys.

1. GROWTH AS THE IDEOLOGY OF MODERN SOCIETIES

The couplet growth–development originates in biology, particularly in the work of Darwin. Georges Canguilhem, the French philosopher of science, has observed:

> Distinguishing between growth and development, Darwin contrasted the adult with the embryo as far as both size and structures are concerned. Everything living can continue to grow by ceasing to develop. Like an adult in weight and volume, it will remain unchanged at one level or another of its specific childhood in its relationships with development.[1]

Applied to the social field, development is the modified growth of the economic organism. Thus, by definition, development is a growth that is corrected, regulated, healthy – therefore a good growth; while growth, as we shall see, is already the achievement of the Good.

Development is good growth

If industrialization had been carried out since the nineteenth century through purely quantitative growth, the result would have been monstrous and absurd. The world would have been covered with steam engines; there would be no more coal; and pollution would have killed off all life. Through force of circumstance, a physical, technical and ecological self-regulation process was set in motion which brought fundamental qualitative changes in its train. There was thus a process of self-correction, and the energetic pursuit of this corrected growth brought with it, more or less spontaneously, a process of social regulation. One could define economic development as the trickle-down effect of industrial growth. This term simply means that, above a certain threshold, growth has some social effects. It cannot but benefit everyone, to a greater or lesser degree. In a World Bank report of 1991, we read: 'During its first two decades of existence, the World Bank tended to identify development with economic growth. The benefits of growth were assumed to trickle down, the poor automatically benefiting from the creation of jobs and the increase in goods and services.'[2]

In the developed countries, even the most liberal ones, there was no increase in the poor, like those of Victorian England as described by Dickens and denounced by Marx. Wealth was disseminated to all. And here, still, development corrected growth and was in itself a good thing. With the Keynesian–Fordist policies of the consumer societies, a further step was taken along the way towards 'the good'. Strengthening the positive effects, this method of social and political regulation tended to distribute high salaries and social income in function of regular gains in productivity. Strong demand, in turn, maintained the whole equilibrium at a high level. This system of mass production and consumption functioned well for the industrialized countries during the Thirty Glorious Years (1945–75): it was, in a way, the apotheosis of development.

Could one perhaps go even further? And affirm, like Pope Paul VI, that: 'Development cannot be reduced to simple economic growth. To be authentic, it must be integrated: in other words it must promote all men and the whole man.'[3] That would be going too far and is not helpful. It would be to put in doubt the ethical value of growth which, in itself, is the good and the beauty of modernity.

Growth as 'good'

Since 1949 and the beginning of the race towards the highest GNP per capita, human society has set itself the target of raising living standards. That it is a good thing is unquestioned, as the term 'well-being' bears unequivocal witness. Industrialization and technology are means which, abstractly, could serve the bad as well as the good, but increasing these means becomes an aim in itself. Furthermore, they are considered to be the only means of achieving the good. It is as if, before the industrial age, civilization had not been able to provide a satisfactory life for its members!

The Edouard Parker Report to the Highway Forum, approved by the OECD in 1991 and recently published under the title *Objective: 10 per cent,*

provides a striking illustration of this.[4] It demolishes all the criticisms of growth and proposes nothing less than a target of 10 per cent in annual growth for the Third World. Why such a growth rate? Because it already needs to be 2 to 3 per cent in order not to stagnate and to compensate for demographic increases. There needs to be another 4 per cent to improve the standard of living and another 3 per cent to reduce underemployment. At this rate the famous trickle-down effect will make itself felt: growth will become development. We shall then, according to the authors, enter into the no less famous 'demographic transition': well-being will bring about a considerable reduction in the birth rate. At this rhythm, people can allow themselves the luxury of fighting against pollution and conserving their culture. As one French commentator put it: 'We expect to see an Algeria proud of being Muslim at 4,800 dollars a head as from the year 2000, taking its present level into account.'[5] Otherwise humanity will be racing towards a planetary Dachau!

The Parker report is no exception to the rule. On various points it is close to the approach already taken in 1977 by the Bariloche report to neutralize the alarmist effects of the Club of Rome's conclusions.[6] '"Because of the high rate of population growth, the African countries should have a growth of at least ten per cent a year", as Mr Edward Jaycox, until recently the "World Bank's Mr Africa", recalled in Paris not long ago.'[7]

The actress Mae West used to say: 'When I am good, I am good, but when I am bad, I am even better!' It is the same with growth. Good or bad, technology and growth are always good as they increase possibilities, create jobs (even while they are getting rid of others) and offer solutions to all the problems that they cause. Pollution or military expenditure thus become positive, because they stimulate the economy; the first because it triggers off new expenditure to remedy the effects of more GNP growth, the second because it generates demand through the income distributed, without there being a corresponding supply. Armaments, like large works of infrastructure, do not compete with the production of consumer goods. According to Keynesian logic, they can act as a jump-start for relaunching the economy.  Both pollution and military expenditure can become a fruitful source of exports and can help the balance of payments.

The call of 269 Nobel prizewinners, known as the Heidelberg Appeal, which was made during the Earth Summit in 1992, is yet another illustration of the strong belief in the blessings of science, technology, progress and growth.

Finally, what makes economic growth an indisputable good in the eyes of most people is that it is the result of behaviour that, in itself, is also moral. The utilitarian principle of justice found in the dominant morality (even including an author like John Rawls) can be reduced to: that is right which maximizes, first the GNP, and second the quantity of life itself. According to the analysis of Max Weber,[8] the take-off of the Western economy was a result of the generalization of an ethic: one of work and the entrepreneurial spirit, practised with scrupulous honesty, of enjoyment in making an effort, of rectitude, of punctuality, of renouncing sensual pleasures, and of the habit of saving. Unlimited material accumulation bears clear testimony to the accentuation of merits and the irrefutable proof of divine blessing. In spite of the repeated and striking failures of development projects in the Third World during the last four decades, the spectacle of 'mal-development' in numerous countries, they still seem to be incapable of challenging the model. It is true, as Marie-Dominique Perrot has said, that 'by systematically transforming nature and social relations into the marketing of goods and services … development seems to be the greatest and most comprehensive undertaking of dispossession and expropriation for the benefit of the dominating minorities that has ever happened.'[9]

However, all these well-founded criticisms gloss over the hardened and impermeable myth of good development and good growth. The reality of the 'good' of well-being, which is proposed as an objective, is not the quality of life but the quantity of gadgets considered as useful by the mere fact that they are being produced and consumed. Growth is a collection of 'things'; well-being is nothing else but 'well-having'. Development disenchants the world by expelling the values from things. By reducing the universe of creatures to the production of utilities, economic growth degrades ethics itself. Well-being is saturated by goods and, in the process, becomes confused with them. There is no escaping from vulgar utilitarianism.

Morality is more a hypocritical façade than a reality: in fact, deceit is everywhere. Business ethics exalts the will to power and egoism, and scorns the weak and the losers.[10] It falls back glibly into Social Darwinism when it is caught red-handed. Too bad for the losers! The advocates of 'good' development know all this and admit it. But the spectacle of the fantastic power of technical society inhibits all fundamental questioning – proof of its totalitarianism. And recourse is made to growth to dress the wounds that it has inflicted in the first place.

'The word development', wrote Bertrand Cabedoche, concluding his book, *Chrétiens et le Tiers Monde*, 'has perhaps lost its attraction as the result of too many disappointing experiences. It remains, however, the only word shared by all human beings to express their hope.'[11] May the planet perish, as long as development remains intact!

2. THE PARADOXES OF GROWTH

The claim of economic growth to be the basic objective of human society is therefore mainly based on the famous trickle-down effect, magnified by the euphoria of the myths of modernity. However, this seductive formulation cannot stand up to a serious examination. So many paradoxes beset the reasoning that the miracle effect, in fact, turns out to be the mirage effect.

The Poverty of Growth

We think of ourselves as an incredibly rich country, but we are beginning to realize that we are also a desperately poor country – poor in most of the things that throughout the history of mankind have been cherished as riches.

Charles A. Reich, *The Greening of America*, Random House, New York, 1970, p. 13.

The paradox of the creation of needs

It is through the creation of psychological tensions and frustrations that economic growth claims to satisfy the basic needs of humanity. It seems that economics cannot stand on its feet without using poverty as a crutch. Not only has the economic imagination literally invented 'scarcity', but the experience of poverty constitutes a condition of growth. The pressure of necessity serves as an engine for putting people to work, while the creation of the indispensable mass demand occurs by exacerbating new needs. The traditional systems for protecting people against poverty are, directly or indirectly, seen as obstacles, brakes and resistance to development and denounced as such by the experts. Simultaneously, the same economic theory makes growth a condition for eliminating poverty.

Thus, since the CFA franc has been devalued in Africa, the prospects for exporting meat open up for certain countries like Burkina Faso. The meat of the Sahel is now competitive with that of Argentina or the surpluses of the Common Market. The World Bank finances projects for developing livestock in this country. However, the experts tear their hair out when they meet herders who really don't see the need to increase their flocks beyond what is necessary, just to make money. 'What shall we do with all that money?' they ask. Such disappointments are quite frequent in the Third World; many similar anecdotes could be recounted.

Therefore, no growth without need, no remedy to poverty without plunging the population into indigence. True, this could be an example of a dialectical process, but it is not proven and the paradox gives rise to suspicion. As for the question of poverty, growth does not seem able to escape this major contradiction. Its attenuation during *Les Trentes Glorieuses* in the countries of the North, thanks to the trickle-down effect and the generalized diffusion of the fruits of growth: has it not been achieved, in fact, by exporting poverty to the South?[12]

The paradox of accumulation

Growth is presented, thanks to the trickle-down effect, as the miraculous remedy for inequalities. It enables difficult reforms of structures, such as agrarian reform, to be circumvented, and softens social conflict. The general idea is that rather than disputing the shares in a small cake it would be better to agree on making the cake bigger so that everyone has more and all have enough. It is a very attractive proposition but, at the same time, economists are unanimous in agreeing that accumulation cannot be achieved without a large inequality in incomes. Here, again, we have a new dialectic. To solve the inequality of conditions you must start by increasing the inequality. This is necessary if there are to be enough savings for investment to take place and ensure the take-off of the economy. Redistribution among the community, which often saves the poor in the South from plummeting into indigence, is the black sheep of the economists. In most development models, a certain inequality is, quite cynically, a necessary precondition of accumulation.

The ecological paradox of growth

This obsession with the GNP means that all production and all expenditure is positive – including those that are harmful and those that the latter renders necessary to neutralize their effects. 'All remunerated work', notes Jacques Ellul, 'is considered as added value, a generator of well-being, while investment in the anti-pollution industry does not add to well-being at all – at best it allows well-being to be conserved. No doubt it sometimes happens that the increase in value to be deducted is greater than the increase in value added.'[13] This is more and more likely.

In 1991, the USA spent $115 billion – that is, 2.1 per cent of the GNP – for the protection of the environment, and that is not all. It is calculated that the new 'Clean Air Act' is going to increase this cost by $45 to $55 billion a year.[14] True, the evaluations of the cost of pollution or the cost price of de-pollution are extremely delicate, problematic and, of course, controversial (see the discussions of the G7 meeting in Naples on the bill for Chernobyl). It is estimated that the greenhouse effect could cost an annual amount of between $600 and $1,200 billion in the years to come: that is, between 3 and 5 per cent of the world GNP.

The World Resources Institute, for its part, has tried to evaluate the reduction in rates of growth if there were to be a levy off natural capital from the viewpoint of sustainable development. For Indonesia, for example, the average yearly rate of growth between 1971 and 1984 would be brought down from 7.1 per cent to 4.0 per cent – and that takes only three resources into consideration: the destruction of forests, the draining of petrol and natural gas reserves, and soil erosion. The German economist W. Schultz has calculated, on the basis of a non-comprehensive list of pollution sources, that the damage incurred by the Federal Republic of Germany in 1985 would amount to 6 per cent of the GNP.[15] Could one even then be sure of having compensated for all the losses in 'natural capital'? It would be like saying that, in these conditions, growth is a myth!

What invalidates the whole ideology of growth is the fact that the trickle-down effect is an imposture. It has apparently functioned relatively well in the industrialized countries, particularly in the Thirty Glorious Years. But, with the globalization of the economy and the uncertainties in the Western economies since 1974, especially in employment, already things are not going very well. While, at the planetary level, the mechanism never functioned anyway. Between 1950 and 1987, according to the World Bank's own statistics, while the world's revenues multiplied by 2.5, the gap between the richest and the poorest fifths of the population grew from 30:1 to 60:1. All evaluations agree on this. 'In 1960', says a UNDP report, '20 per cent of the richest inhabitants of the planet disposed of revenues that were 30 times greater than the 20 per cent of the poorest. In 1990, the revenues of the richest 20 per cent were 60 times greater.'[16]

In the final analysis, growth depends on faith in progress and in techno-science. Self-growth is in a way part of its very concept, as is the case of technology, according to Jacques Ellul's analysis. We are confronted with an insane drive forward which has no other aim or motivation than a desperate escape from the present. This exhausting and endless rush is trampling more and more innocent flowers along the wayside, at the same time as endangering the survival of the planet. Such unlimited growth, at the rate of 10 per cent a year, will lead to 736 times more production within a century. One might well wonder if its very excess will not deprive it of any meaning. What could that mean, living 736 times better?

NOTES

1. Georges Canguilhem, *Études d'histoire et de philosophie des sciences,* Vrin, Paris, 1970, p. 115.
2. World Bank *Report* (Lawrence Salmen), Washington DC, 1991, p. 4.
3. Papal Encyclical, *Populorum progressio*, 1967.
4. Edouard Parker, *Objectif 10%,* Criterion, Paris, 1994.
5. As reported by Paul Fabra, '10% de croissance pour le Tiers Monde?', *Le Monde*, 3 December 1991.
6. Amilcar Herrera, *Un Monde pour tous,* Presses Universitaires de France, Paris, 1977.
7. Jean-Pierre Tuquoi, 'L'Afrique un peu moins pauvre', *Le Monde,* 8 November 1994.
8. *The Protestant Ethic and the Rise of Capitalism,* Charles Scribner, New York, 1958.
9. Marie-Dominique Perrot, 'Les empêcheurs du développement en rond', *Revue Ethnies*, vol. 6, no. 13, 1991, p. 5.
10. See Serge Latouche, *La Planète des Naufragés,* La Découverte, Paris, 1991, especially ch. 3.
11. Karthala, Paris, 1990, p. 255.
12. See Serge Latouche, 'Si la misère n'existait pas, il faudrait l'inventer', in *Il était une fois le développement*, Editions d'En Bas, Lausanne, 1986.
13. Jacques Ellul, *Le Bluff technologique*, Hachette, Paris, 1988, p. 76.
14. Figures given by *Le Monde,* 22 November 1991.
15. Hervé Kempf, *L'Économie à l'épreuve de l'écologie,* Hatier, Paris, 1991, p. 52.
16. UNDP, *World Report on Human Development*, UNDP, New York, 1992.

Translated by Victoria Bawtree

13

THE AGONY OF THE MODERN STATE

Rajni Kothari

RAJNI KOTHARI founded the Centre for the Study of Developing Societies in New Delhi in 1963. Among many other initiatives, he founded Lokayan and the important intellectual journal *Alternatives*. He is a former co-chairman of the International Foundation for Another Development (IFDA), which, thanks to its president, Marc Nerfin, was for many years one of the most important forums for voicing new ideas about the development process. A recipient of the Right Livelihood Award, Rajni Kothari is one of India's most eminent intellectuals and widely regarded as a leading critic of the modern state's tendencies to pursue authoritarian and anti-people development policies. His many books include *Poverty: Human Consciousness and the Amnesia of Development* (Penguin Books, New Delhi and Zed Books, London, 1995). The following text was written specially for this Reader.

The state in modern times has been a source of both law and legitimacy, of authority and monopoly over coercive power (or so it was presumed, and in that presumption lay its power), a source also of security for the people, of systems of justice, equity and accountability, and through them all, of conditions of freedom and creativity, the arts and the pursuit of excellence. It has been the premier institution through which the multiplicity and plurality of the civil domain has been ordered in both perception and reality.

The modern state began as both a philosophical idea and a political construct to deal with a widespread condition of chaos and uncertainty, and to provide conditions of peace, order and security in their place. So germane was it to the human enterprise at that stage (towards the end of the Middle Ages) that it soon became institutionalized, playing the role of international actor for the promotion of the same ideas of peace and security, now on a world scale, even though the 'world' was still a limited geograpical concept, confined as it was to the early Englishmen and Europeans. However, the process was further consolidated with the adoption of the nation-state format by a large array of newly emergent countries after the Second World War. The nation-state on the one hand, and the state system on the other, provided

The Birth of a Kleptocracy

The national bourgeoisie that took on the baton of rationalisation, industrialisation, bureaucratisation in the name of nationalism, turned out to be a kleptocracy. Their enthusiasm for nativism was a rationalisation of their urge to keep the national bourgeoisies of other nations – and particularly the powerful industrialised nations – out of their way.

Kwame Anthony Appiah, *In My Father's House: Africa in the Philosophy of Culture*, Methuen, London, 1992.

the fulcrum around which the world was organized. Even the superimposition of the two superpowers and the emergence of power blocs – or of the UN for that matter – did not reduce the importance of the state as the basic unit of organization and identity in the world. Insisting on the identity it creates being prior to all other identities, the state has either reduced all other corporate identities to individualized subjects or, to the extent it admitted the existence of the former in the form of a complex called civil society, it has purported to be both the embodiment and the protector of such civil society – including the embodiment of cultures, at once their plurality and their mono-cultural form called the nation or territory or region.

It is out of this search for centrality and legitimacy in the modern world, despite so much diversity all around, that a series of theoretical models defining the relationship between the state and the individual or the state and the citizen emerged. These models also reflect shifting perspectives on the state following the quickening of the historical process in Europe and beyond – the two world wars, the great depression following the collapse of the business cycle, the revolt of the masses ever since the French Revolution and leading up to the communist revolution, as well as the social-democratic alternatives to it, the rise of fascism on the one hand and Soviet-style totalitarianism on the other, the end of old-style imperialism and the redefinition of the economic *problématique* in our time, giving rise to new questionings, alternative models and hypotheses. We have had the bourgeois democratic liberal institutional model of the state based on the theory of accountability. Different but at times complementing it has been the social-democratic model of the state assuming responsibility for social transformation and the welfare of the people. We have had the Marxist model which has considered the bourgeois state as a committee of the dominant classes, but one that also supervises relations of production that by their very logic create contradictions that lead to a protracted class struggle ending in a revolutionary takeover by a vanguard party representing the proletariat. The transformation launched

under the Communist Party was meant, in stages, to usher in socialism and the ultimate withering away of the bourgeois state as we have known it.

In recent decades, with the growing sensitization in the human dimensions to the state and its policies, and realization of its increasingly repressive and exploitative thrust (in both bourgeois and communist countries), there has emerged a somewhat different conception of radicalism in the form of a liberal-cum-neo-Marxist model of the state as a space in which the struggle for civil and democratic rights is being waged with a view to ushering in a decentralized 'sustainable' and people-centred structure of institutions that would promote social transformation. This is the broad conception that what are known as the new social movements, together engaged in an attempt to create an alternative model of both development and democracy, have in mind.[1] There is also the Gandhian model of the state as trustee and arbiter between conflicting arenas of interest, from the perspective of serving the deprived strata of a society, the poor and the socially ostracized, through modes of decentralization and people's empowerment. My own idea (not yet a model) of the state is that of a plural arena which, while it displays growing use and misuse of the coercive apparatus and sinews of repression and terror, nevertheless continues to be a mediator among contending groups. Some of these claim the 'rights' of diverse citizen groups, and others the 'privileges' of a less diverse yet differentiated structure of entrenched interests and classes and bureaucracies. I think of it as an increasingly problematic yet still relevant arena encompassing the large diversity of both contending and coalescing populations and interests within a context of historic transformation based on the democratic aspirations of countless millions of people round the world.

Each of these models of the role and significance of the state is in transition, facing as it does new forces that are on the horizon (to which we shall presently return). While on the one hand there still exists a considerable degree of faith in the state, especially among common people, particularly the *dalits*, the general mass of the poor and the oppressed, the minorities and women,[2] which produces a kind of mystification of the state, on the other hand there is growing scepticism and doubt about its efficacy, producing a demystification and decline in both the aura and prestige that it once enjoyed. Instead of centrality and a dominant status, we face a combination of growing marginalization in the state's role and status in civil society, accompanied by growing myopia, dehumanization and brutalization in its relationship with that civil society. Interestingly, the marginalization of the state that seems to be proceeding apace is a result of both overextension and shrinkage. The international order itself, which was long based on the state system (even the capitalist development model had accepted the state as a key instrumentality), faces an era of uncertainty, following the Reaganite–Thatcherite reaction to the right, some of which may now be wearing off, though the basic mind-set continues and conditions the entire functioning of the world system. The so-called 'new world order' and the new Pax Americana represent ominous developments for hopes of a stable and predictable world. But no less serious is the new backlash in civil society, at the 'grass roots', representing new stirrings of consciousness and new assertions of power based, on the one hand, on class and ethnicity and, on the other, on nationality and religious identity. Thus the state as an institution is under severe strain. In consequence, it faces a variety of bids to take it over and undermine it in the name of the economy, world security, religion, ethnicity and notions of self-determination, of 'nations' and regions. These have especially grown since the collapse of the Soviet model of state hegemony in the ordering of social and economic relationships and the decline of the post-colonial movements of nation-building seeking both autonomy and legitimacy of the state in large parts of the Third World.

THE COLLAPSE OF THE SOVIET UNION: IMPLICATIONS FOR THE FUTURE OF THE STATE

In a way the collapse of the Soviet Union provides us with a historical vantage point from which to appreciate the growing erosion and marginalization of the state, in particular through its very overextension. Paradoxical as it may appear, while the Soviet Union was the ultimate in the wielding of state power, it also produced, over time, its erosion and delegitimization, a growing admission of the incapacity of the instrumentalities of state and party and loss of faith in them among both rulers and ruled. While we are still too close to events in the former Soviet Union, the full significance of which is still unravelling, there is little doubt that what we witnessed at the end of the 1980s was in many ways unique in modern history and cannot be explained except by reference to the hollowness of the whole corpus of the state within it. The phenomenon of Gorbachev and what happened under him[3] has been pushed to the background following the coup against him and the rise of Yeltsin, whose wholly adventurist politics, intended to refurbish the Soviet state – in which task he is not likely to succeed – have received the sustained backing of the USA.

The Gorbachev phenomenon, seen as an attempt to dismantle an overgrown state, presents a fascinating case history of marginalization through overextension. Never before had a leadership in control of so much power and such an array of instrumentalities to wield that power (the army, the scientific estate, immense nuclear power, the position of a superpower) itself dismantled the whole apparatus, allowed its vassals to go their own ways, completely shifted its ideological moorings, admitted that the entire edifice was unsuited to the needs of the people, and proceeded to disperse the whole framework of power and authority and the sinews of the state. Never before had so much change been brought about almost wholly non-violently – and that in a society that had never accepted the creed of non-violence.

Pierre Bungener:
Torture as a Normal Instrument of Power

There are thresholds which, when crossed, condemn any cause. When this situation is reached it is, indeed, a sign that the cause has ceased to be a good one. Man, by becoming like an animal, cannot claim to save man.

Torture is a cultural fact, carried out according to the level of our technologies:

- artisanal torture (bad treatment and police commissariats);
- more technical torture (requiring instruments) and also very refined ones; rejuvenated techniques, thanks to a highly developed technology, thanks to computers, thanks to electronics, thanks to the qualifications of torturers, who are electricians, doctors, psychologists and engineers.

Torture is practised, not only in difficult conditions as in war, but in peacetime, in order to maintain order.

Torture becomes a normal instrument of power.

From the handwritten notes of Pierre Bungener, read out during a conference of Amnesty International at the University of Geneva, 15 May 1978. Bungener was a great humanist and an early 'developer' who had the courage and lucidity to question different aspects of the new ideology. He was a director of the African Institute of Geneva (1962) and the president of the first Swiss section of Amnesty International (1970). The text is included in a posthumously published book: Pierre Bungener, *Le développement in-sensé*, Editions L'Age de l'Homme, Lausanne, 1978, p. 46. See also Darius Rejali in Suggested Readings.

And never had a such a society so sharply reduced its military might and its machinery of surveillance, intelligence and security, and that in a state whose major source of strength lay in its armed forces and its worldwide security and intelligence apparatus, or so drastically clipped the power of an all-pervasive party in whose structure of centralized control and institutional power the state had relied so much for more than seventy years.[4] What the long offensive of American imperial power and its worldwide network had failed to achieve over forty-five years was achieved by the play of ideas and the force of conviction of a few individuals occupying strategic positions. (At a time when doctrines of the 'end of ideology' and the 'end of history' have been advanced, it is notable that major changes in the global structure of power have taken place basically through the power of ideas.) And this quite clearly without any powerful and widespread movement from below.

The 'movement' that did take place was led by a unique set of intellectuals – Solzhenitsyn and his *Gulag*, Sakharov and his powerful dissent, the sufferings and voices of many other opponents of the Soviet state. What has happened is nothing short of an elite giving up its enormous power in order to impel their country toward political and social change.[5] The future of the former Soviet Union remains highly uncertain, but its dissolution has produced waves that will continue to have an impact on the state system as we have known it since the Second World War, as well as on the centralized nation-state as it has operated over large areas of the modern world for a still longer period. We have by no means arrived at a stage where we are willing to write off the modern state.[6] But that it faces increasing challenge, above all from the very dialectic it has let loose upon itself through the playing out, or over-playing, of its own (internal) inherent logic, there is no doubt. The challenge is by no means limited to this dialectic. It could have been contained and dealt with if that had been the case. The crisis is accentuated by the rise of new and powerful forces that have emerged outside the main arena of the state, threatening its status and survival as an institution, its role and position in human affairs.

NEW CHALLENGES THREATENING THE SURVIVAL OF THE STATE

The modern state, and particularly the nation-state as a centralized structure, faces serious challenges from at least three major sources. First, over the last few decades, technology seems to be replacing politics and socio-economic factors in the functioning of modern society, and this is seriously affecting the role of the state in civil society. It is leading to a process of de-politicization, to displacement of the civil servant accountable to elected bodies and the people at large by the technocrat accountable only to his peers, and to a momentum generated by the rise of the micro-chip and the computer and by impersonal forces that were always there but were somehow held in check by ideological and political factors in a system that was competitive, pluralistic and open to debate and controversy. It is not as if technology – and the rise of the machine in the affairs of man – was not there or was not there in an important way in earlier periods of history. The Industrial Revolution and its spread round the world was never without a major technological concomitant. But it was still technology as an instrument of man and of nations, including those (one imperial power after another) that had taken upon themselves the task of organizing the whole world in their own image.

The significant change that has now come about is that this organizing of the whole world is being taken up not so much by some imperial power or powers, but by technology and its own inner logic and dynamics, which are under no man's or nation's control. Indeed, not even the scientists and the technologists as individuals or associations know what the next step in the technological enterprise is likely to be. What we have is the dawn of an age of technological fixes without any identifiable fixer. Technology, whether in the field of military R&D (the leading sector in setting the global agenda for some time now),[7] informatics, medicine or agriculture (not to speak of genetics, eugenics and cloning) is assuming an autonomy of its own and subjecting the whole of mankind and civilization to a captive status. It is homogenizing diverse cultures and social sectors and marginalizing the political process. Naturally, in a technologically determined world, where there is little scope for real choices of a socio-political kind, the state loses its importance and governance itself undergoes a radical transformation. The fast changing nature of world capitalism to no small extent draws upon this primacy of modern technology (itself undergoing major transmutations) and has in consequence provided a system of global management to which 'there is no alternative' (the TINA hypothesis). This has further deeply affected the nature of governance in our time. (The recent debate in conservative circles about governments losing control over the governed reflects a condition in which the term 'governance' itself has changed its meaning.) If there is a widespread sense of insecurity round the world, including among those who are supposed to be in charge, it is primarily due to this condition created by modern technology and its institutional catalysts (the multinational corporations) towards which civil society, lay citizens and the state are being pushed.

However, precisely at a time when the state is being rendered weak and disembodied before the advance of technology, it is facing another major challenge from a source which is the polar opposite of technology and its homogenizing mission. That is the assertion of cultures, ethnicity, nationalities, pluralism with a vengeance, when entire societies are bursting at their seams in so many regions of the world, while the tension and violence generated by the cult of consumerism is spreading and destabilizing social arrangements. The resulting state of anomie is precipitating the violence of terrorism and fundamentalism, and the modern state, as we have known it, is ceasing to be able to contain either or to mediate between the two. With this, it is also ceasing to be an embodiment of civil society and a protector of the poor, the weak and the oppressed. The critique of the state as an arena of repression and terror is wholly valid as an empirical description of the relationship between the state and the citizen, but it must take cognizance of the fact that it is also a state that has become powerless before the onslaught of the deep dialectic of technology and culture in our time. The state is ceasing to be a state. It is becoming something else, which we as spectators facing the end of one millennium and the dawn of another must try to fathom but have so far been unable to do so.

This brings us to the third major source of challenge to the modern state, namely, the emergence of a new ideology, or rather a mind-set that is being proposed as a way out of all our problems and crises, including the crisis of the state. It is a mind-set that, far from rejecting the role of modern technology, is proposing to make it the new 'god' of man – away from the old ideologies of liberty, equality and fraternity, away from the role of the state in promoting these values: that is proposing to marginalize both god and the state, making human greed and avarice the prime movers of men and societies, and yet is coming forward and offering to mankind a new utopia – of globalization. It is a utopia that holds out the promise of a new integration of the human enterprise, of joining diverse cultures and civilizations into one single marketplace, nudging along governments and elites, and indeed the masses as well to catch up with this new fantasy. It is not integration based on diversity and of diverse entities finding a common ground, but rather one based on cut-throat competition and rivalry, using whichever means work, giving a new lease of life to the old idea of survival of the fittest. This had been contained by the rise of alternative visions and ideologies but, with the recent almost universal acceptance of the 'new world order', 'new society' and 'new democracy', now seems to offer a way out to all but the poor and the already dispossessed, who are in any case considered to be a surplus that can be dispensed with.[8]

As was mentioned in the beginning, the modern state emerged as a philosophical idea to deal with the situation of growing chaos and uncertainty, promising both order and justice. It seems that while the state as an institutional artefact may yet survive, the idea of the state that was so conceived may well be ending as a project of the modern age, exposing the world once again to chaos and uncertainty and without either order or justice.

NOTES

1. See the various issues and special numbers of the bi-monthly *Lokayan Bulletin* for documentation of the 'new social movements'. For a detailed critique of the Lokayan perspective and a major effort at providing a theoretical rationale for these movements, with emphasis in particular on peasant movements, see Gail Omvedt's ambitious *Reinvesting Revolution: New Social Movements and the Socialist Tradition in India*, M.E. Sharpe, New York, 1993.

2. I attempted to lay this out and to suggest that it leads to a quite different model of radicalism than found in the new social movements, in my 'Rise of the *Dalits* and the Renewed Debate on Caste', *Economic and Political Weekly*, Bombay, 25 June 1994.

3. For an early, and critical, appraisal of the Gorbachev phenomenon, see my 'The New Detente: Some Reflections from the South', *Alternatives*, vol. 14, no. 3, July 1989.

4. See my 'Soviet Developments in Wider Perspective', *Mainstream,* Annual Number, 1991.

5. For a highly perceptive analysis of Gorbachev's contribution in taking his country along a path that almost completely departed from the Soviet Union's established ideological as well as strategic positions, without at the same time renouncing its socialist commitments, see Bhupinder Brar's important study, *Explaining Communist Crises*, Ajanta, Delhi, 1994, especially ch. 7 on 'Perestroika, Powercentrism and the Hegemonic Universe'.

6. Indeed, there are signs of renewed legitimacy of the state in many parts of the world following the adverse results of privatization in the Third World, the return to power of former communist parties in some eastern European countries, and the decline

in romanticism about regional zones based on free trade and the economic prosperity resulting from it (including in Europe itself). Nevertheless there continues to be scepticism about the state enjoying a monopoly of power, and we have witnessed a steady growth in globalization of trade, technology and finance capital, as well as in the consumerist drives of the post-modern world. I have discussed the revival of interest in and legitimacy of the state in my article 'Under Globalisation, Will the Nation State Hold?', *Economic and Political Weekly*, Bombay, 1 July 1995, as well as in an earlier piece entitled 'State and Statelessness in our time', *Economic and Political Weekly*, Bombay, Annual Number, vol. 26, no. 11–12, March 1991.

7. I have discussed the idea of the military being a lead sector in global affairs largely as a result of ever new technological breakthroughs in 'Peace as a Technology Fix', paper presented at conference on conflict resolution at Dunedin, New Zealand, 1987, published in my *Transformation and Survival: In Search of Humane World Order*, Ajanta, Delhi, 1988.

8. On the dispensability thesis, see my 'Of Humane Governance', *Alternatives* 12, 1987, also published in *State against Democracy: In Search of Humane Governance*, Ajanta, Delhi, 1988.

14

EDUCATION AS AN INSTRUMENT OF CULTURAL DEFOLIATION: A MULTI-VOICE REPORT

Joseph Ki-Zerbo, Cheikh Hamidou Kane, Jo-Ann Archibald, Edouard Lizop and Majid Rahnema

Five voices are heard in this presentation. They come from very different parts of the world. Although they have all been 'schooled', they seem to share similar views on the ways the new imported educational systems are now focused on transforming their users into becoming 'developed' versions of an uprooted *homo oeconomicus*.

Ki-Zerbo was the first to use the terms 'insular' and 'culturally defoliant' to describe the imported colonial school. For him, this institution could also be compared to a sacred wood where only a few initiated people would enter to perform esoteric rites beyond ordinary people.

JOSEPH KI-ZERBO is a well-known educator and historian from Burkina Faso. His book *Histoire de l'Afrique Noire*, published by Hatier in 1978, is already a classic. He was a major contributor to the UNESCO-sponsored *General History of Africa* (7 vols), and director of the first volume, *Methodology and African Prehistory*. He was also a member of the Executive Board of UNESCO in the late 1970s.

CHEIKH HAMIDOU KANE is from Senegal. He is an economist by profession and a former Planning Minister. However, it is through his penetrating autobiographical novel, *L'Aventure ambiguë*, that he established himself as a great African writer.

JO-ANN ARCHIBALD is the director of the First Nation House of Learning at the University of British Columbia, Vancouver, Canada. Her research interests include First Nations' education curricula, higher education and story-telling.

EDOUARD LIZOP, who died in 1995, was an educator of great imagination and integrity. He was the principal founder of the Schools for Collective Promotion (Écoles de Promotion Collective), an initiative launched in Africa in the 1950s,

Modern Education and the Creation of Discontinuities

Primitive education was a process by which continuity was maintained between parents and children ... Modern education includes a heavy emphasis upon the function of education to create discontinuities – to turn the child of the peasant into a clerk, of the farmer into a lawyer, of the Italian immigrant into an American, of the illiterate into the literate.

Margaret Mead, from 'Our Education Emphases in Primitive Perspective', in *Education and the Cultural Process*, reprinted from the *American Journal of Sociology*, XLVIII, May 1943, p. 9.

which aimed at finding a creative alternative to the imported model of schooling. Like the Gandhian Nai Taleem, it was warmly welcomed by the first generation of African educators, but nipped in the bud by the bureaucrats within the ministries of education.

MAJID RAHNEMA was Minister for Science and Higher Education in Iran from 1967 to 1971. He is the co-author, with Edgar Faure, of the UNESCO Commission Report *Learning to Be* (Fayard/UNESCO, Paris, 1972), and was a member of the Executive Board of UNESCO from 1974 to 1978.

JOSEPH KI-ZERBO

The 'insular school' is a dangerous cyst and a 'soul-eater'

[School] is a temple of knowledge accessible only to the neophytes, and those who enter there are to accomplish a sort of interplanetary voyage: they encounter a strange decoration, scenery composed of travel agency leaflets.... Here, it is a beech tree in its autumn sumptuousness, which contrasts cruelly with the shaggy and easy-going baobab tree that one stares at distractedly through the window. There, it is a cow from Brittany sitting enthroned on a wall, apparently the first to wonder at its presence there.

It is also a school for uprooting ... a dangerous cyst, a tumor which might only too often prove to be cancerous... [It is socially uprooting, for] once you are selected [to be part of it], you are considered by your own parents as a sort of raw material destined to come out of the process as a very clean-looking and well-esteemed clerk. And the mentality of the pupil himself changes similarly...

[The modern school tends to rob the student of his historic memory. There, one is trained to lose one's personality, no longer being able to recognize one's father or mother or home.] As children are cut off from their historic roots, entire populations risk losing their personality... One learns the dictionary by heart, perhaps to read Tacitus in the original text, but one becomes unable to speak naturally to one's own mother... [They become] 'cultural proletarians, victims of *zombification*', to use Depestre's words. The '*zombi*', in Haitian Creole, is a person whose soul and spirit have been stolen from him, leaving him just his body and his labour power. In Africa, too, we know of 'soul eaters' [*mangeurs d'âmes*]. This process of depersonalization is such that many an African academic whose mind has been moulded by the training country's camp out amongst their own people as agents of technical assistance... For one Senghor, how many millions of obscure *zombies*! For one Césaire, how many a *zombi* who will never write or, even less, live the experience of the *Cahiers d'un retour au pays natal*...[1]

[On another plane, the imported school leads to an economic dead-end and a social powder keg.] One wonders whether school does not create more problems than it solves. It is the origin of this general exodus which is common to all underdeveloped countries, particularly in Africa... The student with a primary school certificate goes to the little town, the one with a high-school diploma to the capital, the graduate and the postgraduate to rich countries. Rural zones which have paid for the expenses of education thus end up by being punctured, with their vitality, their capacity to progress and even to survive pumped out of them. Living in the cities, they are nothing but wrecks. They become like uprooted trees which cannot be replanted elsewhere. They are literally cut off, carried on a river that often has no port.

Finally, school tends to be increasingly anti-democratic. Perceived as a source of upward social mobility, it is desired by everyone, but it actually serves people who are already 'educated', thus becoming the preserve of a small minority.[2]

CHEIKH HAMIDOU KANE

The New School: The Cannon and the Magnet

A hundred years ago our grandfather, along with all the inhabitants of this countryside, was awakened one morning by an uproar arising from the river. He took his gun and, followed by all the elite of the region, he flung himself upon the newcomers. His heart was intrepid, and to him the value of liberty was greater than the value of life. Our grandfather, and the elite of the country with him, was defeated. Why? How? Only the newcomers know. We must ask them: we must go to learn from them the art of conquering without being in the right. Furthermore, the conflict has not yet ceased. The foreign school is the new form of the war which those who have come here are waging...[3]

[But] the country of the Diallobé was not the only one which had been awakened by a great clamour early one day. The entire black continent had its moment of clamour.

Strange dawn! The morning of the Occident in black Africa was spangled over with smiles, with cannon shots, with shining glass beads. Those who had no history were encountering those who carried the world on their shoulders. It was a morning of *accouchement*: the known world was enriching itself by a birth that took place in mire and blood.

From shock, the one side made no resistance. They were a people without a past, therefore without memory. The men who were landing on their shores were white, and mad. Nothing like them had ever been known. The deed was accomplished before the people were even conscious of what had happened.

Some among the Africans, such as the Diallobé, brandished their shields, pointed their lances, and aimed their guns. They were allowed to come close, then the cannon were fired. The vanquished did not understand…

Others wanted to parley. They were given a choice: friendship or war. Very sensibly, they chose friendship. They had no experience at all.

The result was the same, nevertheless, everywhere.

Those who had shown fight and those who had surrendered, those who had come to terms and those who were obstinate – they all found themselves, when the day came, checked by census, divided up, classified, labelled, conscripted, administered.

For the newcomers did not know only how to fight. They were strange people. If they knew how to kill with effectiveness, they also knew how to cure, with the same art. Where they had brought disorder, they established a new order. They destroyed and they constructed. On the black continent it began to be understood that their true power lay not in the cannons of the first morning, but rather in what followed the cannons.

Thus, behind the gunboats, the clear gaze of the Most Royal Lady of the Diallobé had seen the new school.

The new school shares at the same time the characteristics of cannon and magnet. From the cannon it draws its efficacy as an arm of combat. Better than the cannon, it makes conquest permanent. The cannon compels the body, the school bewitches the soul. Where the cannon has made a pit of ashes and of death, in the sticky mold of which men would not have rebounded from the ruins, the new school establishes peace. The morning of rebirth will be a morning of benediction through the appeasing virtue of the new school.

From the magnet, the school takes its radiating force. It is bound up with a new order, as a magnetic stone is bound up with a field. The upheaval of the life of man within this new order is similar to the overturn of certain physical laws in a magnetic field. Men are seen to be composing themselves, conquered, along the lines of invisible and imperious forces. Disorder is organized, rebellion is appeased, the mornings of resentment resound with songs of a universal thanksgiving.

Only such an upheaval in the natural order can explain how, without either of them wanting it, the new man and the new school come together just the same. For neither of them wants the other. The man does not want the school because in order that he may live – that is, be free, feed and clothe himself – it imposes upon him the necessity of sitting henceforth, for the required period, upon its benches. No more does the school want the man because in order to survive – that is, extend itself and take roots where its necessity has landed it – it is obliged to take account of him...[4]

It is certain that nothing pervades our lives with such clamour as the needs of which their school permits the satisfaction. We have nothing left – thanks to them – and it is thus that they hold us. He who wants to live, who wants to remain himself, must compromise...[5]

The chief [of the Diallobé] remained silent for a moment.

'If I told them to go to the new school,' he said at last, 'they would go *en masse*. They would learn all the ways of joining wood to wood which we do not know. But, learning, they would also forget. Would what they learn be worth as much as what they would forget? I should like to ask you: can one learn *this* without forgetting *that*, and is what one learns worth what one forgets?'...[6]

'The school in which I would place our children [concluded the Most Royal Lady] will kill in them what today we love and rightly conserve with care. Perhaps the very memory of us will die in them. When they return from school, there may be those who will not recognize us. What I am proposing is that we should agree to die in our children's hearts and that the foreigners who have defeated us should fill the place, wholly, which we shall have left free.'[7]

JO-ANN ARCHIBALD

The Effects of Schooling on the First Nations of America[8]

During the 1900s, First Nations leaders throughout British Columbia voiced their concerns about the negative effects of education upon their children, families and communities. Children were returning home as strangers to their cultural ways, and critical of the family and community way of life. The late George Manuel condemned the residential schools for devastating the family unit and denigrating the students' culture:

> Our values were as confused and warped as our skills. The priest had taught us to respect them by whipping us until we did what we were told. Now we would not move unless we were threatened with a whip. We came home to relatives who had never struck a child in their lives. These people, our mothers and fathers, aunts and uncles and grandparents, failed to represent themselves as a threat, when that was the only thing we had been taught to understand. Worse than that, they spoke an uncivilized and savage language and were filled with superstitions. After a year learning to see and hear only what the priests and brothers wanted you to see and hear, even the people we loved came to look ugly.[9]

School as a Factor of Division and Disintegration

European school, which was perhaps a factor of national union and unification in Europe, appears to be a factor of national division in Third World countries. Its role is to separate and to select. While it was a means of social integration in Europe, it has proved to be here a means of disintegration. While this same school had participated in the *creation* of a identity and of national consciousness, here it leads to the *imitation* of the identity and of the national consciousness of other peoples.

Jean-Pierre Lepri: *Quelle Ecole pour la Guinée-Bissau?*, mimeographed report for UNESCO, June 1985, p. 63 (translated by Majid Rahnema). Jean-Pierre Lepri was a UNESCO consultant in Guinea-Bissau in the 1980s. In close collaboration with his Guinean counterparts, he developed an intimate knowledge of the country's educational questions, which were reflected in his reports to the government and to UNESCO. Most of them remained in the drawers of their respective archives. See, in particular, his highly illuminating book: *Education et Nationalité en Guinée-Bissau: Contribution à l'étude de l'endogénéité de l'éducation*, Se Former+, Lyon, 1989.

EDOUARD LIZOP

Schools as Instruments of Humiliation

The people of Africa are endowed with a grace of communication and participation that our younger generations seek, sometimes with anguish, sometimes with happiness, sometimes bordering on the grotesque... One can finish a long and brilliant university training without ever having been provoked to dance, to sing, to paint or to talk... As soon as a school is opened, it creates around itself a zone of cultural depression, as it were. Ask an African school teacher what the cultural resources of his village are. He will answer: the school – and nothing else... Maybe the missionary, but often because he, too, is imported. But the market, the palaver tree, the dance, the song, the language of the tam-tam, the tales and the proverbs, the historical and legendary stories, the potter, the blacksmith, the weaver are not for him sources of culture. School acts as an instrument of humiliation. It establishes its empire upon the destruction of whatever it is not, whereas its mission should be to reveal to everyone all the riches and gifts they represent...

A missionary was no longer wanted by a village. Bishop Zoa of Yaoundé was entrusted with a mission of reconciliation. He explained to the population that, by opening his school, the missionary was only inspired by a spirit of devotion to the population. An old man intervened: 'It is not a service that the Father has rendered to us. On the contrary, he has done us the greatest wrong.

Because, when there was no school here, we could go to our plantations with our children: now they cannot come, and they have nothing to do.'

This anecdote impressed the Lord Bishop of Yaoundé to such an extent that, long after the old man had spoken to him, he said to me: 'Imagine if the old man had been able to talk like that to a Minister of Education... Something wonderful might perhaps have happened.'[10]

MAJID RAHNEMA

The Excluding Processes of the School System[11]

The school system, introduced by colonialism in countries under their rule, was soon co-opted by the emerging nation-states. It became one of the most important vehicles of development strategy, being presented to the excluded as the answer to all the problems of their 'underdevelopment', the redeeming genie which could henceforth save their children from misery and shame.

In reality, schools served other purposes. They acted as a rather efficient channel for sieving out, into the Power Establishment, their most ambitious customers. They sometimes did serve as a cultural medium for some exceptionally bright individuals who succeeded in taking advantage of the learning resources for liberating ends. Yet, as a whole, they fostered unprecedented processes of exclusion against the poor and the powerless, despite their claims to serve as a new instrument of democratization.

These excluding processes operated at a number of levels. In relation to the society at large, they destroyed all previously established systems of cultural reference. As the only recognized providers of education, they systematically discredited all previously established mechanisms that different cultures had created throughout their histories for fostering knowledge and culture. The old days described by Julius Nyerere, when 'every adult was a teacher', were over. Now, only those certified by the school system, according to its self-devised criteria, had the right to teach; and only those whose abilities were recognized by the latter could be admitted to learn.

Education thus became a scarcity. And the same system which had created this scarcity was asked to deal with it. The management and the further production of this scarcity reinforced the new economistic perception of reality, entailing a broad range of new exclusions. Literacy campaigns often turned out to be campaigns *against* the non-literate, rather than helping the oral populations to educate themselves and learn as they had always done. For, on the one hand, the adoption of one or two official languages at the national level – either that of the former colonial ruler, or that of the larger dominant ethnic group – excluded all the vernacular and spoken languages that had hitherto served as the main instruments of learning. On the other hand, the absence or the scarcity of any useful printed material in such languages (these often being reduced to propaganda publications by the authorities) further marginalized the non-literate and the unschooled. On the whole, such campaigns ended up creating new classes of social drop-outs.

As to the imported 'modern' schools, they acted as yet another instrument of exclusion by allowing only a small minority of their clients to acquire social recognition. Besides their own army of drop-outs (2–10 per thousand students in the case of Guinea-Bissau), all adults, peasants, women, working people of all ages, and all other learners who, for some reason, could not afford to spend long periods of their life at school, were equally excluded.

Another aspect of the schools' excluding and divisive action has been extensively analysed: the separation of students from their parents and their cultural milieu. The instilling in them, in homeopathic doses, of new alienating values, attitudes and goals, drives them gradually to reject or even despise their own cultural and personal identity. They acquire a false sense of superiority, which turns them away from manual work, from real life and from all unschooled people, whom they tend to perceive as ignorant and underdeveloped.

Thus, a 'cultural gap' develops fast between the newly schooled 'elites' and the rest of the population, a phenomenon that has been largely responsible for the well-publicized rural exodus. The most 'successful' students abandon their village folk and leave, often for good, first for the big cities, later for foreign lands, fostering the process known as the 'brain drain'. As a result, the poor and the excluded pay the cost of an educational system that not only deprives them of any possibility of educating themselves but also severs them forever from some of the most potentially valuable elements of their community, from people who could have acted as their best teachers and friends in all matters concerning their liberation. As to the 'uprooted', they are set adrift, in many cases without ever being able to find new roots for themselves.

As such, the newly reformed 'national' school followed, in terms of its societal goals, the same as those assigned to the old colonial school. According to Albert Moumouni,[12] one Brevie, then governor general of France in French Africa, had summed up these goals as follows:

> Political and economic interests have imposed a two-fold task on our work in education. On the one hand, we must train indigenous cadres to become our auxiliaries in every area and assure ourselves of a meticulously chosen elite. We must also educate the masses to bring them closer to us and transform their way of life. From the political standpoint we must make known our intention of bringing people to the French way of life; from the economic viewpoint we must train the producers and consumers of to-morrow.

This consistency of the producer/consumer approach to education, conceived as an instrumental commodity, is seen in all the 'educational strategies' inspired by the development discourse. In such a context, one can better understand the statement of a former US ambassador and president of the American University of Cairo, when explaining his idea of what constituted an educational 'success'. In his memoirs,[13] he mentions that he regards one of his AUC students as 'a great success because he ended up practically owning the Coca Cola concession in Khartoum'.

NOTES

1. The last part of this paragraph is translated from Ki-Zerbo's article, 'L'Education permanente et l'Afrique', in *Orientations* (Essais et recherches en éducation), no. 43, July 1972, p. 16.
2. Excerpts translated in the last three paragraphs are taken from a speech Ki-Zerbo made in Paris on 5 December 1969, as the secretary general of CAMES (Conseil Africain et Malgache de l'Enseignement Supérieur, Upper Volta – now Burkina Faso).
3. Excerpts from Cheikh Hamidou Kane, *Ambiguous Adventure*, trans. Katherine Woods, Heinemann, London, 1972, p. 37. The 'collage' that makes up this presentation has been taken from parts of the book where Cheikh Hamidou Kane talks about the traditional and the new school.
4. Ibid., pp. 49–50.
5. Ibid., p. 10.
6. Ibid., p. 34.
7. Ibid., p. 46.
8. Extracted from a mimeographed paper entitled, 'Educational Perspectives, Challenges of First Nations Education in the Year 2000', delivered at the Faculty of Education, Simon Fraser University, Vancouver.
9. George Manuel and Michael Posluns, *The Fourth World: An Indian Reality*, Collier-Macmillan, Toronto, 1974, p. 65.
10. Extracted from Edouard Lizop, *Chroniques*, CODIAM (Comité pour le Développement des Investissements Intellectuels en Afrique et à Madagascar), Paris, 1973, pp. 49-50, 21.
11. Excerpts from a lecture at Stanford University (16 April 1985), entitled: 'Education as Participation or Exclusion?' The full text of the lecture was published in Spanish in *El Gallo*, Mexico, 25 August 1985.
12. Albert Moumouni, *Education in Africa*, trans. Phyllis Nauts, Praeger, New York; André Deutsch, London, 1968.
13. John Badeau, *The Middle East Remembered*, The Middle East Institute, Washington DC, 1983.

15

WESTERN SCIENCE AND ITS DESTRUCTION OF LOCAL KNOWLEDGE

Vandana Shiva

The following text is taken from the second chapter, 'Science, Nature and Gender', of the book *Staying Alive: Women, Ecology and Development* (Zed Books, London, 1989). The book examines the position of women in relation to nature – the forests, the food chain and water supplies – linking the violation of nature with the violation and marginalization of women, especially in the Third World. Both arise from assumptions in economic development, which the author argues should be more aptly described as 'maldevelopment'. One result is that the impact of science, technology and politics, along with the workings of the economy itself, are inherently exploitative. The author suggests that there is only one path to survival and liberation for nature, women *and* men, and that is the ecological path of harmony, sustainability and diversity.

VANDANA SHIVA – physicist, philosopher and feminist – is director of the Research Foundation for Science, Technology and Natural Resource Policy, in Dehradun, India. She has been very active in citizens' action against environmental destruction and is highly critical of current agricultural and reproductive technologies. Her other books include *The Violence of the Green Revolution: Third World Agriculture, Ecology and Politics* (Zed Books, London, 1991), and *Monocultures of the Mind: Perspectives on Biodiversity and Biotechnology* (Zed Books, London and Third World Network, Penang, 1993).

Maldevelopment is intellectually based on, and justified through, reductionist categories of scientific thought and action. Politically and economically, each project which has fragmented nature and displaced women from productive work has been legitimized as 'scientific' by operationalizing reductionist concepts to realize uniformity, centralization and control. Development is thus the introduction of 'scientific agriculture', 'scientific animal husbandry', 'scientific water management' and so on. The reductionist and universalizing tendencies of such 'science' become inherently violent and destructive in a world which is inherently interrelated and diverse. The feminine principle becomes an oppositional category of non-violent ways of conceiving the world, and of acting in it to sustain all life by maintaining the interconnectedness and diversity of nature. It allows an ecological transition from violence to non-violence, from destruction to creativity, from anti-life to life-giving processes, from uniformity to diversity, and from fragmentation and reductionism to holism and complexity.

It is thus not just 'development' which is a source of violence to women and nature. At a deeper level, scientific knowledge, on which the development process is based, is itself a source of violence. Modern reductionist science, like development, turns out to be a patriarchal project which has excluded women as experts, and simultaneously excluded ecological and holistic ways of knowing that understand and respect nature's processes and interconnectedness *as science.*

MODERN SCIENCE AS PATRIARCHY'S PROJECT

Modern science is projected as a universal, value-free system of knowledge which has displaced all other belief and knowledge systems by its universality and value-neutrality, and by the logic of its method arrived at objective claims about nature. Yet the dominant stream of modern science, the reductionist or mechanical paradigm, is a particular response of a particular group of people. It is a specific project of Western man which came into being during the fifteenth, sixteenth and seventeenth centuries as the much-acclaimed Scientific Revolution. During the last few years feminist scholarship has begun to recognize that the dominant science system emerged as a liberating force, not for humanity as a whole (though it legitimized itself in terms of universal betterment of the species), but as a masculine and patriarchal project which necessarily entailed the subjugation of both nature and women. Harding has called it a 'Western, bourgeois, masculine project',[1] and according to Keller, 'Science has been produced by a particular sub set of the human race, that is, almost entirely by white, middle-class males. For the founding fathers of modern science, the reliance on the language of gender was explicit; they sought a philosophy that deserved to be called 'masculine', that could be distinguished from its ineffective predecessors by its 'virile' powers, its capacity to bind Nature to man's service and make her his slave.'[2]

Bacon (1561–1626) was the father of modern science, the originator of the concept of the modern research institute and industrial science, and the inspiration behind the Royal Society. His contribution to modern science and its organization is critical. From the point of view of nature, women and marginal groups, however, Bacon's programme was not humanly inclusive. It was a special programme benefiting the middle-class European male entrepreneur through the conjunction of human knowledge and power in science.

In Bacon's experimental method, which was central to this masculine project, there was a dichotomizing between male and female, mind and matter, objective and subjective, rational and emotional, and a conjunction of masculine and scientific dominating over nature, women and the non-West. His was not a 'neutral, 'objective', 'scientific' method – it was a masculine mode of aggression against nature and domination over women. The severe testing of hypotheses through controlled manipulations of nature, and the necessity of such manipulations if experiments are to be repeatable, are here formulated in clearly sexist metaphors. Both nature and inquiry appear conceptualized in ways modelled on rape and torture – on man's most violent and misogynous relationships with women – and this modelling is advanced as a reason to value science. According to Bacon, 'the nature of things betrays itself more readily under the vexations of art than in its natural freedom'.[3] The discipline of scientific knowledge and the mechanical inventions it leads to do not 'merely exert a gentle guidance over nature's course; they have the power to conquer and subdue, to shake her to her foundations'.[4]

FRANCIS BACON

In *Tempores Partus Masculus* or The Masculine Birth of Time, translated by Farrington in 1951, Bacon promised to create a blessed race of heroes and supermen who would dominate both nature and society.[5] The title is interpreted by Farrington as suggesting a shift from the older science, represented as female – passive and weak – to a new masculine science of the scientific revolution which Bacon saw himself as heralding in New Atlantis. Bacon's Bensalem was administered from Solomon's House, a scientific research institute, from which male scientists ruled over and made decisions for society, and decided which secrets should be revealed and which remain the private property of the institute.

Science-dominated society has evolved very much in Bensalem, with nature being transformed and mutilated in modern Solomon's Houses – corporate labs and the university programmes they sponsor. With the new biotechnologies, Bacon's vision of controlling reproduction for the sake of production is being realized, while the green revolution and the bio-revolution have realized what, in New Atlantis, was only a utopia.

> We make by act trees and flowers to come earlier or later than their seasons, and to come up and bear more speedily than by their natural course they do. We make them by act greater, much more than their nature, and their fruit greater and sweeter and of differing taste, smell, colour and figure from their nature.[6]

For Bacon, nature was no longer Mother Nature, but a female nature, conquered by an aggressive masculine mind. As Carolyn Merchant points out, this transformation of nature from a living, nurturing mother to inert, dead and manipulable matter was eminently suited to the exploitation imperative of growing capitalism. The nurturing earth image acted as a cultural constraint on the exploitation of nature. 'One does not readily slay a mother, dig her entrails or mutilate her body.' But the mastery and domination images created by the Baconian programme and the scientific revolution removed all restraint and functioned as cultural sanctions for the denudation of nature:

The Mind that Has No Anchor

When the world is confronted with something totally new, all our old answers, codes, traditions are inadequate.

...There are two attitudes in the world. These are the only states of mind that are of value, the true religious spirit and the true scientific mind.

...The scientific mind is very factual. Discovery is its mission, its perception. It sees things through a microscope, through a telescope; everything is to be seen actually as it is; from that perception, science draws conclusions, builds up theories. Such a mind moves from fact to fact.

...Then there is the religious mind, the true religious mind that does not belong to any cult, to any group, to any religion, to any organized church. The religious mind is not the Hindu mind, the Christian mind, the Buddhist mind, or the Muslim mind. The religious mind does not belong to any group which calls itself religious. Nor is it a religious mind that holds to certain forms of beliefs, dogmas. The religious mind is completely alone. It is a mind that has seen through the falsity of churches, dogmas, beliefs, traditions. Not being nationalistic, not being conditioned by its environment, such a mind has no horizons, no limits. It is explosive, new, young, fresh, innocent. The innocent mind, the young mind, the mind that is extraordinarily pliable, subtle, has no anchor. It is only such a mind that can experience that which you call god, that which is not measurable.

A human being is a true human being when the scientific spirit and the true religious spirit go together. Then human beings will create a good world.

Krishnamurti, excerpts from talks with students in Rishi Valley, in *On Education*, Krishnamurti Foundation Trust, Madras, 1974, pp. 173, 24–6.

> The removal of animistic organic assumptions about the cosmos constituted the death of nature – the most far-reaching effect of the scientific revolution. Because nature was now viewed as a system of dead, inert particles moved by external, rather than inherent forces, the mechanical framework itself could legitimate the manipulation of nature. Moreover, as a conceptual framework, the mechanical order had associated with it a framework of values based on power, fully compatible with the directions taken by commercial capitalism.[7]

Modern science was a consciously gendered, patriarchal activity. As nature came to be seen more like a woman to be raped, gender too was re-created. Science as a male venture, based on the subjugation of female nature and female sex, provided support for the polarization of gender. Patriarchy as the new scientific and technological power was a political need of emerging industrial capitalism. While on the one hand the ideology of science sanctioned the denudation of nature, on the other it legitimized the dependency of women and the authority of men. Science and masculinity were associated in domination over nature and femininity, and the ideologies of science and gender reinforced each other. The witch-hunting hysteria, which was aimed at annihilating women in Europe as knowers and experts, was contemporaneous with two centuries of scientific revolution. It reached its peak with Galileo's *Dialogue* concerning the Two Chief World Systems and died with the emergence of the Royal Society of London and the Paris Academy of Sciences.[8]

> The interrogation of witches as a symbol for the interrogation of nature, the courtroom as model for its inquisition, and torture through mechanical devices as a tool for the subjugation of disorder were fundamental to the scientific method as power. For Bacon, as for Harvey, sexual politics helped to structure the nature of the empirical method that would produce a new form of knowledge and a new ideology of objectivity seemingly devoid of cultural and political assumptions.[9]

The Royal Society, inspired by Bacon's philosophy, was clearly seen by its organizers as a masculine project. In 1664, Henry Oldenberg, Secretary of the Royal Society, announced that the intention of the Society was to 'raise a *masculine philosophy*... whereby the Mind of Man may be ennobled with the knowledge of solid Truths.'[10] And for Glanvill, the masculine aim of science was to know 'the ways of captivating Nature, and making her subserve our purposes, thereby achieving the Empire of Man Over Nature.'[11] Glanvill advocated chemistry as one of the most useful arts, for 'by the *violence* of its artful fires it is made to confess those latent parts, which upon less provocation it would not disclose.'[12] The 'de-mothering' of nature through modern science and the marriage of knowledge with power was simultaneously a source of subjugating women as well as non-European peoples. Robert Boyle, the famous scientist who was also the Governor of the New England Company, saw the rise of mechanical philosophy as an instrument of power not just over nature but also over the original inhabitants of America. He explicitly declared his intention of ridding the New England Indians of their ridiculous notions about the workings of nature. He attacked their perception of nature 'as a kind of goddess', and argued that 'the veneration wherewith men are imbued for what they call nature has been a discouraging impediment to the empire of man over the inferior creatures of God.'[13]

Today, with new ecological awareness, ecologists the world over turn to the beliefs of native American and other indigenous peoples as a special source for learning how to live in harmony with nature. There are many today from the ecology and women's movements who see irrationality in Boyle's impulse for the empire of white man over nature and other peoples, and who see rationality in the words of Indian Chief Smohalla when he cried out: 'You ask me to plough the ground: shall I take a knife and tear my mother's bosom? You ask me to cut grass and make hay and sell it and be rich like white men, but how dare I cut off my mother's hair?'[14]

Chief Seattle's letter, which has become a major inspiration for the ecology movement, states:

> This we know – the earth does not belong to man, man belongs to the earth. All things are connected like the blood which unites one family. Whatever befalls the earth befalls the sons of the earth. Man did not weave the web of life; he is merely a strand in it. Whatever he does to the web, he does to himself.

The ecological and feminist alternatives to reductionist science are clearly not the first attempt to create a science of nature that is not gendered and disruptive. The period of the scientific revolution itself was full of alternatives to the masculine project of mechanistic, reductionist science, and it was also full of struggles between gendered and ungendered science. Bacon and Paracelsus are the leading exponents of the two competing trends of modern science in seventeenth-century Europe.[15] The Paracelsians belonged to the hermetic tradition, which did not dichotomize between mind and matter, male and female. The mechanical tradition, represented by Bacon, created dichotomies between culture and nature, mind and matter, and male and female, and devised a conceptual strategy for the former to dominate over the latter. The two visions of science were also two visions of nature, power and gender relations. For Paracelsus, the male did not dominate over the female, the two complemented each other; and knowledge and power did not arise from dominating over nature but from 'cohabiting with the elements',[16] which were themselves interconnected to form a living organism. For the Paracelsian, 'The whole world is knit and bound within itself: for the world is a living creature, everywhere both female and male', and knowledge of nature is derived through participating in these interconnections.[17]

With the formation of the Royal Society and in the context of emerging industrial capitalism, the contest between the mechanical and hermetic traditions was won by the masculine project, which was the project of a particular class. Paracelsus and Bacon did not merely differ in their ideology of gender and science; they were also differently rooted in the politics of class, with Bacon committed to middle-class values (finally becoming Lord Chancellor and Baron Verulam in 1618 in the reign of James I) and identifying with capitalists, merchants and the state in his scientific project, and Paracelsus on the side of the peasants in their uprising in the Tyrol.[18] Reductionist science became a major agent of economic and political change in the centuries to follow, dichotomizing gender and class relations and man's relationships with nature. 'Given the success of modern science, defined in opposition to everything female, fears of both Nature and Woman could subside. With the one reduced to its mechanical substrata, and the other to her sexual virtue, the essence of *Mater* could be both tamed and conquered.'[19]

For more than three centuries, reductionism has ruled as the only valid scientific method and system, distorting the history of the West as well as the non-West. It has hidden its ideology behind projected objectivism, neutrality and progress. The ideology that hides ideology has transformed complex pluralistic traditions of knowledge into a monolith of gender-based, class-based thought, and transformed this particular tradition into a superior and universal tradition to be superimposed on all classes, genders and cultures which it helps in controlling and subjugating. This ideological projection has kept modern reductionist science inaccessible to criticism. The parochial roots of science in patriarchy and in a particular class and culture have been concealed behind a claim to universality, and can be seen only through other traditions – of women and non-Western peoples. It is these subjugated traditions that are revealing how modern science is gendered, how it is specific to the needs and impulses of the dominant Western culture, and how ecological destruction and nature's exploitation are inherent to its logic. It is becoming increasingly clear that scientific neutrality has been a reflection of ideology not history, and science is similar to all other socially constructed categories. This view of science as a social and political project of modern Western man is emerging from the responses of those who were defined into nature and made passive and powerless: Mother Earth, women and colonized cultures. It is from these fringes that we are beginning to discern the economic, political and cultural mechanisms that have allowed a parochial science to dominate, and how mechanisms of power and violence can be eliminated for a de-gendered, humanly inclusive knowledge.

NOTES

1. S. Harding, *The Science Question in Feminism*, Cornell University Press, Ithaca, N.Y., 1986, p. 8.
2. Evelyn F. Keller, *Reflections On Gender And Science*, Yale University Press, New Haven, Conn., 1985, p. 7.
3. F.H. Anderson, ed., *Francis Bacon: The New Organon and Related Writings*, Bobbs-Merrill, Indianapolis, 1960, p. 25.
4. *The Works of Francis Bacon* (reprinted), edited by J. Spedding et al., vol. V, F.F. Verlag, Stuttgart, 1963, p. 506.
5. Quoted in Keller, *Reflections*, pp. 38–9.
6. Carolyn Merchant, *The Death of Nature: Women, Ecology and the Scientific Revolution*, Harper & Row, New York, 1980, p. 182.
7. Ibid., p. 193.
8. Brian Easlea, *Science and Sexual Oppression: Patriarchy's Confrontation with Woman and Nature*, Weidenfeld & Nicolson, London, 1981, p. 64.
9. Merchant, *The Death of Nature*, p. 172.
10. Easlea, *Science and Sexual Oppression*, p. 70.
11. Ibid.
12. Merchant, *The Death of Nature*, p. 189.
13. Easlea, *Science and Sexual Oppression*, p. 73.
14. Ibid.
15. J.P.S. Oberoi, *The Other Mind of Europe: Goethe as a Scientist*, Oxford University Press, Delhi, 1984.
16. Keller, *Reflections*, p. 48.
17. Merchant, *The Death of Nature*, p. 104.
18. Oberoi, *The Other Mind of Europe*, p. 21.
19. Keller, *The Death of Nature*, p. 60.

16

COLONIZATION OF THE MIND

Ashis Nandy

The following text is made up of extracts from *The Intimate Enemy* (Oxford University Press, Bombay, 1987, pp. ix–xii, 1–4, 7, 10, 100–102). The book consists of two lengthy essays: 'The Psychology of Colonialism: Sex, Age and Ideology in British India', and 'The Uncolonized Mind: A Post-colonial View of India and the West'. The author explores the myths, fantasies and psychological defences that went into the colonial culture, particularly the polarities that shaped the colonial theory of progress: the male versus the female, the adult versus the child, the scientific versus the irrational, and the historical versus the ahistorical. These secular hierarchies gave new legitimacy to modern oppression, defining the modern West as the model of all social change, and Western man as the ideal for the despotic Oriental. They also identified as 'genuine' the non-West, which, even in opposition, conformed to Western norms of dissent.

Ashis Nandy also describes the undercurrent of resistance that broke the rules of 'proper' Westernized dissent and protected the indigenous vision of an alternative future. He shows how India's cultural options were kept open through critical traditionalism rather than through Western modernism.

ASHIS NANDY is a prolific writer and a scholar of great vision, well known for his penetrating analyses of the impacts of modernity and colonialism on the people of subject societies. His major books include *The Intimate Enemy* (Oxford University Press, Bombay, 1987), *Traditions, Tyranny and Utopias* (Oxford University Press, Bombay, 1987) and *The Illegitimacy of Nationalism* (Oxford University Press, Delhi, 1993). He is currently the director of the Centre for the Study of Developing Societies, Delhi.

Modern colonialism won its great victories not so much through its military and technological prowess as through its ability to create secular hierarchies incompatible with the traditional order. These hierarchies opened up new vistas for many, particularly for those exploited or cornered within the traditional order. To them the new order looked like – and here lay its psychological pull – the first step towards a more just and equal world. That was why some of the finest critical minds in Europe – and in the East – were to

The Colonization of the Imaginary in Mexico

Serge Gruzinski's book on the role of the Church in 'the colonization of the imaginary' in Mexico should be read in connection with Ashis Nandy's article. In this important study, the author shows how the Church set out to use the emotions, the fear, the anguish of populations by instilling into their minds the concepts of sin and damnation. Ritual techniques such as confession and penitence led to the full assimilation of the Christian themes of salvation and redemption. For Gruzinski, although this colonization seldom succeeds in destroying the springs of indigenous creativity, it does succeed more than often in weaving indissoluble ties between indigenous cultures and the imported ones. See Suggested Readings.

feel that colonialism, by introducing modern structures into the barbaric world, would open up the non-West to the modern critical-analytic spirit.

Like the 'hideous heathen god who refused to drink nectar except from the skulls of murdered men', History, Karl Marx felt, would produce out of oppression, violence and cultural dislocation not merely new technological and social forces but also a new social consciousness in Asia and Africa. It would be critical in the sense in which the Western tradition of social criticism – from Vico to Marx – had been critical and it would be rational in the sense in which post-Cartesian Europe had been rational. The ahistorical primitives would one day, the expectation went, learn to see themselves as masters of nature and, hence, as masters of their own fate.

Many, many decades later, in the aftermath of that marvel of modern technology called the Second World War and perhaps that modern encounter of cultures called Vietnam, it has become obvious that the drive for mastery over men is not merely a by-product of a faulty political economy but also of a world-view which believes in the absolute superiority of the human over the non-human and the sub-human, the masculine over the feminine, the adult over the child, the historical over the ahistorical, and the modern or progressive over the traditional or the savage. It has become more and more apparent that genocides, eco-disasters and ethnocides are but the underside of corrupt sciences and psychopathic technologies wedded to new secular hierarchies, which have reduced major civilizations to the status of a set of empty rituals. The ancient forces of human greed and violence, one recognizes, have merely found a new legitimacy in anthropocentric doctrines of secular salvation, in the ideologies of progress, normality and hyper-masculinity, and in theories of cumulative growth of science and technology.

This awareness has not made everyone give up his theory of progress, but it has given confidence to a few to look askance at the old universalism within which the earlier critiques of colonialism were offered. It is now possible for some to combine fundamental social criticism with a defence of non-modern cultures and traditions. It is possible to speak of the plurality of critical traditions and of human rationality. At long last we seem to have recognized that Descartes is not the last word on reason, nor Marx that on the critical spirit.

The awareness has come at a time when the attack on the non-modern cultures has become a threat to their survival. As this century with its blood-stained record draws to a close, the nineteenth-century dream of one world has re-emerged, this time as a nightmare. It haunts us with the prospect of a fully homogenized, technologically controlled, absolutely hierarchized world, defined by polarities like the modern and the primitive, the secular and the non-secular, the scientific and the non-scientific, the expert and the layman, the normal and the abnormal, the developed and the underdeveloped, the vanguard and the led, the liberated and the saveable.

This idea of a brave new world was first tried out in the colonies. Its carriers were people who, unlike the rapacious first generation of bandit-kings who conquered the colonies, sought to be helpful. They were well-meaning, hard-working, middle-class missionaries, liberals, modernists, and believers in science, equality and progress. The bandit-kings, presumably like bandit-kings everywhere, robbed, maimed and killed; but sometimes they did so without a civilizing mission and mostly with only crude concepts of racism and *untermensch*. They faced – and expected to face – other civilizations with their versions of middle kingdoms and barbarians; the pure and the impure; the *kafirs* and the *moshreks*; and the *yavanas* and the *mlecchas*. However vulgar, cruel or stupid it might have once been, that racism now faces defeat. It is now time to turn to the second form of colonization, the one which at least six generations of the Third World have learnt to view as a prerequisite for their liberation. This colonialism colonizes minds in addition to bodies and it releases forces within the colonized societies to alter their cultural priorities once and for all. In the process, it helps generalize the concept of the modern West from a geographical and temporal entity to a psychological category. The West is now everywhere, within the West and outside; in structures and in minds.

This is primarily the story of the second colonization and resistances to it: after all, we are concerned with a colonialism which survives the demise of empires. At one time, the second colonization legitimized the first. Now, it is independent of its roots. Even those who battle the first colonialism often guiltily embrace the second. They caution us that conventional anti-colonialism, too, could be an apologia for the colonization of minds.

The idea of psychological resistance to colonialism should be taken seriously. But that implies some new responsibilities, too. Today, when 'Westernization' has become a pejorative word, there have reappeared on the stage subtler and more sophisticated means of acculturation. They produce not merely models of conformity but also models of 'official' dissent. It is

Amilcar Cabral: Culture and People's Roots

Whatever may be the ideological or idealistic characteristics of cultural expression, culture is an essential element of the history of a people. Culture is, perhaps, the product of this history just as the flower is the product of a plant. Like history, or because it is history, culture has as its material base the level of the productive forces and the mode of production. Culture plunges its roots into the physical reality of the environmental humus in which it develops, and it reflects the organic nature of the society, which may be more or less influenced by external factors. History allows us to know the nature and extent of the imbalances and conflicts (economic, political and social) which characterize the evolution of a society; culture allows us to know the dynamic syntheses which have been developed and established by social conscience to resolve these conflicts at each stage of its evolution, in the search for survival and progress.

Just as happens with the flower in a plant, in culture there lies the capacity (or the responsibility) for forming and fertilizing the seedling which will assure the continuity of history, at the same time assuring the prospects for evolution and progress of the society in question. Thus it is understood that imperialist domination, by denying the historical development of the dominated people, necessarily also denies their cultural development. It is also understood why imperialist domination, like all foreign domination, for its own security requires cultural oppression and the attempt at direct or indirect liquidation of the essential elements of the culture of the dominated people.

The experience of colonial domination shows that, in the effort to perpetuate exploitation, the colonizers not only create a system to repress the cultural life of the colonized people; they also provoke and develop the cultural alienation of a part of the population, either by so-called assimilation of indigenous people, or by creating a social gap between the indigenous elites and the popular masses. As a result of this process of dividing or of deepening the divisions in the society, it happens that a considerable part of the population, notably the urban or peasant *petite bourgeoisie*, assimilates the colonizer's mentality, considers itself culturally superior to its own people and ignores or looks down upon their cultural values. This situation, characteristic of the majority of colonized intellectuals, is consolidated by increases in the social privileges of the assimilated or alienated group, with direct implications for the behaviour of individuals in this group in relation to the liberation movement. A reconversion of minds – of mental set – is thus indispensable to the true integration of people into the liberation movement. Such reconversion – re-Africanization, in our case – may take place before the struggle, but it is completed only during the course of the struggle, through daily contact with the popular masses in the communion of sacrifice required by the struggle.

Extracts from a speech on 'National Liberation and Culture', delivered on 20 February 1970 at Syracuse University, New York. Translated from the French by Maureen Webster.

Edward Said on a Teaching of Hugo of St Victor

To Gain the Independence and Detachment of Someone Whose Homeland is 'Sweet', but Whose Actual Condition Makes It Impossible to Recapture that Sweetness

Those people compelled by the system to play subordinate or imprisoning roles within it emerge as conscious antagonists, disrupting it, proposing claims, advancing arguments that dispute the totalitarian compulsions of the world market. Not everything can be bought off.

All these hybrid counter-energies, at work in many fields, individuals and moments provide a community or culture made up of numerous anti-systemic hints and practices for collective human existence (and neither doctrines nor complete theories) that is not based on coercion or domination…

I find myself returning again and again to a hauntingly beautiful passage by Hugo of St. Victor, a twelfth-century monk from Saxony:

> It is, therefore, a source of great virtue for the practised mind to learn, bit by bit, first to change about in visible and transitory things, so that afterwards it may be able to leave them behind altogether. The person who finds his homeland sweet is still a tender beginner; he to whom every soil is as his native one is already strong; but he is perfect to whom the entire world is as a foreign place. The tender soul has fixed his love on one spot in the world; the strong person has extended his love to all places; the perfect man has extinguished his.

Erich Auerbach, the great German scholar who spent the years of World War Two as an exile in Turkey, cites this passage as a model for anyone – man *and* woman – wishing to transcend the restraints of imperial or national or provincial limits. Only through this attitude can a historian, for example, begin to grasp human experience and its written records in all their diversity and particularity; otherwise one would remain committed more to the exclusions and reactions of prejudice than to the negative freedom of real knowledge. But note that Hugo twice makes it clear that the 'strong' or 'perfect' person achieves independence and detachment by *working through* attachments, not by rejecting them. Exile is predicated on the existence of, love for, and a real bond with one's native place; the universal truth of exile is not that one has lost that love or home, but that inherent in each is an unexpected, unwelcome loss. Regard experiences then *as if* they were about to disappear: what is it about them that anchors or roots them in reality? What would you save of them, what would you give up, what would you recover? To answer such questions you must have the independence and detachment of someone whose homeland is 'sweet', but whose actual condition makes it impossible to recapture that sweetness, and even less possible to derive satisfaction from substitutes furnished by illusion or dogma, whether deriving from pride in one's heritage or from certainty about who 'we' are.

> No one today is purely *one* thing. Labels like Indian, or woman, or Muslim, or American are not more than starting-points, which it followed into actual experience for only a moment are quickly left behind. Imperialism consolidated the mixture of cultures and identities on a global scale. But its worse and most paradoxical gift was to allow people to believe that they were only, mainly, exclusively, white, or black, or Western, or Oriental. Yet just as human beings make their own history, they also make their cultures and ethnic identities. No one can deny the persisting continuities of long traditions, sustained habitations, national languages and cultural geographies, but there seems no reason except fear and prejudice to keep insisting on their separation and distinctiveness, as if that was all human life was about. Survival in fact is about the connections between things; in Eliot's phrase, reality cannot be deprived of the 'other echoes [that] inhabit the garden'. It is more rewarding – and more difficult – to think concretely and sympathetically, contrapuntally, about others than only about 'us'. But this also means not trying to rule others, not trying to classify them or put them in hierarchies, above all, not constantly reiterating how 'our' culture or country is number one (or *not* number one, for that matter). For the intellectual there is quite enough of value to do without *that*.
>
> **From *Culture and Imperialism*, Vintage Books, New York, 1994, pp. 335–6.** **(See Box on p. 178 for Edward Said.)**

possible today to be anti-colonial in a way which is specified and promoted by the modern world-view as 'proper', 'sane' and 'rational'. Even when in opposition, that dissent remains predictable and controlled. It is also possible today to opt for a non-West which itself is a construction of the West. One can then choose between being the Orientalist's despot, to combine Karl Wittfogel with Edward Said, and the revolutionary's loving subject, to combine Camus with George Orwell. And for those who do not like the choice, there is, of course, Cecil Rhodes' and Rudyard Kipling's noble, half-savage, half-child, compared to whom the much-hated Brown Sahib seems more brown than sahib. Even in enmity these choices remain forms of homage to the victors. Let us not forget that the most violent denunciation of the West produced by Frantz Fanon is written in the elegant style of a Jean-Paul Sartre. The West has not merely produced modern colonialism; it informs most interpretations of colonialism. It colours even this interpretation of interpretation....

The first differentia of colonialism is a state of mind in the colonizers and the colonized, a colonial consciousness which includes the sometimes unrealizable wish to make economic and political profits from the colonies, but other elements too. The political economy of colonization is of course important, but the crudity and inanity of colonialism are principally expressed in the sphere of psychology, and, to the extent the variables used to describe the states of mind under colonialism have themselves become politicized since the entry of modern colonialism on the world scene, in the sphere of political psychology. The following will explore some of these psychological contours of colonialism in the rulers and the ruled and try to define colonialism as a shared culture which may not always begin with the establishment of alien rule in a society and end with the departure of the alien rulers from the colony. The example I shall use will be that of India, where a colonial political economy began to operate seventy-five years before the full-blown ideology of British imperialism became dominant, and where thirty-five years after the formal ending of the Raj, the ideology of colonialism is still triumphant in many sectors of life.

Such disjunctions between politics and culture became possible because it is only partly true that a colonial situation produces a theory of imperialism to justify itself. Colonialism is also a psychological state rooted in earlier forms of social consciousness in both the colonizers and the colonized. It represents a certain cultural continuity and carries a certain cultural baggage.

First, it includes codes which both the rulers and the ruled can share. The main function of these codes is to alter the original cultural priorities on both sides and bring to the centre of the colonial culture subcultures previously recessive or subordinate in the two confronting cultures. Concurrently, the codes remove from the centre of each of the cultures subcultures previously salient in them. It is these fresh priorities which explain why some of the most impressive colonial systems have been built by societies ideologically committed to open political systems, liberalism and intellectual pluralism. That this split parallels a basic contradiction within the modern scientific-rational world-view, which, while trying to remain rational within its confines, has consistently refused to be rational vis-à-vis other traditions of knowledge after acquiring world dominance, is only the other side of the same explanation.[1] It also explains why colonialism never seems to end with formal political freedom. As a state of mind, colonialism is an indigenous process released by external forces. Its sources lie deep in the minds of the rulers and the ruled. Perhaps that which begins in the minds of men must also end in the minds of men.

Second, the culture of colonialism presumes a particular style of managing dissent. Obviously, a colonial system perpetuates itself by inducing the colonized, through socio-economic and psychological rewards and punishments, to accept new social norms and cognitive categories. But these outer incentives and disincentives are invariably noticed and challenged: they become the overt indicators of oppression and dominance. More dangerous and permanent are the inner rewards and punishments, the secondary psychological gains and losses from suffering and submission under colonialism. They are almost always unconscious and almost always ignored. Particularly strong is the inner resistance to recognizing the ultimate violence which colonialism does to its victims, namely that it creates a culture in which the ruled are constantly tempted to fight their rulers within the psychological limits set by the latter. It is not an accident that the specific variants of the concepts with which many anti-colonial movements in our times have worked have often been the products of the imperial culture itself, and, even in opposition, these movements have paid homage to their respective cultural origins. I have in mind not only the overt Apollonian codes of Western liberalism that have often motivated the elites of the colonized societies but also their covert Dionysian counterparts in the concepts of statecraft, everyday politics, effective political methods and utopias which have guided revolutionary movements against colonialism....

Crucial to this cultural co-optation was the process psychoanalysis calls identification with the aggressor. In any oppressive situation, the process became the flip side of the theory of progress, an ontogenetic legitimacy for an ego defence often used by a normal child in an environment of childhood dependency to confront inescapable dominance by physically more powerful adults enjoying total legitimacy. In the colonial culture, identification with the aggressor bound the rulers and the ruled in an unbreakable dyadic relationship. The Raj saw the Indians as crypto-barbarians who needed to further civilize themselves. It saw British rule as an agent of progress and as a mission. Many Indians in turn saw their salvation in becoming more like the British, in friendship or in enmity. They may not have fully shared the British idea of the martial races – the hyper-masculine, manifestly courageous, superbly loyal Indian castes and subcultures mirroring the British middle-class sexual stereotypes – but they did resurrect the ideology of the martial races latent in the traditional Indian concept of statecraft and gave the idea a new centrality....

In such a culture, colonialism was not seen as an absolute evil. For the subjects, it was a product of one's own emasculation and defeat in legitimate power politics. For the rulers, colonial exploitation was an incidental and regrettable by-product of a philosophy of life that was in harmony with superior forms of political and economic organization. This was the consensus the rulers of India sought, consciously or unconsciously. They could not successfully rule a continent-sized polity while believing themselves to be moral cripples. They had to build bulwarks against a possible sense of guilt produced by a disjunction between their actions and what were till then, in terms of important norms of their own culture, 'true' values. On the other hand, their subjects could not collaborate on a long-term basis unless they had some acceptance of the ideology of the system, either as players or as counterplayers. This is the only way they could preserve a minimum of self-esteem in a situation of unavoidable injustice.

When such a cultural consensus grows, the main threat to the colonizers is bound to become the latent fear that the colonized will reject the consensus and, instead of trying to redeem their 'masculinity' by becoming the counter-players of the rulers according to the established rules, will discover an alternative frame of reference within which the oppressed do not seem weak, degraded and distorted men trying to break the monopoly of the rulers on a fixed quantity of machismo. If this happens, the colonizers begin to live with the fear that the subjects might begin to see their rulers as morally and culturally inferior, and feed this information back to the rulers.[2] Colonialism minus a civilizational mission is no colonialism at all. It handicaps the colonizer much more than it handicaps the colonized....

GANDHI: THE UNCOLONIZED MIND

Gandhi was one of the few who successfully articulated in politics the consciousness which had remained untamed by British rule in India. He transformed the debate on Indian hypocrisy into a simultaneous text on British self-doubt. In spite of his occasionally strident moralism, he recognized that once the hegemony of a theory of imperialism without winners and losers was established, imperialism had lost out on cognitive, in addition to ethical, grounds. To the Kiplings this was a threat. They liked to see colonialism as a moral statement on the superiority of some cultures and inferiority of others. For this reason, they were even willing to accept that some had the right to speak of the superiority of Indian culture over the Western. Cultural relativism by itself is not incompatible with imperialism, as long as one's culture's categories are backed by political, economic and technological power.

Gandhi queered the pitch on two planes. He admitted that colonialism was a moral issue and took the battle to Kipling's home ground by judging colonialism by Christian values and declaring it to be an absolute evil. On the second plane he made his 'odd' cognitive assessment of the gains and losses from colonialism a part of his critique of modernity and found the British wanting in both ethics and rationality. This threatened the internal legitimacy of the ruling culture by splitting open the private wound of every Kipling and quasi-Kipling to whom rulership was a means of hiding one's moral self in the name of the higher morality of history, in turn seen as an embodiment of human rationality. A naive French imperialist once said in the context of Africa. 'I know that I must take pride in my blood. When a superior man ceases to believe himself, *he actually ceases to be superior* ...When a superior race ceases to believe itself a chosen race, it actually ceases to be a chosen race.'[3] Gandhi attacked both the cognitive and moral frames of this insecure, fragile sense of chosenness.

In this respect, he differed from the other anti-Kiplings to whom colonialism was a moral statement. The final morality to them, too, was 'history', and the immorality of colonialism for them, too, was mitigated by the historical role of colonialism as an instrument of progress. Either through a cultural renaissance set off by the impact of a more vigorous culture (as many of the nineteenth-century social and religious reformers in India and recent modernists in our times have described it) or through the growth of modern capitalism on the way to the full-blown liberalism or communism (*à la* utilitarians and Karl Marx), the modern idea of history has implicitly accepted the cultural superiority – or at least the more advanced cultural state – of the colonizing power.[4] It has thus endorsed one of the major axioms of the colonial theory the Kiplings advanced. As against this, Gandhi reaffirmed an autonomous world-view which refused to separate facts from values and refused to see colonialism as an immoral pathway to a valued state of being. Instead of meeting the Western criterion of a true antagonist, he endorsed the non-modern Indian reading of the modern West as one of the many possible lifestyles, which had, unfortunately for both the West and India, become cancerous by virtue of its disproportionate power and spread.

NOTES

1. On this other contradiction, see Paul Feyerabend, *Science in a Free Society*, NLB, London, 1978. In the context of India and China this point emerges clearly from Claude Alvares, *Homo Faber: Technology and Culture in India, China and the West*, 1500–1972, Allied Publishers, New Delhi, 1979. See also Ashis Nandy, 'Science, Authoritarianism and Culture: On the Scope and Limits of Isolation Outside the Clinic', M.N. Roy Memorial Lecture, 1980, Seminar, May 1981; and Shiv Viswanathan, 'Science and the sense of Other', paper written for the colloquium on New Ideologies for Science and Technology, Lokayan Project 1982, Delhi, mimeograph.
2. I have briefly dealt with this in my 'Oppression and Human Liberation: Towards a Third World Utopia', in *Tradition, Tyranny and Utopias*, Oxford University Press, Bombay, 1987; see an earlier version in *Alternatives*, vol. 4, no. 2, 1978–9, pp. 165–80. On this theme see the sensitive writing of Albert Memmi, *The Colonizer and the Colonized*.
3. Psichari-Soldier-of-Africa, quoted in Aimé Césaire, *Discourse on Colonialism*, trans. Joan Pinkham, Monthly Review Press, New York, 1977, p. 29.
4. Among Indians, elements of such an awareness can be found for example in Rammohun Roy, *The English Works*, vols I–VI, edited by Kalidas Nag and Debojyoti Burman, Sadharon Brahmo Samaj, Calcutta, 1945–8; Bankimchandra Chatterji, *Racanavali*, Vols 1 and 2, Sahitya Samsad, Calcutta, 1958 (see especially 'Anandamath', pp. 715–88); Swami Vivekananda, *Pracya O Pascatya*, Advaita Ashrama, Almora, 1898; and Nirad C. Chaudhuri, *The Autobiography of an Unknown Indian*, Macmillan, London, 1951.

Edward Said on Frantz Fanon

Fanon's brilliant analysis of the liberationist tendency opens Chapter 2 [of *The Wretched of the Earth*], 'Spontaneity: Its Strength and Weakness', the basis of which is a time lag and rhythm difference (*décalage*) 'between the leaders of a nationalist party and the mass of the people'. As the nationalists copy their methods from Western political parties, all sorts of tensions develop within the nationalist camp – between country and city, between leader and rank-and-file, between bourgeoisie and peasants, between feudal and political leaders – all of them exploited by the imperialists. The core problem is that, although official nationalists want to break colonialism, 'another quite different will [becomes apparent]: that of coming to a friendly agreement with it.'...

Far from leading 'the colonized people to supreme sovereignty at one fell swoop, that certainty which you had that all portions of the nation would be carried along with you at the same speed and led onward by the same light, that strength which gave you hope: all now are seen in the light of experience to be symptoms of a very great weakness.'

Precisely that power to convey 'the light of experience' is located in the illegal tendency animating the liberationist party. This party shows to all that racialism and revenge 'cannot sustain a war of liberation'; hence the native makes 'the discovery' that in 'breaking down colonial oppression he is automatically building up yet another system of exploitation', this time giving it 'a black face or an Arab one', so long as the mimic men lead....

Fanon was the first major theorist of anti-imperialism to realize that orthodox nationalism followed along the same track hewn out by imperialism, which while it appeared to be conceding authority to the nationalist bourgeoisie was really extending its hegemony. To tell a simple national story therefore is to repeat, extend, and also to engender new forms of imperialism.

Edward Said, *Culture and Imperialism*, Vintage Books, New York, 1994, pp. 272–3; the references are to Frantz Fanon, *The Wretched of the Earth*, Grove Press, New York, 1968, pp. 107, 59.

Edward Said is Parr Professor of English and Comparative Literature at Columbia University, New York. In 1976 his book *Beginnings: Intention and Method* (Basic Books, New York, 1975) won the first annual Lionel Trilling Award given at Columbia University. Yet it was his remarkable study of *Orientalism* (Vintage, New York, 1978), followed by *Culture and Imperialism* (Vintage, New York, 1994) and other works, which brought him world-wide recognition. As a Palestinian, Professor Said has been a major voice in advancing the cause of his country. He might be seen as a living example of the person who, in the words of Hugo of St Victor, 'achieved independence and detachment by *working through* attachments, not by rejecting them'.

17

THE ONE AND ONLY WAY OF THINKING

Ignacio Ramonet

Reproduced below is an English translation by Victoria Bawtree of the editorial in *Le Monde Diplomatique*, January 1995. *Le 'Diplo'*, as it is affectionately known to its subscribers, is one of the most important journals in the world in terms of its in-depth coverage of economic, political, social and cultural affairs. In addition to the original French, there are editions in Arabic, German, Italian, Portuguese and Spanish – oddly enough it is not brought out, even partially, in the English language.

IGNACIO RAMONET is Professeur Agrégé and chief editor of *Le Monde Diplomatique*.

In today's democracies, more and more free citizens feel bogged down, stuck in a sort of glutinous doctrine which imperceptibly wraps itself around all rebellious thinking, inhibiting, disrupting, paralysing and finally suppressing it. This doctrine is the one and only way of thinking, the sole one authorized by an invisible and ubiquitous opinion police. After the fall of the Berlin Wall, the collapse of the Communist regimes and the demoralization of socialism, the arrogance, the effrontery and the insolence of this new Gospel have reached such heights that one can, without exaggeration, describe this ideological frenzy as modern dogmatism.

What is the one and only way of thinking? It is the translation into ideological terms that claim to be universal of economic interests, particularly those of international capital. It could be said that it was formulated and defined from 1944 onwards, at Bretton Woods. Its principal sources are the great economic and financial institutions – the World Bank, the International Monetary Fund, the Organization for Economic Co-operation and Development, the General Agreement on Tariffs and Trade, the European Commission, the Banque de France, and so on – which, in order to diffuse their ideas throughout the world, finance various research centres, universities and foundations, which in turn refine and disseminate the holy writ.

This anonymous discourse is taken up and reproduced by the leading purveyors of economic information and especially by the 'bibles' of investors

The Corruption of Our Faculty to Perceive

The world appears to be in the grip of a fast-spreading disease which, by now, has assumed almost global dimensions. In the individual the symptoms of disorder manifest themselves by a progressive corruption of his faculty to perceive, with corrupted language being the pathogene, that is the agent that makes the disease so highly contagious.

Heinz von Förster, *Observing Systems*, Intersystems Publications, Seaside, Calif., 1981, p. 192.

and stockbrokers – *The Wall Street Journal*, *The Financial Times*, *The Economist*, *The Far Eastern Economic Review*, *Les Echos*, Reuters, etc., which are often the property of the big industrial or financial groups. Almost everywhere, faculties of economics, journalists, writers, and politicians end up imbibing the main commandments of these new legal tablets, and, through the networks of the mass media, they are repeated *ad nauseam*. As we all know, in our media-oriented societies repetition is as good as proof.

The first principle of the one and only way of thinking is all the more convincing in that an inattentive Marxist would in no way deny it: economics is more important than politics. It is on the basis of such a principle that, for example, an instrument as important in the hands of the executive as the Banque de France was, without any real opposition, made independent in 1994 and, to some extent, 'protected from political vagaries'. 'The Banque de France is independent, a-political and transpartisan' stated its governor, M. Jean-Claude Trichet, who added, however: 'We demand that the public debt be reduced', and 'we follow a stable currency strategy.'[1] As if these two objectives were not political!

In the name of 'realism' and 'pragmatism', the economy is put in charge. As M. Alain Minc put it: 'Capitalism cannot collapse, it is the natural state of society. Democracy is not the natural state of society. The market is.'[2] An economy, it goes without saying, that has been stripped of any social concern, which is a sort of pathetic dross, weighing us down, causing regression and crisis.

The other key concepts of the one and only way of thinking are well known: the market, an idol whose 'invisible hand corrects the quirks and dysfunctionalities of capitalism', and particularly the financial markets, whose 'signals direct and determine the general movement of the economy'; competition and competitiveness, which 'stimulate business and make it dynamic, leading to permanent and beneficial modernization'; free exchange, without boundaries, 'a factor in the uninterrupted development of trade, and therefore of societies'; globalization, both of the production of manufactured goods and of financial flows; the international division of labour, which 'moderates union claims and lowers the cost of wages'; strong currencies, 'a stabilizing factor'; deregulation; privatization; liberalization, and so on. Always, it is 'less of the State' and a constant arbitration in favour of revenue returning to capital to the detriment of labour. And indifference as to ecological costs.

Constant repetition, in all the media, of this catechism[3] by almost all politicians, from right to left,[4] gives it such an intimidating force that it stifles all attempts at free thinking and makes it very difficult to resist this new obscurantism.[5]

One almost gets to the point of believing that 17.4 million unemployed Europeans, the urban chaos, the general precariousness of life, the corruption, the suburbs aflame, the ecological pillage, the return to racism, integralism and religious extremism, and the rising tide of the marginalized: that all these are just mirages, reprehensible hallucinations in this best of all possible worlds which is constructing, for our anaesthetized consciousness, the one and only way of thinking.

NOTES

1. *Le Monde*, 17 December 1994.
2. *Cambio* 16, Madrid, 5 December 1994.
3. An exemplary model of this dominant way of thinking is *La France de l'an 2000*, report to the Prime Minister, Odile Jacob publishers, Paris 1994.
4. Many will remember the reply of M. Dominique Strauss-Kahn, Socialist Minister for Industry, to the question: 'What is going to change if the right takes over?' He answered: 'Nothing. Their economic policy will not be very different from ours' (*Wall Street Journal* – Europe, 18 March 1993).
5. Is this the reason why, in the last few weeks, several intellectuals, including Guy Debord, have committed suicide?

18

THE NEW CULTURAL DOMINATION BY THE MEDIA

James Petras

The following text is an abbreviated version of an article that appeared in the Indian journal (published in Bombay) *Economic and Political Weekly*, 6 August 1994.

JAMES F. PETRAS has been Professor of Sociology at the State University of New York at Binghamton since 1972. He also served as director of a project on public administration and agrarian reform in Chile and Peru at Pennsylvania State University. He has written extensively on the global role of the United States, and on cultural imperialism. His recent books include *Latin America in the time of Cholera: Electoral Politics, Market Economics and Permanent Crisis* (Routledge, London, 1992), and *Empire or Republic? American Global Power and Domestic Decay* (Routledge, London, 1994).

In past centuries, the church, educational system and public authorities played a major role in inculcating native peoples with ideas of submission and loyalty in the name of divine or absolutist principles. While these 'traditional' mechanisms of cultural imperialism still operate, new model instrumentalities rooted in contemporary institutions have become increasingly central to imperial domination. The mass media, publicity, advertisement and secular entertainers and intellectuals play a major role today. In the contemporary world, Hollywood, CNN and Disneyland are more influential than the Vatican, the Bible or the public-relations rhetoric of political figures.

Cultural penetration is closely linked to politico-military domination and economic exploitation. US military interventions in support of the genocidal regimes in Central America which protect its economic interests are accompanied by intense cultural penetration. US-financed evangelicals invade Indian villages to inculcate messages of submission among the peasant-Indian victims. International conferences are sponsored for domesticated intellectuals to discuss 'democracy and market'. Escapist television programmes sow illusions from 'another world'. Cultural penetration is the extension of counter-insurgency warfare by non-military means.

Contemporary cultural colonialism (CCC) is distinct from past practices in several senses: (i) It is oriented toward capturing mass audiences, not just converting elites. (ii) The mass media, particularly television, invade the household and function from the 'inside' and 'below' as well as from 'outside' and above. (iii) CCC is global in scope and homogenizing in its impact: the pretence of universalism serves to mystify the symbols, goals and interests of the imperial power. (iv) The mass media as instruments of cultural imperialism today are 'private' only in the formal sense: the absence of formal state ties provides a legitimate cover for the private media projecting imperial state interests as 'news' or 'entertainment'. (v) Under contemporary imperialism, political interests are projected through non-imperial subjects. 'News reports' focus on the personal biographies of mercenary peasant-soldiers in Central America and smiling working-class US blacks in the Gulf war.[1] (vi) Because of the increasing gap between the *promise* of peace and prosperity under unregulated capital and the reality of increasing misery and violence, the mass media have narrowed even further the possibilities of alternative perspectives in their programmes. Total cultural control is the counterpart of the total separation between the brutality of real-existing capitalism and the illusory promises of the free market. (vii) To paralyse collective responses, cultural colonialism seeks to destroy national identities or empty them of substantive socio-economic content. To rupture the solidarity of communities, cultural imperialism promotes the cult of 'modernity' as conformity with external symbols. In the name of 'individuality', social bonds are attacked and personalities are reshaped according to the dictates of media messages. While imperial arms disarticulate civil society and banks pillage the economy, the imperial media provide individuals with escapist identities.

Cultural imperialism provides devastating demonological caricatures of revolutionary adversaries, while encouraging collective amnesia of the massive violence of pro-Western countries. The Western mass media never remind their audience of the murder by anti-communist pro-US regimes of 100,000 Indians in Guatemala, 75,000 working people in El Salvador, 50,000 victims in Nicaragua. The mass media cover up the great disasters resulting from the introduction of the market in Eastern Europe and the ex-USSR, leaving hundreds of millions impoverished.

PROPAGANDA AND CAPITAL ACCUMULATION

The mass media constitute one of the principal sources of wealth and power for US capital as it extends its communication networks throughout the world. An increasing percentage of the richest North Americans derive their wealth from the mass media. Among the 400 wealthiest Americans, the percentage deriving their wealth from the mass media increased from 9.5 per cent in 1982 to 18 per cent in 1989. Today almost one out of five of the richest

> **The Market Itself Is a Product**
>
> Nothing demonstrates so well that the market itself is a product than the press and the television. They sell the consumers during real time: in fact, it could be said that this has become the main profession of the media conglomerates. What is a newspaper today? It is a group of reader-consumers that are sold to the advertisers: it is part of the market rented for the period of a programme or reading time. The show is at the service of the product and the product is at the service of the show. This is the case for the specialized press, for the television and also, to a certain extent, for the general press.
>
> **Philippe Thureau-Dangin, from *La Concurrence et la mort*, Syros, Paris, 1995, p. 107. Translated by V.B.**

North Americans derive their wealth from the mass media. Cultural capitalism has displaced manufacturing as a source of wealth and influence in the USA.

The mass media have become an integral part of the US system of global political and social control, as well as a major source of super profits. As the levels of exploitation, inequality and poverty increase in the Third World, Western-controlled mass communications operate to convert a critical public into a passive mass. Western media celebrities and mass entertainment have become important ingredients in deflecting potential political unrest. The Reagan presidency highlighted the centrality of media manipulation through highly visible but politically reactionary entertainers, a phenomenon which has spread to Latin America and Asia.

There is a direct relation between the increase in the number of television sets in Latin America, the decline of income and the decrease in mass struggle. In Latin America, between 1980 and 1990, the number of television sets per inhabitant increased 40 per cent, while the real average income declined 40 per cent, and a host of neo-liberal political candidates heavily dependent on television images won the presidency.

The increasing penetration of the mass media among the poor, the growing investments and profits by US corporations in the sale of cultural commodities, and the saturation of mass audiences with messages that provide the poor with vicarious experiences of individual consumption and adventure, define the current challenge of cultural colonialism.

US media messages are alienating the Third World people in a double sense. They create illusions of 'international' and 'cross-class' bonds. Through television images a false intimacy and an imaginary link is established between the successful subjects of the media and the impoverished spectators in the *barrios*. These linkages provide a channel through which the discourse of individual solutions for private problems is propagated. The message is clear.

The victims are blamed for their own poverty; success depends on individual efforts. Major television satellites, US and European mass-media outlets in Latin America, avoid any critique of the politico-economic origins and consequences of the new cultural imperialism that has temporarily disoriented and immobilized millions of impoverished Latin Americans.

POLITICS OF LANGUAGE

Cultural imperialism has developed a dual strategy to counter the Left and establish hegemony. On the one hand, it seeks to corrupt the political language of the Left; on the other, it acts to desensitize the general public to the atrocities committed by Western powers. During the 1980s the Western mass media systematically appropriated basic ideas of the Left, emptied them of their original content and refilled them with a reactionary message. For example, the mass media described politicians intent on restoring capitalism and stimulating inequalities as 'reformers' or 'revolutionaries', while their opponents were labelled 'conservatives.' Cultural imperialism sought to promote ideological confusion and political disorientation by reversing the meaning of political language. Many progressive individuals became disoriented by this ideological manipulation. As a result, they were vulnerable to the claims of imperial ideologues who argue that the terms 'Right' and 'Left' lacked any meaning, that the distinctions have lost significance, that ideologies no longer have meaning. By corrupting the language of the Left and distorting the content of the Left and Right, cultural imperialists hope to undermine the political appeals and political practices of the anti-imperialist movements.

The second strategy of cultural imperialism was to desensitize the public; to make mass murder by the Western states routine, acceptable activities. Mass bombings in Iraq were presented in the form of video games. By trivializing crimes against humanity, the public is desensitized from its traditional belief that human suffering is wrong. By emphasizing the modernity of new techniques of warfare, the mass media glorify existing elite power – the techno-warfare of the West. Cultural imperialism today includes 'news' reports in which the weapons of mass destruction are presented with human attributes while the victims in the Third World are faceless 'aggressors or terrorists'.

Global cultural manipulation is sustained by the corruption of the language of politics. In Eastern Europe, speculators and mafiosi seizing land, enterprises and wealth are described as 'reformers'. Contrabandists are described as 'innovating entrepreneurs'. In the West, the concentration of absolute power to hire and fire in the hands of management and the increased vulnerability and insecurity of labour is called 'labour flexibility'. In the Third World, the selling of national public enterprise to giant multinational monopolies is described as 'breaking up monopolies'. 'Reconversion' is the euphemism for

Television and Dependency on the Charity of Strangers

On the one hand, television has contributed to the breakdown of the barriers of citizenship, religion, race, and geography that once divided our moral space into those we were responsible for and those who were beyond our ken. On the other hand, it makes us voyeurs of the sufferings of others, tourists amid their landscapes of anguish.

One of empathy's pleasures is to forget one's moral inconsistencies. Yet the claim that moral empathy at this distance is nothing more than self-deceiving myth relies tacitly on a moral myth of its own: that full moral empathy – full 'suffering with,' based on commonality of experience – is possible only among persons who share the same social identity, for example, the same class. Class identity, however, is no less mythic, no less imagined, than universal human brotherhood. The ethics that derive from it must divide the world into us and them, friends and enemies... 'Weeding out the class enemy' has been the moral *mot d'ordre* for the atrocities committed in the van of the Soviet and partisan armies after World War II, not to mention in the rice paddies of Kampuchea.

Famine, like genocide, destroys the capillary system of social relations that sustain each individual's system of entitlements. In so doing, *genocide and famine create a new human subject – the pure victim stripped of social identity* – and thus bereft of the specific moral audience that would in normal times be there to hear his cry. In these conditions, the family, the tribe, the faith, the nation no longer exist as a moral audience for these people. If they are to be saved at all, they must put their faith in that *most fearful of dependency relations: the charity of strangers.*

The moral empathy mediated by television has a history – the emergence of moral universalism in the Western conscience; this universalism has always been *in conflict* with the intuition that kith and kin have a moral priority over strangers; the twentieth-century inflection of moral universalism has taken the form of an anti-ideological and anti-political ethic of siding with the victim; the moral risk entailed by this ethic is misanthropy, a risk and temptation heightened by television's visual insistence on consequences rather than intentions.

The myth sustaining the news is that it is a picture of what happened to 'the nation' and 'the world' in a given time period, usually the time since the last bulletin. Millions of households look out through the screen *in search of their collective identity* as a national society and as citizens of one world. The media now play the decisive role in *constituting the 'imagined community' of nation and globe, the myth that millions of separate 'I's find common identity in a 'we.' The fiction is that all events depicted have somehow happened to 'us.'* News editors act as ventriloquists of this 'we,' serving up a diet of information that is legitimized as being what 'we' need to know; in fact what we get to know is what fits the visual and chronological constraints of the genre. In this circular process, the news is validated as a system of authority, as a national institution with a privileged role as purveyor of the nation's identity and taker of its pulse.

Michael Ignatieff, 'Is Nothing Sacred? The Ethics of Television', *Daedalus* 114, 1985, pp. 63–4, 65, 70, 71.

reversion to nineteenth century conditions of labour stripped of all social benefits. 'Restructuring' is the return to specialization in raw materials or the transfer of income from production to speculation. 'Deregulation' is the shift in power to regulate the economy from the national welfare state to the international banking, multinational power elite. 'Structural adjustments' in Latin America mean transferring resources to investors and lowering payments to labour. The concepts of the Left (reform, agrarian reform, structural changes) were originally oriented toward redistributing income. These concepts have been co-opted and turned into symbols for reconcentrating wealth, income and power into the hands of Western elites. And, of course, all the private cultural institutions of imperialism amplify and propagate this Orwellian disinformation. Contemporary cultural imperialism has debased the language of liberation, converting it into symbols of reaction.

CULTURAL TERRORISM

Just as Western state terrorism attempts to destroy social movements[2] and revolutionary governments,[3] and disarticulate civil society,[4] economic terrorism as practised by the IMF and private bank consortia destroy local industries, erode public ownership and savage wage and salaried households. Cultural terrorism is responsible for the physical displacement of local cultural activities and artists. Cultural terrorism, by preying on the psychological weaknesses and deep anxieties of vulnerable Third World peoples, particularly their sense of being 'backward', 'traditional' and oppressed, projects new images of 'mobility' and 'free expression', destroying old bonds to family and community, while fastening new chains of arbitrary authority linked to corporate power and commercial markets. The attacks on traditional restraints and obligations are a mechanism by which the capitalist market and state becomes the ultimate centre of exclusive power.

Cultural imperialism in the name of 'self-expression' tyrannizes Third World people fearful of being labelled 'traditional', seducing and manipulating them by the money images of classless 'modernity'. Cultural imperialism questions all pre-existing relations that are obstacles to the one and only sacred modern deity: the market. Third World people are entertained, coerced, titillated to be 'modern', to submit to the demands of the capitalist market, to discard comfortable, traditional loose-fitting clothes for ill-fitting, unsuitable tight blue jeans.

Cultural imperialism functions best through colonized intermediaries, cultural collaborators. The prototype imperial collaborators are the upwardly mobile Third World professionals who imitate the style of their patrons. These collaborators are servile to the West and arrogant to their people, prototypical authoritarian personalities. Backed by the banks and multinationals, they wield immense power through the state and local mass media. Imitative of the

West, they are rigid in their conformity to the rules of unequal competition, opening their country and peoples to savage exploitation in the name of free trade. Among the prominent cultural collaborators are the institutional intellectuals who deny class domination and imperial class warfare behind the jargon of objective social science. They fetishize the market as the absolute arbiter of good and evil. Behind the rhetoric of 'regional co-operation', the conformist intellectuals attack working-class and national institutions which constrain capital movements.

Today, throughout the Third World, Western-funded Third World intellectuals have embraced the ideology of *concertación* (class collaboration). The notion of interdependence has replace imperialism. And the unregulated world market is presented as the only alternative for development. The irony is that today, as never before, the 'market' has been least favourable to the Third World. Never have the USA, Europe and Japan been so aggressive in exploiting the Third World. The cultural alienation of the institutional intellectuals from the global realities is a by-product of the ascendancy of Western cultural imperialism. For those critical intellectuals who refuse to join the celebration of the market, who are outside the official conference circuits, the challenge is once again to return to the class and anti-imperialist struggle.

One of the great deceptions of our times is the notion of 'internationalization' of ideas, markets and movements. It has become fashionable to evoke terms like 'globalization' or 'internationalization' to justify attacks on any or all forms of solidarity, community and/or social values. Under the guise of 'internationalism', Europe and the USA have become dominant exporters of cultural forms most conducive to depoliticizing and trivializing everyday existence. The images of individual mobility, the 'self-made persons', the emphasis on 'self-centred existence' (mass-produced and distributed by the US mass-media industry) have become major instruments in dominating the Third World.

Neo-liberalism continues to thrive not because it solves problems, but because it serves the interest of the wealthy and powerful and resonates among some sectors of the impoverished self-employed who crowd the streets of the Third World. The North Americanization of Third World cultures takes place with the blessing and support of the national ruling classes because it contributes to stabilizing their rule. The new cultural norms – the private over the public, the individual over social, the sensational and violent over everyday struggles and social realities – all contribute to inculcating precisely the egocentric values that undermine collective action. The culture of images, of transitory experiences, of sexual conquest, works against reflection, commitment and shared feelings of affection and solidarity. The North Americanization of culture means focusing popular attention on celebrities, personalities and private gossip – not on social depth, economic substance and the human condition. Cultural imperialism distracts from power relations and erodes collective forms of social action.

NOTES

1. Personal images mask mass state killings, just as technocratic rhetoric rationalizes weapons of mass destruction ('intelligent bombs'). Cultural imperialism in the era of 'democracy' must falsify reality in the imperial country to justify aggression – by converting victims into aggressors and aggressors into victims. Hence in Panama the US imperial state and mass media projected Panama as a drug threat to young people in the USA as it dropped bombs on working-class communities in Panama.
2. The experience of El Salvador and Guatemala in the 1980s is illustrative.
3. Nicaragua's Sandinista government in the 1980s and Chile under Allende in the 1970s are emblematic.
4. Witness the cases of Uruguay and Argentina in the 1970s and 1980s under the military regimes.

Claude Roy: On the Corruption of Language

If language only served to *say* something, words would be rarer, silence more frequent. Words are not used only to transmit a message, to inform about a fact, to create a feeling, to express a thought. They are also used to prevent communication, to put people off the track, to put up a noisy, chattering screen between human beings. In our society, where lies are considered as one of the fine arts of power, and falsification one of the natural instruments of profit, talking in order to say nothing has developed in every field…

One might think that, in a company, the person called the director of communications would be responsible for transmitting everyday news from the CEO to the storekeeper and from the representative to the client, an engineer for ensuring transparency, a magician of contacts, responsible for circulating the right words. Error: the director of communications is the new name for the chief of publicity. As can be seen every day, publicity has nothing to do with transparency or truth.

Another significant title, which expresses what it is not, is the director of human resources. It is difficult to imagine a designation so overwhelmingly rich in graces, virtues, gifts of spirit and heart. This 'director' is supposed to draw generously on the treasure of the human species, on the inexhaustible source of 'all that is human'. He who is responsible for human resources should be on a peak of spiritual power. However, the description of this rising prince of humanity turns out to be the tired old officer, once modestly known as the chief of personnel, a sort of general inspector, superior foreman: a good bloke or embittered watchdog, according to his character or that particular moment, caught between the trunk of management and the bark of the waged workers.

Claude Roy, 'Du mensonge comme l'un des beaux-arts' (The Lie: One of the Fine Arts), in *Le Nouvel Observateur*, 4–10 November 1993. (Translated by M.R.) Claude Roy is a well-known French writer, poet and essayist.

19

HOW THE UNITED NATIONS PROMOTES DEVELOPMENT THROUGH TECHNICAL ASSISTANCE

Pierre de Senarclens

La Crise des Nations Unies (Presses Universitaires de France, Paris, 1988), the book by Pierre de Senarclens from which the following extracts have been taken, is a most instructive analysis of United Nations politics, particularly in the formative decades after the Second World War. The book was published one year before the fall of the Berlin Wall and the subsequent collapse of the Soviet and Eastern European regimes; the UN crisis, however, is now more dramatic than ever. What gives the book its special interest is the way the author traces the origins of many of the problems faced today by the United Nations back to the early years of its existence. In no field is this more striking than in the whole system of technical assistance set up in the early 1950s to promote the 'development' of the Third World countries, which has so spectacularly failed to contribute to the well-being of their populations. These extracts were translated by Victoria Bawtree.

PIERRE DE SENARCLENS has been Professor of International Relations at Lausanne University since 1974. From 1980 to 1983 he was director of the Human Rights Division in UNESCO. He is a specialist in the theory of international relations and is currently writing a book on the political implications of globalization.

THE DEVELOPMENT MISSION

While the first debates at the Economic and Social Council (ECOSOC) and the UN General Assembly were above all devoted to economic and social issues related to the industrialized states and to their reconstruction needs, the development of the 'backward' countries was not long in taking centre stage among the concerns of the United Nations. Already in 1946 the Temporary Social Commission on Social Affairs was stating:

Professional Elites Formulate and Finance Development Policies

Development as it has been practised throughout most of the twentieth century has systematically undermined the self-maintenance abilities of small-scale peasant communities, leaving them highly vulnerable to outside exploitation. While the primary ideological justification for externally planned development was that it would ultimately raise rural living standards, the outcome of decades of development suggests that a fundamental re-assessment of the entire issue is called for. The barriers to progress are more likely to lie beyond, rather than within, local communities...

In 1988, near the end of the Third United Nations Development Decade, there were more impoverished people in the world than ever before...

Global poverty has been consistently treated as a technological problem partly because professional elites who are far removed from the daily realities of poverty formulate and finance development policies. Development is much more than a humanitarian concern; it has become a thoroughly institutionalized and highly complex industry with important political and economic functions for the wealth donors, which may be unrelated to the needs of the poor.

John Bodley, 'The Impoverished World', in *Cultural Anthropology: Tribes, States, and the Global System*, Mayfield Publishing, Mountain View, Calif., 1994, pp. 328, 337, 339. John Bodley is Profesor of Anthropology at Washington State University. His books (see Suggested Readings) are essential reading for students concerned with the 'victims of progress' in different lands.

> At least half the peoples of the world are living, by no fault of their own, under such poor and inadequate conditions that they cannot, out of their own scanty resources, achieve decent standards of living. The deep gulfs existing between the standards of living of different nations and peoples are, in the opinion of the Commission, a main source of international discontent, unrest, crisis and, in the last resort, are causes of wars ultimately endangering and devasting countries of high as well as low standards of living...[1]

This concern became generalized, as US government circles declared loud and long that poverty was a threat to world peace and to the interests of the United States. The Marshall Plan, launched in 1947, aimed at containing the communist threat and Soviet ambitions in Europe: economic aid became political strategy. But this transfer of resources aroused envy in other regions. At the General Assembly and ECOSOC the Latin American representatives, who were under strong social pressures and worried about communist upsurge, demanded that they too should benefit from an economic aid programme.

The logic of imperialism required that development be taken on as a burden of the metropolitan powers and this is reflected in the first discussions at the Trusteeship Council. The delegates of France and the United Kingdom were continually defending the efforts that their countries were making on behalf of development, 'to realize the potential of the countries under trusteeship'. In 1947 M. Laurentie, the French delegate, expressed his satisfaction in seeing his country bring 'a Western mode of reasoning' to the populations of Africa.[2] This education process was a complex, long-term job. As Mr Lamb, the British representative in Tanganyika, explained in 1950: the Trusteeship Authority must in certain cases and in certain circumstances take the decision that seemed best to correspond to the interests of the territory, exactly like a mother or father, whose decisions concerning the education of a child must not be influenced by the child's fears and misgivings.[3] The 'civilizing mission' of the West was prolonged thanks to the efforts being made to achieve the potential of the trusteeship territories as well as to the investment of capital and economic and technical aid. In 1951, the American delegate to the Assembly, Mike Mansfield, described this policy as a continuation of missionary activities.[4]

Development thus implied pursuing the social and cultural evolution of the industrialized countries. This perception emerged clearly from the questionnaire concerning the the non-autonomous territories that was approved by the Assembly. The information requested implied a wholesale transfer of the Western development model to the non-autonomous territories: questions ranged from the most complex agrarian and industrial matters to unemployment statistics, including social benefits for the aged and disabled.[5] This ethnocentric perspective also explained the terminological shifts in the notion of underdevelopment. At the Assembly and ECOSOC, in the official UN documents, countries or regions were referred to at one and the same time as 'backward', 'retarded', 'insufficiently developed', or 'insufficiently advanced', or 'little developed', less 'evolved', or again 'developing'. All these concepts reflect the image of historical phases of the model of the industrialized countries, stages which are to be passed through, following the dominant countries and thanks to their 'assistance'.

The development imperative naturally expressed itself in comparative terms. The difference was emphasized between the United States, where the average annual per-capita revenue at the time was over $1,400, and the other countries in the world, particularly those in the poorest regions where the yearly income was often way below $100.[6] This comparison was of course absurd, as the economic and social realities were completely different. It also overlooked the social dimensions of development and revealed nothing of the distribution of wealth or the nature of economic structures. Nevertheless it gave an impression of authority with its statistics and technical know-how.

It was inevitable that these criteria were to prove irrelevant. As the developed countries were the points of reference for development, the gap was already enormous – and continued to grow. The theme of the widening gap between the developed countries and the less developed countries, linked to that of the growing interdependence between the different parts of the world, did in fact appear in the very first documents about development and technical assistance produced by the Secretariat. The gravity of the problem and its alarming nature were stressed as well as the challenges it posed to the international community. Variations on the theme multiplied over the following years.

In the 'backward' regions, the economy is based on agriculture. Productivity is low, health and hygiene conditions are dramatic, illiteracy widespread, and the low level of education and technical training make progress problematic. Action on a broad front was required to create conditions favourable to economic and social progress: development was seen as a global process aimed at transforming the world in the image of the industrially advanced societies. At the Assembly, as in ECOSOC, there was frequent criticism of the internal structures of the underdeveloped countries, stressing the economic consequences of certain cultural traditions and the social disparities that they encouraged. The report of the famous expert group of 1951, 'Measures for the Economic Development of Underdeveloped Countries' brought it out clearly: the emphasis was on the institutional processes, the requirements of a rationalist and materialistic culture, the values and educational norms that favour the progress of science and technology and the role of the public authorities.[7]

The concept of development as presented at the United Nations at that time covered all aspects of society. It implied agrarian reform, planning, reduction in social inequalities. It required the creation of a modern state, an effective administration. The first UN technical assistance programmes were drawn up along these lines. It was thought that the change from a 'semi-feudal and traditional' administration to more 'rational' management methods was a necessary condition for progress. In 1948, the Assembly authorized the creation of an International Institute for Public Administration. The following year it allocated funds for training fellowships. But if the governments of the less 'evolved' countries were to take initiatives in all economic and social fields, they needed an administrative system capable of creating the conditions necessary for development. UN documents of this period harped on the importance of governmental stability, the maintenance of public order and respect for the law.[8] Clearly, 'qualified' personnel were required: administrators, economists and technicians – particularly in those countries where the Europeans were leaving.

At that time no issue turned up more frequently in the work of the United Nations – this is still the case today – than the ability of science and technology to leapfrog over the classic stages from backwardness to development. This trust in the effectiveness of the new production tools explains the strategy that developed in the ECOSOC reports from 1947. In order to achieve the 'conditions of stability and well-being', great importance was given to 'the modernization of production methods', which meant, above all, 'bringing the tools of modern technology within the reach of all the people'. It was believed that, in order to arrive at this, it was necessary to ensure a 'rational, effective and comprehensive utilization of labour, tools, technical means, energy and capital': industrialization was to play a decisive role in this process.[9] It was also thought that material progress would encourage the blossoming of the cultural and institutional conditions necessary for development.

ASSISTANCE TO THE POOR COUNTRIES

Immediately after the Second World War, the United Nations limited itself to propagating the need for development. Some years went by before the challenge posed by the poor countries was taken up and concrete measures put forward. It was then believed that reconstruction, economic growth based on higher industrial and agricultural productivity, the expansion of international trade, free access to raw materials, the return to monetary stability, anti-cyclical policies carried out by governments to fight unemployment and recession must necessarily bring about an improvement in the living conditions of the international community as a whole. In other words, the return of growth was counted upon to bring about the development of all regions of the world. It was therefore necessary for countries to create an 'economic climate' favourable to development, which meant, in fact, establishing an environment that helped to promote capitalism.

In 1949, during his inaugural speech, President Truman launched his famous Point IV Programme, a technical-assistance project for underdeveloped countries. This project was part of the American anti-communist strategy that aimed at curbing nationalistic tendencies and applying the Marshall Plan policy to the rest of the world. Not long afterwards, the United Nations launched the Technical Assistance Programme (TAP). Modelled on the US initiative, it involved the whole of the United Nations.

Point IV aspired to the dissemination of the American model by showing the way to a future of 'abundance and liberty'. It proposed sharing 'knowledge and capacities'; sending advisers or missions of experts to governments and business; participating in the financing and administering of public services; creating research centres and laboratories, as well as pilot projects, training researchers and university graduates; promoting the exchange of students; distributing publications and films – in short, propagating the American social and cultural system through the dissemination of the knowledge and techniques that enabled it to function.

For the Americans, the technical-assistance policy was useful for three reasons. First of all, it helped to disseminate the liberal model; it could also be kept closely under control, in that the experts had to come mostly from the Western countries. It did not cost very much. And it could even be a source of substantial benefits in that the experts or the techniques proposed would prime the pump for larger investments, which the American companies were anxious not to lose out on.

Western history has unfolded according to laws as rigorous as those of gravitation, so that it was natural that foreign aid should be seen in terms of technical assistance. The need for socio-cultural transformation did in fact explain the role attributed to experts in the development process. The notion of technical assistance was based on the assumption of a universal paradigm, of an economic, social, cultural and institutional norm applicable to all peoples on earth. The expert replaced the missionary of former times in achieving the potential of the newly independent states. He goes 'on mission'. He is sent 'into the field'. He helps towards 'realizing the potential' of the countries concerned. The language of the official reports on assistance was totally infused by the new messianism. It was impossible to convey what the programme 'really represents in the life of the peoples of the world'. It was a wonder to behold 'with what respect and gratitude the governments and the peoples of these countries welcome those who perform its works.'[10]

The projects that inspired such emotion and gratitude were highly diverse. They included advice given to governments for making an inventory of their resources, for helping them create a 'good administration', for setting up a legislative structure, employment services, teaching and public-health systems, agricultural programmes and the management of civil aviation. They involved the sending out of an army of technicians to give training and the allocation of fellowships. All the Specialized Agencies have been involved in these assistance programmes, particularly ILO, FAO, WHO and bodies like the Regional Economic Commissions and UNICEF.

As technical assistance demanded profound social, cultural and institutional changes in the countries concerned, it was obvious that the application of these 'rational' and 'technical' norms had political implications. There has been a tendency, however, to deny the relationships between this technical logic and the political order that produces it – in other words, not to acknowledge the sociological conditioning of these norms considered to be universal. Attempts are still being made to present technical assistance as if its purpose transcended ideological and political options. The notion of development and its ensuing strategy mixes, in the same discourse, the irrepressible logic of technical reasoning with that, infinitely more contradictory, of politics.

This assistance mentality derives from the technocratic bias of those in power. It therefore attracts the governments in developing countries whose representatives at the UN belong, by definition, to a governing elite that shares the ideas that give strength and authority to the advantages and benefits of this form of aid. The United Nations thus produces a discourse that claims to be ahistorical and apolitical on subjects as varied as planning and investments, agrarian reform and public administration, as if the understanding or management of these development elements could be conceived in terms that are universally beyond challenge. Fortunately, from the secretariat viewpoint, the technical assistance option allows the problem of development strategies to be avoided to a certain extent. It enables the specialized institutions to be mobilized through the institutional fragmentation of the system, thus postponing reflection on a more global policy.

In fact, the technical assistance projects of the UN never had much funding, the budget being only $7 million in 1955. As for the Technical Assistance Programme, which was financed by voluntary contributions, its resources were also quite limited: $15 million in 1954. This was a far cry from the approximately $14 billion invested in Europe under the Marshall Plan. Development belonged more to the realm of ideological needs and demands than to concrete realities.

It is true that from 1946 certain voices were raised among the Latin American representatives, associating underdevelopment with relationships of exploitation and domination, contesting the structures of international trade and demanding another form of economic aid. In 1949, Mr M.K. Rao submitted to the Sub-Commission on Economic Development a project which would create a UN Administration for Economic Development. In 1952, the representative of Chile, Mr Hernán Santa Cruz, asked the Assembly to create a Development Fund.

The United States was opposed to this. They refused to listen to any discussion about such a fund, for which they would have the entire financial responsibility. They preferred the mechanisms of the World Bank, which they controlled, and continued to insist on the need to create a climate favourable to investment in the developing countries. Certainly, the international situation at that time did not favour a genuine development policy. Military budgets escalated because of the Korean War, the decolonization conflicts and the East–West confrontation.

The United States therefore never really seriously intended to support the United Nations' work in economic and social development. But it took them several years to 'kill' the project for a Development Fund, which was finally buried in 1957, after innumerable studies had been carried out, expert committees having met and resolutions having been passed. The author of this 'perfect crime' was Mr Paul Hoffman, the former Administrator of the Marshall Plan and the future Director of the United Nations Development Programme (UNDP).[11] Nevertheless, in 1958 the United States did permit the creation of an 'expanded technical assistance programme' (ETAP), with some funds at its disposal to finance pre-investment activities. In 1965 this programme was amalgamated with the Technical Assistance Programme to form the UNDP....

THE DEVELOPMENT DECADE

While they did not take all the initiatives, the Western countries did exercise a decisive influence on the aid projects to the developing countries elaborated by the United Nations. They provided the resources and defined the practical modalities for distributing them. Their concern about development was conditioned by the growing national independence movements and the rapid accession of the Third World to the front of the world stage. The economic and social situation in the 'developing countries' – according to the terms that were used at that time – was more than ever associated by the cabinets of the rich countries' governments with the crises and conflicts that troubled the world order.

At the end of the 1950s, it was the United States that once again took the lead. As the balance of fear obliged the superpowers to play out their conflicts in Third World countries, President Kennedy launched the Alliance for Progress project in Latin America, which was soon reinforced by the Peace Corps. It was mainly a question of wiping out the advance of 'Castroism' south of the Rio Grande and promoting economic and social change, democracy and the growth of the transnationals. A little later, on 9 December 1961, again on the initiative of President Kennedy, the Assembly proclaimed the First Development Decade.[12]

This resolution is strongly imbued with the ideas that were in vogue in the American administration at the time. There are several references to the idea of 'self-sustaining growth' and it also established a distinction between the less developed countries, those which 'are newly developing', and the 'more developed' countries. It supported the economic and social projects spelt out by Washington in the context of the Alliance for Progress: diversifying the economies of the countries concerned, their rapid industrialization, the establishment of highly productive agricultural sectors and agrarian reform programmes.

Its materialistic orientation is striking: development is seen according to the logic of international capitalism's expansion. The first objective is defined in terms of growth, each country having to attain, as a minimum aim, an annual increase in GDP of 5 per cent by the end of the Decade. This was to be made possible through international trade, notably the export of the natural resources of the developing countries. And it was to be based on the internal savings of these countries, as well as the support of foreign capital, private and public. The Decade especially recommended states 'to adopt measures which will stimulate the flow of private investment capital for economic development', and therefore to create a climate favourable to the expansion of the capitalist system. Once again, the need was emphasized for elaborating 'well-conceived and integrated country plans', a proposition consonant with the technocratic ideas fashionable at that time, both in the governments of the Third World and in those of the industrialized countries. It gave the same importance as before to the traditional objectives of technical assistance: eradication of illiteracy, hunger and disease – conditions 'which seriously affect the productivity [*sic*] of the people of the less developed countries'.[13]

The Specialized Agencies made their objectives conform to the needs for growth propagated by the Decade. FAO fixed as an objective a daily intake of 2,300 calories and 10 grammes of animal protein per individual in the Far East and 2,470 calories and 20 grammes of animal protein per individual in the Near East: these targets were to be attained towards the end of the Decade. UNESCO's minimal objective was ten copies of a newspaper, five radio sets and two cinema seats per hundred inhabitants.[14]

On the whole, this development project was well received by the governments of the Third World. It corresponded to the image that the ruling classes had of the attributes of state power and to their political ambitions, as well as to the interests of the urban classes who had diverted the benefits of independence to their own account. It envisaged governments with broad responsibilities, therefore an extended administration, able to plan and mobilize all a country's resources in order to stimulate growth. This is the era when Nasser made speeches about progress that were clearly influenced by the economic 'take-off' theme. Almost everywhere the correlation was made between economic growth and political development. Paradoxically, the enlargement of the United Nations coincided with the triumph of this development ideology.

While the development resources of the United Nations were almost always devoted to technical assistance, since the early 1960s they were extended to include 'pre-investment' activities. 'Experts' continued to be sent into the field by the United Nations and priority was given to private and public investment that furthered the expansion of the capitalist system, particularly through the transnational corporations, whose growth was one of the dominant characteristics of the period.

The UNDP was the agent of this policy. It prolonged the 'colonial' mode of development, as a former UNDP expert clearly demonstrated in 1970.[15] This can be seen in the UN documents concerning technical assistance: they are still impregnated with the paternalistic fervour for great colonial 'adventures'. The WHO cites Disraeli to illuminate the meaning of its action. UNESCO insists on its 'moral' mission. Experts educate, train, advise and give meaning to development plans.[16]

In 1969, the Jackson Report marked the culminating point of these technocratic conceptions of development as propagated by the United Nations. Jackson's dream can be summed up as the search for a 'super brain' able to ensure a perfectly rational management of all the capacities of the United Nations, to mobilize all the resources of science, technology and planning on behalf of development. Its objective was based on the assumption of an incontrovertible, irresistible economic rationality. The governments were in principle responsible for their planning, but UNDP had to be involved in the conceptualization and implementation phases of these national plans. The recommendation for decentralization and 'country programming' which was contained in the Jackson Report is just one of the methods proposed for an effective management of development.

And supposing national policies contradicted the ideological and political foundations of this universal rationality? If, in other words, governmental proposals favoured development projects that conflicted with respect for human rights or the social objectives of the United Nations? If, by chance, cultural traditions, political practices and social customs all ran counter to this logic of assistance, to the 'mission' of the dedicated experts? The Jackson Report evaded these contradictions, which, however, often confronted UNDP officials in their daily work.

In theory, the concept of development defended by the United Nations maintained its social objectives. The process continued to be associated with the need for profound cultural and social transformation, and the importance of educational training and community participation were emphasized. ILO continued to push consistently for the objectives and programmes helping to improve working and living conditions, fulfilling the potential of human resources, developing social institutions and promoting international work standards, all of which conformed with its constitutional aims and conventions. It accordingly gave priority to the developing countries. In 1969, on the occasion of its fiftieth anniversary, it launched a 'World Employment Programme', aiming to make employment one of the most important objectives in national and international development policies. It was especially concerned about the massive underemployment and unemployment accompanying the economic growth and increase in national production of certain developing countries. In 1970, the director general's Report was devoted to world poverty and to minimum living standards. It indicted the exodus of the populations of 'primitive' rural areas towards the degradation of the city slums in various regions of the Third World. It also defined the special measures to be taken on behalf of the most underprivileged, particularly the aboriginal populations and the nomads. It supported the notion of an 'integrated rural development' that included agrarian reforms for raising the living standards of agricultural workers.

In general, the secretariat of the United Nations, strongly influenced by the milieu of its origins, appeared equally concerned about the institutional and structural dimensions of development. In 1968, reacting against the optimism and economistic tendencies of the Decade, the World Economic Survey, published regularly by the UN, deplored that development was all too often compounded with economic growth. It recommended that the emphasis be on changing the level, composition and redistribution of production in order to combat the existing inequalities between regions, racial groups and social classes.

The welfare state, which had been developed in Europe thanks to the strength of the social-democratic movement, remained a model that was above all questioning. Almost everywhere it was a point of reference: its authority was considerable. After having adopted the Covenants on Economic, Social and Cultural Rights in 1966, the General Assembly pronounced, in 1969, the Declaration on Social Progress and Development, which advocated highly advanced social concepts. Not content with reaffirming the ideals of human rights, as they were spelt out in the Declaration and the Convenants on Human Rights, it consisted of a catalogue of projects, from the supply of free health services for the whole population to the setting up of crèches for small children to help working parents, including a whole range of measures for education and professional training. It thus encouraged the states to aim at setting up a complete, coherent system for social security and protection.

How was this design to be carried out? The 1969 Declaration put its faith in the benefits of planning. It recommended a 'maximum mobilization of all national resources and their rational and efficient utilization'. To this end, it proposed the 'mobilization of public opinion' to ensure the 'dissemination of social information, at the national and international levels'. The United Nations thus diffused the model of a state that efficiently organized all economic and social resources for development. This ideological framework, which could be considered as the response of the advanced capitalist countries to the disintegration of traditional community structures, was evidently not adapted to the needs of the young states.

In fact, at the very moment when the Assembly adopted these advanced ideas, the United Nations was unable to define a development policy that could integrate the essential elements of its ideological project. No conceptual or operational linkages were made between the different aspects of development – for example, between its quantitative economic objectives and its social and cultural aspirations. The UNDP continued to send out its geologists, engineers, nutritionists, agronomists, technicians of all kinds, and went on supplying resources for ports, roads and irrigation channels. But it hardly ever concerned itself with the social aspects of development.

The technical assistance programmes of the United Nations do in fact reflect the fragmentation of the advanced industrial countries and the anomie that results from the way that their societies are organized. The programmes thus pass on the productivist logic of the industrial societies and help destroy the meaningful networks and cultural communication, a necessary prerequisite for the division of labour and 'modern' civilization in general. They also continue to reproduce the functionalist design that dominated the constitution of the United Nations system right from the beginning.

This lack of coherence invariably stemmed from the gap between the ideological functions of the United Nations and the means that the system disposes to achieve its objectives. UNDP's resources increased fairly regularly, but, towards the middle of the 1960s, its budget was still only $50 million – less than half the budget of the Canton and City of Geneva for a population of some 300,000 inhabitants. There is indeed an abyss between the aims proclaimed by the United Nations and its resources for action, between the ambitiousness of its programmes and the reality! The fact is that the situation in the so-called developing countries has been progressively worsening, and infinitely greater efforts would be needed to stop this process.

The Decade was an ideological declaration, a propaganda device. The economic policies that really affect development are being worked out on the fringes of the organization, outside the Specialized Agencies, particularly at the IMF, the World Bank, GATT and within the regional institutions for economic and political co-operation, such as OECD or the European Economic Community (*sic*). The governments also give much greater importance to bilateral public assistance, which bring them obvious economic and political advantages.

NOTES

1. Economic and Social Council, Official Records, First Year, Second Session, p. 227.
2. Trusteeship Council, Official Records, Second Session, p. 395.
3. Ibid., Fourth Year, Sixth Session, p. 214.
4. General Assembly, Official Records, Sixth Session, Second Commission, 147th Meeting, p. 18.
5. Resolution 142 (II).
6. *Technical Assistance for Economic Development*, Report prepared by the Secretary General, 1949, p. 4.
7. Report by a Group of Experts Appointed by the Secretary General of the United Nations, New York, 1951, p. 108.
8. United Nations, *Standards and Techniques of Public Administration with Special Reference to Technical Assistance for Undeveloped Countries*, 1951, p. 66.
9. Report of the Working Group for Asia and the Far East, Temporary Sub-Commission on Economic Reconstruction of Devastated Areas. Doc. E/307/Rev.1, p. 47.
10. ECOSOC, Official Records, Twentieth Session, Supplement No. 4, Report of the Committee on Technical Assistance, New York, 1955, p. 1.
11. Hernán Santa Cruz, *El Dilema de la Comunidad Mundial: Cooperer o perecer*, 1941–1970, GEL, Buenos Aires, 1984, t.1, pp. 430–38.
12. Resolution 1710 (XVI).
13. United Nations, *The UN Development Decade: Proposals for Action: Report of the Secretary General*, New York, 1962, pp. 1–2.
14. Ibid., pp. 49–50, 80.
15. S.S. Zarkovich, Le Programme des Nations Unies pour le Développement, PUF, Paris, 1970, especially pp. 155ff.
16. United Nations, *Expanded Technical Assistance Programme: 150,000 Experts in 15 Years*, New York, pp. 99, 115.

NGOs: A Trojan Horse

International programmes of technical and financial aid, or economic and scientific co-operation (green revolution, technology transfer, etc.) have multiplied, contributing to the destruction or the dependency of regional and national economies, but without being able to affect the more isolated rural communities or the indigenous communities more resistant to integration. And it is here that the defenders of the free market and of monetary theories leave the floor to the non-governmental organizations (NGOs). They, in fact, use capital that is not subject to the immediate need of profitability and are free from the constraints of capitalist production. Even more than credit, this can therefore at least partially be likened to investment that does not recover its outlay; in other words, it represents a gift.

The NGOs can all claim to be donors or protectors. More than their economic efficacy, these titles explain their credit and success in the aid and co-operation programmes of Western countries. Recognition of prestige, which is necessarily linked to the gift by indigenous communities, establishes them as political authorities. It is possible to distinguish between the donor NGOs and the technical assistance NGOs who do not have their own funds and economic power. The donor NGOs may have their own technicians like certain national organizations for bilateral co-operation. Or they use the technical assistance NGOs as intermediaries to manage, control or redistribute the funds of development aid.

The indigenous and peasant organizations challenge this supervision. After having requested direct contact with the funding NGOs and control over the NGO technicians, they are now trying to get contracts based on direct reciprocity with the 'professionals' or reciprocal partnerships. In other words, they want to control the orientation and definition of development programmes and replace the Western technicians by their own. Obviously, neither the funding nor the technical NGOs have accepted this kind of control or contract. Confronted by these claims from the indigenous or peasant organizations, the NGOs prefer to look for national partners, outposts of technical or national NGOs, who present themselves as the new intermediaries, legitimized in the name of national independence…

Certain NGOs claim to defend the indigenous cultures and even call for anthropological prudence. But it is easy to see that, under this pretext of respect for the indigenous culture, what they are really interested in is to dissociate the indigenous population from their economy based on reciprocity. To achieve this, they define the local political economy in Western terms (the production of exchange value). As there is usually no such economy in the indigenous world, they refer to the anthropological thesis according to which the exchange economy is really hidden, masked or integrated. This thesis thus authorizes Western technicians to discover, unmask or, rather, invent by re-interpreting the indigenous categories in Western terms – and by so doing, justifying their own intervention. As for the cultural anthropologists, they are interested in becoming authorities on the indigenous culture itself. One claims to be a specialist in its cultural aspects, another in the economy. They share out the community, or the ethnic group, one the body and the other the soul: each according to his or her speciality. But this way of dissociating the indigenous culture from the economy that underlies it, by refusing to admit that there are other economic systems than the one based on exchange, enables the Westerners to develop production for exchange under the guise of respect for the indigenous culture. This can only be called a 'cut flower' policy.

The activities of the NGOs … on the economic level … *consist of substituting reciprocity infrastructure by an exchange infrastructure. This is what I call economicide*. It is the fundamental and systematic function of Western NGOs… Economicide … consists of destroying the communities' economic bases of reciprocity, to impose either privatization or collectivization. Today this economicide is the most secret but perhaps the most effective weapon: it is the most cleverly disguised one used by the West in the Third World countries.

Dominique Temple, 'Les ONG comme cheval de Troie', *IFDA Dossier* 60, July/August 1987. Translated by V.B.

The works of Dominique Temple focus on the understanding of those dimensions of non-Western and 'archaic' societies that are generally overlooked or devalued by developers. In addition to his many incisive articles on such topics as gift, reciprocity and 'economicide', he is the author of three important books (in Spanish and French): *La Dialectica del don* (Editions Hisbol, La Paz 1986), *La Estructura comunitaria y reciprocidad: del quiproquo historico al economicido* (Editions Hisbol e Chitacolla, La Paz, 1989), and (with Mireille Chabal), *La Reciprocité et la naissance des valeurs* (L'Harmattan, Paris, 1995).

PART FOUR

DEVELOPMENT IN PRACTICE

20

HOW THE POOR DEVELOP THE RICH

Susan George

The following text is taken from the Introduction to *The Debt Boomerang: How Third World Debt Harms Us All* (Pluto Press, London and the Transnational Institute, Amsterdam, 1992, pp. xiii–xix). The author shows how countless lives have been devastated by the so-called structural adjustment imposed by the International Monetary Fund and the World Bank in a misguided attempt to deal with the problem of debt in the Third World. In particular she stresses how ordinary people in the First World are also victims of the present crisis: although not to the same degree as the populations directly concerned, they too must pay the price of World Bank and IMF policies that have accelerated deforestation, encouraged mass migrations, fuelled an expanding drugs trade, and heightened global instability and conflict. The banks' irresponsible and short-sighted loan policies, which are underwritten by taxpayers' money, sustain the downward spiral of global indebtedness.

SUSAN GEORGE is an associate director of the Transnational Institute and the author of a number of books on North–South issues, including *How the Other Half Dies: The Real Reasons for World Hunger* (Penguin, Harmondsworth, 1986), *A Fate Worse than Debt* (Penguin, Harmondsworth, 1988), and *Ill Fares the Land: Essays on Food, Hunger and Power* (Penguin, Harmondsworth, 1990). She also serves on the International Board of Greenpeace.

If the goals of official debt managers were to squeeze the debtors dry, to transfer enormous resources from South to North, and to wage undeclared war on the poor continents and their people, then their policies have been an unqualified success. If, however, their strategies were intended – as these institutions always claim – to promote development beneficial to all members of society, to preserve the planet's unique environment, and gradually to reduce the debt burden itself, then their failure is easily demonstrated.

One obvious aspect of this failure, or success, dependent on one's point of view, is financial. From the onset of the debt crisis in 1982 through to 1990 (at the time of writing, the last year for which complete figures are available),

Africa Funding the World Bank

Two facts emerge from the World Bank's accounts. The first is that Africa is paying this institution more than it receives from it. Which means that, contrary to the received wisdom, African poverty is financing the long-term wealth of the rich countries. The second fact is that the Bank, on a global level, is in financial difficulties. It is therefore thanks to our repayments that it manages to survive.

Abdoulaye Wade (Minister of State in Senegal), 'Afrique entre arrimage et trou noir économique', *Le Monde*, 14 July 1994.

each and every month, for 108 months, debtor countries of the South remitted to their creditors in the North an average US$6.5 billion in interest payments alone. If payments of principal are included in the tally, then each of the 108 months from January 1982 through December 1990 witnessed payments from debtors to creditors of, on average, $12.45 billion.

What happened to this money, remitted to private banks, state creditors and international public institutions, thanks to the toil and tears of hundreds of millions? Theoretically, the Third World's interest payments alone could have provided every man, woman and child in North America and Europe with either $1,000 or £500 sterling during this nine-year period.[1] Practically speaking, of course, ordinary citizens in the North obtained no such advantages, in spite of the unprecedented haemorrhage flowing from the less developed to the wealthy countries. On the contrary, these Northern citizens paid, as we intend to show, huge and varied penalties to compensate for the foolish lending policies of their own banks and governments.

Another aspect of the success/failure story has been the opportunity debt has provided to intervene in the management of dozens of debtors' economies. The International Monetary Fund and the World Bank, acting on behalf of the creditor countries that are their major stockholders, have undertaken this task. Their job is simple: to make sure that the debt is serviced. Thus a chief goal of their economic management must be the accumulation of enough hard currency to ensure levels of payments like those just cited. Since the average citizen of a low-income debtor country is fifty-five times poorer, and the average citizen of a middle-income debtor country is nine times poorer than the average citizen of an OECD creditor country, this process has been justifiably likened to extracting blood from a stone.[2]

To accumulate hard currency one must increase exports and reduce government outlays; we will not elaborate here on the specific measures which are supposed to allow governments to 'earn more and spend less'. The problem for the debtor country is that it must remit most or all of its debt service before it is free to engage in any other pursuits. Most debtor countries

A Penalty of £1,000 for the Poor

On 28 May 1994 British Prime Minister John Major reiterated a statement he had made earlier on the damage that the poor were doing to the tourist industry. He recommended that every citizen report beggars to the police, under laws that provide for a fine of a up to £1,000 pounds – to be paid by the poor living on the streets. For John Major, people sleep rough not out of necessity, but out of choice – it had, he believed, become a lifestyle.

A similar theme was taken up again more recently by David Maclean, the Home Office minister (as reported in the *Guardian*, 11 January 1997). He said: 'There are no genuine beggars. Those who are in need have got all the social benefits they require. Every time we go and check, we find they won't go into hostels. Beggars are doing so out of choice because they find it more pleasant.'

These attitudes epitomize the essence of the various programmes for 'the eradication of poverty'. See Georg Simmel, 'The Poor', *Social Problems*, vol. 13, 1965, pp. 117–40; and Philippe Sassier, *Du Bon usage des pauvres: Histoire d'un thème politique (XVIe–XXe)* (Fayard, Paris, 1990).

have for years co-operated, and forced their peoples to co-operate, with the draconian policies of the IMF and the World Bank. Much good it has done them.[3] A decade has passed since the Third World debt crisis first erupted; yet, in spite of harsh measures faithfully applied, this crisis is today more intractable than ever.

At the behest of the Bank and the Fund, debtor countries have deprived their people – particularly the poorest among them – of basic necessities in order to provide the private banks and the public agencies of the rich countries with the equivalent of six Marshall Plans. This unprecedented financial assistance to the rich from the poor may be startling but it is none the less arithmetically true.

According to the OECD, between 1982 and 1990 total resource flows to developing countries amounted to $927 billion. This sum includes the OECD categories of Official Development Finance, Export Credits and Private Flows – in other words, all official bilateral and multilateral aid, grants by private charities, trade credits plus direct private investment and bank loans. Much of this inflow was not in the form of grants but was rather new debt, on which dividends or interest will naturally come due in the future.

During the same 1982–90 period, developing countries remitted *in debt service alone* $1,345 billion (interest and principal) to the creditor countries. For a true picture of resource flows, one would have to add many other South-to-North outflows such as royalties, dividends, repatriated profits, underpaid raw materials and the like. The income–outflow difference between $1,345 and $927 billion is thus a much understated $418 billion in the rich countries' favour. For purposes of comparison, the US Marshall Plan transferred $14 billion 1948 dollars to war-ravaged Europe, about $70 billion in 1991 dollars. Thus in the eight years from 1982 to 1990 the poor have financed six Marshall Plans for the rich through debt service alone.

Have these extraordinary outflows at least served to reduce the absolute size of the debt burden? Unfortunately not: in spite of total debt service, including amortization, of more than $1.3 trillion from 1982 to 1990, the debtor countries as a group began the 1990s *fully 61 per cent more in debt than they were in 1982.* Sub-Saharan Africa's debt increased by 113 per cent during this period; the debt burden of the very poorest – the so-called LDCs, or 'least developed countries' – was up by 110 per cent.

Clearly, the economic policies imposed on debts by the major multilateral agencies – policies packaged under the general heading of 'structural adjustment' – have cured nothing at all. They have, rather, caused untold human suffering and widespread environmental destruction while simultaneously emptying debtor countries of their resources; rendering them each year less able to service their debts, let alone invest in economic and human recovery. The World Bank and the IMF structural adjustors have now had a generous period to impose their plans and cannot complain that their measures have not been given enough time to work. Had these public debt management officials been corporate executives, with so little to show for themselves, their shareholders would have doubtless sacked them long ago for incompetence. Had they been politicians, they would have been trounced at election time and sent back to where they came from.

Corporate managers and local or national public office-holders can be dismissed for poor performance. No such accountability applies to the international bureaucrats acting on behalf of the creditor governments. The international debt managers need never submit to the judgement of their victims. They answer only to their own equally unaccountable superiors, and, at the top of the bureaucratic tree, to a Board of Governors reflecting the majority voting strength of the richest creditor countries. These lavishly compensated international civil 'servants' are consequently still to be found in Washington and throughout the Third World, living exceedingly well.[4]

The international debt managers, whose requirements include higher levels of exports and radical cutbacks in government spending, do not feel the effects of the massive unemployment, depressed wages and drastically reduced public services which quite naturally follow. The social dislocation they have encouraged has not even bought economic health – the debt managers would be hard pressed to point to a single Third World success story. Economically, socially and ecologically speaking, 'structural adjustment' has been a disaster, but the Fund and the Bank are undeterred.

Their perseverance can be at least partly explained by the unequivocal encouragement they have received from certain quarters. The ultimate verdict on IMF and World Bank activities depends entirely on who serves on the jury. For corporations operating in debtor countries – both local and transnational – structural adjustment has reduced both wages and the power of unions, thus enhancing corporate profitability. For many international banks, debt service payments at unusually high interest rates in the early 1980s helped to fuel several years of record earnings. From the corporate or banking perspective, the World Bank and the IMF pass the test with flying colours.

Nor have Third World elites much cause for complaint. They have weathered the 'lost decade of the 1980s' with relative ease and have sometimes profited handsomely from it. They, too, benefit from plummeting wages and their money is often in safe havens outside their own countries, in US dollars or Swiss francs. Each time the IMF requires a devaluation of the national currency to encourage exports, those whose holdings are in foreign currencies automatically become richer at home. And although public services may deteriorate or close down, rich people can afford private ones. Thus it is not surprising that Third World governments have failed to unite and to demand debt reduction. Each debtor country sits down alone to negotiate, across the table from a united creditor front.

The debtors' lack of unity ensures the draining of their economies and a continuing South-to-North resource flow on a scale far outstripping any the colonial period could command. The debtor governments have from time to time made mild remonstrances and called for debt reliefs, but have never collectively confronted the creditors. Even if they suddenly tried to do so, the historic opportunity they might once have seized has passed: the banks are far less vulnerable to pressure than they were until 1987.

As a reward for docility, the creditors have allowed most debtor country elites to maintain their links to the world financial system, providing them with at least a trickle of fresh money and offering them frequent opportunities to purchase local assets at bargain prices through so-called 'debt-for-equity swaps' or privatization programmes. Third World debt should not, therefore, be seen as a straightforwardly 'national' problem. Different social classes in debtor countries have vastly divergent interests and are unequally affected. Although debt has visited unprecedented pain on the vast majority of Third World people, the crisis is not necessarily a crisis for everyone.

While the topmost layers of Third World societies remain largely insulated from debt distress, ordinary people in the South sacrifice to pay back loans they never asked for, or which they even fought against, and from which they derived no gain. Knowledge of their plight is by now fairly widespread in the developed, creditor countries, thanks to the efforts of thousands of concerned people patiently explaining the human and ecological consequences of the debt crisis in the Third World. Yet, despite the best efforts of such people, pressures exerted by dozens of non-governmental organizations in both North and South have so far failed to alter basic debt-management policies. Although the Fund and the Bank now claim they seek to 'mitigate the social costs of adjustment', official response to the crisis advances at a calculated snail's pace, inching from one feeble and ineffective 'Plan' to the next, while leaving the status quo essentially untouched.

Until now, those in the North, including many TNI/IPS Fellows,[5] who have tried to change the debt-management strategies of their governments, the World Bank and the IMF, have rightly based their arguments on ethical and humanitarian grounds. The social and ecological disaster debt has brought upon people in the South, particularly the poorer among them, provides ample justification for this approach.

The impact of Third World debt fallout in the North is much less well known – doubtless because the consequences of debt are more serious and life-threatening in the South than in the North. Nonetheless, we believe it is vital to show how such a seemingly distant phenomenon in fact harms nearly everyone in the North. We view *the debt boomerang* as one way to bridge the information gap; to demonstrate that ordinary citizens of debtor and creditor countries have every interest in joining forces to demand an entirely new approach to Third World debt. Although people in the South are far more grievously affected by debt than those in the North, in both cases a tiny minority benefits while the overwhelming majority pays.

Rarely in human affairs can one show a linear, one-to-one causal link between events; the consequences of the debt crisis are no exception. Thus nowhere do we claim that Third World debt is the *only* cause of, say, increased illegal drug exports to the United States and Europe, or of accelerated deforestation hastening the greenhouse effect. We do, on the other hand, try to show that debt is, at the very least, an aggravating factor in these negative trends. Thus we stress feedbacks more than linear connections and tend to see debt and its multiple consequences as mutually reinforcing. For example, debt-burdened Latin American governments become hooked on dollars from their coca-producing regions. This severely dampens their incentive to encourage legal crops. Increased drug exports, in turn, escalate the costs of law enforcement and contribute to social breakdown in the North.

These harmful effects did not, so to speak, suddenly spring fully armed from the head, or the belly, of the World Bank. They result from a conscious set of policies aimed at promoting a particular kind of development. During the late 1960s and throughout the 1970s, borrowing financed an expensive, capital-intensive, energy-intensive, unsustainable development model favourable only to Third World elites, Northern banks and transnational corporations. This model marginalized the majority, which could not hope to partake of the fruits of a spurious 'growth' based on human exploitation and natural resource depletion.

Not surprisingly, massive overborrowing (encouraged by the creditors, welcomed by the borrower governments) coupled with high interest rates led to the debt crisis. This crisis in turn provided official debt managers in the 1980s and 1990s with a perfect lever, immediately used, to entrench the very development model which had caused the original problem. Relying on unbridled free-market forces and export-led growth, they have devastated the unprotected – poorer, more vulnerable groups and the environment. They are still doing it, and, quite simply, they have to be stopped.

NOTES

1. Almost all debt figures in this study are taken directly or derived from OECD, *Financing and External Debt of Developing Countries*, 1989 and 1990 surveys, OECD, Paris, 1990 and 1991. We generally use this source in preference to the World Bank's *Debt Tables* because OECD figures include short-term debt – for many countries a fairly large proportion of total borrowings – whereas the World Bank's do not. The above calculations are based on total interest payments of US$706 billion for the nine calendar years from 1982 to 1990, divided by 108 months or by 600 million Northern citizens. If payments of principal (amortization) of long-term debt are included, total payback from South to North for the same period was $1,345.3 billion. In that case each of these 600 million Northern citizens would have theoretically received an average $2,242.

2. According to World Bank statistics, the average GNP per capita (1988 dollars) for Low Income Countries is $320, for Middle Income Countries $1,930, for OECD countries $17,470.

3. For greater detail on these measures and their human costs, see Susan George, *A Fate Worse Than Debt*, Penguin, Harmondsworth and Grove Press, New York, 1988.

4. In early 1991, the author was seated on an airplane next to a supervisor of an international construction firm. An old Africa hand, he was on his way to the desperately poor African country Guinea (life expectancy 43 years; illiteracy 72 per cent, according to World Bank figures). There his company was constructing the country's largest swimming pool to enhance the charms of the villa occupied by the World Bank mission chief. According to this informant, the Bank – that is, you, me and the Bank's bondholders – was footing the bill. As of 1 August 1991, salaries for the heads of the World Bank and the IMF were raised to $285,000 per annum. The pay ceiling for their top staff is $190,000.

5. Transnational Institute/Institute for Policy Studies.

21

TO BE LIKE THEM

Eduardo Galeano

The following text was translated from the French by Victoria Bawtree from an article entitled 'Etre comme eux', which was published in *Le Monde Diplomatique* in October 1991 in a translation by Pierre Guillaumin from the original Spanish.

EDUARDO GALEANO originates from Montevideo, Uruguay. A journalist on the well-known weekly, *Marcha*, he had to go into exile to Argentina, then to Spain, during the military dictatorship (1973–85). His best-known book is *The Open Veins of Latin America* (Monthly Review Press, New York, 1973). Among subsequently published works is a passionate review of the continent's tragic history, *Memory Of Fire* (trans. Cedric Belfrage, Pantheon Books, New York and Methuen, London, 1985–88; originally published 1982–86 by Siglo XXI, Madrid). In January 1992 Messidor published a collection of his essays under the title *Contempt: The Destiny Of Latin America*.

It was the promise of the politicians, the justification of the technocrats, the illusion of the outcast. The Third World will become like the First World – rich, cultivated and happy if it behaves and does what it is told, without saying anything or complaining. A prosperous future will compensate for the good behaviour of those who died of hunger during the last chapter of the televised serial of history. WE CAN BE LIKE THEM, proclaimed a gigantic illuminated board along the highway to development of the underdeveloped and the modernization of the latecomers.

But, 'what can't be, can't be, and more than that is impossible', as Pedro el Gallo, the bullfighter so rightly said. If the poor countries reached the levels of production and waste of the rich countries, our planet would die. Already it is in a coma, seriously contaminated by the industrial civilization and emptied of its last drop of substance by the consumer society.

IMPOSSIBLE HOPES

During the last twenty years, while the human race increased threefold, erosion has destroyed the equivalent of the whole cultivable area of the United States. The world, which has become a market for merchandise, loses 15 million hectares of forest a year, of which 6 million become desert. Humiliated nature has been made over to the service of capital accumulation. Soil, water and air are being poisoned so that money produces ever more money, without a fall in the rate of profit. He who makes the most money in the shortest time is the efficient one.

Acid rain from industrial fumes is killing the woods and lakes of the world, while toxic wastes are poisoning the rivers and seas. In the South, imported agro-business prospers, uprooting trees and human beings. In the North and the South, the East and the West, man is sawing off the branch on which he is sitting with feverish enthusiasm.

From woodland to desert: modernization, devastation. The continuous Amazonian bonfire burns an area half the size of Belgium each year on behalf of the civilization of greed, and all over Latin America land is being cleared and becoming arid. *Each minute*, in Latin America, 23 hectares of wood are being sacrificed, most of them by companies who produce meat or wood on a large scale for foreign consumption. The cows of Costa Rica become MacDonald hamburgers in the USA. Half a century ago, trees covered three-quarters of this little country; there are very few left now and, at the end of this century, at the current rate of deforestation, Costa Rica will be completely bare. This country exports meat to the United States and imports from it pesticides that the US bans on its own soil.

A small number of countries are squandering the resources that belong to everyone. The crime and madness of the wasteful society: 6 per cent of the richest populations are devouring one-third of the total energy available and one-third of all the world's natural resources in use. According to the statistics, one average North American consumes as much as fifty Haitians. Obviously these averages do not apply to someone from Harlem or to Baby Doc Duvalier, but it is important to ask: what would happen if the fifty Haitians suddenly consumed as much as fifty North Americans? What would happen if the huge populations of the South could devour the world with the unpunished voracity of the North? What would happen if the luxury articles, cars, refrigerators, television sets, nuclear and electric power stations increased at this crazy pace? All the world's oil would be burnt up in ten years.

And what would happen to the climate which, with the warming of the atmosphere, is already close to catastrophe? What would happen to the soil – the little that erosion spared us? And to the water which, contaminated by nitrates, pesticides and industrial wastes of mercury and lead, is being drunk by one-quarter of humanity? What would happen? Nothing would be left. We would have to change planets. Our own, already so exploited, could no longer stand it.

The precarious equilibrium of the world, which is poised on the brink of an abyss, depends on the perpetuation of injustice. The deprivation of the majority is necessary so that the waste of a few is possible. In order that a few may consume still more, many must continue to consume still less. And so that everyone stays in their place, the system increases its military weapons. Incapable of fighting poverty, it fights the poor, while the dominant culture, a militarized culture, worships the violence of power.

The American way of life, based on the privilege of waste, can only be practised by the dominant minorities of the dominating countries. If it were generalized, it would mean the collective suicide of humanity. It is therefore impossible – but is it even desirable?

In a well-organized ant colony, there are a few queen ants and innumerable worker ants. The queens are born with wings and can procreate. The workers, who do not fly or procreate, work for the queens; the police ants watch over the workers, but also the queens.

'Life is something that happens when one is busy doing something else', remarked John Lennon. In our era, in which ways and means are so often confused, we do not work to live; we live to work. Some work all the time so that they can satisfy their needs. And others work more and more in order to waste.

An eight-hour work day in Latin America is pure fiction. Though it is seldom acknowledged by the official statistics, two jobs are the reality for a mass of people who have no other way of keeping hunger at bay. But, where development is at its apogee, is it normal that people work like ants? Does wealth lead to liberty, or does it increase the fear of freedom?

THE ABERRATIONS OF MODERNITY

To be is to have, says the system. And the problem is that those who have the most want still more; and that, when all is said and done, people end up by belonging to things and working under their orders. The model of life in the consumer society, which these days is imposed as a model at the universal level, converts time into an economic resource which is increasingly rare and expensive. Time is sold and hired. But who is the master of time? The car, the television set, the video, the personal computer, the portable telephone and other pass-cards to happiness, which were developed to 'save time' or to 'pass the time', have actually taken time over. The car, for example, not only occupies urban space, but also human time. In theory the car serves to economize time, but in practice it devours it. A considerable proportion of work time goes to pay the transport for getting to work, which takes more and more time because of the traffic jams in these modern Babylons.

There is no need to be an economic expert. Good common sense is enough to see that technological progress, by increasing productivity, reduces working time. Good common sense, however, did not foresee the fear that 'free time' could bring, or the trap of consumption, or the manipulating power of publicity. In Japanese cities they have been working forty-seven hours a week for the last twenty years, while in Europe the number of work hours has been reduced, but very slowly, at a rhythm that has nothing to do with the accelerated development of productivity. In the automated factory there are ten workers where there used to be a thousand. But technological progress leads to unemployment instead of increasing the spaces of freedom. Freedom to squander one's time: the consumer society does not allow such waste. One's very holidays, organized by agencies which industrialize tourism, have become an exhausting activity. Killing time: modern beaches reproduce the dizziness of everyday life in the urban ant colonies.

Anthropologists teach us that our palaeolithic ancestors did not work more than twenty hours a week. Newspapers inform us that at the end of 1988 a referendum was organized in Switzerland proposing to reduce the working week to forty hours – a reduction of hours without loss of salary. The Swiss voted against it.

Ants communicate among themselves by touching their antennae. The television antennae communicate with the power centres of the contemporary world. The small screen encourages the thirst for possession in us, the frenzy to consume, the exacerbation of competition and avidity for success, in the same way that Christopher Columbus offered glass to the Indians. What the publicity does not say, however, is that the USA consumes, according to the World Health Organization, 'almost half the tranquillizers that are sold in the world'. During the last twenty years, the work day has increased in the USA. During this same period, the number of people affected by stress has doubled.

'A peasant is worth less than a cow and more than a chicken', I heard in Caaguazu, in Paraguay. And in north-east Brazil: 'He who plants has no land and he who has no land, plants.'

TOWNS AS GAS CHAMBERS

The countryside is being deserted; the Latin American towns are becoming hells the size of countries. Mexico City is growing at the rate of half a million people and 30 square kilometres *a year*. It already has a population five times that of Norway. Soon, at the end of the century, the capital of Mexico and the Brazilian city of São Paulo will be the biggest cities in the world.

The great cities of the South of the planet are like the great cities of the North, but seen through a distorting mirror. The Latin American capitals have no bicycle alleys, or filters for toxic gases. Pure air and silence are such rare and expensive commodities that there is no one left who is rich enough to buy them.

The Brazilian plants of Volkswagen and Ford make cars with filters and export them to Europe and to the USA and cars without filters to sell in Brazil. Argentina produces leadless petrol for export. For its internal market, though, it produces poisoned petrol. In all Latin America cars are allowed to spit out lead copiously from their exhaust pipes. From the car point of view, lead raises the octane level and increases the rate of profit. From the human

The Shame of a Nation

In the year nineteen hundred and sixty-four, in the richest nation of the world, six hundred people in NY and four hundred in Washington DC – half of them under ten – were bitten by rats in slum tenements; a family of twelve in the nation's capital, unable to find a low-rent house that would accept nine children, lived – and spent Christmas – in a basement furnace room.

Philip M. Stern, and George de Vincent, *The Shame of A Nation*, Ivan Obolensky, New York, 1965.

point of view, lead damages the brain and the nervous system. The cars, masters of the cities, do not listen to the troublemakers.

Year 2000, picture of the future: people with oxygen masks, birds that cough instead of sing, trees that refuse to grow. In Mexico City today you can see appeals to 'Leave the walls alone' and requests, 'Don't bang the door please'. One can't yet read 'You are advised not to come in'. How soon will there be advice on public health? Each day cars generously spew 11,000 tonnes of poisonous petrol fumes into the atmosphere. Thick fog fills the air and children are born with lead in their blood. Dead birds fall like rain on to the city which, only fifty years ago, was 'the place that had the cleanest air'. Now the cocktail of carbon monoxide, sulphur dioxide and nitrogen oxide has reached three times the tolerance level for human beings. What will the threshold of tolerance be for urban inhabitants?

Five million cars: the city of São Paulo has been likened to an old man suffering from a heart attack. A cloud of gaseous fumes spreads over it. From the surrounding countryside you can only see the most developed city of Brazil on Sundays. Each day, along the avenues in the centre, lighted panels keep the inhabitants informed of the situation. In 1986 the meteorological stations showed that the air was polluted, or very polluted, for 323 days in the year.

In June 1989, on days without wind or rain, Santiago, Chile, was competing with São Paulo for the title of the world's most polluted city. Mount San Cristóbal, in the very centre of town, could not be seen at all, it was so hidden by smog. The brand new democratic government of Chile took some half-hearted measures against the 800 tonnes of gas fumes that were being expelled into the city's atmosphere. Car drivers and businesses then howled that these restrictions violated freedom of enterprise and constituted an attack on human rights. The freedom of money, which distrusts all other freedoms, suffered no restrictions during the dictatorship of General Pinochet and contributed considerably to the general pollution. The right to contaminate is a basic attraction for foreign investment, almost as important as the right to pay minuscule wages. General Pinochet, in fact, never denied the right of Chileans to breathe shit.

The consumer society which consumes everyone obliges people to consume, while television gives courses in violence both to the educated and to the illiterate. Those who have nothing may live far away from those who have everything, but every day they can spy on them on the box. Television provides the obscene spectacle of an orgy of consumption and, at the same time, teaches people the art of shooting their way out.

Reality copies television: violence on the streets is another way of extending what is projected on the screens. Street children take the initiative without criminal intent: it is the only place where they can express themselves. Their only human rights are the rights to steal and to die. Little animals, left to their fate, go hunting. At the first bend in the street, they sharpen their claws and run. Life is soon over for them, worn out by glue-sniffing and other drugs to forget hunger, cold and loneliness. Life can also end suddenly, with a bullet.

THE TOWN AS PRISON

To walk in the streets in the big Latin American cities becomes a high-risk activity. To stay at home, too. The town as prison: those who are not prisoners of need are prisoners of fear. Those who have something, however little, feel threatened, in constant fear of the next attack. Those who have a lot live shut up in security fortresses. The big buildings, the residential estates, are the feudal castles of the electronic age. They only lack moats full of crocodiles. Although they do not have the majestic beauty of the castles of the Middle Ages, they *do* have the huge drawbridges, high walls, the keeps and armed guards.

The state, which is no longer paternalistic but a police state, does not practise charity. That happened in a past that is over and done with: the age of rhetoric, in which those who had gone astray were domesticated by the virtues of study and work. Now that the market economy has become dominant, the army of the outcast are eliminated through starvation and bullets. The children on the street, children of the marginal workforce, are not and cannot be useful to society. Education belongs to those who can pay: repression is used against those who cannot buy it.

According to the *New York Times*, the police have killed more than forty children in the streets of Guatemala City. They are beggar children, petty thieves, rubbish pickers, whose bodies have been found without tongues, without eyes, without ears, and thrown into the garbage. In 1989, according to Amnesty International, 457 children and adolescents were executed in the cities of São Paulo, Rio de Janeiro and Recife. These crimes, committed by the death squads and other paramilitary forces, were not perpetrated in backward rural areas but in the largest cities of Brazil. They have not been committed where capitalism is lacking, but where there is too much of it. Social injustice and contempt for life increase with economic development.

Earning Certificates of Inferiority

Indians in Oaxaca who formerly had no access to schools are now drafted into school to 'earn' certificates that measure precisely their inferiority relative to the urban population. Furthermore – and this is again the rub – without this piece of paper they can no longer enter even the building trades. Modernization of 'needs' always adds new discrimination to poverty.

Ivan Illich, *Toward A History of Needs*, Pantheon Books, New York, 1977, p. 12.

In countries where the death penalty does not exist, it is applied every day to defend property rights, while every day the opinion-makers find excuses for crime. In mid-1990, in the city of Buenos Aires, an engineer shot and killed two young thieves who were escaping after having stolen the cassette player in his car. Bernardo Neustadt, the most influential Argentinian journalist, made the following statement on television: 'I would have done the same thing.' Afanasio Jazadji won a seat as deputy for the state of São Paulo. He had one of the most comfortable majorities in the history of Brazil and has become immensely popular on the radio. His programme loudly defended the death squads, advocating torture and the elimination of delinquents.

In the civilization of unrestrained capitalism, the right to property is more important than the right to life. People are worth less than things. In this context, the laws of immunity are revealing: they absolve the state terrorism exercised by the military dictatorships in the three countries of the Southern Cone, and pardon crime and terrorism, but do not pardon attacks on property rights (Chile: Decree No. 2191 in 1978; Uruguay: Law No. 15,848 in 1986; Argentina: Law No. 23,521 in 1987).

AND HOW'S THE DOLLAR DOING?

February 1989, Caracas. The price of transport suddenly goes up, the price of bread triples and the wrath of the population explodes. Three hundred, five hundred – who knows how many dead people are lying in the streets?

February 1991, Lima. The cholera epidemic hits the Peruvian coast, rages in the port of Chimbote and in the wretched shantytowns round the capital, killing a hundred people in a few days. In the hospitals there is neither serum nor salt. Rigorous economic policy has dismantled the little that remained of public health services and has doubled in no time the number of Peruvians living in acute poverty, who earn less than the minimum wage, which is $45 a month.

The wars of today, the electronic wars, take place on the screens of the video games. The victims are neither seen nor heard. The laboratory economy neither sees nor hears those who are hungry or the earth that has been devastated. Telecommanded weapons kill without remorse. The international technocracy, which imposes its development programmes and its structural adjustment plans on the Third World, also kills from the outside and from far away.

Over a quarter of a century ago Latin America started to dismantle the fragile barriers that had been constructed to oppose the all-powerful influence of money. Bank creditors bombarded these barrages with infallible extortion measures, while the military or the politicians in power helped to destroy them, dynamiting them from within. Thus fell, one by one, the protection barriers put up by the state in previous periods. And today the state is selling its public enterprises for next to nothing or less than nothing, as they are being bought up by those who are selling them. Our countries deliver the keys and all the rest to the international monopolies, known as 'factors that determine the prices' and turn themselves into free markets. The international technocracy, which teaches us how to make injections in wooden legs, says that the free market is the talisman of wealth. But why, then, is it not practised by the rich countries, those who are recommending it? The free market, which humiliates the weak, is the most successful export product of the powerful. It has been constructed for the use of the poor countries: no rich country has ever practised it.

Talisman of wealth, for how many? Here are official statistics from Uruguay and Costa Rica, countries where once social conflict used to be less violent: one Uruguayan in six lives in a state of extreme poverty, while two families out of five in Costa Rica are poor.

The dubious marriage of supply and demand, in a free market which hits the poor and serves the despotism of the powerful, gives rise to a speculative economy. Production is discouraged, work is despised, consumption deified. Stock-exchange boards are gazed at as if they were cinema screens and people talk about the dollar as though it were a human being.

THE 'SOCIAL COST' OF PROGRESS

Tragedy repeats itself as farce. In the era of Christopher Columbus, the development of foreign capital was experienced by Latin America as its own tragedy. Now everything has started again – as farce. It is the caricature of development: a dwarf pretending to be a child.

Technocracy sees statistics, not people. But it only sees the statistics that it wants to see. At the end of this long quarter of a century, some successes of 'modernization' have been celebrated. The 'Bolivian miracle', for example, achieved thanks to drug money: the exploitation of tin ended and, with it, the mining centres and unions that were the most combative in the country. Now the village of Llallagua has no water, but there is an antenna with a television dish on the summit of Mount Calvario. Or the 'Chilean miracle', created by the magic wand of General Pinochet, a successful product that is sold as a potion to the countries of Eastern Europe. But what is the price of the Chilean miracle? Who are the Chileans who have paid for it – and are still paying? Who are the Poles, Czechs and Hungarians who are going to pay for it? In Chile, the statistics proclaim the abundance of bread and, at the same time, admit the increase in the numbers of the hungry. The cock is crowing victory, but the rooster is suspect. Has failure not gone to his head? In 1970, 25 per cent of Chileans were poor; now the poor constitute 45 per cent of the population.

Statistics admit, but do not repent. In the last resort, human dignity depends on cost–benefit analysis, and the sacrifice of the poor is nothing but the 'social cost' of Progress.

What would be the value of this 'social cost' if it could be measured? At the end of 1990 the magazine *Stern* made a meticulous calculation of the damage created by the development of present-day Germany. The magazine evaluates, in economic terms, the human and material costs resulting from car accidents, traffic jams, air and water pollution, the contamination of food, the deterioration of the green belts and other factors. It arrived at the conclusion that the value of all this damage was equivalent to a quarter of the German national product. The increase in poverty, obviously, was not included in these estimates of damage as, for many centuries, Europe has been nourishing its wealth with foreign poverty. But it would be interesting to know what the figure would be if a similar estimate were to be made of the dramatic consequences of 'modernization' in Latin America. Furthermore, the German state does control and limit, to a certain extent, the system's negative effects on people and the environment. What would be the damage estimate in countries like ours, which believe in the free market fable and allow money to roam about freely, like an uncaged wild beast? The damage that this causes us and will continue to cause us; this system that bombards us with artificial needs so that we forget our real ones – how can we possibly measure it? Can we measure the mutilation of the human soul, the escalation of violence, the degradation of everyday life?

ON THE ALTAR OF PRODUCTIVITY

The West is living in a triumphant euphoria. The collapse of the East provides it with a perfect alibi: in the East it was worse. One should, instead, wonder whether it was fundamentally different. In the West, justice is sacrificed on the altar of the goddess Productivity in the name of liberty. In the East, liberty was sacrificed on the altar of the goddess Productivity in the name of justice. In the South we can still ask ourselves if this goddess is worth our lives.

22

DEVELOPMENT AND BUREAUCRATIC POWER IN LESOTHO

James Ferguson

The following text, reproduced from *The Ecologist* (vol. 24, no. 5, September–October 1994), is a summary by James Ferguson and Larry Lohmann of some of the main arguments set out in James Ferguson's book *The Anti-Politics Machine: 'Development', Depoliticization and Bureaucratic Power in Lesotho* (Cambridge University Press, Cambridge, 1990; University of Minnesota Press, Minneapolis, 1994). *The Ecologist* is one of the world's leading journals on ecology (see also the remarks of Gustavo Esteva on pp. 284ff).

JAMES FERGUSON is an associate professor at the Department of Anthropology at the University of California at Irvine.

In the past two decades, Lesotho – a small landlocked nation of about 1.8 million people surrounded by South Africa, with a current gross national product (GNP) of US$816 million – has received 'development' assistance from twenty-six different countries, ranging from Australia, Cyprus and Ireland to Switzerland and Taiwan. Seventy-two international agencies and non- and quasi-governmental organizations, including CARE, the Ford Foundation, the African Development Bank, the European Economic Community, the Overseas Development Institute, the International Labour Organization and the United Nations Development Programme, have also been actively involved in promoting a range of 'development' programmes. In 1979, the country received some $64 million in 'official' development 'assistance' – about $49 for every man, woman and child in the country. Expatriate consultants and 'experts' swarm in the capital city of Maseru, churning out plans, programmes and, most of all, paper, at an astonishing rate.

As in most other countries, the history of 'development' projects in Lesotho is one of 'almost unremitting failure to achieve their objectives'.[1] Nor does the country appear to be of especially great economic or strategic importance. What, then, is this massive and persistent international intervention all about?

CONSTRUCTING A 'DEVELOPER'S' LESOTHO

To 'move the money' they have been charged with spending, 'development' agencies prefer to opt for standardized 'development' packages. It thus suits the agencies to portray developing countries in terms that make them appropriate targets for such packages. It is not surprising, therefore, that the 'country profiles' on which the agencies base their interventions frequently bear little or no relation to economic and social realities.

In 1975, for example, the World Bank issued a report on Lesotho that was subsequently used to justify a series of major Bank loans to the country. One passage in the report – describing conditions in Lesotho at the time of independence from Britain in 1966 – encapsulates an image of Lesotho that fits well with the institutional needs of 'development' agencies:

> Virtually untouched by modern economic development ... Lesotho was, and still is, basically, a traditional subsistence peasant society. But rapid population growth resulting in extreme pressure on the land, deteriorating soil and declining agricultural yields led to a situation in which the country was no longer able to produce enough food for its people. Many able-bodied men were forced from the land in search of means to support their families, but the only employment opportunities [were] in South Africa. At present, an estimated 60 per cent of the male labour force is away as migrant workers in South Africa ... At independence, there was no economic infrastructure to speak of, industries were virtually non-existent.[2]

THE INVENTION OF 'ISOLATION'

To a scholar of Lesotho, these assertions appear not only incorrect but outlandish. For one thing, the country has not been a 'subsistence' society since at least the mid-1800s, having entered the twentieth century as a producer of 'wheat, mealies, Kaffir corn (*sic*), wool, mohair, horses and cattle' for the South African market.[3] Nor were the local Basotho people isolated from the market. When they have had surpluses of crops or livestock, the people have always known how to go about selling them in local or regional markets. According to *The Oxford History of South Africa*:

> In 1837 the Sotho of Basutoland ... had grain stored for four to eight years; in 1844 white farmers 'flocked' to them to buy grain. During 1872 [after the loss of their most fertile land west of the Caledon] the Sotho exported 100,000 *muids* [185 lb bags] of grain ... and in 1877 when the demand for grain on the diamond fields had fallen, 'large quantities' were held by producers and shopkeepers in Basutoland.[4]

Livestock auctions, meanwhile, have been held throughout the country since at least the 1950s, and animals from central Lesotho have been sold by the Basotho as far afield as South Africa for as long as anyone can remember. Far from being 'untouched' by modern 'development', at the time of independence, colonial rule had established a modern administration, airports, roads, schools, hospitals and markets for Western commodities.

The decline in agricultural surpluses, moreover, is neither recent nor, as the Bank suggests, due to 'isolation' from the cash economy. More significant is the loss by the Basotho of most of their best agricultural land to encroaching Dutch settlers between 1840 and 1869. Nor is migration a recent response of a pristine and static 'traditional' economy to 'population pressure'. As H. Ashton, the most eminent Western ethnographer of the Basotho, noted in 1952, 'labour migration is ... nearly as old as the Basuto's contact with Europeans'[5] – indeed, throughout the colonial period to the present, Lesotho has served as a labour reservoir exporting wage workers to South African mines, farms and industry.

Large-scale labour migration, moreover, preceded the decline in agriculture by many years and may even have contributed to it. Even in years of very good crop production, from the 1870s on intermittently into the 1920s, workers left the country by the thousand for work. In the early stages, it seems, migration was not related to a need to make up for poor food production but to buy guns, clothing, cattle and other goods, and, from 1869, to pay taxes.

LESOTHO REALITY

In fact, far from being the 'traditional peasant society' described by the Bank, Lesotho comprises today what one writer describes as 'a rural proletariat which scratches about on the land'.[6]

Whilst the World Bank claims that 'agriculture provides a livelihood for 85 per cent of the people',[7] the reality is that something in the order of 70 per cent of average rural household income is derived from wage labour in South Africa, while only 6 per cent comes from domestic crop production.[8] Similar myth-making pervades a joint FAO/World Bank report from 1975, which solemnly states that 'about 70 per cent of (Lesotho's) GNP comes from the sale of pastoral products, mainly wool and mohair'. A more conventional figure would be 2 or 3 per cent.[9]

Also false is the 'development' literature's picture of Lesotho as a self-contained geographical entity whose relation with South Africa (its 'rich neighbour') is one of accidental geographic juxtaposition rather than structural economic integration or political subordination, and whose poverty can be explained largely by the dearth of natural resources within its boundaries, together with the incompleteness with which they have been 'developed'. If the country is resource-poor, this is because most of the good Sotho land was taken by South Africa. Saying, as USAID does in a 1978 report, that 'poverty in Lesotho is primarily resource-related' is like saying that the South Bronx of New York City is poor because of its lack of natural resources and the fact that it contains more people than its land base can support.

REARRANGING REALITY

A representation which acknowledged the extent of Lesotho's long-standing involvement in the 'modern' capitalist economy of Southern Africa, however, would not provide a convincing justification for the 'development' agencies to 'introduce' roads, markets and credit. It would provide no grounds for believing that such 'innovations' could bring about the 'transformation' to a 'developed', 'modern' economy which would enable Lesotho's agricultural production to catch up with its burgeoning population and cut labour migration. Indeed, such a representation would tend to suggest that such measures for 'opening up' the country and exposing it to the 'cash economy' would have little impact, since Lesotho has not been isolated from the world economy for a very long time.

Acknowledging that Lesotho is a labour reserve for South African mining and industry rather than portraying it as an autonomous 'national economy', moreover, would be to stress the importance of something which is inaccessible to a 'development' planner in Lesotho. The World Bank mission to Lesotho is in no position to formulate programmes for changing or controlling the South African mining industry, and it has no disposition to involve itself in political challenges to the South African system of labour control. It is in an excellent position, however, to devise agricultural improvement projects, extension, credit and technical inputs, for the agriculture of Lesotho lies neatly within its jurisdiction, waiting to be 'developed'. For this reason, agricultural concerns tend to move centre stage and Lesotho is portrayed as a nation of 'farmers', not wage labourers. At the same time, issues such as structural unemployment, influx controls, low wages, political subjugation by South Africa, parasitic bureaucratic elites, and so on, simply disappear.

TAKING POLITICS OUT OF 'DEVELOPMENT'

One striking feature of the 'development' discourse on Lesotho is the way in which the 'development', agencies present the country's economy and society as lying within the control of a neutral, unitary and effective national government, and thus almost perfectly responsive to the blueprints of planners. The state is seen as an impartial instrument for implementing plans, and the government as a machine for providing social services and engineering growth.

'Development' is, moreover, seen as something that only comes about through government action; and lack of 'development', by definition, is the result of government neglect. Thus, in the World Bank's view, whether Lesotho's GNP goes up or down is a simple function of the current five-year 'development' plan being well implemented or badly implemented: it has nothing to do with whether or not the mineworkers who work in South Africa get a raise in any particular year. Agricultural production, similarly, is held to be low because of the 'absence of agricultural development schemes' and, thus, local ignorance that 'worthwhile things could be achieved on their land'. In this way, an extraordinarily important place is reserved for policy and 'development' planning.[10]

Excluded from the Bank's analysis are the political character of the state and its class basis, the uses of official positions and state power by the bureaucratic elite and other individuals, cliques and factions, and the advantages to them of bureaucratic 'inefficiency' and corruption. The state represents 'the people', and mention of the undemocratic nature of the ruling government or of political opposition is studiously avoided. The state is taken to have no interests except 'development': where 'bureaucracy' is seen as a problem, it is not a political matter but the unfortunate result of poor organization or lack of training.

Political parties almost never appear in the discourse of the Bank and other 'development' institutions, and the explicitly political role played by development institutions such as Village Development Committees (VDCs), which often serve as channels for the ruling Basotho National Party (BNP), is ignored or concealed. 'The people' tend to appear as an undifferentiated mass, a collection of 'individual farmers' and 'decision-makers', a concept which reduces political and structural causes of poverty to the level of individual 'values', 'attitudes' and 'motivation'. In this perspective, structural change is simply a matter of 'educating' people, or even just convincing them to change their minds. When a mission is sent out to 'develop the farmers' and finds that 'the farmers' are not much interested in farming, and in fact do not even consider themselves to be 'farmers', it is thus easy for it to arrive at the conclusion that 'the people' are mistaken, that they really are farmers and that they need only to be convinced that this is so for it to be so.

In fact, neither state bureaucracies nor the 'development' projects associated with them are impartial, apolitical machines which exist only to provide social services and promote economic growth. In the case of the Canadian- and World Bank-supported Thaba-Tseka Development Project, an agricultural programme in Lesotho's central mountains, Sesotho-language documents distributed to villagers were found to have slogans of the ruling BNP added at the end, although these did not appear in any of the English-language versions. Public village meetings conducted by project staff were peppered with political speeches, and often included addresses by a high-ranking police officer on the 'security threat' posed by the opposition Basutoland Congress Party. Any money remaining after project costs had been repaid went to the BNP's Village Development Committees – leading one villager to note caustically, 'It seems that politics is nowadays nicknamed 'development'.'

Tellingly, when I interviewed the Canadian co-ordinator of the Thaba-Tseka Project in 1983, he expressed what appeared to be a genuine ignorance of the political role played by VDCs. The project hired labour through the committees, he stated, because the government had told them to. 'We can't afford to get involved with politics', he said. 'If they say "hire through the Committees", I do it.'

It seems likely that such apparent political naiveté is not a ruse, but simply a low-level manifestation of the refusal to face local politics, which, for institutional reasons, characterizes the entire 'development' apparatus.

INEVITABLE FAILURE

Because the picture of Lesotho constructed by the Bank and other 'development' agencies bears so little resemblance to reality, it is hardly surprising that most 'development' projects have 'failed' even on their own terms. Thus, after years of accusing local people of being 'defeatist' or 'not serious' about agriculture, and even implying that wage increases at South African mines were 'a threat' to the determination of farmers to become 'serious', Thaba-Tseka project experts had to concede that local people were right that little beside maize for local consumption was going to come out of their tiny mountain fields, and that greater investment in agriculture was not going to pay handsome rewards.[11]

Casting themselves in the role of politically neutral artisans using 'development' projects as tools to grab hold of and transform a portion of the country according to a pre-determined plan, 'development' officials assumed that the projects were givens and all they had to do was 'implement' them. In the case of the Thaba-Tseka project, for example, planners assumed that it would be a relatively simple matter to devolve much of the decision-making to a newly constituted Thaba-Tseka district, in order to increase efficiency, enable the project to be in closer touch with the needs of 'the people', and avoid its becoming entangled in government bureaucracy. But what the planners assumed would be a simple technical reform led – predictably – to a whole range of actors using the reforms for their own ends.

The project's Health Division, for example, was partly appropriated as a political resource for the ruling Nation Party. Power struggles broke out over the use of project vehicles. Government ministries refused to vote funds to the project and persisted in maintaining their own control over their field staff and making unilateral decisions on actions in the district. An attempt to hire a Mosotho to replace the project's expatriate Canadian director was rejected since, as long as the programme's image remained 'Canadian', there could be no danger of bringing about a real 'decentralization' of power away from Maseru, Lesotho's capital.

Instead of being a tool used by artisans to resculpt society, in short, the project was itself worked on: it became like a bread crumb thrown into an ant's nest. Plans for decentralization were thus abandoned in 1982. Yet Thaba-Tseka's planners continued to insist that the project's failure resulted somehow from the government's failure to understand the plan, or from the right organizational chart not having been found. Needing to construe their role as 'apolitical', they continued to see government as a machine for delivering services, not as a political fact or a means by which certain classes and interests attempted to control the behaviour and choices of others.

A DIFFERENT KIND OF PROPERTY

Another example of 'failure' stemming from the 'development' discourse's false construction of Lesotho is that of livestock 'development'. 'Development' planners have long seen Lesotho's grasslands as one of the few potentially exploitable natural resources the country possesses,[12] and the country's herds of domestic grazing animals as an inertia-ridden 'traditional' sector ripe for transformation by the dynamic 'modern' cash economy. What is required, according to planners, is to develop 'appropriate marketing outlets', control grassland use to optimize commercial productivity through destocking and grazing associations, introduce improved breeds, and convince 'farmers to market their non-productive stock'.[13]

Far from being the result of 'traditional' inertia, however, the Basotho's reluctance to treat livestock commercially is deeply embedded in, and partly maintained by, a modern capitalist labour reserve economy. In Lesotho's highly monetarized economy, an item such as a transistor radio or a bar of soap may be subject to the same market mechanisms of price, supply and demand as it is anywhere else. Cattle, goats and sheep, however, are subject to very different sorts of rules. Although cash can always be converted into livestock through purchase, there is a reluctance to convert grazing animals to cash through sale, except when there is an emergency need for food, clothes or school fees.

This practice is rooted in, and reinforced by, a social system in which young working men are away in South Africa supporting their families for ten or eleven months of the year. (Mines hire only men, and it is very difficult for women from Lesotho to find work in South Africa.) If a man comes home from the mines with cash in his pocket, his wife may present him with a demand to buy her a new dress, furniture for the house or new blankets for the children. If, on the other hand, he comes home with an ox purchased with his wages, it is more difficult to make such demands.

One reason that men like to own large numbers of livestock is that they boost their prestige and personal networks in the community, partly since they can be farmed out to friends and relatives to help with their field work. They thus serve as a 'placeholder' for the man in the household and the community, symbolically asserting his structural presence and prestigious social position, even in the face of his physical absence. After he has returned to the household because of injury, age or being laid off from the South African mines to 'scratch about on the land', livestock begins to be sold in response to absolute shortages of minimum basic necessities. Grazing animals thus constitute a sort of special 'retirement fund' for men which is effective precisely because, although it lies within the household, it cannot be accessed in the way cash can.

Hence a whole mystique has grown up glorifying cattle ownership – a mystique which, although largely contested by women, is constantly fought for by most men. Such conflict is not a sign of disintegration or crisis: it is part of the process of re-creating a 'tradition' which is never simply a residue of the past. If the cultural rules governing livestock in Lesotho persist, it is because they are made to persist; continuity as much as change has to be created and fought for.

Investment in livestock is thus not an alternative to migrant labour but a consequence of it. If livestock sellers surveyed by 'development' experts report no source of income other than agriculture, this does not mean that they are 'serious stock farmers' as opposed to 'migrant labourers'; they may simply be 'retired'.

However useful and necessary they may be, moreover, livestock in Lesotho is less an 'industry' or a 'sector' than a type (however special) of consumer good bought with wages earned in South Africa when times are good and sold off only when times are bad. The sale of an animal is not 'off-take' of a surplus, but part of a process which culminates in the destruction of the herd. A drop in livestock exports from Lesotho is thus not, as the 'development' discourse would have it, a sign of a depressed 'industry', but of a rise in incomes. For instance, when wages were increased in South African mines in the 1970s, Basotho miners seized the opportunity to invest in cattle in unprecedented numbers, leading to a surge in import figures from 4,067 in 1973 to 57,787 in 1978. Over the same period, meanwhile, cattle export figures dropped from 12,894 to 574. A boom in exports, on the other hand, would be the mark of a disaster.

Not surprisingly, attempts to 'modernize' Lesotho's 'livestock sector' have met with resistance. Within one year of the Thaba-Tseka project attempting to fence off 15 square kilometres of rangeland for the exclusive use of 'progressive', 'commercially minded' farmers, for example, the fence had been cut or knocked down in many places, the gates stolen, and the area was being freely grazed by all. The office of the association manager had been burned down, and the Canadian officer in charge of the programme was said to be fearing for his life.

This resistance was rooted in more than a general suspicion of the government and the 'development' project. To join the official 'grazing association' permitted to use the fenced-in land, stock owners were required to sell off many poor animals to buy improved ones, ending up with perhaps half as many. Such sales and restrictions in herd size were not appealing for most Basotho men. Joining the association not only meant accepting selection, culling and marketing of herds. It also meant acquiescing in the enclosure of both common grazing land and (in so far as any Mosotho's livestock are also a social, shared domain of wealth) animals. It thus signified a betrayal of fellow stock-owners who remained outside the organization, an act considered anti-social. Prospective association members also probably feared that their animals – which represent wealth in a visible, exposed and highly vulnerable form – might be stolen or vandalized in retaliation.

THE SIDE-EFFECTS OF 'FAILURE'

Despite such disasters, it may be that what is most important about a 'development' project is not so much that which it fails to do but that which it achieves through its 'side-effects'. Rather than repeatedly asking the politically naive question 'Can aid programmes ever be made really to help poor people?', perhaps we should investigate the more searching question, 'What do aid programmes do *besides* fail to help poor people?'

Leftist political economists have often argued that the 'real' purpose of 'development' projects is to aid capitalist penetration into Third World countries. In Lesotho, however, such projects do not characteristically succeed in introducing new relations of production (capitalist or otherwise); nor do they bring about modernization or significant economic transformations. Nor are they set up in such a way that they ever could. For this reason, it seems a mistake to interpret them *simply* as 'part of the historical expansion of capitalism' or as elements in a global strategy for controlling or capitalizing peasant production.

Capitalist interests, moreover, can only operate through a set of social and cultural structures so complex that the outcome may be only a baroque and unrecognizable transformation of the original intention. Although it is relevant to know, for instance, that the World Bank has an interest in boosting production and export of cash crops for the external market, and that industrialized states without historic links to an area may sponsor 'development' projects as a way of breaking into otherwise inaccessible markets, it remains impossible simply to read off actual events from these known interests as if the one were a simple effect of the other. Merely knowing that the Canadian government has an interest in promoting rural 'development' because it helps Canadian corporations to find export markets for farm machinery, for example, leaves many of the empirical details of the Canadian role in Thaba-Tseka absolutely mysterious.

Another look at the Thaba-Tseka project, however, reveals that, although the project 'failed' both at poverty alleviation and at extending the influence of international capital, it did have a powerful and far-reaching impact on its region. While the project did not transform livestock-keeping, it did build a road to link Thaba-Tseka more strongly with the capital. While it does not bring about 'decentralization' or 'popular participation', it was instrumental in establishing a new district administration and giving the government a much stronger presence in the area than it had ever had before.

As a direct result of the construction of the project centre and the decision to make that centre the capital of a new district, there appeared a new post office, a police station, a prison and an immigration control office; there were health officials and nutrition officers and a new 'food for work' administration run by the Ministry of Rural Development and the Ministry of Interior, which functioned politically to regulate the power of chiefs. The new district centre also provided a good base for the 'Para-Military Unit', Lesotho's army; and near the project's end in 1983, substantial numbers of armed troops began to be garrisoned at Thaba-Tseka.

In this perspective, the 'development' apparatus in Lesotho is not a machine for eliminating poverty that is incidentally involved with the state bureaucracy. Rather, it is a machine for reinforcing and expanding the exercise of bureaucratic state power, which incidentally takes 'poverty' as its point of entry and justification – launching an intervention that may have no effect on the poverty but does have other concrete effects.

This does not mean that 'the state', conceived as a unitary entity, 'has' more power to extract surplus, implement programmes, or order around 'the masses' more efficiently – indeed, the reverse may be true. It is, rather, that more power relations are referred through state channels and bureaucratic circuits – most immediately, that more people must stand in line and await rubber stamps to get what they want. 'It is the same story over again', said one 'development' worker. 'When the Americans and the Danes and the Canadians leave, the villagers will continue their marginal farming practices and wait for the mine wages, knowing only that now the taxman lives down the valley rather than in Maseru.'[14]

At the same time, a 'development' project can effectively squash political challenges to the system, not only through enhancing administrative power but also by casting political questions of land, resources, jobs or wages as a technical 'problem', responsive to the technical 'development' intervention. If the effects of a 'development' project end up forming any kind of strategically coherent or intelligible whole, it is as a kind of 'anti-politics' machine, which, on the model of the 'anti-gravity' machine of science-fiction stories, seems to suspend 'politics' from even the most sensitive political operations at the flick of a switch.

Such a result may be no part of the planners' intentions. It is not necessarily the consequence of any kind of conspiracy to aid capitalist exploitation by incorporating new territories into the world system or working against radical social change, or bribing national elites, or mystifying the real international relationships. The result can be accomplished, as it were, behind the backs of the most sincere participants. It may just happen to be the way things work out. On this view, the planning apparatus is neither mere ornament nor the master key to understanding what happens. Rather than being the blueprint for a machine, it is a *part* of the machine.

NOTES

1. C. Murray, *Families Divided: The Impact of Migrant Labour in Lesotho*, Cambridge University Press, New York, 1981, p. 19.
2. World Bank, *Lesotho: A Development Challenge*, World Bank, Washington DC, 1975, p. 1.
3. 'Basutoland', *Encyclopaedia Britannica*, London, 1910.
4. M. Wilson, and L. Thompson, eds, *The Oxford History of South Africa*, Vol. 1, Oxford University Press, New York, 1969.
5. H. Ashton, *The Basuto: A Social Study of Traditional and Modern Lesotho*, 2nd edn, Oxford University Press, New York, 1967, p. 162.
6. Murray, *Families Divided*, p. 1.
7. FAO/World Bank, *Draft Report of the Lesotho First Phase Mountain Area Development Project Preparation Mission*, Vols 1 and 2, FAO, Rome, 1975, Annex 1, p. 7.
8. A.C.A. Van der Wiel, *Migratory Wage Labour: Its Role in the Economy of Lesotho*, Mazenod Book Centre, Mazenod, 1977.
9. FAO/World Bank, *Draft Report*, Annex 1, p. 7.
10. World Bank, *Lesotho*, p. 9.
11. See 'Appraisal of Project Progress during the Pilot Phase and Review of Plans to Expand Agricultural Programmes in Phase II of Project Operations', CIDA, Ottawa, 1978, p. 39.
12. See, for example, FAO/World Bank, *Draft Report*, Annex 1, pp. 10–12. For a related South African history of government intervention into 'traditional' livestock keeping, see W. Beinart and C. Bundy, 'State Intervention and Rural Resistance: The Transkei, 1900–1965', in M. Klein, ed., *Peasants in Africa*, Sage, Beverley Hills, 1981.
13. 'Appraisal of Project Progress', p. 11.
14. Quoted in B. Murphy, 'Smothered in kindness', *New Internationalist*, no. 82, 1979, p. 13.

23

TRANSMIGRATION IN INDONESIA: HOW MILLIONS ARE UPROOTED

Graham Hancock

Graham Hancock's book *Lords of Poverty* (Macmillan, London, 1989; Mandarin paperback, London, 1991), from which the following extract is taken, caused quite a stir when it was first published. Many 'development' projects could have been singled out for consideration here: this has been chosen as it is one of the most succinct presentations of a project that, in terms of sheer numbers, has wreaked immense damage to the people and the environment of Indonesia. An update details recent developments in the programme, particularly in Western Papua.

GRAHAM HANCOCK was formerly East Africa correspondent of *The Economist*, co-editor of *New Internationalist*, and editor of *Africa Guide*. He received an award for his humanitarian work in Ethiopia during the 1984–85 famine – but became deeply disillusioned with the aid business.

In Indonesia, the world's largest-ever exercise in human resettlement is currently under way – an exercise that is similar in many respects to the Polonoroeste scheme in Brazil and that has attracted multi-million-dollar backing from the World Bank. Known as the 'transmigration programme', it is transferring peasant farmers from overcrowded Java to the more thinly populated outlying islands of the vast archipelago. At least six million people have already been moved,[1] and several million more are scheduled for relocation by 1994.[2]

The Bank first became involved in 1976. By 1986 it had committed no less than $600 million directly to support the transmigration programme – some 20 per cent of all its lending to Indonesian agriculture during this decade. In addition, a further $680 million has been committed to the linked Nucleus Estate and Smallholder scheme – a long-term project which is settling some 95,000 families, of whom about one-quarter are transmigrants.[3] USAID, the government of the Netherlands, the government of France and the government of the Federal Republic of Germany have also been generous in providing funds and technical assistance for resettlement, as have the EEC, UNDP, FAO, the World Food Programme and Catholic Relief Services.[4]

Such unquibbling backing from so large and respectable a group of Western bilateral, multilateral and voluntary agencies is difficult to explain or understand – particularly in the context of the experience of Polonoroeste, which illustrated most starkly the dangers of resettlement in rainforest areas. Like Polonoroeste, furthermore, transmigration in Indonesia has entailed a breathtaking combination of human rights abuses, environmental destruction and bad development. To give some examples:

- Land rights enjoyed under traditional law by the tribal people on outlying islands like Irian Jaya, Sulawesi and Kalimantan have been subordinated to transmigration. The relevant clause in Indonesian government legislation reads as follows: 'The rights of traditional-law communities may not be allowed to stand in the way of the establishment of transmigration sites.'[5]

- Transmigration to the island of Irian Jaya has fuelled a growing conflict between the Indonesian armed forces and nationalist Irianese. According to Marcus Colchester of Survival International: 'Local resistance to the takeover of traditional lands has been met with brutal violence by the Indonesian military.' Indeed, the violence has been so extreme that more than 20,000 Irianese have so far fled their homes and sought refuge in neighbouring Papua New Guinea.[6]

  The World Bank seems unconcerned: its principal internal policy document on transmigration states unequivocally that 'well-planned settlement ... must be encouraged' in Irian Jaya.[7] The document adds that there is a clear need for the Indonesian government to be 'sensitized to the rights of isolated and unassimilated people'. What we are not told, however, is how this is to be achieved.[8] Nor does it seem likely that it will be an easy task: Irianese refugees report that their villages have been bombed by the Indonesian air force, that their settlements have been burned by the military, that women have been raped, that livestock has been killed or driven off, and that numbers of people have been indiscriminately shot while others have been imprisoned and tortured.[9]

- Meanwhile the Indonesian government continues to implement a policy of 'sedentarizing' and 'assimilating' into the mainstream all of Indonesia's tribal peoples. According to the Minister of Transmigration: 'The different ethnic groups' of Indonesia 'will in the long run disappear ... and there will be one kind of man.'[10] This rather chilling objective has been described by one Australian critic as 'the Javanese version of Nazi Germany's *Lebensraum*'.[11] To achieve it, Indonesian government plans call for Irian Jaya's entire indigenous population of 800,000 tribal people to be moved – forcibly if necessary – from their traditional homesteads and villages into resettlement sites on the island by 1998; this programme of 'internal transmigration' is being carried out at the rate of approximately 13,000 families per year.[12]

'Apart from causing severe conflicts over land rights', says Marcus Colchester, international transmigration – which is also taking place on several other islands – 'has proved socially and economically catastrophic for the tribal communities involved. Many communities have faced the double indignity of having their lands taken over for the creation of transmigration sites and then of being forcibly resettled back on their own lands where they find themselves a minority, despised for their 'primitive' customs such as eating sago and pigs.'[13]

- According to a report presented to the United Nations by the London-based Anti-Slavery Society, at least one supposedly vacant island given to migrants was actually already inhabited; the Indonesian army cleared land for the settlers by burning the indigenous people's crops.[14]

- East Timor – seized by the Indonesian army in 1975 – has since been made the target of considerable resettlement from Java. An estimated 150,000 of the 700,000 indigenous inhabitants of East Timor have been killed in the subsequent fighting, or have died of hunger.[15]

- In addition to the human damage that it has done, the resettlement programme has also been responsible for much destructive clearing of Indonesia's unique and extensive tropical rainforest. This forest, as the World Bank tells us in its own policy document on transmigration, 'is one of the most biologically diverse areas in the world and has more than 500 species of mammals, 1,500 species of birds, and a botanical diversity which includes 20,000 species of trees. For this reason, Indonesia's forests and wildlife are a matter of international interest, and Indonesia's stewardship of them a matter of utmost importance.'[16]

In the light of this remark the Bank's continued support for the transmigration programme seems grotesque. An authoritative survey recently carried out by the Indonesian government's own Forestry Department (jointly with the Washington-based International Institute for Environment and Development) concludes that transmigration is 'the single sectoral activity with the greatest potential to advance forest destruction [and] can only have negative implications for forest resources.'[17]

Sulawesi and Sumatra – both major focuses of transmigration – have suffered particularly badly. On the latter, 2.3 million hectares of land formerly under canopy forest are today defined as 'critical' – that is, so degraded that they are unable to sustain even subsistence agriculture or to fulfil normal soil functions such as absorbing water. More than 30 per cent of Sulawesi has been reduced to this same 'critical' state as a result of transmigration.[18] Over Indonesia as a whole, current plans envisage the destruction of a great many more millions of hectares of irreplaceable rainforest to make way for resettlement sites.[19]

Despite these and other profoundly negative aspects of transmigration in Indonesia, the long-term involvement of the World Bank and other donors would perhaps be comprehensible if the programme was achieving its own stated objectives – that is, if it were greatly improving the quality of migrants' lives, or, at the very least, making them less poor than they were before they left their original homes. Tragically, however, this is not the case.

A principal reason why – as aid agencies acquainted with Polonoroeste could not have failed to realize from the outset – is that the soils of new settlements that have been hacked and cleared out of rainforest cannot support sustained agriculture. The result, observes United States Republican Senator Robert Kasten – who has strongly opposed American financial support for transmigration – is that the migrants, after a few short years, 'are left with little choice but to move back to the cities, or to begin illegal logging and slash-and-burn farming, which destroys even more forest lands'.[20]

The move back to the cities is already well advanced. There are documented cases of migrant families attempting to sell their children in order to raise the money to pay for a return to Java.[21] Meanwhile, on Irian Jaya alone, more than 7,000 settlers are known to have abandoned transmigration sites and to have flocked to towns such as Jayapura and Sorong in search of urban employment – which is often not available. Prostitution and the spread of venereal disease are growing social problems which have been directly linked to the failure of transmigration to provide a sustainable economic base for settlers.[22] Nationwide, some 300,000 people are now estimated to be living in 'economically marginal and deteriorating transmigration settlements' and are recognized by the Indonesian government itself as 'a potential source of serious political and social unrest in the future'.[23]

These 300,000, however, are probably just the visible tip of a much larger iceberg of settlers who have found their farms disappointingly unproductive. 'Dumped on deforested land without tools, without a community', in the words of one former aid worker, 'the migrants have been unable to make a go of it'.[24] As a result, they are presently obliged to rely on 'off-farm' work for up to 80 per cent of their incomes[25] – a precarious state of affairs since, as the World Bank admits, these off-farm earnings will fall when 'wage-income associated with site development ceases'.[26] The Bank also notes the probability that any further 'slowdown in government investment in receiving areas … could result in declining migrant incomes and employment opportunities'.[27]

The cumulative effect of factors like these – in a period that has indeed seen reduced spending by the Indonesian government – has been considerable. Despite all the emotional cost, stress and upheaval of leaving their homelands, by far the majority of the migrants have *not* had their dreams for a better life or their aspirations for higher incomes fulfilled. On the contrary,

The 'Toxic Memo' of the World Bank

Just between you and me, shouldn't the World Bank be encouraging *more* migration of the dirty industries to the LDCs? ... The measurement of the costs of health-impairing pollution depends on the forgone earnings from increased morbidity and mortality. From this point of view a given amount of health-impairing pollution should be done in the country with the lowest cost, which will be the country with the lowest wages. I think the economic logic behind dumping a load of toxic waste in the lowest-wage country is impeccable and we should face up to that ... I've always thought that unpolluted countries in Africa are vastly *under*polluted, their air quality is probably vastly inefficiently lower than Los Angeles or Mexico City...

This memo was written, in December 1991, by Lawrence H. Summers, then World Bank Chief Economist and Vice-President for Development Economics, a position he held until he became the US Under-Secretary of the Treasury in 1993. Among the worldwide reactions following its 'leaking' and publication, Susan George and Fabrizio Sabelli's comments are particularly incisive: see Chapter 5, 'The Fundamentalist Freedom Fighter', *Faith and Credit: The World Bank's Secular Empire* (Penguin, Harmondsworth and Westview Press, Boulder, Colo., 1994).

as the Bank makes clear in its confidential *Transmigration Sector Review*: 'Migrant incomes in the settlement area are, on average, slightly lower than those in rural Java and significantly lower than those in the rural outer islands.'[28] Worryingly, the lowest incomes are not found amongst the least experienced settlers on the newest sites – which might be expected – but, rather, in places where migrants have been settled for six years or more.[29]

Because of such disturbing findings, and also in a long-overdue response to protests from environmentalists and human rights groups, some Western donors have reassessed the scope and nature of their involvement in the transmigration programme. Since 1987, for example, the World Bank has been claiming that it is no longer *directly* financing the movement of people: its money is going instead into planning and preparing the sites to which settlers will be moved and into upgrading existing sites. A case in point is the Transmigration Second Stage Development Project, which has received two loans from the World Bank, the first for $160 million and the second – in 1988 – for $120 million.[30] According to a letter dated 6 May 1988 from Russel Cheetham, a senior Bank officer, this project aims through the 1990s to 'improve the incomes and welfare of transmigrant families and local people living in the immediate surroundings [of transmigration sites] by upgrading infrastructure, improving food-crop production, introducing cash crops and improving social and environmental aspects.'[31]

Likewise, in a telex that I received on 30 June 1988 from the chief of the Bank's Agriculture Operations Division, I was told that the latest transmigration project to receive a loan 'does not have a settlement component. It addresses the economic, social and environmental aspects of transmigration through extensive studies for settlements, as well as technical assistance for planning, construction, environment and land tenure issues.'[32]

While such assurances are welcome, there are elements of sophistry in the Bank's attempts to detach the particular operations that it now finances from the murky underbelly of resettlement in Indonesia: arguably support for *any* aspect of transmigration must be helpful in a fairly direct and tangible way to the programme as a whole, particularly when large sums of hard currency are involved. By the summer of 1988 the simple fact was that the Bank had cancelled only $63 million out of a total lending programme well in excess of $1 billion and had already disbursed $324 million in support of transmigration.[33]

Disbursements on this very large scale continue, justified by a virtual blizzard of reassuring statements to the effect that tribal communities will in future be protected and that the Indonesian authorities are now 'showing sensitivity'.[34] Meanwhile, however, Dyaks on Central Kalimantan are tricked into giving up their land rights by signing blank pieces of paper,[35] and the governor of Irian Jaya describes the indigenous Irianese as 'living in a stone-age-like era'.[36] Having launched a programme to separate Irianese children from their parents,[37] this flamboyant individual called, in December 1987, for a further *two million* Javanese migrants to be sent to Irian Jaya so that 'backward' local people could intermarry with the incomers – thus 'giving birth to a new generation of people without curly hair'.[38]

Likewise, while the Bank tells us that its advocacy is helping the Indonesian government to pay more 'attention to the environment, including forests',[39] the truth is that transmigration continues to cause immeasurable ecological damage. In late 1987 forest fires, set off by transmigrants and loggers, raged unchecked over large parts of Kalimantan, Sumatra and Sulawesi – with an estimated 2 million hectares destroyed by October.[40] Meanwhile, on East Kalimantan, logging alone had resulted in the destruction of a further 2.9 million hectares of forest by September 1987.[41] Associated with site development for transmigration, much of this work continues to be carried out in a very careless and ill-disciplined way, leaving logged areas strewn with debris. The result is that when fires get out of control in densely settled areas, they spread rapidly through the logging zones. In addition, rubbish and discarded logs dumped in dried-up stream beds have turned even these natural firebreaks into fire hazards.[42] 'In these circumstances,' says Stephen Corry, Director of the respected British charity Survival International, 'the promotion of further transmigration into Kalimantan would seem highly irresponsible.'[43]

In 1988 Corry put this concern to Barber Conable, the World Bank's President.[44] The reply, however, was that there was no intention of withdrawing 'assistance at this crucial stage'. On the contrary, Corry was told, the Bank's 'continued dialogue with the Government' will 'lead to a better-managed programme'.[45]

There are good reasons to doubt this optimism regarding the effectiveness of 'dialogue' – particularly since the Bank admits in its own internal documents that the Ministry of Transmigration, with which the so-called dialogue is in fact being conducted, has only 'limited capacity to influence policies' in Indonesia.[46] Furthermore, whatever the future holds, the fact remains that many hundreds of millions of dollars have *already* been disbursed by the Bank and other donors, thus inextricably associating Western taxpayers with a spectacularly expensive scheme that appears to have contributed virtually nothing to Indonesia's long-term development. On the contrary, at great cost to human rights and to the environment, transmigration's only 'success' has been to export poverty from Java – where it is visible – to the remote outer islands where it is hidden from view.

UPDATE

In the mid-1980s, international attention was drawn to the devastating effects of the greatest transmigration programme in history carried out in the name of development: the transferring of millions of Javanese peasants to the outer islands of the Indonesian archipelago. One of the most exhaustive enquiries was featured in *The Ecologist* in 1986 (vol. 16, no. 2–3) when Marcus Colchester and others investigated in detail the disastrous human and ecological consequences of the programme, which, because of Indonesia's strategic position and natural wealth, had been receiving massive financial backing from the World Bank and other agencies. Space limitations, however, made us select this shorter piece, which was included in Graham Hancock's book *Lords of Poverty* (Mandarin Paperback, London, 1991). Also, we were unable to identify a comprehensive account that has appeared recently. However, organizations like Survival International (11–15 Emerald Street, London WC1N 3QL) and publications such as the *TAPOL Bulletin* and *Down to Earth* (produced by APPEN, the Asia–Pacific People's Environment Network) are continuing to monitor the transmigration programme. It ploughs on, although at a somewhat reduced rhythm and without direct funding from the World Bank (who supported it for nearly a decade; while the British, US, German, French, Canadian, Australian and Japanese governments still provide funds for the programme through the consultative Group on Indonesia which meets in Paris each year to distribute aid to Indonesia).

In 1994, the World Bank's Operations Evaluation Department concluded that it still had an obligation and responsibilities towards indigenous peoples 'uprooted and severely impacted by projects undertaken in those years', especially the Kubu people of Sumatra. In fact, the Kedung Ombo dam in central Java caused the transmigration of some two hundred farmers to West

Sumatra, where they met all sorts of problems like poor quality soil, insufficient transport for marketing their crops, and conflicts with the local people over their ancestral claims to the land. The World Bank's completion report on the Kedung Ombo dam (which, like most WB documents, is confidential) described the resettlement programme as a complete failure (see *Down to Earth*, no. 26, October 1995). That year saw the end of the first twenty-five years of the programme, which, according to the Indonesian government, moved some 7 million people.

If transmigration has been cut down from its ambition of settling 20 million people, it is far from being abandoned. While it remains in the governmental domain, an increasing number of the projects have become part of private investments – for example, to supply a workforce for the huge Barito Pacific plywood factory on Mangole island, owned by Indonesia's biggest timber tycoons. In fact there is a shift away from creating agricultural plots in rural areas towards the creation of new villages and towns to provide cheap labour for agro-business, the lumber industry and mining. However, reports continue to come in about thousands of transmigrants leaving their sites because of infrastructural problems, lack of support, poor soil, lack of water, food shortages and the hostility of the local population.

The focus of organizations like Survival International is now on West Papua, which the Indonesians call Irian Jaya. This has always been a prime target of the transmigration programme. During the 1980s it came under heavy criticism, not only for its effects on the Javanese migrants but also for its negative impact on the environment and on the culture and livelihood of the indigenous peoples, who number about a million. By 1996 there were 800,000 transmigrants and others still arriving every day by plane. According to a report from West Papua, there is great bitterness among the peoples of West Papua against the transmigrants, who are given relatively privileged treatment so far as jobs are concerned. Cultural tensions between the two communities continue to grow, causing a change in policy whereby they are not being integrated in the same sites any more. This is unlikely to be a long-term solution.

The West Papuans have not only to put up with an inundation of people from Java, for whom transmigration sites are often prepared by the forcible appropriation of their land. As has been reported in the internationl press over the last year, local ethnic groups like the Amungme are also suffering from human rights atrocities and environmental damage from the mining giant Freeport – supported, of course, by the Indonesian armed forces. One of the world's largest, this copper, gold and silver mining complex rips almost 120,000 tonnes of ore a day from mountains once sacred to local indigenous peoples. The Amungme, supported by ecological and human rights groups, are calling for an end to the 'suffering, misery and injury' brought about by the presence of the huge mine in their territory, and Freeport is obviously concerned about its image.

NOTES

1. See the following: *Wall Street Journal*, New York, 24 December 1986 (4.3 million people had been moved by this date); *Indonesia, Transmigration Sector Review*, Report No. 6508-IND, World Bank, Washington DC, 24 October 1986. The resettlement target for financial year 1986–87 was reduced from 100,000 to 36,000 fully-sponsored families; *Jakarta Post*, Jakarta, 6 January 1988. An increase of 56 per cent in the target for financial year 1987–88 was raised to 160,000 families.

2. *Indonesia, Transmigration Sector Review*, Report No. 6508-IND, executive summary, paragraph 83.

3. Ibid., p. 156.

4. *The Ecologist*, vol. 16, no. 2–3, 1986.

5. Basic Forestry Act, Clarification Act. No. 2823 of 1967.

6. *The Ecologist*, vol. 16, no. 2–3, 1986.

7. Indonesia, Transmigration Sector Review, Report No. 6850-IND, executive summary, paragraph 62.

8. Ibid.

9. *The Ecologist*, vol. 16, no. 2–3, 1986, quoting relief workers and UNHCR sources.

10. Speech of 20 March 1985, reported in *The Ecologist*, vol. 16, no. 2–3, 1986.

11. Kenneth Davidson, writing in *The Melbourne Age*, Melbourne, 1 June 1986.

12. Ibid.

13. Ibid.

14. Reported by James Bovard in *The World Bank vs the World's Poor*, Cato Institute Policy Analysis, Washington DC, 29 September 1987.

15. *Wall Street Journal*, New York, 30 September 1985.

16. *Indonesia, Transmigration Sector Review*, Report No. 6580-IND, Chapter 5, paragraph 23.

17. *Forest Policies in Indonesia: The Sustainable Development of Forest Lands* (4 vols), Government of Indonesia/International Institute for Environment and Development, Washington DC, 1985.

18. Ibid.

19. *Five Year Plan 1984–1989.* See Graham Searle, *Major World Bank Projects*, Wadebridge Ecological Centre, Camelford, Cornwall, 1985.

20. Letter to the Honourable M. Peter McPherson, Administrator, USAID, Washington DC, 11 June 1986.

21. Searle, *Major World Bank Projects*, p. 151.

22. *Information Pack On World-Bank Financed Transmigration In Indonesia*, Environmental Defense Fund, Washington DC (regularly updated).

23. *Forest Policies In Indonesia.*

24. Interview with David Deppner.

25. *Indonesia, Transmigration Sector Review*, Report No. 6580-IND, executive summary, paragraph 44(a).

26. Ibid., paragraph 44(b).

27. Ibid., paragraph 10.

28. Ibid., paragraph 6.

29. Ibid., paragraph 44(b).

30. *List of Upcoming MDB Projects with Possible Environmental Issues*, The Bank Information Center, Washington DC (enclosure in letter to Friends of the Earth, UK, dated 22 March 1988).

31. Letter dated 6 May 1988 to Stephen Corry, Director, Survival International, from Russel J. Cheetham, Director, Country Department 5, Asia Region, World Bank.

32. Telex (Ref. AS 5AG) from World Bank to author, dated 30 June 1988. The Bank

took more than a month to reply to my repeated telexed requests for clarification of the scope and purpose of the Indonesia transmigration loans.

33. Ibid.

34. Letter dated 6 May 1988, from Russel Cheetham to Stephen Corry.

35. *Indonesia: World Bank Maintains Support for Transmigration*, Survival International Occasional Report No. 8, London, January 1988.

36. *Indonesia: News And Views* VI (21), Indonesian Embassy, Washington DC, 1986.

37. Ibid.

38. *Jakarta Post*, 15 December 1987, plus various statements cited in Survival International Occasional Report No. 8.

39. Letter dated 6 May 1988 from Russel Cheetham to Stephen Corry. In the classic tradition of digging holes, and then filling them in again, the World Bank decided in April 1988 to provide $34 million to assist a 'Natural Resource Conservation Project' in Indonesia. One of the main purposes of this project is to mitigate the 'forest depletion' caused by the transmigration programme – which, of course, the Bank also supports. The loan announcement comments on the 'movement' of large numbers of Javanese 'to the outer islands' and the damage done by subsequent 'settler encroachment' into forested areas (see News Release No. 88/63, World Bank, Washington DC, 6 April 1988).

40. Survival International Occasional Report No. 8.

41. Ibid.

42. Ibid.

43. Ibid.

44. Letter dated 6 May 1988 from Russel Cheetham, to Stephen Corry.

45. Ibid.

46. *Indonesia: Transmigration Sector Review*, Report No. 6580-IND, p. 95, paragraph 5.18.

24

'WOMEN IN DEVELOPMENT': A THREAT TO LIBERATION

Pam Simmons

The following text originally appeared in *The Ecologist*, vol. 22, no. 1, January–February 1992 – a special issue on 'Feminism, Nature and Development', for which the author was guest editor.

PAM SIMMONS works with the Foundation for Women, Bangkok, Thailand.

No amount of talk about 'consultation', 'partnerships' and 'empowerment' can alter the fact that the principal effect of Third World development, as it is generally practised, is to impose an economic and political system beneficial to a relatively small elite. Indeed, the language of participation only serves to disguise the imbalance of power inherent in conditional transfers of money, technology or education. 'Development' today implies a linear, evolutionary process – a single 'progressive' path along which countries are graded, according to per-capita income, gross domestic product or, more recently, literacy levels and child mortality rates. One path, one scale, one world. This is not the sort of 'liberation' women had envisaged and fought for.

INTEGRATING WOMEN INTO DEVELOPMENT

The negative effects of development on women and their significant but unrecognized role in economic production was first documented by Ester Boserup in 1970.[1] Five years later, the UN Conference on Women held in Mexico denounced the fact that women had been ignored in development policies. The logical answer to women's continued slide into economic poverty was therefore seen to lie in making them more central to development projects and planning. If this was done, the benefits supposedly accruing to men in the Third World would also flow to women. Rarely was the possibility raised that the 'feminization of poverty' was a direct result of women's *inclusion* in the development process.[2]

Women In and Against Development

A Development professional … had just returned from carrying out an evaluation of an adult education programme in a Third World country. Once in the field, she had found that the programme she was to evaluate actually consisted of political conscientization in opposition to the Government. Returning to her university, she became concerned that she possessed information which would enhance her career but might well endanger the people from whom she had learned it. Her thesis would be sent to the funding agency and from there to the 'host country', where it might be used to threaten the work and even the lives of the people who had made themselves available to her study. Her responsibility, as she saw it, was to the people whose political commitments she had come to respect. She decided she could not write of what was actually going on. Instead she chose to write a standardized evaluation of the adult education programme. And this is the thesis that sits on the library shelf at her university and is an item in the agency's data bank. It has become part of what is known about adult education in that country, ready to be picked up in subsequent bibliographies for future adult education projects, each backing off one further step from the actualities of people's lives in this setting.

This instance brings to attention the irreparable disjuncture between interests represented in the centralized information systems of ruling institutions on the one hand, and, on the other hand, the interests of those who are its objects. It also points to the many ordinary ways through decisions professionals make as they carry out their regular work practices, as well as methods of social science and bureaucratic reports, that Women in Development discourse comes to be locked into the capitalist world order.

Adele Mueller, extract from 'Women In and Against Development', mimeo, 1991.

The conclusion that women's poverty could be alleviated by targeting development programmes at women was clearly of benefit to the major development institutions and their backers. Many economists believed that women's productivity was being 'wasted' because it mostly flowed through informal channels, unaccounted for and unexploited by the world market. In relation to women, the World Bank states that, 'no country can afford to underutilize and underequip more than half of its human resources.'[3] For the Bank, women's productivity exists only in relation to its market value. Its version of integrating women into development is a means to channel women's labour and produce through national and international businesses.

Production for the world market was supposed to provide women with economic security and a better standard of living, the same argument that had been used for the previous three or four decades in relation to rural societies generally. That it had failed to achieve the promised advances in wealth and food security was clear. But this did not prevent development experts from advocating its expansion. And, sadly, it did not stir women in the First World to oppose the spread of this form of economic development.

The attempt to integrate women into development, which began as a genuine effort by women to raise the issues of discrimination and inequality, is based on a number of false assumptions. First, that economic growth is synonymous with development and improved standards of living for all. Second, that women were *not* part of the postwar development process. Third, that all women want to be (and have the time to be) part of the international economy. Fourth, that economic growth and the aims of women's movements are compatible. And finally, that women in the developed world have progressed further than women in the Third World towards equality with men.

ECONOMIC GROWTH AND UNDERDEVELOPMENT

The belief in economic growth as the one concrete solution to poverty, inequality and hardship is slowly being disassembled. Millions of people in the South who know first hand of its false promises need no convincing. In the privileged North, it will take a little longer. A great deal has already been written about the dependency of the Western economic system on exploiting poor people, wherever they are, and on depleting natural resources. Yet development programmes are still based upon increasing the productivity of nations in the global economy.

Integrating women into development is approached by the international agencies purely from the dimension of increasing women's market-determined productivity. Thus the World Bank states that using modern high-response seed varieties is advantageous to women because they raise the demand for hired female labour: 'They usually require more labor per acre – particularly in tasks typically done by women, such as weeding, harvesting, and postharvest work.'[4] This incredible assertion ignores the fact that many women have been displaced from their own land by discriminatory land reform policies and the expansion of cash crops, and now have no other option than to work as labourers for less than subsistence wages.[5] It also neglects to consider that women may not actually have the time to do the extra weeding and harvesting, when more and more of their time is taken up in attempting to grow food for their families on degraded lands.

The development projects most often discussed at international fora focus on 'income generation', the provision of credit to women and an improvement in their access to paid employment. While calls for income-generation projects are sometimes linked to suggestions for improvements in subsistence production and land reform for women, these positive elements are always subordinated to the aim of raising women's market-determined productivity.

These projects do not tackle the exploitation of women in export-processing zones, the sex tourism industry or agribusiness. They do not question the basic sexual division of labour or the international division of labour, in both of which women are placed at the bottom. Nor do they suggest that women might be better off resisting producing goods for international markets over which they have no control. There may be considerable advantages for women in having their own source of income, but this cannot be divorced from the social and political relations within which they must work.

In *The Lacemakers of Narsapur*, Maria Mies draws a vivid picture of the outcome for women of a supplementary income-generation business which encouraged them to produce handicrafts for export. In 1977, in the villages around the Indian town of Narsapur, there were about 150,000 women crocheting small lace pieces, later joined together to make tablecloths, shirts and dresses. The industry had first been introduced by missionaries as a compensatory income for newly converted Christians who had been ostracized by their communities. It is now run by Indian export businesses. Poor women supposedly used their 'leisure time' in the home to provide extra income for their families. They were considered to be housewives, not workers. However, they worked up to fourteen hours a day, seven days a week, for which they received an average of 4 rupees a week (approximately 50 US cents).[6] The women did a double job every minute of the day, looking after the household and children while crocheting lace. Working at home meant that the women were isolated from one another, which made organizing to improve their working conditions difficult, and enforced their lack of mobility and their dependence upon men. In these ways, income-generation schemes can too easily reinforce oppression in the home and in the workforce.

Some credit schemes are successful in assisting women to establish a sound and independent economic base, but this is only in a few rare instances where the participants have real control over the conditions of credit and production. In most cases, the administration of the credit remains in the hands of the creditor and is given in instalments. It has to be used for pre-arranged inputs (often sold by the creditor) and labour processes, and the producers are obliged to sell to a specific wholesaler, at a fixed price. Responsibility for production errors or crop failures stays with the producers, while the capacity to use market-price fluctuations for extra profit lies with the entrepreneurs and creditors.[7] No responsibility is accepted by the creditors – in effect, the 'employers' – for adequate incomes, land ownership problems or a social-security system. And as individual debts mount, so manipulation and exploitation of the producers become even easier.

Improving women's access to paid employment can smooth the way to further exploitation, poverty and social dislocation as well. In the export-processing zones in Asia, for example, up to 85 per cent of the workforce are women whose wages are on average 20–50 per cent lower than those paid to men in comparable jobs.[8] The women occupy the lowest levels of the factory hierarchy. Housed in barracks next to the factories, the women workers often find both their working and their dormitory lives controlled by their employers. Sexual harassment and sexual exploitation of these women is rife. As one observer of life at Kaohsiung, Taiwan, recounts, 'every evening foremen and managers at the [export processing zone], along with many shopkeepers and businessmen from town...drive up to the dorms in cars and motorcycles and pick up a bored, lonely and overworked woman for an evening of pleasure.'[9] With no private transport of their own and no entertainment nearby, the women have little choice but to accompany these men as a means of escape from their factory life. Improving access to paid employment is no guarantee that women workers will be treated fairly, or be free from harassment, rape and injury. Indeed, in cases such as the above, the opposite is more likely.

INVISIBLE WORKERS

Implied in the call to integrate women into development is the suggestion that they had previously been excluded. This is blatantly false. What is more accurate is that they were invisible to development planners, policy-makers, government officials and foreign 'experts'. Development projects were planned for men, but it was women's unpaid and low-paid labour that provided the base for 'modernization'. When men were enticed away from their homes to work in industrial centres or on plantations, it was women who took over subsistence production and often cash-crop production as well. In Lesotho and Kenya, 40–60 per cent of married women in the country live as wives of absent migrants at any one time.[10] When men were persuaded to turn over their land to cash crops in the hope of providing a better standard of living for their families, women continued to produce the family food on smaller plots of land. Daughters also moved to urban areas to work as factory employees, domestic workers and prostitutes. All of this is, by now, well acknowledged. The proposed solution, however – to make the women 'visible' by including them in development projects – is merely to propose a failed 'remedy' as a solution for the 'side-effects' caused by that very remedy in the first place.

Development depends upon absorbing all profitable national and regional economies within a global one and smoothing the way for the further penetration of capital and corporations into peoples' lives and livelihoods. Development promotes the hegemony of Western culture, and relegates other cultures to being 'traditional' (quaint and preserved) or 'exotic' (weird and entertaining). The fact that development has left many millions of people worse off than before should lead to a questioning of development and the cultural and political ideologies it stems from, not to a proposal for more of the same.

The Feminization of Poverty

The women, by virtue of present-day social and economic processes, are increasingly bearing the brunt of being poor in America. According to the National Advisory Council on Economic Opportunity, 'All other things being equal, if the proportion of the poor in female-householder families were to continue to increase at the same rate as it did from 1967 to 1987, the poverty population would be composed solely of women and children before the year 2000' (*Fiscal Report – The American Promise: Equal Justice and Economic Opportunity*, National Advisory Council, Washington DC, 1981, p. 46).

Sharon N. Skog, 'Reaganomics, Women, and Poverty', in F. Jimenez, *Poverty and Social Justice*, Tempe, Ariz., 1987.

WOMEN RESISTING DEVELOPMENT

The complaint that women had been excluded from development first occurred in the midst of the new wave of feminism which swept across the USA and Europe in the 1970s. What was being demanded at that time was equal rights – equal opportunities, equal pay, the right to be regarded as fully 'human', and the right to be heard in public.

At the conclusion of the UN Women's Decade in 1985, the position of women in both the Third and the First Worlds had worsened. But Third World women's opposition to imposed 'solutions' was gaining strength. Who, then, took up the call to 'integrate'? Not those Third World women, nor all of the women from the First World either, particularly if they themselves had lived in the shadow of Western 'progress'. It was development institutions which adopted the slogans and the cause. Women's units were created, women's projects funded and women's advocates were appointed to advisory positions. As one development policy officer put it: 'Women have … taken on another role, another perception in our minds, particularly in the minds of project managers: the idea that women are good to have around if you are involved in project development.'[11] It was a whole new lease of life for the flagging development establishment.

At the receiving end of these projects and plans, however, people were loudly protesting. They were screaming out for an end to the schemes that had flooded their land, destroyed their forests, separated children from parents and grandparents, divided men from women, and ridiculed their religions, philosophies and ways of life. The women in these movements were not demanding the right to be included. They wanted to be allowed to decide for themselves what was wrong and how to put it right. In India, women such as Hima Devi, Bimla Behn, Gauri Devi and many others in the

Himalayan region of Garwhal led the famous Chipko movement against further forest 'development'.[12] In southern Africa, women formed their own co-operatives to cope with the absence of men and to resist the spread of cash crops. In Maputo, Mozambique, 'Green Zones', small independent gardens run co-operatively by women, were set up to deal with food shortages.[13] In Brazil, Ação Democrática Feminista Gaucha (Democratic Feminist Action of Rio Grande do Sul) was founded to fight against the imposed agricultural and economic system propounded by the state and the multilateral development banks. Development Alternatives with Women for a New Era (DAWN) was established in 1984 by a group of mostly Third World women researchers and activists with the aim of providing alternative ideas and methods for achieving justice, peace and development.[14] Every day, thousands of other women are taking individual action to fight the spread of Western development. The key to their success is self-definition: the antithesis of a development model that measures every country and every citizen on one single line of progress.

ECONOMIC GROWTH AND PATRIARCHY

Among the broad aims of the women's movements are the achievement of peace, equality and justice. Many feminists criticize the inequities inherent in the dominant economic system. Some, like Maria Mies, Vandana Shiva and Bina Agarwal, explicitly link the expansion of capitalism with the further entrenchment of patriarchy.[15] While, in theory, economic growth in a capitalist system could be made non-discriminatory, in practice the evidence points to the contrary. Introducing equal opportunity legislation in industrialized countries has not altered the ideology that instructs women to work for 'love' in the household, to be content with their role as 'second-income' providers, or to collude in exploiting other women and men in the Third World by purchasing cheap imported goods.

Economic growth in these countries has resulted in a disproportionate number of women being 'dumped' every time there is a slump and being blamed for the ensuing poverty. Every recession sees a renewed pressure on women to leave the formal labour force, either voluntarily or by retrenchment.[16] Concurrently, there are attacks by conservative governments on the welfare system that supports poor women, albeit inadequately. And worse, modernization has changed the culture of violence directed at women only in that it has made it more widespread.[17]

If sustained economic growth is dependent on the increasing exploitation of limited resources, then competition to use these resources can only become more frenzied. In these circumstances, all oppressive systems – including colonialism, racism and sexism – will be increasingly necessary to defend the status quo. If women go on defending economic growth, then they are also, by default, defending patriarchal privilege. The growth that has occurred in industrialized countries is built on the 'slave' labour of women in the North and women and men in the South. Without it, these countries' economies would have floundered.

WOMEN'S EQUALITY IN THE NORTH

Some journalists have referred to the contemporary period as a post-feminist era. If they are correct, then heaven help our daughters. Women currently receive 10 per cent of the world's income and own 1 per cent of the world's wealth as a reward for doing two-thirds of the work.[18] In the North, where 'real progress' has supposedly taken place, the picture is the same as on the global level, if of a different hue. Feminists often face the self-righteous indignation of men who supported equal rights legislation in the 1970s and 1980s, only to find that 'women want more'. They want more, not only because the legislation was never intended to be the whole answer, but also because it has proved much less of a solution than was first thought. Women still receive only 60–70 per cent of men's wages overall in most industrialized countries.[19] In the USA and the UK in particular, women are watching the rapid erosion of hard-won legal rights and benefits in the areas of abortion, social security and health. Sexual harassment, rape and domestic violence appear to be on the increase.[20] Women-headed households constitute the vast majority of those families living in poverty.[21]

The ideological pressure to conform to a male-defined femininity seems as strong as ever. Women's magazines are filled with features on 'keeping your man' or 'how to look ten years younger'. Social problems, such as youth homelessness and children's delinquency, are explained as being due to the 'breakdown of the family', and by implication the failure of the woman to hold things together. Although the causes of these problems are extremely complex, women are a convenient scapegoat when it comes to assigning blame for social disruption. Is it any wonder that women elsewhere do not want this brand of 'equality'? But the assumption behind expanding the development model is that women are somehow better off in the First World. Materially, many of them are, as they share in the takings from the Third World, but socially and emotionally they have made little headway.

SOMETHING DIFFERENT

International development is steeped in patriarchal traditions, not only because all of the major institutions are strongholds of power wielded by men but also because of what development represents.[22] By implying that the Third World is underdeveloped, the development ideology establishes hierarchy; and by making use of unjust terms of trade and debt to control national policies, it enforces exploitation. Development promotes over all other cultures a single culture which has shown itself to be both destructive and unjust. It reinforces the ideology that a woman's place is marginal to public life through such schemes as supplementary income-generation and through the suggestion that women's voices will only be heard through retargeted development projects. By reinforcing the strength of the international commercial sector, one of the stalwarts of male control, development encourages the further entrenchment of patriarchy.

A different approach is possible – and it is not a new development model. It can begin by acknowledging that a mistake was made in attempting to define what women should aspire to, be it earning cash incomes or studying modern agricultural or medical practices. This is not to say that these should be denied to women, but rather that the choice should be real. And it goes much further than consultation and participation and empowerment, which smack of condescension when spoken by those in power. To be real, the choice must be totally under women's control, and the value of other forms of knowledge must not be ridiculed. Economic and social self-sufficiency is surely a better option than integration. Exchange of ideas and goods can still take place but without the threat of disadvantage or manipulation by the party which holds the ideological or economic strings. Too often, cash incomes and modernization are fundamentally linked to oppressive structures such as the international market, which is increasingly controlled by transnational companies, and a violent world order dominated by a powerful group of men – the very same structures that oppress women in the 'privileged' First World.

These shared oppressive structures surely provide the key to the direction that could be taken. Perhaps the best efforts of women in the developed world should be put into resisting the spread of Western-style patriarchy and fighting its source closer to home. It is, after all, mostly men in the First World who own the major companies, control the international organizations, dominate the ideological 'think-tanks', visit the brothels in Third World sex-tourism centres, and expect deference from anyone they financially 'support'.

Combating domination 'at home' does not mean an end to co-operation. Indeed, it is the beginning. Sudha Murali in India writes to me, 'tell me, how do we practically go about delinking the community-based village economy from the market?'[23] We both have a similar problem. Her work with the women's *sanghams* in the drought-affected villages of Mehaboobnagar district aims to regenerate the land and forests and resist the encroachment of development officials who would have the women grow cash crops instead of food. The work of First World activists in resisting the influence and dominance of large companies is partly motivated by concern for women in India, but, importantly, also for themselves. Sudha Murali does not expect them to tell her what to do. An exchange of ideas, though, would be useful for all.

When Maria Mies organized a 'Women and Development' course in the Netherlands, she introduced women from the Third World to Dutch women.

'Third World women learned that First World women, in spite of their education, their higher income, their greater access to paid jobs, their modern lifestyle, were not liberated but suffered from sexist violence and were sometimes ideologically more fettered to the housewife/mother/lover image than they themselves. The Dutch women, on the other hand, learned that Third World women are not all poor and uneducated, that some were more educated than they were and above all less dependent on the ideology of romantic love and hence less emotionally oppressed.'[24] As one Filipina student put it, 'I have always thought that Western values are good for Western people and Eastern values are good for Eastern people. Now I have realized that Western values are also not good for Western people.'

Alliances between women's groups, such as the ones formed to combat sex tourism, or the abuse of reproductive technologies, may do much more towards securing respect and equality for women (in both hemispheres of the globe) than will hundreds of women's projects devised by the development industry.[25] These alliances are formed, not through the established channels of Third World aid and assistance, but by way of personal contact between groups or individuals. One approach is based on superiority and authority, the other on recognition of a mutual oppression.

NOTES

Thanks to the following for helpful comments on the first draft of this article: Paola Sylva, Ecuador; Maria Mies, Germany; Andrea Finger-Stich, France; Fourouz Jowkar, USA; Essma Ben Hamida, Tunisia; Larry Lohmann, UK; Clare Flenley, UK; Sudha Murali, India; Vandana Shiva, India; Moira O'Leary, Australia; Mal Simmons, Australia; Wendy Rees, UK. The responsibility for the article is the author's alone.

1. E. Boserup, *Women's Role in Economic Development*, St Martin's Press, New York, 1970.
2. Some authors, such as Vandana Shiva, Maria Mies, Veronika Bennholdt-Thomsen, Claudia von Werlhof, Diane Elson, Ruth Pearson, Bina Agarwal and the Development Alternatives with Women for a New Era (DAWN) group have written about women's poverty being a direct result of their inclusion in the development process.
3. World Bank, *Annual Report*, Washington DC, 1990, p. 62.
4. World Bank, *World Development Report: Poverty*, Oxford University Press, Oxford, 1990, p. 61.
5. B. Rogers, 'The Power to Feed Ourselves: Women and Land Rights', in L. Caldecott, and S. Leland, eds, *Reclaim the Earth: Women Speak Out for Life on Earth*, The Women's Press, London, 1983; C.E. Sachs, *The Invisible Farmers: Women in Agricultural Production*, Rowman & Allanheld, Totowa, N.J., 1983, p. 122; E. Trenchard, 'Rural Women's Work in Sub-Saharan Africa and the Implications of Nutrition', in J.H. Momsen, and J. Townsend, eds, *Geography of Gender in the Third World*, Hutchinson, London, 1987, p. 166; J.K. Henn, 'Women in the Rural Economy: Past, Present and Future', in M.J. Hay, and S. Stichter, eds, *African Women South of the Sahara*, Longman, London, 1984, pp. 12, 14.
6. M. Mies, *The Lacemakers of Narsapur: Indian Housewives Produce for the World Market*, Zed Books, London, 1982. For a similar study in Sri Lanka, see C. Risseeuw, *The*

Wrong End of the Rope: Women Coir Workers in Sri Lanka, Research Project: Women and Development, University of Leiden, 1980.

7. V. Bennholdt-Thomsen, '"Investment in the Poor": An Analysis of World Bank Policy', in M. Mies, V. Bennholdt-Thomsen and C. von Werlhof, *Women: The Last Colony*, Zed Books, London, 1988.

8. W. Bello, 'The Spread and Impact of Export-Oriented Industrialization in the Pacific Rim', unpublished paper prepared for the 1991 People's Forum in Bangkok, October 1991, p. 11; F. Frobel, J. Heinrichs and O. Kreye, *Die Neue Internationale Arbeitsteung*, Reinbek bei Hamburg, 1977, used in D. Elson and R. Pearson, 'The Latest Phase of the Internationalization of Capital and its Implications for Women in the Third World', Discussion Paper, IDS, University of Sussex, June 1980, p. 13.

9. R. Kagan, 'The Miracle of Taiwan', unpublished manuscript, Institute for Food and Development Policy, San Francisco, 1982, p. 168, cited in Bello, 'The Spread and Impact', p. 12.

10. E. Gordon, 'An Analysis of the Impact of Labour Migration on the Lives of Women in Lesotho', in N. Nelson, ed., *African Women in the Development Process*, Frank Cass, London, 1981, p. 60.

11. J. Davidson, 'An Overview of Women, Environment and Development', unpublished paper prepared for the NGO Workshop on Women, Environment and Development, UN Non-Governmental Liaison Service, Geneva, 22 March 1991.

12. V. Shiva, *Staying Alive: Women, Ecology and Development in India*, Kali for Women, New Delhi and Zed Books, London, 1988, p. 68.

13. B. Rau, *From Feast to Famine: Official Cures and Grassroots Remedies to Africa's Food Crisis*, Zed Books, London, 1991, pp. 170, 181.

14. G. Sen, and C. Grown, *Development, Crises, and Alternative Visions: Third World Women's Perspectives*, Monthly Review Press, New York, 1987, p. 9.

15. M. Mies, *Patriarchy and Accumulation on a World Scale*, Zed Books, London, 1986; Shiva, *Staying Alive*; and B. Agarwal, ed., *Structures of Patriarchy: State, Community and Household in Modernising Asia*, Zed Books, London, 1988.

16. See *The Economic Role of Women in the ECE Region*, UN Publications, New York, 1980; D. Werneke, 'The Economic Slowdown and Women's Employment Opportunities', *International Labour Review*, vol. 117, no. 1, 1978.

17. V. Bennholdt-Thomsen, 'The Future of Women's Work and Violence Against Women', in Mies, Bennholdt-Thomsen and von Werlhof, *Women: The Last Colony*; I. Illich, *Gender*, Pantheon Books, New York, 1982, pp. 31–3.

18. UN Conference on Women, Copenhagen 1980.

19. The average annual earnings of the full-time employed woman still hovers at around the ratio of 60 per cent of a man's average earnings – the same percentage as a hundred years ago (see Illich, *Gender*, pp. 24–6, 29–30); Australian women workers earn 30 per cent less than men,(V.A. Brown, and M.A. Switzer, 'Where Have All the Women Gone? The Role of Gender in Sustainable Development', unpublished paper, Australian National Unversity, Canberra, 1991); in Canada the gap is 34 per cent (E. Smockum, 'Tipping the Scales of Injustice', *Guardian*, 28 May 1991). In the USA in 1981, women earned 56–59 per cent of what men earned (A. Dworkin, *Right-Wing Women: The Politics of Domesticated Females*, The Women's Press, London, 1983, p. 65).

20. The number of reported cases of sexual violence and harassment is on the increase. However, official statistics are a poor indicator of the true extent of incidence owing to large-scale under-reporting. It is therefore difficult to make statements about increasing or decreasing rates of violence with absolute confidence. For further reading on this topic, see Bennholdt-Thomsen, 'The Future of Women's Work'; *Dignity of Women at Work: Report on the Problem of Sexual Harassment in the Member States of the European Community*, HMSO, London, 1989; R. Hall, *Ask Any Woman: London Inquiry into Rape*

and Sexual Assault, Falling Wall Publications, London, 1986; J. Scutt, *Even in the Best of Homes*, Penguin, Australia, 1983; Dworkin, *Right-Wing Women*; S. Brownmiller, *Against Our Will: Men, Women and Rape*, Penguin, Harmondsworth, 1977.

21. In Australia, women make up 70 per cent of those whose incomes fall below the poverty line (Brown and Switzer, 'Where Have All the Women Gone?'). In the US, 78 per cent of all people living in poverty are women and children under 18 (J. Seager and A. Olson, *Women in the World: An International Atlas*, Pan Books, London, 1986, map 28).

22. In 1990, all of the twenty-two executive directors and eighteen presidential staff at the top of the World Bank's hierarchy were men. In the mid-1980s, 5 per cent of senior staff in the World Bank were women; in the US Agency for International Development, only 7 per cent of executives on international assignments were women. In the UN Secretariat, 94 per cent of assistant secretary-generals and directors were men; and at the conference to mark the end of the UN Decade for Women in 1985, one-third of the delegates were men. One delegation (North Korea) consisted entirely of men (Seager and Olson, *Women in the World*, map 38).

23. S. Murali, personal communication.

24. M. Mies, 'Gender Relations and Development in the "Third World"', unpublished paper presented at the annual meeting of the Danish Development Researchers, Copenhagen, December 1989, p. 3.

25. These alliances include the International Feminist Network Against the Trafficking of Women, the Alliance Against Sex Tourism, and the Feminist International Network of Resistance to Reproductive and Genetic Engineering.

25

TEHRI: A CATASTROPHIC DAM IN THE HIMALAYAS

Peter Bunyard

The following text appeared as an article in *Resurgence* (no. 146, May–June 1991). The author gives a moving account of what the construction of the Tehri dam – which, when completed, will be the highest dam in Asia – will mean for the lives of over 85,000 rural people who will be displaced by its waters. An update gives information on recent developments on this dam, which international protest has succeeded in halting – but for how long?

Resurgence is a bi-monthly magazine that keeps its readers informed about current ideas and debate in ecology, philosophy, spirituality, education, science and the arts.

PETER BUNYARD is a founder editor of *The Ecologist*. His most recent work is *Putting Life into Climate* (Editions du Chêne, Paris, 1997).

The Bhagirathi river flows through the western Himalayas into the Ganges, pushing its waters on through the sacred city of Hardwar with its Hindu temples and down into the plains of Uttar Pradesh. Several thousand metres high, beyond the small town of Tehri, a valley broadens out, its slopes a patchwork of beautifully maintained terraces that carry down to the edge of the river. The fields look green, plush with rice and other crops; here and there a lonely figure encourages a small, compact mountain buffalo to make the tight turns that set up the plough for the return furrow.

Such a scene has all the semblance of time-old tranquillity, barely disturbed by the mad rush of the industrial age. But all that labour, all that industrious care, is soon to be washed away and buried for ever in the waters of the Bhagirathi as they rise behind the 260-metre-high Tehri dam, now in its early stages of construction. A stretch of 45 kilometres will be drowned along the Bhagirathi and 35 kilometres along its tributary, the Bhilanguna, the two rivers meeting each other at Tehri, at the dam itself. The Tehri, when completed, will have the dubious distinction of being the largest dam in the whole of Asia.

Ever since the world's first massive dam, the Hoover, built on the Colorado in the 1930s, engineers, aided and abetted by politicians and planners, have looked for rivers to tame. All that water rushing to waste as it follows the natural incline down to the ocean is too much for modern engineers to bear, when it can be used for generating electricity and water for irrigation. The Himalayas, with their tight valleys and torrential rivers, are seen as a godsend, and the Tehri dam as a means to provide drinking water as well as electricity to Delhi, 200 kilometres to the south. It will also be used to irrigate the lands of the wealthier farmers in the plains, thus sustaining the high yields of the Green Revolution. Some critics claim that the real beneficiaries in Delhi will be those intent on keeping their lawns green and their swimming pools filled.

The planners are not particularly concerned at the loss of land in the Himalayas. Why worry over a couple of Himalayan valleys, with their marginal agriculture, when the plains, given a sure supply of water throughout the year, are not only amenable to mechanization but will yield far more, thus making up for the land drowned beneath the waters of the reservoir?

That, then, is the logic behind moves to shift more than 85,000 people from some twenty-three villages and from the town of Tehri to make way for the reservoir. Those whose homes and land will vanish are entitled to compensation, but, with all claims having to be in prior to the rising of the waters, any who accept compensation will be seen as for the dam rather than against. The planners have therefore put those against the dam in a tricky predicament in which they might be forfeiting their right to compensation.

In recent times dramatic changes have taken place in the rivers flowing down from the high Himalayas. The village of Sirain overlooks the Bhagirathi as it sweeps around the valley on its way to Tehri, a few kilometres upstream. Over the past twenty years, but with growing intensity, the river has gouged out its bed, depositing enormous boulders and silt along its route. The giant water wheels that used to pump water onto the surrounding pastures have now disintegrated, having been left like stranded whales as a result of the river bottom having fallen by several metres from its earlier depth. The river level now fluctuates violently between the monsoon and the dry season, with as much as a 1,000 times difference between the extremes. Compare this with Bhutan, which kept its forests intact and which therefore has only a sevenfold difference in the volume of water passing down the river at the height of the rainy and dry seasons.

As Sunderlal Bahuguna of the Chipko movement said, 'When I was a young man, some fifty years ago, the natural forests covered all the slopes that you now see denuded and barren. The women had no need to go much further than a couple of hundred yards to gather firewood and fodder for the animals, and in those days each village had many more buffaloes and cattle than it can support today.' 'When we saw the forests being systematically logged, we didn't think to protest,' he told me, 'We had no idea how much their vanishing would affect the rivers and our lives. We did not benefit from the logging; those who did were mainly from outside, but we now realize what a catastrophe it has brought upon us.'

One of the first indications of change came when the springs used for irrigating the wheat and paddy began to dry up and the yields began to drop drastically. Moreover, pasture by the river became increasingly out of reach of the flowing water as the river dwindled and its level fell. The men could no longer live on the produce of the village and the majority left for seasonal work in the cities, leaving their women behind to do the work in the fields. The trees that provided the basket-maker vanished and he too was out of work, as also was the ancient system of bartering rice and other produce with the craftspeople in the village. Instead, money had to be earned, mostly from outside, to try and purchase the goods that the village could no longer provide. Self-sufficiency began to crumble, just like the denuded slopes.

The ecology of the dammed areas, the needs of the local people, and the way their cultures and traditions have grown symbiotically with their surroundings, are all but forgotten in the modern zeal for utilizing every last drop of nature in what amounts to a spurious pursuit of efficiency. Forgotten, too, is the role of the natural forests in conserving soil and making it fertile, in holding back the rainwater and preventing run-off. The attrition and spoliation began decades ago, spurred on after India's independence, when money-making and profiteering became equated with development. One has only to look upward, to the higher slopes of the Himalayan foothills, to see them shorn of trees, raw with the scars of gully erosion, to realize the awful extent of deforestation, for the most part the result of clear-felling for logs.

For millennia the villagers of the Himalayas have revered the evergreen oak forests of the mountains for the fertility of soil and for the fresh water they brought to them. The Vedic legend goes that the Goddess Ganga was a stormy creature who roamed the heavens like a black cloud. Then came a king, Bhagirat, who needed water for the Earth and its creatures. He called on Ganga to come down and follow him, but she threatened to drown the Earth and carry all away in her fury. Then Shiva rose up from the Earth and caused the water tumbling from the heavens to be distributed in a mass of rivulets, their force softened by the hairs on his head.

The oak of the mountains, in particular *Quercus ingana*, which can grow at altitudes of 10,000 feet, is considered to be holy, the very hair of Shiva. Where the oak grows, there water is to be found, the oak being considered the fount of fertility and of life itself. When the oak and juniper forests were still intact, wild game, including leopards, tigers, deer and bears all abounded, but with the trees gone, the water from the monsoons hurtles freely down the slopes, carrying away chunks of hillside and leaving the hills barren and waterless. As if to make the point, in 1987 the heavy monsoons of that year carried away nine bridges in the region of north-east Garwhal in Uttar

Pradesh, sweeping more than twenty-five busloads of pilgrims to their deaths in the torrents below.

The peoples of the Himalayas, right up to recent times, managed to achieve a remarkable balance between the intricate network of terraced fields and the natural forest on the higher slopes and around the watersheds of the rivers. Indeed, the religions of India are concerned never-endingly with the relationship between humans and nature, nature being sanctified in numerous ways. A classic precedent for the fight to save the trees comes from the Bishnoi people of Rajasthan, who, two centuries before, hugged the trees when the king's woodcutters started chopping the forest down so as to make a new palace. After some villagers, predominantly women, had been killed by the king's men, the king was conscience-stricken and ordered his men away. He then decreed that the forest should be given over to the villagers. Today, that forest still stands, a sacred grove, and one of the few green areas left in the whole of Rajasthan.

Like their predecessors and apparently totally unaware of the precedent, the Chipko people have been prepared to sacrifice themselves to save their remaining forests, for, like the Bishnoi, they know full well that without the forests the environment will rapidly degrade and they will not be able to survive for long.

Today, some 7,000 feet up in the Garwhal region, along a valley that runs diagonally into that of the Tehri dam, the villagers, including the schoolchildren, now regularly take part in out-of-doors discussions on the current state of affairs in the hills and the campaign to re-green them. The women are now preventing further annihilation of the forest. One additional benefit has been the dramatic change in their status in Hindu society.

The logging of vast tracts of forest has put intense pressure on the remaining forests, apart from anything else leading to shortages of fodder. Such shortages mean that fewer buffalo can be kept for working the fields, so reducing the area that can be tilled. The reduction in cattle also results in less fertilizer for the crops, which anyway are being starved of water because of a breakdown in the traditional systems of water retention, including small dams and tanks. Such systems have fallen into disuse because of the destruction of forest and changes in run-off patterns and rainfall.

The women do most of the work. In addition to tilling the fields and harvesting the crops, they bring in firewood from the slopes around, carry the water up from the springs, all while raising children and preparing food, which entails the dehusking of rice. In Sirain, Sunderlal's village, to be washed away in six years' time when the Tehri dam fills, many of the men have had to go away to earn a subsistence wage so as to support their women and children in the village. The onus on the women to hold the village together has grown in proportion to the degradation of the environment. Indeed, it is the women who have suffered most from the deforestation. They are the ones who have to walk 5 or more kilometres to get firewood and then back again with their heavy loads. As Vandana Shiva points out, the situation has now reached breaking point: survival is close to impossible, with no hours left in the day or night to get the basic chores done. Not surprisingly, since the work falls primarily on their shoulders, the women are the ones who have taken the initiative to try and save the forests and even to replant the denuded slopes with useful local trees, including those that would provide fodder and fuelwood. The natural forests traditionally provided food, fodder, fibre, fertilizer and firewood.

Sunderlal has now returned to the village of his fathers to pit himself against the dam and to drown in its reservoir should stupidity prevail. The alternatives to the Tehri dam are obvious to anyone with sensitivity to the environment. For instance, small check dams could be refurbished high up in the slopes to hold back the water in irrigation tanks so that the forest would be coaxed back in areas which have now dried out. Small hydroelectric schemes could be installed to provide power for pumps and electricity for the villages, so helping regenerate the hills.

The construction of dams goes hand in hand with irrigation projects as well as flood control, and more than 2,400 dams with a height of over 30 metres have been built. By 1930 the first concrete dam was built at Mettur, ushering in the age of large dams. By 1950, almost one hundred large dams with reservoirs having a 'culturable command area' exceeding 10,000 hectares had been built in India; the Hirakud and Bhakra-Nangal dams, for instance, becoming the symbols of economic progress, for with their construction came employment, irrigation, flood control and electricity. But then the Machhu dam collapsed in Gujarat, while in 1962 the Panshet and Khadakwasla dams burst in Maharashtra. In fact, forty dams collapsed or failed between 1874 and 1974, giving India a record of 9.2 per cent dam failures compared to a world average of 5.9 per cent.

Big dams are not solving India's water problems; on the contrary, they mop up resources that would be far more effectively spent on rehabilitating degraded lands and on trying to make effective use of the water that to date is lost from the irrigation channels. Indeed, the misguided obsession with prestigious projects such as large dams is missing the point that denuded lands urgently need rehabilitation. In 1972 the annual loss of topsoil in India was put at 6,000 million tonnes. Less than twenty years later, those soil losses were believed to have doubled through poor land management. At the very minimum, annual run-off losses are likely to be 10 per cent of total annual precipitation, those losses being equivalent to as much as 35 million hectare metres.

The irony, given all the disturbing facts on the rate of degradation of the Indian subcontinent, is that the very resource that India has in abundance is subject to abuse and mistreatment. The villagers, who still make up 80 per cent of the Indian population, have the knowledge and wisdom to rehabilitate the lands that the government has taken over and ruined. Equally important, they have the determination and enthusiasm to bring life back to the hills. Given the state of the Himalayan slopes, the threats to move people to make way for dams of dubious value and potentially of great danger, such as the Tehri, must be seen as acts of criminality against both humans and the environment. Furthermore, there is evidence, admittedly circumstantial, that in regions where the environment is still reasonably intact and where villagers can continue to subsist in traditional ways, the rate of population growth is relatively low. That does not mean that technological improvements have no place; on the contrary, if properly focused and adapted to real needs they can be of great service. The message is clear: give people security in land use, give them the means to prevent their lands from becoming degraded through conserving forests and watersheds, and the population problem may begin to vanish. But continue on the path of unrestrained exploitation and the problems will abound, whether in the countryside or in the towns. The big dams, so beloved of engineers and politicians, should not even be low on the list of priorities; they should never be allowed to leave the drawing boards.

UPDATE

Since this article appeared, nearly six years ago, in the magazine *Resurgence* (UK), the controversy around the Tehri dam has continued to hit national and international headlines, thanks largely to the fasts of Sunderlal Bahuguna, as well as other well-known acrivists like Vandana Shiva, who has defended Bahuguna from accusations of being an environmental terrorist, levelled at him by the powerful interests that are pressing for the dam to be completed. Vandana declared that the Tehri dam was 'a totally illegitimate project on several counts', going on to say that 'Neither Bahuguna, nor any of those he has inspired, deserves the label of environmental terrorist. That label belongs to those who are responsible for crimes against nature – to contractors and to the politicians, engineers and administrators they manage to corrupt.'

A few months after Peter Bunyard's article was published, in October 1991, an earthquake (6.6 on the Richter scale) devastated the area on both sides of the dam. There was a public outcry, and a mass of scientific evidence was cited to prove that it was extremely dangerous to build the high dam at Tehri, while the claimed benefits were being grossly exaggerated. The local people, who had been apprehensive for nearly two decades about the consequences of the dam and who had made numerous but unsuccessful efforts to stop its construction, decided to take action once again in 1992. They effectively managed to stop the work of the earthmovers – and were jailed for their pains. In protest, Mr Bahuguna went on an indefinite fast, which was only broken on the 45th day when Prime Minister P.V. Narasimha Rao assured him that there would be a review of the dam. (As a consequence of a previous review, published in 1988, the Ministry of Environment and Forests recommended that the project be abandoned despite the enormous sums that had already been spent on it.) The promised review was never carried out and after two years the bulldozers and trucks were on the move again.

In May 1996 Sunderlal Bahuguna started a second fast, which was finally broken on the 49th day in the presence of Prime Minister H.D. Deve Gowda, who promised to have the dam reviewed by a committee of four experts nominated by Sunderlal. The *Hindustan Times*, in reporting the event, quoted Bahuguna as saying:

> I am a humble son of the Himalayas. We are all Mahatma Gandhi's soldiers and should spread his word. I live in a small village with my wife and do not ask for much from life. My main concern is for saving the environment and giving our children a pollution-free, ecologically balanced world. The Prime Minister has taken the right decision to review the Tehri Dam project, as thousands of lives depend on it.

Another excellent article on the Tehri dam was published by *The Ecologist*, also in 1991 (vol. 21, no. 3, May–June). Its author, Fred Pearce, concluded:

> The Gandhian tradition in India, exemplified by Bahuguna, will always be implacably opposed to vast projects such as the Tehri dam. Its case does not rest on seismology, still less on cost–benefit analysis, but on an entirely different philosophy from the mainstream about economic and social development and the relationship between humans and the natural world. But the economic and seismological uncertainties surrounding Tehri have now grown so great that even the state technocrats, the inheritors of the traditions of Gandhi's successor, Nehru, who famously called large dams 'the temples of modern India', may want to call a halt. They may, to cover their retreat, invoke the sanctity of science, of the sacred Ganga or of the balance sheet. But for the majority of the people of the Bhagirathi valley it matters only that the dam be halted.

However, according to a FIAN International Update (11 July 1996), it is all too possible that the recent promises may turn out as vain as the previous ones and that work on the main dam structures will be continued as soon as the public pressure is off and the real environmental terrorists return to pressing their interests – helped, of course, by institutions like the World Bank, which has firmly declared that many countries still need big dams. To help sell this questionable view, which is being contested all over the world, the World Bank affirms that a billion or more people lack sewage systems and piped potable water – and that this causes the deaths of two to three million infants a year. Ergo, who is against big dams is against children!

26

THE DEVELOPMENT GAME

Leonard Frank

The following text originally appeared in *Granta* 20, 'In Trouble Again: A Special Issue of Travel Writing', Winter 1986. It is written under a pseudonym.

Development, as in Third World Development, is a debauched word, a whore of a word. Its users can't look you in the eye. Among biologists, the word means progress, the realization of an innate potential. The word is good, incontestable, a cause for celebration. In the mouths of politicians, economists and development experts like myself, it claims the same approval, but means nothing. There are no genes governing the shape of human society. No one can say of a society, as a gardener can of a flower, that it has become what it should be. It is an empty word which can be filled by any user to conceal any hidden intention, a Trojan horse of a word. It implies that what is done to people by those more powerful than themselves is their fate, their potential, their fault. A useful word, a bland word, a wicked word, a whore of a word. Development in the mouths of Americans has a lot in common with psychotherapy in the mouths of Russians.

No. This is nonsense. There is nothing sinister about 'development'. It is simply a useful word to describe the achievement of desirable goals: higher incomes, better nutrition and so on. There are no serious disagreements about what is desirable, and by repeated use the word has achieved a validity of shared understanding. That is all.

I'm happy. I'm alone. I am sitting on a balcony with my feet up, perfectly relaxed. My left arm grills in the sun; my right, in the shade, is still cold from the night. Up here, there is not enough air to filter the light from the sun nor enough to store its heat. I am crossed by a sharp diagonal shadow, happily divided. On a low table by my elbow is a pot of green tea, brought to me by a slavish servant. Next to it are papers and an unopened report. Beyond this rest-house are mountains: mountainsides, mountain valleys, mountain peaks, snow, high passes, the Himalayas, the roof of the world.

There are few perfect moments for a man like me, and now I shiver at the perfect moment. I am here, but not here. I am suspended between these mountain tops. I have arrived, but no one knows I have arrived. The officials have not been informed; the other mission members have not yet caught up. For a moment I am free.

'You don't want Botswana. You want Pakistan!' The Korean man calling from Geneva had an explosive way of talking. 'Pakistan. North-west Frontier. Beautiful place. Mountains. It's a good place for a person like you. Famous place for you Westerners. The Great Game and all that. Never mind Botswana: you want Pakistan. Next week. Before the snows come. Very beautiful.'

It sounded like a good idea. There are so many developmental people in Botswana, you can't find anything to finance any more. I asked about the Afghan war.

'No, no. No war. Forget about the war. These people are very poor. Nobody has done anything for them. No development. They need development. You have to go before the snows.'

I don't want to know about the war next door. They don't want me to know. Or about the opium traffic. These are two things I don't want to know too much about. And politics. I don't want to know about politics either.

We are six on the mission to the North-west Frontier: an old Japanese, a Korean, an American, a Bangladeshi, a Dutch girl, me. I'm Canadian with a French mother. None of us has been here before. None of us has previously met. The Korean who brought us together does not know us either. He got my name from an Indian I once worked with in Manila and he phoned me at my Paris number.

How did the world get this way? It's all quite rational but it's too complicated to think about. OK: the Japanese, because Japanese money is becoming important; a Bangladeshi, because they are cheap and brown; a Korean, because the mission organizer is Korean; an American to punch statistics; a Dutch girl sociologist for the soft and warm. A mix of people because this time it's an international agency. I'm in charge; I make the big decisions. We've four weeks to come up with a project for, say, thirty million dollars. Routine.

This job is a question of damage limitation. Damage to yourself. You spend your time in places you don't want to know with people you would not choose. I would not choose them; they would not choose me. You get canny: you don't notice anything you don't need to notice; you schedule work so you can stay at international hotels. You keep the conversation bland. The American is a racist but I am ignoring it. The Korean is upset because his marriage is failing, but I don't want to know. People were not meant to go to a different country every month and live intimately with a group of strangers. When people and places change too much your mind can't cope. You become confused and your memory goes. Once I proposed marriage to a woman in France, but by the time I had visited Venezuela, New Guinea and Zanzibar, I had forgotten.

There is something disturbing about the people in this valley: they look just like me. They are poor peasants, but they look just like me. They have fair complexions, rosy cheeks and straight noses. Some of them are blonde with blue eyes. I am used to my target group being browner. I saw two little blonde girls playing, and they could have been from California, except for their dirty faces. Perhaps the children have dirty faces because it rarely rains and the water from the melted snow is too cold for washing. There is no one I would ask about this.

Their dogs are just like ours. Cocker spaniels seem most popular. The people like to sit in garden chairs on the grass under the trees, and fondle their dogs. They grow apricots and apples. Apples! People in my projects grow mangoes, paw-paws, bananas, passionfruit. They don't grow apples. I suspect an elaborate joke is being played.

Tomorrow we go to another valley, the next day another. We are looking for valleys to develop.

The old Japanese is related to the emperor of Japan. My father managed a supermarket. Last night we shared a room. He snores. I found myself trying to trace the invisible hand which took him from his childhood and me from mine and brought us together on the North-west Frontier. I stopped myself. At breakfast we talked about golf courses in Japan, women in Manila, and the relative merits of Intercontinental and Holiday Inn Hotels.

These people are very poor. They may look like me but the truth is that they are very poor people. They scratch a living without enough land or water. They can't feed themselves. Every year the government distributes subsidized wheat at great expense, but many of them are too remote to be reached. The men have to leave their homes to look for work elsewhere. The ecology is collapsing. There are no longer enough trees to provide firewood for the long winters. Because the trees have been destroyed there are deadly mud-slides which bury villages, and floods which destroy crops.

Three-and-a-half million Afghan refugees make the situation worse – but they are not our concern. The refugees are under separate administration and for us they hardly exist. We pass their camps and caravans, and the officials direct our attention elsewhere. The bases of mujahedin fighters do not exist for us at all. We are skilled at not seeing.

The peasants here sell nothing and buy little. There are no markets; they hardly deserve the name peasant. For half the year they are cut off by snow; for the other half transport is too expensive to be worthwhile. These people are wretched. Only the lightest and most valuable crops are worthy of investment. Opium poppies are ideal, but we have decided that, for us, opium poppies do not exist.

In summary, these people have a resource constraint, a market constraint, an infrastructure constraint and a technical possibility constraint. They are a suitable target group. Their appearance is deceptive.

'OK, but if we define it as an opium-producing region the project will have to come under the US-assisted OEDD programme to co-ordinate it with other international funding for opium poppy substitution. If we do that, the terms of the US money mean we'll be stuck with a law enforcement component. And that means we'll have to channel funds through the NPSEB of the Federal Government. Bad news. Better to define the region as free of opium poppies and make the project part of the SDD without enforcement so we can bypass the OEDD and locate it directly in the DCD of the PG. It will facilitate disbursement no end. Of course the Americans and UNCAD will be pissed off at not getting a piece of the action, but there's no shortage of co-financing agencies. Everyone wants a part of the North-west Frontier these days.'

'Right.'

How did the world get this way? It's simple enough. Let me remember the story. Towards the end of the Second World War, the rich countries, seeing a need for reconstruction in Europe and safeguards against economic instability, brought into being the International Monetary Fund and the International Bank for Reconstruction and Development – the World Bank. With the introduction of America's Marshall Plan for Europe, the World Bank was free to turn its attention to the poorest countries of the world. By providing scarce capital on favourable terms it permitted investment beyond the existing resources of these countries. Moreover, the World Bank was able to provide the missing expertise. The success of these pioneering efforts led to a network of international development banks working under the World Bank's fatherly eye. Nowadays Third World nations can call upon a wide range of international and bilateral agencies to support them in their development efforts, and multinational missions of experienced 'development professionals' can be readily assembled in response to particular needs. There! Now I can sleep.

Except you could say – I've heard it said – that the World Bank is, in reality, an American organization, and its origins were not idealistic but opportunistic. It has loaned money to make the poorest countries import manufactured goods and export their raw materials. It has sought to tie the world to it with the intimate bond of debtor to creditor. It has insisted on projects designed by its own people to enforce its politics at the expense of local needs. It has made the great postwar political discovery: development finance is cheaper than colonialism but just as effective – the difference between a wonder-drug and gross surgery. We are the missionaries representing America's moment of vision, now far removed from us. Restless capital is seeking out the remotest Himalayan valleys, made interesting by heroin on New York streets, by the Russians across the border and by the need of a friendly dictatorship to survive an election. We are all foreigners, but we are all Americans. None of us knows Pakistan but we all know what is good for it.

Now I can't sleep.

The truth is that money is simply the way of our world. We are the honest brokers who stand between the ignorant poor and the powerful rich.

The Development Concept Should Be Radically Relativized

Today, some people attempt to substitute for the term 'development' other symbols representing what is good, what is desirable, the realizing of human potential, personal and collective. At the workshop on intercultural cooperation, held at Marlagne (Namur, Belgium), the participants devoted one full session to the search for 'homeomorphous equivalents' to the term 'development'. The expression comes from Raimon Panikkar and stems from his attempts to understand, from the viewpoint of a given culture, ideas formulated by another. What is meant by such 'equivalents' is not analogies but functional equivalence in different cultural systems. Among the suggestions voiced during the session let us retain, to replace the term 'development', the expression 'a good life'. Achieving the necessary conditions to lead 'a good life' may be a less Eurocentric and more universal exercise than promoting 'development'. Be that as it may, the choice of terminology matters little. The real interest of such research is to 'relativize' radically the concept of development.

From Thierry G. Verhelst, *No Life without Roots: Culture and Development*, Zed Books, London, 1990, p. 63. Translated by Bob Cumming.

We control capital with careful planning; we guarantee that governments will not use aid for selfish or despotic ends. We stand in the path of an irresistible force and try to keep it decent.

Now please let me sleep.

'It's absolutely amazing. They are the most fantastic people. Do you know that their culture is tied up with the Persians and the Chinese? They don't really belong with the rest of Pakistan at all. You should talk to the people in the villages. They know exactly what they want. They are very well organized, very articulate. Sociologically it's amazing. The whole community is devoted to building these incredible irrigation works. Have you been up in the mountains to look at them? They build these stone channels high on the mountainsides – sometimes water has to travel five miles along sheer rock faces before it reaches a patch of soil. They could give Western engineers some lessons. And the social structure is completely intact and self-sufficient. All the labour is organized by the community and they make sure everyone shares the benefits. These people are geniuses! All the trees and livestock are managed on a community basis too. And have you seen how dignified they are? They smile because they don't feel belittled by the outside world yet. We have to be very careful here; they have something very valuable. We should go gently. Otherwise I can't agree with development here.'

I expect the Dutch girl's right. But where does it get us? The government wants to spend lots of money fast; the agency wants to lend it. She's naive.

She burdens me. She does not understand the simplest fact of a bank's life: a return next year is worth having but a return in ten years' time isn't worth the trouble of calculation. Capital and care don't mix, and she had better decide who is paying her, the agency or the peasants.

I find the beauty sickening. I sit on the veranda with five companions not of my choosing. Some of them read reports, pretending to work. All of us have run out of safe things to say. In front of the veranda are mountain flowers, then the big river, then the mountains. If I look up, it's all snow-capped peaks, like meringue-topping. I don't want it. It's like a deceit, a sneer. The people are poor, the mountains a logistical nightmare. Everything is vertical instead of horizontal. Road building will cost twice the average. The sky here is an absurd blue, totally clear. It draws you up into it. Thank God we are returning to the Intercontinental in Peshawar tomorrow.

At least two people in the mission are mad. They have made the mistake of confusing what they say they are doing with what they are doing. The American carries his own computer around with him and is entering all the official statistics he can find. He wants to calculate the impact of all our possible investments in the region. The madness takes the form of obsessive scrupulousness about the data and analytical techniques. If two figures contradict each other – as they always do – he sweats over reconciling the difference and weighting the averages. He is trying to create a single economic model which will go from the daily milk consumption of migrant pastoralists in winter to the indirect macro-economic benefits of oil import substitution. His eyes are glued to his computer; it is impossible to get him to attend meetings any more. He only leaves his chair to go jogging, returning as dead-eyed and haggard as when he left. I tell him to relax. I tell him – exaggerating slightly – that half the statistics come from village clerks who made them up and the other half are manipulated by the government for policy purposes. And anyway, the figures don't matter very much. There will be a project: they want to borrow; we want to lend. His economic calculations will just be the window-dressing. It's politics, not economics, I tell him. At this he flies into a fury, standing up and knocking over his chair. He insists that he is a professional and that I should respect his expertise and integrity. I drop the subject. He's an experienced expert; I know that in the end he will convince himself that the convenient figures are the right ones.

The Korean is also mad. He is 40, has had half his stomach removed, drinks a bottle of whisky every night and compresses his leisure into immense bouts with the pornography he carries around with him. At home his wife has given up on him because he is never there. He fawns on the old Japanese who treats him like a servant, requiring him to prepare food and give massages in addition to his duties as an agriculturalist. His problem is that he genuinely likes the peasant farmers and, astonishingly, speaks enough Urdu to talk to them. This sympathy conflicts with his method of work, which is to start with what he thinks the peasants should be doing in ten years' time and work backwards. Each time he follows this line of thinking he discovers that the peasants would have to be forced to change their lives in ways they would not like. His inability to reconcile the idea of the peasants becoming Korean with the idea of them being happy sends him to the whisky, the pornography and, on one occasion, to my room at four in the morning. There he drunkenly asserted that he was a simple man, a peasant educated by accident, not like the aristocratic old Japanese whom he must respect but secretly disliked.

I've learned more about the Korean than any of the others. During the long night I came close to being involved in his emotions and caring about his problems. I only saw the danger with the coming of the dawn, when I understood it would be best to take a firm line and give him a deadline for his overdue report. After he left I felt dizzy, like a man walking on a cliff edge.

The old Japanese is not mad. His life is the game and he plays it well. The Dutch girl is not mad because she isn't in the game yet. I'm not mad; I know the rules.

'We are very interested in the mountain area. We want to do something for our people quickly. We don't want your six-year project; we want two years, three years. The people up there hardly know the government exists. They wonder what the government is doing for them. They see the refugees receiving all sorts of international aid and they wonder why they are not getting anything. It is a restless place. You should not think so small. We want to make an impact. You should join these people to the rest of Pakistan. You should be building tunnels through the mountains and making truckable roads right up to the border areas. There are huge barren areas you could irrigate with large-scale irrigation schemes. Take our word for it. If you give us money we can do it. We can move people from the crowded areas to these new schemes. We can open up the region to new crops and industries. You are too timid. Agricultural research and improved farming are not enough. We want results. It's a priority area. The government is ready to move. We know what we have to do; you do not need to work it out in detail. Just release the money and we will do the rest.'

My head aches. We are back from the Himalayas. Do not disturb me in my Intercontinental room. I close the curtains. The hotel rooms in Pakistan have videos because there is nowhere to go. No bars, no nightclubs, no women. Not officially. The film is *On Golden Pond*, about a cranky old American played by Henry Fonda and a crusty old woman played by an actress whose name I used to know. Every month I learn the names of a hundred new people and a hundred new places and then forget them. Like a prostitute, I am a master of forgetting, but it's an inexact science. In the film I notice that, one, the couple have plenty of money; and, two, they've got a lot of time on their hands. I turn it off in favour of going through the pile of reports from which I will make my report.

In Peshawar they have blown up the PIA office, the railway station, the Khyber Mail Express, a bazaar, the Afghanistan office and the third best hotel – twice. At our hotel someone shot a white woman by the swimming pool, but I am told that the killing was religious not political. I ask my government guide whether the Intercontinental is likely to be blown up, us in it. For some reason he imagines me an ally and launches into a reckless analysis of the situation. The official line is that the Russian-backed Afghan government is responsible, even though on one occasion they seem to have bombed themselves. The imputed motive is that the bombings will stir up resentment among the Pakistan populace against the Afghan refugees, who are already disliked for taking over the most profitable businesses. If the refugees become unwelcome, Pakistan will no longer be able to support effectively the mujahedin fighters who mingle with them. My confidant is not convinced by this version. He tells me that he is a supporter of Benazir Bhutto and a rapid return to democratic government. He believes that his own government is bombing itself to create a security crisis which will give it an excuse to continue martial law.

There are more complexities. He is very indiscreet. I've no idea whether he is right or wrong. Finally he notices my indifference and stops talking, embarrassed. I ask him again whether he thinks our hotel will be blown up. I tell him it is a management consideration. He replies that I need not worry, the bombers seem interested in killing only local people.

I don't like change but there is one new fact I must accept. Japan. The Japanese asks me quietly about vacant posts in international organizations. Can I help him place his men? He is sad about Japan's apologetic posture in the development world. The war is long over but, although Japanese money is important, his country has not been given the influence to match its contribution. It is a humiliation. He wants to change things softly, softly. I encourage him and the inevitable. He has invited me to Japan and I am ready to stop being American and to become Japanese. I'm tired of new places but I suppose I will go.

The Dutch girl is a nuisance. What are they doing sending a young woman to a Muslim country anyway? The officials do not listen to her, and her inexperience is a problem for the rest of us. For her it is an important discovery that the official world does not match the real one. She visits villages and reports back to us at dinner that the irrigation schemes are not working the way the government says they are, or that the veterinary employees are selling drugs they should give away. She tells us that money for building primary schools has gone into the pockets of contractors and local politicians. The official figures on truck transport are wrong because they neglect the Afghanis who own most of the trucks. And so on. She's like a detective excited at uncovering a vast conspiracy. We make non-committal replies and try to change the subject. The older Japanese says nothing and finds an excuse to leave the table.

You have to make a choice about the world you live in – the real world or the official world. Nowadays I live in the official world. The real world is infinitely complex, and even the people who are part of it don't understand it. And we are here for only four weeks, most of that in office meetings. When you discover that the official world does not correspond to the real world, you can either accept the official version or make your own judgement. It's always best to take the government figures. That way you save yourself work and don't tread on the toes of anyone who matters. We are here, after all, as guests.

'Look, we want to lend you the money you are talking about, but one valley is not enough. One valley doesn't have the absorption capacity. We need a minimum of two, and preferably three, valleys. We want at least a million people. Otherwise Geneva won't like it. Frankly, they will say it was not worth the expense of sending out a mission. We want to give you a project but you'll have to take away some valleys from someone else and give them to us.'

I spend my life in other people's offices. Here the officials are polite and intelligent, and invariably insist on tea and biscuits. In this case it's an administrator in the British mould – a cultured, literate generalist. I employ my usual technique of letting the man speak while I doodle in my notebook pretending to note his views. We are getting along well when three French people are shown in to pick up their tourist authorizations. The occasional bombing of the border area by Russian MiGs had not inhibited the promotion of tourism by a government department not responsible for defence matters.

The two Frenchmen and one woman seem unduly taken aback by my presence and offer me a confusion of greetings. They look unlikely mountain trekkers: two of them, a middle-aged couple, are overweight, while the third is a fit young man. For French people on an expensive holiday, they are oddly un-chic. The woman's hair is poorly cut and her make-up is clumsy. All of them are cheaply dressed. They look away from me in order to avoid conversation; I'm convinced they are not French. While the official signs the papers and talks about snow leopards and the rare hawks to be found in the mountains, I examine their shoes. They look like Adidas and Nikes but in fact they are cheap imitations. Now I am convinced they are Russians posing as tourists; no wealthy Frenchman would wear imitation brands.

After they leave, the official returns to our conversation apologetically, explaining that he has been told to encourage tourism. I shrug and tell him I understand.

'We have decided we can give you two more valleys. We will give you an American valley and one which was going to the Germans. We want to reduce bilateral funding in favour of international donors. But we have to have assurances that you will release the money fast.'

'No problem. I'll tell Geneva.'

Someone always gets sick on these trips. Foreign food, foreign bugs, unhealthy hotel life. Usually it's the stress that does it. People were not meant to live this way. First it was the old Japanese with his aches and pains, now it's the Bangladeshi. It will not be the American, who is too dry for any disease to take, and the Dutch girl has vitality on her side. I am saving myself and I doubt it will be me. The Bangladeshi has some sort of burning in his stomach and is vomiting all the time. Last week he told me he was homesick and missed his children. What could I say? Illness is an embarrassment to everyone and, in a way, unprofessional. We all have to work harder. If it gets serious it becomes a management problem. We'll have to decide whether to evacuate him to the American hospital or send him home. Either way he doesn't get paid and will probably not be hired again.

I'm tired of this mission. I don't like Muslim countries: they make your life difficult. All over the world men are much the same: you can unwind with them in bars, talk about money and politics and women. Here they don't drink in public and don't admit to lust. The will of Allah suddenly comes into the middle of a business discussion. A meeting stops because it's time for the chief secretary to pray. The whole place seems slightly out of focus. The same government which uses sophisticated economic analysis is also keen on cutting the hands off criminals and public floggings. You hardly see a woman on the streets and, when you do, she is covered from the top of her head to her toes. I caught myself trying to catch a glimpse of an ankle just to check whether the woman was young or old, fat or slim. Next month it's the Gambia where the hotels are full of English women holidaymakers going topless.

'OK, what we'll do is this. We'll keep the six-year concept but make a four-year first phase to satisfy the government. We'll go for a small-farmer development package, with increased government staff and transport in the region, but we'll include pre-feasibility studies for the large construction projects so they can't say we ignored them. Logistically and socially the large-scale projects are bad news. We'll include them in the total package but auction them off separately to co-financing agencies. There are plenty of development agencies who would be happy to pick them up. Pakistan is a success story, don't forget: it can pay its debts. And this is the hottest region right now. We'll put in a good-size road component, but we can't touch the ecological problems – too long-term. We'll put in something for research to cover our critics. And I want something on the soft and warm – an appendix on social factors. OK? We're getting there. We're in business.'

We've done the Himalayas, we've done the provincial government and we've cleared the federal government in Islamabad. After twenty-seven nights together, the mission has dispersed. The old Japanese and the American have taken the report to Geneva. The Korean has gone to Korea, the Dutch girl is staying on to do some research of her own. Research for research's sake. The Bangladeshi was sent home four days early. I've shed them; I'm alone in the Karachi Sheraton. So tired. My job is over and I have five nights to kill before I need to be in Washington for a briefing on the Gambia mission. I try – not very hard – to remember the names of officials in Peshawar and I am pleased to find that already I cannot.

I take a long hot bath and wrap myself in an extravagance of towels. Then I take a walk around the hotel's restaurants and cafes, looking at the foreign women without focusing my attention on any particular one. Probably I am smiling. I don't need company; I've had enough of company. Back upstairs, I phone room service to order beer and something simple and Western to eat. They are showing *Close Encounters of the Third Kind* on the video and I settle back on the bed to watch. I have lots of pillows and the dinner tray on the bed next to me. I run a calculation through my mind to see how much I've earned, then I get lost in the film. Then I fall asleep.

PART FIVE

TOWARDS THE POST-DEVELOPMENT AGE

Go to the people. Live among them. Learn from them. Love them. Start with what you know. Build on what they have. But of the best leaders when their task is done, the people will remark: 'We have done it ourselves.'

Chinese poem

27

FROM GLOBAL THINKING TO LOCAL THINKING

Gustavo Esteva and Madhu Suri Prakash

A revised and expanded version of the following text appeared in *Interculture*, vol. 29, no. 2, Summer/Fall 1996. This, in turn, constituted the Prologue and Chapter 1 of the book by the same authors, *Grassroots' Post-modernism: Beyond Human Rights, the Individual Self, the Global Economy* (Peter Lang, New York, 1996).

GUSTAVO ESTEVA is an economist, journalist and former editor of the Mexican newspaper *El Gallo Ilustrado* and of *Opciones*, a bi-weekly supplement of the newspaper *El Nacional*. He defines himself as a de-professionalized intellectual and a non-partisan political activist working with urban and rural grassroots groups in Mexico. Over the past years, he has been a key figure in the founding of several Latin American and international NGOs and networks. He is head of the People's Tribunal in Oaxaca, author of a book on the Zapatistas, and member of the Comision National de Justicia para los Pueblos Indigenos de Mexico.

MADHU SURI PRAKASH is professor-in-charge of the Educational Theory and Policy program at Pennsylvania State University and a recipient of the Eisenhower Award for Distinguished Teaching.

'Think globally, act locally': the slogan supposedly formulated by René Dubos some decades ago is not only a popular bumper sticker today; it increasingly captures the moral imagination of millions of people across the globe. Several 'certainties' support this slogan's moral injunction: first, the modern age forces everyone to live today in a global village; second, therefore, across the globe, people face shared predicaments and common enemies, like Cargill, Coca Cola, the World Bank and other transnational corporations, as well as oppressive nation-states; third, only a clear awareness of the global nature of such problems could help forge the coalitions of 'human solidarity' and 'global consciousness' needed for struggling successfully against these all-pervasive global enemies; fourth, this global consciousness includes the recognition that every decent human being must be morally committed to the active global defence of 'basic needs' or universal human rights (schooling,

> Wanting to reform the world without discovering one's true self is like trying to cover the world with leather to avoid the pain of walking on stones and thorns. It is much simpler to wear shoes.
>
> **Lao Tzu, *Tao Te Ching***

health, nutrition, housing, livelihood, etc.) and human freedoms (from torture, oppression, etc.).

The slogan simultaneously rejects the *illusion* of engaging in global action. This is not mere realism: ordinary people lack the centralized power required for 'global action'. It is a warning against the arrogance, the far-fetched and dangerous fantasy of 'acting globally'. It urges respect for the limits of 'local action'. It resists the Promethean lust to be godlike – omnipresent. By clearly defining the limits of intelligent, sensible action, it encourages decentralized, communal power. To make 'a difference', actions should not be grandiosely global but humbly local.

Our paper attempts to extend the valuable insights contained in the second part of the slogan to the first part. We urge the replacement of 'global thinking' with 'local thinking'. We begin by presenting a synopsis of Wendell Berry's well worked-out argument, warning not only against the dangerous arrogance of 'global thinkers', but also of the human impossibility of this form of thought.[1] From there, we attempt to debunk the other 'certainties' that today pressure millions of modern, developed 'global citizens' into believing that they have the moral obligation to engage in global thinking.

Contemporary globalists also uphold the 'certainties' that disparage their injunction 'think locally'. The latter centre around another modern illusion: that local thinking must necessarily be not only ineffective in front of the global Goliath, but also *parochial*, taking mankind back to the Dark Ages when each was taught only to look after his/her own, and 'the devil take the hindmost'. In rejecting these charges, we will try to show both the parochialism of 'global thinking' and the open nature of 'local thinking'.

GLOBAL THINKING IS IMPOSSIBLE

The modern 'gaze' can distinguish less and less between reality and the image broadcast on the television screen.[2] To fit the Earth conveniently into the modern mind, the latter has shrunk it to a little blue bauble, a mere Christmas-tree ornament; and invited modern men and women to forget how immense, grand, unknown and mysterious it is, warns Wendell Berry. If we forget this, we succumb to the arrogance of thinking that we can also overcome the limits of human intelligence. Like the Gods, we can know the globe; and, knowing it, engage in 'thinking globally' to manage planet Earth.

We can only think wisely about what we actually know well. And no person, however sophisticated, intelligent and overloaded with the information-age state-of-the-art technologies, can ever 'know' the Earth – except by reducing it statistically, as all modern institutions tend to do today, supported by reductionist scientists.[3] Since none of us can ever really know more than a minuscule part of the Earth, 'global thinking' is at best only an illusion and at worst the ground for the kinds of destructive and dangerous actions perpetrated by global 'think-tanks' like the World Bank, or their more benign counterparts – the watchdogs in the global environmental movement.

In bringing his contemporaries 'down to Earth' from out of space and space 'thinking', in teaching us to stand once again on our own feet as did our ancestors, Wendell Berry helps us to rediscover the immensity, grandeur and mystery of the Earth in the face of human finiteness, and to debunk another 'fact' of television-manufactured reality: the 'global village'. The transnational reach of *Dallas* and the sexual escapades of the British royal family or the Bosnian bloodbath, like the international proliferation of McDonald's, Benetton or Sheraton establishments, confirm the modern prejudice that we all live in 'one world'.[4] McLuhan's unfortunate metaphor of the 'global village' now operates as a 'fact', a pre-formulated judgement, completely depleting critical consciousness. Modern arrogance suggests that modern man can know the globe, just as pre-moderns knew their village. To rebut this nonsense, Berry confesses that he still has much to learn in order to 'husband' with thought and wisdom the small farm in his ancestral Kentucky that he has tilled and harvested for the past forty years. His honesty about his ignorance in caring for his minuscule piece of our Earth renders naked the dangerousness of those who claim to 'think globally' and aspire to monitor and manage the 'global village'.

THE WISDOM OF 'THINKING LITTLE'

In the tradition of Gandhi, Illich, Leopold Kohr and his disciple Fritz Schumacher, Berry warns of the many harmful consequences of 'thinking big': pushing all human enterprises beyond the human scale. Exemplifying the humility that comes with an appreciation of the genuine limits of human intelligence and capacities, Berry celebrates the age-old wisdom of 'thinking little': on the scale that humans can really understand, know and take care of the consequences of their actions and decisions upon others.

Afraid that local thinking weakens and isolates people, localizing them into parochialism, the alternative global thinkers[5] forget that Goliath did in fact meet his match in David. And, forgetting this biblical moral insight, they place their faith in the countervailing force of a competing Goliath of their own: global thinking or 'planetary consciousness'. By framing their local efforts within the context of global thinking – transmitted internationally through e-mail, CNN and other networks – they seek the global ban of DDT, nuclear power or torture; and the global dissemination of schools, vaccines, hospitals, roads, flush toilets and other 'basic amenities' of modern life to every village on Earth. Hunger in Ethiopia, bloody civil wars in Somalia or Yugoslavia, human rights violations in Mexico thus become personal concerns for all good, non-parochial citizens of Main Street, supposedly complementing their local involvement in reducing garbage, homelessness or junk food in their own neighbourhoods. Most global Samaritans fail to see that when their local actions are informed, shaped and determined by the global frame of mind, they become as uprooted as those of the *other* globalists they explicitly criticize.

To relearn how to think little, Berry recommends starting with the 'basics' of life: food, for example. He suggests discovering ways to eat which take us beyond 'global thinking and action' towards 'local thinking and action.'

Global thinkers and think-tanks, like the World Bank, disregard this wisdom both at the level of thought and at that of action. Declaring that current food problems, among others, are global in their nature, they seek to impose global solutions. Aware of the threats perpetrated by such 'solutions', the proponents of 'think globally, act locally' take recourse to the tradition of Kohr et al. only at the level of action. By refusing to 'think little', they thus actually support and function on their enemies' turf.

The question is how to defeat the five Goliath companies now controlling 85 per cent of the world trade in grains and around half of its world production. Or the four controlling the American consumption of chicken. Or those few that have cornered the beverage market. Any change will wait forever if the challenge to the food Goliaths is delayed until equally gigantic transnational consumers' coalitions are forged, whether inspired by Ralph Nader or informed by a global consciousness about the right way to eat.

All global institutions, including the World Bank and Coca Cola, have to concretize their transnational operations in actions that are always necessarily local; they cannot exist otherwise. Since 'global forces' can only achieve concrete existence at some local level, it is only there at the grassroots that they can most effectively and wisely be opposed.

Thousands of small grassroots groups are realizing that there is no need to 'think big' in order to begin releasing themselves from the clutches of the monopolistic food economy; that they can free themselves in the same voluntary ways as they entered it. They are learning simply to say 'No' to Coke and other junk food, while looking for local alternatives that are healthy, ecologically sound, and decentralized in terms of social control. Among the more promising solutions is the movement towards Community Supported Agriculture (CSA), inspired by both local thinking and action. It involves urban consumers supporting small local farmers who farm with wisdom and care for local soils, waters and intestines. And who, in doing so, simultaneously ensure that unknown farmers from far-away places like Costa Rica or Brazil are not exploited with inhuman wages and left sick with cancer or infertility. By taking care of our own local food, farms and farmers, those of us who are members of CSAs are slowly learning to overcome the parochialism of 'industrial eaters' – those who are 'educated' to be oblivious to the harm done by supporting multinationals and others who 'think big', destroying millions of small family farms across the globe.

Those of us supporting CSAs are trying to abandon the global thinking with which industrial eaters enter their local grocery stores: buying 'goods' from any and every part of the Earth, motivated solely by the desire to get the 'best' return for their dollar. Of course, those of us who are now trying to think locally about food (among other 'basics') are also frugal: we do want the best return for our dollar. But for us this means much more than maximizing the pounds of eggs or the gallons of milk with which we can fill our grocery bags. We are interested in knowing about the kinds of lives lived by the hens whose eggs we eat; we want to know what type of soil our lettuce springs from. And we not only want to ensure that the animals and plants we bring to our palate were treated well; we are also educating ourselves about our eating habits so that the farmers who work for us will not die of deadly diseases or become infertile because of the chemicals they were forced to spray on their fields. We have now read enough to know why these ills occur every time we buy grapes from California, or bananas from Costa Rica. We also know that when our food comes from so far away, we will never know the whole story of suffering perpetrated unintentionally by us, despite the valiant efforts of journals like *The Ecologist* or scholars like Frances Moore Lappé; nor, for that matter, once we get a partial picture, will we be able to do much about it. Therefore by decreasing the number of kilometres we eat, bringing them closer and closer to our local homes, we know we are 'empowering' ourselves to be neither oppressed by the big and powerful, nor oppressors of these *campesinos* and small farmers who live across the globe; and we are also educating ourselves to look after the well-being of members of our local community, who, in their turn, are similarly committed to our well-being. In doing so, we are discovering that we are also saving money, while being more productive and efficient.

THE STRENGTH OF THINKING AND ACTING LOCALLY

Local initiatives, no matter how wisely conceived, seem *prima facie* too small to counteract the 'global forces' now daily invading our lives and environments. The whole history of economic development, in its colonialist, socialist or capitalist forms, is a history of violent interventions by powerful forces 'persuading' small communities to surrender with the use of weapons, economic lures and 'education'.

Countless such cases give ample proof that local peoples often need outside allies to create a critical mass of political opposition capable of stopping those forces. But the solidarity of coalitions and alliances does not call for 'thinking globally'. In fact what is needed is exactly the opposite: people thinking and acting locally, while forging solidarity with other local forces that share this *opposition* to the 'global thinking' and 'global forces' threatening local spaces. For its strength, the struggle against Goliath enemies demands that there be no deviation from local inspiration and firmly rooted local thought. When local movements or initiatives lose the ground under their feet, moving their struggle into the enemy's territory – global arenas constructed by global thinking – they become minor players in the global game, doomed to lose their battles.

The Earth Summit is perhaps the best contemporary illustration of this sequence. Motivated by global thinking, thousands of local groups flew across the world to Rio de Janeiro only to see their valuable initiatives transmogrified into nothing more than a footnote to the global agreements conceived and now being implemented by the big and the powerful. Prescient of this failure of 'thinking big/global', Berry predicted that the global environmental movement, by following the grand highways taken by the peace and civil rights movements, would lose its vitality and strength, uprooted from its natural ground: the concrete spaces of real men and women who think and act locally.

CHALLENGING UNIVERSALISM

The strongest support for 'global thinking' is proffered by those with full faith in the universal declaration of human rights. Even those rejecting most varieties of 'global thinking' propound the moral imperative to struggle for universal rights, perceived by many to represent a Western conquest on behalf of every human on Earth. Most fail to see why any conception of universal rights – to education, for example – is controversial and a colonial tool for domination. That is why most cannot comprehend Gandhi's resistance to those educational rights which called for the importation of schools into India, prescient as he was of the cultural damage the universal right to these institutions would do to well-rooted, local, pre-colonial, indigenous approaches to education/cultural initiation.

In recent years, ordinary peoples and radical thinkers of many cultures have been challenging, on different grounds, the very notion of human rights – both their nature and their universality. Given their individualist underpinnings, these rights entail dissolving the very foundations of cultures which are organized around the notions of communal obligations, commitment and service. In most Latin American, Asian or African villages, collective or communal rights have clear priority over *personal* or *individual* rights; legitimate hierarchies (of the elders, for example) have primacy over equality (which in the real world always means illegitimate hierarchies); and concrete customs, rather than abstract universalizable laws, support communal bonds and organize social support.

The Problem of Pluralism

Once upon a time ... it was Mankind's dream (a dream which seems somehow built into the heart of man) to build one single tower, one big ladder to heaven, one great construct. And the Lord – who seems here to be perhaps envious, or wants to keep his prerogatives, or is playing a nasty game – the Lord appears not to favor such human enterprises and, once upon a time, time and again, Nebuchadnezzar falls, the *augustus imperator* dies, the colossal empires collapse, the great hordes fade away ... And yet we go on dreaming the same dream of a big city enclosing everything. Perhaps, after all, the Lord God knew better: that the nature of Man is not gregarious, collective, but each human being is a king, a microcosm and the cosmos is a pluriverse and not a universe. God, as the symbol for the infinite, seems to be in his proper role when he is destroying all human endeavors towards comfortable finitudes.

In any case, after sixty centuries of human memory in the historical realm, is there no way for us to awaken to the futility of this dream? What would happen if we simply gave up wanting to build this tremendous unitarian tower? What if instead we were to remain in our small beautiful huts and houses and homes and domes and start building roads of communication (instead of just transportation), which could in time be converted into ways of communion between and among the different tribes, life-styles, religions, philosophies, colors, races, and all the rest? And even if we cannot quite give up the dream of a unitarian Mankind – this dream in the monolithic system of the tower of Babel which has become our recurring nightmare – could it not be met by just building roads of communication rather than some gigantic new empire, ways of communion instead of coercion, paths which might lead us to overstep our provincialisms without tossing us all into a single sack, into a single cult, into the monotony of a single culture?

Raimon Panikkar, 'The Myth of Pluralism: The Tower of Babel – A Meditation on Non-violence', *Cross Currents*, Summer 1979, pp. 199–200.

Alienating individualism is essential to the very conception of universal human rights, assert their cultural critics. In radical contrast, real communal rights of peoples to their commons often come with moral codes and traditions that imply dissolving or contradicting individual rights, to avoid their inherent individualism. Facts such as these challenge the universality of human rights, revealing that individualism, as a perception defining and shaping both human nature and human rights, is a peculiar Western construction, assumed only by an increasing, but still minor, percentage of people on Earth. Most other cultures of the world's social majorities have definitions of human well-being that either do not require or reject the notion of individual human rights. Two-thirds of the world's people do not possess the concept of individual human rights. Given their emphases on communal duties and obligations,[6] the notion that an individual can possess abstract rights is inconceivable to them.

What for some people is a 'right', for some others is a 'torture', and vice versa. Schooling, homes for 'senior citizens', sewage or prisons, on the one side, and community service, religious practices or common rituals, on the other, offer good cases for radical cultural opposition and pluralism. In some cultures (like those of the majority of Mexico's indigenous peoples, for example), crimes call for compensation 'paid' with services to the community. Economic responsibility must be assumed by killers for the families of the men killed, according to some cultural obligations. These forms of compensation require freedom from jail and a real opportunity for social rehabilitation. Jails, which do not represent a violation of human rights in Western cultures, in the former cultural contexts are tantamount to inhuman tortures. Analogously, sewerage and flush toilets, assumed as a 'right' and a 'basic need' in some cultures, are recognized by an increasing number of people as a real threat; while dry latrines and other locally designed technologies are seen by these groups as the only responsible methods for 'taking care of our own shit', to use a culturally specific colloquialism. Institutionalizing old and young people rather than including them in all aspects of communal and family life is perceived as a right within some cultures; while others conceive such institutionalization as inhumane and a form of torture.[7]

Human rights were born in particular cultural contexts, conceived in the course of legitimate struggles against abuses of power. They express the reality of the individuals created by modern Europe, legitimately reacting against abuses by modern states. Far from assuming that the behaviour of the individual or *homo oeconomicus* defines human nature for all times and cultures, critics of universal human rights are finally recognizing facts well documented by Western scholars: that both individualism and *homo oeconomicus* are historical Western creations, and not ahistorical traits of our species. Whatever their merits and successes in industrial societies, these 'rights' contaminate many communities, particularly in the South, introducing within them the virus of *homo oeconomicus*: the possessive individual first fashioned in Europe.

Opposition to human rights is entirely compatible, therefore, with an active struggle to oppose all abuses of power, both pre-modern and modern, in all their forms. And it explicitly includes abuses which still justify the 'global thinking' that increasingly invades the lives and environments of people with schools, highways, prisons, flush toilets, Chemlawn and other poisonous pesticides, plastic garbage bags or junk food.

ESCAPING PAROCHIALISM

Our arguments against 'thinking big' do not deny the reality of the internationalization of the economy, now in its final phases, and increasingly reflected in the system of global mass media. Equally real is the homogenization of ways of living of large minorities in both North and South. Such phenomena and other related aspects of modern reality have been used as empirical support for the illusion that all people on Earth are being 'globalized' – a prospect that some perceive as a threat and others as a promise. Whether threat or promise, 'realists' who tend to see 'upwards' while contaminating the worlds of people who try to live 'down to earth', also argue for the unavoidability of globalization. They remain blind to the fact that, far from being 'globalized', the real lives of most people on Earth are clearly *marginalized* from any 'global' way of life. The social majorities of the world will never, now or in the future, have access to these so-called global phenomena, if the Club of Rome report, and other studies that followed it, including the Worldwatch State of the World annual reports, are to be trusted. The world's social majorities will never eat in McDonald's, have access to schools and hospitals, check into a Sheraton or drive family cars. Globalists will have depleted the world's resources long before that could ever happen.

Global proposals are necessarily parochial: they inevitably express the specific vision and interests of a small group of people, even when they are formulated in the interest of humanity.[8] In contrast, local proposals, if they are conceived by communities rooted in specific places, reflect the *radical pluralism* of cultures and the unique *cosmovision* that defines every culture: an awareness of the place and responsibilities of humans in the cosmos.[9] For those who think locally do not twist the humble satisfaction of belonging to the cosmos into the arrogance of pretending to know what is good for everyone and attempting to control the world. There is a legitimate claim to universality intrinsic in every affirmation of truth. However, local people do not identify the limits of their own vision with that of the human horizon itself.

While some of the people marginalized from the amenities of modernity are still struggling to be part of the world's 'globalized' minorities, many more have recently started to abandon such illusions. In doing so, they are rediscovering their own culturally specific, alternative definitions of 'a good life', feasible in their own local spaces. Besieged by 'global' pressures and aggressions, which generate uncertainty, destruction and discrimination, they are less bedazzled by global solutions to their concrete local predicaments. Renouncing universal definitions of 'the good life' (like 'the American dream') imposed across the world by global economic development, they are starting to protect themselves from the threats of modernity by rooting themselves more firmly in their soils, their local commons – cultural space that belongs to them and to which they belong. Even the most superficial observation of what is really happening among the social majorities, particularly in the South, allows us to see the proliferation of localized initiatives, rooted in the concrete world that shapes the daily life of communities. They are not ignoring 'global phenomena' that continually intrude upon their lives, but delinking with ingenuity and effectiveness from the 'global thinking', plans and proposals that marginalize them from the operations of the global economy. They are escaping the globalization of their marginality by turning to localization.

Growing coalitions of local thinkers/activists are learning to counteract effectively the damage of global thinking and action through a shared rejection. Their shared 'No's' to their 'common enemies' (whether a nuclear plant, dam or Walmart) simultaneously affirm their culturally differentiated perceptions and locally rooted initiatives and modes of being. Their motives and arguments for saying 'No' are as different as the variety of local settings that they are trying to protect through their shared rejection. When these shared 'No's' interweave cross-cultural agreed commitments, they retain their plurality, without falling into cultural relativism. They successfully oppose *globalism* with *radical pluralism*, conceived for going beyond Western monoculturalism – now made up and disguised as 'multiculturalism' inside as well as outside the quintessentially Western educational setting: the classroom. And they find, in their concrete practices, that all 'global powers' are built on shaky foundations (as the Soviet Union so ably demonstrated in the recent past), and may, therefore, be effectively opposed through modest local actions.

EPILOGUE

Surely, there must be some beneficial varieties of global thinking? Not all forms of global thinking should be seen as harmful just because some of them have terrible consequences? Questions like these have been raised by many readers of the earlier drafts of our article – and especially those readers who for many years of their lives have been consciously and deliberately committed to the ideals of global thinking. Does your paper not exemplify a beneficial variety of global thinking, these readers have asked us. Does not the example of *The Ecologist*, for many years committed to the cause of saving the Narmada river in India, the agricultural lands of Costa Rica, or the Brazilian rainforest, from its headquarters in England, amply demonstrate all the worldwide beneficial effects of good global thinking? These questions compel us to conclude this article by distinguishing 'global thinking' from different varieties of 'local thinking married to local action'.

The Ecologist, it seems to us, offers a prime case for distinguishing between these two varieties of thought. For decades, its readers have been educated about the initiatives of local groups struggling against the horrors perpetrated by global Goliaths like the World Bank, MacDonalds, Cargill or Coca Cola. The editors of this journal, while living and working in England, have amply demonstrated their solidarity with local initiatives, struggling for the cultural and ecological survival of their regional spaces all over the earth. In fact, this journal has played a key role in forging solidarity between small local groups which would not otherwise have known of like-minded communal action far flung across the vast planet. This solidarity, when misunderstood, can be mistaken for both global thinking and global action. The mistake rests in conflating global thinking (whether married to local or global action) with a commitment to the pluralism inherent in a wide variety of human contexts of local-scale thought/action across the world. An extended commitment to local thought in all its diversity and radical pluralism should not be mistaken for the arrogance, grandiosity and homogeneity of global thought....

The time has come to recognize, with the late Leopold Kohr, that the true problem of the modern age lies in the inhuman size or the scale of many contemporary institutions and technologies. Instead of trying to counteract such inherently unstable and damaging global forces through government or civic controls that match their devastating scale, the time has come 'to reduce the size of the body politic which gives them their devastating scale, until they become once again a match for the limited talent available to the ordinary mortals of which even the most majestic governments are composed'. In other words, said Kohr,

> instead of centralization or unification, let us have economic cantonization. Let us replace the oceanic dimension of integrated big powers and common markets by a dike system of inter-connected but highly self-sufficient local markets and small states in which economic fluctuations can be controlled, not because national or international leaders have Oxford or Yale degrees, but because the ripples of a bond, however animated, can never assume the scale of the huge swells passing through the united water masses of the open seas.[10]

This is sound advice: not only for dealing with GATT, the European Union, NAFTA or the World Bank in the political arena, but also to put public pressure on governments with regard to the reorientation of their policies. It applies equally to every local struggle. Kohr's utopia cannot be constructed from the top down, creating gigantic dikes to stop such oceanic waves, or struggling to 'seize' such powers in order to give them a different orientation or to dismantle them. In the struggle against such forces, there is a need to keep all political bodies at a human scale.

The Ecologist once again offers an example: a dozen journalists working with a few thousand people in the interest of sharing the knowledge and experiences of local groups which are struggling at the local level; and thereby developing solidarity with other local people confronting similar predicaments.

It is more than a metaphor to say that *The Ecologist* or the 'Zapatista journals' are contemporary commons, to which others freely have access. For no material in *The Ecologist* has a restricted use, and there are no royalties paid for its reproduction. Neither type of journal has any global pretension, any all-embracing ideology, any global thinking. The plurality of their sources and audiences is not reduced to an abstract common denominator, constructed by the editors. Instead, they are offered for what they are: subjective, local accounts or recollections, from which others may draw some important lessons, to be applied in local terms through the lenses of their own subjectivities.

There may be some globalists among those campaigning to save the Narmada; or among those thousands of people using e-mail to disseminate all over the world the manifestos of the Zapatistas; or among those travelling thousands of miles and confronting severe risks to break the siege imposed upon them by the army, in order to make them submit by threatening hunger; or among those campaigning against the World Bank, poisonous pesticides, nuclear plants, dams or genetic engineering; or among those struggling for human rights, biodiversity or a cleaner environment.

Fortunately, however, many more have perceived that 'global forces' or 'global enemies' can only exist at the local level in the real world. And that is the only level at which real men and women can effectively struggle. To succeed, all local struggles should distinguish between truly local phenomena and local incarnations of 'global forces'. If local people think that they are struggling against a specific restaurant, without perceiving what it means to be a MacDonald's, or against this specific local officer or police force, without perceiving what it means to have the backing of the World Bank, they will probably fail to understand the nature of their struggle. Clearly, knowing the local nature of global institutions is a prerequisite to success. Sharing information among local peoples struggling against the same kinds of predicament and the giving and receiving of solidarity have become increasingly indispensable to the effectiveness of local struggles. In no way do these forms of transnational sharing transmogrify local people into globalists.

NOTES

1. To study the different reasons Wendell Berry offers for opposing 'global thinking', see Wendell Berry, 'Out of Your Car, Off Your Horse', *Atlantic Monthly*, February 1991; 'Nobody Loves This Planet', *In Context*, no. 27, Winter 1991; 'Think Little', in *A Continuous Harmony: Essays Cultural and Agricultural*, Harcourt Brace Jovanovich, New York, 1972. See also Madhu Suri Prakash, 'What Are People For? Wendell Berry on Education, Ecology and Culture', *Educational Theory*, vol. 44, no. 2, Spring 1994, pp. 135–7. For other critiques of 'global thinking', see Wolfgang Sachs, ed., *Global Ecology*, Zed Books, London, 1993.

2. For the past three years at Pennsylvania State University we have been studying with Ivan Illich how, for the many millions raised on television, Mickey Mouse has become as real as Ronald Reagan: that, worse still, both are in fact larger than 'real' life itself – as are television phenomena like Michael Jackson and Madonna. For his discussion of the destruction of the senses in the age of 'La Technique', see Ivan Illich, 'An Address to Master Jacques', *Bulletin of Science, Technology and Society*, vol. 14, no. 2, 1994; and 'Guarding the Eye in the Age of Show', *Science, Technology and Society*, Working Paper No. 4, Science, Technology and Society, University Park, Pa., 1994.

3. For a classic exploration of reductionism in science, see Carolyn Merchant, *The Death of Nature: Women, Ecology and the Scientific Revolution*, Harper & Row, San Francisco, 1980.

4. Wolfgang Sachs, 'One World', in *The Development Dictionary: A Guide to Knowledge as Power*, edited by Wolfgang Sachs, Zed Books, London, 1992.

5. We are calling 'alternative global thinkers' all those theoreticians and practitioners

who explicitly oppose conventional global thinking, epitomized by the World Bank, while committed to global alternatives to it. The Worldwatch Institute, David C. Korten, James Robertson, and Greenpeace exemplify such alternatives. David C. Korten is the founder and chair of the People-Centered Development Forum (14E 17th St, Suite 5, New York, NY 10003, USA), which disseminates a regular column and promotes seminars, global campaigns, etc. on alternative developments. His books include *Getting to the 21st Century: Voluntary Action and the Global Agenda*, Kumarian Press, West Hartford, Ct., 1990; and *When Corporations Rule the World*, Kumarian Press, West Hartford, Ct., and Berret-Koehler Publishers, San Francisco, 1995. James Robertson is an active member of The Other Economic Summit, developing the 'Schumacher School' of economics. He publishes a newsletter, *Turning Point 2000* (The Old Bakehouse, Cholsey, Oxon OX10 9NU, UK). His books include *Health, Wealth and the New Economics: An Agenda for a Healthier World*, TOES, London, 1985; and *Future Work: Jobs, Self-Employment and Leisure after the Industrial Age*, Temple Smith/Gower, London, 1985.

6. For a radical critique of human rights as a concept that is transcultural and universal, see Robert Vachon, *Human Rights and Dharma*, mimeo, distributed by the Intercultural Institute of Montreal (4971 St Urbain, Montreal, P.Q. Canada, H2T 2W1). See also Raimon Panikkar, 'La Notion des droits de l'homme est-elle un concept occidental?', in *Diogene* (UNESCO), no. 120, 1982, pp 87–115; published in English and French editions, with debate, in *Interculture*, pp. 82–83, 2–78.

7. See Gustavo Esteva, 'A New Source of Hope: The Margins', *Interculture*, vol. 26, no. 2, Spring 1993, pp. 2–62; see also Leroy Little Bear, 'A Concept of Native', *Native People and Justice in Canada*, vol. 5, no. 2–3, pp. 71–99; Robert Vachon, 'The Mohawk Nation and Its Communities', *Interculture*, vol. 24, no. 4, Fall 1991, pp. 1–35, and vol. 25, no. 1, Winter 1992, pp. 1–27; Pat Lauderdale, 'Indigenous North American Alternatives to Modern Law and Punishment: Lessons of Nature', mimeo, University of Innsbruck, 1991.

8. See Vandana Shiva, 'The Greening of Global Reach', in Sachs, ed., *Global Ecology*, pp. 2–62.

9. See Raimon Panikkar, 'The Religion of the Future', *Interculture*, vol. 23, no. 3, Summer 1990. For his discussion of radical pluralism, see Raimon Panikkar, 'The Myth of Pluralism: The Tower of Babel – Meditation on Non-violence', *Cross Currents*, no. 29, 1979, pp. 197–230.

10. Leopold Kohr, *The Academic Inn*, Y Lolfa, Talybont, Dyfed, 1993, pp. 10, 11.

28

THE NEED FOR THE HOME PERSPECTIVE

Wolfgang Sachs

The following text is an abbreviated version of an article published in *Interculture,* vol. 29, no. 1, Winter 1996 – an issue devoted to 'The Post-Modern Era', which includes articles by Ashis Nandy ('Development, Science and Colonialism') and Raimon Panikkar ('The Contemplative Mood: A Challenge to Modernity').

We have had to leave out two parts of the original article for reasons of space. The first deals with the fortress perspective, which works on the silent assumption that development will have to remain spatially restricted, but can be made sustainable for the richer parts of the world. The second considers the astronaut's perspective, which recognizes that development is precarious in time and seeks to turn the planet into an object of global management, through an efficiency revolution, making minimal use of nature. We have here concentrated on the home perspective, which understands sustainability as being that of communities, through resistance to development: the quest for justice must, then, delink from development, and all ideas of development in its conventional sense must be abandoned.

WOLFGANG SACHS has long been active in the German and Italian green movements. He is particularly concerned with how ecology has changed recently from being a knowledge of opposition to being a knowledge of domination. He is the author of *For Love of the Automobile: Looking Back into the History of our Desires* (University of California Press, Berkeley, 1992); the editor of *The Development Dictionary: A Guide to Knowledge as Power* (Zed Books, London, 1992); and the editor of *Global Ecology: A New Arena of Political Conflict* (Zed Books, London, 1993). Currently based at the Wuppertal Institute for Climate, Wolfgang Sachs is Chair of the Board of Greenpeace, Germany.

After forty years of development, the state of affairs is dismal. The gap between frontrunners and stragglers has not been bridged; on the contrary, it has widened to the extent that it has become unimaginable that it could ever be closed. The aspiration to catch up has ended in a blunder of planetary proportions. The figures speak for themselves: during the 1980s, the contribution of developing countries, where two-thirds of humanity live, to the world's GNP has shrunk to 15 per cent, while the share of the industrial countries, with 20 per cent of the world's population, has risen to 80 per cent.[1] To be sure, upon closer inspection the picture is far from homogeneous, but neither the Southeast Asian showcases nor the oil-producing countries affect the conclusion that the development race has ended in disarray. The world may have developed, but it has done so in two opposite directions.

This is all the more true if one considers the destiny of large majorities of people within most countries: the polarization between nations repeats itself in each case. On the global as well as on the national level, there is a polarizing dynamic at work, which creates an economically vigorous middle class on the one side and large sections of socially excluded population on the other side. The best one can say is that development has created a global middle class of those with cars, bank accounts and career aspirations. It is made up of the majority in the North and small elites in the South and its size equals roughly that 8 per cent of the world population which owns an automobile. They are, beyond all national boundaries, increasingly integrated into the worldwide circuit of goods, communication and travel. An invisible border separates in all nations, in the North as well as in the South, the rich from the poor: entire categories of people in the North – like the unemployed, the elderly and the economically weak – and entire regions in the South – like rural areas, tribal zones and urban settlements – find themselves increasingly excluded from the circuits of the world economy. 'North' and 'South' are therefore less and less geographical categories but rather socio-economic ones, referring to the line which divides the strong world market sectors from the competitively weak, economically superfluous sectors in society.[2] A new bipolarism pervades the globe and reaches into every nation; it is no longer the East–West division which leaves its imprint on every society, but the North–South division.

THE CRISIS OF NATURE

A second product of the development era has dramatically come to the fore in recent years. It has become evident that the racetrack leads in the wrong direction. President Truman first defined the poorer countries as 'underdeveloped areas' in his inaugural speech before Congress on 20 January 1949 and he could still take it for granted that the North was at the head of social evolution. Now, this premiss of superiority has been fully and finally shattered by the ecological predicament. For instance, much of the glorious growth in productivity is fuelled by a gigantic throughput of fossil energy which requires mining the earth on the one side and covering her with waste on the other. By now, however, the global economy has outgrown the capacity of the earth to serve as mine and dumping ground. After all, the world economy increases every two years by about the size ($60 billion) it had reached by 1900 after centuries of growth. Although only a small part of the world's regions has experienced economic expansion on a large scale, the world economy already weighs down nature to an extent that she has in part to give in. If all countries followed the industrial example, five or six planets would be needed to serve as 'sources' for the 'inputs' and 'sinks' for the waste of economic progress. A situation has thus emerged where the certainty which ruled two centuries has been exposed as a serious illusion: that growth is a show with an open end. Economic expansion has already come up against its bio-physical limits; recognizing the finiteness of the Earth is a fatal blow to the idea of development as envisaged by Truman.

After five hundred years, the North's protected status seems to be drawing to an end. Europe's journey to the ends of the Earth, initiated in the fifteenth century and completed in the twentieth, has lifted history to new heights, but has at the same time produced a configuration of conflicts which will inevitably shape the face of the twenty-first century. A world divided and a nature ill-treated is the heritage which casts its shadow forward. It is not that these conflicts as such are news, but that their impact potentially spreads worldwide, as the pace of globalization accelerates. For the unification of the world increasingly shows its seamy side; the globalization of goodies is accompanied by the globalization of troubles. What is new, in fact, is that the North is less and less protected by spatial and temporal distances from the unpleasant long-term consequences of its actions.

For several centuries the North could avoid dealing with the reality of a divided world, since the suffering occurred far away. Long distances separated the places of exploitation from the places of accumulation. However, as distances shrink, so the distance between victims and winners shortens, exposing the North to the threats of a divided world. Globalization not only joins the haughty North to the South, but also the chaotic South to the North. Likewise, the bitter consequences of the ill-treatment of nature make themselves felt. Many generations could afford to neglect the limits of nature as a source and a sink; the costs of the present have been transferred to the future. The more the rate of exploitation increases, however, the faster the finiteness of nature makes itself felt on a global scale. Since the distance in time, which for so long bolstered industrialism against its effects, is shrinking, the bio-physical limits of nature have forcefully emerged in the present. For these reasons, time and space, delay and distance, have ceased to provide a protective shell for the world's rich; as globalization promises the simultaneity and ubiquity of goodies, so also is the simultaneity and ubiquity of troubles to be expected.

THE HORNS OF THE DILEMMA

'Development', as a way of thinking, is on its way out. It has slowly become common sense that the two founding assumptions of the development promise have lost their validity. For the promise rested on the belief, first, that development could be universalized in space, and, second, that it would be durable in time. In both senses, however, development has revealed itself as finite, and it is precisely this insight which constitutes the dilemma that has pervaded many international debates since the UN Conference on the Environment in Stockholm in 1972. The crisis of justice and the crisis of nature stand, with the received notion of development, in an inverse relationship to each other. In other words, any attempt to ease the crisis of justice threatens to aggravate the crisis of nature. And the reverse: any attempt to ease the crisis of nature threatens to aggravate the crisis of justice. Whoever demands more agricultural land, energy, housing, services, or, in general, more purchasing power for the poor, finds himself in conflict with those who would like to protect the soils, animals, forests, human health or the atmosphere. And whoever calls for less energy or less transport and opposes clear-cutting or input-intensive agriculture for the sake of nature, finds himself in conflict with those who insist on their equal right to the fruits of progress. It is easy, however, to see that the base upon which the dilemma rests is the conventional notion of development; for if there was a development that used less nature and included more people, a way out of the dilemma would open up. It is small wonder, therefore, that in the last two decades committed minds from all corners of the world have been calling for an 'alternative model of development'.

The comet-like rise of the concept 'sustainable development' is to be understood against this background. It promises nothing less than to square the circle: to identify a type of development that promotes both ecological sustainability and international justice. Since the time of the Club of Rome study Limits to Growth, two camps of political discourse had emerged, one under the banner of 'environment' and the other under the banner of 'development'. The voices from the North mostly emphasized the rights of nature, while the voices from the South tended to bring claims for justice to the fore.[3] In 1987, the World Commission for Environment and Development (the Brundtland Commission) appeared to have succeeded in building a conceptual bridge between the two camps, offering the definition which has become canonical: sustainable development is development 'that meets the needs of the present without compromising the ability of future generations to meet their own needs'.[4]

However, a quick glance reveals that the formula is designed to maximize consensus rather than clarity. As with any compromise, that is no small achievement, because the definition works like an all-purpose cement which glues all parts together, friends and foes alike. The opponents of the 1970s and 1980s find themselves pinned down to a common ground, and since then everything has revolved around the notion of 'sustainable development'. Nevertheless, the price of this consensus was considerable. Dozens of definitions are being passed around among experts and politicians, because many and diverse interests and visions hide behind the common key idea. As so often happens, deep political and ethical controversies make the definition of the concept a contested area.

The formula is based upon the notion of time. It invites the reader to raise his eyes, to look at the future, and to pay due consideration to the generations of tomorrow. The definition officially confirms that the continuity of development in time has become a world problem. The egoism of the present is under accusation – an egoism which sells off nature for short-term gain. In a way, the phrase reminds one of the words by which Gifford Pinchot, the steward of Theodore Roosevelt's conservation programme, sought to bring utilitarianism up to date: 'conservation means the greatest good for the greatest number for the longest time'. But, upon closer inspection, one will note that the definition of the Brundtland Commission does not refer to 'the greatest number', but focuses instead on the 'needs of the present' and those of 'future generations'. While the crisis of nature has been constitutive for the concept of 'sustainable development', the crisis of justice finds only a faint echo in the notions of 'development' and 'needs'. In the definition, the attention to the dimension of time is not counterbalanced by an equal attention to the dimension of space. It is, therefore, no exaggeration to say that the canonical definition has resolved the dilemma 'nature versus justice' in favour of nature. For two crucial questions remain open. What needs? And whose needs? To leave these questions pending in the face of a divided world means to sidestep the crisis of justice. Is sustainable development supposed to meet the needs for water, land and economic security or the needs for air travel and bank deposits? Is it concerned with survival needs or with luxury needs? Are the needs in question those of the global consumer class or those of the enormous numbers of have-nots? The Brundtland report remains undecided throughout and therefore avoids facing up to the crisis of justice.[5]

Environmental action and environmental discourse, when carried on in the name of 'sustainable development', implicitly or explicitly position themselves with respect to the crisis of justice and the crisis of nature. Different actors produce different types of knowledge; they highlight certain issues and underplay others. How attention is focused, what implicit assumptions are cultivated, which hopes are entertained, and what agents are privileged depends on the way the debate on sustainability is framed. What is common to all these discourses, I would submit, is the hunch that the era of infinite development hopes has passed, giving way to an era in which the finiteness of development becomes an accepted truth. What renders them deeply different, however, is the way they understand finiteness: either they emphasize the finiteness of development in the global space and disregard its finiteness in terms of time, or they emphasize the finiteness of development with regard to time and consider irrelevant its finiteness in terms of global space. In [what follows], I would like to sketch out three different perspectives of 'sustainable development' which differ in the way they implicitly understand finiteness.

The *fortress perspective* works with the silent assumption that development, unfortunately, will have to remain spatially restricted, but can be made durable for the richer parts of the world. It neglects the fact that the range of harmful effects produced by the North now covers the entire globe and limits the responsibility of the North to its own affairs. The *astronaut's perspective* takes a different view. It recognizes that development is precarious in time and seeks global adjustment to deal with the crisis of nature and the crisis of justice. As a response to the global reach of harmful effects, it favours the extension of the range of responsibility, until it covers the entire globe. The *home perspective*, in turn, accepts the finiteness of development in time and suggests delinking the question of justice from the pursuit of development. It draws a different conclusion from the fact that the range of effects produced by the North has vastly outgrown the radius of Northern responsibility, and advocates reducing the effects until they remain within the given radius of responsibility. It is very possible that the relative strength of these perspectives will shape the future of North–South relations.

[The author then presents, in greater detail, the characteristics of the fortress perspective and the astronaut's perspective, before passing to the home perspective.]

THE HOME PERSPECTIVE

The world was surprised and responded to the events in Mexico with irritation, as hundreds of armed *indios* all of a sudden occupied the city of San Cristóbal de Las Casas. On the very day that the NAFTA agreement became effective, a hitherto unknown liberation movement emerged from the forests of Chiapas and challenged the Mexican government. What did the rebels want? Where were they coming from? In the following days, a long letter from subcomandante Marcos was published in the press, which began:

> Suppose you want to travel to the South East of the country and suppose you find yourself on one of the three roads which lead to the state of Chiapas … Our wealth leaves this land not just on these three roads. Chiapas is bleeding to death in a thousand ways: through oil and gas pipelines, power supply lines, railway coaches, banking accounts, trucks, ships and airplanes, clandestine paths and paved roads. This land continues to pay its tribute to the empire: oil, electricity, cattle, coffee, maize, honey, tobacco … Primary resources, several billion tonnes with various destinations, flow out to … the USA, Canada, Holland, Germany, Italy, Japan, but always with the same destination – the empire.[6]

The Chiapas rebellion was a sudden signal. It pulled back the veil of oblivion from those indigenous and rural populations in the hinterland of the global middle classes who are largely excluded from the fruits of the unification of the world. They are to be found everywhere, in innumerable villages and on all continents: peasants and landless workers, migrants and tribals, the periphery of the world market. Despite their many differences, they generally share the fate of being threatened by the claims urban-industrial developers make on their resources. However, when water sources dry up, fields get lost, animals vanish, forests dwindle and harvests decrease, the basis of their livelihood is undermined, and they are pushed onto the market, for which they do not have sufficient purchasing power. In such circumstances, the growth economy threatens life-support systems in two ways: that of people immediately and that of the biosphere in the long run. The crisis of nature and the crisis of justice coincide for large parts of the world population in the experience of being marginalized by expansionist 'development'.

THE NORTH AS ARENA OF ECOLOGICAL ADJUSTMENT

The proud declarations from Chiapas give voice to the ordeals of the great majority of the world's population. There is not, however, much reason to believe that this division of the world – the international consumer classes on the one hand, the urban poor on the other – can be overcome by accelerating the course along the racetrack of 'development'. On the contrary, an exponential growth of the world economy will most likely increase the pressure on the hinterland with its resources of nature and labour power, a pressure which constantly threatens to push the mini-economies beyond the islands of affluence into disintegration. It is understandable, in this context, that for many communities 'sustainability' means nothing else but resistance against development.[7]

It is one of the unelaborated assumptions of the home perspective that, conceptually speaking, the quest of justice needs to be decoupled from the pursuit of conventional development. This insight arises from the struggles of many communities, be it in Chiapas or in the Narmada Valley. But not only that: such an insight also arises forcefully from the limits of development in terms of time. Since the crisis of nature blocks the universalization of development, it is also in the name of justice that the conventional development idea should be abandoned. The crisis of justice, according to this perspective, cannot be dealt with by redistributing 'development', but only by getting off people's backs, limiting the development pressures emanating from the various 'Norths' in the world.

This approach links those activists, NGOs, politicians and dissident intellectuals – the social base of the home perspective – in the North who are concerned about justice with those who are concerned about nature. Both groups converge in expecting the North to retreat from utilizing other people's nature and to reduce the part of the global environmental space it occupies. After all, most of the Northern countries leave what W. Rees has called an 'ecological footprint' on the world which is considerably larger than their territory. They occupy foreign soils to provide themselves with tomatoes, rice, feedstuff or cattle; they carry away raw materials of any kind; and they utilize the global commons – like the oceans and the atmosphere – far beyond their share. By way of example, Germany – not to mention the USA – uses seven times more energy per capita than Egypt, fourteen times more aluminium than Argentina, and 130 times more steel than the Philippines.[8] As everyone knows, the Northern use of globally available environmental space is excessive; the style of affluence in the North cannot be generalized around the globe, it is oligarchic in its very structure. The protagonists of the home perspective conclude that those who want more fairness in the world will work towards reducing the 'ecological footprint' which their society leaves on others.

For this way of thinking, the North is called upon to reduce the environmental burden it puts on other countries, and to repay the ecological debt accumulated from the excessive use of the biosphere over decades, indeed centuries. The principal arena for ecological adjustment is thus neither the Southern hemisphere nor the entire globe, but the North itself. It is the reduction of the global effects of the North to the radius of real responsibility that is at the centre of attention, not the extension of Northern responsibility to coincide with the radius of the effects. The home perspective believes in making room for others by an orderly retreat; it proposes a new kind of rationality, which could be called 'the rationality of shortened chains of effect' for meeting the crisis of justice and of nature. Neither the astronaut's perspective nor the fortress perspective shape this perception, but rather the ideal of a good global neighbourhood. It requires a reform of home, out of a cosmopolitan spirit.

EFFICIENCY AND SUFFICIENCY

Yet the reform of home is a major challenge. Level-headed consideration of the necessary reduction in demands made on nature gives rise to doubts about the wisdom of reducing ecology to efficient resource management. For the magnitude of reduction required if nature is to be used in an ecologically sound and internationally just way makes the head spin. According to a current rule of thumb, only a cutback of between 70 and 90 per cent in the throughput of energy and materials in the forty to fifty years ahead would do justice to the seriousness of the situation. Only a daring optimist will believe that such a target could be achieved merely by improvements in efficiency. An efficiency revolution will not be enough.

Therefore the home perspective hesitates to overemphasize efficient resource management, and attempts to focus the social imagination on the revision of goals, rather than on the revision of means. That this caution makes sense is also logically clear. Over the longer term, saving effects are invariably swallowed up by the quantity effects involved, if the overall dynamics of growth are not slowed down. Consider the fuel-efficient car.

Today's automobile engines are definitely more efficient than in the past; yet the relentless growth in the number of cars and miles driven has cancelled out that gain. And the same logic holds across the board, from energy saving to pollution abatement and recycling. What really matters, in fact, is the overall physical scale of the economy with respect to nature, not simply the efficient allocation of resources. Herman Daly has made a telling comparison: even if the cargo on a boat is distributed efficiently, the boat will inevitably sink under too much weight – even though it may sink optimally! Thus efficiency without sufficiency is counter-productive: the latter has to define the boundaries of the former.

A society in balance with nature can, in fact, only be approximated through a twofold approach: through intelligent rationalization of means and prudent moderation of ends. In other words, the 'efficiency revolution' remains directionless if it is not accompanied by a 'sufficiency revolution'. Nothing is ultimately as irrational as rushing with maximum efficiency in the wrong direction. A 'sufficiency revolution', however, can neither be programmed nor engineered; it involves a mixture of subtle and rapid changes in the cultural outlook and the institutional setup of society. Therefore this environmental discourse focuses its attention on values and institutional patterns – in short, on the symbolic universe of society, while both the fortress and the astronaut's perspectives highlight the physical energy processes – in short, the world of material quantities. Obviously, it is here that the home perspective becomes somewhat lofty: its discourse amounts to an invitation, not a strategy.

NEW MODELS OF PROSPERITY

Fortunately for these environmentalists, wealth is no longer what it used to be. Annually, enormous resources of nature and intelligence are invested to increase an already immeasurable economic strength by several per cent. After all, humankind – which essentially means the global consumer classes – has consumed as many goods and services since 1950 as the entire previous period of history.[9] But is it to be taken for granted that an increase in well-being corresponds to an increase in GNP? Meanwhile, there are some indications that industrial societies passed a threshold in the 1970s, after which growth in GNP no longer relates to growth in the quality of life.[10] This is good news for the home perspective, because it encourages these voices to assume that even a shrinking volume of production would not necessarily lead to a shrinking well-being: on the contrary, even a growth in well-being may be imagined.

Given that the negative consequences of economic growth seem to have increased faster than the positive consequences for the last twenty years, the home perspective view counts on the emergence of counter-motives to the growth philosophy of the ever 'faster, farther and more'. Consider, for instance, the energy-intensive urge for acceleration. If pursued thoroughly enough, acceleration demonstrates the unfortunate tendency to cancel itself out. One arrives faster and faster at places at which one stays for ever shorter periods of time. Acceleration shows, beyond a certain level, a counter-productive tendency; it is therefore not so surprising that a renewed interest in slowness is developing beneath the veneer of enforced acceleration. What would an advanced transportation system look like if it were not shaped by the imperative of acceleration? As with time, so with space: after distance-intensive life-styles have become widespread, a new appreciation for one's place and community is now growing. What would politics look like if it centred on the regeneration of places? A similar sensibility might be growing regarding the possession of things. The resource-intensive accumulation of goods, the thousand brands and fashions, increasingly congest everyday life, making it difficult to keep afloat. As a consequence, the ideal of lean consumption becomes more attractive, because a wealth of goods is at odds with a wealth of time. How would things look if they were designed with a view to quality, durability and uniqueness?

Such questions are being raised. All of them reveal a fundamental concern of the home perspective: the search for a society which is capable of remaining on an intermediary level of performance. In other words, a society which is able not to want what it would be capable of providing. Self-limitation always implies a loss of power, even if it is sought in the name of a new prosperity. However, in what way a renunciation of power for the sake of the common good could be reconciled with the question of individual liberty remains the conundrum of the home perspective. At any rate, both the crisis of justice and the crisis of nature suggest looking for forms of prosperity that would not require permanent growth. For the problem of poverty lies not in poverty but in wealth. And, equally, the problem of nature lies not in nature but in overdevelopment. It is likely that Aristotle was well aware of these interconnections when he wrote: 'The greatest crimes are committed not for the sake of necessities, but for the sake of superfluities. Men do not become tyrants in order to avoid exposure to the cold.'[11]

NOTES

1. W. Kuhne, 'Deutschland vor neuen Herausforderungen in den Nord-Sud-Beziehungen', *Aus Politik Und Zeitgeschichte*, Supplement to *Das Parlament*, no. 46, 1991, p. 6.

2. See, for instance, the telling title of Rajni Kothari, *Growing Amnesia: An Essay on Poverty and Human Consciousness*, Penguin, New Delhi, 1993.

3. For an overview of the international discussion, see John McCormick, *Reclaiming Paradise: The Global Environmental Movement*, Indiana University Press, Bloomington, 1989; Hans-Jurgen Harbordt, *Dauerhafte Entwicklung Statt Globaler Selbstzerstorung: Eine Einfuhrung in das Konzept des 'Sustainable Development'*, Berlin, 1991; Peter Moll, *From Scarcity to Sustainability. Future Studies and the Environment: The Role of the Club of Rome*, P. Lang, Frankfurt am Main and New York, 1991.

4. World Commission on Environment and Development, *Our Common Future*, Oxford University Press, Oxford, 1987, p. 8.

5. Paul Ekins, 'Making development sustainable', in Wolfgang Sachs, ed., *Global Ecology: A New Arena of Political Conflict*, Zed Books, London, 1993, p. 91, suggests a similar reading.

6. *Perfil de la Jornada*, Mexico City, 27 January 1994 (author's translation).

7. Yash Tandon synthesizes the experience of peasant movements in sub-Saharan Africa in this way. See his 'Village Contradictions in Africa', in Sachs, ed., *Global Ecology*, p. 221.

8. Raimund Bleischutz and Helmut Schutz, *Unser Trugerischer Wohlstand*, Wuppertal Institut fur Klima, Umwelt, Energie, 1993, p. 5.

9. Alan T. Durning, *How Much Is Enough*?, Earthscan, London, 1992, p. 38.

10. See the discussion on the Index of Sustainable Economic Welfare in Herman E. Daly and John B. Cobb, *For The Common Good*, Beacon Press, Boston, Mass., 1989, pp. 401–55.

11. Aristotle, *Politics*, 1267a.

David Clark, *Basic Communities: Towards an Alternative Society*

This book (published by SPCK, London, 1977) considers different groups and movements trying to build communities under modern conditions. The author gives examples of 'communities of interest' who try to live differently. 'Alternative communities', he says, 'have arisen before in history, given content and form by the era in which they have emerged. What makes those of our generation particularly important is their extent (for the phenomenon is world-wide), their variety (for they have arisen within every sector of society), the ethos and organization of their group life and their steady growth in number and stability, in spite of the fact that the first flush of enthusiasm which characterized the birth of many in the 1960s and early 1970s has long since faded.'

The examples of the present 'communities of interest' described by David Clark are in general limited to Britain, in particular those of a Christian inspiration. 'There has emerged the commune movement trying to discover an alternative to the present shape of the family; those involved in conservation opposed to our squandering of the earth's natural resources; the alternative-technology movement seeking to find a means to small-scale, manageable ways of handling the modern discoveries of science; groups concerned with the full participation of workers in industrial management; those disillusioned with the way we educate people and looking for a new relationship between teacher and student; groups attempting to meet far more adequately the needs of the disadvantaged; those challenging the injustices of a world still at the mercy of arrogance, prejudice, and greed. And there are people, too, searching for a fresh and dynamic spirituality which can give meaning and vitality to lifeless forms of public worship and private prayer.'

M.R.

A most useful annotated list of over 170 basic communities of this type, spread all over the world, is given at the end of the book. As the list stops in the year 1977, the author recommends that persons interested in their development or in the newly established ones consult the periodical *Community* edited by David Clark (Westhill College, Woeley Park Road, Birmingham B29 6LL) or contact the resource centre of magazines and articles about community in Britain, through Joy Hasler, 126 Oak Tree Lane, Selly Oak, Birmingham B29 6HY.

29

BASTA! MEXICAN INDIANS SAY 'ENOUGH!'

Gustavo Esteva

The following text originally appeared in *The Ecologist*, vol. 24, no. 3, May–June 1994.

At midnight on 1 January 1994, NAFTA (the North American Free Trade Agreement between Mexico, the USA and Canada) came into force. Barely two hours later, thousands of Indians armed with machetes, clubs and a few guns occupied four of the main towns in Chiapas, a province on Mexico's southern border with Guatemala, and declared war on the Mexican government. Two dozen policemen and an unknown number of rebels died in the assault. The following day, Mexican President Carlos Salinas dismissed the uprising as the work of 'a local group of professionals of violence, probably foreigners' and launched a massive attack upon the rebels, using tanks, Swiss airplanes, US helicopters and 15,000 troops. Nobody knows the full extent of the violence that followed but there were reports of civilian killings, torture, summary executions and unlawful detentions.

The rebels soon revealed, however, that they were Indians of different ethnic groups calling themselves Ejército Zapatista de Liberación Nacional (EZLN). Rebelling not only against the president and the army, they appealed for an end to 500 years of oppression and 40 years of 'development', expressing the hope that a coalition of political parties would organize free elections and allow the Indians to reclaim their commons and to regenerate their own forms of governance and the 'art of living and of dying'. It was time to say 'Basta! Enough!'...

The Chiapas uprising – and the support given to it throughout the nation – came as a shock to the government. The revolt was not a response to a lack of development – a call for cheaper food, more jobs, more health care and more education – or to poverty or misery. It was a dignified reaction to too much development. It arose because people opted for a more dignified form of dying.

There has been a constant allusion to death in the communiqués of the EZLN. Alluding to the federal army, one of the captains said, 'Let's see who is more ready to die, they or us.' It is not a mere slogan. Expelled from their lands, oppressed by a violent structure of power, with death visiting their children every day, they chose dignity. They knew they were confronting forces infinitely superior and that there was no hope of a military victory. They expected massive and brutal retaliation, killing most of them, perhaps all of them.

Yet this apparently futile gesture caught the imagination of millions of people throughout Mexico. The EZLN was not prepared for such solid support and neither was the government. In the hiatus, a moment arose for dialogue and negotiation and the EZLN seized the opportunity to launch an eloquent and unprecedented attack upon the process of development. Rather than demanding the expansion of the economy, either state-led or market-led, the EZLN wish to expel it from their domain. They are pleading for protection of the 'commons' they have carved out for themselves in response to the crisis of development: ways of living together that limit the economic damage and give room for new forms of social life. Within their traditional forms of governance, they keep alive their own life-support systems based on self-reliance and mutual help, informal networks for direct exchange of goods, services and information, and an administration of justice which calls for compensation more than punishment. They are challenging the social imagination to conceive political controls that allow these post-economic initiatives to develop.

To challenge the rhetoric of development, however, is not easy. Mexico's economic growth, the promise of prosperity tendered by the IMF and the World Bank, the massive investment in modernity as an integral element of the war against poverty – these have been cast as truths beyond question. But the EZLN has dared to question them – it announced to the world that development as a social experiment has failed miserably in Chiapas.

The unexpected support for the EZLN movement lies in the fact that it encapsulates new aspirations. As such, it is hard to categorize. It has no one leader, and its collective leadership of elected representatives from 1,000 communities consciously resists any form of personality cult. It owes little to the classic model of a Marxist guerrilla group since it eschews any political platform or ideology. It is not a fundamentalist or messianic movement: its members come from different Indian peoples, profess different religions, and are explicitly ecumenical. Nor is it a nationalist movement: it shows no desire for Chiapas to become a small state, an indigenous republic, or an 'autonomous' administrative district, in line with the demands of minorities in some other countries. The EZLN refuses to change the nature of the movement by becoming a political party, for example. 'Nothing for us, everything for all' they respond to such proposals.

The movement does, however, owe something to that long tradition of peasant and Indian rebellions that have had such an influence upon Mexico's history: to Pancho Villa, who inspired the EZLN's military strategy, and

Emiliano Zapata, from whom the EZLN take their name and their claim for land and freedom. Villa and Zapata are renowned, not simply for occupying the Presidential Palace at the head of victorious peasant armies in the 1920s, but also for immediately abandoning it as they did not want to seize power and govern Mexico, but only to reclaim the peasant commons. Yet the EZLN is at the same time a contemporary movement, using modern means of communication and adopting a political style and direction that might be termed 'postmodern'. It is born from disillusionment with the ballot box and party-political apathy, and from popular resistance to conventional forms of participation.

The Chiapas uprising signals the efflorescence of a wider movement that until now has been gathering momentum beneath the surface of social awareness both in Mexico and elsewhere. It comprises networks of groups – coalitions of discontent – which share certain characteristics: they are deliberately open and allow for the participation of different ideologies and classes; they distrust leaders and centralized political direction; they consciously avoid any temptation to lead or control the social forces they activate. They opt instead for flexible organizational structures, which they use for concerted action, rather than for channelling demands; they explicitly detach themselves from abstract ideologies, preferring to concentrate on specific campaigns (for example, against a dam, a road, a nuclear plant or the violations of human rights); and they exhaust all democratic means and legal procedures available before resorting to direct action or revolt.

The EZLN has manifested all these traits in its political stance, as have its supporters. For example, when the national government attempted to isolate the EZLN by convening 280 Indian and peasant organizations of Chiapas, the groups responded by publicly adopting the EZLN claims as their own in support of its struggle. Another illustration of conflict being turned around was on the second day of the uprising when the EZLN captured, tried and convicted one of the most hated men in Chiapas, former governor and army general Absalón Castellanos. Many expected that he would be shot as an exemplary punishment. Instead the EZLN sentenced him to work in a community for the rest of his life – and then handed him back to the president in good health. Such tactics are conciliatory rather than divisive and help explain the EZLN's remarkable ability to act as a social nucleus for diverse coalitions of discontents throughout the country whilst at the same time avoiding ideological and political rivalries and sterile polemics.

Almost a year after this article was published, on 1 April 1995, the French newspaper *Le Monde* reproduced a letter from Subcomandante Marcos of the Zapatista movement, from which the following translated excerpts have been taken.

Letter from Subcomandante Marcos, Chiapas, Mexico

Globalization So they talk to us about globalization. And we realize that this is what they call this absurd order, where there is only one country – the country of money. Where the frontiers will disappear, not as a result of brotherhood, but through the haemorrhage that fattens the powerful who have no nation.

Lies, the universal currency Lies have become the universal currency, and, in our country, the dream of happiness and prosperity of a few have been woven out of the nightmares of almost everyone else.

Poverty and wealth We were poor and we covered up our indigence by wealth. The lie was so overwhelming that we ended up by believing it ourselves.

Suffering death and neglect Suffering death is nothing compared with the agony of being forgotten. A country that forgets itself in this way is a sad country. A country that forgets its past cannot have a future.

Paradoxes Look at how things are turning out. In order for people to see us we have masked our faces. So that we are given a name, we have chosen to be anonymous. To have a future, we have put our present in jeopardy; and, in order to live, we are dead.

Women A third of our fighting forces is now composed of women, who have shown their courage and strength through 'convincing' us to accept their laws. They participate on an equal level in the military and civil organization of our struggle and we consider this a good thing.

Laws: To win and to convince We wish to convince, while the government wants to win. We say that a law that must use arms in order to be applied is not worthy of being called a law.

The nation-state and its legality People from the government have come and they have said that legality has been re-established in Chiapas. They came with their bullet-proof vests and tanks, but they did not stay long as they soon got tired of making their speeches in front of chickens, pigs, dogs, cows, horses and a stray cat … The government has also waged war against the other Mexicans. Only, instead of using tanks and planes, they carry out an economic programme which will kill them all the same, but more slowly.

A flower And we would like to say to you all, thank you. We say that we would like to offer you a flower … But with this letter you can make a flower out of paper which you can put in your buttonhole or your hair, whatever is appropriate. That will be charming if you go out and dance … On that note, I leave you, because another plane is arriving and I must extinguish the light – but not the hope!

30

THE QUEST FOR SIMPLICITY: 'MY IDEA OF SWARAJ'

Mahatma Gandhi

Earth provides enough to satisfy every man's needs but not for every man's greed.

I do not believe that multiplication of wants and machinery contrived to supply them is taking the world a single step nearer its goal... I whole-heartedly detest this mad desire to destroy distance and time, to increase animal appetites and go to the ends of the earth in search of their satisfaction. If modern civilization stands for all this, and I have understood it to do so, I call it Satanic.

It is a theft for me to take any fruit that I do not need, or to take it in a larger quantity than is necessary. We are not always aware of our real needs, and most of us improperly multiply our wants and thus unconsciously make thieves of ourselves.

True economics is the economics of justice. People will be happy in so far as they learn to do justice and be righteous. All else is not only vain but leads straight to destruction. To teach the people to get rich by hook or by crook is to do them an immense injustice.

My idea of the village *swaraj* is that it is a complete republic, independent of its neighbours for its vital wants and yet interdependent for many others in which dependency is a necessity... In a structure composed of innumerable villages ... life will not be a pyramid with the apex sustained by the bottom, but it will be an oceanic cycle whose centre will be the individual... The outmost circumsphere will not wield power to crush the inner circle but will give strength to all within and derive its own strength from it.

You must not imagine that I am envisaging our village life as it is today. The village of my dream is still in my mind. After all, every man lives in the world of his dreams. My ideal village will contain intelligent human beings.

They will not live in dirt and darkness as animals. Men and women will be free and able to hold their own against anyone in the world. There will be neither plague, nor cholera, nor smallpox; no one will be idle, no one will wallow in luxury. Everyone will have to contribute his quota of manual labour. It is possible to envisage railways, post and telegraph … and the like…

What I object to is the craze for machinery, not machinery as such. The craze is for what they call labour-saving machinery. Men go on 'saving labour' till thousands are without work and thrown on the open streets to die of starvation. I want to save time and labour, not for a fraction of mankind, but for all. I want the concentration of wealth, not in the hands of a few, but in the hands of all. Today, machinery merely helps a few to ride on the backs of millions. The impetus behind it all is not the philanthropy to save labour, but greed. It is against this constitution of things that I am fighting with all my might.

The end to be sought is human happiness combined with full mental and moral growth. I use the adjective moral as synonymous with spiritual. This end can be achieved under decentralization. Centralization as a system is inconsistent with a non-violent structure of society.

31

THE SEARCHERS AFTER THE SIMPLE LIFE

David E. Shi

The following text is extracted from *The Simple Life: Plain Living and High Thinking in American Culture* (Oxford University Press, New York and Oxford, 1986, pp. 3–36). The author explains how he has treated the simple life both as a sentimental ideal and as an actual way of living, revealing in the process the personal implications for many of those who have tried to live that way.

DAVID E. SHI is President of Furman University, Greenville, South Carolina. His other publications include *Facing Facts: Realism in American Thought and Culture, 1850–1920*, Oxford University Press, New York, 1995.

The precise meaning of the simple life has never been fixed. Rather, it has always represented a shifting cluster of ideas, sentiments and riches, a reverence for nature and a preference for rural over urban ways of life and work, a desire for personal self-reliance through frugality and diligence, a nostalgia for the past and a scepticism towards the claims of modernity, conscientious rather than conspicuous consumption, and an aesthetic taste for the plain and functional. Over the years, individuals and groups have varied in the emphasis placed on these attitudes. As a result, there have been, and still are, many *forms* of simple living representing a wide spectrum of motives and methods. Their common denominator has been the core assumption that the making of money and the accumulation of things should not be allowed to smother the purity of the soul, the life of the mind, the cohesion of the family, or the good of the commonweal. As I have employed the concept, therefore, the simple life represents an approach to living that self-consciously subordinates the material to the ideal.

Of course, such a philosophy of living is by no means distinctively American. The primacy of the spiritual or intellectual life has been a central emphasis of most of the world's major religions and philosophies. The great spiritual teachers of the East – Zarathustra, Buddha, Lao-Tse and Confucius – all stressed that material self-control was essential to the good life, and many Americans, particularly Thoreau and the 'hippies' of the 1960s, drew much of their inspiration for simple living from its Oriental tradition. By far, however, the most important historical influence on American simplicity has been the combined heritage of Greco-Roman culture and Judeo-Christian ethics. Most Greek and Roman philosophers were emphatic in their praise of simple living, as were the Hebrew prophets and Jesus.

Socrates was among the first to argue that ideas should take priority over things in the calculus of life. 'Men are to be esteemed for their virtue, not their wealth', he insisted. 'Fine and rich clothes are suited for comedians. The wicked live to eat; the good eat to live.' Socrates advocated a golden mean between poverty and wealth, and so, too, did his famous pupil Plato. But it was in Aristotle's writings that this classical concept of leading a carefully balanced life of material moderation and intellectual exertion was most fully articulated. 'The man who indulges in every pleasure and abstains from none', Aristotle observed, 'becomes self-indulgent, while the man who shuns every pleasure, as boors do, becomes in a way insensible: temperance and courage, then, are destroyed by excess and defect, and preserved by the mean.'

A similar theme of simple living coupled with spiritual devotion runs through the Old Testament, from the living habits of tent dwellers of Abraham's time to the strictures of the major and minor prophets against the evils of luxury – in terms both of material excess and of excessive sophistication in thought. As the author of Proverbs prayed, 'Give me neither poverty nor wealth, but only enough.' Likewise, the career of Jesus represented, from start to finish, a protest against Greek sophistication and luxury. Jesus repeatedly warned of the 'deceitfulness of riches', noting that superfluous wealth too easily led to hardness of heart toward one's fellows and deadness of heart toward God. Experience had shown, he argued, that it was 'easier for a camel to go through the eye of a needle than for a rich man to enter into the kingdom of God'. Jesus therefore urged his followers to seek their 'treasures in heaven' rather than on Earth.

So much for the ideal. In practice the simple life prescribed in classical philosophy and early Christian thought has proven far more complex, protean and volatile than such summary descriptions imply. The necessarily ambiguous quality of a philosophy of living that does not specify exactly how austere one's mode of living should be has produced a welter of different practices, several of which have conflicted with one another. The same self-denying impulse that has motivated some to engage in temperate frugality has often led others to adopt ascetic or primitive ways. During the classical period, for instance, there were many types of simple living, including the affluent temperance of the Stoics, Cicero, Seneca and Marcus Aurelius; the more modest 'golden mean' of Socrates, Plato, and Aristotle; the ascetic primitivism of Diogenes, and the pastoral simplicity of Virgil and Horace. An equally wide spectrum of practices developed among early Christians. In asserting the superiority of spiritual over worldly concerns, some gave away all of their possessions and went to the desert to live as hermits. Others joined monasteries and a few engaged in prolonged stints of abstinence and mortification. Yet, at the same time, many officials of the early Catholic Church preached Christian simplicity while themselves living in considerable comfort and even luxury.

Since ancient times similarly diverse versions of the simple life have been practised by poets and priests, businessmen and philosophers, monarchs and scientists. Simplicity has been an especially salient theme in Western literature. Chaucer repeatedly reminded readers of Christ's life of voluntary simplicity. Boccaccio took cheer in an open-air search for the spontaneous; Dante called upon his readers to 'see the king of the simple life'; and Shakespeare offered the happiness of the greenwood tree. The Romantics of the eighteenth and nineteenth centuries likewise promoted a simplicity modelled after the serene workings of nature.

...There have been many through the centuries who have practised simplicity rather than played at it. The names of St Francis, Thomas More, John Milton, William Blake, Blaise Pascal, John Wesley, Prince Kropotkin, Leo Tolstoy, Albert Schweitzer, Toyohiko Kagawa, Mahatma Gandhi, E.F. Schumacher and Mother Teresa come readily to mind. For them, simplicity frequently entailed what the English poet William Wordsworth called 'plain living and high thinking'. The degree of plainness differed considerably from individual to individual, as did the nature of the 'high thinking'. They simplified their lives in order to engage in a variety of enriching pursuits: philosophy, religious devotion, artistic creation, revolutionary politics, humanitarian service, or ecological activism.

American practitioners of simple living have displayed a similar diversity in putting the ideal into practice. Simplicity has been advocated for both religious and secular reasons. In addition, class biases, individual personality traits and historical circumstances have combined to produce many differing versions of the simple life in American culture. Several enthusiasts have been quite affluent, a few have been almost primitive. Some have espoused the simple life as a conservative, even reactionary, instrument of social control, finding in it an ideological means of preserving the status quo by impressing upon the masses the virtues of hard work, social stability and personal contentment. Others have viewed simple living as an explicit rejection of the prevailing social and economic order or as a refreshing therapeutic or recreational alternative to the hedonistic demands of the consumer culture. In addition, some proponents have felt the need to withdraw from the larger society, while others have tried their best to sustain their personal ethic in the midst of a tempting and complex world...

...The simple life has been both a myth of social aspiration and a guide for individual living. In both respects it has experienced frustrating failures. Yet it has displayed considerable resiliency over the years. Like the family, simplicity is always said to be declining but never disappears. No sooner do advocates in one era declare it dead than members of the next proclaim its revival.

32

THE INFRAPOLITICS OF SUBORDINATE GROUPS

James C. Scott

The following text is an abridged version of Chapter 7 of *Domination and the Arts of Resistance: Hidden Transcripts* (Yale University Press, New Haven, Conn. and London, 1990), a book that studies power relations from the viewpoint of subordinate groups in society. Yet, asks the author, can we make such studies when the powerless often have to adopt a strategic pose in the presence of the powerful, while the latter may overdramatize their own mastery? James Scott is therefore interested in a different approach to the study of power relations, one which uncovers the contradictions and tensions – and their immanent possibilities. For this purpose he makes a comparison between the 'hidden transcript' through which subordinate groups express a critique of the powerful, with the 'public transcript' of the powerful, the dominant forces in society. He shows how such comparisons can lead to substantially new ways of understanding resistance to domination. As he says, the hidden transcript is often expressed openly, although in a disguised form.

> I suggest, along these lines, how we might interpret the rumours, gossip, folktales, songs, gestures, jokes and theatre of the powerless as vehicles by which, among other things, they insinuate a critique of power while hiding behind anonymity or behind innocuous understandings of their conduct. These patterns of disguising ideological insubordination are somewhat analogous to the patterns by which, in my experience, peasants and slaves have disguised their efforts to thwart material appropriation of their labour, their production and their property: for example, poaching, foot-dragging, pilfering, dissimulation, flight. Together, these forms of insubordination might suitably be called the infrapolitics of the powerless.

Mrs Poyser, to whom there is reference in this chapter, first appears in Chapter 1. The author uses an episode from George Eliot's *Adam Bede*, in which Mrs Poyser, wife of a tenant farmer, after suffering a series of impositions and threats from the landlord, Squire Donnithorne, ends up by openly defying him, expressing the feelings of many others in the parish. In this way, the hidden transcript becomes a public one, with all the risk that this entails for her and her husband.

JAMES C. SCOTT is the Eugene Meyer Professor of Political Science and chairman of the Council of Southeast Asia Studies at Yale University. His major books are *The Moral Economy of the Peasant* (Yale University Press, New Haven, Conn., 1976), *Weapons of the Weak: Everyday Forms of Peasant Resistance* (Yale University Press, New Haven, Conn., 1987), and *Domination and the Arts of Resistance* (Yale University Press, New Haven, Conn., 1990).

> The cultural forms may not say what they know, nor know what they say, but they mean what they do – at least in the logic of their praxis.
>
> Paul Willis, *Learning to Labour*

> [The supervision of gleaning] exasperated morale to the limit; but there is such a void between the class which was angered and the class that was threatened, that words never made it across; one only knew what happened from the results; [that peasants] worked underground the way moles do.
>
> Honoré de Balzac, *Les Paysans*

In a social science already rife – some might say crawling – with neologisms, one hesitates to contribute another. The term *infrapolitics*, however, seems an appropriate shorthand to convey the idea that we are dealing with an unobtrusive realm of political struggle. For a social science attuned to the relatively open politics of liberal democracies and to loud, headline-grabbing protests, demonstrations and rebellions, the circumspect struggle waged daily by subordinate groups is, like infrared rays, beyond the visible end of the spectrum. That it should be invisible ... is in large part by design – a tactical choice born of a prudent awareness of the balance of power....

The term *infrapolitics* is, I think, appropriate in another way. When we speak of the infrastructure for commerce we have in mind the facilities that make such commerce possible: for example, transport, banking currency, property and contract law. In the same fashion, I mean to suggest that the infrapolitics we have examined provides much of the cultural and structural underpinning of the more visible political action on which our attention has generally been focused. The bulk of this chapter is devoted to sustaining this claim.

First, I return briefly to the widely held position that the offstage discourse of the powerless is either empty posturing or, worse, a substitute for real resistance. After noting some of the logical difficulties with this line of reasoning, I try to show how material and symbolic resistance are part of the same set of mutually sustaining practices. This requires re-emphasizing that the relationship between dominant elites and subordinates is, whatever else it might be, very much of a material struggle in which both sides are continually probing for weaknesses and exploiting small advantages. By way of recapitulating some of the argument, I finally try to show how each realm of open resistance to domination is shadowed by an infrapolitical twin sister who aims at the same strategic goals but whose low profile is better adapted to resisting an opponent who could probably win any open confrontation.

THE HIDDEN TRANSCRIPT AS POSING?

A sceptic might very well accept much of the argument thus far and yet minimize its significance for political life. Isn't much of what is called the hidden transcript, even when it is insinuated into the public transcript, a matter of hollow posing that is rarely acted out in earnest? This view of the safe expression of aggression against a dominant figure is that it serves as a substitute – albeit a second-best substitute – for the real thing: direct aggression. At best, it is of little or no consequence; at worst it is an evasion. The prisoners who spend their time dreaming about life on the outside might instead be digging a tunnel; the slaves who sing of liberation and freedom might instead take to their heels. As Barrington Moore writes, 'Even fantasies of liberation and revenge can help to preserve domination through dissipating collective energies in relatively harmless rhetoric and ritual.'[1]

The case for the hydraulic interpretation of fighting words in a safe place is, as we have noted, perhaps strongest when those fighting words seem largely orchestrated or stage-managed by dominant groups. Carnival and other ritualized, and hence ordinarily contained, rites of reversal are the most obvious examples. Until recently, the dominant interpretation of ritualized aggression or reversal was that, by acting to relieve the tensions engendered by hierarchical social relations, it served to reinforce the status quo. Figures as diverse as Hegel and Trotsky saw such ceremonies as conservative forces....

Perhaps the most interesting thing about the safety-valve theories in their many guises is the most easily overlooked. They all begin with the common assumption that systematic subordination generates pressure of some kind from below. They assume further that, if nothing is done to relieve this pressure, it builds up and eventually produces an explosion of some kind. Precisely how this pressure is generated and what it consists of is rarely specified. For those who live such subordination, whether Frederick Douglass [a slave in the antebellum US South – ed.] or the fictional Mrs Poyser, the pressure is a taken-for-granted consequence of the frustration and anger of being unable to strike back (physically or verbally) against a powerful oppressor. That pressure generated by a perceived but unrequited injustice finds expression, we have argued, in the hidden transcript – its size, its virulence, its symbolic luxuriance. In other words, the safety-valve view implicitly accepts some key elements of our larger arguments about the hidden transcript: that systematic subordination elicits a reaction and that this reaction involves a desire to strike or speak back to the dominant. Where they differ is in supposing that this desire can be substantially satisfied, whether in backstage talk, in supervised rituals of reversal, or in festivities that occasionally cool the fires of resentment.

The logic of the safety-valve perspective depends on the social psychological proposition that the safe expression of aggression in joint fantasy, rituals or folktales yields as much, or nearly as much, satisfaction (hence, a reduction in pressure) as direct aggression against the object of frustration. Evidence on this point from social psychology is not altogether conclusive, but the preponderance of findings does not support this logic. Instead, such findings suggest that experimental subjects who are thwarted unjustly experience little or no reduction in the level of their frustration and anger unless they are able to injure directly the frustrating agent.[2] Such findings are hardly astonishing. One would expect retaliation that actually affected the agent of injustice to provide far more in the way of catharsis than forms of aggression that left the source of anger untouched. And, of course, there is much experimental evidence that aggressive play and fantasy increase rather than decrease the likelihood of actual aggression. Mrs Poyser felt greatly relieved when she vented her spleen directly to the squire, but presumably was not relieved – or not sufficiently – by her rehearsed speeches and the oaths sworn behind his back. There is, then, as much, if not more, reason to consider Mrs Poyser's offstage anger as a preparation for her eventual outburst than to see it as a satisfactory alternative.

If the social-psychological evidence provides little or no support for catharsis through displacement, the historical case for such an argument has yet to be made. Would it be possible to show that, other things being equal, dominant elites who provided or allowed more outlets for comparatively harmless aggression against themselves were thereby less liable to violence and rebellion from a subordinate group? If such a comparison were undertaken, its first task would be to distinguish between the effect of displaced aggression *per se* and the rather more material concessions of food, drink, charity and relief from work and discipline embedded in such festivities. In other words the 'bread and circuses' that, on good evidence, are often political concessions *won* by subordinate classes may have an ameliorating effect on oppression quite apart from ritualized aggression.[3] An argument along these lines would also have to explain an important anomaly. If, in fact, ritualized aggression displaces real aggression from its obvious target, why then have so many revolts by slaves, peasants and serfs begun precisely during such seasonal rituals (for example, the carnival described by Le Roy Ladurie) designed to prevent their occurrence?[4]

THE HIDDEN TRANSCRIPT AS PRACTICE

The greatest shortcoming of the safety-valve position is that it embodies a fundamental idealist fallacy. The argument that offstage or veiled forms of aggression offer a harmless catharsis that helps preserve the status quo assumes that we are examining a rather abstract debate in which one side is handicapped rather than a concrete material struggle. But relations between masters and slaves, between Brahmins and untouchables, are not simply a clash of ideas about dignity and the right to rule; they are a process of subordination firmly anchored in material practices. Virtually every instance of personal domination is intimately connected with a process of appropriation. Dominant elites extract material taxes in the form of labour, grain, cash and service, in addition to extracting symbolic taxes in the form of deference, demeanour, posture, verbal formulas and acts of humility. In actual practice, of course, the two are joined inasmuch as every public act of appropriation is, figuratively, a ritual of subordination.

The bond between domination and appropriation means that it is impossible to separate the ideas and symbolism of subordination from a process of material exploitation. In exactly the same fashion, it is impossible to separate veiled symbolic resistance to the ideas of domination from the practical struggles to thwart or mitigate exploitation. Resistance, like domination, fights a war on two fronts. The hidden transcript is now just behind-the-scenes griping and grumbling; it is enacted in a host of down-to-earth, low-profile stratagems designed to minimize appropriation. In the case of slaves, for example, these stratagems have typically included theft, pilfering, feigned ignorance, shirking or careless labour, foot-dragging, secret trade and production for sale, sabotage of crops, livestock and machinery, arson, flight, and so on. In the case of peasants, poaching, squatting, illegal gleaning, delivery of inferior rents in kind, clearing clandestine fields and defaults on feudal dues have been common stratagems.

To take the question of slave pilfering as an illustration, how can we tell what meaning this practice had for slaves?[5] Was the taking of grain, chickens, hogs and so on a mere response to hunger pangs; was it done for the pleasure of adventure,[6] or was it meant to chasten hated masters or overseers? It could be any of these and more. Publicly, of course, the master's definition of *theft* prevailed. We know enough, however, to surmise that, behind the scenes, theft was seen as simply taking back the product of one's labour. We also know that the semiclandestine culture of the slaves encouraged and celebrated theft from the masters and morally reproved any slave who would dare expose such a theft: '(To) steal and not be detected is a merit among [slaves] … And the vice which they hold in the greatest abhorrence is that of telling upon one another.'[7] Our point is not the obvious one that behaviours are impenetrable until given meaning by human actors. Rather, the point is that the discourse of the hidden transcript does not merely shed light on behaviour or explain it; it helps constitute that behaviour.…

A penetrating study of forest poaching in early eighteenth-century England and the draconian death penalties enacted to curb it reveals the … link between a sense of popular justice that cannot be openly claimed and a host of practices devised to exercise those rights in clandestine ways.[8] In this period, the titled owners of estates and the Crown began in earnest to restrict local customary rights to forest pasturage, hunting, trapping, fishing, turf and heath cutting, fuel wood gathering, thatch cutting, lime burning and quarrying on what they now insisted was exclusively their property. That yeomen, cottagers and labourers considered this breach of customary law to be an injustice is abundantly clear. Thompson can thus write of yeomen with a 'tenacious tradition of memories as to rights and customs … and a sense that they and not the rich interlopers, owned the forest.'[9] The term *outlaws* as applied to those who continued to exercise these now-proscribed rights has a strange ring when we recall that they were certainly acting within the norms and hence with the support of most of their community.

And yet, we have no direct access to the hidden transcript of cottagers as they prepared their traps or shared a rabbit stew. And of course there were no public protests and open declarations of ancient forest rights in a political environment in which all the cards were stacked against the villagers in any sustained, open confrontation. At this level we encounter almost total silence – the plebeian voice is mute. Where it does speak, however, is in everyday forms of resistance in the increasingly massive and aggressive assertion of these rights, often at night and in disguise. Since a legal or political confrontation over property rights in the forest would avail them little and risk much, they chose instead to exercise their rights piecemeal and quietly – to take in fact the property rights they were denied in law. The contrast between public quiescence and clandestine defiance was not lost on contemporary authorities, one of whom, Bishop Trelawny, spoke of 'a pestilent pernicious people … such as take oaths to the government, but underhand … labour its subversion'.[10]

Popular poaching on such a vast scale could hardly be mounted without a lively backstage transcript of values, understandings, and popular outrage to sustain it. But that hidden transcript must largely be inferred from practice – a quiet practice at that. Once in a while an event indicates something of what might lie beneath the surface of public discourse: for example, a threatening anonymous letter to a gamekeeper when he continued to abridge popular custom, or the fact that the prosecution couldn't find anyone within a radius of five miles to testify against a local blacksmith accused of breaking down a dam recently built to create a fish pond. More rarely still, when there was nothing further to lose by a public declaration of rights, the normative content of the hidden transcript might spring to view. Thus two convicted 'deer-steals', shortly to be hanged, ventured to claim that 'deer were wild beasts and that the poor, as well as the rich, might lawfully use them.'[11]

The point of this brief discussion of poaching is that any argument which assumes that disguised ideological dissent or aggression operates as a safety-valve to weaken 'real' resistance ignores the paramount fact that such ideological dissent is virtually always expressed in practices that aim at an unobtrusive renegotiation of power relations. The yeomen and cottagers in question were not simply making an abstract, emotionally satisfying backstage case for what they took to be their property rights; they were out in the forests day after day exercising those rights as best they could. There is an important dialectic here between the hidden transcript and practical resistance.[12] The hidden transcript of customary rights and outrage *is* a source of popular poaching providing that we realize, at the same time, that the practical struggle in the forests is also the source for a backstage discourse of customs, heroism, revenge and justice. If the backstage talk is a source of satisfaction, it is so in large part owing to practical gains in the daily conflict over the forests. Any other formulation would entail an inadmissible wall between what people think and say, on the one hand, and what they do, on the other.

Far from being a relief-valve taking the place of actual resistance, the discursive practices offstage sustain resistance in the same way in which the informal peer pressure of factory workers discourages any individual worker from exceeding work norms and becoming a rate-buster. The subordinate moves back and forth, as it were, between two worlds: the world of the master and the offstage world of subordinates. Both of these worlds have sanctioning power. While subordinates normally can monitor the public transcript performance of other subordinates, the dominant can rarely monitor fully the hidden transcript. This means that any subordinate who seeks privilege by ingratiating himself to his superior will have to answer for that contact once he returns to the world of his peers. In situations of systematic subordination such sanctions may go well beyond scolding and insult to physical coërcion, as in the beating of an informer by prisoners. Social pressure among peers, however, is by itself a powerful weapon of subordinates. Industrial sociologists discovered very early that the censure of workmates often prevailed over the desire for greater income or promotion. We can, in this respect, view the social side of the hidden transcript as a political domain striving to enforce, against great odds, certain forms of conduct and resistance in relation with the dominant. *It would be more accurate, in short, to think of the hidden transcript as a condition of practical resistance rather than a substitute for it.*

One might argue perhaps that even such practical resistance, like the discourse it reflects and that sustains it, amounts to nothing more than trivial copying mechanisms that cannot materially affect the overall situation of domination. This is no more real resistance, the argument might go, than veiled symbolic opposition is real ideological dissent. At one level this is perfectly true but irrelevant since our point is that these are the forms that political struggle takes when frontal assaults are precluded by the realities of power. At another level it is well to recall that the aggregation of thousands upon thousands of such 'petty' acts of resistance have dramatic economic and political effects. In production, whether on the factory floor or the plantation, it can result in performances that are not bad enough to provoke punishment but not good enough to allow the enterprise to succeed. Repeated on a massive scale, such conduct allowed Djilas to write that 'slow, unproductive work of disinterested millions … is the calculable, invisible and gigantic waste which no communist regime has been able to avoid.'[13] Poaching and squatting on a large scale can restructure the control of property. Peasant tax evasion on a large scale has brought about crises of appropriation that threaten the state. Massive desertion by serf or peasant conscripts has helped bring down more than one *ancien régime*. Under the appropriate conditions, the accumulation of petty acts can, rather like snowflakes on a steep mountainside, set off an avalanche.[14]

TESTING THE LIMITS

> In any stratified society there is a set of limits on what … dominant and subordinate groups can do … What takes place, however, is a kind of continual probing to find out what they can get away with and discover the limits of obedience and disobedience.
>
> Barrington Moore, Jr, *Injustice: The Social Basis of Obedience and Revolt*

Rarely can we speak of an individual slave, untouchable, serf, peasant or worker, let alone groups of them, as being either entirely submissive or entirely insubordinate. Under what conditions, however, do veiled ideological opposition and unobtrusive material resistance dare to venture forth and speak their name openly? Conversely, how is open resistance forced into increasingly furtive and clandestine expression?

The metaphor that promises to serve us best in understanding this process is that of guerrilla warfare. Within relations of domination, as in guerrilla warfare, there is an understanding on both sides about the relative strength and capacities of the antagonist and therefore about what the likely response to an aggressive move might be. What is most important for our purposes, though, is that the actual balance of forces is never precisely known, and estimates about what it might be are largely inferred from the outcomes of previous probes and encounters. Assuming, as we must, that both sides hope to prevail, there is likely to be a constant testing of the equilibrium. One side advances a salient to see if it survives or is attacked and, if so, in what strength. It is in this no-man's-land of feints, small attacks, probings to find weaknesses, and not in the rare frontal assault, that the ordinary battlefield lies. Advances that succeed – whether against opposition or without challenge – are likely to lead to more numerous and more aggressive advances unless they meet with a decisive riposte. The limits of the possible are encountered only in an empirical process of search and probing.[15]

The dynamic of this process, it should be clear, holds only in those situations in which it is assumed that most subordinates conform and obey

The Rebellion of the Chorus

What is happening now is that daily life is beginning to rebel. This does not take the form of epic events, like the storming of the Bastille or the assault on the Winter Palace, but manifests itself in less spectacular ways – though also more frequently.

The chorus is now talking out of turn: while maintaining its own identity, it is moving out of the place that was assigned to it. The symbol *par excellence* of this rebellion is the women's liberation movement, precisely because women have always represented the quintessence of everyday life. Men who have fought for their people or acted as their political representatives are now being taken by surprise because their womenfolk are saying that their work in washing dirty clothes and bringing up children can no longer be taken for granted. But the disorder in the libretto is even more general: the ethnic minorities, the old, the homeless, the handicapped, the homosexuals, the marginalized, the young – above all the young – are also violating the rituals of discretion and good manners. They are putting themselves at the centre of the stage and demanding to be heard.

José Nun, *La Rebelión del Coro: estudios sobre la racionalidad política y el sentido común*, Nueva Visión, Buenos Aires, 1989. Translated by V.B.

not because they have internalized the norms of the dominant, but because a structure of surveillance, reward and punishment makes it prudent for them to comply. It assumes, in other words, a basic antagonism of goals between dominant and subordinates that is held in check by relations of discipline and punishment. We may, I believe, routinely suppose this assumption holds in slavery, serfdom, caste domination and in those peasant–landlord relations in which appropriation and status degradation are joined. Such assumptions may also hold in certain institutional settings between wardens and prisoners, staff and mental patients, teachers and students, bosses and workers.[16]...

While the pressure driving everyday resistance varies with the needs of subordinate groups, it is rarely likely to disappear altogether. The point is that any weakness in surveillance and enforcement is likely to be quickly exploited; any ground left undefended is likely to be ground lost. Nowhere is this pattern more evident that in the case of repetitive appropriations such as rents or taxes. Le Roy Ladurie and others, for example, have charted the fortunes of tithe collections (in principle, one-tenth of the grain harvest of cultivators) over nearly four centuries.[17] Because it was so rarely devoted to the local religious and charitable purposes for which it was originally intended, the tithe was bitterly resented. Resistance, however, was less to be found in the open protests, petitions, riots and revolts that did occasionally erupt but rather in a quiet but massive pattern of evasion. Peasants secretly harvested grain before the tithe collector arrived, opened unregistered fields, interplanted titheable and non-titheable crops, and took a variety of measures to ensure that the grain taken by the titheman was inferior and less than one-tenth of the crop. The pressure was constant, but at those rare moments when enforcement was lax the peasantry would take quick advantage of the opportunity. When a war stripped a province of its local garrison, tithe collections would plummet; full advantage would be taken of a new tithe collector, unfamiliar with all the techniques of evasion. The most dramatic example of exploiting the openings available came with the redemption payments accorded the clergy just after the French Revolution in order to phase out the tithe gradually. Sensing the political opening and the inability of the revolutionary government to enforce the payments, the peasantry so effectively evaded payment as to abolish the tithe forthwith.[18]

Ideological and symbolic dissent follows much the same pattern. Metaphorically we can say, I believe, that the hidden transcript is continually pressing against the limit of what is permitted on stage, much as a body of water might press against a dam. The amount of pressure naturally varies with the degree of shared anger and indignation experienced by subordinates. Behind the pressure is the desire to give unbridled expression to the sentiments voiced in the hidden transcript directly to the dominant. Short of an outright rupture, the process by which the limit is tested involves, say, a particularly intrepid, angry, risk-taking, unguarded subordinate gesturing or saying something that slightly breaches that limit. If this act of insubordination (disrespect, cheek) is not rebuked or punished, others will exploit that breach and a new, *de facto* limit governing what may be said will have been established incorporating the new territory. A small success is likely to encourage others to venture further and the process can escalate rapidly. Conversely, the dominant may also breach the limit and move it in the opposite direction, suppressing previously tolerated public gestures.[19]

Ranajit Guha has argued convincingly that open acts of desacralization and disrespect are often the first sign of actual rebellion.[20] Even seemingly small acts – for example, lower castes wearing turbans and shoes, a refusal to bow or give the appropriate salutation, a truculent look, a defiant posture – signal a public breaking of the ritual of subordination. So long as the elite treat such assaults on their dignity as tantamount to open rebellion, symbolic defiance and rebellion do amount to the same thing.

The logic of symbolic defiance is thus strikingly similar to the logic of everyday forms of resistance. Ordinarily they are, by prudent design, unobtrusive and veiled, disowning, as it were, any public defiance of the material or symbolic order. When, however, the pressure rises or when there are weaknesses in the 'retaining wall' holding it back, poaching is likely to escalate into land invasions, tithe evasions into open refusals to pay, and rumours and

Resisting with Laughter and Silence

Laughter, meaningful silences, humour and the African's art of ridiculing political personalities are forms of struggle that currently show there is neither unawareness nor resignation. To this must be added the power of secrecy. Many Africans operate under cover of secret societies, even in politics. They carry on the struggle using every aspect of their culture. This is true of various Third World countries.

Jean-Marc Ela, as quoted by Thierry G. Verhelst, in *No Life Without Roots: Culture and Development*, trans. Bob Cumming, Zed Books, London, 1987.

jokes into public insult. Thus, the offstage contempt for the Spanish church hierarchy that was, before the Civil War, confined to veiled gossip and humour, took, at the outset of the war, the more dramatic form of the public exhumation of the remains of archbishops and prioresses from the crypts of cathedrals, which were then dumped unceremoniously on the front steps.[21] *The process by which Aesopian language may give way to direct vituperation is very much like the process by which everyday forms of resistance give way to overt, collective defiance.*

The logic of the constant testing of the limits alerts us to the importance, from the dominant point of view, of making an example of someone. Just as a public breach in the limits is a provocation to others to trespass in the same fashion, so the decisive assertion of symbolic territory by public retribution discourages others from venturing public defiance. One deserter shot, one assertive slave whipped, one unruly student rebuked: these acts are meant as public events for an audience of subordinates. They are intended as a kind of pre-emptive strike to nip in the bud any further challenges to the existing frontier (as the French say, *pour decourages les autres*) or perhaps to take new territory.

Finally, a clear view of the 'micro' pushing and shoving involved in power relations, and particularly power relations in which appropriation and permanent subordination are central, makes any static view of naturalization and legitimation untenable. A dominant elite under such conditions is ceaselessly working to maintain and extend its material control and symbolic reach. A subordinate group is correspondingly devising strategies to thwart and reverse that appropriation and to take more symbolic liberties as well. The material pressure against the process of appropriation is, for slaves and serfs, nearly a physical necessity, and the desire to talk back has its own compelling logic. No victory is won for good on this terrain: hardly has the dust cleared before the probing to regain lost territory is likely to begin. The naturalization of domination is always being put to the test in small but significant ways, particularly at the point where power is applied.[22]

Domination and Resistance

	Material domination	*Status domination*	*Ideological domination*
Practices of domination	Appropriation of grain, taxes, labour, etc.	Humiliation, disprivilege, insults, assaults on dignity	Justification by ruling groups for slavery, serfdom, caste, privilege
Forms of public declared resistance	Petitions, demonstrations, boycotts, strikes, land invasions and open revolts	Public assertion of worth by gesture and/or open desecration of status symbols of the dominant	Public counter-ideologies propagating equality, revolution, or negating the ruling ideology
Forms of disguised, low-profile, undeclared resistance: infrapolitics	Everyday forms of resistance, e.g. poaching, squatting, desertion, foot-dragging. Direct resistance by disguised resisters, e.g. masked appropriations, threats, anonymous threats	Hidden transcript of anger, aggression and disguised discourses of dignity, e.g. rituals of aggression, tales of revenge, use of carnival symbolism, gossip, rumour, creation of autonomous social space for assertion of dignity	Development of dissident sub-cultures, e.g. millennial religions, slave 'hush-arbors', folk religion, myths of social banditry and class heroes, world-upside-down imagery, myths of the 'good' king or the time before the 'Norman Yoke'

RESISTANCE BELOW THE LINE

We are now in a position to summarize a portion of the argument. Until quite recently, much of the active political life of subordinate groups has been ignored because it takes place at a level we rarely recognize as political. To emphasize the enormity of what has been, by and large, disregarded, I want to distinguish between the open, declared forms of resistance, which attract most attention, and the disguised, low-profile, undeclared resistance that constitutes the domain of infrapolitics (see Table above). For contemporary liberal democracies in the West, an exclusive concern for open political action *will* capture much that is significant in political life. The historic achievement of political liberties of speech and association has appreciably lowered the risks and difficulty of open political expression. Not so long ago in the West, however, and even today for many of the least privileged minorities and marginalized poor, open political action will hardly capture the bulk of political life. Nor will an exclusive attention to declared resistance help us understand the process by which new political forces and demands germinate before they burst on the scene. How, for example, could we understand the open break represented by the Civil Rights Movement or the Black Power Movement in the 1960s without understanding the offstage discourse among black students, clergymen, and their parishioners?

Taking a long historical view, one sees that the luxury of relatively safe, open political opposition is both rare and recent. The vast majority of people have been and continue to be not citizens, but subjects. So long as we confine our conception of *the political* to activity that is openly declared we are driven to conclude that subordinate groups essentially lack a political life, or that what political life they do have is restricted to those exceptional moments of popular explosion. To do so is to miss the immense political terrain that lies between quiescence and revolt, and that, for better or worse, is the political environment of subject classes. It is to focus on the visible coastline of politics and miss the continent that lies beyond.

Each of the forms of disguised resistance, of infrapolitics, is the silent partner of a loud form of public resistance. Thus, piecemeal squatting is the infrapolitical equivalent of an open land invasion: both are aimed at resisting the appropriation of land. The former cannot openly avow its goals and is a strategy well suited to subjects who have no political rights. Thus, rumour and folktales of revenge are the infrapolitical equivalent of open gestures of contempt and desecration: both are aimed at resisting the denial of standing or dignity to subordinate groups. The former cannot act directly and affirm its intention and is thus a symbolic strategy also well suited to subjects with no political rights. Finally, millennial imagery and the symbolic reversals of folk religion are the infrapolitical equivalents of public, radical, counter-ideologies: both are aimed at negating the public symbolism of ideological domination. Infrapolitics, then, is essentially the strategic form that the resistance of subjects must assume under conditions of great peril.

The strategic imperatives of infrapolitics make it not simply different in degree from the open politics of modern democracies; they impose a fundamentally different logic of political action. No public claims are made, no open symbolic lines are drawn. All political action takes forms that are designed to obscure their intentions or to take cover behind an apparent meaning. Virtually no one acts in his own name for avowed purposes, for that would be self-defeating. Precisely because such political action is studiously designed to be anonymous or to disclaim its purpose, infrapolitics requires more than a little interpretation. Things are not exactly as they seem.

The logic of disguise followed by infrapolitics extends to its organization as well as to its substance. Again, the form of organization is as much a product of political necessity as of political choice. Because open political activity is all but precluded, resistance is confined to the informal networks of kin, neighbours, friends and community rather than formal organization. Just as the symbolic resistance found in forms of folk culture has a possibly

Breaking the Monopoly of Knowledge

Anyone's self-development starts, as it must, with one's self-understanding to guide one's own action, and is a process in which self-understanding develops as action is taken and reviewed. Formal efforts at social 'development' have however been in the hands of elites who have in general considered themselves wiser than the people, and instead of seeking to promote the people's self-enquiry and understanding have sought to impose their own ideas of 'development'. In doing this they have promoted their own 'self-development' in some ways, while bringing the world to the dismal state in which we find it today. In any case this had to be at the cost of people's self-development, for one cannot develop with somebody else's ideas. This has been, I suggest, also the single most important intellectual error in many otherwise committed efforts toward social change for people's liberation, which seek to *indoctrinate* the people in a vertical relation with them, and give priority to structural change over liberation of the mind. Only with a liberated mind which is free to enquire and then conceive and plan what is to be created, can structural change release the creative potential of the people. In this sense, liberation of the mind is the primary task, both *before* and *after* structural change.

This implies breaking the monopoly of knowledge in the hands of the elites – i.e. giving the people their right to assert their existing knowledge to start with, giving them the opportunity and assistance, if needed, to advance their self-knowledge through self-enquiry as the basis of their action, and to review themselves and their experiences from action to further advance their self-knowledge. In this reflection–action–reflection process of the people (people's praxis), professional knowledge can be useful only in a dialogue with people's knowledge on an equal footing through which both can be enriched, and not in the arrogance of assumed superior wisdom. Altering thus the relations of knowledge, to produce and advance 'organic knowledge' as a part of the very evolution of life rather than abstract (synthetic) knowledge produced in academic laboratories to be imposed upon life, is a central commitment of what is being termed as 'participatory research'.

Anisur Rahman, 'People's Self-development', *Journal of the Asiatic Society of Bangladesh (Hum.)* vol. 34, no. 2, December 1989.

Anisur Rahman was for many years the Co-ordinator of the Programme on Participation of the Rural Poor in Development in the International Labour Organization, Geneva. He has been Economics Professor at Dhaka University, and in the post-independence period he was a member of the Bangladesh Planning Commission.

innocent meaning, so do the elementary organizational units of infrapolitics have an alternative, innocent existence. The informal assemblages of market, neighbours, family and community thus provide both a structure and a cover for resistance. Since resistance is conducted in small groups, individually, and if, on a larger scale, it makes use of the anonymity of folk culture of actual disguises, it is well adapted to thwart surveillance. There are no leaders to round up, no membership lists to investigate, no manifestos to denounce, no public activities to attract attention. These are, one might say, the elementary forms of political life on which more elaborate, open, institutional forms may be built and on which they are likely to depend for their vitality. Such elementary forms also help explain why infrapolitics so often escapes notice. If formal political organization is the realm of elites (for example, lawyers, politicians, revolutionaries, political bosses), of written records (for example, resolutions, declarations, news stories, petitions, lawsuits), and of public action, infrapolitics is, by contrast, the realm of informal leadership and non-elites, of conversation and oral discourse, and of surreptitious resistance. The logic of infrapolitics is to leave few traces in the wake of its passage. By covering its tracks it not only minimizes the risks its practitioners run but also eliminates much of the documentary evidence that might convince social scientists and historians that real politics was taking place.

Infrapolitics is, to be sure, real politics. In many respects it is conducted in more earnest, for higher stakes, and against greater odds than political life in liberal democracies. Real ground is lost and gained. Armies are undone and revolutions facilitated by the desertions of infrapolitics. *De facto* property rights are established and challenged. States confront fiscal crises or crises of appropriation when the cumulative petty stratagems of its subjects deny them labour and taxes. Resistant subcultures of dignity and vengeful dreams are created and nurtured. Counter-hegemonic discourse is elaborated. Thus infrapolitics is, as emphasized earlier, always pressing, testing, probing the boundaries of the permissible. Any relaxation in surveillance and punishment and foot-dragging threatens to become a declared strike; folktales of oblique aggression threaten to become face-to-face defiant contempt; millennial dreams threaten to become revolutionary politics. From this vantage point infrapolitics may be thought of as the elementary – in the sense of foundational – form of politics. It is the building block for the more elaborate institutionalized political action that could not exist without it. Under the conditions of tyranny and persecution in which more historical subjects live, it *is* political life. And when the rare civilities of open political life are curtailed or destroyed, as they so often are, the elementary forms of infrapolitics remain as a defence-in-depth of the powerless.

NOTES

1. Barrington Moore, Jr, *Injustice: The Social Bases of Obedience and Revolt*, M.E. Sharpe, White Plains, N.Y., 1987, p. 459n.

2. Leonard Berkowitz, *Aggression: A Social Psychological Analysis*, McGraw Hill, New York, 1962, pp. 204–27.

3. This perspective is suggested by the monumental work of Paul Veyne, *Le Pain et le Cirque*, Editions du Seuil, Paris, 1976. Veyne treats the bread and circuses of classical Rome as something as much *wrung* from elites as conferred by them to neutralize anger. As he claims, 'The government does not provide the circus to the people to depolitize them but, certainly, they would be politicized against the government if it refused them the circus' (p. 94).

4. The coincidence by itself does not, of course, prove that such rituals, as rituals, were a provocation to revolt. Here one would have to distinguish between the effects of ritual symbolism on the one hand, and the mass assembly of subordinates on the other.

5. I have benefited greatly here from Alex Lichtenstein, 'That Disposition to Theft, with which They Have Been Branded: Moral Economy, Slave Management and the Law', *Journal of Social History*, Spring 1988.

6. As Charles Joyner (*Down by the Riverside*, University of Illinois Press, Urbana, 1984, p. 177) notes, the trickster in Afro-American folktales took particularly great satisfaction in taking his food from more powerful (cited in Lichtenstein, 'That Disposition to Theft', p. 418.

7. Charles C. Jones, The Religious Institution of the Negroes In The United States, pp. 131, 135; cited in Lichtenstein, 'That Disposition to Theft,' p. 422.

8. E.P. Thompson, *Whigs and Hunters*, Penguin Books, Harmondsworth, 1975.

9. Ibid., p. 108.

10. Ibid., p. 124.

11. Ibid., p. 162.

12. A comparable dialectic, moreover, joins the practices of domination to the hidden transcript. The predations of game wardens, arrests and prosecutions, new laws and warnings, the losses of subsistence resources would continually find their way into the normative discourse of those whose earlier rights to the forest were being curtailed.

13. Milovan Djilas, *The New Class*, Praeger, New York, 1957, p. 120. One is also reminded of the East European adage: 'They pretend to pay us and we pretend to work.'

14. This argument is made at much greater length in James C. Scott, *Weapons of the Weak: Everyday Forms of Resistance*, Yale University Press, New Haven, Conn., 1987, ch. 7.

15. The initiation of some forms of rebellion can be understood along these lines.

16. The most obvious empirical test of this assumption is to observe what happens when surveillance or punishment is relaxed.

17. For a review of this literature and an argument about the importance of this form of resistance, see my 'Resistance without Protest and without Organization', *Comparative Studies in Society and History*, vol. 29, no. 3, pp. 417–52.

18. Revolutionary vacuums have aided more than one peasantry in this fashion. In the months after the Bolshevik seizure of power but before the new state made its presence felt in the countryside, the Russian peasantry did on a larger scale what they had always attempted on a smaller scale. They opened up new fields in what had earlier been woodland, gentry pastures and state land and didn't report it; they inflated local population figures and *de*flated arable acreage in order to make the village seem as poor and untaxable as possible. A remarkable study of this period by Orlando Figes suggests

that, as a result of these self-help measures, the 1917 census underestimated the arable land in Russia by 15 per cent (*Peasant Revolution, Civil War: The Volga Countryside in Revolution*, Clarendon Press, Oxford, 1987, ch. 3).

19. Primary- and secondary-school teachers share a lore about how important it is to establish a firm line and enforce it lest a pattern of verbal disrespect become established, leading, presumably, to more daring acts of lèse-majesté. Similarly, referees of basketball games may punish even trivial fouls at the outset of a game simply to establish a line that they may later relax slightly.

20. *Elementary Forms of Peasant Insurgency*, Oxford University Press, Delhi, 1989, ch. 2.

21. Bruce Lincoln, 'Revolutionary Exhumations in Spain, July 1936', *Comparative Studies in Society and History*, vol. 27, no. 2, pp. 241–60.

22. This, I believe, is the missing element in the theories of legitimation to be found in John Gaventa's otherwise perceptive book, *Power and Powerlessness: Quiescence and Rebellion in an Appalachian Valley*, University of Illinois Press, Urbana, 1980, especially ch. 1. See also Stephen Lukes, *Power, a Radical View*, Macmillan, London, 1974.

On Aztec and Hindu Forms of Resistance?

I remember Ivan Illich once recounting how a group of fifteenth-century Aztec priests, herded together by their Spanish conquerors, said in response to a Christian sermon that if, as alleged, the Aztec gods were dead, they too would rather die. After this last act of defiance, the priests were dutifully thrown to the war dogs. I suspect I know how a group of Brahman priests would have behaved under the same circumstances. All of them would have embraced Christianity and some of them would have even co-authored an elegant *prasasti* to praise the alien rulers and their gods. Not that they would have become good Christians overnight. Most probably their faith in Hinduism would have remained unshaken and their Christianity would have looked after a while dangerously like a variation on Hinduism. But under the principle of *apaddharma* or the way of life under perilous conditions, and the principle of oneness of every being – the metaphysical correlate of what a well-intentioned Freudian modernist has called projective extraversion born of extreme narcissism – they would have felt perfectly justified in bowing down to alien gods and in overtly renouncing their culture and their past. ...

Ever since the modern West's encounter with the non-Western world, the response of the Aztec priests has seemed to the Westernized world the paragon of courage and cultural pride; the hypothetical response of the Brahman priests hypocritical and cowardly. But the question remains why every imperialist observer of the Indian society has loved India's martial races and hated and felt threatened by the rest of India's 'effeminate' men willing to compromise with their victors? What is it in the latter that has aroused such antipathy? Why should they matter so much to the conquerors of India if they are so trivial? Why could they so effortlessly become the antonyms of their rulers? Why have so many modern Indians shared this imperialist estimation? Why have they felt proud of those who fought out and lost, and not of those who lost out and fought?

On one plane the answer is simple. The Aztec priests after their last act of courage die and they leave the stage free for those who kill them and then sing their praise; the unheroic Indian response ensures that part of the stage always remains occupied by the 'cowardly' and the 'compromising' who may at some opportune moment assert their presence....

But another answer to the question can also be given. It is that the average Indian has always lived with the awareness and possibility of long-term suffering, always seen himself as protecting his deepest faith with the passive, 'feminine' cunning of the weak and the victimized, and surviving outer pressures by refusing to overplay his sense of autonomy and self-respect...

In order to truly live, the inviolable core of Indianness seems to affirm, it might sometimes be better to be dead in somebody else's eyes, so as to be alive for one's own self. In order to accept oneself, one must learn to hold in trust 'weaknesses' to which a violent, culturally barren and politically bankrupt world some day may have to return.

My concerns here are unheroic rather than heroic, and empirical rather than philosophical. The argument is that when psychological and cultural survival is at stake, polarities such as the ones discussed here do break down and become partly irrelevant, and the directness of the experience of suffering and spontaneous resistance to it come through on all planes. When this happens, there emerges in the victim of a system a vague awareness of the larger whole which transcends the system's analytic categories and/or stands them on their head. Thus, the victim may become aware that, under oppression, the parochial could protect some forms of universalism more successfully than does conventional universalism; that the spiritualism of the weak may articulate or keep alive the values of a non-oppressive world better than the ultra-materialism of those who live in visionless worlds; and that the non-achieving and the insane may often have a higher chance of achieving their civilizational goal of freedom and autonomy without mortgaging their sanity. I imply that these paradoxes are inevitable because the dominant idea of rationality is the first strand of consciousness to be co-opted by any successful structure of institutionalized oppression. When such co-optation has taken place, resistance as well as survival demands some access to the larger whole, howsoever self-defeating that process may seem in the light of conventional reason and day-to-day politics. This, I suspect is another way of restating the ancient wisdom – which for some cultures is also an everyday truism – that knowledge without ethics is not so much bad ethics as inferior knowledge.

Ashis Nandy, *The Intimate Enemy: Loss and Recovery of Self under Colonialism*, Oxford University Press, Delhi, 1983, p. 113.

33

ALTERNATIVES FROM AN INDIAN GRASSROOTS PERSPECTIVE

D.L. Sheth

D.L. SHETH is well known for his studies of grassroots movements in India and their concern to reconcile micro-forms of regenerative action and resistance with macro-spaces which tend to co-opt them for their own ends. He is a co-editor of the quarterly journal *Alternatives*, which since its establishment in 1975 has regularly published some of the most incisive and thought-provoking articles on questions of social transformation and human governance. He is also a member of the Centre for the Study of Developing Societies (29 Rajpur Road, Delhi, India). The following text is an extract from a forthcoming study.

The grassroots movements in India have depended for over two decades on the global discourse on alternative development. This dependence has been particularly marked since the ending of the Cold War. The movements find it increasingly difficult to relate to the global alternativist discourse in which, the danger of a nuclear holocaust having receded, the issues of alternative development are no longer articulated in terms of humanity's 'common future'.

The global ecological movements no longer view their role in terms of pressing the politics of an alternative paradigm: that of organizing the economy and social-cultural life locally and globally. Instead, the issue is being recast in terms of international relations, conceding to criteria of 'tolerable limits' and 'admissible costs' of environmental damage entailed in the development process.

The issue of human rights has been entangled with the foreign-policy considerations of the rich and powerful countries and has been added to the list of conditionalities of the world financial agencies – dissociating, in the process, the thinking on human rights from issues of removing poverty, fulfilling basic human needs and social justice. Poverty is increasingly being seen as poor peoples' own failure to create wealth. In other words, the global discourse on human rights has ceased to be a discourse regarding social and political transformation; it has, instead, become a discourse about indexing conditions in which the power of some 'developed' countries could be and should be used over other countries to bring about a global legal regime of rights – as if a global civil society and global citizenship is already in place!

In the global feminist discourse, the sensitivity about the social, economic and cultural impediments faced by women in poor countries in securing their rights has greatly receded; in its place, the metropolitan concern about women's rights in a consumerist society have acquired prominence. Even if these propositions cannot be demonstrated to flow directly from the normativist critiques of development, there is little doubt that they have overpowered the global discourse on movements.

What, then, is the politics of alternative development that the grassroots movements in India can pursue in the post-Cold War world? Some patterns of their politics are becoming visible.

First, there seems to be a return to an earlier assumption that a political action for alternative development should not be derived deductively from a received theory, not even the theory based on the global alternativist critiques of development. Instead, it should emerge from the concrete and specific struggles of the people themselves. Consequently, the emphasis is placed on such issues as decision-making – not only in choosing means, but in defining goals of development. The emphasis is once again being laid on social justice and equity, as well as on citizenship rights and even the rights of the unborn.

Second, the issue of development is being increasingly viewed in political terms, engaging the movements in the larger issue of democratization – not only of the policy (state) but also of economic organization (work and work place) and social organizations (ranging from the national society to the family). Thus, remaining sensitive to the gender, ecological, cultural and human rights aspects involved in redefining development, the concrete struggles are political in nature; they are primarily about confronting the hegemonic structures of power – locally, nationally and globally. The strategies of action have so far been in the form of protests, but they also emphasize withdrawal of legitimation to the prevalent structures of domination and resistance, to an imposed homogeneity of attitudes, tastes and life-styles – whether these are imposed by the market or through an ideology of majority nationalism, or by the state acting on behalf of the national and global interests of the metropolitan elites.

By readjusting their activities to the changed national and global economic context of the post-Cold War world, the grassroots movements in India are thus articulating the idea of alternative development in terms of concrete political struggles waged against various programmes of structural adjustment being devised by the state. This is evident in their assessment of the new market model of development.

FACING THE NEW MARKET MODEL OF DEVELOPMENT

While the grassroots movements concede that the economy is growing in volume, they find its impact in removing poverty and unemployment to be negligible. In their view, it continues to operate on the principle of the social and cultural exclusion of groups from the ranks of the middle classes. Over the last decades, the Indian middle class has indeed grown in magnitude, incorporating the erstwhile poor households of the higher social strata in its composition. But it is still a class by and large consisting of the upper castes of the *dwijas.* Seen in secular terms, the prevalent economic growth model has little to offer to the vast multitudes in the 'unorganized' and 'informal' sector; the model simply holds them to ransom for cheap and perennial labour supply as and when needed by the organized economy. Whatever benefits were supposed to trickle down to them have stopped half way. On the other hand, the model offers ever-increasing standards of living to those with some entitlements (land, education, social privileges) and by virtue of which they form a part of the small organized sector in the economy. For those outside the organized sector, malnutrition, destitution and semi-starvation prevail. The dividing line is drawn quite firmly now and looks as though it cannot be obliterated.

The new market model of development increasingly perceives rural development as a problem of *sectoral development*, monitored through an input–output calculus, where inputs are made in the rural economy for obtaining outputs for use in the urban-industrial sector. The index for measuring rural development has thus become one of growing dependency (its euphemism being 'integration') of the rural production system on the urban-industrial economy, which regulates the markets, monitors supplies and demands, commands the policy and thereby lays down priorities not only for the economy but for the lives of vast, dependent populations. The activists of the movements find it astounding that the market economy allows, even encourages a colonial-type exploitation of the primary producers (tribals, artisans, small and marginal farmers and landless labour) by a small urban-industrial elite, and its client class of a dependent rural elite. In other words, it seems to them that the market economy, instead of making a dent in the social structure, is being absorbed by it.

Worse still, millions among the rural population continue to be deprived of even the doubtful privilege of being 'dependents' of the organized economy. Their need to survive cannot become an effective demand in the market for they have practically no purchasing power. They are exposed to a state of destitution, semi-starvation and chronic malnutrition, a long period of physical and psychological stunting, and slow death. For them, the problem is sheer physical survival, not 'development'.

The state and the political process having lost a commanding position vis-à-vis the economy, intervention on behalf of the poor to restrain the market forces from destroying the local subsistence economies and their natural environs (which at least provided food and shelter to the poor) is becoming less and less effective. The state is also unable to replace such destruction with any credible system of welfare, and the 'integrating' national economy has no place for the displaced and the uprooted. So, they swarm as destitutes into the cities. The huge numbers of people affected adversely by development are unable to make a sufficiently forceful demand on the mainstream democratic process, either because the polity has begun to move along the fringes of the market or because it has itself acquired the character of a market. Moreover, the destitute people are made up of occupationally disparate and socially fragmented populations (often belonging to opposite camps in the local social structure): groups which simply cannot be organized into trade unions like the industrial workers.

The combined impact of all this on the poorest of the poor is that they are not entitled to become full wage-earners in the economy or fully fledged citizens in the polity. For them, in the present economic and political framework of development, there is no transitional path in sight. They cannot graduate from penury to any liveable standard or from subjecthood to citizenship, or from an endemic state of starvation, disease and destitution to basic needs satisfaction. They do not have enough of a material base to enable them to reflect on their condition and to acquire radical consciousness. Also they have lost the security of the traditional social order, which has been shaken to its very roots. In proportional terms, their number may have decreased, but the 'left-outs' of development and the market still constitute a staggering figure in absolute numbers – roughly 150 million. More significant is that their exclusion is social rather than purely economic in nature, a large majority of this population being constituted by the tribals, the dalits and the lower rungs of the former Sudra communities and sections of minorities. The established economic and political institutions, often aided by the analyses of social scientists, have, however, docketed their problem as being one of 'overpopulation' or (when they create trouble, only to be ruthlessly repressed) of 'law and order'.

The grassroots movements thus mainly work for and with the people at the bottom, who are written off by development, as well as by organized politics. The emphasis of their programmes varies widely, from raising the level of material life, to raising consciousness, to demanding a rightful share in the national cake, to working for self-reliant economic, social and cultural development in local or regional settings. But almost all grassroots activists are, in their different ways, in search of an alternative to the present model of development: one in which the people at the bottom can find their rightful place as producers in the economy and citizens in the polity.

NEW STRATEGIES OF ACTION

It is in this context that new strategies of action are being worked out by several grassroots movements and organizations to counter both the state and the market models of development. Such new thinking and action strategies are being carried out in various local milieux and in response to problems of specific population groups with whom and for whom the grassroots organizations are working. These initiatives have not yet acquired a durable macro-formation. But they are showing a clear departure from the old statist, as well as from the new market-democracy, model of development.

The new agents of change and the grassroots organizations do not view poverty as a purely economic problem, one of enlarging the national cake through capital accumulation and growth so that the benefits of such economic development automatically trickle down to the bottom. Instead, they see poverty as a function of the structural locations of the poor in society, which meet with barriers that separate the world of development (with all its legal, political and economic immunities and insulations) from the world of poverty (with all its vulnerabilities and exposure to exploitation). Their perception of these barriers is not primarily in terms of economic classes, and their strategies of action are not, therefore, purely in terms of class struggle. They believe that the new socio-political formations of the poor and the deprived, being grounded in caste and ethnic structures which divide the world of the poor along different socio-cultural lines, make it difficult to organize movements based purely on class. Hence their emphasis is first on organizing the social categories, such as the backward castes, the dalits, the tribals, and also the women, and only then evolving strategies for joint fronts. Accordingly, their activities oppose not only the economic exploitation of the poor but also the new forms of social and cultural exploitation. This is especially evident in their work among the dalits, the tribals and women.

The grassroots groups also reject the 'inputs' view of rural development as a partial and lopsided view. A large majority of the population lacks any economic and organizational capacity to receive and use credit, seeds, fertilizers, irrigation, and so on. These inputs are simply swallowed up by the upper stratum of rural society. The groups focus more on creating various capabilities among the rural poor than merely presenting them with different packages of inputs dispensed by the development establishment.

The general approach of the grassroots groups is not to work for such administrative units as a revenue village, a block or a district. They prefer working with specific vulnerable groups within – and across – these units. Instead of working as the middlemen of development, they prefer to work directly among the poor, relying increasingly on the internal resources – economic, social, cultural and political – of the people themselves.

Rural development is not viewed as a problem of the efficient implementation of given schemes and programmes, but essentially as a *struggle* to establish the economic and political rights of the poorest among the poor – these are necessary for their very survival. Thus they demand direct institutional intervention – on the part of the state, the judiciary and the 'fourth estate' – to protect the rights of the poor, which is a precondition to improving their situation. At the same time, they organize the people for struggles against the state institutions whenever these impede people's own empowerment.

The continuing attempts by the bureaucratic and technocratic elites to depoliticize the development process are resisted. For the grassroots groups, it is only through the politicization of the poor that development can reach them. The poorest of the poor, having no purchasing power, cannot create an 'effective' demand in the economic market, so the demand has to be made politically effective. By and large, political parties have failed to achieve this for the poor. Even the need for votes gets them only temporary benefits around election times – if at all. (On the whole, though, even these go to the intermediaries.) The new agents of change and action groups are therefore devoting themselves progressively to organizing the vulnerable groups politically through struggles on specific issues. Through this process they are building a new political credibility for themselves, which they do not seek for electoral purposes but to create a long-term impact on the nature of Indian politics.

As the development administration has failed to link the policies and programmes of the government with the felt needs of the people (especially the poorest), the scope for grassroots initiatives in this regard has enormously increased. But this role cannot be performed without giving a political content to their economic schemes. It is in this way that the economic activities they organize and promote for extremely poor populations differ from the development programmes being implemented by the state bureaucracy.

The decline of the political process (parties and elections) has made the state less and less accountable vis-à-vis its development expenditures. The growing desperation of the poor, on the other hand, is pushing them into more and more chaotic and violent actions. To overcome this counter-productive trend, the agents of change at the grassroots are devising new forms of political action: militant but non-violent protests against the so-called development projects which involve the massive displacement of the poor. They engage in continuous pressure on public opinion regarding the adverse effects (economic, cultural and ecological) of such projects. And they organize mutual learning and the training of cadres through dialogue and interaction among them, as well as a long-term process of building a shared identity of language and lifestyle between agents of change themselves and the people. They are, in the process, redefining economic demands in terms of political and cultural rights. It is through this process that they seek to mediate between the coercion of the haves and the anarchy of the have-nots.

As the new agents of change and activist groups are not convinced by the logic of capturing state power as a precondition for social transformation, they are more inclined to work with long-term perspectives, emphasizing the decentralization of economic and political power. This helps them to integrate the hitherto neglected social and cultural issues in formulating their economic and political programmes. All this allows them greater flexibility and openness, experimentation and innovation in planning their actions and choosing issues. Health, environment, education, the role of science, technology and other such issues have all simultaneously become developmental and political issues for them.

In sum, the grassroots initiatives in India today constitute both a critique and a protest against the prevailing model of development. Their long-term goal is to evolve an alternative approach to development that is more holistic, transcends economism and is self-consciously political – political on behalf of those sections of society whom modern 'development' has rendered destitute and starving.

34

THE POWER OF THE POWERLESS: CITIZENS AGAINST THE STATE IN CENTRAL EASTERN EUROPE

Václav Havel

The following text is an extract from an essay, 'The Power of the Powerless', which was written in 1978 and included in the book *Open Letters: Selected Writings, 1965–1990* (Vintage, New York, 1992). Other essays include 'On Evasive Thinking', 'Politics and Conscience', 'Stories and Totalitarianism', 'Farce, Reformability and the Future of the World', and 'A Word about Words'.

VÁCLAV HAVEL is the President of the Czech Republic. He is the author of many plays, among them *The Garden Party*, *The Memorandum*, *Largo Desolato*, *Temptation*, and three one-act plays, *Audience*, *Private Views* and *Protest*. In 1979 he was sentenced to four-and-a-half years in prison for his involvement in the Czech human rights movement: out of this came his book of letters to his wife, *Letters to Olga* (1988).

The manager of a fruit and vegetable shop places in his window, among the onions and the carrots, the slogan: 'Workers of the World, Unite!' Why does he do it? What is he trying to communicate to the world? Is he genuinely enthusiastic about the idea of unity among the workers of the world? Is his enthusiasm so great that he feels an irrepressible impulse to acquaint the public with his ideals? Has he really given more than a moment's thought to how such a unification might occur and what it would mean?

I think it can safely be assumed that the overwhelming majority of shopkeepers never think about the slogans they put in their windows, nor do they use them to express their real opinions. That poster was delivered to our greengrocer from the enterprise headquarters along with the onions and carrots. He put them all into the window simply because it has been done that way for years, because everyone does it, and because that is the way it has to be. If he were to refuse, there could be trouble. He could be reproached for not having the proper 'decoration' in his window; someone might even accuse him of disloyalty. He does it because these things must be done if one is to get along in life. It is one of the thousands of details that guarantee him a relatively tranquil life 'in harmony with society', as they say.

Obviously the greengrocer is indifferent to the semantic content of the slogan on exhibit; he does not put the slogan in his window from any personal desire to acquaint the public with the ideal it expresses. This, of course, does not mean that his action has no motive or significance at all, or that the slogan communicates nothing to anyone. The slogan is really a *sign*, and as such it contains a subliminal but very definite message. Verbally, it might be expressed this way: 'I, the greengrocer XY, live here and I know what I must do. I behave in the manner expected of me. I can be depended upon and am beyond reproach. I am obedient and therefore I have the right to be left in peace.' This message, of course, has an addressee: it is directed above, to the greengrocer's superior, and at the same time it is a shield that protects the greengrocer from potential informers. The slogan's real meaning, therefore, is rooted firmly in the greengrocer's existence. It reflects his vital interests. But what are those vital interests?

Let us take note: if the greengrocer had been instructed to display the slogan 'I am afraid and therefore unquestioningly obedient', he would not be nearly as indifferent to its semantics, even though the statement would reflect the truth. The greengrocer would be embarrassed and ashamed to put such an unequivocal statement of his own degradation in the shop window, and quite naturally so, for he is a human being and thus has a sense of his own dignity. To overcome this complication, his expression of loyalty must take the form of a sign which, at least on its textual surface, indicates a level of disinterested conviction. It must allow the greengrocer to say, 'What's wrong with the workers of the world uniting?' Thus the sign helps the greengrocer to conceal from himself the low foundations of his obedience, at the same time concealing the low foundations of power. It hides them behind the façade of something high. And that something is *ideology*.

Ideology is a specious way of relating to the world. It offers human beings the illusion of an identity, of dignity, and of morality while making it easier for them to *part* with them. As the repository of something 'supra-personal' and objective, it enables people to deceive their conscience and conceal their true position and their inglorious *modus vivendi*, both from the world and from themselves. It is a very pragmatic, but at the same time an apparently dignified, way of legitimizing what is above, below, and on either side. It is directed towards people and towards God. It is a veil behind which human beings can hide their own 'fallen existence', their trivialization and their adaptation to the status quo. It is an excuse that everyone can use, from the greengrocer, who conceals his fear of losing his job behind an alleged interest in the unification of the workers of the world, to the highest functionary, whose interest in staying in power can be cloaked in phrases about service to the working class. The primary excusatory function of ideology, therefore, is to provide people, both as victims and pillars of the post-totalitarian system,[1] with the illusion that the system is in harmony with the human order and the order of the universe.

The smaller a dictatorship and the less stratified by modernization the society under it, the more directly the will of the dictator can be exercised. In other words, the dictator can employ more or less naked discipline, avoiding the complex processes of relating to the world and of self-justification which ideology involves. But the more complex the mechanisms of power become, the larger and more stratified the society they embrace, and the longer they have operated historically, the more individuals must be connected to them from outside, and the greater the importance attached to the ideological excuse. It acts as a kind of bridge between the regime and the people, across which the regime approaches the people and the people approach the regime. This explains why ideology plays such an important role in the post-totalitarian system: that complex machinery of units, hierarchies, transmission belts and indirect instruments of manipulation which insure in countless ways the integrity of the regime, leaving nothing to chance, would be quite simply unthinkable without ideology acting as its all-embracing excuse and as the excuse for each of its parts.

Between the aims of the post-totalitarian system and the aims of life there is a yawning abyss: while life, in its essence, moves towards plurality, diversity, independent self-constitution and self-organization, in short, towards the fulfillment of its own freedom, the post-totalitarian system demands conformity, uniformity and discipline. While life ever strives to create new and 'improbable' structures, the post-totalitarian system contrives to force life into its most probable states. The aims of the system reveal its most essential characteristics to be introversion, a movement towards being ever more completely and unreservedly *itself*, which means that the radius of its influence is continually widening as well. This system serves people only to the extent necessary to ensure that people will serve it. Anything beyond this, that is to say, anything which leads people to overstep their predetermined roles is regarded by the system as an attack upon itself. And in this respect it is correct: every instance of such transgression is a genuine denial of the system. It can be said, therefore, that the inner aim of the post-totalitarian system is not mere preservation of power in the hands of a ruling clique, as appears to be the case at first sight. Rather the social phenomenon of self-preservation is subordinated to something higher, to a kind of blind *automatism* which drives the system. No matter what position individuals hold in the hierarchy of power, they are not considered by the system to be worth anything in themselves, but only as things intended to fuel and serve this automatism. For this reason, an individual's desire for power is admissible only in so far as its direction coincides with the direction of the automatism of the system.

Ideology, in creating a bridge of excuses between the system and the individual, spans the abyss between the aims of the system and the aims of life. It pretends that the requirements of the system derive from the requirements of life. It is a world of appearances trying to pass for reality.

The post-totalitarian system touches people at every step, but it does so with its ideological gloves on. This is why life in the system is so thoroughly permeated with hypocrisy and lies: government by bureaucracy is called popular government; the working class is enslaved in the name of the working class; the complete degradation of the individual is presented as his or her ultimate liberation; depriving people of information is called making it available; the use of power to manipulate is called the public control of power, and the arbitrary abuse of power is called observing the legal code; the repression of culture is called its development; the expansion of imperial influence is presented as support for the oppressed; the lack of free expression becomes the highest form of freedom; farcical elections become the highest form of democracy; banning independent thought becomes the most scientific of world-views; military occupation becomes fraternal assistance. Because the regime is captive to its own lies, it must falsify everything. It falsifies the past. It falsifies the present, and it falsifies the future. It falsifies statistics. It pretends not to possess an omnipotent and unprincipled police apparatus. It pretends to respect human rights. It pretends to persecute no one. It pretends to fear nothing. It pretends to pretend nothing.

Individuals need not believe all these mystifications, but they must behave as though they did, or they must at least tolerate them in silence, or get along well with those who work with them. For this reason, however, they must *live within a lie.* They need not accept the lie. It is enough for them to have accepted their life with it and in it. For by this very fact, individuals confirm the system, fulfil the system, make the system, *are* the system.

We have seen that the real meaning of the greengrocer's slogan has nothing to do with what the text of the slogan actually says. Even so, this real meaning is quite clear and generally comprehensible because the code is so familiar; the greengrocer declares his loyalty (and he can do no other if his declaration is to be accepted) in the only way the regime is capable of hearing; that is, by accepting the prescribed *ritual*, by accepting appearances as reality, by accepting the given rules of the game. In doing so, however, he has himself become a player in the game, thus making it possible for the game to go on, for it to exist in the first place.

If ideology was originally a bridge between the system and the individual as an individual, then the moment he or she steps on to this bridge it becomes at the same time a bridge between the system and the individual as a component of the system. That is, if ideology originally facilitated (by acting outwardly) the constitution of power by serving as a psychological excuse, then from the moment that excuse is accepted, it constitutes power inwardly, becoming an active component of that power. It begins to function as the principal instrument of ritual communication *within* the system of power.

The whole power structure (and we have already discussed its physical articulation) could not exist at all if there were not a certain 'metaphysical' order binding all its components together, interconnecting them and subordinating them to a uniform method of accountability, supplying the combined operation of all these components with rules of the game, that is, with certain regulations, limitations and legalities. This metaphysical order is fundamental to, and standard throughout, the entire power structure; it integrates its communication system and makes possible the internal exchange and transfer of information and instructions. It is rather like a collection of traffic signals and directional signs, giving the process shape and structure. This metaphysical order guarantees the inner coherence of the totalitarian power structure. It is the glue holding it together, its binding principle, the instrument of its discipline. Without this glue the structure as a totalitarian structure would vanish; it would disintegrate into individual atoms chaotically colliding with one another in their unregulated particular interests and inclinations. The entire pyramid of totalitarian power, deprived of the element that binds it together, would collapse in upon itself, as it were, in a kind of material implosion.

As the interpretation of reality by the power structure, ideology is always subordinated ultimately to the interests of the structure. Therefore, it has a natural tendency to disengage itself from reality, to create a world of appearances, to become ritual. In societies where there is public competition for power and therefore public control of that power, there also exists quite naturally public control of the way that power legitimates itself ideologically. Consequently, in such conditions there are always certain correctives that effectively prevent ideology from abandoning reality altogether. Under totalitarianism, however, these correctives disappear and thus there is nothing to prevent ideology from becoming more and more removed from reality, gradually turning into what it has already become in the post-totalitarian system: a world of appearances, a mere ritual, a formalized language deprived of semantic contact with reality and transformed into a system of ritual signs that replace reality with pseudo-reality.

Yet, as we have seen, ideology becomes at the same time an increasingly important component of power, a pillar providing it with both excusatory legitimacy and an inner coherence. As this aspect grows in importance, and as it gradually loses touch with reality, it acquires a peculiar but very real strength. It becomes reality itself, albeit a reality altogether self-contained, one that on certain levels (chiefly inside the power structure) may have even greater weight than reality as such. Increasingly, the virtuosity of the ritual becomes more important than the reality hidden behind it. The significance of phenomena no longer derives from the phenomena themselves, but from their locus as concepts in the ideological context. Reality does not shape theory, but rather the reverse. Thus power gradually draws closer to ideology than it does to reality; it draws its strength from theory and becomes entirely dependent on it. This inevitably leads, of course, to a paradoxical result; rather than theory, or rather ideology, serving power, power begins to serve ideology. It is as though ideology had appropriated power from power, as though it had become dictator itself. It then appears that theory itself, ritual itself, ideology itself, makes decisions that affect people, and not the other way around.

If ideology is the principal guarantee of the inner consistency of power, it becomes at the same time an increasingly important guarantee of its *continuity*. Whereas succession to power in classical dictatorships is always a rather complicated affair (the pretenders having nothing to give their claims reasonable legitimacy, thereby forcing them always to resort to confrontations of naked power), in the post-totalitarian system power is passed on from person to person, from clique to clique and from generation to generation in an essentially more regular fashion. In the selection of pretenders, a new 'king maker' takes part: it is ritual legitimation, the ability to rely on ritual, to fulfil it and use it, to allow oneself, as it were, to be borne aloft by it. Naturally, power struggles exist in the post-totalitarian system as well, and most of them are far more brutal than in an open society, for the struggle is not open, regulated by democratic rules, and subject to public control, but hidden behind the scenes. (It is difficult to recall a single instance in which the First Secretary of a ruling Communist Party has been replaced without the various military and security forces being placed at least on alert.) This struggle, however, can never (as it can in classical dictatorships) threaten the very essence of the system and its continuity. At most it will shake up the power structure, which will recover quickly, precisely because the binding substance – ideology – remains undisturbed. No matter who is replaced by whom, succession is only possible against the backdrop and within the framework of a common ritual. It can never take place by denying that ritual.

Because of this dictatorship of the ritual, however, power becomes clearly anonymous. Individuals are almost dissolved in the ritual. They allow themselves to be swept along by it and frequently it seems as though ritual alone carries people from obscurity into the light of power. Is it not characteristic of the post-totalitarian system that, on all levels of the power hierarchy, individuals are increasingly being pushed aside by faceless people, puppets, those uniformed flunkies of the rituals and routines of power?

The automatic operation of a power structure thus dehumanized and made anonymous is a feature of the fundamental automatism of this system. It would seem that it is precisely the *diktats* of this automatism which select people lacking individual will for the power structure, that it is precisely the *diktat* of the empty phrase which summons to power people who use empty phrases as the best guarantee that the automatism of the post-totalitarian system will continue.

Western Sovietologists often exaggerate the role of individuals in the post-totalitarian system and overlook the fact that the ruling figures, despite the immense power they possess through the centralized structure of power, are often no more than blind executors of the system's own internal laws – laws they themselves never can, and never do, reflect upon. In any case, experience has taught us again and again that this automatism is far more powerful than the will of any individual; and should someone possess a more independent will, he or she must conceal it behind a ritually anonymous mask in order to have an opportunity to enter the power hierarchy at all. And when the individual finally gains a place there and tries to make his or her will felt within it, that automatism, with its enormous inertia, will triumph sooner or later, and either the individual will be ejected by the power structure, like a foreign organism, or he or she will be compelled to resign his or her individuality gradually, once again blending with the automatism and becoming its servant, almost indistinguishable from those who preceded him or her and those who will follow. (Let us recall, for instance, the development of Husák or Gomulka.) The necessity of continually hiding behind and relating to ritual means that even the more enlightened members of the power structure are often obsessed with ideology. They are never able to plunge straight to the bottom of naked reality and they always confuse it, in the final analysis, with ideological pseudo-reality. (In my opinion, one of the reasons the Dubček leadership lost control of the situation in 1968 was precisely because, in extreme situations and in final questions, its members were never capable of extricating themselves completely from the world of appearance.)

It can be said, therefore, that ideology, as that instrument of internal communication which assures the power structure of inner cohesion is, in the post-totalitarian system, something that transcends the physical aspects of power, something that dominates it to a considerable degree and, therefore, tends to assure its continuity as well. It is one of the pillars of the system's external stability. The pillar, however, is built on a very unstable foundation. It is built on lies. It works only as long as people are willing to live within the lie.

Why, in fact, did our greengrocer have to put his loyalty on display in the shop window? Had he not already displayed it sufficiently in various internal or semi-public ways? At trade-union meetings, after all, he had always voted as he should. He had always taken part in various competitions. He voted in elections like a good citizen He had even signed the 'anti-Charter'. Why, on top of all that, should he have to declare his loyalty publicly? After all, the people who walk past his window will certainly not stop to read that, in the greengrocer's opinion, the workers of the world ought to unite. The fact of the matter is, they don't read the slogan at all, and it can be fairly assumed they don't even see it. If you were to ask a woman who had stopped in front of his shop what she saw in the window, she could certainly tell you whether or not they had tomatoes today, but it is highly unlikely that she noticed the slogan at all, let alone what it said.

It seems senseless to require the greengrocer to declare his loyalty publicly. But it makes sense nevertheless. People ignore his slogan, but they do so because such slogans are also found in other shop windows, on lamp posts, bulletin boards, in apartment windows, and on buildings; they are everywhere, in fact. They form part of the panorama of everyday life. Of course, while they ignore the details, people are very aware of that panorama as a whole. And what else is the greengrocer's slogan but a small component in that huge backdrop to daily life?

The greengrocer had to put the slogan in his window, therefore, not in the hope that someone might read it or be persuaded by it, but to contribute, along with thousands of other slogans, to the panorama that everyone is very much aware of. This panorama, of course, has a subliminal meaning as well: it reminds people where they are living and what is expected of them. It tells them what everyone is doing, and indicates to them what they must do as well, if they don't want to be excluded, to fall into isolation, alienate themselves from society, break the rules of the game, and risk the loss of their peace and tranquillity and security.

The woman who ignored the greengrocer's slogan may well have hung a similar slogan just an hour before in the corridor of the office where she works. She did it more or less without thinking, just as our greengrocer did, and she could do so precisely because she was doing it against the background of the general panorama and with some awareness of it, that is, against the background of the panorama of which the greengrocer's shop forms a part. When the greengrocer visits her office, he will not notice her slogan either, just as she failed to notice his. Nevertheless their slogans are mutually dependent; both were displayed with some awareness of the general panorama and, we might say, under its *diktat.* Both, however, assist in the creation of that panorama, and therefore they assist in the creation of that *diktat* as well. The greengrocer and the office worker have both adapted to the conditions in which they live, but in doing so they help to create those conditions. They do what is done, what is to be done, what must be done, but at the same time – by that very token – they confirm that it must be done, in fact. They conform to a particular requirement and in so doing they themselves perpetuate that requirement. Metaphorically speaking, without the greengrocer's slogan the office worker's slogan could not exist, and vice versa. Each proposes to the other that something be repeated and each accepts the other's proposal. Their mutual indifference to each other's slogans is only an illusion: in reality, by exhibiting their slogans, each compels the other to accept the rules of the game and to confirm thereby the power that requires the slogans in the first place. Quite simply, each helps the other to be obedient. Both are objects in a system of control, but at the same time they are its subjects as well. They are both victims of the system and its instruments.

If an entire district town is plastered with slogans that no one reads, it is on the one hand a message from the district secretary to the regional secretary, but it is also something more: a small example of the principle of social *auto-totality* at work. Part of the essence of the post-totalitarian system is that it draws everyone into its sphere of power, not so they may realize themselves as human beings, but so they may surrender their human identity in favour of the identity of the system, that is, so they may become agents of the system's general automatism and servants of its self-determined goals, so they may participate in the common responsibility for it, so they may be pulled into and ensnared by it, like Faust with Mephistopheles. More than this, so they may learn to be comfortable with their involvement, to identify with it as though it were something natural and inevitable and, ultimately, so they may – with no external urging – come to treat any non-involvement as an abnormality, as arrogance, as an attack on themselves, as a form of dropping out of society. By pulling everyone into its power structure, the post-totalitarian system makes everyone instruments of a mutual totality, the auto-totality of society.

Everyone, however, is in fact involved and enslaved, not only the greengrocers but also the prime ministers. Differing positions in the hierarchy merely establish differing degrees of involvement: the greengrocer is involved only to a minor extent, but he also has very little power. The prime minister, naturally, has greater power, but in return he is far more deeply involved. Both, however, are unfree, each merely in a somewhat different way. The real accomplice in this involvement, therefore, is not another person, but the system itself. Position in the power hierarchy determines the degree of responsibility and guilt, but it gives no one unlimited responsibility and guilt, nor does it completely absolve anyone. Thus the conflict between the aims of life and the aims of the system is not a conflict between two socially defined and separate communities; and only a very generalized view (and even that only approximative) permits us to divide society into the rulers and the ruled. Here, by the way, is one of the most important differences between the post-totalitarian system and classical dictatorships, in which this line of conflict can still be drawn according to social class. In the post-totalitarian system, this line runs *de facto* through each person, for everyone in his or her own way is both a victim and a supporter of the system. What we understand by the system is not, therefore, a social order imposed by one group upon another, but rather something which permeates the entire society and is a factor in shaping it, something which may seem impossible to grasp or define (for it is in the nature of a mere principle), but which is expressed by the entire society as an important feature of its life.

The fact that human beings have created, and daily create, this self-directed system through which they divest themselves of their innermost identity is not therefore the result of some incomprehensible misunderstanding of history, nor is it history somehow gone off its rails. Neither is it the product of some diabolical higher will which has decided, for reasons unknown, to torment a portion of humanity in this way. It can happen and did happen only because there is obviously in modern humanity a certain tendency towards the creation, or at least the toleration, of such a system. There is obviously something in human beings which responds to this system, something they reflect and accommodate, something within them which paralyses every effort of their better selves to revolt. Human beings are compelled to live within a lie, but they can be compelled to do so only because they are in fact capable of living in this way. Therefore not only does the system alienate humanity, but at the same time alienated humanity supports this system as its own involuntary masterplan, as a degenerate image of its own degeneration, as a record of people's own failure as individuals.

The essential aims of life are present naturally in every person. In everyone there is some longing for humanity's rightful dignity, for moral integrity, for free expression of being and a sense of transcendence over the world of existences. Yet, at the same time, each person is capable, to a greater or lesser degree, of coming to terms with living within the lie. Each person somehow succumbs to a profane trivialization of his or her inherent humanity, and to utilitarianism. In everyone there is some willingness to merge with the anonymous crowd and to flow comfortably along with it down the river of pseudo-life. This is much more than a simple conflict between two identities. It is something far worse: it is a challenge to the very notion of identity itself.

In highly simplified terms, it could be said that the post-totalitarian system has been built on foundations laid by the historical encounter between dictatorship and the consumer society. Is it not true that the far-reaching adaptability to living a lie and the effortless spread of social auto-totality have some connection with the general unwillingness of consumption-oriented people to sacrifice some material certainties for the sake of their spiritual and moral integrity? With their willingness to surrender higher values when faced with the trivializing temptations of modern civilization? With their vulnerability to the attractions of mass indifference? And in the end, is not the greyness and the emptiness of life in the post-totalitarian system only an inflated caricature of modern life in general? And do we not in fact stand (although in the external measures of civilization, we are far behind) as a kind of warning to the West, revealing to it its own latent tendencies?

Let us now imagine that one day something in our greengrocer snaps and he stops putting up the slogans merely to ingratiate himself. He stops voting in elections he knows are a farce. He begins to say what he really thinks at political meetings. And he even finds the strength in himself to express solidarity with those whom his conscience commands him to support. In this revolt the greengrocer steps out of living within the lie. He rejects the ritual and breaks the rules of the game. He discovers once more his suppressed identity and dignity. He gives his freedom a concrete significance. His revolt is an attempt to *live within the truth*.

The bill is not long in coming. He will be relieved of his post as manager of the shop and transferred to the warehouse. His pay will be reduced. His hopes for a holiday in Bulgaria will evaporate. His children's access to higher education will be threatened. His superiors will harass him and his fellow workers will wonder about him. Most of those who apply these sanctions, however, will not do so from any authentic inner conviction but simply under pressure from conditions, the same conditions that once pressured the greengrocer to display the official slogans. They will persecute the greengrocer either because it is expected of them, or to demonstrate their loyalty, or simply as part of the general panorama, to which belongs an awareness that this is how situations of this sort are dealt with, that this, in fact, is how things are always done, particularly if one is not to become suspect oneself. The executors, therefore, behave essentially like everyone else, to a greater or lesser degree: as components of the post-totalitarian system, as agents of its automatism, as petty instruments of the social auto-totality.

Thus the power structure, through the agency of those who carry out the sanctions, those anonymous components of the system, will spew the greengrocer from its mouth. The system, through its alienating presence in people, will punish him for his rebellion. It must do so because the logic of its automatism and self-defence dictate it. The greengrocer has not committed a simple, individual offence, isolated in its uniqueness, but something incomparably more serious. By breaking the rules of the game, he has disrupted the game as such. He has exposed it as a mere game. He has shattered the world of appearances, the fundamental pillar of the system. He has upset the power structure by tearing apart what holds it together. He has demonstrated that living a life is living a lie. He has broken through the exalted façade of the system and exposed the real, base foundations of power. He has said that the emperor is naked. And because the emperor is in fact naked, something extremely dangerous has happened: by his action, the greengrocer has addressed the world. He has enabled everyone to peer behind the curtain. He has shown everyone that it *is* possible to live within the truth. Living within the lie can constitute the system only if it is universal. The principle must embrace and permeate everything. There are no terms whatsoever on which it can coexist with living within the truth, and therefore everyone who steps out of line *denies it in principle and threatens it in its entirety.*

This is understandable: as long as appearance is not confronted with reality, it does not seem to be appearance. As long as living a lie is not confronted with living the truth, the perspective needed to expose its mendacity is lacking. As soon as the alternative appears, however, it threatens the very existence of appearance and living a lie in terms of what they are, both their essence and their all-inclusiveness. And at the same time, it is utterly unimportant how large a space this alternative occupies: its power does not consist in its physical attributes but in the light it casts on those pillars of the system and on its unstable foundations. After all, the greengrocer was a threat to the system not because of any physical or actual power he had, but because his action went beyond itself, because it illuminated its surroundings and, of course, because of the incalculable consequences of that illumination. In the post-totalitarian system, therefore, living within the truth has more than a mere existential dimension (returning humanity to its inherent nature), or a noetic dimension (revealing reality as it is), or a moral dimension (setting an example for others). It also has an unambiguous *political* dimension. If the main pillar of the system is living a lie, then it is not surprising that the fundamental threat to it is living the truth. This is why it must be suppressed more severely than anything else.

In the post-totalitarian system, truth in the widest sense of the word has a very special import, one unknown in other contexts. In this system, truth plays a far greater (and, above all, a far different) role as a factor of power, or as an outright political force. How does the power of truth operate? How does truth as a factor of power work? How can its power – as power – be realized?

Individuals can be alienated from themselves only because there is *something* in them to alienate. The terrain of this violation is their authentic existence. Living the truth is thus woven directly into the texture of living a lie. It is the repressed alternative, the authentic aim to which living a lie is an inauthentic response. Only against this background does living a lie make any sense: it exists *because* of that background. In its excusatory, chimerical rootedness in the human order, it is a response to nothing other than the human predisposition to truth. Under the orderly surface of the life of lies, therefore, there slumbers the hidden sphere of life in its real aims, of its hidden openness to truth.

The singular explosive, incalculable political power of living within the truth resides in the fact that living openly within the truth has an ally, invisible to be sure, but omnipresent: this hidden sphere. It is from this sphere that life lived openly in the truth grows; it is to this sphere that it speaks, and in it that it finds understanding. This is where the potential for communication exists. But this place is hidden and therefore, from the perspective of power, very dangerous. The complex ferment that takes place within it goes on in semi-darkness, and by the time it finally surfaces into the light of day as an assortment of shocking surprises to the system, it is usually too late to cover them up in the usual fashion. Thus they create a situation in which the regime is confounded, invariably causing panic and driving it to react in inappropriate ways.

It seems that the primary breeding ground for what might, in the widest possible sense of the word, be understood as an opposition to the post-totalitarian system is living within the truth. The confrontation between these opposition forces and the powers that be, of course, will obviously take a form essentially different from that typical of an open society or a classical dictatorship. Initially, this confrontation does not take place on the level of real, institutionalized, quantifiable power which relies on the various instruments of power, but on a different level altogether: the level of human consciousness and conscience, the existential level. The effective range of this special power cannot be measured in terms of disciples, voters or soldiers, because it lies spread out in the fifth column of social consciousness, in the hidden aims of life, in human beings' repressed longing for dignity and fundamental rights, for the realization of their real social and political interests. Its power, therefore, does not reside in the strength of definable political or social groups, but chiefly in the strength of a potential, which is hidden throughout the whole of society, including the official power structures of that society. Therefore this power does not rely on soldiers of its own, but on the soldiers of the enemy as it were – that is to say, on everyone who is living within the lie and who may be struck at any moment (in theory, at least) by the force of truth (or who, out of an instinctive desire to protect their position, may at least adapt to that force). It is a bacteriological weapon, so to speak, utilized when conditions are ripe by a single civilian to disarm an entire division. This power does not participate in any direct struggle for power; rather it makes its influence felt in the obscure arena of being itself. The hidden movements it gives rise to there, however, can issue forth (when, where, under what circumstances, and to what extent are difficult to predict) in something visible: a real political act or event, a social movement, a sudden explosion of civil unrest, a sharp conflict inside an apparently monolithic power structure, or simply an irrepressible transformation in the social and intellectual climate. And since all genuine problems and matters of critical importance are hidden beneath a thick crust of lies, it is never quite clear when the proverbial last straw will fall, or what that straw will be. This, too, is why the regime persecutes, almost as a reflex action preventively, even the most modest attempts to live within the truth.

Why was Solzhenitsyn driven out of his own country? Certainly not because he represented a unit of real power, that is, not because any of the regime's representatives felt he might unseat them and take their place in government. Solzhenitsyn's expulsion was something else: a desperate attempt to plug up the dreadful wellspring of truth, a truth which might cause incalculable transformations in social consciousness, which in turn might one day produce political debacles unpredictable in their consequences. And so the post-totalitarian system behaved in a characteristic way: it defended the integrity of the world of appearances in order to defend itself. As long as it seals off hermetically the entire society, it appears to be made of stone. But the moment someone breaks through in one place, when one person cries out, 'The emperor is naked!' – when a single person breaks the rules of the game, thus exposing it as a game – everything suddenly appears in another light and the whole crust seems then to be made of a tissue on the point of tearing and disintegrating uncontrollably.

When I speak of living within the truth, I naturally do not have in mind only products of conceptual thought, such as a protest or a letter written by a group of intellectuals. It can be any means by which a person or a group revolts against manipulation: anything from a letter by intellectuals to a workers' strike, from a rock concert to a student demonstration, from refusing to vote in the farcical elections to making an open speech at some official congress, or even a hunger strike, for instance. If the suppression of the aims of life is a complex process, and if it is based on the multifaceted manipulation of all expressions of life then, by the same token, every free expression of life indirectly threatens the post-totalitarian system politically, including forms of expression to which, in other social systems, no one would attribute any potential political significance, not to mention explosive power.

The Prague Spring is usually understood as a clash between two groups on the level of real power: those who wanted to maintain the system as it was and those who wanted to reform it. It is frequently forgotten, however, that this encounter was merely the final act and the inevitable consequence of a long drama originally played out chiefly in the theatre of the spirit and the conscience of society. And that somewhere at the beginning of this drama, there were individuals who were willing to live within the truth, even when things were at their worst. These people had no access to real power, nor did they aspire to it. The sphere in which they were living the truth was not necessarily even that of political thought. They could equally have been poets, painters, musicians, or simply ordinary citizens who were able to maintain their human dignity. Today it is naturally difficult to pinpoint when and through which hidden, winding channel a certain action or attitude influenced a given milieu, and to trace the virus of truth as it slowly spread through the tissue of lies, gradually causing it to disintegrate. One thing, however, seems clear: the attempt at political reform was not the cause of society's reawakening, but rather the final outcome of that reawakening.

I think the present also can be better understood in the light of this experience. The confrontation between 1,000 Chartists and the post-totalitarian system would appear to be politically hopeless. This is true, of course, if we look at it through the traditional lens of the open political system, in which, quite naturally, every political force is measured chiefly in terms of the positions it holds on the level of real power. Given that perspective, a mini-party like the Charter would certainly not stand a chance. If, however, this confrontation is seen against the background of what we know about power in the post-totalitarian system, it appears in a fundamentally different light. For the time being, it is impossible to say with any precision what impact the appearance of Charter 77, its existence, and its work has had in the hidden sphere, and how the Charter's attempt to rekindle civic self-awareness and confidence is regarded there. Whether, when and how this investment will eventually produce dividends in the form of specific political changes is even less possible to predict. But that, of course, is all part of living within the truth. As an existential solution, it takes individuals back to the solid ground of their own identity; as politics it throws them into a game of chance where the stakes are all or nothing. For this reason, it is undertaken only by those for whom the former is worth risking the latter, or who have come to the conclusion that there is no other way to conduct real politics in Czechoslovakia today. Which, by the way, is the same thing: this conclusion can be reached only by someone who is unwilling to sacrifice his or her own human identity to politics, or rather who does not believe in a politics that requires such a sacrifice.

The more thoroughly the post-totalitarian system frustrates any rival alternative on the level of real power, as well as any form of politics independent of the laws of its own automatism, the more definitely the centre of gravity of any potential political threat shifts to the area of the existential and the prepolitical: usually without any conscious effort, living within the truth becomes the one natural point of departure for all activities that work against the automatism of the system. And even if such activities ultimately grow beyond the area of living within the truth (which means they are transformed into parallel structures, movements, institutions, they begin to be regarded as political activity, they bring real pressure to bear on the official structures and begin in fact to have a certain influence on the level of real power), they always carry with them the specific hallmark of their origins. Therefore it seems to me that not even the so-called dissident movements can be properly understood without constantly bearing in mind this special background from which they emerge.

The profound crisis of human identity brought on by living within a lie, a crisis which in turn makes such a life possible, certainly possesses a moral dimension as well: it appears, among other things, as *a deep moral crisis in society*. A person who has been seduced by the consumer value system, whose identity is dissolved in an amalgam of the accoutrements of mass civilization, and who has no roots in the order of being, no sense of responsibility for anything higher than his or her own personal survival, is a *demoralized* person. The system depends on this demoralization, deepens it, as in fact a projection of it into society.

Living within the truth, as humanity's revolt against an enforced position, is, on the contrary, an attempt to regain control over one's own sense of responsibility. In other words, it is clearly a moral act, not only because one must pay so dearly for it, but principally because it is not self-serving: the risk may bring rewards in the form of a general amelioration in the situation, or it may not. In this regard, as I stated previously, it is an all-or-nothing gamble, and it is difficult to imagine a reasonable person embarking on such a course merely because he or she reckons that sacrifice today will bring rewards tomorrow, be it only in the form of general gratitude. (By the way, the representatives of power invariably come to terms with those who live within the truth by persistently ascribing utilitarian motivations to them – a lust for power or fame or wealth – and thus they try, at least, to implicate them in their own world, the world of general demoralization.)

If living within the truth in the post-totalitarian system becomes the chief breeding ground for independent, alternative political ideas, then all considerations about the nature and future prospects of these ideas must necessarily reflect the moral dimension as a political phenomenon. (And if the revolutionary Marxist belief about morality as a product of the 'superstructure' inhibits any of our friends from realizing the full significance of this dimension and, in one way or another, from including it in their view of the world, it is to their own detriment: an anxious fidelity to the postulates of that world-view prevents them from properly understanding the mechanisms of their own political influence, thus paradoxically making them precisely what they, as Marxists, so often suspect others of being – victims of 'false consciousness'.) The very special political significance of morality in the post-totalitarian system is a phenomenon that is at the very least unusual in modern political history, a phenomenon that might well have … far-reaching consequences.

NOTE

1. In a previous passage, the author clarifies this term, which he uses to describe the political regimes of the Eastern bloc (at the time of writing in the late 1970s). He distinguishes these regimes from traditional dictatorships in a number of ways. In the latter, power is usually wielded by a small group of people who take over the government by force and it is usually temporary, lacking historical roots, and practises a certain amount of improvisation. However, none of these characteristics applies to the political regimes of Eastern Europe over the past decades. Václav Havel calls them 'post-totalitarian' regimes, explaining: 'I do not wish to imply by the prefix 'post' that the system is no longer totalitarian; on the contrary, I mean that it is totalitarian in a way fundamentally different from classical dictatorships, different from totalitarianism as we usually understand it.'

Wisdom as Power

This process toward social autonomy and regionality involves a different way of doing politics. Of course, it is not new; indeed, it is as old as Zarathustra, the first of the Indian Magi who recommended and relied on familial and folk beliefs for the survival of societies. But it amounts to a return to ancestral values and to the controllable, local dimensions of day-to-day life. It responds to a yearning to live decently in a type of society where power is no longer the monopoly of a chosen, centralized few, but distributed through relatively small organized communities and regions whose representatives respond collectively and directly to their constituents.

The main factors of this trend are *social movements* – not political parties as traditionally understood and conceived – with a concern for public issues which range from ecology to education, recreation and civic action. Their guiding principle is to proceed from *the grassroots upwards*, rather than from the top down, as occurs in the classic power structure which tends to disregard the views of the masses. Their most effective weapons for mobilization are based on *popular culture*, rather than on elitist referents. Their greatest ontological challenge is the *practical rationality* of traditional knowledge; that is, the rediscovery of forms of wisdom which have become obscured or discarded by Cartesian methods and Kantian empirical presuppositions. Their goal is political in the old sense of the word: *the achievement of power* to exercise a superior philosophy of life in which there is no role for old and present terrors.

...This is a practical and reflective rhythm in the grassroots that invites us to participate in alternative and probably better visions of the world. In fact it is a counterdiscourse to current 'development', which hinges on the idea of 'people's participation'.

...The common people and their organic intellectuals in the many places throughout the world where this rediscovery has taken place (especially in the Third World) have remembered (if they had ever in fact forgotten it) that knowledge is power. Through the contribution of their wisdoms they are creating a new and more comprehensive paradigm in which practical rationality combines with academic and Cartesian *ratio*, and where the means to produce knowledge are seen to be equally as important as those of material production.

...Such a scientific and political transformation at the grassroots, as well as on the scientific level, presupposes a change in the cast of social actors: in the resulting participatory type of community it is the civil sector which takes over the helm of society, not the military establishment or other power groups. And a truly participatory type of democracy replaces the current version of representative democracy which is in crisis in many parts of the world. Thus far, two social groups are assuming leading roles in such struggles and movements in the Third World: women and the marginal young literates. This is understandable, if we remember they have been victimized most cruelly by historical forces.

Such extended people's participation and atomized power at all levels of society (the true democratization of power) are nourished by an existential idea of *viviencia* or *Erlebnis;* that is, learning how to live and let live. It does not seek power to control and dominate through violence, but to rule by accord, pluralistic tolerance and direct democracy, although it does want to dismantle presently destructive centres of force, manipulation and monopoly. It means a return to the common people's core values rooted in original praxis, communal living and co-operation, and the humble respect of nature and man. It requires less of Machiavelli and Locke and more of Kropotkin and Althusius, and it signals a renewed interest in venerable anarchistic premisses (in the philosophical sense).

...Is a new comprehensive participatory paradigm or model now in the making? If it is, let us keep on trying. Let us lift the dust from our ancestral wisdoms; let us give new life to our gregarious impulses and inbred empathy, so that we can end the rule of Leviathan and Mars as the justifiers of the existence of nations and states.

Orlando Fals Borda, *Development: Seeds of Change* (SID), no. 3, 1983, pp. 66–7.

Orlando Fals Borda is a Colombian sociologist, dean and professor emeritus at the National University of Bogotá, former deputy to the Colombian National Constituent Assembly and Vice-Minister of State. He has been a major architect of the Participatory Action Research (PAR) concept in Latin America. See, in particular, the volume he edited, *Challenge of Social Change* (Sage, London, 1985), his *Knowledge and People's Power: Lessons with Peasants in Nicaragua, Colombia and Mexico* (ILO, Geneva, 1985), and, with Anisur Rahman, eds, *Action and Knowledge: Breaking the Monopoly with Participatory Action Research* (Apex Press, New York, 1991).

35

PROTECTING THE SPACE WITHIN

Karen Lehman

KAREN LEHMAN is a Senior Fellow at the Institute for Agriculture and Trade Policy, Minneapolis. She wrote an article on the disastrous consequences of the agricultural policies followed by Mexico, entitled 'The Great Grain Robbery of 1996', *Development: Seeds of Change* (SID), no. 4, 1996.

> Thirty spokes share the wheel's hub;
> It is the centre that makes it useful.
> Shape clay into a vessel;
> It is the space within that makes it useful.
> Cut doors and windows for a room;
> It is the holes that make it useful.
> Therefore profit comes from what is there;
> Usefulness from what is not there.
>
> Lao Tzu

At the centre of this discussion of what is economy and what is not is the simple relation or lack of it between what is profitable and what is useful. Many of our social institutions, at their best, were built as windows, vessels and spokes around a space which all knew was important but which none could name. Had the relationship between the space within and the structure around it remained pleasing, perhaps there would not be the desire, that temptation, to try to describe and give form to the space within.

The space within is itself, something apart. There is danger in trying to use a nail to pierce it, a plant to build a bridge across it, and to assume that in some way one has touched it. Many, in their efforts to protect or make the space within socially valuable, have attempted to do just this. Women's work, for example, should be made visible and valuable by placing a market value on child-rearing and housekeeping and by paying women wages to carry out this labour.

Yet to attempt to make visible that which is seen, institutional that which is informal, valuable that which is priceless, profitable that which is useful, and to structure that which is related, is to shrink the space within, destroying its beauty and its usefulness.

What happens in the space within cannot be simply described as 'gift' or 'non-economic life'. Yet if we think of it as something which has had a historic relation to economy, without being subsumed in it, we will be close to the truth. The market, and secondly money, were created as means to deal with the stranger – those not within the family, the tribe, household or village. Different rules were in effect for these relations with the outside than for those which governed the space within, however diversely this has been defined in different cultures. Within these realms, men and women had discrete and often equally important spheres, that of the man not always economic, nor that of the woman always and solely domestic. Men as well as women maintained the space within, not only through subsistence work, but through other things as well.

There are some things, even in industrialized societies, which do not, cannot and should not 'pay for themselves'. Things like fiesta, faith, child-rearing, mourning and celebration are those which nourish the community and the people in it. If the market economy is based on the assumption of scarcity, the space within and its activities are shaped by faith in the cornucopia. The market economy is structured to contend with the physical world, the finite. Its accountability is to quantity which is measurable. The space within, on the other hand, is concerned with the spiritual, the emotional, the social, and is the realm where real care and creation of social bonds is found. The accountability of the space within is to quality, which can only be experienced.

There are those who cannot imagine that something can be useful and beautiful without at the same time being profitable. Their industrious transformation of social life has shrunk the space within dramatically, to the extent that some believe it was never necessary in the first place, that its only purpose was to give shape to the frame around it, and that it is right and good that the frame should eventually cover or replace it.

The history of the movement from producing for subsistence to producing for the market parallels the shrinking of the useful but not profitable space within. Yet the two are distinct. Beneath the basic analysis of the change from subsistence activity to production for the market is the implicit assumption that people do what they do only to provide for their survival. Therefore, when people abandon their religious practices, their communal forms of governance, and a host of other customs, they do so because they no longer have survival value. But there is another possibility: that as economy invades subsistence activities, it captures and transforms customs and social relations, turning them with a new ideology to the service of the new form of production; unless, that is, they are vigorously defended.

The invasion of the space within by economy has several interesting characteristics. First, because the space within is visible only to those who participate in it, it is invisible to the logic of economy; yet the activities that were carried out within it become universally visible when they are captured

> What is most necessary for man, and what is given him in great abundance, are experiences, especially experiences of the forces within him. This is his most essential food, his most essential wealth. If man consciously receives all this abundance, the universe will pour into him what is called *life* in Judaism, *spirit* in Christianity, *light* in Islam, *power* in Taoism.
>
> **Ismail Al-Faruqi, 'On the Ethics of the Brethren of Purity', *Muslim World*, vol. 50, July 1960, p. 196.**

and professionalized. Something new is apparently created out of nothing, yet the consequences for the space within remain invisible in themselves, their effects being interpreted in the market economy as the need for new services to fix social disruption.

Second, based as it is on abundance, the space within carries much more of the activity and work of a society than can perhaps be imagined. The crisis of both the welfare state and the developing nation is that of an economy based on scarcity which tries to absorb and manage a world based on abundance. It is the dilemma of the large fish, who, after swallowing an apparently smaller one, realizes in horror that the 'little one' is actually much larger than himself (if less visible) and therefore utterly indigestible. The market economy cannot function if it attempts to perform the work of the space within using the measure of scarcity – cash. The money literally cannot stretch around it. In our technological societies, we have acted as if it can, and now that the true size of the beast becomes apparent, we scream for fiscal reform and cutbacks in social services. In the Third World, women are the ones trying to stretch themselves around the double burden, men's entrance into the global economy having proven insufficient to provide the cash necessary in the newly economized context. Women can hardly be expected to succeed where men failed, under the circumstances.

The implication of the economization of life is that the space within shrinks. The stranger enters the house and becomes its core. Television and the road mark the trail by which the people were carried off from the space within to that outside – without leaving home.

A BALANCE?

What if, instead of assuming the inevitability of economy and development, and therefore the necessity for women to take unattractive places within it, we look at things slightly differently? What if we imagine that the point is not to arrange the space within to fit the economy, but to defend a kind of relation between the two that supports both and damages neither?

On Saturday and Sunday afternoons in Mexico City, half a million people flock to the markets of Tepito, a 'popular' neighbourhood near the centre of the city. Tepito promotes its reputation as a centre for smuggled goods, a tough neighbourhood that can defend itself from the inside out, with its own justice for thieves analogous to tarring and feathering, and an orientation to city government that recognizes the threat of the wrecking ball and has resolve to halt it. Here in Tepito, the men appear to be the leaders of the myriad of organizations which co-operate, without co-ordination, around the religious hub of the community; but most will admit that a group of women exercises the real leadership of the community, planning the strategy and calling the shots. This they do from the more than 12,000 vending stalls in the streets of Tepito and from their '*vecindades*', clusters of up to forty housing units constructed around a central courtyard, the patio. In Tepito, 'the body is the home of the soul, the house is the home of the body, and the patio is the home of the people'. Everything moves from this literal 'space within' outward into the marketplace which physically rings the *vecindades*.

What is important here is that Tepiteños are firmly within economy, there being no sharper vendors than those of Tepito. Yet because both men and women support both the space within and economic life, they have succeeded in forging a relation between the two which ensures that the marketplace feeds the stomach but doesn't replace the heart.

Through the process of development, men have become increasingly economized, leaving women alone to maintain the space within. As women become economized, the space within is left to fend for itself and, in many cases, to die. What are the upwardly mobile professionals' homes and communities if not places where everything is paid for, from child care to mental health to dinner *à la* microwave?

Public policies have systematically eliminated possibilities for a fusion of the space within and economy closer to the hearth. The consumer protection movement, with the intent of protecting people from the irresponsibilities of corporate industry, resulted in the outlawing of many of the means of subsistence available to families, particularly women, in the USA during the Great Depression – home beauty parlours, boarding houses and the like.

If we allow ourselves to see the space within, to hear the wind blowing through it, instead of imagining it as invisible and silent, we will see what women, and until recently men, have been doing when not engaged in economic labour. For too long we have been looking at the window and not at the view. Women are now at the centre of the vista; increasingly, by necessity and misguided policy, they are being nailed into the framework, a position from which escape requires heroic effort.

To Find a Language for Our Need for Belonging

We recognize our mutual humanity in our differences, in our individuality, in our history, in the faithful discharge of our particular culture of obligations. There is no identity we can recognize in our universality. There is no such thing as love of the human race, only the love of this person for that, in this time and not in any other. These abstract subjects created by our century of tyranny and terror cannot be protected by abstract doctrines of universal human needs and universal human rights, and not merely because these doctrines are words, and whips are things. The problem is not to defend universality, but to give these abstract individuals the chance to become real, historical individuals again, with the social relations and the power to protect themselves... Woe betide any man who depends on the abstract humanity of another for his food and protection. Woe betide any person who has no state, no family, no neighbourhood, no community that can stand behind to enforce his claim of need.

...Our task is *to find a language for our need for belonging* which is not just a way of expressing nostalgia, fear and estrangement from modernity. Our political images of civic belonging remain haunted by the classical *polis*, by Athens, Rome and Florence. Is there a language of belonging adequate to Los Angeles? Put like that the answer can only seem to be no. Yet we should remember the ninteenth-century city and the richness of its invention of new forms and possibilities of belonging. Those great cities – Manchester, New York, Paris – were as strange to those who had to live in them for the first time as ours may seem to us. Yet we look back at them now as *a time of civic invention* – the boulevard, the public park, the museum, the café, the trolley car, street lighting, the subway, the railway, the apartment house. Each of these humble institutions created a new possibility for fraternity among strangers in public places.

Michael Ignatieff, *The Needs of Strangers*, The Hogarth Press, London, 1984, pp. 52–3, 139–40.

36

BIRTH OF THE INCLUSION SOCIETY

Judith A. Snow

The following text formed Judith Snow's Preface to the *Whole Community Catalogue*, edited by David Wetherow, Communitas Inc. (Box 374, Manchester, Connecticut 06040, USA) with Gunnars & Campbell Publishing, Winnipeg, Manitoba, 1990.

JUDITH A. SNOW is a visiting scholar at the Centre for Integrated Education and Community, Toronto, Ontario. Severely physically handicapped herself, she has been a source of inspiration and hope for others suffering mental and physical disabilities.

There is in the world today a vibrant new culture. It is young and rough, but its birth has been true and with proper nurture its life and growth promise to be dramatic. It is the culture of inclusion.

The culture of inclusion begins in the affirmation that all human beings are gifted. This statement sounds strange to many ears because our traditional world reserves the adjective 'gifted' for only a chosen few whose talents and abilities, usually in very circumscribed ways, impress, enlighten, entertain or serve the rest of us. The inclusion culture views giftedness much differently.

We affirm that giftedness is actually a common human trait, one that is fundamental to our capacity to be creatures of community. Gifts are whatever we are, whatever we do or whatever we have that allow us to create opportunities for ourselves and others to interact and do things together – interactions that are meaningful between at least two people. For example, if you are interested in an evening's fun playing softball and you have six people on your team, you have an opportunity to offer to several people, including some bystanders who might just end up watching. But you can't play softball without at least seven people per team. So when the seventh person comes along, that person's presence is a gift to other people, even if she or he doesn't play very well. Our presence is the fundamental gift that we bring to the human community. Presence is the foundation of all other opportunities and interactions – of everything that is meaningful in our lives.

What About the Children in the Post-Development Age?

In most 'development' projects, children are the last to be consulted or heard in decisions that ultimately affect *their* lives more than anybody else. Paradoxically, the ideology of 'progress' helped institutionalize processes of infantilization, rather than encourage more creative and meaningful responses to the universe of the younger generations.

Children and The Environment is the name of an unusually far-reaching project started by the California Wellness Foundation, in close collaboration with the University of California in Berkeley, which constitutes one of the few exceptions to this trend. For its promoters, 'children's environments include all the physical places where children go, or are placed – in homes, child care, streets, schools, parks, churches, malls, courts, or jails. [That includes] what happens to them in these places, and their relationships with other people there. They also comprise the food they eat, the drugs they consume, the TV programs they watch, the air they all breathe and the political and commercial climate in which decisions affecting all these are made.'

'Of the 8 million children 18 years and under in [the state of California]', says the last report of the project, 'two million come from families living in poverty, lacking adequate food, without health insurance, often in physically and socially toxic environments. If current trends continue, as many as one-third of our children will live in poverty and hunger by the year 2000 … Moreover, the public discourse around vital children's issues, in science, government and through media, is nearly always framed by adult experts. Even though children, with their families and in communities, live in closest contact to the problems that affect them, children's subjective experience is rarely taken into account. Children, like women a century ago, are for the most part unheard.'

For the report, 'Western norms of development, reflected in children's legal status, have worked against the recognition of the young as social and political agents in their own right. In most cases children are still not consulted at all about their "best interests", since they are marked as "not yet fully being", as underdeveloped.'

'Nineteenth-century assumptions of backwardness and progress underlie the dominant research in child *development*. There is an implicit notion that children must be "civilized" through socialization, and a deeply embedded presupposition that they are socialized "to" an independent, pre-existing and stable environment. Children's development is always in relation to discourses and practices around family, school, the media environment, childhood professionals, everday life, cultural traditions, peer groups, and the "natural" and the built world. Our approach commits us to respect the fact of children's subjectivity, so that they are seen in their capacity as producers of the world they inhabit, and not simply passive products of it.'

Inspired by children's movements in Latin America and Europe, the initiative is a most interesting signpost on the post-development road. It proposes to help children create for their activities autonomous 'safe spaces' where they would be able to give shape to their dreams of a different world. New forms of partnership and participation are already emerging that provide evidence that children can be much better experts for finding solutions to their problems. We hope that more adults will be found everywhere to imagine such and other new forms of partnership, so that people of all ages can discover the joy of learning from each other, free from the stereotyped images they have of each other.

M.R.

The report *Children and Environment: Planning Project Report* (Draft 3, dated 17 January 1996) was prepared for the California Wellness Foundation by a multicultural, interdisciplinary group of researchers and activists under the overall direction of Dr Michael Schwab, Community Health Specialist at the School of Public Health of the University of California at Berkeley.

Also fundamental to each person's presence is each person's difference. In fact presence is not possible without difference since even on a very simplistic level difference is essential to life. For example, none of us would be here if the male and female difference did not exist. Meaning depends on difference as well, since if we were all the same there would be nothing to share or contribute to one another. Therefore, not sameness but presence and difference are fundamental to life and community.

In addition to our presence, each of us has a grab bag of other ordinary gifts that allow for us to create and participate in daily opportunities. From getting up, making breakfast, washing dishes or loading a dishwasher, talking on a telephone, writing on a piece of paper, listening to another person, getting from one place to another, enjoying some music, expressing an opinion, going to a meeting, playing with a baby or having fun with a friend, a variety of simple activities taking place in ordinary places on ordinary streets make up the fabric of the vast majority of our work, family life, private life and public contribution.

Beyond ordinary giftedness there is extraordinary giftedness, the kind that extends opportunity for interaction and meaning to a large number and variety of people. One person is not just nice to be with but is a truly funny comedian; another doesn't just get around but dances on skates beautifully; another not only shows up for the Parents and Teachers Association but has ideas that are engaging and changing the face of the local school board.

Each person has a variety of ordinary and extraordinary gifts. The people whom we call handicapped are people who are missing some typical ordinary gifts. However, such people also have a variety of other ordinary and extraordinary gifts capable of stimulating interaction and meaning with others. In fact it is not just that walking is a gift, and not walking is not a gift, or that knowing how to put your clothes on right is a gift and not knowing how is not a gift. Rather, walking is a gift and not walking is also a gift; knowing how to dress is a gift and not knowing how to dress is also a gift. Each creates the possibility of meaningful interaction.

The affirmation of giftedness creates the need for us to organize our homes, schools, workplaces and other establishments differently and this is what has given birth to the inclusion culture. In the past we became efficient at separating people into classifications of supposed sameness. Now we are struggling to build our community life up from the foundation of our enriching differences.

In North America the Canada geese fly south every fall and north in the spring, covering thousands of miles each way. The birds fly in a V-formation, with one bird in front followed by two diverging lines of fliers. The lead bird breaks the wind resistance for the two behind who in turn are shields for the birds behind each of them, down to the end of the line. But in the course of each flight the leader drops out of position to go to the end of the line and to be replaced by one of the following birds, over and over again. In this way no one bird is ever leader so long as to be exhausted or to deny opportunity to another bird. In turn, each bird is the guide. This is a model of organizing a community so that the gifts of all benefit everyone.

In some schools we see classrooms of creative learning being founded on the support that children and teachers can offer to each other in the spirit of co-operation. In housing we see people forming inclusive, mutually supportive developments where vulnerable people anchor circles of caring. In decision-making bodies we see people taking leadership in turns, based on their energy, experience, desire and availability, and able to give way to one another at the right time.

Of course these efforts at inclusive community are isolated and foundationally weak. But the seed has been well sown. These efforts support each other and inspire others to change. The story of inclusion has a vigorous beginning and promises a very creative future.

Why We Sing
(Por que cantamos)

If each hour brings its death
if time is a den of thieves
the breezes carry a scent of evil
and life is just a moving target

you will ask why we sing

if our finest people are shunned
our homeland is dying of sorrow
and the human heart is shattered
even before shame explodes

you will ask why we sing

if the trees and the sky remain
as far off as the horizon
some absence hovers over the evening
and disappointment colours the morning

you will ask why we sing

we sing because the river is humming
and when the river hums the river hums
we sing because cruelty has no name
but we can name its destiny
we sing because the child because everything
because in the future because the people
we sing because the survivors
and our dead want us to sing

we sing because shouting is not enough
nor is sorrow or anger
we sing because we believe in people
and we shall overcome these defeats

we sing because the sun recognizes us
and the fields smell of spring
and because in this stem and that fruit
every question has its answer

we sing because it is raining on the furrow
and we are the militants of life
and because we cannot and will not
allow our song to become ashes.

Mario Benedetti, Uruguay, 1979.
Translated by D'Arcy Martin.

37

REINVENTING THE PRESENT: THE CHODAK EXPERIENCE IN SENEGAL

Emmanuel Seni N'Dione, Philippe de Leener, Jean-Pierre Perier, Mamadou Ndiaye and Pierre Jacolin

Increasingly, Africa appears to the outsider as the land of the doomed. For a couple of centuries, its people were submitted to some of the most visibly shocking crimes ever perpetrated by the 'developed' world: slavery and colonialism at its worst. However, what occurred after their political independence proved to be even worse. African politicians who had headed their people's struggle for independence replaced the colonial rulers and set up new nation states with a view to transforming the old systems of repressive governance into new instruments of liberation. Yet most of them only illustrated Frantz Fanon's metaphor of 'Black skins, white masks'. In half a century, their total betrayal of their people caused the latter untold miseries and indignities. The 'development' which was proposed to them as the key to their liberation ended up creating millions of newly excluded people and refugees. Institutions set up to reinforce people's independence either helped the emerging indigenous 'elites' to establish new forms of slavery at home, or served to pump out the 'educated' in the form of 'brain drain'. Last but not least, the new slaves were forced to honour the debts which their masters had taken, in their name, from the World Bank and other foreign institutions, in order to maintain their repressive power.

Yet, once again, the rarest pearls seem to be found in the darkest depths of the oceans. The text which follows is the account of a very 'small', yet highly inspiring, exercise of regenerative co-action, undertaken by the members of an African community and their friends, outside the development paradigm. The experience known as Chodak has already been mentioned in some articles in this Reader, in particular that of Hassan Zaoual, who stresses the importance of exploring the specificities of human sites and provides interesting clues for understanding the new approaches being tried by Chodak. But only a careful reading of the whole book by the ENDA-GRAF team, *Réinventer le présent*, can render the full richness of this experience in Senegal. It is, however, hoped that the following excerpts, selected from the book and translated from the French for this Reader by Victoria Bawtree, will provide enough material for those interested in the many ways in which the people at the grassroots are preparing the post-development era. Such interest may even provoke a demand for an English translation of the book: it is symptomatic that there are few English-language presentations of the work of Emmanuel N'Dione and his friends, although *Dynamique urbaine d'une société en grappe: un cas, Dakar* was published by ENDA-Tiers Monde as long ago as 1987. However, Intermediate Technology Publications, with ENDA-GRAF, have published a first English presentation of the Chodak experience, under the title *The Future of Community Lands: Human Resources* (London, 1995).

EMMANUEL SENI N'DIONE has a doctorate in Sociology. He is the director of the ENDA-GRAF Programme, ENDA-Tiers Monde, Dakar, Senegal. His friends have given him the appellation 'barefoot researcher'.

BIRTH OF A FRIENDSHIP IN THE PLURAL

Our adventure began in February 1975, in the periphery of Dakar, at Grand-Yoff to be exact. We had counted on the proverbial cohesiveness of African communities on which to build our efforts to strengthen the activities of the grassroots.

The ideological yoke we had made for ourselves weighed heavily on us. It hindered us from appreciating the dense, diversified social fabric that was staring us in the face. For a long time we had preferred to strengthen peasant initiatives outside their original institutional niches, for fear of losing our soul and monopoly over those initiatives – all privileges which, paradoxically, we secretly wanted to keep.

Fortunately the facts won out over our obstinacy. In fact, the associations which we had helped to create – in the fields of health programmes, re-integrating idle young people, improving the standard of living and various economic activities – had all broken up. Members did not take to group methods of operating: they preferred the security of groups made up of families or clans, social networks, *mbotayes*, *tontines*, street gangs … They found that our way of confronting reality resulted only in isolating individuals from their own social space and thus increased their insecurity.

The need to survive and to justify our existence in the district brought us to our senses. We became more attuned to what the people were doing. At the same time, we had abandoned our habit of always relating the facts, observations, people's attitudes and behaviour to our own framework of reference. We recognized that we lacked a lot of information, which hindered us in understanding the coherences and incoherences of people's actions. It was absolutely vital to get hold of this missing information.

Surveys, research into the local milieu or feasibility studies could not provide this missing information, nor would they help to create and expand the indispensable climate of confidence and collaboration between us and the peasants and shanty-town dwellers with whom we wanted to work in a synergetic way. In the usual methods of information gathering, individuals are pre-eminent, while what we needed to know was exactly how relative their importance was. Groups and associations of all kinds seemed to be the best interlocutors and to provide natural spaces for participation. It thus became necessary to identify them in order to know what their projects were, and to negotiate our own participation in lines of action that had already been determined by them.

Our initial plans of action thus largely depended on the itinerary followed by grassroots actors. By these, we mean the living populations as opposed to masses, who tend to be passive and manipulated. They are seen as an ideal framework for reciprocal communication, questioning and apprenticeship as well as for continuing negotiations. In this way we were led to share adventures together in different fields. We developed activities in such diverse sectors as fisheries, health, local land planning, village irrigation, drainage, agricultural, rural and urban forestry, recycling and treatment of garbage, commercial and non-commercial exchanges, environmental education…

We also collaborated with different partners: the *mbotayes* in the urban areas, women, young people in the streets, girls and women in difficulty, people's enterprises, artisans, grain processors, savings groups (men and women), traditional health practitioners, village associations, farmers, herders, fishermen, tree farmers … We were concerned to identify activities that reinforced the capacities of the people and that promoted reciprocal apprenticeship and the acquisition of new skills. Above all, while our symbolic opening up was going on and enabling us to take on board other values, we wanted to acquire more hands-on experience for researching individuals and groups and for promoting mutual benefits. And later on, to make a place for them amongst us, if they so wished.

Thanks to this approach and the lessons we learned along the way, we developed various methods of working and accumulated a genuinely meaningful experience. Through action, we continued to make discoveries, dictated by circumstances and unforeseen situations. Sometimes, when confronted with two possible lines of action we made certain choices, justifying them according to our intuition, sensitivities and subjectivities. We learnt from these experiences to the extent that we had been lucid enough in understanding the terrains which we had explored and the paths we had taken. Sometimes it was the desire to know more that caused us to get lost.

Our minds thus began to be enriched by new concepts, born out of the pains of successive disillusionments and deconstructions, of constructed or revitalized myths, enabling us to see unexpected realities and new categories of people, animals and things. While they seemed random enough at the beginning, these new beliefs, thanks to our imaginary world, found their place in a symbolic space which gave them consistency and legitimacy. After initial confusion, we reorganized the pieces of our puzzle and quite naturally developed a capacity to circumscribe and project a social or political space in which we hoped the poor would occupy a privileged position. We assumed that they were the indispensable resource able to respond to the challenges of the future.

DEVELOPMENT: A POVERTY-GENERATING IDEOLOGY

The outstanding events in recent world history had shaken our certainties, questioning the simplistic formula of 'progress for everyone' and brought to light what should disappear for ever in a 'developing' world, particularly the phenomena of exclusion and impoverishment. It is only too obvious that the world around us does not integrate everyone. On the contrary, a minority seems to pull through by creating the conditions for excluding the majority, amongst whom are the people with whom we work in the urban and the rural areas. More and more, a culture dominated by the values of a monetary economy is spreading and substituting all other kinds of thinking, to the point that only transactions bearing the seal of money seem worthwhile. As we thought about it, were we not, after all, helping to create the poor, through our practices, promoting values and perceptions of things which encouraged impoverishment, domination or exclusion and which consolidated this development culture?[1]

This was a key moment in our itinerary. Without realizing it and with the best of intentions, we were thus inviting the penetration of the dominant economic logic, to the extent that we were supporting a whole set of viewpoints on what should or should not be done, what should be thought and how – for example by proposing ways of organizing which purported to be democratic and egalitarian, or by introducing the biased criteria of profitability.[2] We were making the same comments when we started up production projects to improve the income of individuals or groups.

We then realized that we were looking at the grassroots population from the standpoint of our own descriptive categories, particularly the way in which we would view situations and what the solutions should be. We had the illusion that we could see the reality, in all its objectivity. We claimed to base our positions on the so-called 'logic of things', whereas it was only our own vision – a vision which was natural for us, given our culture and our constraints.

Impoverishment and domination are linked to the way we see reality in the function of ourselves and of our own projections…

IMPOVERISHING THE VERNACULAR CONCEPT OF RICHES

There are many development models, some of which claim to be alternative. Every aid agency, every organization almost, has its own philosophy in this respect. To simplify matters, but at the risk of seeming reductionist, we shall be speaking here about the development model in the singular, as we feel that, apart from a few differences which admittedly can at times be very obvious, these models all share certain common denominators, which we would like briefly to consider.

At present, the development culture, which engenders impoverishment and loneliness, promotes the following:

- an economic conception of time;
- the cult of statistics and competition between individuals;
- the universalizing claims of the development model;
- a certain image of individual success which development culture transmits as a value;
- money as a universal yardstick for deciding what people and things are worth;
- the commodification of people and goods;
- the compartmentalization of life, specialization carried to extremes;
- the hegemony of international languages in explaining the world.

How is it possible not to question the values conveyed by this type of development, while refusing to consider life as a spectacle to be consumed? The idea of a development based on impoverishing the concept of wealth is simply unacceptable; in particular when it degrades the human quality of relationships among people and their relationships with their environment.

We find it absurd to accumulate an increasing heap of material 'riches'. We find it equally absurd to claim that such riches, one day, will be the lot of a humanity that is constantly growing in number. As the wealth of a few develops, the poverty of the majority increases: a growing number of men and women become incapable of surviving on their own. As we see it, what could be expected from this type of development is that it excludes the largest number of people from the processes which serve the interests, the good and the power of a few. It serves to create poverty and exclusion, when it is redistribution that should take precedence.

Indeed, the systems that dominate the world base the legitimacy of development in the belief that what is valid for them must necessarily be valid for everyone. If they have been able to accumulate a certain quantity of goods through industrialization and have received a certain satisfaction from it, then this model must, according to them, be universally adopted.

To reject this vision of development is not only to refuse a model or a concept; it is to distance oneself from a whole host of references, practices and ways of reasoning. This is not to deny, of course, that in certain sectors an accumulation of resources and the consequent investments are necessary…

By depreciating the capacity to be self-sufficient and being satisfied with local resources, the development ideology is creating poverty. From this viewpoint, the expression 'subsistence economy' to describe the non-commercial economies is very revealing: these economies and the people who are involved in them are only subsisting, in the sense that they are only meeting their needs. The development ideology implies – and therein lies its fraudulence – that development can bring something else, something more than life – something which today is lacking and which is the explanation of poverty. That something is nothing but the avalanche of goods and the spectacle provided by their consumption. It is no longer enough to live; it is necessary to consume.

As soon as this view is rejected and its logic turned upside down, wealth can be identified, not in objects or in purchasing power but in the level of integration of people in their natural and spiritual environment, in the quality of their relationships with the society around them. If we were to evaluate the wealth of a society by its level of independence or autonomy vis-à-vis the foreigner, the far-off, the unknown; if we were to assess it according to its capacity to integrate and 'include' the greatest number of people; if we also assessed its capacity to redistribute – one would be led to conclude that many in the West live in a state of poverty and precariousness. The slightest tremor on Wall Street throws thousands of people, whole families, on to the street, without resources and without access to resources, isolated in their solitude. However, regardless of what happens in New York or Tokyo, there are still numerous groups of people throughout the world who can live without fear of the feverish movements of the Dow Jones or Nikkei stock-exchange indexes. For these groups depend above all on their relations with their neighbours and their integration into the immediate natural environment. Poverty is above all a cultural phenomenon: individuals are poor if they see themselves as such, as are those who do not realize their own wealth.

All this makes us refuse economic evaluations that are based on purchasing power, the gross national product, the level of consumption and the creation of money as absolute and universal references.

TOWARDS A NEW DEFINITION OF WEALTH

What seems important now is to re-create a dynamic at the margins of development, breaking with everything that we have just been denouncing. Such a rupture would start with a new appreciation of what wealth really is and the perhaps irreconcilable concepts underlying it. Everything has a value, not only that which is bought or sold. Wealth, therefore, has many dimensions. One becomes rich by taking advantage of the many canals that irrigate and diversify knowledge and wisdom, and stimulate mutual discoveries and recognition. People themselves are the main means for making this synergy work: hence the importance of supporting dynamic processes that rehabilitate people in all their dimensions, and that also rehabilitate relationships between themselves and their surroundings.

At the moment, it is essentially the laws of the market which establish the values of things and people, that define the relative spaces and give sense to social practices. For example, wage-earners establish the value of human resources: those who have a job, and therefore a wage, have access to material wealth and relationships; the others are excluded. Unemployment is not only lack of income; it is above all the absence of a place, of a *raison d'être* in society. Those who accept this process become the accomplices of exclusion and all forms of impoverishment. We must resort to other references and reinforce ways of behaving that encourage people to recognize each other's worth.

Recreating the social ties that convey the sense of collectivity

One of the basic mechanisms of domination seems to be the way a 'sense of exclusivity' is produced: our everyday parlance is contaminated by terms or concepts that manufacture poverty and exclusion. Typical of this phenomenon are the dichotomies literate/illiterate, experts/uninitiated, science/people's knowledge, modern/traditional, and so on. We have already talked about the concept of poverty: if the currently dominant meaning is accepted, i.e., if the wealthy are defined as those who accumulate large quantities of goods or monetary wealth for their private benefit, then the poor are obviously those who are not in this situation, like most of the people with whom we are working. Looking at agricultural producers in this light, it is tempting to categorize as rich the French farmer who is a member of the 100 quintals club [1 quintal equals 100 kilos] and the Sahelian cereal-producing peasant as poor, if only material production is considered as capital. On the one hand a few tools, and on the other machines that fill buildings as vast as railways stations. But if we look at the definition in the opposite way and, for example, consider as rich the producer who has a large network of mutual aid on which he can count, it is probable that the Sahelian cereal producer will seem very wealthy compared with French or American farmers, isolated as they are in their immense landholdings.

This is why we consider this capital of relationships as the main wealth of the poor. It therefore seems essential to support all initiatives that make the most of peoples' social networks – for example, through promoting meetings between popular leaders and experts.

Rediscovering the sense of the practical

Changing human beings means changing their way of seeing the world and especially the way they see the world *in* which and *off* which they live. We must not impose our own ways of seeing; instead we must be able to recognize the meaning that people give to what they do or to their own lives, and enable them to rediscover their capacity to make sense of it all.

Look at children. They are constantly faced with the dilemma: to create or to conform? Contemporary artists teach us how to rediscover symbolic creativity through a critical analysis of conformity. Recognizing the meaning people give to things and to their lives is to recognize the different pairs of glasses that are used to perceive the world, whether it is close by or far away. The significance, the profound meaning, of what we see and of the life we live mostly depends, in the ultimate analysis, on how we see things and the words we use in speaking about them. To recognize this way of seeing and the words expressing what is seen seems to be a basic principle, an inescapable point of departure.

This is what we mean by rediscovering the sense of things: to help bring to light those 'signifiers' that create exclusion, that devalue the resources and abilities of the people themselves, and to replace them with things that, rather, rehabilitate them – what we call the 'inclusive sense'. This is a necessary condition for promoting 'the inclusion' of the majority; that is, their integration into a system of life that they can handle and which assimilates them instead of excluding them.

The rediscovery of the relevant sense of the expression *here and now* can only be carried out by the poor themselves. Our role, as we see it today, is to work with this inclusive sense, with a view to facilitating the processes aimed at rediscovering it. It is also to bring the dominant system to value this perception. We have no pretensions to being new interpreters, or to substituting a new prophecy for the dominant one. We feel that the very process of rediscovery is a liberating one. The truth, *one's own* truth, is not received from outside: it is discovered in the very process of one's own liberation. The same things holds for the 'real' sense of things and life.

Reciprocity as an alternative to free exchange

Many African societies still live according to the model of reciprocity. 'I receive, therefore I exist. I give, therefore I am respected.' According to this logic, the gift is the main point of reference: the act of giving, which is in fact redistributing the surplus that has been created, confers respectability and prestige. What is determinant is the social context which legitimizes the gift so that it is never an isolated act: the gift creates or reinforces the social ties; it calls for a counter-gift which is never spelt out, either for its content or for its expiry date.

The exchange logic that the development model is trying to make universal aims at satisfying the individual needs that each person may have to assure his or her personal well-being. The exchange takes place on a note of 'I give you what you don't have and, in exchange, you give me what I don't have, in proportion to the value of my contribution.' The emphasis is put on the thing and on its possession, according to a logic of accumulation ('The more I have, the more I am'). The value of what is exchanged is subjective and relative, fixed by the law of scarcity: only what is rare has value. Everything can be classified according to a scale of values and sanctioned by money.

Everywhere it spreads, this development logic tends to substitute the relationships of reciprocity by economic relationships imposed by the yardstick of free exchange, bringing with it a decomposing of the social tissue and a disintegrating of the ties of solidarity. In places where an *economy of sufficiency* prevailed, the logic of free exchange now talks of the *subsistence economy*. Quite simply, it is no longer enough to be; to be more, it is necessary to have more and more, on pain of merely subsisting.

Four orientations

We have chosen four strategic lines of action to reconstruct the original sense of *here and now*, to re-create the social ties that reinforce the feeling of collectivity and to rehabilitate popular reciprocity and expertise. They have the following objectives:

- utilizing the spaces of tension;[3]
- regenerating the value of popular creativity;
- regenerating the value of cultural contributions and the sense (or meaning) of symbolic spaces;
- making a critique of 'bastions'[4] and promoting popular expertise.

Our allies in this strategy are *the victims* of the present dominant system, in particular those who have been excluded from their symbolic wealth and, inside each of them, especially the rebel, the creator, the seeker and the inventor who are lying dormant. Like those who are dominated, we too are learning to discern the wealth, resources and values which are denied, ignored or rejected by the dominant system. In the rural areas, for example, we are interested in what others have devalued and what the villagers consider to be hopeless, such as the spaces abandoned because they are not productive enough, the species which are in the process of disappearing because they are being overexploited or abandoned altogether, the plants and phytotherapeutic practices which are associated with them, the religious acts that are linked with agro-pastoral activities...

DISCOVERING NEW WAYS OF INTERPRETING REALITY

Social and economic practices make up a culture as much as gestures, attitudes and behaviour. They result from ways of 'living in the world' on a day-to-day basis. We have noticed a loss of meaning which is caused by increasing recourse to foreign systems of explaining things to people. Things are no longer true or false because they have been tested by people themselves, or because people close to them have experienced or accepted them as such, but because they coincide with an explanation that has been legitimized by foreign authorities: Science, Religion, Reason … When people are dispossessed of their capacity to explain the reason for things, they become culturally dominated and disposed to accept their own exclusion.

In practice, the loss of meaning comes from expropriation, both at the level of resource management and that of cultural transmission. That is what happens, for example, when the care of trees is assigned to an administration that redefines the rules and, through them, imposes the definition of what a tree or a forest is. It is the same thing for projects that support women with savings and credit schemes. They often emphasize the management of the money and the size of individual profit, whereas, from the viewpoint of the women, it is the redistribution and new relationships that enable the access to credit. To re-create the meaning of people's real lives, it is more appropriate to talk about 'relational economies', as 'projects' often focus, sometimes exclusively, on the monetary economy or accounting techniques.

Start out with life itself and evolving situations, rather than problems or needs

Real change, we feel, comes from within societies and is characterized by movement towards a greater integration of all dimensions of life. It is what creates synergies and the sense of inclusion.

The world is not only a universe of problems and emergencies. Difficulties and needs are beyond measure. However, these needs and problems must not cover up the really basic concerns, which only the poor can identify and legitimize. They must not overshadow the search for cohesion and coherence, which are of permanent concern for many groups of people who are being impoverished by the dominant system. Thus, to empty granaries, or to commemorate funerals in between seasons, should not be considered as 'unreasonable', as certain people deplore when talking about the peasants that they are supporting. 'A replete stomach does not fill either the heart or the soul, while the soul and the heart that are at peace can await the harvest in all serenity', as Mossi peasants in Burkina Faso explained to us. This kind of experience has taught us to be wary of such notions as 'needs' and 'problems'.

Development ideology is entirely based on the idea that needs must be satisfied, at all costs. So much so that one could define development as an enterprise that aims at the progressive satisfaction of needs that are less and less related to subsistence. From this viewpoint, the more developed ones are those who have satisfied their primary needs – to drink, eat, look after their health, and so on, and who now seek to satisfy new needs through consuming products that are less necessary. In fact, the satisfaction of one need gives rise to dissatisfaction because of ten or a hundred other needs, and so it goes on for ever. To use needs as a point of departure, we felt, led to an impasse. Needs are alienating, in the sense that they drive the individual to look further and further afield, outside of himself, far away and outside of his reference community. The only really essential need would seem to be a sense and a harmony in one's life, in the place where one is living, with those around one. This is a need that cannot be the object of trade. 'I have nothing, therefore I don't need anything', says the Moroccan proverb.

To stick to what is close by does not mean excluding what is further away, so long as the latter does not cause destruction and rootlessness. The need for more, for some other thing, elsewhere, is part of life: it creates temporary or lasting migrations, the complexities of which we should one day try to understand better.

Rather than relying on a controversial ideology of development, we prefer to base our work on *situations*. It may be that we create these situations as a consequence of our actions, or it may be that these situations exist independently of us and that we utilize them. Both approaches, if they exclude alternatives, raise questions. Any situation can serve as a point of departure for reflection – both our own, but also and above all on the part of those with whom we are interacting, in the town or in the countryside. All situations can be used as opportunities to look into issues which can lead to action or to learning processes, as well as serving as a springboard to question one's certainties. As long as they are part of everyday life, situations present opportunities to stimulate grassroots reflection.

But the here and now should not make us lose sight of external relationships. We now live in the 'global village' and we should not be indifferent to what is going on in the centre or in other peripheries. On the contrary, we should seek out collaboration both at the local and global levels. We do not want to intone the refrain 'excluded of the world, unite!', but a knowledge and understanding of what is going on at the national or the international level can help us work out local priorities. Being local doesn't mean being isolationist.

OF BELIEFS AND KNOWLEDGE

The statements on which beliefs are based reflect the personality and culture of the observer. Concepts do not thus represent the so-called perceived objects or realities, as the act of observation is a projection of the mental universe of the person who is observing that which is external to himself/herself. The representations, ideas, conceptions, convictions – in sum, all that follows the observations – are beliefs: in other words, things one believes to be true.

In this way beliefs are born. They are necessary for our own security – because we need to believe in things to live. They are also indispensable in our relationships with others, in the sense that we subdue them if they adopt our beliefs, or we let ourselves be dominated by them if we adopt their beliefs. In fact power, which is at the centre of all social relations, rests on the market of beliefs.

The dominant beliefs become universal when they are no longer linked to the people who have proclaimed them, or to the situations and struggles that activated them, or to their perceptions, but are claimed to be brought about by things; they pass for being objective, they insidiously become the viewpoint of things ('it's like that'), they become 'knowledge'. It is here, too, that the symbolic places, the sites of beliefs of one and everyone, become the epistemological sites of knowledge for everyone. Social control also works through the control of beliefs, and therefore the control of souls.

From this it follows that those who do not know are those whose beliefs have not been endorsed as tools or bases on which to construct and conduct society. The poor are precisely those who have no opportunity to make known their beliefs or to have them recognized, or to reproduce them: those whose beliefs cannot be elevated into knowledge, or who have no possibility of 'selling' the product of their imaginary on the belief market. Clearly, what is true is what the powerful believe or say to be true: the truths of the poor or of those without rank are only beliefs that come up against the knowledge of those who hold the levers of power.

This is why the relationship between knowledge and power must, we feel, be clarified if one wants change. To recognize the value of the know-how and the beliefs of the poor somehow ends up by becoming a political act: it amounts to attacking the bases of legitimacy of the dominant power.

Working with the underprivileged means, first of all, rehabilitating the status of their beliefs and promoting them on the belief market. And, at the same time, it means giving them the right to recognition. The beliefs that the dominant have set up as knowledge for all occasions, to hold good for everyone else, must be brought down from their pedestals. Thus, we feel that the search for a more just society must start out by legitimizing all beliefs (which is not the same thing as subscribing to all beliefs).

For that which we believe to be knowledge is only learned from others through education and mechanisms of identification. This is why all knowledge systems should be made relative: they are knowledges pertaining to a particular group of humans, in a given epoch and space. By accepting the limit of our knowledge, it is possible for us to open ourselves up to the riches of all knowledge and beliefs.

NOTES

1. There are proposals by certain organizations which seem to be solutions. For example, some experiences developed by the ILO, namely through its policy of supporting small and medium-sized enterprises, have their attractions, but unfortunately they favour the penetration of the dominant economic logic.

2. This certainly does not mean that we reject the concept of profitability. What we are against are the reductionist, simplistic and impoverished interpretations that are

transmitted by capitalists. For us, profitability includes the long term, the creation of relationships, exchange and the conservation of the environment.

3. These 'spaces of tension' are both 'physical' and 'relational', according to the authors. The first group includes 'socio-spatial' spaces, such as the urban peripheries threatened by the expansion of cities, precarious neighbourhoods, with squatter populations, and the rural spaces from which their populations have been evicted (such as classified forests, natural reservations, etc.). To these should be added the spaces of social tension opposing the administration to the population, landowners to tenants, holders of formal power to informal power, bosses to employees, old to young, men to women [Eds].

4. Bastions are those institutions that produce and impose on everyone the 'right' fashion for understanding the world and the way it functions. As such, they tend to legitimize the current practices that lead to excluding most of humanity. Schools, universities, administrations, banks are, in our view, some of these bastions.

AFTERWORD

TOWARDS POST-DEVELOPMENT: SEARCHING FOR SIGNPOSTS, A NEW LANGUAGE AND NEW PARADIGMS

Majid Rahnema

Truth is perhaps the most important name of God. In fact it is more correct to say that Truth is God, than to say God is Truth.... Therefore the pursuit of Truth is true *bhakti* (devotion). It is the path that leads to God. There is no place in it for cowardice, no place for defeat. It is the talisman by which death itself becomes the portal to eternal life. In this connection it would be well to ponder over the lives and examples of Harishchandra, Prahlad, Ramachandra, Imam Hassan and Imam Husain, the Christian saints, etc. How beautiful it would be, if all of us, young and old, men and women, devoted ourselves wholly to Truth in all that we might do in our waking hours, whether working, eating, drinking and playing, till dissolution of the body makes us one with Truth.

...Some ancient seeker after Truth realized that he who went on destroying others did not make headway but simply stayed where he was, while the man who suffered those who created difficulties marched ahead, and at times even took the others with him. The first act of destruction taught him that the Truth which was the object of his quest was not outside himself but within. Hence the more he took to violence, the more he receded from Truth. For in fighting the imagined enemy without, he neglected the enemy within.

Mahatma Gandhi[1]

My point is not that everything is bad, but that everything is dangerous, which is not the same thing as bad. If everything is dangerous, then we always have something to do... I think that the ethico-political choice we have to make every day is to determine which is the main danger.

Michel Foucault[2]

I

The first generation of schooled elites who started building their newly 'independent' nations belonged to the strange universe that Matthew Arnold once described as being 'between two worlds, one dead, the other powerless to be born'. For centuries, their people had been overrun, aggressed, mutilated and humiliated in their minds and bodies, and their countries plundered in the name of progress and civilization. The 'elites' were actually among the few who had received 'proper' education, often combined with social and economic privileges. These turned out, however, to be a poisonous gift, for they carried with them an HIV-type legacy. The founding elites of the emerging nations were, quite often, harbouring within their cells some of the 'genes' of their former masters.

Like them, many of those elites now believed, deep in their hearts, that only the model of society incarnated by the North – and the kind of power associated with it – could now allow their populations to wipe out the consequences of their 'underdevelopment'. Thus they shared with their former masters, at least, two certainties, which formed the cornerstones of the emerging construct of development: (a) that, regardless of the many 'positive', though outdated, aspects of indigenous cultures, everything composing their present life was bad, and that they were no longer in a position to address the complexities of the modern world without a sustained programme of development; and (b) that the only way for their people to re-emerge as dignified human beings was to prepare them for all the sacrifices necessary to 'catch up with the West'.

The facts and testimonies gathered in this Reader show that development did not prove to be the panacea those elites believed it to be. Despite the new governments of the 'Third World' according it absolute priority for fifty years, at least in their official discourse, the great majority of them soon realized that the objectives they had set for themselves were unrealistic and impossible to achieve. As it stands now, they have also to admit that not only did development fail to resolve the old problems it was supposed to address, but it brought in new ones of incomparably greater magnitude. Not only did development prove to be simply a myth for the millions it was destined to serve; the very premisses and assumptions on which it was founded were misleading. Teodor Shanin's analysis of the idea of Progress; Marshall Berman's metaphor of Faust as the first developer; and Arturo Escobar's analysis of the development discourse – all offer insights as to why the development discourse was bound, from the beginning, to cause the tragedies it did in fact bring about.

Had development achieved its ends...

The authoritative and often well-documented books listed at the end of this Reader show that the failures of development can no longer be attributed solely to the inability of the governments, institutions and people in charge of implementing it. In fact, if they had been successful in fulfilling all the promises they made to their peoples, and had there been enough money and resources to bring about the development of *all* the so-called underdeveloped countries of the world to the level of the 'most advanced', the resulting deadlocks and tensions would perhaps have taken an even more dramatic turn. For example, it has been estimated that a single edition of the *New York Times* eats up 150 acres of forest land.[3] Other figures suggest that, were the rest of the world to consume paper, including recycled paper, at the same rate as the United States (with 6 per cent of the world's population), within two years not a single tree would be left on the planet. Moreover, considering that the number of private cars in the USA by far exceeds its population, an efficient development machine, capable of taking the levels of newspaper reading and car ownership in China and India up to those of the USA, would pose to those countries (and perhaps the rest of the world) problems of traffic, pollution and forest depletion on a disastrous scale. It is thus perhaps a blessing that the machine was actually *not* as efficient as its programmers wanted it to be![4]

The issue is, therefore, not that development strategies or projects could or should have been better planned or implemented. It is that development, as it imposed itself on its 'target populations', was basically the wrong answer to their true needs and aspirations. It was an ideology that was born and refined in the North, mainly to meet the needs of the dominant powers in search of a more 'appropriate' tool for their economic and geopolitical expansion. As such it could, at best, transfer on to the new nation-states the contradictions of their own socio-economic systems. In fact, the ideology helped a dying and obsolete colonialism to transform itself into an aggressive – even sometimes an attractive – instrument able to recapture lost ground.

Was everything so bad in the old world?

The tragedies and traumas that have resulted from the launching of development world-wide have helped many of the earlier believers to revise their positions. The studies contained in this Reader are testimony to the fact that a new generation of thinkers and 'doers' – particularly those whose personal field experience has led them to see things from the perspective of the peoples most concerned – have now come to question many of their previous ideological certainties. More people realize that everything in the old, 'non-developed' world was not so bad. After all, to paraphrase Foucault, there were perhaps as many 'bad' things there as in modern societies, the difference being that the latter's 'bad' things are often potentially much more perilous.

Marshall Sahlins is no longer alone in proposing that in many ways people's lives had previously been more joyful and much less tense.[5] They had no cars, no Internet and none of the consumer goods to which modern men and women are now addicted. They had no laws and no social security to protect them, no 'free press', no 'opposition party', no 'elected leaders'. But they had no less time for leisure, or, paradoxically, were no less economically 'productive' for the things they needed. And, contrary to the racist clichés in vogue, they were not always governed by cannibals and tyrants.

On Sustainability

The existing system has taken the word 'sustainability' to its heart, and now employs it at every turn, but in a context which deprives it of its meaning. For sustainability is the most basic form of conservatism. It means not taking from the earth, from the world, from society, from each other, from life, more than we give back. But when industrial society uses the word, it means the sustaining of itself, no matter what the cost. It means sustaining privilege, sustaining poverty, sustaining abuse of the earth, sustaining inequality, sustaining starvation, sustaining violence. To sustain the existing system, to defend the status quo, is neither conservative nor sustainable. It is not even a status quo. For what is called the status quo is a form of continuous depletion, of entropy. And such conservatism will perish if it is not subjected to a radical revaluation.

Here we see the fundamental contradiction of a conservatism that has attached itself to a system that subverts all values and practices that we want desperately to conserve. Those so-called conservatives who piously and ingenuously ask nothing more than to be allowed to continue with things as they are, to be permitted to maintain our tried and trusted ways of doing things, are actually grave-diggers, preparing for the funeral rites, not only of economic systems, but also of the earth itself. What a sad and bitter irony that those who were predicted to be the grave-diggers of capitalism, the Western working class, have become, to a considerable extent, the foot soldiers in this war against the planet.

Naturally, this new militant role has been hidden from the working class ('We have a right to what we've got'), as were their earlier roles in an exploitative system, as factory or cannon fodder, and equally in its projected overthrow, as the vanguard of history. We have constantly been pressed into the service of warmongers, whether the war of all against each, class war, or war against the planet, wars for the most part never formally declared, and prosecuted without consultation.

It would be a central characteristic of the new radicalism that the people should determine their own role and function in bringing about social change and safeguarding human continuities. This would necessarily require a keener recognition of the covert role we are playing in the current conflict over control of planetary resources. For, once more, we find that the common people, the masses, the working classes, the popular forces, and rank and file, have been enlisted under false colours. And this time, it is a war even more dreadful than the ghastly conflicts which have preceded it.

Trevor Blackwell and Jeremy Seabrook, *Revolt against Change: Towards a Conserving Radicalism*, Vintage, London, 1993, pp. 96–7.

Effective personal and collective moral obligations often took the place of legal provisions.

If there is any message implicit in the contributions to this Reader, it is that the development discourse on the inability of the 'underdeveloped' countries to govern themselves is an aberration. Many modern societies still have much to learn from them. This is not to say that they were 'better', or that we should go back to a 'state of Nature' – a prospect that would be neither desirable nor feasible. Nevertheless, a deeper and unbiased knowledge of how different cultures have solved their problems and of what they learned to cherish or dislike through the ages would be instructive for all those in search of alternatives to our own dilemmas.

Throwing the baby out with the bathwater?

In their attempts at exploring 'the other side of the moon', most contributors to this Reader have come to the conclusion that development was indeed a poisonous gift to the populations it set out to help. For it introduced a paraphernalia of mirages into their natural environment, and at the same time dispossessed them of most of the things that gave meaning and warmth to their lives.

This view is certainly not shared by the institutions, the experts and the politicians involved in 'technical assistance', for whom development is still a sacred cow, to be preciously nurtured for all the underprivileged of the world. They are ready to concede some of its failures, and agree on the need to give it 'a human face', to have the 'target populations' participate in planning the programmes and implementing them. Yet they take strong objection to all attempts to 'throw the baby out with the bath water'. It is dangerous, they argue, to suggest that in the name of perfectionism even the present tiny amount of assistance should be stopped or diverted to other, often much more questionable, ends. The metaphor may be catchy, but to point up its misleading irrelevance to the real issues one might ask these people why is it they continue to wash the baby in dangerously polluted water. In this context I would like to offer the following comments.

To rephrase Foucault, I am not personally of the view that all development projects are bad. Some of them could even be presented as 'models' in their own specific fields, technically speaking. My own experience as the UN Resident Representative in Mali, and as the co-ordinator of the Alashtar programme in Iran, is that certain projects have been, at least for a while, beneficial to people, with little negative impact on their lives after completion. I am therefore sensitive to the feelings of friends who, equally, have known of such 'good' projects. This is all the more relevant in a world where the bulk of world 'resources' are being ravaged to meet the unquenchable greed of arms producers and dealers, and of national and international pirates and their conmen, and where support is being given to the new neo-liberal

Reasserting the Primacy of Small Communities

At the core of the idea of community – and of the embryonic communitarianism – are three basic principles which are not only important, but also helpful in thinking about a more sustainable politics for the next century.

The first is the simple recognition of people's social nature, and one might add, of the sociability, sense of fairness, sympathy and duty that evolutionary psychologists now see as hardwired into our genetic make-up. Two hundred years of history have done much to nurture institutions for freedom and equality, but very little for the fraternity and solidarity that hold societies together. Yet this softer value – a social capital that enables people to work together, to trust each other, to commit to common causes – has proved absolutely critical to societal success, whether in narrow economic terms or in terms of well-being.

The second principle is about scale. Community is deliberately a different word from society. It may refer to neighbourhoods or workplaces, but to be meaningful it must imply membership in a human-scale collective: a scale at which it is possible to encounter people face to face ... [and] to nurture human-scale structures within which people can feel at home. Social science is ill at ease with such ideas. Strangely there is very little theory about the importance of scale and form in economics and sociology (unlike in biology where thinkers like D'Arcy Thompson long ago made the connection).

The third principle is a reassertion of ethics – the recognition that any viable politics needs to be prepared to make judgments about behaviour, and about what types of behaviour work against the common interest and against the interest of future generations. Without a strong sense of personal ethics, societies require an unacceptable level of policing and contracts; and without a strong sense of personal responsibility it is inevitable that costs will be shunted out on to the natural environment and on to future generations...

Bookchin, Illich and Schumacher have reasserted the primacy of small communities taking responsibility for their own condition of life. Across a range of disciplines thinking has turned to biology, the nature of living systems, and to principles of self-organization as the only viable way to cope with change and complexity.

This long-run development of an alternative paradigm of organization – one that is radically different from the dominant models of the industrial age – has briefly coincided with a much shorter swing of the pendulum away from the particularly ferocious free-market individualism that dominated the UK and the USA in the 1980s. The appetite for a politics of community in these countries reflects the fact that policies of deregulation have gone furthest in disrupting the sense of belonging, fuelling a public mood of anxiety about the decay of social order. Rising crime, bad behaviour and the decline of traditional forms of authority are all taken as symptoms of a society that is out of balance. In some respects this is nothing new: a century ago there was no shortage of thinkers and politicians warning that new industries and cities were destroying old communities and corroding people's sense of moral values. The writings of people like Émile Durkheim sound remarkably familiar. But the sheer pace of change of recent years, driven forward by rapid globalization and declining deference, has given such fears new force.

Geoff Mulgan, 'A Sense of Community', *Resurgence*, no. 172, pp. 18–19. Geoff Mulgan is director of Demos, 9 Brideswell Place, London EC4V 6AP.

mafias that control the governments of repressive states. It is indeed a painful fact that many plausible arguments against development can be used to appropriate funds set aside for development and direct them to other, nefarious, ends. There appears, 'strategically speaking', to be some validity in the argument that says: better to spend on good agricultural projects, on education, on food and shelter for the destitute (however questionable such spending may be from a philosophical point of view), than on military, police or 'security' projects.

The question at stake is, however, that the two are often impossible to disentangle from each other. Militaristic or police states that need money and 'aid' for their own repressive apparatuses can obtain them much more easily when they can bolster their demands with a list of 'good' developmental projects. Habyarimana's Rwanda or Mobutu's Zaïre are good examples of the use of development projects to attract money for the ends of such corrupt leaders.

I remember Joseph Ki-Zerbo talking about a similar question at the Executive Board of UNESCO. He used the metaphor of a train which is in fact going nowhere. It crosses a drought-stricken region whose people believe it might take them to a better place. At each station, hundreds of people try to board it, such that in the resultant overcrowding everyone risks being suffocated. Thus, for the travellers and for those in charge of the train, the main problem becomes that of meeting their immediate physical needs. No one seems interested in knowing where the train is taking them, and why they are on it. Obviously, in the situation created for the passengers on the train, anything that would relieve some of their urgent needs is welcome. Yet food and water are of no use if no attempt is made to change the direction of the train. The basic point raised by most of the contributors to this Reader is that there is no point in mobilizing spectacular relief operations for the passengers on the development train. That can only postpone the day of reckoning. If the train continues on the same old tracks, it will result in a disaster that would be beyond the help of such relief operations.

The contributors generally agree that the people whose lives have often been traumatized by development changes do not refuse to accept change. Yet what they seek is of a quite different nature. They want change that could help people to enhance their inborn and cultural capacities: change that would enable them to blossom 'like a flower from the bud' (a good definition in Webster's dictionary for what development should be!); that could leave them free to *change the rules and the contents of change*, according to their own culturally defined ethics and aspirations.

The balance sheet of development from the losers' perspective

The hidden – yet clear – message that every development project has carried to the people at the grassroots has been that their traditional modes of living, thinking and doing have doomed them to a subhuman condition; and that nothing less than a fundamental change in their ways of confronting modern realities will allow them to emerge from that condition and earn the respect of the civilized world. Moreover, these projects have also served to subject them to a new breed of bureaucrats and people alien to the community. Even when their 'managers' were of their own country and shared the native tongue, they nevertheless spoke a strange new language which the local populations had difficulty in understanding.

As a result, the old convivial and familiar spaces which gave the people life were, at best, reduced to 'commercial centres' where money became the main instrument for social recognition and survival. Compared to life in the new, modern urban agglomeration, the traditional community indeed lacked many of the consumer goods and social services that were introduced to attract the needy and the modernized poor. Yet those living there had seldom felt alone before, or like strangers to each other. They had little, but they did not consider themselves poor. Even when the human niche of the group felt constraining to those who dreamt of living elsewhere or differently, there was almost always someone who could respond to somebody else's suffering. 'Needs' adapted themselves to the laws of necessity, often finding comforting responses in the traditions of solidarity: the culture of gifts, hospitality and reciprocity which linked people together.

The development ideology shattered this familiar universe where human relations predominated and where the strong desire to tackle common needs together formed part of the language of mutual help and hope. Particularly amongst the younger people, the ideology produced new kinds of dreams, especially where technological breakthroughs had raised their expectations to unprecedented levels. The craziest fantasies seemed to be within reach. But what actually happened was quite different, and gave new meaning to the myth of Tantalus. While the ambrosia that Tantalus had stolen from the Heavens did actually allow him to enter and live in the paradise of his dreams, it only subjected him to the most unimagined tortures. The condemned king was now surrounded by streams and trees groaning with fruit, to which, however, he was forever denied access.

At the local or 'national' level, it soon appeared to many that the development idea carried with it new forms of domination and exclusions they had never previously known. They were programmed to become rich and have greater *purchasing* power. However, even in the few cases where this happened, people's actual power to take autonomous decisions concerning their own lives was considerably reduced, as all the power centres moved towards the modern techno-political and economic apparatuses set up around the capitals of the new nation-states. And these began to develop unprecedented forms of control and subjugation over their populations.

On another level, however, while these national governments were increasing their domination and repressive powers over their own people, they became weaker and more dependent on foreigners. As the need for money to strengthen their repressive apparatuses increased, and with national resources often far below developmental needs, most had to accept the drastic conditions that were imposed on them by their former colonial masters – now called their partners in development. As a result, the new nation-state, which the population had originally welcomed as an institution to protect them against foreign predators, itself became a permanent threat to everyone, and any questioning of its relevance taboo – subject to both censorship and self-censure, if not outright repression and extermination.

II

The arguments in favour of development

A major argument advanced in favour of development is that it is, after all, a generous and helpful response to the needs of millions who want and ask for it. As long as the 'haves' and the 'developed' countries are able to afford it, it is their duty and moral obligation to help. In fact, development is beneficial not only to the 'underdeveloped' but also to the 'developed' nations, to the extent that it can also create new markets for their economies, as well as facilitating access to raw materials in the former countries. This argument is questionable on three main counts.

The decisive factors and motivations that have prompted the governments and aid-providing institutions of the North to support development activities have, to date, had little or nothing to do with the desires or needs of their so-called 'target populations'. To use the terms coined by James Scott, the humanitarian and 'helping' arguments used here are the 'public transcript' of the development deal. Its 'hidden transcript' is quite different. The wishes of the people in need are a myth, well maintained by foreign and national authorities for their political, economic, military and sometimes geopolitical objectives.

Couldn't States Be Given a Human Size? The Insights of a Forgotten Pioneer

The size of everything is determined by the function it fulfils. The function of the state is to furnish its members with the protection and certain other social advantages which could not be obtained in a solitary pioneer existence. This indicates that a state composed, let us say, of only five or six families, might indeed be too little. But we have already seen that this constitutes no serious problem, for whenever things, be they physical or social atoms, are too small or lack density, they begin to form aggregations and 'run together naturally for mutual help and readily coalesce to form stable tribes and communities'. The question is, when does a community become stable?...

From a political point of view, it begins to fulfil its purpose at a population figure that may conceivably be lower than a hundred. Any group that can form a village, can form a stable and sovereign society. A country such as Andorra, with a present population of less than seven thousand, has led a perfectly healthy and undisturbed existence since the time of Charlemagne. However, a community has not only political purposes. It has also a cultural function to perform. While it may produce an ideal democracy at its smallest density, this is not sufficient to provide the variety of different individuals, talents, tastes, and tasks to bring out civilization as well. From a cultural point of view, the optimum size of a population must therefore be somewhat larger. Economically, it is big enough when it can furnish food, plumbing, highways, and fire trucks; politically, when it can furnish the tools of justice and defence; and, culturally, when it can afford theatres, academies, universities and inns. But even if it is to fulfil this extended purpose, a population needs hardly to number more than ten or twenty thousand to judge from the early Greek, Italian, or German city-states. With a population of less than one hundred thousand, the Archbishopric of Salzburg produced magnificent churches, a university, several other schools of higher learning, and half a dozen theatres in its little capital city alone....

From a political as well as a cultural point of view, ... the ideal limit to the size of a state [is what] provides a population large enough 'for a good life in the political community' and yet small enough to be well governed since it 'can be taken in at a single view'. [Plato, from whom this passage is quoted, thought a population of 5,040 was the best.] It is this kind of state that exists in a number of Swiss cantons where alone we can still find the old and cherished institution of direct democracy. They are so small that their problems can be surveyed from every church tower and, as a result, be solved by every peasant without the befuddling assistance of profound theories and glamorous guessers. However, modern techniques have given some elasticity to the concept of what can be taken in at a single view, extending the population limit of healthy and manageable societies from hundreds of thousands to perhaps eight or ten million. But beyond this, our vision becomes blurred and our instruments of social control begin to develop defects which neither the physical nor the social sciences can surmount.

A small-state world, by dividing our universal, permanent, impersonal miseries into small, discontinuous, and personal incidents, returns us from the misty sombreness of an existence in which we are nothing but ghostly shadows of meaningless issues, to the bliss of reality which we can find only in our neighbours and our neighbourhoods. There alone, love is love, and sex is sex, and passion is passion. If we hate a man, it is not because he is a communist but because he is nasty, and if we love him it is not because he is a patriot but because he is a gentleman.

Only in a time of crisis has unity sense, when individuals and peoples are bound to live in a 'military alliance' and many of our ideals must temporarily be suspended. But in all other periods unity, which is the great ideal of totalitarians and collectivists, is the principal danger confronting democrats. They do not want to have single parties, but several parties, not single states but many states. Their principles are based on diversity and balance, not on unity and its natural concomitant, tyranny.

Leopold Kohr, *The Breakdown of Nations* (1957), Dutton, New York, 1978, pp. 106–8, 111, 113.

The work of Leopold Kohr in the early 1950s was to inspire such pioneers as Schumacher and Illich in many of their most innovative and radical thoughts on certain aspects of progress and development. The much talked-about formula 'Small Is Beautiful', which is associated with Schumacher's philosophy, was actually coined by this exceptionally incisive thinker, whose three main books, *The Breakdown of Nations*; *Development Without Aid: The Translucent Society* (Christopher Davies, Llandybie, Camarthenshire, 1973); and *The Overdeveloped Nations* (Simon & Schuster, New York, 1978) are, strangely, unknown even now to many students of development studies. Some of Kohr's statements may be questioned on various grounds, but that does not at all diminish his originality, particularly if one considers that such thoughts were published at a time when they appeared totally opposed to the mainstream thinking of the time. As such, Kohr belongs to the family of such great precursors as Jacques Ellul and Lewis Mumford.

It is a fact that all requests for development assistance are made, as a rule, by national governments or organizations that are controlled by them. Similarly, at the donor end of the line, it is up to the official authorities to agree to such requests. The 'target populations' rarely have any say in these agreements. Hence, it is true that development is wanted by governments. But as the overwhelming majority of the governments in the South do not consider themselves accountable to their people, the banner of development is generally used by them for obtaining credits of another kind. To take a recent dramatic example, Rwanda was supplied with one of the highest per-capita supplies of arms and ammunition on the grounds that the country had been recognized as a particularly 'successful' model of development. The deals between France and Rwanda that followed might be taken to indicate that both governments were committed to development. Yet the fact that the government of Rwanda was in favour of that kind of development could hardly be used as proof that the people wanted it too.

On the myth of 'the people' and their claim for development

What if the people were to express, openly and 'democratically', their wish to receive development aid? This argument is now particularly supported by those who hope that a different, participatory version of development, based on the real support of the population, could restore to the institution its lost legitimacy.

As already stated, it may be true that the majority of people whose standard of life has in fact greatly deteriorated do want change. Yet it is hard to imagine that, under the political and socio-economic pressures to which populations are generally submitted, at both the national and the international level, a truly democratic system could be found which could reconcile the requirements of modern development with the people's free choice, and even less with the needs of grassroots communities.

In the first place, in those communities that are now so torn apart by conflicting interests and currents created by their exposure to modernity, it is not easy to determine who wants what. Not only are there different ideas about what the needs are, but the perception of what could satisfy them is often changing and confused. A 'voting' process alone cannot determine what a group actually needs as a whole, and any decision coming out of that mechanical process will not necessarily represent what is good and desirable for that group. In this context, the modern idea of equality has further complicated the search for a change that is both 'democratic' and ultimately 'good' and beneficial for all. For it tends to valorize an idea of freedom that is purely quantitative.

Teodor Shanin, an eminent contributor to this Reader, is quoted as saying: 'If the people can express themselves democratically, most of them tend to vote for things that good socialists would consider *petit bourgeois* preferences: some pornography, some sports, more TV than reading – what usually appears in a popular newspaper.'[6] This statement points up the ambiguous uses currently made of the modern construct of 'the people' and their 'opinion', which often serves the major interests vested *in* the people much more than the people themselves.

Vernacular societies had a much more realistic view of things. Not blinkered by the myth of equality, they believed that the good of the community was better served by those of its members it considered to be the wisest, the most virtuous, and hence the most 'authoritative' and experienced persons of the groups – those who commanded everyone's respect and deference. This belief, it is true, was not always upheld in practice by those who exercised power or who lacked the moral qualities expected of them. There were as many unscrupulous and vain persons as exist in modern 'democratically' elected societies. Yet, because of their size or perhaps the nature of relationships within small communities, their arts of governance suffered less from the hypocritical ideological illusions that affect modern systems of governance.

On another plane, the conviction that the members of a society were *different*, and that such a fact had to be acknowledged by all, often induced them to perceive society in a hierarchical fashion. This perception did not necessarily result in discrimination against the 'lower' persons in each particular hierarchy. Rather, it imposed special and additional obligations on those persons at the top. In the *de facto* hierarchies of power, knowledge and wealth that control the modern societies of 'equals', those at the top do not consider that they have any particular obligation at all to those at the bottom.

Confucius on the 'good' and 'bad' people in the village

Confucius, for example, thought that every society consisted of two basic categories of persons, the 'masses' (the *min*) and the 'good and authoritative persons' (the *jen*).[7] The designation of 'the masses' (*min*) is derived from 'closed eyes', and one of the first pictographs for it seems to illustrate an eye which lacks a pupil, while the *jen* is drawn like the kernel of a fruit.[8] The *chün tzu*, or 'exemplary persons', were the most revered among the *jen*, as they represented the highest forms of excellence in human qualities – in particular humility, social effacement and deep love for the weakest and the 'lowest' persons.[9] People who commanded deference and respect were never 'elected' by the others. Neither was their 'authority' dependent on their likes and dislikes. The following parable beautifully expresses the qualities expected of a true *jen*:

> Tzu-kung inquired. 'What do you think about someone whom everyone in the village likes?'
>
> Confucius replied: 'That is not enough.'
>
> 'What if everyone in the village disliked him?'
>
> Confucius replied. 'That is still not good enough. Better if all good people in the village were to like him and all of the bad people were to dislike him.' (*Analects*, 13/24)

In the mind of Confucius, these distinctions were not to be interpreted so as to grant the 'authoritative persons' any right to take advantage of their condition, to humiliate or to mistreat others. Quite the contrary. Their recognition was, rather, intended to establish the foundation of an *aesthetic* order based on the pursuit of good and harmony among differences (13/23). Later, we shall take up his conception of an *aesthetic order,* as opposed to a purely *logical*, a *rational*, order.

Extending the Confucian distinction to more 'modern' societies, it could

The Wisdom of Restraint

The wisdom proper to philosophy comes from its restraint. If the latter builds up a universalizing world, art borders it with a margin of reserved beauty. Philosophers, do your work with accuracy and suffer in silence that you be treated as poets: those who are ordinarily excluded from the city. It is better that way. Build a great work where shall be found, precisely located, all things of the world, rivers, seas, constellations, the rigours of formal science, models, structures, neighbourhoods, approximate accuracies of experimentation, turbulences or percolations, fluctuations of history, crowds, times, small gaps, fables of language and tales of the good people, but build it so beautifully that its very beauty restrains it. Restrains it in singularity. Defines it. Preserves it from excess. Luckily and by definition, the inimitable does not find imitators and therefore neither expands itself nor propagates.

All beautiful, all new.

The beautiful contains the true; that is, it retains it, limits its expansion, closes up its furrow when it passes, shapes its features. The true requires a limit and demands it from beauty.

When science and reason would have attained beauty, we shall run no risk. When philosophy reaches beauty, it brushes aside all danger.

When the true is beautiful, it forgets to advance in space. The beautiful is the true at peace with itself: restrained truth…

To enjoy power and not take advantage of it, that is the beginning of wisdom. Of civilization.

The political philosophy of restraint: the only thinkable equality henceforth presupposes poverty, not as a lack of riches, but as a positive value.

The Third World precedes us.

Let's get started.

Michel Serres, *Le Tiers Instruit*, Editions François Bourin, Paris, 1991, pp. 191–3. Translated by M.R.

be said that they all represent a mix of *min*- and *jen*-like individuals. Some – usually a minority – are indeed wise, virtuous and compassionate persons commanding authority, respect and deference, while others, at the opposite end of the spectrum, could personify the worst meanings of the Chinese character *min* – that is, those who are blind, confused, 'mentally dark', if not simply stupid, or wicked. With regard to contemporary societies, one should add to both these categories the 'leaders' and manipulators of all kinds – the profit-makers, the envious or greedy power-seekers, the professional 'revolutionaries' whether red or black, the modern salesmen of hopes and expectations, not to forget the pusher-dealers of all kinds of addictive consumer goods and services.

A voting system represents, at best, a purely mechanistic addition to all the evasive and confused opinions produced by the impact of such – often contradictory – factors. At worst – which is often the case in most current 'developing' countries – it represents a fraudulent operation performed by the state simply to give it a 'democratic' justification. In any case, it would be naive to interpret the results of such 'consultations' as a true expression of what the people want, or as somehow serving the good of the community.

A number of objective facts are, however, clear. These must be taken into account if there is to be a regeneration of the people's arts of self-governance. Development has failed to meet the needs and preoccupations of those at the bottom of the social ladder. Often, it has turned them into their own enemies, once they have internalized the developers' perception of what they need. This has served to exacerbate social tensions everywhere. It has made the bad rich richer and the good poor poorer. It has destroyed the old fabric of communal societies. And it has created needs, envies and services that can only make people more dependent on development, while systematically dispossessing the excluded from their means of sustenance.

III

If the post-development era is to be free of the illusions, ideological perversions, hypocrisy and falsehoods that pervaded the development world, the search for signposts and trails leading to a flow of 'good life' (the *fidnaa*[10] in Dadacha's language) should be informed by an entirely new rationale and set of assumptions. This should help, at the local and transnational levels, the *jen* and the *min* to rediscover themselves, to learn from each other, to explore new possibilities of dialogue and action, and to weave together relationships of a different kind, transcending the present barriers of language, and thereby going beyond the paradigms that the development era has so persistently maintained for the last fifty years.

The search for new possibilities of change

The end of development should not be seen as an end to the search for new possibilities of change, for a relational world of friendship, or for genuine processes of regeneration able to give birth to new forms of solidarity. It should only mean that the binary, the mechanistic, the reductionist, the inhumane and the ultimately self-destructive approach to change is over. It should represent a call to the 'good people' everywhere to think and work together. It should prompt everyone to begin the genuine work of self-knowledge and 'self polishing' (as the *ahle sayqal* do, according to Rûmi), an exercise that enables us to listen more *care*fully to others, in particular to friends who are ready to do the same thing. It could be the beginning of a long process aiming at replacing the present 'dis-order' by an 'aesthetic order' based on respect for differences and the uniqueness of every single person and culture.

On powerlessness and the 'mask of love'

A first condition for such a search is to look at things *as they are*, rather than as we want them to be; to overcome our fears of the unknown; and, instead of claiming to be able to change the world and to save 'humanity', to try saving ourselves from our own compelling need for comforting illusions.

The *hubris* of the modern individual has led him or her to believe that the existential powerlessness of humankind can usefully be replaced with compulsive 'actomania'. This illusion is similar to the modern obsession with fighting death at all costs. Both compulsions tend, in fact, to undermine, disfigure and eventually destroy the only forms of power that define true life. Paradoxically, it is through fully experiencing our powerlessness, as painful as that may be, that it becomes possible for us to be in tune with human suffering, in all its manifestations; to understand the 'power of the powerless' (to use Václav Havel's expression); and to rediscover our oneness with all those in pain.

Blinkered by the Promethean myth of Progress, development called on all the 'powerless' people to join in a world-wide crusade against the very idea of powerlessness, building its own power of seduction and conviction on the mass production of new illusions. It designed for every taste a 'mask of love' – an expression coined by John McKnight[11] to define the modern notion of 'care' – which various 'developers' could deploy when inviting new recruits to join the crusade.

It is because development incarnated a false love for an abstract humanity that it ended up by upsetting the lives of millions of living human beings. For half a century its 'target populations' suffered the intrusion in their lives of an army of development teachers and experts, including well-intentioned field workers and activists, who spoke big words – from conscientization to learning from and living with the people. Often they had studied Marx, Gramsci, Freire and the latest research about empowerment and participation. However, their lives (and often careers) seldom allowed them to enter the intimate world of their 'target populations'. They were good at giving people passionate lectures about their rights, their entitlements, the class struggle and land reform. Yet few asked themselves about the deeper motivations prompting them to do what they were doing. Often they knew neither the people they were working with, nor themselves. And they were so busy achieving what *they* thought they had to do *for* the people, that they could not learn enough *from* them about how actually to 'care' for them, as they would for their closest relatives and friends whom they knew and loved.

My intention in bringing up this point is not to blame such activists or field workers – many of them may have been kind and loving persons. It is, rather, to make the point that 'the masks of love' to which they became addicted prevented them discovering the extraordinary redeeming power of human powerlessness, when it opens one's soul to the world of true love and compassion.

Similar 'masks of love' have now destroyed the possibilities of our truly 'caring'. Thus, when we hear about the massacres in Algeria, Rwanda, Zaïre, the Middle East or Bosnia, or the innumerable children, women and men dying from starvation, or being tortured and killed with impunity, we feel comforted and relieved when we send a cheque to the right organization or demonstrate on their behalf in the streets. And although we are fully aware that such gestures are, at very best, like distributing aspirin pills to dying people whom nothing can save; although we may have doubts as to whether our money will reach the victims, or fears that it might even ultimately serve those governments, institutions or interests who are responsible for this suffering; we continue to do these things. We continue to cheat ourselves, because we consider it not decent, not morally justifiable, not 'politically correct', to do otherwise.

Such gestures, which we insist on calling acts of solidarity rather than 'charity', may however be explained differently: by the great fear we have of becoming fully aware of our powerlessness in situations when nothing can be done. And yet this is perhaps the most authentic way of rediscovering our oneness with those in pain. For the experiencing of our powerlessness can lead us to encounter the kind of deep and redeeming suffering that provides entry to the world of compassion and discovery of our true limits and possibilities. It can also be the first step in the direction of starting a *truthful* relationship with the world, as it is. Finally, it can help us understand this very simple tautology: that no one is in a position to do more than one can. As one humbly recognizes this limitation, and learns to free oneself from the egocentric illusions inculcated by the Promethean myth, one discovers the secrets of a power of a different quality: that genuine and extraordinary power that enables a tiny seed, in all its difference and uniqueness, to start its journey into the unknown.

For the 'right' size and proportions

Respect for the 'right size' of everything is another aspect of the need to recognize our limits and possibilities. That recognition can help us understand that life is not a linear, endless and wild growth, but rather a wheel-like movement which takes the same unique seed along its journey to become a flower, a fruit and a new seed again, its 'seedness' allowing it to maintain, through its many lives-and-deaths and ends-and-beginnings, its 'right' sizes and proportions. The ideas of Progress and Development had disastrous consequences for the lives of vernacular societies, because they deliberately overlooked the vital importance of preserving their right size.

On another level, a shift of focus from bigness and quantity to the right size and quality could help us to understand that a small, human-sized and familiar group of friends, who know and trust one other, is often the ideal place for them to learn from each other, to act in truth and eventually to change the only worlds they can truly love and care for. In such concrete and recognizable worlds, people are no longer abstractions to each other. Each is the fruit of genuine experiences that he or she can share with the other, without fear of being ideologically wrong, 'politically incorrect', or heretical in the eyes of their religion. And as one group of friends relates to another, participants in these relationships cease to see other people only through ideologically constructed images.

For parallel communities of 'good' men and women

The post-development period will distinguish itself from the preceding one if it is able to bring about the 'good, the compassionate and the authoritative' – if the *jen* everywhere cultivate new relationships of friendship, and thereby discover themselves and each other, and learn the arts of listening and being attentive (i.e. to *attend*) to each other.

Confucius was right to emphasize the particular responsibility of the *jen* in every group. This recognition that all humans are not, in real life, endowed with the same qualities of wisdom and character differs from the illusions created by modern ideologies. The latter postulate an abstract equality between people, while actually fostering the worst types of hierarchy among them. It is right to imagine that in the post-development age the direction, the quality and the content of changes desired by each community would result from a constant dialogue, particularly amongst the *jen* or the most trusted members of a community. Such relationships could allow the younger and the more active members in each group to combine their greater knowledge and sensitivity to the 'modern' world with the wisdom inherited from tradition, the listening and inspiring qualities of those older. The more a community can rediscover its possibilities for action, taking full advantage of its cultural legacy and those technological advances of modernity that can be used autonomously, the less it would need any developmental type of assistance or intervention from outside.

When the subjugated reach the limits of their possibilities

In a world where the managers of the 'global village' are everywhere set to 'normalize' and to integrate all spaces of life which might otherwise escape their control, the main obstacle to the creative autonomy of smaller communities is the invisible force of economy and technology carried by different institutionalized agencies: the major Powers, the transnational and multinational corporations, the official and the mafia-like networks of arms dealers, the institutions of technical and financial assistance, and so on. The manipulative, destructive and dissuasive power of these institutions is often immensely out of proportion to the small, though resilient, life forces that come from grassroots communities wanting to preserve their autonomy.

It is exactly at this point that the subjugated – in particular the grassroots populations exposed to that power – reach the limits of their capacity for self-reliance. It then becomes impossible for them, by themselves, to stop or even meaningfully reduce the negative effects of the forces out to destroy them. At that stage, they certainly need friends – reliable and trustworthy friends – not just at home but wherever those forces are operating.

Towards new forms of co-action and 'helping'

Such friends are particularly useful in countries where the centres of power are located, and where there are more free spaces for action – through the media, civil-rights and grassroots associations, and more recently e-mail and Internet facilities. The spontaneous support given lately by millions of Americans to the Zapatistas through such spaces is a magnificent example of such forms of co-action and solidarity. The world-wide network of another organization, Amnesty International, is another example of the same type of action.

For some, *positive subversion*, in the sense that Cardinal Arns of São Paulo talks about,[12] could be a way of stopping the threat to the populations concerned. This form of action was effectively used by the Theology of Liberation movement in Latin America when some 'good people' from the Church used it for serving other defenceless 'good people' in their struggles for justice. Subversion *from above* has become a common, almost built-in, practice for top-placed executives, who often use their power to direct their organizations to act against the moral principles officially upheld by them. Under these circumstances it is natural, and indeed moral, for anyone working within such institutions to use the free spaces not yet controlled by the system to subvert them *from within*.

Such modes of positive subversion have in fact been used, in various forms, by all subjugated peoples throughout history, and it has often helped them attain their goals without undue violence. The practice continues, particularly in countries where those whose job it is to keep the law are its most systematic violators.

On intervention: its dangers, ethical dilemmas, limits and possibilities

This leads us to the question of intervention. Who are we – who am I – to intervene in other people's lives when we know so little about any life, including our own? Even in the case where we intervene because we think we love and care for others, how is it possible to say in advance that our intervention will not eventually produce a result opposite to that expected?

Sincerity is Subversive

If the First World has no alternatives to offer in the present poverty crisis, we in the Third World beseech you to *at least* respect our own choices of alternatives. We have an old political joke in Brazil: we were at the brink of an abyss and now we have taken a great step forward. International poverty is an abyss. And the fear of national alternatives in the Third World is exactly this great step forward.

The wealth of the nations has always been seen in the context of ever newer frontiers. In colonial times, Europe knew great wealth because of the 'new' worlds that it explored in East and West. And the United States became wealthy as they conquered frontiers in North America. Today there are few colonies in the old sense of the term. And few countries in the First and Second Worlds still have frontiers to conquer. But the concept has remained in economics and politics. The Third World, no longer as colonies, but as ideological blocs, is the 'new frontier' for the wealthy countries. Our raw materials and our cheap labour become the incubators of new wealth for the already wealthy.

I have been told, even by European theologians, that if this system causes hunger and death in Brazil, that is just too bad. Those people have to die so that the system can go on. But I do not accept this. I *cannot* accept it. An economic system cannot be judged only by what it does *for* people, but also by what it does *to* people. An economic system cannot have as a by-product the creation of a sub-race or the death of millions. And the worst of this situation is that anyone who calls attention to it is considered subversive. But subvert only means to turn a situation around and look at it from the other side. I respectfully submit to you that this situation *has* to be looked at from the other side.

Cardinal Paulo Evaristo Arns, Archbishop of São Paulo, Brazil, *Development: Seeds of Change* (SID), no. 3, 1985, pp. 3–5.

It is because of its unknown and unpredictable effects that, in my view, intervention should be considered as an act bordering on the *sacred*. Consider the spontaneous, compassionate gesture of the Good Samaritan, who, without harbouring any *project* of intervention in his mind, goes to the aid of an apparently wounded and dying man in the road. That act could hardly be called intervention, in the sense used in the modern aid vocabulary. It has no ulterior motive, and hence is an act of love and compassion, a 'right action' in Buddhist terms. Here, the actor does not ask himself whether the person about to receive help will some day be useful to him, whether he is a saint, a friend or an enemy, or a would-be criminal. That is why the Good Samaritan's act borders on sacred territory.

The case is different with a *project of intervention*, which is prepared and developed somewhere, often in an institutional framework, with a view to changing the lives of other people, in a manner useful or beneficial to the intervener. Hence the need for the latter to be aware that he or she is launched on an adventure fraught with considerable danger. Such awareness makes it necessary for interveners to start examining the whys and wherefores of their actions. Exceptional personal qualities are needed to prevent 'well-intentioned' interventions producing results contrary to those planned – as has been the case in most 'developmental' and many 'humanitarian' instances.

Before intervening in other people's lives, one should first intervene in one's own; 'polishing' oneself to ensure that all precautions have been taken to avoid harming the objects of intervention. Many questions should be explored first. What prompts me to intervene? Is it friendship, compassion, the 'mask of love', or an unconscious attempt to increase my powers of seduction? Have I done everything I could to assess the usefulness of my intervention? And if things do not proceed as I expect them, am I ready to face the full consequences of my intervention? To what extent, that is, am I seriously committed to the intervention?

As institutions are, by definition, inanimate and seldom able to transform themselves from within, while the objects of their intervention are often living human beings, the more rigid and unchecked by counter-powers they are, the more their interventions tend to produce different results. The ex-Soviet Union is a striking example: seventy years of scientifically planned interventionism aimed at destroying capitalism ended up by producing exactly the opposite result. There is no reason to believe that other interventionist regimes based on developmental or religious ideologies will not meet similar fates.

Rethinking 'wu-wei'

Great Chinese thinkers like Lao Tzu and Confucius clearly sensed most of the unethical and senseless aspects of intervention inasmuch as they introduced the concept of *wu-wei*, a term that has been translated sometimes as 'non-intervention', sometimes as 'action through non-action'.[13]

The idea underlying the concept is that the 'accomplished leader, far from exercising coercive power over his people, grounds his pursuit of order in the richness of diversity and orchestrates his subjects' impulses toward the direction of an aesthetic harmony that harmonizes their possibilities of creativity.' In other words, if the political order emerges from the grassroots, the *wu-wei* ruler needs none of the coercive or repressive activities to which the incompetent, the unjust and the undeserving ruler has recourse. For the *wu-wei* posture is itself a function of the ruler's respectfulness and tolerance.

Going back to Confucius, one realizes how the arts of governance have regressed with the advance of Progress! And how painful it is to reflect that the modernized 'elites' of the many countries where such arts were known did

The Key to Our Future Survival: Native Societies?

We surely need to abandon all values that place emphasis on commodity accumulation as something desirable in life.

Growth economics, the profit motive, and the market economy, all counterproductive to a sustainable future, must be regarded as short experiments that have failed miserably, and must be abandoned as such; there is no more room for them on Earth. (Simultaneously, world population needs drastic steady reduction, even among Western industrial nations, where each individual consumes twenty to thirty times the resources of a person in a nonindustrial nation. A more equitable allocation of the already available resources is also an obvious necessity.)

A long list of technologies and technical systems must be re-examined from a holistic, systemic perspective … Those found incompatible with sustainability and diversity on the planet must be abandoned.

Finally, we need to rethink our relationship with nature and with native peoples. This includes relearning history and grappling with the forces that caused this history to occur. And we need to directly support the struggles of native people to recover and maintain their land base and sovereignty, wherever this battle occurs.

There is no denying that all of this amounts to considerable adjustment, but it's not as if there were much choice. Truly, such change is inevitable if sanity and sustainability are to prevail. To call this adjustment 'going back' is to conceive of it in fearful, negative terms, when the changes are actually desirable and good. In fact, it is not really going back; it is merely getting back on track, as it were, after a short unhappy diversion into fantasy. It is going *forward* to a renewed relationship with timeless values and principles that have been kept alive for Western society by the very people we have tried to destroy.

As for whether it is 'romantic' to make such a case, I can only say that the charge is putting the case backwards. What is romantic is to believe that technological evolution will ever live up to its own advertising, or that technology itself can liberate us from the problems it has created. So far, the only people who, as a group, are clear-minded on this point are the native peoples, simply because they have kept alive their roots in an older, alternative, nature-based philosophy that has proven effective for tens of thousands of years, and that has nurtured dimensions of knowledge and perception that have become opaque to us. It is the native societies, not our own, that hold the key to future survival.

Jerry Mander, *In the Absence of the Sacred: The Failure of Technology and the Survival of the Indian Nations*, Sierra Club Books, San Francisco, 1991, pp. 383–4.

not try to learn from them, but instead copied the imported dominant models of governance, which proved to have so little relevance to their people. The only hope now, for post-development times, is that the failure of such models – including the triumphalist model of neo-liberal 'democracy' in the United States, with its increasing problems of violence, *de facto* unrepresentativeness and systemic discrimination against those excluded and considered 'dispensable' – will lead the new generations to rethink modern governance in the spirit of *wu-wei* and other teachings of the great old sages of 'underdeveloped' nations.

Towards a bottom-up aesthetic order

The orchestrated launching of the 'global village', with its discoverers hoping to sing their requiem on the demise of History, produced quite understandable fears in those for whom a real village is still a unique *domus* for good and convivial humans. As the invention of the 'global village' was of a piece with the other world campaigns aimed at recruits for globalization, the people belonging to real villages all over the world have become oversensitive toward any idea of universalism. In the meantime, profit-makers, money operators, arms dealers, media giants and mafiosi of all kinds who form the global village are pushing hard at the limits of those at the grassroots who have become 'dispensable' for them.

In some countries, the breaking of these limits has already given unscrupulous and dangerous agitators the opportunity of taking up arms and using terrorism and mass killings in the name of their people. As a result, the increasing number of 'good people' who are experiencing the breaking down of the limits of their own resistance and self-reliance find themselves 'between the devil and the deep blue sea', with dramatic consequences. Mass tragedies of a new kind are being prepared, to which it will not be possible to find local solutions, as their causes are to be found deep in the existing so-called world order. It is therefore no longer possible for the friends of victims to be indifferent to their conditions. How, then, can they respond intelligently to the cries for help?

Experience shows that people in distress have many friends, who will do whatever they can to respond to their cries, each according to their conscience and abilities, and using the means available to them. What these expanding circles of friends might do now is see whether and how their action can pave the way for the emergence of a different, an *aesthetic*, order arising from the grassroots.

I use the term 'aesthetic' in the sense attributed to Confucius. According to his commentators, the *aesthetic order* he had in mind challenges the disjunction between the maker of an order and those who enjoy its benefits. It is the opposite of the logical or rational order, which presses toward generality, uniformity and substitutability. 'Whereas rational order permits one to abstract from the concrete particularities of the elements of the order and treat these elements indifferently, aesthetic order is constituted by just those particularities... [And] a complex of elements reaches the maximum of aesthetic disorder with the realization of absolute uniformity. But this is the highest degree of rational *order*.'[14] The way an aesthetic order is construed is similar to the composition of a work of art, where the greatness of the artist is demonstrated by his or her genius in creating a piece which is actually both aesthetic and rational, as 'it is based upon an appreciation of the uniformities (the compositional elements) as well as the diversities (the irreplaceably unique characteristics) that constitute the work.'[15]

The post-development era is in dire need of a commitment from all good men and women to the creation of an aesthetic world order in which new forms of friendship and solidarity will be able to interact in order to stop the evil forces of the 'global village' destroying the last 'good people' struggling to protect themselves from them. It would be up to the emerging circles of friends to explore how the profoundly humane ethics of such an order could be reconciled with the unavoidable needs of a rational order.

Towards new paradigms and a new language

For such an aesthetic order to emerge, new paradigms must be found to replace some of the outdated and irrelevant ones that govern and distort our present perception of reality. Among these will be the *nation-state* as the protector of the people placed under its jurisdiction; *progress* and *development* – both clinging to the sub-paradigms of continuity and linearity; *scarcity* – as the basis and justification of modern economy. Here again, a tremendous creative effort lies ahead for the emerging circles of friendship.

What actually inhibits, even paralyses the work of such circles is the hegemony of a universalist language, which, like the global village, tends to destroy the real languages used by millions of people everywhere to express themselves and their worlds. I refer not only to languages in the sense of 'mother tongues', but to that truly 'universal' language (in French, *langage* rather than *langue*) which allows different people sharing similar fates to understand each other, across different cultural and geographical borders and beyond the particular words used in their mother tongues. Unfortunately, most local and culturally construed terms that define the perception of different communities in those things close to their hearts – such as poverty, conviviality, abundance, freedom, deference, the good and the virtuous – have all been reduced to 'amoebas' or 'plastic' words, called upon to mean the same thing the world over. So long as these words colonize people's languages, it will be difficult – even for the circles of friends – to talk seriously about such problems.

From self-knowledge to the passion of witnessing one's Truth

When one studies some of the significant grassroots movements of recent times (for example, the *Swadhyaya* in India, the *Sarvodaya* in Sri Lanka), which seem to have followed the Gandhian path, it is apparent that a dimension has emerged out of the people's arts of resistance (both at the group and individual levels) that requires a much more attentive reading. I call this the dimension of the inner world, rather than using the more current but ambiguous term 'spirituality'. 'Fundamentalist' populist movements, through which a certain interpretation of religion and spirituality has enabled a new breed of unscrupulous politicians and professional 'revolutionaries' to achieve their own ends, have received wide attention. But less has been learned about the smaller groups of people, or even individuals, who, without any publicity, perceive the meaning of their lives as a dedicated search for the Truth, a search which starts from the deeper layers of their own inner world and manifests itself outwardly in new forms of praxis and co-action, and in friendship and solidarity with others engaged in the same search.

This way of being has firm roots in the traditions of resistance by the weak. In these traditions, 'right action' involving others starts always as a personal work on oneself. It is the fruit of an almost divine kind of exercise, which usually takes place in the solitude of thought and creation. A truth reached in the meditative world of a free searcher can bring him or her to experience the often painful and unpopular act of provoking *dis-sensus*. Yet, if such dissent is not an end in itself, never inspired by an egocentric attitude, it is a cathartic means to bring about new and more serious possibilities of consensus.

On the path to his or her truth and freedom, the seeker after Truth finds solace in the act of witnessing. In modern times, this places intellectuals – those whose thoughts and 'intellect' are the most precious thing they can share with others – in a particular position: that of cultivating their truth with great humility and strength and drawing on the courage necessary to see it through to the end, rather than trying to 'advise' people in positions of power who seek to use such advice for their own ends. In the traditions of my own culture and that to which Gandhiji refers, the word *witness* and its derivatives – in Arabic and Persian, *shâhed*, *shahîd* and *shahâdat*, particularly in their *sûfi* connotation – mean 'to observe', 'to witness', 'to bear testimony', 'to be present at or in', 'to reflect the beauty of truth', but also 'to become a martyr'. The *shâhed* is therefore a person so viscerally engaged in searching for the truth and sharing it with friends that he or she would consider it normal, and indeed a blessing, to commit his or her life to that truth. This is how the great Hallâj,[16] following the examples of other 'witness-martyrs' such as Christ, Imam Hussain and many other saintly figures, experienced the exhilarating joy of witnessing his truth: even when his arms were cut to pieces, he persistently repeated: 'I am the Truth [or God]'.

Unlike the period preceding it, the post-development era should not be focused on merely operational or spectacular 'plans of action' or 'strategies'. It will represent a different age only if it is in harmony with the existential need of all the 'good' people of the world to live differently, to witness their truth, and to cultivate friendship. And this can come about only if we all begin with ourselves, and learn to face our Truth and live with it as an artist does with the object of his or her creation.

It is revealing that, many years after Gandhi, Michel Foucault, a 'modern' and secular seeker of Truth from a totally different culture and set of traditions, has expressed a similar thought, in his own way. When asked about the ethics on which another form of life could be built, he replied:

> What strikes me is the fact that, in our society, art is now only linked to objects, rather than to individuals or to life itself. This kind of art is specialized, or produced by experts who are artists. But couldn't we ourselves, each one of us, make of our lives a work of art? Why should a lamp or a house become the object of art – and not our own lives?

NOTES

This text is a completely revised and abridged version of the Sjef Theunis Memorial Lecture, delivered in Tunis, 17 November 1995.

1. M.K. Gandhi, *From Yeravda Mandir*, Navajivan Trust, Ahmedabad, n.d.
2. Michel Foucault, 'On the Genealogy of Ethics', in H. Dreyfus and P. Rabinow, *Michel Foucault: Beyond Structuralism and Hermeneutics*, University of Chicago Press, Chicago, 1982, p. 231.
3. Figures quoted from G. Schwab in William Wood, S.J., 'An Affluent American Responding to Global Poverty', in Francisco Jiménez, *Poverty and Social Justice*, Bilingual Press, Tempe, Ariz., 1987, p. 120.
4. According to Gustavo Esteva, 'if all countries "successfully" followed the industrial example, five or six planets would be needed to serve as mines and waste dumps' (see 'Development', in Wolfgang Sachs, ed., *The Development Dictionary*, Zed Books, London, 1992, p. 2).
5. See Pierre Clastres, *Society Against State: Essay in Political Anthropology*, Zone Books, New York, 1987; also Diana Lima Handem, 'Etude d'une société sans état: Les Balante de Guinée Bissau', in J.-P. Lepri, *Education et Nationalité en Guinée-Bissau: Contribution à l'étude de l'endogénéité de l'éducation*, Se Former+, Lyon, 1989.
6. Gustavo Esteva, in Intercultural Institute of Montreal, *Living with the Earth: A Report*, Quebec, 30 April–3 May 1992, p. 117.
7. For an excellent introduction to the thinking of Confucius on governance and the notion of aesthetic order, see David Hall and Roger T. Ames, *Thinking Through Confucius*, State University of New York Press, Albany, N.Y., 1987. As for the concept of *jen*, it has been translated into English in many different ways: as benevolence, love, altruism, goodness, compassion, perfect virtue, human-heartedness, humanity. The ambiguity surrounding it may be due to the fact that it somehow represents all those, and, as Hall puts it, is 'a process term denoting qualitative transformation of the person and achievement of authoritative humanity. It is a transformation of self: the disciplining of the "small person" (*hsiao jen*) with his disintegrative preoccupation with selfish advantage, towards the sensibilities of the profoundly relational persons' (p. 115).
8. Contrary to appearance, the 'authoritative person' in Confucian language is not at all 'authoritarian'. He commands authority and respect because he is a self-disciplined and virtuous person who loves others. According to Confucius, he is 'a person who is able to promote the five attitudes in the world: respect, tolerance, living up to one's word, diligence and authority' (*Analects*, 17/6).

9. It is important to emphasize that *Chün Tzu* were considered to be a nobility of refinement rather than blood. For Confucius, social and political distinctions are a reflection of personal cultivation and one's consequent contribution to the socio-political harmony.

10. See G. Dahl and G. Megerssa, 'The Spiral of the Ram's Horn', in G. Dahl and G. Rabo, eds, *Kam-Ap or Take-Off: Local Notions of Development*, Studies in Social Anthropology, Stockholm, 1992, p. 159 (part of this article is reproduced as No. 5 in the present Reader).

11. John McKnight, *The Careless Society: Community and Its Counterfeits*, Basic Books, New York, 1985.

12. See Box on p. 396 above.

13. According to Joseph Needham, *wu-wei* means that 'things have to be left to themselves and one should allow nature to follow its course, rather than go against it, in other words one should learn not to intervene. This was the great Taoïst slogan throughout the ages, the non-taught doctrine and the non-written order' (J. Needham, *La Science chinoise et l' Occident: Le Grand Titrage*, Seuil, Paris, p. 148. See also Hall and Ames, *Thinking Through Confucius*, p. 168.

14. Hall and Ames, *Thinking Through Confucius*, pp. 138, 136.

15. Ibid., p. 137.

16. Mansur Al-Hallâj is a highly revered Persian mystic. Born in 858, he was condemned to death, horribly mutilated and executed in the year 922, for having claimed to incarnate Truth (*Al Haq* or God). A moving account of his passion can be found in Farid al-Din Attar, *Muslim Saints and Mystics: Episodes from Tadhkirat al-Auliya*, trans. A.J. Arberry, Arkana, London, 1990, pp. 264–71. According to Attar, even after his broken limbs were burned, from his ashes came the cry: 'I am the Truth.'

On Garitoy's Death

18 December 1986
Another bullet is fired
Ending another good man.

Garitoy is dead
he is indeed.
One body down
One spirit up.
His passion for MCTN
exceeded his passion for food
He authored friendships
despised deception
blended family and function.

Marawi is silent
the campus is serene
Lake Lanao wails
such loss, such parting
Mindanao is never the same.

Garitoy was an architect
of dreams,
for generations to flesh out
He told me early this month
'I have accepted the fact
that we need not live
to taste the fruits
of our labors.'

Weep not – he died
a composed man
his dreams all
shall live
long enough
in Jib-jib, Borgy, Nits
The Kambays
and us
meant so much.

Fe E. Remotigue, The Philippines, 1987.

MCTN is the Mindanao Community Theatre Network, of which the author of the poem, known to her friends as Pepot, was at one time the chairperson.

SUGGESTED READINGS

The books and articles listed here (some of them annotated) should not be considered a bibliography in the conventional and academic sense of the word. They are rather 'suggested readings' for those whose thirst for a personal understanding of our changing world prompts them to share their thoughts and experiences with others. The books, articles and papers listed below could be random lights for them. They do not claim to cover all, or necessarily the best of what has been written or published on the subjects addressed by the contributors. Neither have they been chosen on an 'objective' basis, giving *all* views an equal chance of being represented.

Three sets of reasons may explain the choice. First, these are to a large extent those texts that, in the past fifty years of my life, have come to my attention, either directly or through friends, colleagues and students who were more or less familiar with my particular interests, curiosity, preoccupations and doubts. Many have affected my thinking, helped me question my certainties and opened up for me new horizons for perceiving the world. They are mostly drawn from the personal indexes or data base I set up for my own learning and for my students. They would be incomplete even if they represented *all* the works that have come to my attention. I therefore sincerely wish and hope that readers will complete the list with further references.

Second, these readings have been chosen on the basis of the same logic as that applied to the choice of contributors. That is, they do not generally belong to the mainstream, even less to the dominant thinking on development. They are rather *human centred*, *radical*, in the etymological sense of the word, and *subversive* in the sense explained in the introduction.

Finally, their *raison d'être* is to invite every reader to use them as an interlocutor to enrich their own dialogue with new ideas and possibilities of action. We apologize, therefore, for not including in the list many important books found in more conventional bibliographies on development. The intention has been to bring to the notice of readers the books we think could be studied for a more enriching encounter with the present and future builders of the post-development era.

M.R.

Achebe, Chinua, *Things Fall Apart*, London: Heinemann, 1958.

Adamson, Peter, 'The Rains: A Report from a Village in Upper Volta', *New Internationalist* 120, 1983.

Agamben, Georgio, *Essays on the Destruction of Experience*, trans. Liz Heron, London, Verso: 1993.

Ahluwalia, Montek S., 'Inequality, Poverty and Development', *Journal of Development Economics*, vol. 3, no. 4, December 1976, pp. 307–42.

Ake, C., *Social Science as Imperialism: The Theory of Political Development*, Lagos: University of Abadan Press, 1979.

Al-Ghazali, *On the duties of Brotherhood*, trans. Muhtar Holland, Woodstock, N.Y.: The Overlook Press, 1976. [Translated from the Classic Arabic. The eight duties of brotherhood by Ghazali: material assistance, holding one's tongue, speaking out, forgiveness, prayer, loyalty and sincerity, informality.]

Almond, G.A., M. Chodorow and R.H. Pearce, eds, *Progress and its Discontents*, Berkeley: University of California Press, 1982. [Divided into five parts, related to the historical, scientific, economic, social and humanistic dimensions, it covers twenty-five different themes by as many authors, such as P. Chaunu, Georges Duby, etc.]

Alvares, Claude, *Technology and Culture in India, China and the West, 1500–1972*, Delhi: Allied Publishers, 1979.

Alvares, Claude, *Science, Development and Violence*, New Delhi: Oxford University Press, 1993.

Amin, Samir, *Neo-Colonialism in West Africa*, Harmondsworth: Penguin, 1964.

Amin, Samir, *Trois Expériences africaines de développement: Le Mali, la Guinée et le Ghana*, Paris: PUF, 1965.

Amin, Samir, *Impérialisme et sous-développement en Afrique*, Paris: Anthropos, 1976.

Amin, Samir, *L'Accumulation à l'échelle mondiale: Critique de la théorie du sous-développement*, Paris: Anthropos, 1981 [1973].

Amin, Samir, *Maldevelopment, Anatomy of a Global Failure*, London: Zed Books, 1990.

Amselle, J.L., *Le Sauvage à la mode*, Paris: Le Sycamore, 1979.

Anderson, B., *Imagined Communities: Reflections on the Origin and Spread of Nationalism*, London: Verso, 1983 [Describes nations/nationalism as products of the social imagination.]

Annis, Sheldon, 'What is Not the Same About the Urban Poor: The Case of Mexico City', in John P. Lewis et al., *Strengthening the Poor: What Have We Learned*, Overseas Development Council, 1988, pp. 133–48.

Apffel Marglin, Frédérique, *Development and Repression: A Feminist Critique*, WIDER Research Project, June 1990.

Apffel Marglin, Frédérique, 'Sacred Grove: Regenerating the Body, the Land, the Community', paper presented at the *Intercultural Institute of Montreal (IIM) Conference Living with the Earth*, April 1992.

Apffel Marglin, Frédérique, ed., *Dominating Knowledge*, Oxford: Clarendon Press, 1990.

Appiah, Kwame Anthony, *In My Father's House: Africa in the Philosophy of Culture*, New York: Oxford University Press, 1992.

Arendt, Hannah, *The Human Condition*, Chicago: Chicago University Press, 1958. [Powerful historical treatise on the meaning of work in Western thought.]

Arendt, Hannah, *On Violence*, San Diego and London: Harvest HBJ, 1969.

Arndt, H.W., *The Rise and Fall of Economic Growth: A Study in Contemporary Thought*, Chicago: University of Chicago Press, 1984.

Asad, T., ed., *Anthropology and the Colonial Encounter*, New York: Humanities Press, 1973.

Ashcroft, B., G. Griffiths and H. Tiffin, eds, *The Post-Colonial Studies Reader*, London: Routledge, 1995. [Contains 86 papers related to the post-colonial era, under the headings: Issues and Debates, Universality and Difference, Representation and

Resistance, Postmodernism and Post-colonialism, Nationalism, Hybridity, Ethnicity and Indigeneity, Feminism and Post-colonialism, Language, The Body and Performance, History, Place, Education, Production and Consumption.]

Attali, Jacques, et al., *Le Mythe du Développement*, Paris: Editions du Seuil, 1977.

Aubrey, Andrès, 'Mexique: Manger, Un acte politique; Stratégie paysanne de la production alimentaire,' *IFDA Dossier* 57/58, January/April 1987.

Auletta, Ken, *The Underclass*, New York: Random House, 1983.

Auster, Richard D. and Morris Silver, *The State as Firm: Economic Forces in Political Development*, The Hague: Martinus Nijhoff, 1979.

Ba, Ampaté H., *Aspects de la civilisation africaine*, Paris: Présence Africaine, 1972.

Bahuguna, Sunderlal, 'CHIPKO: The People's Movement with a Hope for the Survival of Humankind', *IFDA Dossier* 63, January/February 1988, pp. 3–14.

Balandier, Georges, *Sociologie des Brazavilles noires*, Paris: Armand Colin, 1955. [On rural exodus, the notion of *poto-poto*, urban tensions and individual typologies.]

Balandier, Georges, *Afrique Ambiguë*, Paris: Plon, 1957.

Bandyopadhyay, Jayanta, and Vandana Shiva, 'Political Economy of Ecology Movements', *IFDA Dossier* 71, May/June 1989, pp. 37–60.

Barkin, David, 'The Specter of Rural Development', *NACLA Report on the Americas*, vol. 28, no. 1, July/August 1994.

Baudrillard, Jean, 'La Genèse idéologique des besoins', in *Pour une Critique de l'économie politique du signe*, Paris: Gallimard, 1972, pp. 59–94.

Baudrillard, Jean, *La Société de consommation: ses mythes, ses structures*, Paris, Denoël, 1970.

Bayart, Jean-François, *The State in Africa: The Politics of the Belly*, Harlow: Longman, 1966. [Originally published in French in 1988. Achieved instant academic popularity, not least for its provocative discriptions of raw greed, corruption and whoring at the highest levels of most African governments.]

Baybroke, D., 'Let Needs Diminish that Preferences May Prosper', in N. Resher, ed., *Studies in Moral Philosophy*, Oxford: Blackwell, 1968. ['A persuasive statement about the descent of man from the kingdom of preference into the bondage of needs' (Illich).]

Beckman, David, 'The Politics of Hunger', *Christian Century*, vol. 11, no. 14, 28 April 1993. [An interview with David Beckman, head of Bread for the World, who wrote the BFW booklet *Transforming the Politics of Hunger*.]

Bellman, B.L., *The Language of Secrecy: Symbols and Metaphors in Poro Ritual*, New Brunswick, N.J.: Rutgers University Press, 1984.

Ben Abdallah, Taoufik, and Philippe Engelhard, *Quel Avenir pour l'économie populaire en Afrique?*, Dakar: ENDA, 1988.

Berger, Peter, Brigitte Berger and Hansfried Kellner, *The Homeless Mind: Modernization and Consciousness*, New York: Random House, 1974.

Berkes, Fikret, *Common Property Resources: Ecology and Community-based Sustainable Development*, London: Belhaven Press, 1989.

Berman, Marshall, *All That Is Solid Melts Into Air: The Experience of Modernity*, New York: Simon & Schuster, 1982; London: Verso, 1983.

Berman, Marshall, *Coming to Our Senses: Body and Spirit in the Hidden History of the West*, New York: Simon & Schuster, 1989.

Bernard, James, *The Death of Progress*, New York: Alfred Knopf, 1973.

Berry, Wendell, *What Are People For?*, San Francisco: North Point Press, 1990. [Refreshing essays on the many dimensions of a regenerative approach to life, with thoughts on style and grace, 'practical harmony', diversity, local culture, nature, people, women and computers.]

Bhattacharji, Sukumari, 'Economic Rights and Ancient Indian Women', *Economic and Political Weekly*, 2–9 March 1991, pp. 507–12.

Biswas, Asit K., Zuo Dakang, James E. Nicklum and Liu Changming, eds, *Long-Distance*

Water Transfer, A Chinese Case Study and International Experiences, London: Tycooly International Publishing, 1984.

Black, Walter, and Donald Shaw, eds, *Theology, Third World Development and Economic Justice*, Canada: Fraser Institute, 1985.

Blackwell, Trevor and Jeremy Seabrook, *The Revolt Against Change: Towards a Conserving Radicalism*, London: Vintage, 1993. [Thought-provoking book on basic concepts such as change, conservatism and radicalism. Blackwell teaches at Harlow College; Seabrook is an independent writer and journalist, author of *Pioneers of Change* (London: Zed Books, 1993) and *Victims of Development* (see below).]

Blomstrom, Magnus and Björn Hettne, *Development Theory in Transition*, London: Zed Books, 1984.

Blumenberg, H., *The Legitimacy of the Modern Age*, Cambridge, Mass: MIT Press, 1983.

Bodley, John H., *Anthropology and Contemporary Human Problems*, Palo Alto, Calif.: Mayfield Publishing Co., 1985.

Bodley, John H., *Victims of Progress*, Mountain View, Calif.: Mayfield Publishing Co., 1990.

Bodley, John H., ed., *Tribal Peoples and Development Issues*, Mountain View, Calif.: Mayfield Publishing Co., 1988.

Bohannan, P. and G. Dalton, *Markets in Africa: Eight Subsistence Economies in Transition*, Evanston: Northwestern University Press, 1962.

Bohannan, P., 'Concepts of Time among the Tiv of Nigeria', in J. Middleton, ed., *Myth and Cosmos*, Austin: University of Texas Press, 1980 [1953].

Bolter, D., *Turing's Man: Western Culture in the Computer Age*, Chapell Hill: University of North Carolina Press, 1984. [How needs are being recast today as requirements to fit into the mental construct of systems thinking (Illich).]

Bourdieu, Pierre, *La Misère du monde*, Paris: Seuil, 1993. [Hundreds of voices from the 'old' and the 'new' poor expressing their feelings and perceptions. A powerful and illuminating testimony on modernized poverty.]

Bourguignat, Henri, *La Tyrannie des marchés: Essai sur l'économie virtuelle*, Paris: Economica, 1995.

Brandon, Williams, *The Last Americans: The Indian in American Culture*, New York, McGraw Hill: 1974.

Brébant, Brigitte, *La pauvreté, un destin?*, Paris: L'Harmattan, 1984.

Brody, Alan, and Joseph Ascroft, 'Do the Mass Media Cause Poverty? A Return to Traditional Media', Paper presented at the 32nd Annual Conference of the International Communication Association, Boston, Mass, 1–5 May 1982.

Brown, Lester, and S. Postel 'The Thresholds of Change', in *State of the World Reports*, Worldwatch Institute, 1987.

Buchsbaum, Herbert, 'One Night, One City', *Scholastic Update* (Teacher's Edition), vol. 126, no. 11, 11 March 1994. [A small testimony on the desperation of American poverty – and the compassion that helps fellow human beings make it through the night. Particularly focused on the homeless.]

Bungener, Pierre, *Le Développement in-sensé*, Lausanne: L'Age d'Homme, 1978.

Caillé, A., *Critique de la raison utilitaire*, Paris: La Découverte, 1989.

Canguilhem, Georges, et al., *Du Développement à l'évolution*, Paris, PUF, 1962.

Cardoso, Eliana, and Ann Helwege, 'Below the Line: Poverty in Latin America', *World Development*, vol. 20, no. 1, 1992, pp. 19–37.

Cardoso, Fernando Henrique, 'Associated-Dependent Development: Theoretical and Practical Implications', in Alfred Stepan, ed., *Authoritarian Brazil*, New Haven, Conn.: Yale University Press, 1977.

Cardoso, Fernando Henrique, *Autotarisomo e Democratização*, Rio de Janeiro: Paz e Terra, 1975.

Certau, Michel de, *The Practice of Everyday Life*, Berkeley, University of California Press, 1984.

Césaire, Aimé, *Discourse on Colonialism*, New York: Monthly Review Press, 1972.
Césaire, Aimé, *Notebook of a Return to My Native Land*, Newcastle upon Tyne: Bloodaxe Books, 1995.
Chamard, Régent, *Les Tendances de la pauvreté dans les régions du Canada: La situation particulière du Québec*, Direction de la recherche, Ministère de la Main-d'oeuvre, de la Sécurité du revenu et de la Formation professionnelle, May 1991, pp. 1–24.
Chittick, William C., 'Toward a Theology of Development', *Nameh Farhang* (Teheran) 12, Winter 94.
Chomsky, Noam, *Chronicles of Dissent: Interviews with David Barsamian*, Monroe, Maine: Common Courage Press, 1992. [Radical reflections on language in the service of propaganda, terrorism and the politics of language, historical engineering, elite power and the responsibility of intellectuals, the Gulf War, world order and disorder, and the global protection racket.]
Chomsky, Noam, *Deterring Democracy*, London: Vintage, 1992.
Chossudovsky, Michael, 'G7 Creating Global Poverty', *Canadian Dimension*, vol. 29, no. 5, October–November 1995, p. 29. [On the creation of global poverty, manufacturing public debt, the burden of creditors, global financial market instability.]
Christie, Nils, *Crime Control as Industry – Towards Gulags, Western Style*, London: Routledge, 1995.
Cinar, E. Mine, 'Disguised Employment: The Case of Female Family Labor in Agriculture and Small-Scale Manufacturing in Third World Countries, *IFDA Dossier* 59, May–June 1987, pp. 13–18.
Clark, David, *Basic Communities: Towards an Alternative Society*, London: SPCK, 1977.
Clastres, Pierre, *La Société contre l'état*, Paris: Editions de Minuit, 1974.
Clastres, Pierre, *Recherches d'anthropologie politique*, Paris: Editions du Seuil, 1980.
Cleaver, Harry, 'The Chiapas Uprising and the Future of Class Struggle in the New World Order', *Riff-Raff* (Padua), February 1994.
Cohen, Erik '"Christianity and Buddhism in Thailand", the "Battle of Axes" and the "Contest of Power"', *Social Compass*, vol. 38, no. 2, June 1991, pp. 115–40.
Cohn, Bernard S. 'The Command of Language and the Language of Command', in Ranajit Guha, ed., *Subaltern Studies*, New Delhi: Oxford University Press, 1985, vol. 4, pp. 279–29.
Coleman, James Scott, *Nationalism and Development in Africa*, edited by Richard L. Sklar, Berkeley: University of California Press, 1966.
Coser, Lewis, 'The Sociology of Poverty', *Social Problems* 13, 1965, pp. 141–9.
Dag Hammarskjöld Foundation, *Development Dialogue*, Special Issue on 'Autonomous Development Funds', no. 2, Uppsala, 1995.
Dahl, Gudrun, and Gemetchu Megerssa 'The Spiral of the Ram's Horn: Boran Concepts of Development', in G. Dahl and A. Rabo, *Kam-Ap or Take-Off: Local Notions of Development*, Stockholm: Stockholm Studies in Social Anthropology, 1992.
Dahrendorf, Ralf, *The Modern Social Conflict: An Essay on the Politics of Liberty*, Berkeley: University of California Press, 1990. [Contains interesting insights on the modern 'work society', the 'underclass' and the Lumpenproletariat (sometimes translated as the 'social scum'.]
Daley, E. Herman and John B. Cobb, Jr, *For the Common Good: Redirecting the Economy toward Community, the Environment and a Sustainable Future*, Boston, Mass.: Beacon Press, 1989.
Dallape, Fabio, *Enfants de la rue, enfants perdus? Une expérience à Nairobi*, ENDA, Série Études et Recherches, no. 128, Dakar, August 1990.
Dalton, G., ed., *Primitive, Archaic and Modern Economics: Essays of Karl Polanyi*, Boston, Mass.: Beacon Press, 1971.
Danziger, Sheldon H., et al., eds, *Prescriptions for Change*, Cambridge, Mass.: Harvard University Press, 1994. [Collection of essays on poverty in the USA: 'The poor have

gotten poorer, blacker, younger, less economically mobile, less competitive in the job market, less able to pay for health care. No one believes any more that a rising tide of economic growth will lift all boats. The tide is weak and the boats leaky', as James Tobin remarks in his contribution. 'And the United States remains an embarrassment among industrialized nations.']

Das, Amritananda, *Foundations of Gandhian Economics*, Delhi: Allied Publishers, 1979.

Das, V., ed., *Mirrors of Violence: Community, Riots, Survival*, New Delhi: Oxford University Press, 1990. [Highlights the insrumentalization of communal violence under the pretence of secularism.]

Davidson, Art, ed., and the Association of Village Council Presidents, *Does One Way of Life Have to Die So Another Can Live?*, Bethel, Ala.: Yupik Nation, 1974.

Davidson, Basil, *The African Genius*, Boston, Mass.: Little, Brown, 1970.

Davidson, Basil, *The Black Man's Burden: Africa and the Curse of the Nation State*, Oxford: James Currey, 1992.

Davis, D.E., *Ecophilosophy: A Field Guide on the Literature*, San Pedro: Miles, 1989. [A useful reference too on ethics and environment, with an annotated bibliography.]

Depestre, R., *Bonjour et adieu à la négritude*, Paris: Laffont, 1980.

Desmond Clark, J., and S.A. Brandt, eds, *From Hunters to Farmers*, Berkeley: University of California Press, 1984.

Dhar, P.N., 'UN and Development', *Seminar* (Delhi) 314, October 1985, pp. 48–52.

Dharmapal, *Indian Science and Technology in the 18th Century*, New Delhi: Impex, 1971. [Highlights the Indian patrimony of knowledge before colonization.]

Dia, A.M., *Islam, Sociétés africaines et culture industrielle*, Dakar: NEA, 1975.

Dia, A.M., *Essais sur l'Islam*, 3 vols: 1: *Islam et humanisme*; 2: *Socio-Anthropologie de l'Islam*; 3: *Islam et civilisations négro-africaines*, Dakar: NEA, 1977–81.

Diakhate, L., 'Le Processus d'acculturation en Afrique noire et ses rapports avec la négritude', *Présence Africaine* 56, 1965.

Diamond, S., *In Search of the Primitive: A Critique of Civilization*, New Brunswick, N.J.: Transaction, 1987.

Dicko, Ahmadou A., *Journal d'une défaite*, Paris: L'Harmattan/Dag Hammarskjöld Foundation, 1992.

Diop, C.A., *L'Afrique noire précoloniale*, Paris: Présence Africaine, 1960.

Diop, C.A., *Civilisation ou barbarie*, Paris: Présence Africaine, 1981.

Douthwaite, Richard, *The Growth Illusion: How Economic Growth has Enriched the Few, Impoverished the Many and Endangered the Planet*, Dublin: Lilliput Press, 1992.

Dreyfus, H.L., and Paul Rabinow, *Michel Foucault: Beyond Structuralism and Hermeneutics*, with an Afterward and Interview with Michel Foucault, Chicago: University of Chicago Press, 1983.

Dreze, Jean, Amartya Sen and Athar Hussain, eds, *The Political Economy of Hunger: Selected Essays*, Oxford: Clarendon Press, 1996.

Dube, S.C., *Modernization and Development: The Search for Alternative Paradigms*, London: UNU/Zed Books, 1988.

Dubois, Marc, 'The Governance of the Third World: A Foucauldian Perspective on Power Relations in Development', *Alternatives*, vol. 16, no 1, Winter 1991, pp. 1–29.

Dumont, Louis, *From Mandeville to Marx: The Genesis and Triumph of Economic Ideology*, Chicago: University of Chicago Press, 1977 (translated from *Homo Equalis*, I, Paris: Gallimard, 1977].

Dumont, Louis, *Homo Hierarchicus: Le Système des castes et ses implications*, Paris: Gallimard, 1979 [1967].

Dupire, Marguerite, 'The Position of Women in a Pastoral Society: The Fulani WoDaaBe, Nomads of Niger', in Denise Paulme, ed., *Women of Tropical Africa*, Los Angeles: University of California Press, 1963.

Dupuy, Jean-Pierre, and Paul Dumouchel, *L'Enfer des choses: René Girard et la logique de l'économie*, Paris: Editions du Seuil, 1979.
Durning Alan, *How Much Is Enough*, London: Earthscan, 1992.
Durning, Alan, 'Action at the Grassroots: Fighting Poverty and Environmental Decline', *Worldwatch Paper* 88, January 1989.
Duvall, Raymond, and John R. Freeman, 'The Techno-Bureaucratic Elite and Entrepreunial State in Dependent Industrialization', *American Politial Science Review* 77, pp. 569–87.
Edwards, Michael, 'The Irrelevance of Development Studies', *Third World Quarterly*, vol. 11, no. 1, January 1989. [Most development work benefits expatriate development workers – of whom, notes the author, there were 80,000 in Africa in 1985, costing some $4 billion.]
Ekins, Paul, 'Economy, Ecology, Society, Ethics: A Framework for Analysis – Real Life Economics for a Living Society', paper presented at Second Annual International Conference on Socio-Economics, Washington DC, 16 March 1990.
Ekins, Paul, ed., *The Living Economy: A New Economics in the Making*, London: Routledge, 1986.
Ela, J.-M., *Le Cri de l'homme africain*, Paris: L'Harmattan, 1980.
Ellul, Jacques, *The Technological Society*, New York: Knopf, 1964.
Ellul, Jacques, *La Subversion du Christianisme*, Paris: Editions du Seuil, 1984.
Ellul, Jacques, *La Raison d'etre: Méditation sur l'ecclésiaste*, Paris: Editions du Seuil, 1987. ['To be ready for hoping in what does not deceive, one should first lose hope in what deceives.']
ENDA (P. Engelhard, Youba Sokona and Taoufik Ben Abdallah), *A Diagnostic and Strategic Outline of the Approach: Poverty and the Environment in Africa/Esquisse diagnostique et stratégique de l'approche: Pauvreté et environnement en Afrique*, Dakar: ENDA/Tiers Monde, July 1991.
Escobar, A. and S. Alvarez, eds, *New Social Movements in Latin America: Identity, Strategy, and Democracy*, Boulder, Colo.: Westview Press, 1991.
Escobar, Arturo: 'Discourse and Power in Development: Michel Foucault and the Relevance of His Work to the Third World', *Alternatives* 10, Winter 1984–85, pp. 377–400.
Escobar, Arturo, *Encountering Development, The Making and Unmaking of the Third World*, Princeton, N.J.: Princeton University Press, 1995.
Esteva, Gustavo, 'Regenerating People's Space', *Alternatives*, vol. 13, no. 1, 1988.
Esteva, Gustavo, and Madhu Suri Prakash, *Grassroots Post-Modernism: Beyond Human Rights, the Individual Self, the Global Economy*, New York: Peter Lang, 1996. [Drawing on their personal experiences, respectively in Mexico and India, the authors seek to define the first elements of an emerging 'post-modern epics' composed of the thousands of social movements and initiatives of resistance to modernity and its global project. A most valuable and thought-provoking contribution to the discourse and practices associated with the forthcoming post-development era.]
Etzioni, Amitai, 'The Community in an Age of Individualism', *The Futurist*, May–June 1991, pp. 35–9.
Evans, Peter, B., *Dependent Development: The Alliance of Multinational, State and Local Capital in Brazil*, Princeton, N.J.: Princeton University Press, 1979.
Evans, Peter B., *Predatory, Developmental and Other Apparatuses: A Comparative Political Economy Perspective on the Third World State*, Brown University, Center for the Comparative Study of Development, August 1989. [Developmental states: the state as a nexus of exchange; Zaire as an exemplary case of predation; 'klepto-patrimonialism' of Mobutu; the cases of Japan, Korea, Brazil, etc. Very useful bibliography at the end.]
Faber, Mient Jan, 'Grass-Roots Movements and Crisis in Churches' East–West Relations', *Bulletin of Peace Proposals*, vol. 21, no. 2, 1990, pp. 195–203.

Fall, Yoro, 'Colonisation et décolonisation en Afrique: Dimension historique et dynamique dans les sociétés', paper presented at the Seminar on Post Development, Christophe Eckenstein Foundation, Geneva, 5–9 March 1990.

Fals Borda, Orlando, *Knowledge and People's Power*, Delhi: Indian Social Institute, 1988.

Fals Borda, Orlando, ed., *The Challenge of Social Change*, London: Sage, 1985.

Fanon, Frantz, *The Wretched of the Earth*, edited by Constance Farrington, New York: Grove Press, 1966.

Fanon, Frantz, *Black Skin, White Masks*, London: Pluto Press, 1991 (translation of *Peau noire, masques blancs*, Paris: Seuil, 1952).

Feith, Herb, 'Repressive–Developmental Regimes in Asia', *Alternatives* (Delhi), 1981, pp. 491–506.

Ferguson, James, *The Anti-politics Machine: 'Development', Depoliticization and Bureaucratic Power in Lesotho*, Cambridge: Cambridge University Press, 1990.

Fields, K., *Revival and Rebellion in Colonial Central Africa*, Princeton, N.J.: Princeton University Press, 1985.

Finquelievich, Susana, 'Interactions of Social Actors in Survival Strategies: The Case of the Urban Poor in Latin America', *IFDA Dossier* 59, May–June 1987, pp. 19–30.

Forrester, Viviane, *L'Horreur économique*, Paris: Fayard, 1996. [A recent bestseller by a French novelist on her vision of the disasters which, in her view, economy has set out for the future of civilization. More than the content of the essay, its extraordinary popularity has been commented on by the media as representing the revolt of the French people against the economistic phenomenon.]

Foster, George M., 'Peasant Society and the Image of Limited Goods', *American Anthropologist*, vol. 6, no. 7, 1965. [Identifies the 'image of limited good' as the key cognitive orientation in peasant societies. Limited good referred to the assumption that 'all desired things in life … exist in finite and unexpandable quantitites.']

Foster, George M., 'The Anatomy of Envy: A Study in Symbolic Behavior', *American Anthropologist*, vol. 13, no. 5, April 1972.

Foucault, Michel, *The Order of Things*, New York: Pantheon, 1973.

Foucault, Michel, *Power/Knowledge: Selected Interviews and Other Writings 1972–1977*, edited by Colin Gordon, New York: Pantheon, 1980.

Foucault, Michel, *The Archeology of Knowledge*, New York: Pantheon, 1982.

Foucault, Michel, 'On the Genealogy of Ethics', in Paul Rabinow, ed., *The Foucault Reader*, New York: Pantheon, 1984.

Foucault, Michel, 'The Ethic of Care for the Self as a Practice of Freedom', an interview in J. Bernauer and D. Rasmussen, *The Final Foucault*, Cambridge: MIT Press, 1988.

Franke, Richard, and Barbara Chassin, 'Peasants, Peanuts, Profits, and Pastoralists', *The Ecologist*, vol. 11, no. 4, 1981, pp. 156–68.

Friedland, Roger, 'Class Power and Social Control: The War on Poverty', *Politics and Society*, vol. 6, no. 4, 1976.

Friedmann, John, 'From Social to Political Power: Collective Self-empowerment and Social Change', *IFDA Dossier* 69, January/February 1989, pp. 3–14.

Fuchs, Estelle, *The Danish Friskoler and Community Control*, in E.B. Leacock, ed., *The Culture of Poverty: A Critique*, New York: Simon & Schuster, 1971.

Fugelsang, Andreas, *About Understanding: Ideas and Observations on Cross-cultural Communication*, Uppsala: Dag Hammarskjöld Foundation, 1982.

Fukuoaka, M., *The One Straw Revolution*, Hoshangabad (India): Friends' Rural Centre, 1985.

Funiciello, Theresa, *Tyranny of Kindness: Dismantling the Welfare System to End Poverty in America*, New York: Atlantic Monthly Press, 1993.

Gabel, Medard, and Robert Rodale (The Concupia Project), 'Regenerating the United States Economy through Growth in Regional and Local Self-reliance', *IFDA Dossier* 47, May–June 1985, pp. 15–26.

Gaiha, Raghav, 'Are the Chronically Poor also the Poorest in Rural India?', *Development and Change*, vol. 20, no. 2, April 1989, pp. 293–321.

Galbraith, J.K., 'Weapons and World Welfare', *Development Forum*, vol. 15, no. 3, April 1987, p. 6.

Galeano, Eduardo, *We Say No: Chronicles of 1963–1991*, trans. Mark Fried, New York: W.W. Norton, 1992.

Galeano, Eduardo 'The Corruption of Memory', *NACLA Report on the Americas*, vol. 27, no. 3, November/December 1993.

Galtung, Johan, Peter O'Brien and Roy Preiswerk, eds, *Self-Reliance: A Strategy for Development*, Geneva: Institute of Development Studies (IUED), 1980.

Gandhi, Mahatma, 'Hind Swaraj', in *Collected Works of Mahatma Gandhi*, Delhi: Government of India, 1963, 4, pp. 81–103.

Garfinkel, Harold, 'Conditions of Successful Degradation Ceremonies', *American Journal of Sociology* 16, 1956. [The process of transforming an individual's total identity into an identity lower in the group's scheme of social types. Excellent article for understanding the condition of the assisted in modern welfare states.]

Gaupp, Peter, 'Waru Waru: Farming Renaissance at Lake Titicaca', *Swiss Review*, vol. 41, no. 11.

Geertz, Richard, et al., *Meaning and Order in Moroccan Society*, Cambridge: Cambridge University Press, 1979.

George, Henry, *Progress and Poverty*, London: Dent, 1976.

George, Susan, *A Fate Worse than Debt*, Harmondsworth: Penguin, 1988.

George, Susan, *The Debt Boomerang: How Third World Debt Harms Us All*, London: Pluto, 1992.

George, Susan, and Fabrizio Sabelli, *Faith and Credit: The World Bank's Secular Empire*, Harmondsworth: Penguin, 1994.

Geremek, Bronislaw, *Truands et misérables dans l'Europe moderne (1350–1600)*, Paris: Gallimard, 1980.

Geremek, Bronislaw, *Poverty: A History*, Oxford: Blackwell, 1994.

Gerster, Richard, 'How to Ruin a Country: The Case of Togo', *IFDA Dossier* 71, May/June 1989, pp. 25–36.

Ghanshyam (Lok Jagriti Kendra, Madhupur, Bihar), 'Sustainable Development: Going Back to the Roots', paper prepared for the conference on 'Living with the Earth', Intercultural Institute of Montreal, 30 April–3 May 1982.

Giedion, S., *Mechanization Takes Command*, New York: W.W. Norton, 1969. [A classic, according to Otto Ulrich.]

Goneya, Judith, 'The Paradox of the Advantaged Elder and the Feminization of Poverty', *Social Work*, vol. 39, no. 1, January 1944, p. 35. [On the concepts of the advantaged elder and the feminization of poverty. The theoretical shortcomings of both concepts are examined, and a broader model of economic well-being that emphasizes the interactive nature of gender, race, and class is proposed.]

Gourlay, K.A., *World of Waste: Dilemmas of Industrial Development*, London: Zed Books, 1992.

Grall, Paul, and Anne Wery, 'Le Concept de pauvreté: Les diverses facettes institutionnelles de la pauvreté ou les différentes naturalisations de ce concept', *Courrier Hebdomadaire du CRISP* 771, 1977.

Grell, Paul, and Anne Wery, 'La Relativité du concept de pauvreté', *Economie et Humanisme* 254, July–August 1980.

Gronemeyer, Marianne, 'Helping', in Wolfgang Sachs, ed., *The Development Dictionary: A Guide to Knowledge and Power*, London: Zed Books, 1992, pp. 53–69.

Gronemeyer, R., *Hirten und Helfer*, Giwaawn: Focus, 1988. [Bids a sad farewell to nomadic ways of life, which have been devastatingly affected by aid.]

Gruzinski, Serge, *La Colonisation de l'imaginaire: Sociétés indigènes et occidentalisation dans le Mexique espagnol, XVIe-XVIIIe siècle*, Paris: Gallimard, 1988. [Important study on the ways the West, through religion and domination, colonized the people's imaginary. A significant contribution to the history of relations between orality, memory, the image and the writing. Also interesting insights into the way Mexicans organized themselves in order to defend their culture, and how their *epistemé*, including their 'moral economy', helped them develop the socio-cultural networks and the 'niches' necessary for the defence of their immune defence systems.]

Gudeman, S., *Economics as Culture: Models and Metaphors of Livelihood*, London: Routledge, 1986.

Guéhenno, Jean-Marie, *The End of the Nation-State*, Minnesota, University of Minnesota Press, 1995. [The author was France's ambassador to the EU. He argues that nation-states no longer serve a useful purpose, and predicts the rise of a new 'imperial age' in which the world will be controlled by communications networks, the supernational arteries of business and information, rather than by politics. The world is 'capable of building all sorts of 'virtual communities' that will liberate us from the constraints of geography, and from the traditional political structures that have for so long framed our actions.' Also, 'nations – even the most powerful of them all, the US – no longer have the capacity, in a global world, of protecting the people whose destiny they claim to embody from the uncertainties of the outside world... Given competition from faraway countries, given the migration of poverty and terrorism, it has become as impossible to control the world that surrounds us as it is to ignore it.' In the indefinite future, he believes, we will all inhabit a more orderly world 'that is at once unified and without a center'.]

Guha, Ranajit, and G.C. Spivak, *Selected Subaltern Studies*, with a foreword by Edward Said, Oxford: Oxford University Press, 1988.

Guillaume, Henri, *Eloge du désordre*, Paris: Gallimard, 1978.

Guruge, Ananda W.P., 'Identité culturelle et développment: tradition et modernité', *IFDA Dossier* 68, November/December 1988, pp. 51–9.

Hall, David L., and Roger T. Ames, *Thinking through Confucius*, Albany, N.Y.: SUNY Press, 1987.

Halpern, Manfred, 'Choosing Between Ways of Life and Death and Between Forms of Democracy: An Archetypal Analysis', *Alternatives* (Delhi), 1987, pp. 5–35.

Hancock, G., *Lords of Poverty*, London: Mandarin, 1991.

Handler Joel, and Yeheskel Hasenfeld, *The Moral Construction of Poverty*, London: Sage, 1991.

Harries, Patrick, 'Aspects of Poverty in Gazankulu: Three Case Studies', Second Carnegie Inquiry into Poverty and Development in Southern Africa, conference paper no. 67, 13–19 April 1984.

Harrington, Michael, *The New American Poverty*, New York: Viking Penguin, 1985.

Haswell, Margaret, *The Nature of Poverty: A Case-history of the First Quarter-Century after World War II*, London: Macmillan, 1975.

Havel, Václav, *Open Letters: Selected Writings*, New York: Viking Books, 1991.

Hayter, Theresa, *Aid, Rhetoric and Reality*, London: Zwan Pluto, 1985.

Herskovits, M.J., *The Human Factor In Changing Africa*, New York: Knopf, 1962.

Hettne, Björn, 'The Development Strategy of Gandhian Economics', *Journal of the Indian Anthropological Society*, vol. 6, no. 1, April 1971.

Hettne, Björn, 'Three Worlds of Crises for the Nation-State', paper for the UNU Project of Third World and World Development, SID, Delhi, 1988.

Hewitt, W., 'Strategies for Social Change Emloyed in *Communidades Eclesiasis de Base* (CEBS) the Archdiocese of São Paulo, *Journal for the Scientific Study of Religion*, 1986, vol. 25, pp. 16–30.

Hirschman, Albert, *The Passions and the Interests, Political Arguments for Capitalism Before Its Triumph*, Princton, N.J.: Princeton University Press, 1977.

Hirschman, Albert, *Essays in Trespassing: Economics to Politics and Beyond*, Cambridge: Cambridge University Press, 1981.

Hirschmann, David, 'Women and Political Participation in Africa: Broadening the Scope of Research', *World Development*, vol. 19, no. 12, December 1991, pp. 1679–94.

Horton, R., 'African Traditional Thought and Western Science', in B.R. Wilson, ed., *Rationality*, Oxford: Basil Blackwell, 1981.

Hunter, J.D., Stephen C. Ainly et al., *Making Sense of Modern Times: Peter L. Berger and the Vision of Interpretive Sociology*, London: Routledge, 1986.

Huntondji, P., *African Philosophy: Myth and Reality*, Bloomington: Indiana University Press, 1977.

Hurst, Philip, *Rainforest Politics: Ecological Destruction in South-East Asia*, London: Zed Books, 1990.

Hyde, Lewis, *The Gift: Imagination and the Erotic Life of Property*, New York: Vintage, 1983 [1979].

Ibn Khaldun, Al Muqaddimah, *An Introduction to History*, trans. Franz Rosenthal, Princeton, N.J.: Princeton University Press: 1958.

Ignatieff, Michael, *The Needs of Strangers*, London: Chatto & Windus, 1984.

Ignatieff, Michael, 'The Ethics of Television', *Daedalus* 114, 1985.

Iliffe, John, *The African Poor*, Cambridge: Cambridge University Press, 1979.

Iliffe, John, *The Emergence of African Capitalism*, Minneapolis: University of Minnesota Press, 1983. [Illustrates how different cosmologies shape the meaning of production. Includes an article by T. Weiskel, 'Toward an Archaeology of Colonialism: Elements in the Ecological Transformation of the Ivory Coast'.]

Illich, Ivan, *Celebration of Awareness*, London: Marion Boyars, 1971.

Illich, Ivan, *Deschooling Society*, Harmondsworth: Penguin Books, 1971.

Illich, Ivan et al., *Disabling Professions*, London: Marion Boyars, 1977.

Illich, Ivan, *Toward A History of Needs*, New York: Pantheon, 1977.

Illich, Ivan, *The Right to Useful Unemployment and its Professional Enemies*, London: Marion Boyars, 1978.

Illich, Ivan, *Shadow Work*, London: Marion Boyars, 1981. ['The modern age can be understood as that of an unrelenting 500–year war waged to destroy the environmental conditions for subsistence and replace them by commodities produced within the frame of the new nation state. In this war against popular cultures and their framework, the State was at first assisted by the clergies of various churches, and later by the professionals and their institutional procedures. During this war, popular cultures and vernacular domains – areas of subsistence – were devastated at all levels. Modern history, from the point of view of the losers in this war, still remains to be written. The report on this war has so far reflected the belief that it helped the "poor" toward progress. It was written from the point of view of the winners. Marxist historians are usually not less blinded to the values that were destroyed than their bourgeois, liberal or Christian colleagues. Economic historians tend to start their research with categories that reflect the foregone conclusion that scarcity, defined by mimetic desire, is the human condition par excellence.']

Illich, Ivan, *Gender*, Berkeley, Calif.: Heyday Books, 1982. [The book's reflections on the modernization of poverty and the feminization of poverty are important for a deeper understanding of the hidden dimensions of development.]

Illich, Ivan, *In the Mirror of the Past: Lectures and Addresses, 1978–1990*, London: Marion Boyars, 1992. [Contains important contributions on 'Disvalue', on 'The Educational Sphere', 'The History of *Homo Educandus*' and Illich's reflections on 'The Message of Bapu's Hut'.]

Institut Interculturel de Montreal (IIM), *Living with the Earth: Cross-cultural Perspectives on Sustainable Development: Indigenous and Alternative Practices*, The Colloquium Report, Orford, Quebec, 30 April–3 May 1992.

Jacquard, Albert, *J'accuse l'économie triomphante*, Paris: Calmann-Lévy, 1995.
Jacquard, Albert, *Le Souci des pauvres: L'Héritage de François d'Assise*, Paris: Calmann-Lévy, 1996.
Jayal, N.D., 'Destruction of Water Resources – The Most Critical Ecological Crisis of East Asia', London: *The Ecologist*, vol. 15, no. 1–2, 1985.
Jennings, Bruce, *A Grassroots Movement in Bioethics*, Hastings Center Report Special Supplement, June/July 1988.
Jensen Doreen and Cheryl Broks, eds, *In Celebration of Our Survival: The First Nations of British Columbia*, Vancouver: UCB Press, 1991.
Jimenez, Francisco, *Poverty and Social Justice*, Tempe, Ariz.: Bilingual Press, 1987.
Kaboré, Gomkoudougou V., 'Caractère "féodal" du système politique mossi', *Cahiers d'Etudes Africaines* (Paris), vol. 7, no. 3, 1962.
Kassam, K.E., 'The Fertile Past: The Gabra Concept of Oral Tradition', *Africa*, 1986, vol. 56, no. 2.
Kennedy, P., *The Rise and Fall of the Great Powers: Economic Change and Military Conflict from 1500 to 2000*, New York: Random House, 1989.
Ki-Zerbo, Joseph, *La Natte des autres: sur le développement endogène*, Dakar: CODESRIA; Paris: Diffusion, 1991.
Kim Soo Whan, Cardinal Stephen, 'Every Country in the World Neglects the Poor', *IFDA Dossier* 77, May/June 1990, pp. 33–5.
Kim, Eun Mee, 'From Dominance to Symbiosis: State and Chaebol in the Korean Economy, 1960–1985', Ph.D. dissertation, Department of Sociology, Brown University, Providence, R.I., 1987.
Klare, Michael T., *Supplying Repression*, New York: Field Foundation, December 1977.
Kohr, Leopold, *Development Without Aid: The Translucent Society*, Llandybie, Carmarthenshire: Christopher Davies, 1973.
Kohr, Leopold, *The Breakdown of Nations*, New York: Dutton, 1978.
Kohr, Leopold, *The Overdeveloped Nations*, New York: Simon & Schuster, 1978.
Korten, David, C., *When Corporations Rule the World*, London: Earthscan, 1996.
Kothari, Rajni, ed., *State and Nation Building*, New Delhi: Allied Publishers, 1976.
Kothari, Rajni, *Poverty: Human Consciousness and the Amnesia of Development*, London: Zed Books, 1995.
Kothari, Rajni, *Footsteps into the Future: Diagnosis of the Present World and a Design for an Alternative*, Free Press, 1975.
Kothari, Rajni, *Rethinking Development: In Search of Human Alternatives*, Croton-on-Hudson: Apex Press, 1989.
Kothari, Rajni, *State Against Democracy: In Search of Human Governance*, Croton-on-Hudson: Apex Press, 1989.
Kothari, Rajni, 'The NGOs, the State and World Capitalism', *Social Action*, vol. 36, October–December 1986, pp. 359–77.
Kozol, Jonathan, 'Knocking on Heaven's Door', *Teacher Magazine*, vol. 7, no. 2, October 1995. [Surrounded by death and dying, the children of the South Bronx speak with painful clarity about the poverty that has wounded but not hardened them.]
Krishnamurti, J., *The Only Revolution* and *The Urgency of Change*, both in Mary Lutyens, ed., *The Second Penguin Krishnamurti Reader*, London: Penguin Books, 1984 [1973].
Krishnamurti, J., *The Wholeness of Life*. London: Krishnamurti Foundation Trust, 1987 [1982].
Kuper, Hilda, and Selma Kaplan, 'Voluntary Associations in an Urban Township', *African Studies*, no. 3, December 1944, pp. 178–86.
Ladner, G.B., *The Idea of Reform: Its Impact on Christian Thought and Action in the Age of the Fathers*, Cambridge, Mass.: Harvard University Press, 1959.
Lakatos, I., and A. Musgrove, eds, *Criticism and the Growth of Knowledge*, Cambridge: Cambridge University Press, 1970.

Laleye, I., *La Conception de la personne dans la pensée traditionnelle Yoruba*, Berne: Lang, 1970.

Lapierre, Dominique, *City of Joy*, London: Arrow, 1991 (translated from *La Cité de la joie*, Paris: Robert Laffont, 1985). [A novel based on some 200 taped interviews in the poorest district of Calcutta. Gives an idea of how humans exposed to the hardest difficulties and humiliations caused by other humans live however with utmost dignity and grace, providing their own answers to their problems.]

Lappé, Frances, *Taking Population Seriously: The Missing Piece in the Puzzle*, London: Earthscan, 1989.

Latouche, Serge, *Faut-il refuser le développement?* Paris: PUF, 1985.

Latouche, Serge, *La Planète des naufragés. Essai sur l'Après-développement*, Paris: La Découverte, 1991.

Latouche, Serge, *In the Wake of the Affluent Society*, London: Zed Books, 1995.

Laudan, Larry, *Progress and Its Problems: Towards a Theory of Scientific Growth*, Berkeley: University of California Press, 1977. [A challenging book containing many interesting observations on science and its rationality. Refers extensively to Kuhn and Feyerabend, but seems vehemently critical of Foucault.]

Le Goff, Jacques, *Your Money or Your Life (Economy and Religion in the Middle Ages)*, New York, Zone Books: 1988. [Translated from *La Bourse et la vie*, a history of usury and the creation of the purgatory by the famous French medievalist.]

Leacock, Eleanor Burke, ed., *The Culture of Poverty: A Critique*, New York: Simon & Schuster, 1971.

Legasse, Simon, 'La Pauvreté d'après la sagesse profane', in Marcel Viller, F. Cavallera and J. de Gilbert, eds, *Dictionnaire de Spiritualité ascétique et mystique, doctrine et histoire*, Paris: Beauchesne et ses fils, 1937–95.

Lehman, Karen, 'Reflections from the Space Within', *IFDA Dossier* 59, May/June 1987, pp. 3–12.

Leiss, W., *The Limits to Satisfaction: An Essay on the Problems of Needs and Commodities*, Toronto: Toronto University Press, 1976. [Explores the genesis of needs in the transformation of desire into demand for commodities.]

Lélé, Sharachchandra M., 'Sustainable Development: A Critical Review', *World Development*, vol. 19, no. 6, June 1991, pp. 607–21.

Lemarchand, René, 'Power and Stratification in Rwanda: A Reconsideration', *Cahiers d'Etudes Africaines*, vol. 6, no. 24(4), 1966.

Lepri, Jean-Pierre, *Education et Nationalité en Guinée-Bissau: Contribution à l'étude de l'endogénéité de l'éducation*, Lyon: Se Former+, 1989.

Levi, Margaret, 'The Predatory Theory of Rule', *Politics and Society*, 1981, vol. 10, no. 4, pp. 431–65.

Lévy, Jean-Philippe, *The Economic Life of the Ancient World*, Chicago: University of Chicago Press, 1967 (originally published as *L'Economie antique*, Paris: PUF, 1964).

Lewis, John P., et al., *Strengthening the Poor: What Have We Learned*, New Brunswick, N.J.: Transaction Publishers, 1988.

Lewis, Oscar, 'Caste and the *Jajmani* System in a North Indian Village', *Anthropological Essays*, New York: Random House, 1970, pp. 360–86.

Lewis, Oscar, 'Peasant Culture in India and Mexico: A Comparative Study', *Anthropological Essays*, New York: Random House, 1970, pp. 387–409.

Lewis, Oscar, 'The Culture of Poverty', *Anthropological Essays*, New York: Random House, 1970, pp. 64–79.

Liedloff, Jean, *The Continuum Concept*, London: Futura, 1975. [One of the few reports on 'archaic' or 'primitive' societies which has been prepared not by an anthopologist, but by a woman who has lived with them, mainly because she liked the people and wanted to learn from them. The result is a refreshing and inspiring testimony on the Yequana Indians and the way they are still running their lives.]

Lima Handem, Diana, 'Etat d'une société sans état: Les Balante de Guinée Bissao' in Jean-Pierre Lepri, *Education et Nationalité en Guinée-Bissau.*

Linard, André, 'Superbarrio est arrivé, éé!', *La Otra bolsa de valores* (Mexico City), June 1992.

Lipietz, Alain, *Mirages and Miracles: The Crises of Global Fordism*, London: Verso, 1987 (translation of *Mirages et Miracles: Problèmes de l'industrialisation dans le Tiers Monde*, Paris: La Découverte, 1985).

Lipton, M., 'The Theory of the Optimising Peasant', *Journal of Developent Studies*, 1968, pp. 327–51.

Livernash, R, 'The Growing Influence of NGOs in the Development World', *Environment* 34, June 1992, p. 12. [A useful article for technical research on NGOs, but nothing going beyond the UNDP language.]

LOKAYAN, *What Is LOKAYAN? A project of the Centre for the Study of Developing Societies (CSDS)*, published by LOKYAN, 13 Alipur Road, Delhi 110054, 1982. [LOKAYAN has since published a regular Bulletin containing most interesting articles on grassroots experiences.]

Lopezillera, Luis Méndez, 'Organizations of Social Promotion and Endogenous Building of Civil Society', paper for CEPAUR seminar, Bogota, 2–5 August 1988.

Lopreato, Joseph, 'Interpersonal Relations in Peasant Society: The Peasant's View', *Human Organization*, vol. 21, no. 1, Spring 1962, pp. 21–4.

Löwith, K., *Meaning in History*, Chicago: University of Chicago Press, 1949. [A key book on Christianity, secularization and progress.]

Luckham, Robin, 'Militarism: Force, Class and International Conflict', *Bulletin of the Institute of Developmental Studies* (University of Sussex, Falmer), vol. 30, no. 9, July 1977.

Lummis, Charles Douglas, 'Development against Democracy', *Alternatives*, vol. 16, no. 1, Winter 1991, pp. 31–66.

Lummis, Charles Douglas, *Radical Democracy*, Ithaca and London: Cornell University Press, 1996.

MacFarquhar, Emily, et al., 'The War against Women', *US News and World Report*, vol. 116, 28 March 1994, p. 42. ['In much of the world, political and economic "progress" has been dragging them backward.']

Maffesoli, Michel, *La Conquête du présent: Pour une sociologie de la vie quotidienne*, Paris: PUF, 1979.

Mahdi, Muhsin, *Ibn Khaldun's Philosophy of History*, London: Allen & Unwin, 1957; Chicago: University of Chigago Press, 1964.

Manandhar, Ramesh, 'Against Professionalism: Architect or Facilitator? A Life Story from Nepal', *IFDA Dossier*, 47, May/June 1985, pp. 3–14.

Mander, Jerry, *In the Absence of the Sacred*, San Francisco: Sierra Club Books, 1991.

Mandeville, Bernard de, *The Fable of the Bees: or Private Vices, Publick Benefits*, London, 1714.

Manteuffel, Tadeuz, *Naissance d'une hérésie: les adeptes de la pauvreté volontaire au Moyen Age*, Paris: Mouton, 1970.

Marcos, Subcomandante, Frank Bardacke and Leslie Lopez, *Shadows of Tender Fury: The Letters and Communiqués of Subcomandante Marcos and the Zapatista Army of National Liberation*, New York: Monthly Review Press, 1995.

Marcos, Subcomandante, 'Letters from Marcos', Northwestern University, *Triquarterly*, Fall 1994, pp. 89–145.

Mauss, M., *The Gift*, trans. W.D. Hall, New York: W.W. Norton, 1990.

Mazrui, A.A. and M. Tidy, *Nationalism and New States in Africa*, London: Heinemann, 1984.

McDyer, J., *Glencolumbkille Report*, Glencolumbkille, Donegal: Donegal Democrat Ltd, n.d. (1974?). [A report by Father McDyer, who initiated this cooperative and participatory project, following his first publication called 'The Glencolumbkille Story', published some years earlier by the same company. Father McDyer calls himself a Christian communist and advocates 'community communism'.].

McKibben, B., *The End of Nature*, New York: Random House, 1989. [The deeper civilizational issues in the present debate on nature and environment.]

McKnight, John, *The Careless Society: Community and Its Counterfeits*, New York: Basic Books, 1985. [A moving book on the destruction of convivial relations in society, the loss of the 'art of suffering', and the people's natural gift for overcoming difficulties.]

Meer, Fatima, ed., *Poverty in the 1990s: The Responses of Urban Women*, Paris: UNESCO and International Social Science Council, 1994. [A collection of case studies on women's urban poverty and the gender impacts of structural adjustment. Papers are largely empirical and descriptive, revealing commonalities and distinctive differences between poor urban women accross the world.]

Meier, Reinhard, 'Poverty and Pride Among the Sioux', *Swiss Review of World Affairs*, vol. 41, no. 7, October 1991, pp. 23–5.

Memmi, Albert, *The Colonizer and the Colonizer*, Boston, Mass.: Beacon Press, 1966.

Menchú, Rigoberta, *I, Rigoberta Menchú: An Indian Woman in Guatemala*, trans. Ann Wright, London: Verso, 1984.

Merchant, Carolyn, *The Death of Nature: Women, Ecology and the Scientific Revolution*, San Francisco: Harper & Row, 1980. [Recounts the major rupture in Western attitudes and the discontinuities in European history.]

Merchant, Carolyn, *Ecological Revolutions: Nature, Gender, and Science in New England*, Chapel Hill: University of North Carolina Press, 1989. [Documents how the ways of knowing nature have changed from the native Indian to the colonialist and industrialist modes, focusing on evidence from a limited geographical area.]

Messerschmidt, Donald M., and APROSC Gaun Sallah Contract Team, *Gaun Sallah: The 'Village Dialogue' Method for Local Planning in Nepal, A discussion-paper*, Katmandu: SECID/RCUP, 1984.

Mies, M., V. Bennholt-Thomsen and C. Von Worlhof, *Women: The Last Colony*, London: Zed Books, 1988.

Mitchell, Stephen, *Tao Te Ching*, New York: Harper & Row, 1988. [A new English version of Lao Tzu's perennial teachings: 'Whoever can see through all fear/ will always be safe./ Seeing into darkness is clarity./ Use your own light/ and return to the source of light.']

Mokakit: Indian Education Research Association, *Selected Papers from the 1984 Mokakit Conference*, Vancouver: Mokakit Indian Education Research Association, July 1986.

Moore, Barrington, Jr., *Injustice: The Social Bases of Obediance and Revolt*, White Plains, N.Y.: M.E. Sharpe, 1987.

Moore-Lappé, F., J. Collins and D. Kinley, *Aid as Obstacle: Twenty Questions about Our Foreign Aid and the Hungry*, San Francisco: IFDP, 1980.

Morey, Sylvester M. and Olivia Gilliam, *Respect for Life: The Traditional Upbringing of American Indian Children*, New York: The Myrin Institute, 1974.

Morin, Edgar, *Introduction à la pensée complexe*, Paris: ESF Editeur, 1990.

Mottahedeh, Roy P., *Loyalty and Leadership in an Early Islamic Society*, Princeton, N.J.: Princeton University Press, 1980. [A serious study of the ways earlier Islamic societies operated in terms of loyalties, kinships and other links binding members together.]

Mudimbe, V.Y., *L'odeur du père, Essai sur les limites de la science et de la vie en Afrique noire*, Paris: Présence Africaine, 1982.

Mudimbe, V.Y., *The Invention of Africa: Gnosis, Philosophy, and the Order of Knowledge*, Bloomington, Ind.: Indiana University Press, 1988.

Mueller, A., 'The Bureaucratization of Development Knowledge: The Case of Women in Development', Ph.D. dissertation, University of Toronto (OISE), 1987.

Müller, J., *Liquidation or Consolidation of Indigenous Technology: A Study of the Changing Conditions of Production of Village Blacksmiths in Tanzania*, Aalborg: Aalborg University Press, 1980.

Mumford, Lewis, *The Myth of the Machine*, New York: Harcourt Brace Jovanovich, 1964.

Myrdal, Gunnar, *The Challenge of World Poverty*, New York: Pantheon, 1970.

N'Dione, E., P. de Leener, M. Ndiaye, P. Jacolin and J.-P. Perier, *The Future of Community Lands: Human Resources*, London: Intermediate Technology Publications/ENDA GRAF, 1995 [The only English presentation of the Chodak experience in Grand Yoff, Dakar by the ENDA/GRAF team].

N'Dione,Emmanuel S., *Dynamique urbaine d'une société en grappe: Un cas, Dakar*, Dakar: ENDA, 1987.

N'Dione, Emmanuel S., *Le Don et le Recours: Ressorts de l'économie urbaine*, Dakar: ENDA, 1992.

N'Dione, Emmanuel S., *Réinventer le Présent. Quelques jalons pour l'action, Dakar:* ENDA/GRAF Sahel, 1994. [The story of one of the most original approaches to social change, from both theoretical and practical perspectives.]

Nandy, Ashis, 'The Idea of Development: The Experience of Modern Psychology as a Cautionary Tale and as an Allegory', in C. Mallman and O. Nudler, eds, *Human Development in its Social Context*, London: Edward Arnold Overseas, 1986, pp. 248–59.

Nandy, Ashis, 'Cultural Frames for Social Transformation: A Credo', *Alternatives* 12, 1987, pp. 113–23.

Nandy, Ashis, *The Intimate Enemy*, Bombay: Oxford University Press, 1987.

Nandy, Ashis, *Traditions, Tyranny and Utopias*, Bombay: Oxford University Press, 1987.

Nandy, Ashis, ed., *Science, Hegemony and Violence*, Bombay: Oxford University Press, 1988.

Nandy, Ashis, 'Shamans, Savages and the Wilderness: On the Audibility of Dissent and the Future of Civilizations', *Alternatives* 14, 1989, pp. 263–77.

Nandy, Ashis, *The Illegitimacy of Nationalism*, Delhi: Oxford University Press, 1993.

Needham, J., et al., *Science and Civilization in China*, 7 vols, Cambridge: Cambridge University Press, 1954.

Needleman, Jacob, *Money and the Meaning of Life*, New York: Doubleday, 1991.

Negri, Antonio, *The Politics of Subversion*, Cambridge: Polity, 1990.

Nelson, Benjamin, *The Idea of Usury: From Tribal Brotherhood to Universal Otherhood*, London: University of Chicago Press, 1969. [Valuable piece of scholarship for understanding the evolution in the perception of wealth and the permeation of Western culture by a universalist morality conducive to systematic capitalist enterprise.]

Nerfin, Marc, 'The Relationship NGOs–UN Agencies–Governments: Challenges, Possibilities and Prospects', position paper prepared for the First International Meeting of NGOs and UN system agencies, Development, International Co-operation and the NGOs, Rio de Janeiro, 6–8 August 1991.

Nguvulu, A., *L'Humanisme négro-africain face au développement*, Kinshasa: Okapi, 1971.

Nietschmann, Bernard, 'Third World Colonial Expansion: Indonesia, Disguised Invasion of Indigenous Nations', in John H. Bodley, ed., *Tribal Peoples and Development Issues*, Mountain View, Calif.: Mayfield Publishing House, 1988, pp. 191–207.

Norberg-Hodge, Helena, *Ancient Futures: Learning from Ladakh*, San Francisco: Sierra Club Books, 1991.

Ntoane, C.N. and K.E. Mokoetle, 'Major Problems as Perceived by the Community', *Second Carnegie Inquiry into Poverty and Development in Southern Africa*, conference paper, no. 2, 13–19 April 1984.

Nyerere, Julius, *Ujamaa, Essays on Socialism*, Oxford: Oxford University Press, 1968.

Nyerere, Julius, *Freedom and Development*, Oxford: Oxford University Press, 1973.

O'Donnell, Guillermo, *Modernization and Bureaucratic-Authoritarianism: Studies in South American Policies*, Berkeley: Institute of International Studies, University of California, 1973.

Olson, Mancur, *The Rise and Decline of Nations*, New Haven, Conn.: Yale University Press, 1982.

Omo-Fadaka, Jimoh, 'Environment and Development – What Mutual Interests and Safe Guards?', paper presented at the Foundation Christophe Eckenstein Seminar on 'Towards the Post-Development Age', Geneva, 6–9 March 1990.

Ong, A., *Spirits of Resistance and Capitalist Decline*, Albany, N.Y.: SUNY Press, 1987.

P.M., *Bolo'bolo*, New York: Semiotext(e), 1985 (originally published in German, Zurich: Verlag Paranoïa City). [A ludic utopia on how a more creative and humane life could be imagined on planet Earth, where the cultural identity of each *ibu* (child, woman, man) could be respected in his or her *bolo* (one's own chosen community or neighbourhood), through *dala* (local assemblies) and other convivial devices, without any imposed institutional setup inhibiting people's freedom of choice. The booklet is placed under a Brazilian proverb which says: 'If you are alone in dreaming, it is only a dream; if you are many to dream, it is reality which starts.' Regrettably, this utopian dream did not get the attention it deserved.]

Pankhurst, Richard, 'The Great Ethiopian Famine of 1888–1892: A New Assessment', *Journal of the History of Medicine and Allied Sciences* 21, April 1966, pp. 95–124.

Pannikar, Raimon, 'The Contemplative Mood: A Challenge to Modernity', *Cross Currrents*, Fall 1981, pp. 261–72.

Pannikar, Raimon, *The Cosmotheandric Experience*, New York: Orbis, 1993.

Pannikar, Raimon, 'A Nonary of Priorities', *Interculture*, special issue, vol. 24, no. 1, Winter 1996.

Parenti, Michael, *The Sword and the Dollar: Imperialism, Revolution and the Arms Race*, San Diego: St Martin Press, 1989.

Partant, François, *La Fin du développement: Naissance d'une alternative?*, Paris: Maspéro, 1982. [An original thinker whose other books are equally challenging. Among them: *Que la crise s'aggrave*, 1976; *Le Pédalo ivre*, 1981 (a Voltaire-type philosophical tale on the discovery of an ideal society living on an island somewhere on Lac Leman in Switzerland); finally *La ligne d'horizon*, 1982, a posthumous work summarizing the author's political thought.]

Pattnaik, Binay Kumar, 'Distorted Development in Orissa', *Economic and Political Weekly*, 2–9 March 1991, pp. 491–2.

Payer, Cheryl, *The World Bank: A Critical Analysis*, New York: Monthly Review Press, 1982.

Peemans, Jean-Philippe, 'Quelques notes sur la crise et les problèmes actuels de la restructuration de l'accumulation mondiale', *Contradictions* 9, 1976, pp. 63–86.

Perkins, John M., *Beyond Charity*, Grand Rapids, Mich.: Baker Books, 1993. [Perkins is a priest who has chosen to move into one of the most dangerous areas in Northwest Pasadena 'because he wanted to give children other alternatives besides being part of a gang'.]

Perrot, Marie-Dominique, 'Passager clandestin et indispensable du discours: le présupposé', in G. Rist and F. Sabelli, eds, *Il était une fois le développement*, Lausanne: Editions d'En Bas, 1982, pp. 71–9.

Perrot, Marie-Dominique, 'Les Empêcheurs de développer en rond', *Ethnies: droits de l'homme et peuples autochtones*, vol. 13, Spring 1991, pp. 4–11.

Perrot, Marie-Dominique, 'La Fiction et la Feinte: Développement et peuples autochtones, ethnies,' *Survival International*, special issue, no. 13, Spring 1991.

Perrot, Marie-Dominique, 'Réflexions autour de la notion de développement durable', paper presented at the IIM Conference 'Living with the Earth', Orford, Quebec, April 1992.

Perrot, Marie-Dominique, G. Rist and F. Sabelli, *La Mythologie programmée: L'economie des croyances dans la société moderne*, Paris, PUF, 1992.

Polanyi, Karl, Conrad M. Arensberg and Harry W. Pearson, eds, *Trade and Market in the Early Empires*, Glencoe, Ill.: The Free Press, 1957. [Contains Polanyi's article on 'The Economy as Instituted Process'.]

Polanyi, Karl, *The Great Transformation: The Political and Economic Origins of Our Time*, Boston, Mass.: Beacon Press, 1957 (1944).

Polanyi, Karl, *The Livelihood of Man*, New York: Academic Press, 1977. [Both books are now classics for their analysis of the birth of the liberal creed and the processes leading to the emergence of a 'disembedded' economy.]

Pollard, Nigel, 'Appropriate Technology: Really Appropriate or Just a Misfit?', *The Ecologist*, vol. 13, no. 1, 1983, pp. 27–51.

Pomonti, J.C., *L'Afrique trahie*, Paris: Hachette, 1979.

Popkin, Samuel L., *The Rational Peasant: The Political Economy of Rural Society in Vietnam*, Berkeley: University of California Press, 1979.

Pradervand, Pierre, *Listening to Africa: Developing Africa from the Grassroots*, New York: Praeger, 1989.

Prasad, Nageshwar, ed., *Hindi Swaraj: A Fresh Look*, New Delhi: Gandhi Peace Foundation, 1985.

Price, David, 'The World Bank versus Native Peoples: A Consultant's View', *The Ecologist*, vol. 15, no. 1–2, 1985, pp. 73–7.

Procacci, Giovanna, 'Social Economy and the Government of Poverty', in G. Burchell, C. Gordon and P. Miller, eds, *The Foucault Effect*, Hemel Hempstead: Harvester Wheatsheaf, 1991.

Prokash, Om and P.N. Rastogi, 'Development of the Rural Poor: The Missing Factor', *IFDA Dossier* 51, January/February 1986, pp. 4–16. [The paper identifies problems and failures of the developmental process in a village in Uttar Pradesh. It considers the exploitation of the poor by powerful local interests, deploring the lack of a spiritual factor; a lack that, according to the authors, has devitalized and desensitized development, perpetuating exploitation of the poor and their poverty.]

Quid Pro Quo, Journal of the South–North Network Cultures & Development. [Monthly journal published by Thierry G. Verhelst, 174 rue Joseph II, B-1040 Brussels, Belgium.]

Rabinow, Paul, ed., *The Foucault Reader*, New York: Pantheon, 1984.

Radin, P., *Primitive Man as Philosopher*, London and New York: Appleton, 1927.

Rahman, Anisur, 'People's Self-Development', *Journal of the Asiatic Society*, Bangladesh (Hum.), vol. 34, no. 2, December 1989.

Rahman, Anisur, 'Towards an Alternative Development Paradigm', paper given at conference of the Bengladesh Economnic Association, Dhaka, 23 November 1990.

Rahman, Anisur, ed., *Grassroots Paritipation and Self-reliance: Experiences in South and S.E. Asia*, New Delhi: Oxford and IBH Publishing Co., 1984.

Rahnema, Majid, 'Alphabétisation contre les analphabètes?', *IFDA Dossier* 31, September/October 1982.

Rahnema, Majid, 'NGOs: Sifting the Wheat from the Chaff', *Development* (SID) 3, 1985.

Rahnema, Majid, 'Under the Banner of Development', *Development* (SID) 1/2, 1986.

Rahnema, Majid, 'Power and Regenerative Processes in Micro-Spaces', *International Social Scientific Journal*, UNESCO, 1988.

Rahnema, Majid, 'Participatory Action Research, The Last Temptation of Saint Development', *Alternatives* 15, August 1990.

Rahnema, Majid, 'Swadhyaya: The Unknown, the Peaceful, the Silent Yet Singing Revolution of India', *IFDA Dossier* 75/76, January/April 1990.

Rahnema, Majid, *Global Poverty: A Pauperizing Myth*, Montreal: IIM, Interculture, 1991.

Rahnema, Majid, 'Science and Subjugated Knowledges: A Third World Perspective', in Ruth Hayhoe, ed., *Knowledge across Cultures: Universities East and West*, Toronto/Wuhan: OISE Press and Hubei Education Press, 1993.

Rahnema, Majid, 'Beyond the Formal Debates on the U.N. and World Orders', *Development* 4, December 1995.

Rau, Bill, *From Feast to Famine: Official Cures and Grassroots Remedies to Africa's Food Crisis*, London: Zed Books, 1991.

Redfield, Robert, *Papers*, edited by Margaret Redfield, vol. 1: *Human Nature & the Study of Society*; vol. 2: *The Social Uses of Social Sciences*, Chicago: University of Chicago Press, 1962–63. ['To be able to find out what it is that a Zuñi Indian is ashamed of, one must first know what it is to be ashamed.']

Reich, Charles A., *The Greening of America*, New York: Random House, 1970. ['We think of ourselves as an incredibly rich country, but we are beginning to realize that we are also a desperately poor country – poor in most of the things that throughout the history of mankind have been cherished as riches' (p. 13).]

Rejali, Darius M., *Torture and Modernity: Self, Society, and State in Modern Iran*, Boulder, Colo.: Westview Press, 1994. [A Foucault-inspired study of the relations between torture and modernity, which discusses, anong other subjects, the representation of punishment, disciplinary and tutelary practices, Islam and punishment, revolution and terror, and the nature of power in Iranian society.]

Revue du Mauss, Paris: Editions La Découverte. [A quarterly review which questions the utilitarian and economistic bias in social sciences and modern life.]

Rich, Bruce M., 'Multi-lateral Development Banks: Their Role in Destroying the Global Environment', *The Ecologist*, vol. 15, no. 1–2, 1985.

Rich, Bruce M., *Mortgaging the Earth: The World Bank, Environmental Impoverishment and the Crisis of Development*, London: Earthscan, 1994.

Richards, P., *Indigenous Agricultural Revolution: Ecology and Food Production in West Africa*, London: Hutchinson, 1985. [Points out the wisdom of traditional knowledge systems.]

Rigby, P., *Persistant Pastoralists: Nomadic Societies in Transition*, London: Zed Books, 1985.

Ringer, Robert J., *How You Can Find Happiness During the Collapse of Western Civilization*, New York: QED/Harper & Row, 1983. ['Though a paper dollar will buy only 5% of what it could purchase in 1940, an ounce of gold will still buy about the same amount of products and services that it did forty, fifty or even one hundred years ago' (pp. 162–6).]

Rist, Gilbert, *Le Développement: Histoire d'une croyance occidentale*, Paris: Presse des Sciences Po, 1996.

Rist, Gilbert and F. Sabelli, eds, *Il était une fois le développement*, Lausanne: Editions d'En Bas, 1986.

Rist, Gilbert, Majid Rahnema and Gustavo Esteva, *Le Nord perdu: Repères pour l'après-développement*, Lausanne: Editions d'En Bas, 1992.

Robert, Jean, 'After Development: The Threat of Disvalue', paper presented at seminar on Post-Development, Fondation Christophe Eckenstein, Geneva, 5–9 March 1990.

Roby, Pamela, *The Poverty Establishment*, Englewood Cliffs, N.J.: Prentice-Hall, 1974. [Brings together radical articles on the power structure which 'not only creates and maintains poverty programs to regulate the poor, but also preserves inequality by continuously generating schemes to increase the profits and power of the rich.']

Rodney, W., *How Europe Underdeveloped Africa*, Washington DC: Howard University Press, 1981.

Rogers, Susan Carol 'Female Forms of Power and the Myth of Male Dominance: A Model of Female–Male Interaction in Peasant Society', *American Ethnologist*, vol. 2, no. 4, November 1975, pp. 727–56. [Explores the transformation of male dominance from myth to reality during the process of industrialization. Much of the literature on peasant modernization rests on false assumptions regarding the role of women:

only when we stop looking at male roles and forms of power as the norm can we understand how human societies operate.]
Romanyshin, R., *Technology as Symptom and Dream*, London: Routledge, 1989. ['Recounts fascinatingly the cultural dream at the roots of the rise of technology' (Otto Ulrich).]
Rosaldo, Renato, *Culture and Truth: The Remaking of Social Analysis*, Boston, Mass.: Beacon Press, 1989.
Rosecrance, R., *The Rise of the Trading State: Commerce and Conquest in the Modern World*, New York: Basic Books, 1986. [On the secular substitution of economic for military competition.]
Roy, Ramashray, *Against the Current. Essays in Alternative Development*, Delhi: Satvahan Publications, 1982.
Ruwen, Ogien, *Théories ordinaires de la pauvreté*, Paris: PUF, 1983.
Sachs, Ignacy, *La Découverte du Tiers-Monde*, Paris: Flammarion, 1971.
Sachs, Wolfgang, 'The Gospel of Global Efficiency: On Worldwatch and Other Reports on the State of the World', *IFDA Dossier* 68, November/December 1988, pp. 33–9.
Sachs, Wolfgang, 'Global Ecology and the Shadow of Development', paper presented at the IIM Conference 'Living with the Earth', later published in *UNESCO Courier*, September 1992.
Sachs, Wolfgang, ed., *The Development Dictionary: A Guide to Knowledge and Power*, London: Zed Books, 1992.
Sachs, Wolfgang, ed., *Global Ecology: A New Arena of Political Conflict*, London: Zed Books, 1993.
Sahlins, Marshall, *Stone Age Economics*, Chicago: Aldine Publishing Co.: 1972.
Sahlins, Marshall, *Culture and Practical Reason*, Chicago: University of Chicago Press, 1976.
Said, Edward W., *Orientalism*, New York: Vintage Books, 1978.
Said, Edward W., *Culture and Imperialism*, New York: Vintage Books, 1994.
Sale, Kirkpatrick, *Rebels Against the Future*, Reading, Mass.: Addison-Wesley, 1995. [Other books by the same author include: *The Green Revolution*, *The Conquest of Paradise*, *Human Scale*, *The Land and People of Ghana*.]
Sanchez, Enrique E., *Requiem por la modernization: perspectivas cambiantes en estudios del desarrollo*, Mexico: Universidad de Guadalajara, 1986.
Sarvodaya, *Ten Basic Human Needs*, Colombo, Sri Lanka: Community Education Series, 26 Moratuwa, Sri Lanka, 1978.
Sassier, Philippe, *Du Bon Usage des pauvres: Histoire d'un thème politique (XVIe–XXe siècle)*, Paris: Fayard, 1990.
Schroyer, Trent, 'Corruption of Freedom in America', in J. Forrester, ed., *Critical Theory and Public Life*, Boston, Mass.: MIT Press, 1985.
Schuftan, Claudio, 'Foreign Aid and its Role in Maintaining the Exploitation of the Agricultural Sector: Evidence from A Case-study in Africa', *International Journal of Health Services*, vol. 13, no. 1, 1983, pp. 33–48.
Schuftan, Claudio, 'Multidisciplinarity, Paradigms and Ideology in Development Work', *Scandinavian Journal of Development Alternatives*, vol. 7, nos 2 and 3, 1988.
Schuftan, Claudio, 'Development Nemesis', mimeo, Box 40874, Nairobi, 1990.
Schumacher, E.F., *Small Is Beautiful*, London: Blond and Briggs, 1973.
Schumacher, E.F., 'Making Sense', *Whole Earth Review*, Summer 1991, pp. 94–101.
Schwab, G., *Dance with the Devil*, quoted in S.J. William Woods, 'Affluent American Response', in Francisco Jimenez, *Poverty and Social Justice*, Tempe, Ariz.: Bilingual Press, 1987. ['A single edition of the New York Times eats up 150 acres of forest land.']
Schwartz, John E. and Volgy, Thomas J., 'Above the Poverty Line, but Poor', *The Nation* 256, 15 February 1993. [A revealing article on the true number of the economically modernized poor in the USA, arguing that 26 million people should be added to

the 36 million Americans classified by the Census Bureau as officially poor in 1991. 'Because the cost of basic necessities at the minimum standard rose more rapidly than the general price index, the official poverty line fell ever behind economic reality' over the years. Based on numerous Gallup polls of the minimum income needed to live adequately, it puts forward what the authors call 'the real poverty line', some 60 per cent higher than the official one.]

Scott, James C., *The Moral Economy of the Peasant*, New Haven, Conn.: Yale University Press, 1976. [Demonstrates, in the cases of Burma and Vietnam, how the peasants' 'moral economy' allows them to preserve and enrich their culture while at the same time safeguarding their security.]

Scott, James C., *Weapons of the Weak: Everyday Forms of Resistance*, New Haven, Conn.: Yale University Press, 1987.

Scott, James C., *Domination and the Arts of Resistance: Hidden Transcripts*, New Haven, Conn.: Yale University Press, 1990. [A major book for understanding the *problematiques* of domination and resistance, particularly in oral cultures.]

Seabrook, Jeremy, *Victims of Development: Resistance and Alternatives*, London: Verso, 1994. [On how the people themselves view their experiences and struggles. Vivid, first-hand stories ranging from the tenements of São Paulo and the slums of Manila to the inner-city areas of Liverpool and the council estates of rural Cornwall.]

Sen, Amartya, 'Liberty and Poverty', *Current*, May 1994. [Sees 'human beings as people with rights to exercise, not as part of a "stock" or a "population" that passively exists and must be looked after.']

Senghor, Leopold, *Liberté I: Négritude et humanisme*, Paris: Seuil, 1967.

Senghor, Leopold, *Liberté II: Nation et voie africaine du socialisme*, Paris: Seuil, 1971. [A poet and former President of Senegal, created the concept of 'negritude' and published two more books in the same series, respectively in 1977 and 1983: *Liberté III: Négritude et civiliation de l'universel* and *Liberté IV: socialisme et planification*.]

Serres, Michel, *Eclaircissements: Entretiens avec Bruno Latour*, Paris, Flammarion/Champs: 1994.

Seshadri, C.V., *Development and Thermodynamics*, Madras: Murugappar Chettiar Research Centre, 1986.

Shanin, Teodor, *Introduction to the Sociology of 'Developing Societies'*, Harmondsworth: Penguin, 1971.

Shanin, Teodor, *Late Marx and the Russian Road: Marx and the Peripheries of Capitalism*, New York: Monthly Review Press, 1983.

Shanin, Teodor, 'Expolary Economies: A Political Economy of Margins', paper for Colloquium on Alternative Economies in Toronto, May 1988.

Shanin, Teodor and Hamza Alavi, *The Roots of Otherness: Russia as a 'Developing Society'*, London: Macmillan, 1985.

Sharpe, Gene, *The Politics of Nonviolent Action*, Boston, Mass.: Porter Sargent, 1973.

Shayegan, Daryush, *Qu'est-ce qu'une révolution religieuse?*, Paris: Albin Michel, 1991.

Shi, David E., *The Simple Life: Plain Living and High Thinking in American Culture*, New York: Oxford University Press, 1986. [On the history of American movements pursuing the simple life: from the Puritan ethic of hard work, temperate living, and spiritual devotion among settlers of the colonial period, to Jimmy Carter's and Ronald Reagan's contrasting philosophies of what constitutes the good life.]

Shiva, Vandana, *Staying Alive: Women, Ecology and Development*, London: Zed Books, 1989.

Shiva, Vandana, *The Violence of the Green Revolution*, London: Zed Books, 1991.

Simmel, Georg, 'The Poor', *Social Problems* 13, 1965, pp. 117–40.

Sinha, Arun, *Against the Few: Struggles of India's Rural Poor*, London: Zed Books, 1991.

Sivaraksa, Sulak, 'Buddhism and Development', Rome: FAO, *Ideas and Action*.

Sizoo, Edith, 'Wearing Masks in Development', *Culture and Development*, vol. 3, no. 8/9.

Skog, Sharon N., 'Reagonomics, Women, and Poverty', in F. Jimenez, *Poverty and Social Justice*, Tempe, Ariz.: Bilingual Press, 1987. [Women are increasingly bearing the brunt of poverty in America. According to the National Advisory Council on Economic Opportunity, 'All other things being equal, if the proportion of the poor in female-householder families were to continue to increase at the same rate as it did from 1967 to 1987, the poverty population would be composed solely of women and children before the year 2000' (*Fiscal Report – The American Promise: Equal Justice and Economic Opportunity*, Washington DC: National Advisory Council, 1981, p. 46).]

Smith, Page, *Rediscovering Christianity: A History of Modern Democracy and the Christian Ethic*, New York: St Martin's Press, 1994.

Smith, Peter H., *Labyrinths of Power: Political Recruitment in 20th Century Mexico*, Princeton, N.J.: Princeton University Press, 1979.

Soe, Christian, ed., *Comparative Politics*, Guilford, Conn.: Dushkin, 1994.

Somjee, Geeta and A.H. Somjee, 'The Unreached Poor', in *Reaching Out to the Poor: The Unfinished Rural Revolution*, London: Macmillan, pp. 136–47.

Sommers, Christina and Fred, *Vice and Virtue in Everyday Life: Introductory Readings in Ethics*, San Diego: Harcourt Brace Jovanovich, 1989.

Souza, G. de, *La Conception de 'vie' chez les Fons*, Cotonou: Editions du Bénin, 1975.

Soyinka, Wole, 'Of Power and Change', *African Statesman* (Lagos), July–September 1966, pp. 53–64.

Soyinka, Wole, *Collected Plays*, 2 vols, London: Oxford University Press, 1973 and 1974. [Two plays in this outstanding collection by the Nobel prizewinning playwright are particularly relevant to the cultural issues addressed in the Reader: *The Lion and the Jewel* and *Madman and Specialists*, both in volume 2. Students of Africa can feel and understand the truth of Africa through Soyinka's powerful plays much better than by reading most research studies on the continent.]

Springborg, P., *The Problem of Human Needs and the Critique of Civilization*, London: Allen & Unwin, 1981. ['The only monographic attempt at retracing the perception of the analogues of 'need' in Western thoought from the Greeks to the present' (Ivan Illich).]

Starrels, Bould and Nicholas, 'The Feminization of Poverty in the United States', *Journal of Family Issues*, vol. 15, no. 4, December 1994, p. 590. [Contains a useful bibliography on the feminization of poverty.]

Stavenhagen, R., 'Ethnodevelopment: The Hidden Dimension', *UNU Work in Progress*, vol. 9, no. 1, July 1985, p. 13.

Steele, Tom and Richard Taylor, 'Against Modernity: Gandhi and Adult Education', *International Journal of Lifelong Education*, vol. 13, no. 1, January–February 1994, pp. 33–42.

Stern, Philip M. and George de Vincent, *The Shame of A Nation*, New York: Ivan Obolensky, 1965. [Moving photographs showing the daily life of the destitute in the USA.]

Strange, Susan, *Casino Capitalism*, Blackwell: Oxford, 1986.

Subry, Andrès, 'Mexique: Manger, Un acte politique, Stratégie paysanne de la production alimentaire, *IFDA Dossier* 57/58, January/April 1987, pp. 5–14.

Sundquist, James L., ed., *On Fighting Poverty, Perspectives from Experience*, New York: Basic Books, 1969.

Swantz, Marja Liisa, 'The Development Crisis in the North', paper presented at the SID Conference in New Delhi, 1988.

Tevernier, Paul, *The Meaning of Gifts*, trans. John S. Gilmour, Richmond, Va.: John Knox Press, 1963.

Tawney, R.H., *Religion and the Rise of Capitalism*, New York: Penguin, 1947.

Temple, Dominique, 'Les ONGs comme Cheval de Troie', *IFDA Dossier*, 60, July/August 1987, pp. 39–52.

Tevoedjre, Albert, *Poverty, Wealth of Mankind,* Oxford: Pergamon Press, 1979. [Translation of *La Pauvreté, richesse des peuples*, Paris: Editions Ouvrières, 1978.]

Thoreau, Henry D., *The Selected Works of Thoreau*, Boston, Mass.: Houghton Mifflin, 1975.

Thoreau, Henry D., *Walden*, with an introduction by Ramesh K. Srivastava, Delhi: Oxford University Press, 1983. [The great story of a delightful human experience of living differently and simply, free from the tyranny of imputed needs.]

Thureau-Dangin, Philippe, *La Concurrence et la mort*, Paris: Syros, 1995.

Tillard, Jean-Marie R., 'Pauvreté chrétienne' in *Dictionnaire de Spiritualité*, Paris, Beauchesne: 1983.

Tinker, Irène and Monique Cohen, 'Ziguinshor, Manikganj, Iloilo and Bogor: Street foods as income and food for the poor', *IFDA Dossier* 49, September/October 1985, pp. 13–24.

Tournier, Paul, *The Meaning of Gift*, trans. John S. Gilmur, Richmond Va.: John Knox Press, 1963.

Townsend, Peter, 'The Meaning of Poverty', *British Journal of Sociology* 13, 1962.

Tuan, Y.-F., *Topophilia: A Study of Environmental Perceptions and Values*, Englewood Cliffs, N.J.: Prentice Hall, 1974. [Shows the many different ways in which the environment, across history and cultures, figured in human imagination.]

Turnbell, C.M., *The Lonely African*, New York: Simon & Schuster, 1962.

Tutu, D., *Hope and Suffering*, Grand Rapids: W.B. Edermans, 1984.

Vachon, R., Ashis Nandy, Wolfgang Sachs and Raimon Pannikar, 'The Post-Modern Era: Some Signs and Priorities', *Interculture*, special issue, vol. 24, no. 1, Winter 1996.

Vachon, Robert, et al. *Alternatives au Développement*, Montréal: Centre Interculturel Monchanin (presently IIM), 1988.

Vachon, Robert, *Human Rights and Dharma*, paper presented at the IIM Conference 'Living with the Earth, April 1992.

Valentine, Charles A., 'The 'Culture of Poverty': Its Scientific Significance and its Implications for Action', in Eleanor Burke Leacock, ed., *The Culture of Poverty: A Critique*, New York: Simon & Schuster, 1971.

Valentine, Charles A., 'Culture and Poverty: Critique and Counter-Proposals', *Current Anthropology*, April–June 1969, pp. 181–201.

Vansina, J., 'Once Upon a Time: Oral Traditions as History in Africa' in F. Gilbert and S. Grabard, eds, *Historical Studies Today*, New York: W.W. Norton, 1972.

Veblen, Thorstein, *The Theory of the Leisure Class*, New York: Mentor, 1953. [A classic work on conspicuous consumption.]

Verhelst, Thierry G., *Culture and Development*, trans. Bob Cumming, London, Zed Books, 1987.

Verhelst, Thierry G., *No Life Without Roots*, London: Zed Books, 1989.

Visvanathan, Shiv, 'Mrs Brundtland's Disenchanted Cosmos', *Alternatives*, 16, 1991, pp. 377–84.

Wachtel, Paul L., *The Poverty of Affluence: A Psychological Portrait of the American Way of Life*, Philadelphia: New Society Publishers, 1989.

Wagar, W.W., 'Modern Views on the Origins of the Idea of Progress', *Journal of History of Ideas* 28, 1967, pp. 55–70. [Offers a panoramic view of various authors concerned with the subject of secularization, among them the less pessimistic outlook of Maritain.]

Wallerstein, I., *Africa: The Politics of Independence*, New York: Random House, 1961.

Watts, Michael, *Silent Violence: Food, Famine and Peasantry in Northern Nigeria*, Berkeley: University of California Press, 1983. [A must for the understanding of the man-made reasons behind modern African droughts.]

Wax, Murray L., 'Poverty and Interdependency', in Eleanor Burke Leacock, ed., *The Culture of Poverty: A Critique*, New York: Simon & Schuster, 1971.

Weber, Eugen, *Peasants into Frenchmen: Modernization of Rural France, 1870–1914*, Stanford: Stanford University Press, 1976.

Weber, Max, *The Protestant Ethic and the Spirit of Capitalism*, New York: Charles Scribner, 1958. [Quotes many of the writings of Benjamin Franklin defining the hell of modern man – what Weber calls the 'philosophy of avarice'.]

Weil, Simone, *First and Last Notebooks*, trans. Arthur Wills, with an introduction by Gustave Thibon, New York: G.P. Putnam's Sons, 1952.

Weil, Simone, *The Need for Roots: Prelude to a Declaration of Duties Toward Mankind*, trans. Arthur Wills, G.P. Putnam's Sons, 1953 (from *L'Enracinement*, Gallimard, Folio: 1990 [1909]).

Weil, Simone, 'Sketch of Contemporary Social Life', *Oppression and Liberty*, trans. Arthur Wills and John Petrie, with an introduction by F.C. Ellert, Amherst: University of Massachussetts Press, 1973 ('Esquisse de la vie sociale contemporaine', *Oppression et liberté*, Paris: Gallimard, 1955).

Weiler, Hans N., 'The International Politics of Knowledge Production and the Future of Higher Education', paper prepared for meeting 'The New Roles of Higher Education at a World Level', UNESCO-CRESALC, Caracas, Venezuela, 2–3 May 1991.

Weinberg, Bill, *War on Land: Ecology and Politics in Central America*. London: Zed Books, 1991.

Weiskel, T., 'Toward an Archaeology of Colonialism: Elements in the Ecological Transformation of the Ivory Coast', in D. Worster, ed., *The Ends of the Earth*, Cambridge: Cambridge University Press, 1988.

Wickramaarachchi, S.P., 'Keeping the People's Surplus in People's Hands', *Development* (SID) 2, 1984, pp. 26–9.

Wilkinson, Richard G., *Poverty and Progress*, London: Methuen, 1977.

Will, R.E. and H.G. Vatter, *Poverty in Affluence: The Social, Political, and Economic Dimensions of Poverty in the United States*, New York: Harcourt, Brace and World, 1970.

Winner, L. *Autonomous Technology*, Cambridge: MIT Press, 1977. [Thorough study of the modern experience of 'technology out of control'.]

Winner, L., *The Whale and the Reactor: A Search for Limits in the Age of High Technology*, Chicago: Chicago University Press, 1985. [A collection of fine essays on technology.]

Wiredu, J.E., 'How Not to Compare African Thought with Western Thought', in R. Wright, ed., *African Philosophy: An Introduction*, Washington DC: University Press of America, 1977.

Wiser, D.H., *The Hindu Jajmani System: A Socio-economic System Inter-relating Members of a Hindu Village Community in Services*, Lucknow, 1936.

Wolf, E., *Europe and the People without History*, Berkeley: University of California Press, 1982.

Wolpin, Miles D., *Militarization, Internal Repression and Social Welfare in the Third World*, London: Croom Helm, 1986.

Worster, D., ed., *The Ends of the Earth*, Cambridge: Cambridge University Press, 1988.

Wright, Rolland H., 'The Stranger mentality and the culture of poverty', in Eleanor Burke Leacock, ed., *The Culture of Poverty: A Critique*, New York: Simon & Schuster, 1971.

York, Geoffrey, *The Disposessed: Life and Death in Native Canada*, London: Vintage, 1990. [Excellent book on the destruction of Native Americans by development, by a correspondant of the Toronto *Globe and Mail*.]

Young, Crawford, 'The Ideas of Progress in the Third World', in G.A. Almond, M. Chodorow and R.H. Pearce, eds, *Progress and its Discontents*, Berkeley: University of California Press, 1982.

Young, Iris Marion, *Justice and the Politics of Difference*, Princeton, N.J.: Princeton University Press, 1985.

Zaoual, D., *The Religion, Spirituality, and Thought of Traditional Africa*, Chicago: Chicago University Press, 1979.

Zaoual, Hassan, 'Essai sur l'enigme du développement', mimeo, 1986.

Zaoual, Hassan, 'Le Développement 'Désemparé' du tiers-monde: Bilans et perspectives théoriques', seminar at the Institut Universitaire d'Etudes sur le développement, Geneva, 16–17 January 1989.

Zaoual, Hassan, 'La Méthodologie des sites symboliques', I.U.T. Dunkerque–Calais, Université du Littoral, mimeo, 1991.

Zaoual, Hassan, 'La Nature et les cultures', paper presented at the IIM Conference 'Living with the Earth', April 1992.

LIST OF BOXES

INDEX

Page numbers in italics refer to material contained in the boxes